NEW

INSTITUTIONAL
ECONOMICS

INSTITUTIONAL ECONOMICS
Social Order and Public Policy

Wolfgang Kasper

Professor of Economics, University of New South Wales, Canberra, Australia

Manfred E. Streit

Director, Max-Planck-Institute for Research into Economic Systems, Jena, Germany

THE LOCKE INSTITUTE

Edward Elgar
Cheltenham, UK • Northampton, MA, USA

Published by
Edward Elgar Publishing Limited
Glensanda House
Montpellier Parade
Cheltenham
Glos GL50 1UA
UK

Edward Elgar Publishing, Inc.
6 Market Street
Northampton
Massachusetts 01060
USA

A catalogue record for this book
is available from the British Library

Library of Congress Cataloging in Publication Data

Kasper, Wolfgang.
    Institutional economics : social order and public policy /
Wolfgang Kasper, Manfred E. Streit.
    Includes bibliographical references and index.
    "The Locke Institute."
    1. Institutional economics.   I. Streit, Manfred E.   II. Locke
Institute.   III. Title.
HB99.5.K37   1999
330–dc21

                                        98–21249
                                            CIP

ISBN 1 85898 941 8 (cased)

Typeset by Manton Typesetters, 5–7 Eastfield Road, Louth, Lincs, LN11 7AJ, UK.
Printed and bound in Great Britain by MPG Books Ltd, Bodmin, Cornwall

Contents

PART II   APPLICATIONS

List of Figures

List of Tables

Foreword

This book introduces the student, and others with a basic understanding of economics, to the rapidly evolving discipline of institutional economics. The central tenet of this discipline is that a modern economy is a complex, evolving system whose effectiveness in meeting diverse and changing human purposes depends on rules which constrain possibly opportunistic human behaviour (we call these rules 'institutions'). Institutions protect individual spheres of freedom, help to avoid or mitigate conflicts, and enhance the division of labour and knowledge, thereby promoting prosperity. Indeed, the rules that govern human interaction are so decisive for economic growth that the very survival and prosperity of humankind, whose numbers are bound to increase for some time yet, depend on the right institutions and the fundamental human values that underpin them.[1]

Institutional economics differs greatly from modern neoclassical economics, which is based on narrow assumptions about rationality and knowledge and which implicitly assumes the institutions as given. Institutional economics has important connections with jurisprudence, politics, sociology, anthropology, history, organisation science, management and moral philosophy. Because institutional economics is open to intellectual influences from a wide range of social sciences, this book recommends itself not only to the economist interested in economic growth, innovation, development, comparative economic systems and political economy, but also to students of these disciplines.

The realisation that institutions matter has spread rapidly over the past 20 years. This development was recently compared by one observer to the Copernican Revolution, in that it has turned the focus of economics from specific processes and outcomes to universal, abstract rules (M. Deaglio, in *Biblioteca della libertà*, no. 134, p. 3). The trailblazers of this approach were writers such as Friedrich von Hayek and others writing in the Austrian tradition, Ronald Coase, who alerted economists to the consequences of transaction costs, James Buchanan and others of the 'public choice' school, economic historians such as Douglass North, who discovered the importance of institutions by analysing past economic development, and economists such as William Vickery who showed the consequences of people having limited, asymmetric knowledge. The fact that these authors received Nobel Prizes in Economics in 1974 (Hayek), 1986 (Buchanan), 1991 (Coase), 1994 (North) and 1996 (Vickery) indicates that the study of institutional economics is in the ascendancy. The shift to a focus on institutions has also been furthered by theories of complex systems, such as chaos theory and fuzzy logic, which show that actions can frequently have unforeseeable side effects, so that process interventions by policy produce inferior outcomes to reliance on uniform general rules.

Although a growing number of scholars are grappling with the consequences of the complexity of economic life, this insight has in most countries not yet filtered through to public opinion, nor for that matter to many university courses. To be sure, the consequences of complexity are now widely understood in other areas such as ecology. Public opinion in many countries now understands that ecological systems are complex and evolving – and in many respects beyond human comprehension – so that interventions can have unpredictable and dangerous side-effects. Yet, when it comes to policy interventions in equally complex and open economic systems, similar caution is rarely advocated. Indeed, side-effects are routinely ruled out in the teaching of economics by the assumption of *ceteris paribus*.

The recent rise of institutional economics also owes much to events. In the mature industrial economies with electoral democracies, the traditional economic order under the institutions of capitalism has been decaying gradually, often imperceptibly, under the load of the unforeseen consequences of proliferating interventions and an increasing politicisation of economic life. This has led to slower economic growth and given rise to a widespread cynicism about public policy. 'In the last quarter of the Twentieth Century', writes institutional economist Thráinn Eggertsson (1997), 'unexpected difficulties in manipulating Western economic systems ... undermined the optimism of the early post-war era' about what can be achieved by public policy. But these experiences have also triggered more or less consistent attempts at economic reform (for example, privatisation and deregulation). Increasingly streamlined legal-institutional arrangements are seen as crucial to economic and social outcomes. It is accepted by increasing numbers of policy makers that institutions need to be cultivated. Observers in the new industrial countries and the less developed economies have also realised that conventional theories of economic growth excluded important, indeed essential, dimensions of the problem of economic development, in particular institutional development to achieve freedom, economic prosperity and security. The critical role of institutions is certainly evident when we analyse why the growth experiences, say, between countries in East Asian and African economies diverged so widely.

Another development that is drawing attention to the role of institutions is globalisation. In recent decades international competition has increased. To a considerable extent, this is also a competition between different institutional systems. Some rule systems have proved successful in attracting growth-promoting capital and enterprises; and countries which lost out are beginning to emulate the institutions of the successful countries.

Arguably the most powerful impetus to reintegrate the study of institutions and institutional change into economics came with the spectacular failure and collapse of the centrally planned socialist economies. The institutions of socialism had often discouraged citizens from drawing fully on their knowledge. As a consequence, they failed to keep pace with the capitalist market economies. The challenges of transforming the formerly socialist societies has now focused the minds of many economists on the importance of institutions to the exploitation of knowledge and the encouragement of enterprise and exchange. In a similar vein, heavily administered economies with a strong commitment to redistribution and public welfare provision, for example in western Europe, are experiencing a slowdown in innovation, growth and job creation. Many observers there, too, now argue for institutional reforms. To understand their arguments, it is necessary in the first place to integrate institutions explicitly into economic theories. It is, for example, simply not possible to explain satisfactorily why (re-)privatising many economic activities of government, such as welfare provision, will lead to overall gains and why deregulation has advantages, if the explicit analysis of institutions is eliminated from the research.

We belong to those economists who see the search for and testing of useful knowledge as the key driving force behind modern economic growth. Therefore, social devices that help us to economise on the cost of knowledge search are of central interest to economics. When we began to teach economics from this standpoint, we could not find a fully satisfactory introductory text. To be sure, there is no shortage of relevant literature, but most textbooks still suffer from the birth defect of assuming 'perfect knowledge'. This book is an effort to fill the gap.

The book begins with an introductory discussion why institutions matter. We show that the extraordinary growth of the world population and of living standards this century, as well as the dramatic differences between national growth rates, have a great deal to do with certain types of institutions, values and social orders. In Chapter 2, we define key concepts, such as 'institutions', 'economic order', 'coordination costs' and 'public policy'. We then discuss fundamental assumptions about human behaviour and acknowledge that people who act as agents for others may sometimes behave opportunistically and against the interests of the principals (Chapter 3). Although individuals tend to pursue their own purposes, they nevertheless share certain fundamental values with others in their community. For example, they aspire to freedom, security and material wellbeing. These fundamental values help to underpin social cohesion. They are discussed in Chapter 4. Then, we proceed to discuss the nature and role of institutions and the order that certain institutional arrangements facilitate (Chapters 5 and 6).

Whereas Chapters 2–6 are intended to lay the theoretical foundations for an understanding of institutional economics, the remaining chapters deal rather with the applied aspects of institutional economics. In Chapter 7, we analyse the foundations of the capitalist system, in particular private property and freedom of contract. The following chapter is focused on competition, a dynamic process in which entrepreneurial buyers and suppliers discover, develop and test useful knowledge. We shall differentiate between economic competition among sellers and buyers for the favours of the other side of the market and political competition for political influence. We then look at institutional arrangements that underpin economic organisations, such as business firms (Chapter 9). In Chapter 10, we look at the functions of government and the difficulties that arise when economic problems are addressed by collective, political action. We shall also discuss the precautions that need to be taken to prevent politicians and bureaucrats from acting against the interests of the citizens.

What has been learnt up to that point is used to discuss international economic exchanges and how national governments can be restrained from suppressing competitive challenges, and how institutional systems evolve (Chapters 11 and 12). In the final two chapters, we apply the institutional-economics approach to a discussion of some of the most topical issues in contemporary economics: why socialism failed; how the socialist system can be transformed; how the heavily administered, mature welfare states might be reformed to meet the competitive challenges from the new industrial countries; how new industrial countries, for example in Asia, can better protect themselves from crises in their development; and why the continued spread of prosperity around the world will ultimately depend on fostering appropriate institutions.

The development of the main themes in this book from basic premises demands a somewhat patient reader. Impatient readers may want to jump straight to Chapters 7–14, if they wish to find out quickly why property rights and free markets matter for prosperity and innovation, what is essential to the functioning of business and government organisations, and how institutional economics is applied to pressing policy issues. We urge these impatient readers to revise the Key Concepts throughout the earlier chapters, which we have interspersed in the text.

This book is a joint venture between two friends who began their academic careers as 'apprentices' in the same workshop in the mid-1960s: as PhD students and associates of Professor Herbert Giersch at Saarbrücken University, Germany, and as staffers with the German Council of Economic Advisers. Over the past quarter-century, our careers have taken us to far distant places and through differing experiences: the European and the East Asian–Australian life experience respectively. Yet most of our conclusions, and the way in which we reshaped our basic philosophies and the economics we once learnt, moved along similar trajectories. It was therefore not all that hard to engage in the dialogue from which this joint textbook was developed, despite the fact that we probably had very different types of student before the eye of our imagination when conceiving the various chapters. We happily admit that writing this book was even fun!

The reader will learn that it is often useful when discussing public policy to make value judgements about what is desirable and what is not. It behoves us therefore to declare explicitly that we hold certain preferences which some of our readers may not share or with which they clearly disagree. We place a high personal preference on individual freedom and see the individual as the ultimate reference point for all public policy. We do not attribute purposes separate from the individual to some abstract community such as 'the nation', or to non-human phenomena like Nature. We also prefer growing prosperity to contentment with modest material achievement, and hold the view that justice and equity refer to formal rules about treating people in equal circumstances equally – not equal outcomes irrespective of effort or good luck.

It seems to us that one cannot help but take such a position when one observes the transformation of the economy and society in east Germany, where much of this book was first conceived and drafted. The material and moral outcomes of the alternative, collectivist position, and of fuzzy institutional arrangements, become painfully evident when shuttling between various countries and societies. This is also obvious when one compares the quality of life for the broad mass of people in developing countries with differing economic systems, or when one observes the climate in collectivist welfare states and in those regimes that are based primarily on self-reliance, responsibility and initiative. These conclusions of course reveal our personal preferences and value judgements.

Leaving our own value judgements aside, we should also note at the outset that institutions reflect specific values and are instrumental in their pursuit. Values therefore have to be identified and explored as part of institutional economics. This should enable us to arrive at scientific statements about values which may be assessed critically as to their consequences – as distinct from value judgements with which one might agree or disagree.

Since most of institutional economics depends on complex verbal reasoning and reference to diverse disciplines, the reader may find the book harder to follow than a standard text in mainstream economic theory which relies, by and large, on simple mathematics. To make it easier for the reader not to lose the thread, we employ several didactic devices:

- at the beginning of each chapter, there is a short 'Primer' to serve as an appetiser and to draw the reader's attention to the main issues and their relevance;
- at the end of each chapter, we invite the reader to review the material by posing a number of provocative questions; they are intended to help readers check whether they have understood the most important elements of our argument;
- we highlight Key Concepts by interspersing them in the text; the intent is not to offer encyclopedic definitions but rather to ensure that the reader pays due attention to the key ideas which were developed in the preceding paragraphs and which constitute the major tools of institutional economics;
- at some points, we highlight what is said in the main text by offering mini case studies.

A book of this kind is built on the work of many scholars, not all of whom could ever be acknowledged by citing their work. Indeed, we owe much to the intellectual giants who preceded us; the only justification for attempting this work is that even a dwarf can see further when he stands on the shoulders of giants. In writing this book, we ran up a particularly heavy debt to one class of scholars whom we did not quote sufficiently: the many analysts – past and present – of the German economic tradition who paid more attention to institutions than did mainstream Anglo-Saxon economists. The great masters of the past have of course been translated into English and can be cited. But German economics offers a sophisticated and differentiated strand of modern institutional economics whose findings and subtleties have not, as yet, been fully received on the global academic stage. We exploited our comparative and absolute advantages of being able to read German, but did not assume that our average reader would have access to German sources and decided not to make our full academic debts explicit by citing much of the German-language literature.[2]

A particular word of thanks goes to the Foundation for Economic Education in New York for permitting us to reprint Leonard Read's classic piece on the division of labour and knowledge, 'I, Pencil', which is reproduced in the Appendix, and to Paul Johnson, London, the Centre for Independent Studies, Sydney, and the Fraser Institute, Vancouver, for their permission to reproduce passages and materials to which they hold the copyright.

For a part of the time spent on drafting this book, Wolfgang Kasper benefited from a special studies programme of his employer, the University of New South Wales, which freed him from lecturing and administrative routines and gave him a travel grant. On two occasions, he enjoyed the hospitality of the new Max-Planck-Institute for Research into Economic Systems at Jena, Germany, where much of this book was conceived and developed. Both authors owe a debt of gratitude to all those scholars at the Institute who took an active interest in the project, in particular Daniel Kiwit, Stefan Voigt, Oliver Volkart, Antje Funck, née Mangels and Michael Wohlgemuth. The latter two gave generously of their time and knowledge when they commented in detail on an earlier draft. Anna Kasper in Sydney, Mathias Drehmann in London and John W. Wood at Lincoln University in New Zealand also contributed useful comments and criticism. We also owe thanks to Professor Fred Foldvary of the Kennedy School of Business in California for critical comments on an earlier draft. On a more practical level, this book owes much to Mrs Uta Lange in Jena and in particular Mrs Firzia Pepper in Canberra who assisted ably and with great dedication in the production of the manuscript.

Finally we wish to record our appreciation to the editors at Edward Elgar Publishing for numerous professional queries and stylistic improvements.

The major theme pervading this book is that human knowledge is limited, as is, of course, our own knowledge. We therefore accept the usual responsibility for all remaining oversights, mistakes and misinterpretations.

We hope that the reader will enjoy the book and adopt the novel way of looking at life from the angle of economic and social institutions.

WOLFGANG KASPER
MANFRED E. STREIT

On language

'Liberal' and 'liberalism' are used throughout in their original sense, namely, to imply freedom of information, thought, exchange and so on, rather than in the North American sense of 'redistributive-interventionist'.

Notes

1. Throughout the book, we shall use the term 'institutional economics'. In the 1960s and 1970s, when the importance of institutions for economic analysis was rediscovered by a growing number of authors, the term 'new institutional economics' was used to differentiate these modern efforts from the earlier, normally much more descriptive treatment of institutions, both by the German 'historical school' and the American institutionalists in the late nineteenth and early twentieth century.

2. Readers with access to German are in the first instance referred to the journal *Ordo*, which has over the decades been the main market place for German *ordo* liberal writing.

    In addition to Streit (1991 and 1995, cited in the Bibliography), the following books would have been cited repeatedly had our book been written for German speakers:

    W. Eucken ([1952] 1990), *Grundsätze der Wirtschaftspolitik*, Tübingen: Mohr-Siebeck; F. Böhm (1980), *Freiheit und Ordnung in der Marktwirtschaft*, ed. E.-J. Mestmäcker, Baden-Baden: Nomos; E. Streißler and C. Watrin (eds) (1980), *Zur Theorie marktwirtschaftlicher Ordnungen*, Tübingen: Mohr-Siebeck; W. Stützel, Ch. Watrin, H. Willgerodt and K. Hohmann (eds) (1981), *Grundtexte der Sozialen Marktwirtschaft*, Stuttgart and New York: Fischer; V. Vanberg (1982), *Markt und Organisation*, Tübingen: Mohr-Siebeck; A. Schüller (ed) (1983), *Property Rights und ökonomische Theorie*, München: Vahlen; D. Cassel, B. J. Ramb and H. J. Thieme (eds) (1988), *Ordnungspolitik*, München: Vahlen; G. Radnitzky and H. Bouillon (eds) (1991), *Ordnungstheorie und Ordnungspolitik*, Berlin, Heidelberg, New York: Springer; Ernst-Joachim Mestmäcker (1993), *Recht in der offenen Gesellschaft*, Baden-Baden: Nomos.

CHAPTER 1

Introduction:
Why Institutions Matter

All human interaction requires a degree of predictability. Individual actions become more predictable when people are bound by rules (which we shall call institutions). Institutions are of course also needed to facilitate economic life: economic exchanges cannot function in a vacuum. Indeed, the type and quality of institutions make a great difference to how well the members of a community are able to satisfy their economic aspirations and how fast the economy grows.

To begin with an empirical dimension, we review the unprecedented record of global economic growth and the role institutions have played in it. During the second half of the twentieth century, real per capita incomes have grown faster and the experience of rising living standards has reached more people on earth than ever before. And this has been accompanied by unprecedented increases in the world population. This experience was far from uniform, a fact that raises interesting questions about what explains the differences, for example between the fast growth in East Asia and the slow growth or even decline in Africa and the former Socialist bloc: why is it that people in the fast-developing economies marshalled resources more successfully and were more enterprising in meeting material requirements?

A brief survey of theories of economic growth will show that growth is a complex phenomenon. Neoclassical growth theory can only identify proximate conditions of growth, such as capital accumulation and technical change. To explain *why* people save, invest, learn and search for useful knowledge, we have to look at different institutional and value systems behind the successes and the failures. We will also see that there are numerous barriers to growth and that certain types of institution motivate people more than others to overcome existing obstacles to growth.

1

Man's behavior in the market relationship, reflecting the propensity to truck and barter, and the manifold variations ... that this relationship can take; these are the proper subjects for the economist's study.
(*James Buchanan, 'What should economists do?', 1964*)

[After having deposited a considerable sum of money in a bank in a foreign country:] It hit me that I'd handed over my [funds] to a total stranger in a bank I knew nothing about in a city where I knew almost nobody ... in exchange for nothing but a flimsy paper with a scribble in a language I didn't understand. What I had going for me, I reflected, ... was a great web of trust in the honesty of business. It struck me with awe how much that we take for granted in business transactions suspends from that gossamer web.
(*Jane Jacobs, Systems of Survival, 1992*)

Economic growth will occur if property rights make it worthwhile to undertake socially productive activity ... Governments take over the protection and enforcement of property rights because they can do it at a lower cost than private volunteer groups. However, the ... needs of government may induce the protection of certain property rights which hinder rather than promote growth; therefore we have no guarantee that productive institutional arrangements will emerge.
(*Douglass C. North and Robert P. Thomas, The Rise of the Western World, 1973*)

When measured by decades, the economy is always in upheaval. For the past few hundred years, every generation has found more efficient ways of getting work done, and the cumulative benefits have been enormous. The average person today enjoys a much better life than the nobility did a few centuries ago. It would be great to have a king's land, but what about his lice?
(*Bill Gates, The Road Ahead, 1993*)

1.1   Why Do Institutions Matter?

One person cannot interact with another without some shared understanding about how the other will respond and some sanction if the other responds arbitrarily and contrary to agreement. Private individuals and businesses can only buy, sell, employ labour, invest and explore innovations if they can have some confidence that their expectations will be met. Much of the exchange between individuals and firms is based on repetitive operations, and we prefer these to be predictable because that reduces frictions and uncertainties. Just imagine, if your next bill at the check-out in the supermarket came to ten times what you paid for the same basket of goods at the last visit! Or if the bank where you deposited your savings suddenly refused to honour your cheque! Human interactions, including those in economic life, depend on some sort of trust which is based on an order that is facilitated by rules banning unpredictable and opportunistic behaviour. We call these rules 'institutions'.

In our daily lives we interact with numerous people and organisations whom we scarcely know, but in whose predictable behaviour we place great faith. We hand over our hard-earned money to a teller clerk, whose face we may not remember five minutes later, in a bank about whose reserves and management we know nothing. We allow ourselves to be operated upon by surgeons we have hardly met, in hospitals we had never seen from the inside before. We prepay for the delivery of a car made in a foreign country by workers we will never meet. Yet, in all these situations, we trust that we will get worthwhile service and that promises to deliver will be kept. Why? Because all these people have specialised knowledge and skills to offer and because they are bound by institutions – constraints on their opportunistic temptations not to deliver or to short-change us. We are able to assume that selfish breaches of the contracts into which we enter will incur sanctions of one sort or another. Come to think of it, modern economic life depends rather precariously on numerous written and unwritten rules. If they are widely violated – as when society collapses after a lost war or in internal chaos – many of the human interactions on which we depend for our wellbeing are no longer possible; living standards and the quality of life then plummet. The institutions which normally prevent this are thus the very foundations of our living standards and our sense of security and community.

The Institutional Deficit in Economics and Public Policy

The mainstream of twentieth century neoclassical economics has, by and large, assumed that institutions are exogenously given and that agents have perfectly adjusted to them. At best it has treated them as a complication of economic models. The standard assumption is that people transact business without frictions and costs. In defence of this stance, it is argued that all theorising is necessarily based on abstraction, and that one abstracts from phenomena that do not matter to what one wishes to analyse. To give an example: although the phenomenon of gravity is very important to our general understanding of the physical world, we do not explicitly incorporate gravity into the analysis of economic growth.

However, this defence is wholly inappropriate. Institutions reduce the costs of coordinating human actions and therefore are of central importance to understanding human interaction. We can demonstrate this either by plausible, everyday examples or by showing that assuming away institutions has led to critical deficits in economic knowledge.

At the level of everyday life, institutions already matter in the nursery: when children are given their toys as their own personal property, it can be observed that they take care and can be encouraged to be generous in lending their property to their playmates. When, on the other hand, everything belongs to all of them and to no one in particular, they tend to neglect their 'assets' and fight over the possession of specific toys (Alchian, in Henderson, 1993, pp. 73–4). Another example which can show how an institution helps people obtain their goals more effectively is money. When people have to rely on barter to obtain the goods and services they want to consume, but do not produce, they face great uncertainty about whether they will be able to obtain them. Will they find a taker for the vegetables they have grown? Who wants to exchange these for a computer program which they want? More importantly, they may not even find out what they are able or want to buy. If, on the other hand, there is an asset which is generally accepted as a medium of exchange (money) whose supply and uses are bound by institutions, people can have much greater confidence that they will be able to obtain what they desire, and their search and transaction costs are much lower than with barter. Money thus helps to economise on coordination costs.

At the level of practical economic policy, standard neoclassical mainstream economics repeatedly failed in recent years to explain or predict real-world phenomena, because it excluded from its models institutions and the reasons for their existence. The poverty of standard economics became clear, for example, in explaining the growth process. Policy advice in developing countries was often misplaced, because many economic advisers made the habitual assumption that institutions do not matter. In reality, many imported concepts foundered because the institutions in developing countries differed greatly from those in the developed countries and because indigenous institutions had to be adapted if certain policy concepts were to work. The institutional framework in which modern production and trade can flourish can therefore frequently not be taken for granted. And western economists trained in a tradition that does so are ill-prepared to diagnose why sustained growth does not materialise and what might be done to remedy the situation (Olson, 1996). Arguably the most critical test for neoclassical economics came when the command economies in the former Soviet empire stagnated and finally collapsed. Western economists – and international organisations populated by neoclassical economists – failed to predict this epochal event and were at first unable to give sound advice because they ignored institutions. After all, the demise of socialism poses the challenge to create and foster such fundamental institutions as private property rights, contract law and the rule of law in general.

Another way of making the same fundamental point is to draw attention to the high and rising share of coordination costs in the total cost of producing and distributing the national product in modern economies. A large part of the service sector – which now accounts for no less than 66 per cent of the total OECD's economic product – is concerned with facilitating transactions and organising human interaction. The 'coordination sector' of the modern economy is necessary to facilitate the growing division of labour and knowledge on which our living standard is based. To assume, as neoclassical economics does, that there are no transaction costs and hence that there is no need for rules to economise on these costs, pushes more than half of all economic endeavours in advanced economies aside, namely that large and rapidly growing segment of the service sector that deals with transactions and coordination. By underrating the coordination problem, neoclassical economics biases analysis towards production and physical distribution, and therefore becomes less relevant for much of modern business which is concerned with organising and coordinating decisions with suppliers and buyers.

A similar blind spot is the source of failure in diagnosing why the heavily administered welfare economies are experiencing an economic slowdown, high unemployment, growing distrust and widespread voter cynicism. The gradual erosion and decay of essential institutions – such as reliable property rights, self-responsibility and the rule of law – in interest-group dominated democracies has often gone unnoticed. Ways to turn back the clock were not readily discovered because institutional change was not part of what most economists analyse.

It was also discovered long ago by economic historians, if indeed they ever were unaware, that institutional change is an important and exciting part of their discipline (Gibbon, [1776–88] 1996). Nobel Prize winner and economic historian Douglass North put it well when he wrote:

> the neoclassical paradigm is devoid of institutions ... The currently fashionable growth models of economists do not confront the issue of the underlying incentive structure that is assumed in their models. These lacunae in our understanding have been forcefully brought to the attention of economists by the events in Central and Eastern Europe ... where the challenge is to restructure the economies ... in order to create a hospitable environment for economic growth. Can that restructuring be done without deliberate attention to institutions? Delineating the institutional characteristics of such markets is a first step in answering these questions. (North, 1994, p. 257; also see North in Drobak and Nye, 1997, pp. 3–12)

It has also become clear that standard economic theory is only of limited value to business economics. Many practical business people rightly find economic theories barren, abstract and of little relevance to their pursuits. This is why some of the recent revival in institutional economics has come from the study of business history, economic sociology, the 'new organisation science' and 'law and economics'. These disciplines have explicitly incorporated institutions into their models to offer more apposite practical advice.

The Rise of Institutional Economics

Because of mounting dissatisfaction with standard economics and its abstract, arid models, many scholars are now (again) taking up the central proposition of institutional economics, namely that institutions play a crucial part in coordinating individual actions. The analysis of the foundations, evolution, content, consistency and enforcement of rules can tell us a lot about central economic phenomena, such as economic growth or how markets function. It is now increasingly being realised that institutions constitute critical social capital: they are, so to speak, the 'software' that channels the interaction of people and the development of society. Indeed, we are finding that the software is normally more important than the 'hardware' (tangible phenomena, such as physical capital).

As a consequence of these insights, there has been growing interest in institutional economics, a way of looking at real-life economic phenomena which differs considerably from the standard neoclassical approach to economics, focusing on the conditions of allocation of *given* resources to satisfy *given* wants. As we shall see in Chapter 2, the approach of institutional economics does not take resources or human wants as given, but rather focuses on evolution and economic growth through the discovery and utilisation of new wants and new useful resources.

Since institutions are critical to economic growth, we will use the remainder of this chapter to show that the extraordinary postwar economic growth experience cannot be satisfactorily explained without an understanding of institutions.

1.2 The Record of Economic Growth

The Long-term View

The economic experience of humanity over the long term has been characterised by very slow progress in productivity and living standards. Population growth normally matched technical and economic advances, so average living standards remained almost the same over the centuries. Basic criteria of average material living conditions – such as longevity, basic health, child mortality, the incidence of famine and major epidemics – did not change much for the average citizen between the neolithic revolution, which heralded the beginning of agriculture and animal husbandry some 10 000 years ago, and the seventeenth century, when the industrial revolution began (Kahn, 1979, pp. 7–25; Rostow, 1978). European peasants lived with the reality of cold, grime, hunger, disease and early death almost to the same extent as their forefathers had in Roman times, and it is debatable whether the average Chinese peasants in the first half of the twentieth century were any better off than their forebears during the Han dynasty 2000 years earlier. Historians often concentrate on the rulers and the few rich, but they remind us infrequently of the living conditions of the average man or woman.[1]

We have to remind ourselves of the long-term economic experience of mankind to appreciate the revolution which has taken place more recently and to see that the development of growth-facilitating institutions has been central to the spread of prosperity. After many centuries during which living standards had at best risen by almost imperceptible fractions of a per cent per year, first England, then north-west Europe and north America witnessed sustained rises in the living standards of the *average* citizen. This process began in the late eighteenth century and gathered steam during the nineteenth, when three countries – Britain, the US and Germany – were producing two-thirds of all manufactured output in the world. During the nineteenth century, one country after another took off into a process of industrialisation and sustained economic growth. Towards the end of the nineteenth century and in the first half of the twentieth, per capita incomes in the countries now known as OECD countries, that is, the old industrial countries with essentially capitalist market economies, grew on average at an unprecedented 1.4 per cent annually, despite the destructions of two world wars during the first half of the twentieth century (Table 1.1). None the less, at the end of the twentieth century less than one-fifth of the world population are producing four-fifths of world output, so the vast majority of humankind has much scope for catching up with the most productive communities.

Table 1.1   Modern economic growth: per capita income adjusted for inflation (% p.a.)

Period	Old industrial countries (OECD)	Less-developed countries
Up to early 19th century	Virtual stagnation (some take off)	Virtual stagnation
1820–1870	+0.6	↑
1870–1913	+1.4	↓
1913–1950	+1.3	(some take off)
1950–1973	+3.5	+2.7 (great divergence)
1973–present	+2.5	+1.7 (great divergence)

Sources: Maddison (1991) and own updates

At the end of the second world war, many observers depicted the growth record of the nineteenth and early twentieth centuries as a passing phenomenon and predicted secular stagnation. But they were wrong. Not only did average per capita incomes in OECD countries rise by an unprecedented annual average of 3.5 per cent from 1950 to the onset of the oil crisis of 1973, but the phenomenon of economic growth began to spread to the rest of the world, creating developing countries in many parts of the world. Industries had spread outwards from established centres of industry and high income in earlier epochs, but by 1950 modern methods of industrial production were still the almost exclusive possession of European civilisation. The most notable exceptions were Japan and a few regional industrial centres elsewhere, such as Shanghai.

Between 1950 and 1973, the average annual growth rate for the uneven, amorphous average of developing countries was 2.75 per cent, and a subgroup, the 'new industrial economies' of East Asia, grew much faster, beginning to capture world markets for their exports and narrowing the gap to western standards of technology, productivity and income in record time (World Bank, 1993; Kasper, 1993). Since the oil crisis of 1973, global economic growth has slowed a little – to 2.5 per cent per annum on average in the old industrial countries of OECD, and on average 1.7 per cent in the developing countries. But the pace of economic progress is still unprecedented by any long-term historic standard. In the growth-orientated East Asia-Pacific economies, average real per capita incomes have risen by some 8 per cent annually between the late 1960s and mid-1990s – nearly a seven-fold rise within one generation. Such a dynamic growth experience, affecting some 1.75 billion people, is unprecedented in the history of humankind.

If long-term comparisons of living standards are made, as economic historians have long been doing (Rostow, 1978; Maddison, 1991), it has to be concluded that present-day living standards in India are roughly equal to those in Britain after the Napoleonic wars, that average living standards in China in the 1990s compare with American income levels before the first world war, and that living standards of the average inhabitant of the dynamic East Asian market economies now probably approach those which the richest Europeans (the Swiss) enjoyed around 1950.

Demographic Transition

The rise in living standards went along with an unprecedented rise in world population. When modern industry first started in England (say around 1750), the total world population stood at an estimated 790 million. Whereas the number of people on earth is estimated to have increased by 68 per cent during the nineteenth century, it will have gone up by no less than a further 370 per cent by the close of the twentieth (Rostow, 1978, pp. 1–44). Historically, human life expectancy was short. For example, women in France in the 1740s could expect to live on average only about 25 years. Now, the average life span of French women is 81 years. This has much to do with economic growth. It ended the ever-present threat of starvation (there were 16 general famines in France in the eighteenth century alone) and enhanced medical resources (in eighteenth-century London, 10 per cent of all deaths were from smallpox, a disease that vanished completely with general vaccination). About one-quarter of children born in pre-Revolution Paris were abandoned by their mothers. The diet of ordinary people was monotonous and unbalanced. When living standards rose, the gains were often channelled into better health care, famine relief and improved nutrition, so that fewer people died early. In one country after another, mortality rates dropped fairly rapidly after the onset of economic development, whereas birth rates declined with a lag and more slowly, leading to a temporary population explosion. The phenomenon is called 'demographic transition'.

Likewise, the rapid rise in living standards in the Asia-Pacific region since 1970 was accompanied by rapid decreases in mortality rates.

Thus, on average of the one and three-quarter billion population of this region, infant mortality dropped from 77 per thousand in 1970 to 40 per thousand in 1995 (World Bank, 1997, p. 225). This is typical; human life expectancy has invariably risen with living standards. Growth has increased human life spans, a fact that can be illustrated both by data from the US ...

	1901	1995
Income level (in constant US$ per capita)	100	376
Average life expectancy (years)	58.8	77

... as well as with the more recent data from the East Asia-Pacific region:

	1970	1995
Income level (in constant US$ per capita)	100	642
Average life expectancy (men and women, years)	59	68

Source: World Bank

The rapid rise in population growth tends to subside again with continuing economic growth, better education and rising material aspirations (Freeman and Berelson, 1974, pp. 36–7; Kahn, 1979).

The most remarkable aspect of the global economic experience this century has undoubtedly been that most of the rapidly increasing numbers of people on earth are better fed, clad, housed, educated and entertained than their forebears. There are now only relatively few areas where the long-term human experience of misery persists or where material living conditions have deteriorated, most notably in south Asia, Africa and some of the former centrally planned economies.

The secular and global shift from stagnation to growth during the twentieth century has of course not created Utopia on earth. However, in most places and for most of the time, higher income levels have proven to be compatible with the other fundamental values to which people aspire, such as freedom, justice and security.

O Key Concepts

Growth is measured by a sustained rise of the value of goods and services per capita in real terms, that is, after elimination of the effects of inflation.

Some economists have argued for making allowances for other factors, such as environmental amenity. But the measurement difficulties are so intractable that per capita income (or per capita gross domestic product) is still the most widely used measure of growth.

The term **demographic transition** refers to the temporary acceleration of the population growth rate that occurs after take-off into sustained economic growth. It results from the coincidence of a fairly rapid drop in death rates and a lagged fall in birth rates. ●

Some Country Experiences

The global growth experience sketched so far was not uniform. On the whole, countries that were ahead at the beginning of the twentieth century – the US, Britain, Australia – still rank amongst the most wealthy nations: indeed, the societies that were most affluent and productive in 1820 managed to achieve the steepest increase in living standards during the nineteenth century. Most of the countries that were poorest nearly 200 years ago are still lagging behind.

However, there are remarkable exceptions to this general rule: Japan, a poor, isolated country at the beginning of the nineteenth century, caught up with the richest countries in Europe and America in the second half of the twentieth century (Figure 1.1[2]). The East Asian city economies of Hong Kong and Singapore (not shown) have also caught up with the West. A similar catch-up process got under way in other East Asian market economies, such as Korea (see figure). Equally remarkably, the most populous nations in the Asia-Pacific region – China and Indonesia – have grown fast after experiencing near-stagnation in per capita incomes at a very low level during the first half of the twentieth century. As far as the statistics can be trusted, living standards in fast-growing countries such as South Korea, Taiwan, Malaysia and even Thailand have by the mid-1990s overtaken living standards in many countries of eastern Europe (World Bank, various).

In some cases, per capita incomes declined over considerable periods, for example in India and China during the first half of this century, and more recently in Africa (note Ghana and South Africa in Figure 1.1). Likewise, it is apparent that formerly communist countries – such as the USSR/Russia and the Czech Republic in Figure 1.1 – underwent a slowdown in growth and then, as their economic institutions unravelled, an absolute decline. Thus, Russian per capita incomes are estimated by the World Bank to have fallen by 40 per cent between 1985 and 1995 (World Bank, 1997, p. 215). This has had pervasive

Figure 1.1   World economic growth, 1820–1995 (1990 constant international US$)

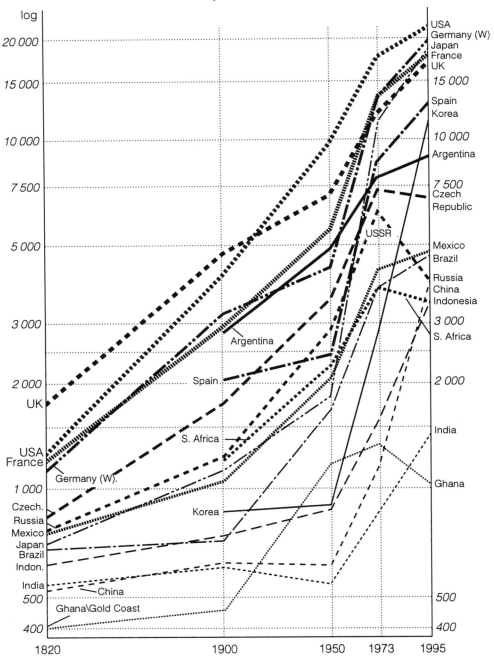

Note: Logarithmic scales, as used here, show a steady rate of growth as a straight line, an acceleration as a steeper gradient than that straight line, and a deceleration of growth as a less-steep gradient.

Source: Maddison (1995) and own updates.

social consequences, for example on life span and health. To cite but one example, the incidence of diphtheria, which was negligible in Russia in the 1980s, rose to about 50 000 in the early 1990s. All this goes to show that economic growth is far from automatic and that the conditions of economic growth need to be cultivated, lest far-reaching economic and non-economic consequences be suffered.

Steep drops in living standards, such as those experienced in Russia, suggest questions about the fundamental causes for such an unusual experience. Even casual analysis points to the lesson that this has much to do with the decay of the institutions of a society. The experience of a messy transition from a failing set of institutions to another socioeconomic order certainly shows that high living standards are not automatic, but that they depend on the coordination rules of the economic game, the institutions (for more on transition problems, see Chapter 13).

Economic stagnation and negative growth, it would seem on *a priori* grounds, are associated with closed economies, civil and international strife, dramatic changes to economic systems and heavy constraints on private initiative and ownership (lack of liberty); whereas fast, sustained growth is associated with secure property rights, competition and openness (Fraser Institute, 1997). This hypothesis certainly deserves detailed exploration and explanation.

More generally, the question arises: what explains economic growth?

1.3   Explaining Economic Growth

The Mobilisation of Production Factors

When economists try to explain the remarkable record of sustained growth in human productivity and incomes, they discover that more and more explanatory factors have to be drawn upon in order to come to grips with this complex phenomenon.

In the 1940s and 1950s, economists emphasised the importance of mobilising capital (K) for long-term growth, assuming that growth depended on capital accumulation (savings, net investment).

> Central factor of growth: K

In modern economies, capital accumulation normally requires two separate acts by different people: (a) the postponement of consumption from current income, the 'savings sacrifice', and (b) the borrowing of savings by enterprises coupled with the installation of productive machinery, buildings and other items of physical capital (investment). The process of capital formation was often depicted as potentially unstable (Harrod–Domar theory).

Some economists of the 1940s and 1950s saw growth as a temporary phenomenon, because they assumed that growing amounts of capital investment would lead to a declining marginal productivity of capital. In that respect, they echoed the nineteenth-century prediction by Karl Marx (1818–83), who had forecast the eventual downfall of the capitalist system because investors would sooner or later run out of ideas for profitable uses of capital, so that the rate of return on capital would drop. As we now know, they were thoroughly wrong.

In the 1950s, the economics profession became uncomfortable with the narrow focus on capital mobilisation as an explanation of the growth process. This happened at a time when growth had resumed vigorously after the war. Economists now drew on the notion of a national production function, a relationship in which inputs such as capital, labour (L) and technology (TEC) are related to predictable amounts of output. Nineteenth-century theories, which had asserted that population growth is a key influence on economic growth, were now revived and related to the growth of the labour force.

A rapid growth of labour supply was normally seen as a positive influence on economic growth. All inputs of production factors were assumed to have positive but decreasing returns to scale (Solow, 1988, summarises earlier writings by himself and others on this type of theory):

> Central factors of growth: K, L, TEC

This neoclassical approach had the advantage of demonstrating that the growth process need not be unstable or run inevitably into declining rates of increase, as Marx had asserted. Technically speaking, economists no longer thought in terms of a *given* production function, but realised that better technology lifted the production function. This means that better technology, for example, enables given flows of capital and labour to be translated into more output. The theory also allowed for the obvious fact that factor prices can change – for example, when increasing capital surpluses reduce capital interest rates – and induce factor substitution: cheaper capital can be used in greater proportions to save on expensive labour. For such labour–capital substitution to be possible, technology has to be recognised explicitly, because substitution requires changing technologies. Indeed, from the 1960s, technical innovation became one of the focal interests of researchers who explored the reasons for economic growth.

The Hardware and the Software of Growth

That quest received a further boost in the 1960s when economists began to stress the important influence of better education and skill acquisition (SK): processes that add to what has come to be known as 'human capital' (Becker, 1964).

> **Central factors of growth: K, L, TEC, SK**

This line of inquiry underlined the insight that better technical knowledge and better skills were needed to ensure that growing capital stocks were used with rising capital productivity. It soon became apparent that improvements in the 'software of development' (skills, technical and organisational knowledge) ensured the better efficiency of the 'hardware of development' (labour, capital).

As the 1960s wore on, other observers emphasised the contribution of natural resources to growth and pointed to a possible eventual exhaustion of some natural resources (NR) (Club of Rome, see Meadows *et al.*, 1972). Yet economists with an understanding of knowhow and technology held the optimistic view that rising scarcity prices for some natural resources would mobilise new knowledge of how to obtain more such resources or how to economise on available resources, so as to open new avenues for growth (Beckerman, 1974; Arndt, 1978).

Data for the 'software factors' were hard to obtain. But it was shown in many quantitative analyses of economic growth (based on the assumption of a neoclassical production function and competitive markets) that these factors were indeed often very important. Often, half or more of the measured rise in living standards could be plausibly attributed to third factors, that is, inputs other than labour and capital (Denison, 1967). In particular, it was found that the differences between slow- and fast-growing economies could often be 'explained' by third factors (Chenery *et al.*, 1986; Barro and Sala-I-Martin, 1995, pp. 414–61).

However, while offering a useful quantitative perception of what mattered to long-term growth performance, the analysis did not really *explain* why certain societies accumulated more physical and human capital than others. All the above-mentioned analyses offered only proximate explanations of growth. It was still not possible to tell *why* people save and invest, exploit natural resources, acquire skills or fail to do so (Giersch, 1980; Harberger, 1984).

Other economists who analysed economic growth in old and new industrial countries focused on an observation already made in the 1930s, namely that the structural composition of economic activity changes systematically with rising income levels. In particular, manufacturing was the 'engine of growth' over a certain range of incomes, growing faster than the economy as a whole (Syrquin, 1988; Rostow, 1978; Fels, 1972). Beyond a certain income level, services tended to grow disproportionately fast. It was also observed that different types of industries flourished at different income levels: labour-intensive industries have the growth edge when incomes (and wages) are low, and more capital- and skill-intensive industries when incomes rise. The structural composition of the national product highlighted the fact that, behind the summary, macroeconomic phenomenon of growth, there were in reality organically evolving microeconomic structures. Economies with a high degree of price flexibility and high factor mobility tended to grow faster than rigid economies (Kasper, 1982, pp. 71–96). Structural change (ΔSTR) therefore is part and parcel of the growth process:

> Central phenomena of growth: K, L, TEC, SK, NR, ΔSTR

It was soon also found that political processes often do much to rigidify economic structures, both in less developed countries (where established interest groups might rule) and developed, democratic economies (where lobbies and self-seeking power groups might capture political and administrative processes to resist structural adjustment to new conditions).

Enterprise, Knowledge and Institutions

This microeconomic focus blended well with a renewed and more sophisticated focus on the central role of knowledge: how is new, useful knowledge best found, tested and applied? What motivates the agents of that process – the entrepreneurs [E] – to mobilise production factors, to risk innovative uses of knowledge and to try out structural changes?

Central processes of growth:
K, L, TEC, SK, NR, ΔSTR

↑

Entrepreneurs

In the 1970s, economic theorists drew on the work done in the first half of the century by writers such as Joseph Schumpeter (1883–1950) and the Austrian school of economics (Ludwig von Mises, 1881–1973; Friedrich August Hayek, 1899–1992), who had studied the role of the entrepreneur in economic progress and the importance of competition as a discovery procedure for useful human knowledge (Hayek, 1937; 1945; 1978; Kirzner, 1960, 1973, 1997; Kilby, 1971; Machlup, 1981–4; Blandy *et al.*, 1985). They held that the evolution of knowledge, technology and the economy was driven by risk-taking agents of knowledge discovery – but only if they had a material incentive to be on the alert and to innovate and if they were exposed to ongoing challenges of competition.

Knowledge can only be exploited and multiplied if people with specialist knowledge can cooperate. A better division of labour – which is in reality a better division and coordination of knowledge – is thus the real source of economic progress. This insight is not new. Scottish economist-philosopher Adam Smith wrote over 200 years ago: 'It is the great multiplication of the productions of all the different arts in consequence of the division of labour which occasions, in a well-governed society, that universal opulence which extends itself to the lowest ranks of the people' (Smith, [1776] 1970–1, p. 10).

Since the mid-1970s, the quest to explain economic growth has also been given considerable impulses by long-term economic history (North and Thomas, 1973, 1977; North, 1992; Jones, [1981] 1987, 1988; Rosenberg and Birdzell, 1986; Hodgson, 1988). These analyses showed why great advances in technical and organisational knowledge had been made in the industrial revolution. These advances did not come about suddenly, but had depended crucially on the gradual evolution of institutions favourable to capital accumulation and exchange in markets (individual civil liberties; property rights; effective protection of contracts under the law; limited government). They demonstrated that capitalist entrepreneurs had not been able to produce sustained economic growth where there was no trust, but relied crucially on economic, civil and political liberties, as well as on the favourable institutional frameworks that underpin mutual trust (Scully, 1991, 1992; Porter and Scully, 1995).

A related line of inquiry asked why the great advances in technical knowledge in non-European cultures had not led to an industrial revolution. In particular, it had long been a puzzle of economic history why China's excellent technology, especially in the Sung dynasty (960–1278), was never translated into an industrial revolution. These analyses pointed to the lack of certain social, political and legal preconditions – in short, institutions – in China and other huge Asian economies. In those large, closed economies, the rulers did not have to compete to attract or retain entrepreneurial, knowledgeable people in their jurisdiction (as was the case in post-medieval Europe). The rulers did not have to cultivate those institutions that mobile capital and enterprise found attractive (Jones, [1981] 1987). After examining alternative explanations for the failure of the Chinese to set off a sustained industrial revolution, a team of economic historians came to the conclusion that:

> [the individual members of Chinese] society could reduce transaction costs only so far, not far enough to put the economy on a course for sustained intensive growth ... Little was provided [by government] in the way of infrastructure or services. Notably, there was no independent legal system, no protection for valuables carried over the roads, no policeman to guard the standing crops ... There were formal courts of law, but they lacked systematic procedures involving such nuisances as real evidence. Contracts were not enforceable ... Business dealings tended to be face-to-face or confined to groups with which the merchants or artisans were already affiliated for non-business reasons.
> (*Jones* et al., *1994, p. 33*)

In other words, deficiencies in institutional development in Asia negated the reaping of the fruits of technical progress and a potentially large market. Douglass North concluded in the same vein: 'The historical study of economic growth is a study of institutional innovations that permit increasingly complex exchanges to be realised by reducing the transaction (and production) costs of such exchanges' (North, in James and Thomas, 1994, p. 258). Sustained differences in economic growth rates cannot be explained without reference to institutions (Olson, 1996).

Institutions – to which Adam Smith had already referred in the quote above when he spoke of 'a well-governed society' – have more recently been again identified as important to the coordination of complex, dynamic economic life by the theory of evolving, complex systems. Mathematicians and natural scientists have shown that broad patterns of behaviour can often be identified, yet even small changes in a variable may have unpredictable, significant side-effects which subsequently evolve into major impacts on the system (chaos theory). The same analytical approach can explicate the uncertainties in economic and business life which evolves within very complex, changing networks. Therefore, human interaction in the economy depends greatly on fairly regular patterns on which people may rely. If these are disturbed by policy interventions, unforeseen side-effects evolve, which makes it impossible to plan precise outcomes. Instead, coordination requires general, abstract and adaptive rules of interaction and coordination – in short, institutions (Parker and Stacey, 1995). Coming from an original historic-comparative background, John Powelson also highlighted the central role of institutions in long-term economic development (Powelson, 1994). Only with the help of such rules can coordination be enhanced and economic efficiency and living standards grow.

These various strands of inquiry added empirical substance to the teachings of the neo-Austrian school (as well as continental European researchers in the *ordo* liberal school and writers in the public-choice tradition) who emphasised the crucial importance of institutions to entrepreneurship in discovering useful knowledge and in marshalling the resources of capital, labour, skills and raw materials, so that new and growing outputs are created (Hayek, 1973, 1976a, 1979a; Eucken, [1940]1992; Buchanan, 1991; also Casson, 1993). Growth is then the statistically measured reflection of the actions of entrepreneurs, consumers, savers, producers and traders to obtain what people value more highly.

Empirical research has also pointed to a further, related aspect, namely the importance of preferences for material betterment, as well as widely shared preferences for a number of fundamental values, such as freedom, peace, justice and security. Appropriate institutions are a necessary, but not sufficient, condition for growth. Entrepreneurs, and people generally, also need to have a preference for honest cooperation and material advancement (for example, choosing work over leisure). In the long term, there is a complex interrelation between people's fundamental values and institutions: if institutions enable wealth creation, people are more likely to develop a taste for the experience, and if they experience growth, they value trust-enhancing institutions (this point was made, for example, by Khalil, 1995; see also Voigt, 1993).

Growth is thus driven by entrepreneurs using knowledge in a deepening division of labour (specialisation). This is only possible with appropriate 'rules of the game' to govern human interaction. Appropriate institutional arrangements are needed to provide a framework to human cooperation in markets and organisations and to make such cooperation reasonably predictable and reliable. A coordinative framework is, for example, provided by cultural conventions, a shared ethical system and formal legal and regulatory stipulations (for details, see Chapters 5 and 6). The result is an understanding of the growth process that ties the macroeconomic analysis to the microeconomics of structural change and the microeconomic foundations of motivation and institutional constraints, in other words, that relate economic growth to sociological factors such as preferences and value systems.

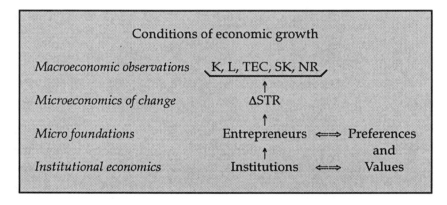

In many ways, the focus on the institutional aspects in the explanation of economic growth amounts to a rediscovery of what early thinkers such as the Scottish social philosophers David Hume and Adam Smith had said, namely that at least three institutions are fundamental to human progress and civilised society: the guarantee of property rights, the free transfer of property by voluntary contractual agreement, and the keeping of promises made (Hume, [1786] 1965). We may also conclude that contemporary economic growth theory is returning to the traditional tie-up with sociology and anthropology, where writers such as Max Weber had placed it before abstraction and mathematisation took hold of it.[3]

We conclude this introductory chapter by saying that institutions underpin the complex web of human interaction across nations and continents, because human interaction depends invariably on very tenuous links of trust – indeed, a 'gossamer web', as it was so aptly put by Jane Jacobs in one of the quotes at the head of this chapter.

O Key Concepts

Physical capital consists of tangible assets that have the potential to raise the capacity of other production factors, such as labour, to produce goods and services. In modern economies, the process of capital formation requires acts of **saving** (not consuming income generated) and acts of **investment** (borrowing to acquire capital assets).

The term **human capital** sometimes relates only to those assets that are embodied in individuals (skills, knowledge, knowhow); other authors have a wider conception of human capital, and include shared, disembodied knowledge, such as shared values, shared conventions, rules, and laws – what we shall cover in this book with the term 'institutions' (see Chapter 2). Human capital, therefore, goes far beyond formal knowledge or what intellectuals know, covering implicit, informal knowhow, aptitudes and basic values, as well as socially shared rule systems.

Entrepreneurs are people who are on the alert for opportunities and ready to exploit them by incurring transaction costs. Economic entrepreneurs are on the look-out for new knowledge and prepared to risk as yet untested combinations of production factors in the hope of material gain. ●

Questions for Review

- Can you say roughly what an institution is? Can you give a few specific examples of institutions?
- Is it at all possible for you to interact with someone else without at least sharing some institutions? Try to think of some interaction with strangers and ask yourself what shared institutions make that specific type of interaction feasible. What would you have to tell an alien visiting from Mars before it (he? she?) could buy something in your local corner store?
- Can you imagine a sport without institutional constraints on the player? Imagine a boxer and a tennis player interacting without a shared understanding of the rules of the intended game? Can you imagine what traffic would be like in your home town if there were no rules restraining drivers?
- In what instances, according to the argument in this chapter and in the opinion of Douglass North, has standard mainstream economics failed to come to grips with economic reality? Can you think of

other instances where one cannot explain to strangers what goes on without explaining the rules (institutional constraints)?

- How do we define economic growth?
- How do we measure economic growth?
- How long would you survive on your own (that is, without any division of labour and knowledge with your fellow human beings) if you lived in the most advantageous spot of uncivilised nature on your continent?
- What is the 'demographic transition'? How can it be explained? What does it mean for population growth in the twenty-first century?
- What factors have economists identified as the main explanations of economic growth?
- Is the statement that 'the economy grows because of fast capital formation' a satisfactory and full explanation of growth? If not, why not?
- What is the role of knowledge in the growth process?
- What is the role of entrepreneurship?
- Can you explain how advances in knowledge and skills have averted Karl Marx's prediction that the capitalist system would sooner or later collapse because it would run out of rewarding investment opportunities?
- Are institutions a sufficient (or only a necessary) condition for growth? Give reasons to explain your answer.
- Why did the industrial revolution, which initiated the process of sustained economic growth, not start in China?
- Can you explain why institutions are important for growth? What role do they play in facilitating or hindering the division of labour?
- Is it possible that decay in institutions leads to a drop in living standards? How might such an experience be reversed, for example in the case of Russia in the late 1980s and 1990s?
- Can you think of a case where your personal future is dependent on tenuous trust in others whom you hardly know? Have you ever paid large sums of money in a similar situation to the quotation from Jane Jacobs at the head of this chapter? If so, what gave you the confidence that you would ever get value in return for the payment? What are the reasons that enable you to entrust the savings for your retirement to others, or to rely on someone's promise of delivery of a prepaid good or service?
- If trust in the financial institutions and the value of money in a country are destroyed, how can people make provision for their old age?

Notes

1. A noteworthy exception is the graphic, insightful description of average living conditions in Europe before the onset of the industrial revolution by Braudel (1981–4).
2. The graph is based on data collated by the experienced observer of long-term economic history, Angus Maddison (1995). They are based on inflation-adjusted national incomes, translated into US dollars with purchase-power equivalents (that is, reflecting how many real goods and services people can buy in their respective countries). Clearly, such long-term international comparisons are based on many assumptions, so the data can only serve as a general guide. None the less, these seem the best data available to document how different societies fared in their long-term quest for material betterment.
3. German economist-sociologist Max Weber (1864–1920) became known in the English-speaking world primarily for his thesis that economic growth depends on capitalist accumulation, which in turn depends on a class of capitalist entrepreneurs, who in turn could only become active if there were the appropriate set of religious values, civic virtues and institutions (Weber, [1927] 1995).

PART I

Foundations

CHAPTER 2

Definitions: Economics, Institutions, Order and Policy

In this chapter the reader will learn what an institution is, how institutions come into existence and how they facilitate the emergence of order (a confidence-inspiring, predictable pattern of behaviour). The reader will also see how institutions and order help in coping with the economic problem, namely overcoming scarcity and discovering new wants and resources. We shall see that institutions assist members of a community when they wish to cooperate, since institutions make it more convenient, less costly and less risky for individuals to rely on each other, in particular when developing and using new knowledge.

We also learn that institutions and their economic consequences are now attracting growing interest – although the basic ideas are not new. Property rights, the freedom of contract, stable money and other such confidence-inspiring certainties, which are based on sound institutions, were analysed by the classical moral philosophers and economists, such as David Hume and Adam Smith, the Austrian school and many other precursors of modern institutional economics. Their contributions will be reviewed briefly.

In building up a scientific picture of the economic world, definitions play an important part.
(Walter Eucken, The Foundations of Economics, *[1950] 1981)*

Law is reason without wishes.
(Aristotle, 384–322 BC*)*

[T]here ... are certain super individual schemes of thought, namely institutions, which ... serve ... to some extent the coordination of individual plans.
(Ludwig Lachmann, Capital, Expectations and the Market Process, *1977)*

2.1   Basic Definitions

This textbook is about economics – the science which aims to explain how people satisfy their diverse human wants by drawing on scarce resources and how people discover new wants and resources – and about the role which institutions play in economic life. Before we can begin to discuss the issues, it is necessary to spell out how we define the most important terms. (Other people, and researchers in other disciplines, do not always attach the same meanings to the terms as we do.)

Institutions

Institutions are defined here as man-made rules which constrain possibly arbitrary and opportunistic behaviour in human interaction. Institutions are shared in a community and are always enforced by some sort of sanction. Institutions without sanctions are useless. Only if sanctions apply will institutions make the actions of individuals more predictable. Rules with sanctions channel human actions in reasonably predictable paths, creating a degree of order. If various related rules are consistent with each other, this facilitates the confident cooperation between people, so that they can take good advantage of the division of labour and human creativity. For example, traffic rules – a set of institutions – impose constraints on individual drivers but allow the generality of people to travel more speedily and safely; and the institutions that establish protected property rights enable people to buy, sell and grant credit to others.[1]

The general presumption is that institutions have a great impact on how well people attain their economic and other objectives and that people normally prefer institutions which enhance their freedom of choice and economic wellbeing. But institutions will not always serve these ends. Certain types of rules may have deleterious consequences for general material welfare, freedom and other human values, and a decay of the rule system can lead to economic and social decline. It is therefore necessary to analyse the content and effect of institutions on choice and prosperity as part of institutional economics.

Order and Economic Life

The key function of institutions is to facilitate order: a systematic, non-random and therefore comprehensible pattern of actions and events. Where there is social chaos, social interaction is excessively costly, confidence and cooperation disintegrate. The division of labour, which is the major source of economic wellbeing, is not possible. We shall therefore focus here on how institutions promote order in economic interaction, that is, the patterns that emerge when individuals try to come to grips with the scarcity of resources. Order inspires trust and confidence, as well as reducing the costs of coordination. When order prevails, people are able to make predictions, are then better able to cooperate with others and feel confident to risk innovative experiments of their own. People then can more easily find the information they need about specialists with whom they can cooperate and to guess what such cooperation is likely to cost and return. More useful knowledge will be used and discovered as a consequence.

As just noted, economics deals with scarcity. This means that a decision in favour of one action inevitably implies a rejection of alternative actions. Such decisions are always subjective: alternatives are evaluated by different individual decision makers. Thus, each reader of this chapter is forgoing other uses of her or his time. We call the valued alternative uses of resources 'opportunity costs', and it is obvious that one reader's opportunity costs may be the attendance at a lecture and another's a holiday on the beach (Buchanan, 1969, foreword). Even where the alternative forgone by a choice is technically the same – for example, that we cannot listen to a rock concert because we are reading this book – the value of the sacrifice will differ among us. You may bear much higher opportunity costs than we do. This point is important: economic decisions should, as far as possible, be left to individuals, who know their subjective opportunities, rather than to collective decision makers, who are less well informed.

Where different people, with different aspirations and capabilities, make these choices and assess their opportunity costs, order and trust are appreciated. Information is then easy to convey to others and a sophisticated division of labour is possible. The content of order-supporting institutions is therefore of great relevance to economic outcomes that satisfy diverse people in a changing environment.

We also need to define institutional economics; this is concerned with the analysis of the impact of coordinative rules, and sets of rules, as well as their enforcement, on economic results. Institutional economics is also concerned with how institutions evolve in the face of changing economic circumstances. In short, institutional economics deals with the two-way relationship between economic life and institutions.

O Key Concepts

Economics is the discipline that is concerned with the ways in which people satisfy their diverse wants with resources that turn out to be scarce and in which they try to overcome scarcity by finding and testing useful knowledge. People tend to increase their wants faster than human knowledge and other resources grow to satisfy them, so scarcity is a prevalent trait of the human condition.

As economics is concerned with choices in the face of scarcity, the concept of **opportunity cost** plays a key role. It highlights that any choice 'costs' several others – alternatives that have to be forgone. In practice, the opportunities forgone are anticipated and are evaluated differently by different people, depending on their subjective appreciation (subjective opportunity costs). Thus, our opportunity costs may differ completely from yours.

Institutions are rules of human interaction that constrain possibly opportunistic and erratic individual behaviour, thereby making human behaviour more predictable and thus facilitating the division of labour and wealth creation. Institutions, to be effective, always imply some kind of sanction for rule violations. The terms 'institution' and **'rule'** will be used interchangeably in this book.

Order prevails if repetitive human interactions follow some kind of discernible pattern. Such patterns can emerge when sets of institutions exist that are sufficiently cohesive to channel human actions so that they are non-random and hence essentially predictable.

Institutional economics covers a two-way relationship between economics and institutions. It is concerned with the effects of institutions on the economy as well as the development of institutions in response to economic experiences. ●

The Origins of Institutions

How do institutions come into existence? One possibility is that rules and entire rule systems are shaped by long-term human experience. People may have discovered certain arrangements that allow them to better meet their aspirations. Thus, it may have proved useful to adopt the custom of greeting the people one meets. Useful rules will become a tradition and will be perpetuated, if adopted by sufficient numbers of people to create a critical mass, so that they are followed community-wide. The rules will be spontaneously enforced and emulated as they gradually emerge and become known throughout a community. Arrangements that fail to satisfy human aspirations will be rejected and discontinued. Thus, most of the rules that matter to our daily lives develop within society in an evolutionary process of gradual feedback and adjustment. And the precise content of most institutions will evolve gradually along a steady path. We call such rules internal institutions. In analysing how internal institutions come about, institutional economics draws frequently on the insights of moral philosophy, anthropology, psychology and sociology.

Other types of institutions come into existence because they are designed, are made explicit in legislation and regulations and are formally enforced by an authority outside society, such as a government. Such rules are designed and imposed by agents who are selected by a political process and who act from outside the society as such. They are ultimately enforced by legitimated means of coercion, for example through the judiciary. We call these institutions external institutions. As soon as institutions are imposed externally by rulers, parliaments or bureaucracies, a fundamental problem arises, namely that the political agents, who should act in the interest of the citizens, tend to exceed their mandate and use rules and rule enforcement for their own benefit. For this and other reasons, political processes themselves need to be subjected to certain rules. The effectiveness of external institutions depends greatly on whether they are complementary to the internally evolved institutions: for example, whether legislation supports a society's morality, its cultural conventions, customs and manners. When analysing external institutions, it is necessary to draw on the political and legal sciences.

O Key Concepts

Internal institutions evolve from human experience and incorporate solutions that have tended to serve people best in the past. Examples are customs, ethical norms, good manners and conventions in trade, as well as natural law in Anglo-Saxon society. Violations of internal institutions are normally sanctioned informally, for example by others in the community when people with bad manners discover that they are not invited again. But there are also formal sanctioning processes to enforce internal institutions (see section 5.2).

External institutions are imposed and enforced from above, having been designed and established by agents who are authorised by a political process. An example is legislation. External institutions are coupled with explicit sanctions which are imposed in formal ways (for example, law courts following procedures of due process) and may be enforced by the legitimated use of force (for example, the police).

Thus, the distinction between internal and external institutions hinges on the origin of the rules. ●

Normative Content and Public Policy

In institutional economics it is often appropriate to analyse values and the effects of values, for institutions determine to a great extent how people attain their own personal objectives and are able to realise their fundamental values. Some institutions are more expedient than others for them. Institutions also impact on the values that people hold and the purposes that they pursue. Institutions thus reflect subjective notions of the relation between one individual and others in a community, and their acceptance and enforcement depend crucially on cultural notions of what society stands for. Shared fundamental values in a community support cohesion and motivate people to act within the institutional framework. Institutional economics therefore has to analyse human values explicitly – more precisely, statements about what people appreciate as valuable – and to participate in moral discourse. In this respect, it draws on moral philosophy.

Institutions – and underlying values – which are widely shared by a community define that community, such as a family, a neighbourhood, a nation or an international professional association. Institutions constitute the 'social cement' that makes and defines a society (to use the term American sociologist John Elster (1989) used in a book title). Individuals may belong to a great variety of different, overlapping communities, obeying differing sets of institutions; some they share with their neighbours in the same geographic area, others with people far away. In the same vein, institutions have an intercommunity dimension. Systems of economic institutions may be more or less open to other communities or nations which share other institutions. Openness here means that border-crossing exchanges of goods and services and flows of people, capital and ideas are possible. Here, institutional economics shares common ground with international law and politics.

We must also distinguish between the theory and the policy of institutional economics. Institutional theory describes, explains and predicts the emergence and the effects of rules, and discusses how changing certain rules may help or hinder certain outcomes or classes of outcomes. In this respect, institutional economics belongs to the realm of positive science and makes a contribution to economic policy.[2] Depending on how well institutional theory works, we may go beyond this and be able to derive policy-orientated knowledge that helps to shape institutions in the real world according to certain objectives. Economists, as scientists, may give policy advice on how particular objectives could be pursued more effectively under alternative sets of institutions. Public policy – the systematic use of political means in the pursuit of certain objectives – normally proceeds within given institutional constraints, but it may also be conducted by trying to alter institutions, either in explicit ways or as a side-effect of policy actions. Institutional economists therefore tend to focus on the interactions between public policy and institutions.

Beyond this, economists, like any other citizens, may also say what they consider to be desirable, good or bad. Then, they adopt a normative stance, in which case they should reveal their personal values and preferences.

O Key Concepts

(Fundamental) values are defined as high preferences revealed, time and again, in human choices and public actions. They are accorded, by most people most of the time, a high rank order. This is demonstrated by the subordination of other preferences to them. Examples of such values are freedom, justice, security and economic welfare.

Public policy is the systematic pursuit, by political, collective means, of certain objectives. Public policy is conducted not only by government agents (parliamentarians, politicians, administrators), but also by representatives of organised groups, such as unions, industry associations, consumer and welfare lobbies, bureaucracies, and certain individuals (industry leaders, academics, press representatives) who influence collective actions, that is, actions that involve agreements between more than two partners, often implicitly between millions of people in a community. ●

2.2   The Precursors of Contemporary Institutional Economics

The Scottish Enlightenment

This brief overview of the key concepts of institutional economics should be rounded off by at least some reference to the precursors of contemporary institutional economics in the history of ideas. As noted, institutions have not been explicitly analysed in most of mainstream twentieth-century economics. Their importance was largely overlooked because of the assumptions commonly made by economists; in particular, analytically convenient – though peculiar – assumptions about 'perfect knowledge' and rational choice between given, known objectives and available, known means.

Differently from modern economic theorists, the classic social scientists, especially the Scottish moral philosophers and economists of the eighteenth century, such as David Hume, Adam Ferguson and Adam Smith, understood the central importance of institutions. Adam Smith's famous 'invisible hand' mechanism – which describes how self-seeking individuals are coordinated by competition in markets – cannot be comprehended as anything other than an ordering institutional system. Adam Ferguson stressed the evolution of institutions over time and David Hume explored the institutional foundations on which the capitalist market economy is built and how these are placed into the intellectual, cultural and political life of a nation. Both aspects are of great import to contemporary institutional economics.

We might even go back 2500 years in history and claim that the Greek statesman-philosopher Solon and his Chinese near-contemporary Confucius were philosophers who emphasised the importance of rules for human interaction in promoting peace and prosperity in a community.

The Austrian School

More recently, institutional economics received a mighty impetus from the Austrian School, in particular Carl Menger and Ludwig von Mises, as well as the neo-Austrians, such as Ludwig Lachmann, Friedrich von Hayek, Murray Rothbard and Israel Kirzner, and the Chicago economists, such as George Stigler and Milton Friedman (see references to these authors in the Bibliography). The Austrian contribution placed the analysis of rules into the context of limited human knowledge, methodological individualism – the insight that only people act, never abstract collectives, such as nations, races, or social classes[3] – and subjectivism – the insight that only individuals are able to read the world subjectively and therefore differ in their ability to understand the world and in their value judgements. From this it follows that interpersonal differences have to be respected and cannot be easily aggregated into collective goals.[4] The Austrian contributions present important analytical and philosophical challenges and suggest a cautious treatment of what we mean by rationality. Ludwig von Mises produced an early critique of the institutions of socialism, which still has not been fully absorbed into the mainstream of political and economic thought; his line of argument was carried further by Hayek, Kirzner and Rothbard. Their inspirational influence on economic institutions and orders will repeatedly be evident in this book (see, in particular, section 5.5 on individualist versus collectivist perceptions of society).

Institutional economics is also based on the conception of the economy as a complex, evolving system. The notion of equilibrium as a durable state or as a normatively desirable condition is alien to this approach. Instead of such ahistorical notions, economic life is seen as being on a path of gradual evolution, with some elements appearing, others disappearing, as people select what suits their diverse purposes (Shackle, 1972; Witt, 1994; Metcalfe, 1989).

O Key Concepts

The term **Scottish Enlightenment** refers to moral philosophers and economists (such as David Hume and Adam Smith) who wrote predominantly in the eighteenth century. They explored what basic institutions a functioning capitalist economy needs, namely the rule of law, private property and the freedom to contract. They castigated the deleterious consequences of Mercantilism (selective trade protectionism and the preferment of specific groups, reliance on public enterprise, powerful coalitions between ruler and established merchant interests). They advocated a minimal state and the self-reliance of the individual citizen.

Neoclassical economics has become the dominant mode of economic analysis in the twentieth century. It centres on the conditions of economic equilibrium and is normally based on the simplifying assumptions:

- that economic agents have 'perfect knowledge';
- that people pursue their purposes rationally and maximise some target variable subject to budget constraints;
- that it is possible to describe representative households, producer-investors and governments;
- that business transactions, for example in markets, are frictionless and cost-free; and
- that the individual preferences of the members of society can somehow be expressed in a social welfare function.

In contradistinction to evolutionary economics (see below), the analysis typically begins with an equilibrium – understood as a situation in which people's plans and expectations are mutually compatible – that is disturbed by one isolated event, and then shows to what new equilibrium the system moves (comparative static analysis, assuming all other things to be equal: the famous *ceteris paribus* clause of economic textbooks). It is often assumed that policy makers are able to design a line of rational action which achieves their objectives. These assumptions facilitate the formulation of mathematical models and econometric analyses. And in turn these suggest that economic policy should be conducted in terms of predetermined goals and instruments, pulling deftly at 'the levers of the economy'.

Austrian economics is a tradition of analysing economic phenomena which started during the nineteenth century in Vienna (Carl Menger, 1840–1921), but is now gaining growing influence in business and policy making. It is based on the understanding that knowledge is imperfect, that people interact in dynamic market processes and that time and evolution are important. Its cornerstones are:

- **methodological individualism** (that economic phenomena are explained by the actions, or inactions, of individuals who try to acquire costly but useful information and are engaged in purposeful action);
- **subjectivism** (that economic phenomena have to be explained by the decisions of people who bring to bear their unique perceptions of reality and hence their unique values, aspirations, knowledge and assessments of costs and benefits, and that people act rationally in their own distinctive self-interest); and
- an emphasis on complex, open-ended **processes of trial and error** which happen in historic time and occur in an environment of uncertainty (and not on static outcomes and equilibrium); economic actions tend to have many unintended and unpredictable side-effects.

Austrian economists concentrate on how people coordinate their individual pursuits and what institutions evolve so that people can better cope with reaching their individual goals even when they lack knowledge. Different from the 'instrumentalist approach' of neoclassical economics, Austrian economists counsel caution in policy and suggest a focus on cultivating and setting universal rules which channel market processes.

For an introduction, see 'Austrian economics' in Henderson (1993, pp. 105–9); Boettke, (1994, pp. 1–6); and Kirzner (1997). ●

Ordo Liberalism, Public Choice and Other Sources

Another tradition in economics and law that focused on institutions is the Freiburg School, sometimes also called the German *ordo* liberal school. It was inspired for decades by Walter Eucken and Franz Böhm, who showed the deleterious effects of the decay of the basic rules of competition in the Weimar Republic (1919–33) and Nazi Germany. They adapted the basic institutions described by the Scottish philosophers to modern industrial mass society, with political parties, self-seeking bureaucracies and organised interest groups.

New Anglo-Saxon impulses to contemporary institutional economics began with the path-breaking work of Ronald Coase; more recently some of these ideas were taken up by 'public choice economics' in the works of writers such as James Buchanan, Gordon Tullock and Mancur Olson. Other insights, which added much empirical content to institutional economics, have been contributed by long-term economic historians, such as Douglass North and Eric Jones, whom we quoted in Chapter 1. They showed how competition amongst communities and jurisdictions led to the evolution of more citizen- and enterprise-friendly rules, such as limited government, property rights, due process and the rule of law. Economic and business historians have had great influence in turning economics again from a comparative-static to an evolutionary discipline. The 'new organisation science' has also added analyses of the effect of institutions on the shape and effectiveness of particular organisations (see authors such as Armen Alchian, Oliver Williamson, Yoram Barzel, Louis de Alessi in the Bibliography).

In the 1980s and 1990s, institutional economics developed into a dynamic, broad field of research focusing on the central importance of institutions in motivating economic action. At present, the field appears to be split into two camps: one group of analysts comes from traditional neoclassical economics and organisation science; they have recognised the importance of institutions (and transaction costs) and have tried to graft these phenomena on to traditional mainstream economics. Another group, to which we belong, has found that fundamental assumptions of institutional economics are incompatible with constituent assumptions of neoclassical welfare economics, such as 'perfect knowledge' and objective rationality. We have taken the hard step of writing off much of our old knowledge capital in order to develop institutional economics afresh from basic presumptions about human values, cognition and behaviour.

This book is an attempt to make the results – albeit imperfect – of this new intellectual venture teachable and to show the far-reaching consequences for public policy.

O Key Concepts

***Ordo* liberalism** (also known as the Freiburg School) refers to a specifically German tradition that began in the 1920s and 1930s. It attributed the economic (and political) failures of the Weimar Republic to political rent-seeking and the government's tolerance of the closure of markets to competitors. The *ordo* liberals recommended supplementing the key institutions that the Scottish Enlightenment had identified (private property, freedom of contract, rule of law) with an active defence of competition by government against organised groups, party interests and bureaucratic egotism. They also demanded that policy should help to create stable expectations and desist from stop–go policies. (For an introduction, see Kasper and Streit, 1993.)

Evolutionary economics designates a school of thought that focuses on the market processes of change and progress, restructuring and innovation through competition, rather than on static equilibrium, which is the main focus of neoclassical economics. It analyses economic phenomena in historic time, that is, with the knowledge that the clock cannot be turned back and that events are irreversible. It is therefore necessary to look at historical paths, for example in technical change. Evolutionary economists reject the unrealistic notion, common in neoclassical analysis, that economic actors make decisions completely anew at the beginning of every period. It deals with open systems which allow individual experimentation by variation, selection and imitation of what people value highly. Thus, evolutionary economics focuses on change, learning and creativity, the complex interplay between technical, societal, organisational, economic and institutional change, paying great attention to the role of creativity and entrepreneurship. Competition is seen as the device that sorts out what is deemed useful by people from what is considered not worth the cost.

In distinction to comparative-static analysis, it is assumed:

* positively, that 'disequilibrium' is normal; and
* normatively, that people thrive in disequilibrium processes ('equilibrium is death!', 'as long as I live, I grow').

Whereas standard neoclassical textbooks assume that people start afresh in each period and plan utility- or profit-maximising outcomes, the evolutionary approach is to analyse a path-dependent sequence of events, where the decisions in earlier periods have great (but not exclusive) influence on what can happen in the next.

To illustrate the point: the standard neoclassical assumption would be that a music student in semester 1 chooses to learn the piano, in semester 2 she starts afresh and decides to learn the trombone, in semester 3 it may be the violin. By contrast, **path dependency** in evolutionary economics assumes that, usually, music students build on their first-semester knowledge. In contrast to comparative-static neoclassical economics, which suggests the pursuit of perfection, the evolutionary policy stance is to look out for pragmatic, ongoing improvements.

For an introduction, see Witt (1994); also Witt (1991); Metcalfe (1989); and Nelson (1995).

Public choice is a tradition of American origin which applies economic principles to the analysis of political decision making. It is based on the observation that politicians and administrators – like all other people – pursue their own goals, not necessarily those of the electorate. In other words, public choice economists operate on the assumption that, when self-seeking knaves are turned into elected officials or bureaucrats, they do not turn into white knights in shining armour. Public choice analysis thus highlights **rent-seeking**, that is, the reallocation of property rights by political action rather than market competition. They show that government agents and industrialists frequently pursue particular interests through redistributive political interventions. Public choice has shown the limits of what can be achieved by political, collective action; it may be labelled the 'economics of politics and collective decision making'.

For an introduction, see 'Public choice', in Henderson (1993, pp. 150–4) and references to 'rent-seeking' in that volume; Buchanan (1991, pp. 29–46); Tullock (1987); 'Public choice', in Eatwell *et al.* (1987); or for a book-length exposé: Mitchell and Simmons (1994, esp. pp. 195–222).

The **old institutional economics** covers the contributions of American and European economists who wrote mainly in the early decades of the twentieth century, analysing institutions and rejecting classical economic theories. In Germany, the 'Historic School' – authors such as Gustav Schmoller – tried to describe economic reality and incorporated the rules of human interaction in their descriptions of economic and social evolution. In the United States, Thorstein Veblen, John Commons and Wesley Mitchell studied the economic role of institutions (for more detail, see articles on 'Institutionalism, "Old" and "New"' in Hodgson *et al.* (1994, pp. 397–402). The new institutional economics, as defined in this book, has little in common with the older institutionalists in America and their 'Historical School' counterparts in Europe. ●

Questions for Review

- The reader should now be aware what an institution is. What are internal and external institutions and how do they come about?
- Can you give a few examples of an internal institution in your community? What functions do they serve? Can you imagine what would happen if the institutions were generally violated and therefore disappeared?
- What would happen if the institution of good manners disappeared in your community? Would it be easier or harder for people like you to cooperate effectively and plan for the future? Think of practical examples.
- By what processes do external institutions (constitutional rules, legislation, regulations) come about in your country? How are they changed?

- Define what an organisation is. Are banks and insane asylums institutions in the sense used here?
- When the clause 'If you shoot someone in the head … ' is completed with

  (a) ' … then the person dies';

  (b) ' … then you are very naughty';

  which is a normative and which a positive statement? Give reasons for your reply.
- List the assumptions on which neoclassical mainstream economics tends to be built. Are they realistic?
- What are the key characteristics of the Austrian School of economics?
- When you read sentences such as 'The global community is obliged to eliminate hunger in the third world', 'The government undertakes to halve unemployment': who is meant to act? Please search for similar abstract-collectivist examples in newspaper columns, political speeches and sermons, and analyse in each case who – if anyone – is intended to act, or whether such statements are meaningless utterances that have no function other than to make people feel good.
- If someone writes to you that 'The University is utterly delighted with your achievement': whose heart (asking from the viewpoint of a 'methodological individualist approach') beats faster?
- Give an example from your experience where something is path-dependent (that is, cannot be reversed without considerable cost).
- The readers should be able to offer many examples from everyday life and politics that illustrate why institutions matter.

Notes

1. The term 'institution' has numerous and conflicting definitions in the literature. Social scientists from different disciplines and ages have imbued the term with so many alternative meanings that it does not seem possible to give a generally valid definition beyond a loose association with regularity in behaviour. However, the definition that we shall use consistently in this book – in the sense of rules with sanctions that have normative influence on human behaviour – appears to have emerged amongst contemporary institutional economists as the consensus definition (see, for example, North, 1990, pp. 3–6; Drobak and Nye, 1997, pp. xv–xx).

   Common English usage often confuses institutions, as defined here, with 'organisations', which are systematic arrangements of resources aimed at achieving a shared purpose or purposes. Thus, firms, banks and government administrations are purposive organisations, whereas the Ten Commandments and the traffic code are sets of institutions.
2. Positive economics extends also to the analysis of human values which are related to institutions. In this case, economists produce scholarly statements about the consequences of certain values, as opposed to making their own value judgements.
3. The founder of Austrian economics, Carl Menger, drove the point home when he wrote (in 1883): 'the phenomena of "national economy" are by no means direct expressions of the life of a nation as such or direct results of an "economic nation".

They are, rather, the results of … innumerable individual economic efforts. [They] must … be theoretically interpreted in this light' (cited in Boettke, 1994, p. 11).

4. The reader is invited to become alert to often-heard non-individualist statements such as: 'the nation has the desire to … ', 'the international community should attend to this problem', 'the government ought to decide', 'the nation requires a population of 100 million', 'the world community must solve the problem of hunger', 'world history will explain', or references to undefined collectives, such as 'poverty should be eradicated by 2020'. It is very educational to ask in each case who specifically the intended individual decision makers are, what their subjective motivations might be and why they are hidden, or hide themselves, behind faceless collectives.

CHAPTER 3

Human Behaviour

In this chapter, we discuss a few basic but far-reaching assumptions about human nature. We shall see that the central problem to overcoming scarcity is ignorance (the knowledge problem). This is at variance with the assumption of 'perfect knowledge' which is so often made by economists.

Bits of useful knowledge are dispersed among people throughout the community. People pursue their own, self-set purposes by drawing on their own knowledge, and that of others if they can be found. In the process, more useful knowledge is discovered, although people have limited capacity, limited resources and limited time to acquire and evaluate new information and to compound it into knowledge. In any event, this is a costly process. People therefore tend to make decisions within the bounds of limited information and learn by trial and error. We shall also see that certain rules assist economic agents to reduce the costs of knowledge search and to inspire confidence in cooperating with others, for example through market exchanges.

We shall also try to find out what motivates human beings to act to the benefit of others. In the family, among friends and in small groups, people frequently act out of love, solidarity or altruism. However, what works well in the small group cannot be transferred to modern mass society or collective action in an entire nation. At that level we act for strangers usually only if we are either coerced or out of self-interest, when we are offered a payment in exchange for our efforts.

We conclude this chapter by pointing to the pervasive problem of how to motivate agents, who act on behalf of others and who are often much better informed about the action than the princi-

pals. In other words, we shall look at the pervasive principal–
agent problem in human interaction.

Man is truly altered by the coexistence of other men; his faculties cannot
be developed in himself alone, and only by himself.
(Samuel T. Coleridge, British poet-philosopher, 1818)

The worth of knowledge cannot begin to be asserted until we have it. But
then it is too late to decide how much to spend on breaching the walls to
encourage its arrival.
(George Shackle, 1972)

Even 200 years after Adam Smith's *Wealth of Nations*, it is not yet fully
understood that it is the great achievement of the market to have made a
far-ranging division of labor possible, that it brings about continuous adaptation of economic effect to millions of particular facts or events which
in their totality are not known and cannot be known to anybody.
(Friedrich Hayek, 1978)

Before we can discuss institutions as such, it seems appropriate to
investigate some basic traits of human behaviour. The need to foster
institutions arises from certain intrinsic qualities of human nature,
such as a limited capacity to absorb and evaluate information and to
retain knowledge. 'Information' is used here to designate an item of
explicit knowledge that everyone can learn. Bits of information are
evaluated and amalgamated into a body of knowledge in which ideas
are systematically related and which is open to new insights. The
word 'information' frequently relates to the act of informing and the
flow of information, whereas 'knowledge' emphasises the personal
state of holding a *stock* of knowledge in one's mind. People who are
aware of much information may not necessarily be able to use it in
interactive, applied and novel ways (information junkies), whereas
knowledgeable people are able to make use of what they know in
applied, novel and creative ways. The science which deals with knowledge and how people arrive at new insights is called epistemology
(after the Greek term *episteme*: knowledge, insight, understanding).

We shall also have to discuss how the actions of individuals in sharing
knowledge are coordinated in a world where coordination costs
resources.

3.1   The Knowledge Problem

On Epistemology

We saw in section 1.2 that the growth of per capita incomes is limited by a lack of knowledge, although competitive buyers and sellers help to utilise the knowledge that exists and to develop further knowledge, whereby they contribute to economic growth. Despite these efforts, the problem of limited knowledge is a central bain of human existence and a constitutional cause of scarcity: if we knew more, we could satisfy human wants better with material resources. Human ignorance and processes to cope with it, albeit imperfectly, are thus absolutely central to economics, the science of how to overcome scarcity. This has become known as the 'knowledge problem'. The problem was introduced into economics by Friedrich August von Hayek who spoke of 'constitutional ignorance', an essential aspect of human existence (Hayek, 1937; 1945, esp. p. 530; also see reference in Henderson, 1993, pp. 791–4). In his 1974 Nobel Prize lecture, Hayek once again returned to the theme. It was entitled 'The Pretense of Knowledge', and showed that much of the economics profession pretended to know what was in reality unknowable, and they therefore risked giving irrelevant advice (Hayek, reprinted in Nishiyama and Leube, 1984, pp. 266–80). The knowledge problem is a central theme of Austrian economics.

When developing a theory about complex reality, admittedly simplifying assumptions must be made – just as a map depicts a simplified model of reality and omits much confusing detail. However, it is not permissible in model building to abstract from *constitutional* criteria, such as the lack of knowledge in explaining scarcity and economic phenomena, because the omission of constitutional criteria leads to nonsense models. To illustrate the point: in developing a theory of ballistics, it is acceptable, in the first instance, to abstract from air temperature and humidity, so that a simplified model is derived which can later be made more realistic by dropping these restrictive assumptions. But nonsensical conclusions are inevitable if at the outset a constitutional element, such as gravity, is assumed away. Likewise, it makes no sense to start developing a theory of human medicine by assuming the head and the nervous system away, or an economic theory by assuming that people have 'perfect knowledge'.

In reality, human beings suffer from two kinds of incompleteness in their knowledge when interacting with others:

(a) they have uncertain knowledge about the future ('future uncertainty'), but they have to make guesses about the future in order to act. They appreciate being given help that reduces uncertainty and inspires confidence;

(b) they have 'sideways uncertainty' about resources and potential exchange partners. as well as their precise characteristics. In particular, when they want to engage others to act for them, they will often not know whether those agents will act honestly, reliably and to the best of their capability, or whether they will shirk their obligations.

The assumption is often made in conventional textbooks that there is a phenomenon such as an 'economic man (or woman)' who has perfect knowledge of the available means and the ends which can be won, and therefore is able to make rational choices to maximise his or her utility now and in the future. Analyses based on this narrow kind of end–means rationalism turn economics into a mere computation exercise. However, they fail to convince practitioners of business, because business people simply know that no one has all the requisite knowledge of the available means and that people are often unsure of their own objectives; indeed, that chasing better information is an essential part of their jobs. They have to operate daily on the premise that individuals have a limited capacity to absorb knowledge, to digest, convey and apply it; expressed technically: human beings suffer from limited cognitive capacity. And this is constitutional.

People carry some of the knowledge they need in their own heads, but most of the time they can only utilise what they know in cooperation with others. In the modern world, people's own knowledge does not go very far in helping them to meet their aspirations. An individual would not even be able to produce something as simple as a pencil. Indeed, no single person on earth has ever made a pencil all alone. It takes graphite miners in Chile, wood cutters in Canada, glue makers in Taiwan, tool makers in Germany, traders in New York, and thousands of unknown others to cooperate and contribute. Much of their knowledge is specific to the place where they work. Since these are people with highly specialised knowledge, they have to rely on the many members of past generations who developed the knowledge about the various specialised production methods. They also have to rely on complex tools and on those who learnt how to organise the numerous trade connections which are necessary for the miracle of the pencil to arrive in our hands (and all this for the price of a few cents!).[1] If producing a pencil seems a task of mind-boggling complexity, think of a standard motor car, which contains about 4000 components made in many different factories, or a modern jet fighter that contains some 750 000 million highly specialised bits and pieces.

For most of what we require to meet our aspirations, we thus have to rely on the cooperation of other people, frequently uncountable numbers of unknown others who have knowledge of which we have not even an inkling and who we shall never meet. To satisfy our wants we depend on the division of labour amongst specialised producers, and that means depending to a considerable extent on the division of specialist knowledge. This specialisation is so complex even to get as simple a product as a pencil into our hands that it cannot be understood completely by any one human mind. Consequently, the big question is: how can all these diverse people around the world be coordinated to produce the desired end result, millions of different goods and services?

Knowledge and Coordination

When individuals interact to draw on the specialised knowledge of their fellows to satisfy their aspirations (or, for that matter, to find out whether their aspirations are at all feasible), they are uncertain about how others will respond to their approaches. They may, in the first instance, not even know whom to approach and how, and what material conditions are important to meeting their aspirations. At the same time, they are uncertain who will approach them, with what demands and how, and they will also be unclear how they themselves might respond to new demands from others. In other words, they face strategic uncertainty.

In this context, we have to distinguish between two different types of knowledge, or rather, ignorance:

(a) economic actors may lack certain kinds of supplementary knowledge, but be roughly aware of the character and content of the information they have to seek. Thus, I may have told you in which suburb I live, and you may want to find me. There are more or less effective search processes: referring to a map, driving around, asking people, for instance. Institutional arrangements can help in the search process, for example the rule that houses should be numbered sequentially. In this case it is appropriate to speak of 'information search';

(b) a totally different type of ignorance exists when we do not even have an inkling of what we do not know. When such knowledge is discovered, the discoverer is totally surprised. In retrospect, the new idea is obvious, and we are often surprised that, prior to the discovery, we did not know it. Since people do not know what to search for, they cannot go about this in rational ways, for example, by trying to minimise the costs of finding something (which they cannot know). An example of this was when Columbus chanced upon the New World, having had no prior knowledge that America existed. In this case, it is appropriate to speak of a 'discovery' (Kirzner, 1997).

The knowledge-search-and-coordination problem is complicated by the fact that the knowledge we carry in our heads is the result of evolutionary selection. People (other than new-born babies) possess knowledge which they have acquired and validated through subsequent experience. If old knowledge is not useful or turns out to be counterproductive because circumstances have changed, it is forgotten or revised. The world changes all the time: people's tastes change; different and more people are born; resources become scarce or are newly discovered; production technologies are innovated, and so on. In the process, everyone has to cope with uncertainty about how the world will change and how others will react to new circumstances. Existing knowledge often loses its usefulness because the world and other people are changing ceaselessly. Most relevant knowledge is thus the result of learning by doing and is acquired by innumerable different human beings in a decentralised selection process of trial and error.

A central tenet of epistemology is that knowledge is not a static concept. Knowledge is always specific to a particular time. People acquire most of their knowledge by a process of *catallaxis*, that is, by interacting with others and exchanging ideas and assets, a concept probably first put forward by British economist Richard Whately (1787–1863) and more recently revived by Ludwig von Mises. They were able to draw on the pioneering work of the British social philosophers John Locke (1632–1704) and David Hume (1711–76) who analysed the problems of human cognition, that is, how human senses receive impressions (sensation) and digest them through thought processes of internal relation-building (reflection).[2] They investigated how a person's ideas are developed by the digestion of impressions in the brain to generate that person's body of knowledge. When people interact and cooperate, they continually discover new sensations and are torn between a conservative instinct to retain familiar knowledge, which they share with others, and an experimental instinct to explore new ideas and overturn what is familiar and shared with others. Thus, producers of a certain good or service have an interest in replicating what they have produced in the past. That saves effort. But this conservative interest may be challenged by the need to take account of customer feedback about deficiencies and hence to redesign the product. The wish to beat the competition drives producers, time and again, to yield to the experimental urge and modify their existing knowledge. They keep learning. Personal preferences and real-life circumstances play a key role in what knowledge is being selected and retained by individuals, so different people will therefore possess different knowledge.

O Key Concepts

Epistemology is the science which investigates how humans gain and convey knowledge. It is one of the main branches of philosophy and is concerned with the nature, origin, scope and limits of human knowledge. The name is derived from the Greek words *episteme* (knowledge) and *logos* (theory): the theory of knowledge.

We speak of **information search** when the general context is known and details have to be found out. This is, for example, done by software developers who want to make a computer program work better. By contrast, we speak of **discovery** when totally new knowledge is found and the discoverer is genuinely surprised. It takes good luck and the quality of enterprise to make such discoveries. ●

New knowledge often comes about by marginal adaptations and variations of existing knowledge. As people interact, small creative steps occur here and there, and stepwise improvements accumulate over time. Thus, much of the improvement in aircraft design since the Wright brothers took off in 1903 is owed to numerous small improvements in aeronautical technology, propulsion and management, and much of it emerged from the interaction between aircraft users and aircraft builders. These steady, adaptive improvements are often overshadowed by creative breakthroughs when major new concepts emerge. Thus, the flight of the Wright brothers was an emergent addition to knowledge in that it initiated motorised flight, as was the introduction of jet propulsion. Whilst such creative breakthroughs capture the imagination and are recorded in the history books, their contribution to economic progress is much less than the broad, gradual adaptive advancement of knowledge in the many areas of human pursuit.

Sometimes, relevant knowledge is put together by systematic design, as in organised industrial research and development or in an architectural plan. Here knowledge does not evolve pragmatically by trial and error inside society, but is constructed systematically by a group which observes matters from the outside. Frequently, groups of such planners are motivated to find perfect 'for-all-eternity solutions', based on precise information. They construct and prescribe an ideal design. As long as the framework for the design remains unchanged, such knowledge may indeed be consistent and effective, but problems arise as soon as the framework evolves. Then, yesterday's perfect solution turns out to be no good for tomorrow's circumstances.

Knowledge may emerge either in a creative act, out of human inspiration and curiosity when people spontaneously try out new ideas, or when they plan a process of research and design to find something new. An example of planned knowledge search is the invention and commercial utilisation of nuclear power; an example of a spontaneous act of creativity which was not planned by a designer was the painting of the *Mona Lisa* which probably reflected how Europeans viewed the human condition in the Renaissance. Much knowledge has been uncovered by chance, by serendipitous ambling or sheer inspiration, by people who were on the lookout and prepared to make discoveries. This is even true in the modern world in which much research and development is organised and conducted by research specialists.

When analysing the evolution of human knowledge, we shall find that much is owed, not to an emergent, major act of creativity, but to adaptive change, to creativity by trial and error, by tinkering and improvement in response to new demands and changing conditions. Adaptive tinkering is often underrated or even overlooked by observers, who tend to be fascinated by the more conspicuous big innovations and emergent acts of creativity. The far-distant ancestor who invented the wheel changed human knowledge by a big and creative step. However, since then the basic idea has been improved upon by millions of users of wheels in millions of adaptive changes to supply us with the tiny wheels in watches and the giant wheels on huge dump trucks in the mining industry. It was a major creative step a hundred years ago when pioneers – the American Wright brothers – invented powered flight. But most of the difference between their aeroplane and a modern jumbo jet is owed to the innumerable adaptive advances in practical knowledge – as well as to numerous aborted ideas that did not work out as expected.

Implicit and Explicit Knowledge

Another aspect of human knowledge worth discussing relates to how relevant knowledge is retained in people's minds and passed on. Certain types of knowledge can easily be put in words, written down and passed on in the form of manuals or textbooks. Much scientific and technical knowledge can, for example, be made explicit and passed on in schools and university lectures. It can also be described in patent applications and sold to businesses that want to utilise it. But such explicit knowledge is far from all that we know and use to enhance our living standards. There is much implicit knowledge, on which we rely tacitly, in our daily lives and our work routines. We often refer to it by using the terms 'knowhow' and 'skills'. It is often surprisingly difficult and costly, even if possible, to make knowhow explicit – just try to write down an instruction for how to tie shoe laces for someone who has never done it!

Implicit (or tacit) knowledge can be acquired in processes of 'learning by doing'. It is internalised in the human mind until people use it without reflection (Polanyi, 1966). Much learning is indeed better done by practising and internalising tacit knowledge. Just think of the young person who will learn the skills of skateboarding with alacrity by imitating friends and going through the same routines time and again, until becoming a champion skateboarder! It would be near-impossible to convey all relevant knowledge in explicit form to a teenager by handing over manuals about gravity, friction, velocity and centripetal forces. Or, as another example, would you entrust your life to a surgeon who has studied all the relevant knowledge for an open-heart operation from books and professors, but without learning the necessary routine skills of surgery by operating on frogs and pig hearts? Yet the leaders of many developing countries have pursued policies of keeping out foreign experts and multinational companies which could convey implicit knowhow and skills, and have instead relied solely on the acquisition of explicit industrial knowledge. The economic record of such countries suggests that underrating the importance of practical routines, skills and knowhow out of a misconception about useful knowledge can have costly and far-reaching consequences. For the same reason, industries which stress hands-on work experience in apprenticeships and engineering studies tend to use technical knowledge better than industries where explicit knowledge is overrated and implicit knowhow, skills and efficient work routines are ignored or downplayed.

O Key Concepts

Knowledge consists of symbols and relations retained in the human mind. Knowledge may be made explicit and communicated formally, or it may consist of implicit knowhow – informal, petty knowledge, often of great complexity and specific to place, circumstance and time – which can probably only be acquired by practice (**learning by doing**). Much relevant knowledge is in tacit (or implicit) form, often called **knowhow**. It is acquired by imitating routines in which all the many small, complex bits of relevant knowledge are absorbed. Whilst some bodies of implicit knowledge can be made explicit –for example, be written down in manuals – much still depends on tacit knowhow.

Knowledge is often generated by the spontaneous interaction of people. It can also be created by design when people get together in an organised way and develop new knowledge through a plan to research and develop useful ideas.

The **knowledge problem** derives from the fact that human beings have only a limited capacity to develop, test and apply knowledge. Ignorance therefore is a constitutional element of human existence, including of economics, that is, how to overcome scarcity. 'Constitutional' here means that it is an essential part of human existence and cannot be assumed away. Knowledge is contained in the human brain, more precisely in the diverse human brains of all the people who live on earth. Only tiny fractions of it can be concentrated in any one mind. Knowledge therefore is used effectively only if mechanisms can be found to draw on the diverse, specialised knowledge of a very large number of people.

The **division of labour and knowledge** allows people to specialise but requires them to cooperate. Thanks to specialisation, people are able to acquire more knowledge and use it to solve problems. With experience, they are likely to chance upon more knowledge. Over time, they become more effective in meeting their own and other people's wants, as they learn new and adapt or discard old knowledge. The division of labour and knowledge therefore is a dynamic, evolving concept.

One has to distinguish between **emergent and adaptive additions to knowledge**: emergent knowledge refers to major creative breakthroughs (for example, the splitting of the atom), whereas the adaptive development of knowledge refers to the steady flow of creativity in which small, stepwise improvements are made in response to opportunities of supply and demand (for example, what makes the difference between the first sputtering motor car of Mr Benz and the sleek limousines on today's motorways would be described as the result of adaptive augmentations to knowledge). Emergent additions are often the result of the **discovery** of ideas that were previously completely unknown, whereas adaptive additions to knowledge are often the result of planned **information search**.

Knowledge evolves in a tension between:

- a **conservative instinct**, which aims to retain what has proved useful and has been appreciated by others; and
- an **experimental instinct**, which derives from curiosity and the desire to meet aspirations better by matching (often changing) circumstances.

Knowledge specific to space and time refers primarily to knowhow which differs from place to place and evolves over time. It is essential to effective human interaction; in economics, it relates primarily to commercial knowledge: where is the cheapest source of supply? who has the skills and connections this year to produce a specific product? how can one obtain a certain service by tomorrow? and so on. ●

'Economic Man' Does Not Exist

Conventional neoclassical economics has pushed the knowledge problem aside by making the simplifying assumption of 'perfect knowledge'. Many economic textbooks make this assumption on page 1 so that they can begin with logical deductions from this and other premises. What this implies in practice is that the preferences of millions of people for trillions of goods, services and satisfactions are known, as well as all the resources on earth and the billions of relevant production techniques. Then it is possible to reduce economics to simply computing how known resources are transformed by known technologies to meet the pre-existing, known preferences of 'economic man'. The elegant mental map of reality, the neoclassical model that one obtains, reduces the most essential questions of economics to a poor, overly abstract construct of the mind. Because of the birth defect of 'perfect knowledge', neoclassical theory often has little relevance to real human existence, which is a constant attempt to know more and test old knowledge.

Our approach to institutional economics is not based on the assumption of 'perfect knowledge'. Rather, the lack of knowledge – ignorance – is taken as part and parcel of human existence. It cannot be eliminated, because it is constitutional. But, as we shall see, the lack of knowledge can be eased by appropriate institutional arrangements which can guide individual decision makers through a complex and uncertain world and can help us to economise on the need to know. This approach may make economic analysis more cumbersome and less elegant, but, we trust, more relevant to understanding reality and more convincing to the practitioners in business and public policy.

3.2 Types of Behaviour, Cognition and Bounded Rationality: Deciphering Reality

Of Symbols and Images

We acquire a 'world view' and we decipher the complex reality around us by attaching meanings to symbols and by relating these symbols, one might say by operating with 'images' (Boulding, [1956] 1997). But thinking with symbols is not a purely private, individual matter. What the human mind constructs as an image of reality is influenced by social, cultural experience, so that different people perceive the world differently. Cultural experiences influence a person's cognition, as does language, since some thought processes make use of linguistic symbols. This makes communication between members of different cultures sometimes difficult, because many 'images of the mind' are not shared and need to be explicated before they are understood (Redding, 1993, pp. 72–7).

Because they create meaningful symbols and relate them in their minds, humans are able to interact with the world in ways that go beyond reflexive behaviour (like the response of the pupil of the eye to bright light), conditioned reflexes (like our mouths salivating when we think of delicious food), and instrumental behaviour (like the use of a stick to push a stone aside). The human mind is able to attach non-intrinsic, abstract meanings to signals and turn these into symbols which often represent meanings that have nothing to do with the original signal. Symbols may depend on a complex context in order to be read correctly (for example, a red light may indicate the need to stop the car or it may signal a red-light district). It is this capacity to work with abstract symbols that forms the 'mental gulf that divides the lowest savage from the highest ape', as the famous British anthropologist Edward Burnett Tylor (1883) once put it last century.

Symbolling constitutes the largest part of the knowledge and information we acquire, but it often influences the more primitive types of behaviour (reflexive and instrumental). Much learning takes the form of 'internalising' concepts that are first consciously acquired as symbols and then, through repeat processes, turned into conditioned reflexes. Thus, we first absorb a chain of symbols to understand how a car is steered. Then, we practise – again and again – till the various actions become almost automatic, conditioned reflexes. Skills and much specific knowledge is acquired by different people in similar ways, to become 'implicit knowledge'. In similar processes of internalisation, we acquire moral standards, which might be called 'ethical skills'.

They are most effectively learnt by repeat practice (observing adults in the family, for example). Thus, we are frequently honest not because we carefully analyse a specific situation through a chain of symbols, but in a conditioned-reflexive way. Such reflexive behaviour speeds up decision processes and enhances the effectiveness of human interaction.

O Key Concepts

Cognition is the invisible (re-)construction of reality as perceived by the senses which takes place in the mind, which operates almost imperceptibly in thought processes and which helps people to decipher reality. Cognition is, to some extent, culturally conditioned, so people from different cultures decipher reality differently. The human mind is informed by social experience: reality for one person is often at variance with reality as perceived by another person who has had different experiences.

We can distinguish between the following **types of behaviour** (moving from primitive to more highly developed forms):

- reflexive (example: contraction of a muscle when pain is inflicted);
- conditioned-reflexive (example: a shudder when you think of being beheaded);
- instrumental (example: use of chopsticks to eat);
- symbolising (creation, combination and digestion of symbols, example: developing an architectural design and using it to construct a building).

A **symbol** is a mental abstract, an image of the mind, which represents a more complex whole. ●

The Information Paradox

Rational decision making requires knowledge and wilful choice between alternatives. The alternatives have to be known to enable a rational choice. However, resources and time to obtain information about alternatives are scarce and costly, so endless information gathering is not possible. 'Information costs are the costs of transportation from ignorance to omniscience, and seldom can a trader afford to take the entire trip' (Stigler, 1967, p. 297). We often choose to remain ignorant because it is too costly to be informed. Otherwise the human race would perish of paralysis by analysis. Therefore, the question arises, to what point will people carry their information search: to the point where the expected marginal cost is equal to the (marginal) expected benefit (Stigler, 1971a), or to a point where experience suggests they probably know enough to decide?

The answer is that individuals cannot know the expected costs and benefits of obtaining certain types of information before they have acquired it, so they are unable to maximise net returns from knowledge not yet acquired. Paradoxically, they would need the very information before they have acquired it, as British economist George Shackle (1903–92) pointed out in the quote at the head of this chapter. This logic point had been called earlier the 'information paradox' (Arrow, 1962). Unlike the production of goods and services, where the knowledge is possessed beforehand about costs and benefits so that resource use can be optimised, the production of information cannot be subjected to such a rational calculus.

We can illustrate the point by thinking of a student who wonders whether it is worth £5 of his money to watch a particular movie. The only way to really know the answer is to spend the money and watch it! Although the risk can be reduced by reading film reviews, it is always possible, with hindsight, that the money would have been better spent on something else, even if a trailer or a film review gives partial knowledge of the movie. In short, when searching for new knowledge, we never know what we shall find and whether the information will be useful and as valuable as expected. Often, we are even completely ignorant of what we are missing until we make a discovery.

There is another peculiarity in the production of knowledge: the costs of knowledge search have to be considered as 'sunk costs'. This means that the costs of knowledge production once incurred have no relevance to the extent to which the information is used, whereas the costs of the production of goods have a bearing on the amount that can be produced with a profit (Streit and Wegner, 1992). In practice, people engage in the search for information until they perceive that they have incurred sufficient expense and then make a decision within the bounds of what they have been able to find out. Experience and individual inclination will guide them in acquiring information which they consider sufficient to make a choice; their experience will save them from wasting excessive effort on information gathering. This does not mean that they will not, in specific instances, make decisions which turn out to be wrong.

Obtaining and analysing new knowledge is costly in terms of time, effort and resources. Therefore, no one will acquire all the knowledge needed for complex operations. People will rather seek to exploit the knowledge of others by interacting with them. Indeed, it is rational for people to acquire only certain bits of information and to remain ignorant of other information, given the high costs and uncertain outcomes of knowledge search (rational ignorance).

Different Kinds of Rationality

What has been said so far has a further important consequence: people who incur the costs of searching for useful knowledge under conditions of uncertainty cannot be all-knowing and often will not be able to make rational choices. They will usually even find it hard to stick rigidly to their preconceived objectives and aspirations. In the process of interacting with others, their aspirations will evolve. If they are disappointed frequently, they peg back what they aspire to. If objectives are reached easily, they may become more ambitious and discover new wants. In other words, people will often display adaptive behaviour, recognising the bounds of what they can attain. But at other times enterprising people will act to break through the constraints which they normally accept as given or will discover new opportunities by chance.

We therefore have to distinguish between three kinds of rationality:

(a) end–means rationality, where the ends and the means to attain them are known, for example from earlier experience;
(b) bounded, adaptive rationality; and
(c) entrepreneurial-creative rationality that, on occasions, breaks out of recognised bounds, makes discoveries and exploits them.

Instances of end–means rationality can be observed when agents have set themselves fixed goals or when others have set those goals for them, and when people use available resources and techniques to maximise the attainment of the goals. When you enter a marathon race, your objective may be to finish in the shortest possible time to win the race. You employ all your resources of physical strength and will power, as well as your knowledge of how to pace yourself, towards attaining that goal. Another instance is a business company that employs all available means to achieve a return on its assets. This sort of rational behaviour underlies neoclassical textbook analysis.

But frequently the other kinds of rationality are prevalent. What if you are not a top long-distance runner but nevertheless want to compete in marathons? You will rationally adjust your objective to your own resources in the light of past performance and get great satisfaction from running a time commensurate to your resources. Instead of following absolute goals, people gradually discover what they can achieve and handle their goal-attainment rationally in an adaptive way. This is so because people are frequently limited in their capacities to absorb and evaluate information. American economist-sociologist Herbert Simon (1976) called this 'bounded rationality' or 'procedural rationality'. Instead of optimising given objectives, people and businesses 'satisfice', he wrote; they adjust their aspiration levels in the light of past experience.

❖ The Knowledge Problem and the Concept of Efficiency

One consequence of the knowledge problem is that extreme care must be taken in using the term 'efficiency'.

It is valid to say that a middle-range car which runs 100 km on 7 litres of petrol is more efficient than one that needs 10 litres. Here, we compare physical outputs (travel over 100 km) with inputs (litres of petrol) between fairly simple technical systems and make statements about **technical efficiency**.

Economic choices, however, require that we put valuations on inputs and outputs, for example market prices for the input of petrol and a valuation for the performance of a 100 km trip. This gives us information about **economic efficiency**. Such statements are valid, as long as we are clear about the valuation and understand the system in which inputs are converted to outputs, when making interpersonal utility comparisons.

Frequently, however, the term 'efficiency' is applied by planners and managers to complex, evolving systems where the valuation of diverse inputs and outputs is not clearly understood and where invalid interpersonal utility comparisons have to be made, about whose basis one really has no knowledge. Indeed, different observers will attach differing values and consider their own, subjective opportunity costs. Then, comparisons to the effect that 'A is more efficient than B' are not valid, because one simply does not know how other people would value inputs and outputs. The point may become clear to the reader when asked: Which is the most efficient motor car in the world? What is best depends on individual, subjective valuations, and a complex machine that can serve a myriad of differing purposes cannot generally be called the best or the most efficient.

The problem becomes even more intractable when we deal with unknowable inputs and outputs. A statement to the effect that 'this is the most efficient way to defend the security of country X' is invalid, because the output 'security' is inherently not known and hence not measurable. Rough-and-ready assumptions that some assumed proxy measures a nation's security, so that decisions can be made on efficiency, are likely to lead to dangerous errors because such assumptions will more likely than not turn out to be wrong.

When considering complex systems, such as national economies, we can only legitimately say that one system is capable of generating more economic growth than another or more innovations than another. This is a statement about the **dynamic efficiency** of a system, an inherent quality to adapt, respond or develop new knowledge.

The term efficiency becomes meaningless when its use implies comparisons between complex reality and an abstract, ideally functioning economic system in which decisions are made on the basis of perfect knowledge which allows decision makers, somehow, to evaluate all possible outcomes of the division of labour with given production techniques and given resources. Such a reference system can nowhere be realised. It is Utopian and hence not a valid reference standard to judge the efficiency of operations in the real world. It has been aptly characterised as a Nirvana approach to economics (Demsetz, 1969).

See R. Cordato, 'Efficiency', in Boettke (1994, pp. 131–7). ◆

At times, a third kind of rationality may be observed. Although people normally accept given constraints and act within them, whether they be constraints of nature and resource supply, of technical knowledge or of institutions, they may at certain junctures decide to tackle these constraints head-on and widen or bypass acknowledged obstacles to their goal achievement (Schumpeter, 1961). Thus, the Wright brothers, and many before them, did not accept the known constraints of gravity. The Wrights finally managed to fly in a powered aircraft. Or, in the Renaissance, some exceptional Europeans refused to accept the man-made constraints over the supply of spices from the East (the supply was constrained by Muslim intermediaries): they sailed directly and discovered the sea routes to India, and chanced on America in the process. In these cases, individuals acted out of a creative and entrepreneurial motivation. People at times also act in creative-entrepreneurial ways when they break institutional constraints, for example by violating conventions and customs, or when they engage in political lobbying to gain support for the change of an institution. We therefore have to recognise as a third type of rational behaviour creative rationality, which propels people to take risks and open up new paths and which keeps them on the alert for new discoveries which is apt to increase human knowledge.

We may go further and acknowledge that a considerable part of our daily human behaviour is not rationally and logically targeted at any identifiable objective. Much human action is coordinated by habits which cannot be explained in any one specific instance by rational calculus: why do people vote in elections, when this act has patently no measurable effect on the conduct of policy, let alone their own lives? Why do people give tips to waiters whom they will never see again? Often people simply follow habitual patterns, imitating others.

O **Key Concepts**

Rationality refers to purpose-directed action, guiding all actions towards the attainment of a goal or goals (or ends).

We can distinguish between:

(a) **end–means rationality**, where the ends are given and actions are taken to attain a given end (example: pursuit of a rate of return by a firm);

(b) adaptive **bounded rationality**, which relates to (in practice frequent) situations when people do not all-knowingly maximise their given objectives, but may adapt their aspirations (goals) in the light of experience to what is more feasible;

(c) **entrepreneurial-creative rationality**, which relates to an approach in which agents try to overcome existing constraints, whether of resource supplies, technological limits or institutional constraints (example: humans overcame the pull of gravity, a physical constraint, eventually in entrepreneurial-creative ways by exploring the lifting capacity of gases and fluid dynamics around fixed wings).

Rational ignorance is the behaviour of people not to acquire certain types of knowledge in the face of the costs and uncertainties of information search. ●

3.3   Motivation: By Love, Command or Self-interest

The Individual and Social Bonds

At this juncture, we have to emphasise the obvious fact that human beings interact with each other and that human behaviour has to be seen in a social context. Indeed, very few people can function well on their own for more than limited periods of time. They need the stimulation and control of how their fellows respond. Humans thrive intellectually, morally, culturally and emotionally only thanks to their personal connections with their fellows. Indeed, most people are at their worst when they are isolated, anonymous and alienated from others.

If we study institutions, by definition we do not adopt a position of 'isolationist individualism', a position of seeing the individual as an island, but rather we conceive of people as 'social animals' who pursue their own ends in cooperation with others. To adopt a position of individualism, as we have, therefore does not mean that we study people as stand-alone individuals. Individualism means instead that individual aspirations are the ultimate measure of social and economic study, but of individuals that live in a social context and are constrained by institutions, which largely define what is 'social'. The institutional-economics approach acknowledges that individuals establish reciprocal relations and indeed need lasting communal bonds. Each association with others gives us a sense of belonging, but it also imposes institutional strictures. Such associations are perceived as deeply satisfying and give people a sense of identity and security (Hazlitt, [1964] 1988, pp. 35–43). Social connections serve, so to speak, to keep our selfish, atavistic, opportunistic individual instincts on a leash, and institutions form a central part in constraining instinct-driven opportunism, as we have seen.

What has been said about social bonds between individuals also applies to groups. If various social groups are sharply delineated and in conflict, sustained economic development is unlikely (Powelson, 1994). What is needed is the open society, in which the poor share power and share rules with the rich and powerful (Popper, 1945). Eric Jones, who studied episodes of economic growth in history, spoke in this context of the 'relative connectedness' of the community as a precondition to creative and effective interaction (Jones, 1988, p. 128).

From recognising these facts of human existence it does not follow that the 'herd' has to be organised by a leader, commanded from the top down and directed to serve some predetermined goal(s). Frequently, social bonds evolve spontaneously, and people usually belong to numerous, overlapping groups, associations and networks which are governed by differing institutions (pluralist society). Thus, we may be members of a family, various clubs, religious communities, differently defined regional entities, such as a local neighbourhood, a city, a province, a nation state, and a transnational cultural community. We normally feel that such diverse and multiple associations best serve to realise our potential.

The social aspect of human behaviour is no doubt deeply embedded in the human heritage. Paleo-anthropologists believe that the gradual evolution of our ancestors from bands of *Australopithecus*, who probably lived in hordes like baboons, had much to do with social interaction when hunting, gathering or sharing the loot in camps. Humans trained their differentiated cognitive abilities by social interaction; they gained evolutionary advantages in coordinating with others and survived better (Leakey, 1994).[3] Evolution thus favoured people with good interactive and coordinative abilities who functioned well in social groups. And tribes which developed institutions which ensured that scarce food resources were shared evenly within a close-knit, small group under a circumspect leader had better survival chances. Thus, a 'tribal mentality' based on social bonding and sharing evolved over millions of years and became deeply embedded in the human psyche (Hayek, 1976a, pp. 133–52; Giersch, 1996). When studying human behaviour, we therefore must not assume that humans are isolated individuals, but rather that they are social creatures whose interaction is essential to them.

This leads us on to the next question: namely, what motivates individuals to act on behalf of others?

Three Types of Motivation

It is a basic premise of human behaviour that individuals normally act in their own self-interest. They may pursue their aspirations in whatever way possible, whether this harms the aspirations of others or not. Thus, the aspiration not to go hungry may be pursued by planting food, by buying and selling, or by theft. Experience shows, however, that theft (and other types of opportunistic behaviour) leads to costly conflicts and is wasteful in that a society of thieves reaches lower satisfaction levels than a society in which people cooperate honestly. We therefore have to ask how individual autonomy to act should be constrained so that such opportunism is controlled. We already know from what was said earlier that this kind of constraint on human behaviour is the function of institutions.

In principle, there are three ways in which people can be induced to make an effort in the interest of others (Boulding, 1969, p. 6; Hazlitt, [1964] 1988, pp. 92–107):

(a) they make the effort to benefit others out of love, solidarity, or other variants of altruism;
(b) they are coerced by someone who threatens them with the use of force (command);
(c) they act out of their own free will, but are motivated out of enlightened self-interest because they can expect a sufficient reward. What they do for others is then the side-effect of their selfishness.

The first motivation works well in small groups such as the family, in a small tribe and among friends. It deserves social recognition and is often rewarded by prestige. It enables the division of labour and knowledge in small communities without high coordination and monitoring costs. As noted above, such motivation has been so essential for the survival of small tribes of our ancestors during hundreds of thousands of generations that most humans have been instinctively conditioned to consider altruism as something noble and praiseworthy.

But what works well in the small group, because of good knowledge about the others and mutual control that is tempered by personal empathy, cannot be transferred to the large group, such as the modern macro-society with industrial mass production and mass communication.[4] Some may regret that large communities such as nations do not work like a family. They may also regret that the baker does not simply provide the bread for free. Yet the evidence is clear: when interacting with strangers, people usually need a motivation other than love and solidarity.

This becomes apparent when the solidarity model of the small group is transferred to society at large by the socialist doctrine. The promise of communal sharing under the slogan 'from each according to ability, to each according to need' leads to massive shirking and hence poor living standards. Efforts to reform people and to create the new socialist man who toils selflessly for others out of mere altruism have failed abysmally. Consequently, people had to be coerced. Representatives of the state, however selected, assumed the power to punish those who did not produce to the targeted norm. Coercion and fear were then the main motivations under socialism to get people to produce something for the benefit of others – and dissimulation and shirking were practised wherever people could get away with it. In the Christian tradition, education and preaching are relied upon to encourage people to treat others with solidarity. This may have worked in small groups in early Christendom but it failed to ensure adequate living standards in bigger societies, where solidarity inevitably declines with social distance.

The third possible motivation is self-interest. It works, for example, through voluntary exchange in the market place. People share knowledge and help others because they want what the others have to offer. The doctor who gets up in the night to attend to a sick child does so for the money. But the beneficial side-effect of his selfish action is that the child's pain is eased. It may be shocking to young people who are educated in the solidarity mode of the family to discover that, in anonymous mass society, others do things that benefit them as a by-product of a selfish pursuit of money. But at least many different people, with different skills and assets, act to their benefit, even if they do not care personally for the people they serve. People are thus guided by 'the invisible hand' to work for the benefit of others. The 'invisible hand' of the market mechanism has in practice to be supplemented by institutional constraints, such as an understanding of professional duty (for example, in the medical profession) and the effort to keep a reputation intact out of a long-term, extended self-interest.

Clearly, people will only be motivated to perform a service for others out of self-interest if the reward they obtain is for them to keep and if they are not forced to share what they have earned with others. This means that people must have the right to private property, including in the use of their own labour. Without a respected and protected right to own property – which also entails the right to exclude others from its use and to dispose of the property as one decides – there will not be sufficient motivation for the many specialists in a modern mass society to produce the goods and services that other people want. The useful knowledge that is held in millions of different human brains will only be exploited to the best of people's abilities if there is a set of institutions (rules) that protect private property.

The President of Uganda, Yoweri Museveni, a former Marxist who ended civil conflict and turned the economy around, expressed the motivation issue brilliantly when he said:

> I think that [collectivism] was a strategic mistake. They [the Marxists] chose a tool which would not get human beings to produce. Do you make [the people] produce by appealing to the altruism which was very much in short supply? Or do you make them produce by making use of their selfishness, which was in abundance?
> (*Reported in* Time, *14 April 1997, p. 43*)

Motivation in Micro and in Macro Societies

At this juncture in the argument, we have reached several very important conclusions:

- love and altruism, which have a very important place in motivating people in small groups, do not work among people in modern mass societies who do not know and cannot control each other directly;
- the alternative of relying on coercion has the important drawback that those in authority often do not have the knowledge necessary to utilise all available resources and that people who are coerced try to shirk their duties when they are able to get away with it;
- the system of utilising available knowledge and accumulating new information, which is at the heart of the economic growth process, requires incentives that appeal to self-interest and rely on voluntary action. The desirable outcomes of such action are often

unintended by-products of the selfish pursuit of people's own purposes.

O Key Concepts

The **information paradox** arises when we want to assess how many resources to dedicate to information search. Whereas we can calculate beforehand how many resources to use in order to obtain a desired output from a farm or factory, given that we have all relevant information on how the farm or factory functions, such a calculus of optimisation cannot be made for the production of knowledge. We simply do not have the necessary information prior to incurring the expense of acquiring it. We can normally only go by past experience and seek limited information before making a decision. And once the knowledge has been acquired, the costs of information search are sunk costs: they have no effect on the further use of the information.

Opportunism describes the short-term maximisation of human satisfaction without regard to the impact of such behaviour on others and without regard to the accepted norms of behaviour in a community. Such behaviour has disintegrating, and hence harmful, long-term consequences and makes human actions less predictable over the long term. Thus, it is opportunistic to satisfy one's appetite by stealing from others, or to forget to repay one's contractual debts. 'By opportunism I mean self-interested seeking with guile. This includes, but is scarcely limited to, more blatant forms, such as lying, stealing, and cheating' (Williamson, 1985, p. 47). It is the role of institutions, which always include sanctions, to suppress opportunism.

Small-group coordination, for example within the family, is based on much implicit knowledge and informal behavioural control, usually by someone in authority whose power is tempered by sympathy. By contrast, **macro-group coordination** requires general institutions because a large number of people have to be coordinated and no one can possess all the specific knowledge and capacity to control everyone and everything by prescriptive command.

Altruism is an attitude that places the interests of others above one's own. It contrasts not only with egotism (ruthless self-seeking), but also with a rational extended self-interest in pursuing own goals in preference to satisfying the poorly known aspirations of others. ●

3.4 The Principal–Agent Problem

Agents and Principals

Since motivation by altruism is normally limited to small groups and coercion is wasteful and ineffectual, a problem arises when people act for others to whom they are not very close. It is common for people to act as agents on behalf of principals; for example, when the owners of a firm employ staff, when managers run the day-to-day operations of a business that belongs to shareholders, or when citizens elect politicians to decide certain tasks on their behalf. In these cases, agents are tempted to act opportunistically in the knowledge that they will get away with it since the principals are not well informed or remain 'rationally ignorant' about the details of the agent's actions. The principals incur high monitoring costs if they want to find out what the agents are really doing (asymmetric information). Consequently, workers may get away with shirking some of their duties when they could work harder. Business managers may prefer the good life and satisfice, whereas it would be in the interest of the owner of the business (the principal) if they behaved in risky, creative-entrepreneurial ways. And citizens, the principals, often do not get from government officials what they want because parliamentarians and officials pursue their own purposes. This is known as the 'principal–agent problem', a consequence of the knowledge problem and the natural limits to solidarity with others.[5]

When people feel they can get away with opportunistic behaviour, because those whom they short-change do not know and will not find out, they fall prey to 'moral hazard'. This term was first used in insurance, when insured persons failed to take full precautions to avoid damage and when only they could know what full precaution meant. Thus, agents are exposed to moral hazard when principals are ignorant or when they are not constrained in their actions by appropriate rules.

The principal–agent problem is often considerable when people are employed in big business and government organisations. They tend to busy themselves with activities they themselves find agreeable, and not necessarily with activities that serve the purpose(s) of the enterprise to sell at a profit for the owners or to achieve other objectives of the principals. This often results in high organisation costs. Managers and other employees in a firm may come up with schemes to organise numerous meetings, research projects, in-service courses and coordination committees that deflect or distribute responsibilities for risk-taking. They may justify the need to travel and a whole host of other seemingly 'essential' activities, many of which occupy their time and add to overheads without making a sufficient contribution to the profit. Yet outsiders, including the owners of the firm and hence their employers, do not know which costs are necessary and which are not.

How to Motivate Agents

Wherever people employ agents to act on their behalf, the motivation of the agents requires attention. The three types of motivation, discussed above, may be employed by principals to ensure that agents act to their best capabilities on their behalf:

(a) Agents can be inspired to make the principals' goals their own out of solidarity. Where only few people are involved, say in a small firm, collaborators can be very loyal to the owner, or owners can use direct appeals to their colleagues to perform on their behalf; even in larger operations collaborators can be educated in habits of loyalty to the principals, which can save on monitoring and other transaction costs.

(b) Agents can be controlled by direct supervision and coercive commands. They can be guided by instructions and be subject to penalties if they do not follow instructions, as long as the principals are informed about the agents' actions and potential scope for action.

(c) Agents can follow general rules which create incentives for them to pursue the principals' interests out of their own self-interest (indirect control). Thus, workers may promote profitability because they want performance pay, even if the principals' profits are of no direct concern to them.

An example for direct control of possibly opportunistic agents is the supervision of workers in a factory to see whether they produce the output quantities that the management has planned. This requires much knowledge on the part of the principals and supervisors and may cause high monitoring costs when the production task becomes complex. The alternative is to appeal – as far as possible – to the self-motivation of the agents by rules and incentives which induce them to do the principals' bidding voluntarily, for example by paying the workers piece rates or by profit-sharing arrangements. Important indirect controls against pervasive agent opportunism also derive from competition: agents perceive that they risk losing their jobs if they do not perform as well as they can to promote the principals' purposes.

Massive principal–agent problems arose in socialism, a doctrine that claimed the moral high ground by rejecting the motive of selfishness. Since solidarity with 'society' turned out to be limited, the principals had to rely on coercion, but found themselves confronted with insurmountable information and monitoring costs. The principals simply could not know what production was possible, what innovations might be feasible and what resources could be saved. Their capacity to coerce and punish 'their' agents was extremely limited, and shirking became almost universal. In the end, the system collapsed because of the failure to cope with the principal–agent problem.

The principal–agent problem is a central concern of institutional economics. As we shall see, it is often addressed by appropriate institutions. Much human effort has gone into finding ways of tackling it (Jensen and Meckling, 1976; Arrow, 1985). In later chapters, we shall discuss the problem in business organisations, which are often run by managers on behalf of the owners, and in government, where politicians and administrators need to be motivated to do the citizens' bidding in circumstances where the citizens simply do not know much about the affairs of government and often prefer to remain ignorant.

O Key Concepts

The **principal–agent problem** arises whenever people act on behalf of others, whom we call principals, and when the agents have better knowledge about the operation than the principals (asymmetric information). It is then possible that agents may act in their own interests and neglect the interests of the principals (shirking, opportunistic behaviour). The problem is prevalent in big business and big government and presents a major management challenge.

When people act opportunistically, we say that they fall prey to **moral hazard**. The term was first used in the analysis of insurance to describe cases where insured individuals failed to undertake all possible steps to avoid damage, knowing that they would be compensated. In a more general sense, moral hazard is now used to describe situations where self-interested individuals are tempted to violate general standards of honesty and reliability because circumstances allow them to get away with it. ●

Questions for Review

● To understand the importance of the division of labour and knowledge, imagine how long you would survive all on your own in a remote wilderness if you could only consume what you yourself have made or are able to gather. Begin by imagining that you are cold and hungry ... and do not cheat by assuming that you brought food or matches from the supermarket! Then think about how your living standard would rise if you could coopt others, so that some of you could specialise. Ask yourself what ten categories of people you would coopt to your wilderness to improve your chances of survival.

- Give examples of (a) adaptive, trial-and-error evolution of knowledge, and (b) creative steps forward (emergent changes).
- Can you find an example from your own life where the conflict between the interest to conserve old knowledge and the interest to experiment with new information was decided in favour of the new? Why did you adopt and utilise new information?
- What is 'rational action'?
- Explicate the differences between (a) ends–means rationality; (b) bounded rationality; and (c) entrepreneurial-creative rationality, by examples from your own personal experience.
- What is meant by 'bounded rationality'? Can you find an example when you made adjustments to your own set goals? Why did you adjust your aspirations?
- What motivates people to perform services for others?
- Why did we write that love and compassion are not sufficient to motivate people who live in a modern industrial society?
- Which motivation underlies the concept of socialism?
- What happens when people lose the right to own what their own labour creates (slavery)?
- Define the principal–agent problem and find an example where you act as an agent for others. What are the devices that motivate you not to act opportunistically?
- Where do others act at your behest? How are they motivated to do their best on your behalf?
- Do you know cases of 'moral hazard' among your associates? Do you recall having fallen prey to the 'moral hazard' temptation yourself?

Notes

1. This fundamental point is made brilliantly in L.E. Read, 'I, Pencil', which we reproduce with permission in the Appendix.
2. John Locke in particular was far ahead of his time. Recent physiological research has confirmed how sensations lead to short-term connections in the brain and are committed to the short-term memory. As a given sensation is reaffirmed by repeat sensations or reflection, hormonal bursts convert the short-term impressions into 'hardwired' connections in our brains, associations that we remember long term.
3. The theory of biological evolution, which Charles Darwin developed, differs from

the evolution of human knowledge and ideas in that new knowledge can be learnt and passed on to other people, whereas biological evolution does in all probability contain a mechanism to incorporate what has been learnt in the genes which are passed on to future generations. Hence, a close analogy between biological and social evolution would be misleading.

4. In western society, most people think of a continuum of ever-wider communities, from the micro- to the macro-groups to which they belong: the nuclear family, the extended family, the local community, the province, the church, the professional group, as well as other intermediate, voluntary groupings of civil society, the nation, the West, the global community. In other societies, perceptions differ. Thus, traditional Chinese society had a much less continuous perception of belonging. One was the member of a distinct, strongly bonded and self-administering micro-society called family and of the macro-society of the nation (Redding, 1993). However, Chinese emigrants quickly developed many voluntary associations that form layers between the micro-level of the family and the macro-universe of the nation and developed a corresponding gradient of solidarity.

5. One aspect of the principal–agent problem, which is not often dealt with, concerns the opportunistic sheltering of principals behind their agents: sometimes the boss hides behind the agents – think of the Mr Big in drug trading – to escape responsibility for his or her actions. This point will not be pursued further in this book.

CHAPTER 4

Fundamental Human Values

Most individuals aspire to certain universal, fundamental values, such as freedom, justice, security, peace and prosperity. These are general, overriding preferences to which most people attach a high priority and to which they subordinate other pursuits. These values underpin societal bonds and motivate people in their life's pursuits. We incorporate considerations about basic human values in our analysis, because they undergird social structures and institutions.

We shall also discuss the meaning of freedom, justice and equity, as well as security, peace and material welfare. We shall see that certain interpretations of justice and equity have the capacity to undermine freedom and security. Next, we shall discuss nature conservation and recent attempts to place the aim of environmental protection above the human-centred values mentioned above.

The point will be made that only human values can serve to coordinate people and that the pursuit of absolute objectives, which are not related to shared human values, is likely to undermine a free society. We acknowledge that conflicts arise when these fundamental values are pursued, but shall also show that conflicts can be attenuated or even turned into complementarities if one thinks long term and relies on general rules rather than arbitrary *ad hoc* interventions.

One may rob an army of its commander-in-chief; one cannot deprive the humblest man of his free will.
(*Confucius (c. 551–479*BC*)*, Analects)

We regard happiness as the fruit of freedom, and freedom as the fruit of courage.
(*Pericles, reportedly in his funeral oration for the dead of the Peloponnesian war, 431*BC*)

All men are created equal ... endowed by their Creator with certain in-alienable rights; that among these are Life, Liberty, and the pursuit of Happiness.
(Bill of Rights, adopted 1790 in the US Constitution)

Political liberty consists in the power of doing whatever does not injure another. The exercise of the natural rights of every man has no other limits than those which are necessary to secure to every other man the free exercise of the same rights; and these limits are determined only by law.
(French National Assembly, Declaration of the Rights of Man, *1789)*

An economy, of course, does indeed consist of technologies, actions, mar-kets, financial institutions and factories – all real and tangible. But behind these, guiding them and being guided by them on a sub-particle level are beliefs ... They shape in aggregate the macro economy ... They are the DNA of the economy.
(W.B. Arthur, Complexity, *1995)*

To preach morality is easy; to give it a foundation is hard.
(A. Schopenhauer, German philosopher, 1788–1860)

4.1   Shared, Underlying Values

Universal Values

When individuals pursue specific purposes of their own, which differ from those of others and vary over time, their actions nevertheless tend to be informed and supported by largely similar underlying values. Whatever their background and culture, most human beings, when given the choice, place a high priority on attaining a number of fairly universal, fundamental values, even at the expense of other, more specific aspirations. The values discussed here are ultimate pur-poses to which people normally aspire; they constitute powerful motivations for human action and have a pervasive influence on daily human actions. Visible economic phenomena are influenced by values in ways analogous to how invisible DNA carries chromosome infor-mation which informs all our visible physiological and psychological traits (see the quote from Brian Arthur at the top of this chapter). Moreover, we can observe that these values are central to what most citizens would consider a good society (Boulding, 1959; Hazlitt, [1964] 1988, pp. 35–43 and 53–61). They are:

(a) individual freedom from fear and coercion, which is reflected in numerous civil and economic liberties. Freedom means that indi-viduals can enjoy a sphere of safeguarded autonomy to pursue their self-chosen purposes, a domain where they are in control of their decisions but of course within constraints set by physical-technical and socioeconomic conditions, particularly those institutions that serve to protect the freedom of others. Freedom without the constraint of rules would be licence, and licence inevitably destroys social harmony and effective cooperation;

(b) justice, which means that people in equal circumstances are treated equally and that restraints are placed on all in equal measure, irrespective of class or person. In practice, this often relates to the demand for the rule of law rather than the (arbitrary) rule of men. This kind of procedural (or formal) justice is closely related to equity, namely that all have the opportunity to pursue their self-set goals without artificial hindrance. Some observers stipulate different interpretations of justice and equity, implying some degree of equality of outcomes irrespective of the starting position, luck or effort (see section 4.2 below);

(c) security, which is the confidence that people will be able to enjoy their life and freedom into the future without experiencing violent and undue interference and unexpected and unmanageable changes in their circumstances. It may refer to one's own personal appreciation of security or to an observer's appreciation of other people's security. Some observers, though most decidedly not the authors of this book, give a different meaning to security, relating it to the protection of acquired socioeconomic positions in the face of change and challenges.

(d) peace, which is the absence of strife and violence inflicted by powerful agents, both within the community (internal peace) and from the outside (external peace). Peace is closely related to security according to the first meaning in the preceding paragraph, but not to security in the sense of conserving acquired socioeconomic positions;

(e) economic welfare (or prosperity), which relates to aspirations for material betterment and for some measure of security of material achievements over time;

(f) a livable natural and man-made environment; this is another value that most people aspire to. It may be considered to a considerable extent as a subset of security (for example, to avoid future environmental catastrophes that could harm human wellbeing). Other observers, though not the authors of this book, postulate nature preservation as an absolute objective, which should take precedence over human aspirations.

These human aspirations take varying concrete forms, depending on past experience and cultural circumstance. They have fairly universal appeal only in their general content. As far as we know, human beings have hardly ever striven to be deprived of freedom, to forgo justice and so on, unless they could see a trade-off with another of the afore-mentioned fundamental values. Therefore fundamental human values – these universally shared preferences of a very high order – are revealed by frequent human choice. 'Where an individual sets the "stopping point", what "ultimate" values he adopts is solely his responsibility, not that of society, although the values prevalent in a given society influence the individual who has grown up there or lives there' (Radnitzky, in Radnitzky and Bouillon, 1995a, p. 7).

Since human beings pursue these values in their actions, it seems appropriate to incorporate the analysis of values – and of how these values affect human action – in the analysis of institutional economics (the reader is referred to our remarks on value judgements in the Foreword). Confining ourselves to a value-free analysis, in the sense of the analyst not referring to her or his values, would deprive the theory of much relevance. The theory would not be able to explicate reality sufficiently.

Interdependencies in Multivalue Systems

When people pursue various fundamental values concurrently, as they normally do, they discover complex interdependencies between them. Sometimes, there are complementarities between values, which means that an advance in achieving one fundamental aspiration also advances the achievement of another. An example of such a complementarity would be a situation where greater prosperity leads to more security because more material resources can be invested in ensuring future freedom. In other cases there are conflicts, for example when greater individual freedom means less peace within a community.

The trade-offs between the various values are often hard to assess because they change with circumstances and because there are so many interdependencies. It is therefore important not to single out one particular value as superior to all others. Admittedly, a single-value approach may often be appealing and easier to understand, but it would only lead to the total neglect of the other values and ultimately a worsening of the human condition. If, for example, the preservation of peace were given absolute priority, individual freedom, material progress and widely shared notions of justice would in all likelihood soon be violated. Likewise, the pursuit of absolute individual freedom, free of all constraints, leads to gross violations of internal and external peace and of what most people consider as just and equitable. The pursuit of specific aspirations is therefore always circumscribed by trade-offs among the multiplicity of values.

Conflicting values tend to be more frequent in the short term. What is a conflict over the short run may turn out to be a complementarity over the longer run. Examples for this are:

- limitations of individual freedom that may promote short-term increases in prosperity, for example, when the freedom to invest abroad is limited. But over the long run freedom of choice of how and where to invest promote prosperity, and growing prosperity is in turn likely to promote liberty, as the experience of the 1980s and 1990s in many countries suggests;
- in the short run, security often conflicts with prosperity, for example when scarce resources are diverted from private investment and consumption to defence spending. But, over the long run, prosperous countries are more secure, and secure countries attract more of the capital and enterprise which are conducive to growing prosperity.

For public policy, this has the practical implication that a long-term focus, coupled with a plea for a measure of tolerance in short-term conflicts, promotes conflict avoidance and a better realisation of people's aspirations.

O Key Concepts

Fundamental values are defined here as the fairly universally held, high preferences of individuals to which more specific aspirations tend to be subordinated. Such values take different concrete shape in different societies, but are in principle universally pursued irrespective of culture. Examples of such fundamental values are freedom, justice, peace, security and prosperity.

Two fundamental values (or goals) are in **conflict** when the promotion of the one detracts from the other (example: more security comes at the expense of freedom). They are **complementary** when the promotion of one value also furthers the attainment of the other (example: more freedom promotes prosperity). Relationships between fundamental values are not static, but depend on the means chosen to attain them and on the time horizon over which the values are pursued – with longer time horizons, conflicts often turn into complementarities. ●

What Defines Decent Society?

Various societies may be judged by the extent to which its members are able to attain these fundamental values and by the extent to which the majority of the population adheres spontaneously to them. It would also seem valid to apply these fundamental, widely held standards as a measuring rod to judge a particular government's policies and actions. In short, individual human values are the norms on which institutions and public policies are normally judged. They describe good society from the viewpoint of the individual and reflect a vision that turns human wellbeing over the longer term into the yardstick for assessing institutions and public policy.

Policy makers sometimes adopt these values as explicit policy goals, even enshrining them in constitutions and political programmes. However, it must be noted that fundamental values are not abstract ends in themselves. They are always anchored in individual human aspirations. Nor are they some societal, communal goals that can be separated from what individuals want or that represent solely what the rulers want. They are always given meaning by what the sovereign, diverse human beings in a community value highly and universally.

The high and universal preferences that we call fundamental values are often internalised. This means they have been deeply ingrained in the human psyche by practice and experience and are often brought to bear without explicit reflection. The process of internalising fundamental values probably begins at a young age and, similar to conventions such as honesty, they are practised within the microcosm of the family before they are applied and refined in contact with the macrocosm of the wider community. They become part of 'culture' and the definition of what makes a society.

If the fundamental values of a society are shared strongly and consistently and, if necessary, are defended with resolve, they constitute a support for that society's institutions, thereby enhancing the chance of social order (Radnitzky and Bouillon, 1995a, 1995b; Scully, 1992). The comparison of the fundamental beliefs and expectations of human beings with the DNA information that shapes the physical appearance of the body seems appropriate as ever-evolving human actions are guided by these universal preferences just as the specifics of biological evolution are guided by the invisible chromosomes (compare the quotation at the head of this chapter). Reasonably stable, universal values and beliefs can make an intractably complex world more manageable for us. They are therefore part of the 'social capital' that enables a community to prosper by the division of labour and they help to augment its material resources. In that sense, fundamental values constitute a production factor that is often more important than physical items, such as machines or transport facilities, as they underpin how smoothly we cooperate. The importance of fundamental values becomes evident when we look at societies that do not share a commitment to them, for example parts of the Balkans as to peace and justice, many African societies as to personal security, and repressive regimes around the world as to individual freedom.

But the relationship between human values and economic life is not a one-way street. Communities with a prospering open economy, in which most people are fairly self-reliant, create a demand for the defence of fundamental values. Such an economy tends to form part of a social environment in which fundamental aspirations to freedom, justice, security and the like are constantly practised, tested and asserted, so that they are held more firmly and uniformly. This can be best seen when we observe what happens in economies that are not competitive and in societies that are subject to totalitarian rule. Here, subservience, dissimulation of basic aspirations and toleration of gross violations of basic human values are common. The community's institutions are then not well supported by fundamental values and do not function well in coordinating human behaviour. As we shall see later, one of the legacies of totalitarian regimes with discriminatory institutions and unfree economies is that basic human values are held and practised in an ill-defined manner. Then, the internal and external institutions are not well supported by individuals ready to defend the basic values spontaneously in the face of rule violations.

4.2   Freedom, Justice and Equity

'Freedom From' and 'Freedom To'

The United Nations human rights declaration begins with the statement that all human beings are born free. Freedom depends on a community consensus that certain actions (by fellow citizens, by governments) must be tolerated and others are prohibited by general, enforceable rules. It is the liberty *from* something, such as coercion or fear (negative liberties), not the freedom *to* do something or lay some claim *to* something (positive liberties). The prohibitions that ensure freedom are directed against all actions that might impede others in their legitimate pursuit of their own happiness. From a slightly different standpoint freedom may be defined in the words of the German philosopher Immanuel Kant (1724–1804) who wrote that freedom relates to the 'conditions under which the arbitrary decisions of the individual are made compatible with the arbitrary decisions of others by a universal law of liberty'. Thus, the protection of the autonomous domain of citizens to the maximum possible extent is the guarantor of freedom. Institutions that proscribe those actions which have in past experience proven to be incompatible with the freedom of all serve to promote freedom. Such institutions have to be universal in that they apply equally to unknown numbers of people and cases (Hayek, 1988, pp. 62–3).

The classical definition of freedom is freedom from interference: to what extent can individuals enjoy protected domains of autonomous decision and self-responsibility? But in the course of the twentieth century, another definition of freedom has been popularised in certain circles: the freedom to claim resources, to work, to health services, and so on. Whereas the classical notion is a negative freedom, denying others control and ensuring self-responsibility, this second notion relates to positive freedoms, claims to (someone's) resources. The argument in favour of these positive freedoms is that negative freedoms cannot be exercised without resources, so poor or unemployed people are not 'free'. This notion has given rise to the contemporary American meaning of 'liberal', which differs from the classical European meaning of the term. The proliferation of open-ended, liberal claims to resources requires coercion and leads to fear, that is, it diminishes freedom as defined by the classical liberal writers. In this book, the term freedom is confined to the classical liberal definition.

Power and Freedom

When people are free, they can pursue their self-set goals according to their own plans. But people may also exercise their free will by trying to influence others so that these others support their goals. Such an influence may be accepted out of voluntary compliance – for example, out of personal empathy or because of a signed contract – or because of a threat of force (coercion). In the first case, the freedom of the other party is not impeded, whereas it is when coercion comes into play. The distinction between voluntary compliance and coercion is, however, less clear-cut than it may appear at first glance. Coercion represents merely the extreme case in which the coerced party has no chance to resist or escape the threatened use of force.

Below a certain threshold, more or less subtle means to exercise coercive power over others exist, even in situations in which people submit in more or less voluntary ways. Power over others, whether exercised by individuals or by organised groups such as industry cartels, unions or government bodies, is a consequence of limited or inferior alternatives which the others have at their disposal to choose from. The alternatives to submitting (more or less freely) may be attractive, for example when there is a psychological dependency on the holder of power. In economic life, power is the result of a lack of competition, that is, a lack of close substitutes between which one may chose. Suppliers may, for example, have market power in the form of a monopoly thanks to a successful innovation, which limits the realistic choices of potential buyers. This limitation of the freedom of choice of buyers tends to be temporary. More durable limits to economic freedom exist when a supplier's market power is the result of private or public restraints of competition, for example by the formation of an industry cartel or through government interference with free trade. Public restraints are based on the power of government to coerce. These few examples should suffice to demonstrate the difficulties that arise whenever we deal with the phenomena of power and freedom in society.

Procedural Justice versus 'Social Justice'

The discussion of freedom also touches on justice. Private coercion is incompatible with individual freedom and tends also to be considered unjust. One of the major reasons for the existence of government is to ensure that all individuals are protected from the exercise of coercion by powerful individuals and groups. Many communities legitimise the exercise of collective force, because experience has shown that the exercise of individual power by violent means leads to injustices or a 'brutish state' of society, as the British philosopher Thomas Hobbes (1588–1679) put it. Where human interactions are determined by the violence potential of thuggish people or groups, ordinary people experience injustice. Indeed, to prevent this is a central concern of collective action (Chapter 10).

Justice may be measured by one of the following standards:

(a) justice of individual behaviour: namely, that individuals and authorities should treat others equally in equal circumstances (no discrimination, procedural justice); or

(b) justice as a social norm: namely, that social positions and the outcomes of interaction should be equal ('social justice' or 'equality of outcomes', which is at the basis of the welfare state and which will be discussed more fully in Chapter 10).

Like 'positive freedom' (claims), 'social justice' is at loggerheads with the attainment of freedom and prosperity, as we shall see below.

The Principle of Non-discrimination

When discussing institutions such as the law, we may ask what content the institutions should have to ensure that the actions of individuals and government are considered as just. At least in the Judeo-Christian and Islamic social traditions, which are based on the notion of the equality of individuals before God, justice in the procedural sense is tied to the concept of equality before the law. Justice is that kings and beggars are subject to equal laws (a key aspect of the rule of law) – a concept that is far from universal and that is in practice widely violated around the world. Procedural justice requires the guarantee of equal basic rights irrespective of race, religion, wealth or connections. It always relates to 'negative liberties', freedoms from unnecessary and unequal restraints, not to 'positive liberties'. In economic life, justice in this sense means that all have, in principle, the same liberties to compete with their diverse assets and to be treated as equals. It does not mean equal luck or equal outcomes from that competition.

When discrimination is proscribed and individuals are not allowed the use of force, then people are compelled to rely on voluntary cooperation with others through contracts. The aim of the (private) law is to ensure that all citizens enjoy equal opportunities to act out of their own free will without unnecessary legal constraints. This is procedural justice. It is the only form of justice which the state can guarantee: equal outcomes can, in any event, not be guaranteed since chance has a hand in determining outcomes. Another reason why government cannot guarantee social justice in the sense of ensuring equal outcomes is that, in modern mass society, a great number of other human beings have an influence on outcomes, many of whom are unknown to the individual actor or the government. Equal outcomes are therefore impossible to imagine, as long as people enjoy the freedom to act and react and as long as that has a bearing on what they earn and own. Like positive liberties, the equality of outcomes ('social justice') requires that property rights are infringed. It must be noted here that inequality is not injustice (Flew, 1989).

'Social justice' – attained by redistribution of material endowments and outcomes to achieve equality after interaction in the market place – relies on collective action to reallocate property rights according to a preconceived standard of equality. This conflicts with the principle of justice in the sense of equal treatment of persons and circumstances, as well as the principle of freedom. The pursuit of 'social justice' therefore poses several fundamental questions: If the formally just treatment of people leads to unequal outcomes, should the treatment of people then become unequal to ensure outcome equality? Or what is to be done if unequal starting positions persist? Then, equalisation by redistributive government intervention has to rely on discrimination against some. Negative freedom is also pushed aside when claims for (positive) material equality are pursued and the traditional concept of procedural justice is violated, as the law is used to discriminate between formally equal citizens. Then, equality before the law gives way to a state of affairs that many would consider unjust (Hayek, 1976a, pp. 62–88).

When government assumes a redistributive function, it can therefore not treat all citizens with formal equality. The classical role of government was only to protect the law and the peace. But when redistribution became a concern of government in western societies, individual liberties and the rule of law were in danger of being undermined (a more detailed analysis of the consequences of the pursuit of 'social justice' will be given in section 10.4).

This conclusion forces us to acknowledge that 'social justice' cannot be achieved by government action over the long term. This is borne out by the evidence of beggars in the streets of even the most elaborate western welfare states and by the evidence of a fairly even income and wealth distribution in the new industrial countries of East Asia, which have not made much of an attempt at redistribution policy (Riedel, 1988, pp. 18–21; World Bank, 1993).

None the less, gross inequalities in incomes and living standards are considered unacceptable to many in Western societies, partly because people identify to some extent with their most vulnerable fellow human beings and partly because they fear deleterious consequences for internal peace and the attainment of other fundamental values (Kliemt, 1993). There is certainly a role for private, voluntary charity on the part of the affluent for the poor. Such voluntary redistribution, instead of coercive state intervention to reallocate property rights, has beneficial effects, also for those who do not participate. It therefore deserves societal acclaim.

4.3   Security, Peace and Prosperity

Security: the Intertemporal Dimension of Freedom

Security is the intertemporal aspect of freedom. It is the confidence that future freedom will not be endangered. Security can be endangered not only by external threats, but also by domestic infringements of freedom and by unforeseen events.

When we deal with security in the face of external coercion or attack, the goal of external peace is closely related to security. It relates to freedom from violence and coercion in international relations. Internal security and peace cover not only the absence of civil war, but also the absence of violent confrontations, such as widespread crime, violent strikes and riots.

Security and peace are defined in relation to the use of violence and arbitrary behaviour by people with power. There is a gradual transition from the normal daily conflicts and disputes which are inevitable in any living society to a situation of genuine insecurity. Small interpersonal conflicts are the inevitable consequence of differences in human values and aspirations as well as of everyone's pursuit of happiness, which of course often has external consequences for the wellbeing of others. The dividing line, where security and peace are endangered, lies where violent and arbitrary means to obtain personal objectives are used, where conflicts are no longer resolved by discourse, private negotiation or mediating third parties and where widely held rules are violated.

When discussing security, it must be established who assesses security: an individual personally assessing his or her own security, or a third party who assesses someone's or a group's security. Given the relation to an inevitably uncertain future, assessments of security vary greatly between individuals, some of whom are confident they can master risks, others who are risk-averse. Security assessments always require much information search and forecasting as well as some evaluation of the capability to respond to unforeseen eventualities. There can of course be no absolute security in a changeable world. The pursuit of absolute security would only endanger other social values and be unsustainable. In an evolving world, security is not rigidity. Indeed, the attempt to avert changes only leads to greater insecurity in the long term, as conditions get further out of kilter with changing reality. Frequently, the best we can do for our security is to maintain a capability of alertness and responsiveness to deal with the unforeseen.

Since security relates to the future, it always has a time dimension. On occasions, this complicates the definition of what is meant by security. As just noted, the pursuit of security for the short term can easily imperil long-term security. Thus, if people elect political leaders who only emphasise securing material living standards for the next term of office and who refuse to take longer-term considerations into account, they opt for great risks to security in the long term. A proper understanding of security therefore requires a variable time horizon and trade-offs between short- and long-term aspirations to security, as well as deductions from maximalist interpretations of what is considered subjectively secure.

When the members of societies pursue their security above all other objectives, they are bound to discover that, after a time, this replaces experimentation and evolution with conservation; the qualities of alertness and adaptability to change are lost and the means to secure future freedom become eroded. When people have lost the taste for change and the capabilities to cope with it constructively, they begin to feel subjectively insecure; they lose confidence. They may then try to control competition and openness, frequent sources of challenge to existing economic and social positions. A growing preference for imposed security then postpones the very adaptations that guarantee long-term security – as judged by an informed, independent observer. Dealing with aspirations to security therefore requires careful assessment and the readiness to cope with certain sources of insecurity, as and when such eventualities arise.

Peace and Security: Competition Depersonalises Conflict

Peace in a community tends to be enhanced when potential conflicts are depersonalised by rules that commit the members of the community to non-violent conflict resolution. One way of depersonalising interpersonal or intergroup conflicts is to reduce to the minimum the areas that are decided by the collective action by governments, namely ensuring that life, the institutions and material assets are protected, as well as funding the administration of this protective function of government. The allocation of incomes and property and production are then left largely to the impersonal mechanisms of market competition. When these functions become politicised, collective antagonism can easily take hold and emotions can be whipped up by political operators to bind political factions together. This is rarely conducive to internal peace.

One important function of economic rivalry in markets is that the power of individual and corporate suppliers and buyers is contested and controlled by their peers. Competition not only controls economic power, but also political power that flows from monopoly positions. Another function of competition in markets is to make the control of performance impersonal: sellers undertake self-seeking but voluntary efforts to satisfy potential buyers. Those sellers who cannot obtain prices sufficient to cover their production and transaction costs – in short, who fail to make a profit – will be inclined to attribute their failure to the anonymous forces of the market, rather than blaming other specific competitors or buyers. This means the depersonalisation of the ever-present conflict between sellers, who want a higher price, and buyers, who want a lower price, a circumstance that makes an important contribution to securing peace, both within countries and in international relations.

An example of how the impersonal institutions of the market can help to defuse conflict is a free, deregulated labour market. If employers are driven by the pursuit of profit, they will hire the workers who offer the best productive value for the cost of the wage. In other words, employers will be blind to race, creed or gender. Those who discriminate, for example on the basis of race, will incur a profit penalty and may eventually have to get out of business. This is typically a more effective way to integrate a diverse society than cumbersome and costly policies to enforce 'positive discrimination', for example on race (a difficult-to-measure quality and one that is based on untenable assumptions of inherent disadvantages; Sowell, 1990, 1996).

People from very different cultural backgrounds and with little in common can interact beneficially and peacefully as long as they deal with each other in markets. With time, they may learn from each other and even gain respect and a liking for each other. By contrast, directives and controls imposed by political processes often emotionalise matters and create divisions which political agents exploit (Sowell, 1990). It was typical that Bosnians, Serbs and Croats who had fought an armed conflict could deal with each other in market places when political reconciliation proved unmanageable. The same holds true internationally: nations whose citizens share growing trading interests and are constrained from imposing political controls (like tariffs) tend to see advantage in keeping the peace.

The depersonalisation of the conflicting economic interests can only occur if competition is widely accepted as an ordering principle, which also means that all its distributional and other consequences are accepted, and if political agents are kept from intervening. Once certain agents intervene to constrain the competitive process (for example, by forming cartels) or use their power to coerce (for example, by setting up barriers to market entry), peace and security are likely to suffer as conflicts become personalised, emotionalised and politicised.

The philosophers of the eighteenth and early nineteenth centuries were very optimistic that the spread of commerce and the shift to motivation by self-interest and voluntary action would enhance morals and the spontaneous adherence to fundamental values, in particular social peace and security (Hirschman, 1977). Subsequently, observers were unable to share this optimism about the depersonalisation of exchange and conflict, as the competition they observed was frequently not among equals, but between powerful and powerless people or groups. Frequently, competition was not even-handed. This created positions of economic and, consequently, political power which was in turn used to further entrench market power. However, to conclude from this that there is no benefit for peace and security from competition would be wrong. Rather, the fostering of competition should be seen as an effective means to control concentrations of power, and with it abuses of power that endanger security, peace and freedom.

Well-functioning competition always has consequences for individual security. Market participants are always exposed to unforeseen changes in supply and demand during the economic process, so they can never expect total security. Moreover, people face the risks of being unable to produce for personal reasons, for example because of illness or old age, and the risks of socioeconomic conflicts. These risks to personal security have to be met by private wealth buffers and insurance, but there may also be a consensus in a community that some of these economic risks should be addressed by collective action (public provision of security, social security). It is, however, not valid to eliminate such insecurities of the market by suppressing competition, because that will only lead in the longer run to much greater insecurities which come from hamfisted political intervention and impose change by convulsion rather than evolution.

Government can also not promise total material security to all citizens, because the entire economic system would become rigid and moral hazard and loafing would spread. The cost has to be borne collectively and anonymously by taxes, whereas the gains in material security are personal. This creates an asymmetry which leads to unlimited, open-ended demands for more and more social provisions of security. Political interests will then drive the process increasingly towards a closer focus on security and away from other fundamental values. This process is illustrated by the experience of medieval corporatist city states in Europe, post-medieval China, the socialist regimes and the welfare states of the twentieth century. In the long run, the securing of personal income and wealth positions by political intervention led in all these cases to eventual societal dislocation, burdens on following generations and intergenerational injustice.

We must therefore conclude that security can only be provided – and should only be demanded and promised – by carefully observing the trade-offs with other fundamental values.

Prosperity

Prosperity or economic welfare also relates to aspects of security, in the first instance to the command over material goods and services to satisfy wants. Prosperity ensures access not only to purely material satisfactions, but also to cultural and spiritual fulfilment, health care, old-age provision and other ingredients that secure a comfortable life. As a first approximation, the attainment of prosperity is measured by real per capita incomes and wealth. But the security of prosperity over time, such as by the control of inflation and a measure of stability of income flows, is also part of what people aspire to under the rubric of material welfare.

The aspiration to prosperity has gained greater priority in the minds of many people around the world with the spreading economic growth experience during the twentieth century (see Chapter 1). In many communities, prosperity now appears to have taken a pre-eminent position, comparable to the pursuit of religious and spiritual aspirations in medieval Europe or parts of present-day India and the Middle East.

As already noted, there are complementarities and trade-offs between security and the aspiration of most people for economic welfare or prosperity. Prosperity, in particular when it allows people to form a buffer of wealth, promotes the security of individuals and enables communities to safeguard their security. After all, insurance, the defence of future freedom against external or domestic strife and the fostering of security-building institutions cost scarce resources. As we saw, there is, however, also conflict when demands for security dominate and endanger future prosperity.

Fortunately, other fundamental aspirations, such as freedom, justice and peace, tend, on the whole, to be promoted by better material conditions. This does not mean that economic prosperity can be equated to happiness, only that it is seen as desirable by large numbers of people throughout the world.

O Key Concepts

Freedom is the opportunity to pursue autonomously within one's domain one's own, self-set purposes without interference. But freedom is circumscribed by the equal freedom of others. It implies the absence of coercion or fear of coercion. Freedom is here always defined as the (negative) freedom from coercion and interference.

Justice means that equal circumstances are treated equally by individuals and authorities and that restraints are placed on all in equal measure (and not according to personal standing or belonging to a particular group). This is the concept of procedural (or formal) justice, which underlies the principle of equality before the law. It has to be distinguished from **social justice**, which is orientated towards the **equality of outcomes** of human interaction, irrespective of starting position, luck and effort. Social justice aims to even out differences in incomes, wealth and other outcomes of human interaction. If it becomes a dominant concern of public policy, it undermines procedural justice and freedom, as well as incentives to compete and perform.

Equity closely relates to justice, namely that all should have access to similar opportunities. It must thus be distinguished from the equality of outcomes.

Security relates to the confidence that people will be able to enjoy freedom into the more or less distant future. It is freedom from fear of violent interference by private or collective agents. Institutions tend to constrain arbitrary and violent behaviour in some, and therefore promote the security of others. In a different meaning, security is used as equal to social justice. As soon as security is orientated towards the protection of acquired social and economic positions it tends to clash with freedom.

Peace means the absence of violence and strife, both within the community (internal peace or harmony) and from the outside (external peace). It relates to security in the first meaning.

Economic welfare or prosperity relates to the availability of goods and services to satisfy (easily growing) material human wants. ●

4.4   Conservation of the Environment

Intergenerational Justice and the Environment

In recent decades, as the number of people on earth and in certain areas has increased, aspirations to conserve the natural and the man-made environment have been on the increase in most countries. Many social critics have claimed environmental conservation as a fundamental human value and hence a basic goal of policy which should be considered equal to, or more important than, individual freedom or prosperity, for example. At one level, this demand can be understood as a reaction to numerous changes in the wake of the unprecedented economic growth of the past fifty years, be it the exhaustion of known or easily accessible stocks of natural resources or the accumulation of hard-to-digest residues from growing production and consumption activities – effluents, waste and congestion. The growth of production and consumption has created external costs, that is, burdens on third parties, and has led to the exhaustion of previously free goods, such as clean water. However, the growing demand for conservation may also reflect resistance to continuing, even accelerating, changes which challenge the individual's capacity to adjust; in a way, conservation may reflect aspirations to greater security.

Some observers have even concluded that economic growth cannot continue, because it runs into limits set by the natural environment, including clean air and water; indeed, that rising and spreading prosperity has to be stopped in the interest of nature conservation. This argument is based on the logic of physics which says that matter is finite and cannot be 'mined' for human use forever. But such a closed-system logic is based on a misunderstanding of what makes for economic growth. Growth occurs in an open system, which means that the system is opened up by innovative knowledge. Rising living standards, as reflected in rising real per capita incomes, do of course require that physical molecules are relocated. But the more important aspect of economic growth is that physical matter, when relocated and combined in certain ways, is given a higher value. Thus, the iron taken from the ground is valued much more highly when converted into a knife. National products rise not so much because natural resources are taken from the ground, but because they are valued much more highly by people. Besides, modern economic growth is becoming much less dependent on the extraction of natural resources, because many resources are being recycled and because the demand is shifting to services. The computer age is making abundant silicon a key raw material. This is why a survey of long-term social trends and possible resource and environmental bottlenecks by a panel of sixty-four leading scientists concluded that there was no unmanageable natural resource constraint on growth (Simon, 1995).

This is not to say that there are not some bottlenecks in the supply of natural resources, in particular in energy supplies and the absorption of waste and emissions from economic activities. But these may be overcome, for example, when scarcity prices send out the signal to economise and substitute for scarce resources or to bring about innovative technologies (Borcherding, in Block, 1990, pp. 95–116). None the less, the question arises whether this is the most appropriate solution to specific environmental problems or whether direct policy action is more appropriate. We shall see later that private and collective solutions – markets or public policy – have to be allowed, depending on the environmental problem at hand.

Many concerns with the natural environment arise because someone's economic activity causes effects on others that cannot be easily compensated (externalities). Other environmental concerns deal with the interests of future generations: how do we ensure that future generations have the freedom to develop without facing sudden, harsh and unmanageable resource bottlenecks or the collapse of the natural system in which they will live? This relates environmental issues to security and intergenerational justice. After all, it would be unjust to leave a devastated environment to future generations. It is certainly appropriate to include the likely interests of future generations among our fundamental values and to ask how they can best be looked after. Nature conservation is therefore a legitimate fundamental concern.

Can We Deal with Extra-human Values?

In the debate about the environment, we sometimes hear an argument that goes beyond what has been said so far. Some in the environmental debate try to place nature above all human interests. They see human beings as an integral part of an interdependent physical system and argue in terms of purely quantitative, physical trade-offs between human demands and the demands of animals, plants and other elements of the physical world. This school of thought, which has been labelled 'eco fundamentalism' (Lal, 1995), rejects the argument in this chapter that human concerns and valuations alone should be the measure of all human activity. Instead, it tries to place the interests of animals and ecosystems on an equal footing with human interests, or even above them. For example, it advocates an extreme interpretation of the 'precautionary principle' in ecology, namely that no harm whatsoever should be done to the natural environment, whatever the consequences to other human aspirations such as prosperity. It is argued that the 'precautionary principle' should apply when damage to the environment is irreversible (for example, extinction of a species), even when the connection between a suspected harmful action and the environmental effect is not (yet) scientifically proven. The conservation of nature should prevail irrespective of possible harm to human aspirations and possible alternatives of human adjustment to environmental damage. This kind of thinking has, for example, become dominant in the discussion of climate change. However, this approach presents fundamental logical difficulties because the design of all policy is a product of the human mind and we can express, assess and compare only human values. Attempts to take away the reliance on human valuations would suppress the very communication and steering mechanisms which coordinate human action and would empower some collective dictatorship.

Once we abandon human valuations as the sole reference system for human action, we have to ask whose valuations are to replace them: maybe the polar bear's for whom humans are food? Humans have no way of entering into communication with other species. All that happens is that some human agent argues on behalf of another species on the pretext that she or he knows what serves that species. When we abandon human valuations and logical discourse about them, the 'interests of Nature' therefore become an excuse for some self-appointed elite to overrule human valuations. The protagonists will claim superior knowledge about what is good for nature conservation and then enforce their decisions against the wishes of the majority of people. The interaction of the many human beings in market decisions – who are concerned with freedom, justice, prosperity, future security, including future resource supplies – is then replaced by the dictatorial directives of an elite, however selected and legitimated. Such an absolutist approach would violate the fundamental individual values that underpin and inform society.

O Key Concepts

Conservation of the environment is concerned with safeguarding environmental amenities and natural resources with regard to the interests of present and future generations. It relates to prosperity, equity, security and intergenerational justice. It is a legitimate concern for moral discourse and public policy.

Eco fundamentalism posits absolute priorities for nature conservation which are not related to fundamental human valuations and which are to override human aspirations, such as freedom, prosperity, security and justice. ●

This brief discussion of eco fundamentalism clarifies an important point about fundamental values: they must always reflect the diverse and conflicting valuations of human beings and relate all human interaction to a humane perspective. A humane society depends crucially on the focus on human valuations, which are, after all, the only language in which the members of the community can communicate their aspirations. Foisting non-human 'values', external to human valuation, on public policy would cause society to disintegrate. This may empower an elite, which would override everyone's interests, but destroy freedom, justice, prosperity, security, peace and the other aspirations discussed here.

Questions for Review

- What is the function of fundamental human values for institutions and the maintenance of a social order?
- Give an example of an action by you that interferes with the freedom of others. What constraints are there in your community to safeguard your fellow citizens' freedom in this case?
- Why does it make sense to restrict the exercise of power to government agents (violence professionals) and to control them by collective rules? What happens to the realisation of the fundamental values discussed in this chapter when Mafia rings and other private violence professionals reign unchecked?
- Why does the availability of alternatives help to protect your freedom?
- Explain the difference between procedural justice and 'social justice' by using examples from the public life of your community.
- Is it just that a supermodel, thanks to inherited good looks, earns 100 times more than a seamstress? If your answer is that this is unjust, how would you rectify the situation? And would that infringe the attainment of freedom and formal justice?
- Is it just that an academically trained expert earns twice as much as the average wage?
- What is the 'just price' for bread in your community? Or does this concept make no sense, because the price of bread is only a signal which ensures that those who want to pay for bread are effectively supplied with it? What would happen if the 'just price' for bread were deemed to be half the market price and was set by the government as the maximum price at which bread could be sold?
- Is it possible to ensure that all can enjoy equal living standards in a community? If everyone is assured of the same income, will people make much of an effort?
- Discuss the consequences for the attainment of other fundamental values in a society that fails to maintain internal peace and harmony. Use countries that are making headlines as examples to illustrate your points.
- In what ways is prosperity compatible with the other fundamental human values? Can you think of ways in which it conflicts?
- Why do most of us aspire to conserving the natural environment?
- What are the costs in terms of fundamental human values of applying an extreme interpretation of the 'precautionary principle' to conservation, regardless of proven causation, costs to humanity and alternatives to cope with environmental or ecological problems?
- What happens if a community equates the perceived interests of an endangered animal or plant with the interests of human beings? How can the interests of an animal or plant be measured? Who

should do the measuring and the comparison with human interests? How is that particular agent legitimated? What would happen if an 'eco police' applied the valuations of polar bears or other non-human species to everything on earth? And how would the 'interest' of one species be reconciled with the valuations done on behalf of other species?

CHAPTER 5

Institutions: Individual Rules

Institutions are generally known, man-made rules to constrain possibly opportunistic human behaviour. They carry some kind of sanction for non-compliance which varies widely as to its character and formality.

We shall discuss a wide range of institutions that have evolved in societies, for example, customs, good manners and the manifold institutional arrangements which merchants and financiers have created and apply to facilitate their trade.

Although much of social and economic life is ordered by such internal institutions, people in more complex societies have invariably found it convenient and effective to supplement internal institutions with external institutions and formal arrangements to enforce them. External rules are designed in political processes and enforced by government agencies carrying out the so-called protective function of the state, including by legitimate uses of force.

Appropriate institutions serve to reduce coordination costs in complex systems, to limit and possibly resolve conflicts between people and to protect individual domains of freedom. To serve these ends, institutions need specific qualities, such as certainty, generality and openness (universality). Rules that are not universal but are designed to obtain specific purposes fail easily in their coordinative, normative function and often overtax the knowledge of the rule makers. Moreover, they easily overtax the cognitive capacity of those whom they are to influence – in plain English: citizens simply cannot know and obey thousands of complex, case-specific rules and regulations.

The obedience to learnt rules has become necessary to restrain those natural instincts which do not fit into the order of the open society.
(Friedrich A. Hayek, Political Order of a Free People, *1979)*

Civil liberty is the status of the man who is guaranteed by law and civil institutions the exclusive employment of all his own powers for his own welfare.
(W.G. Sumner, The Forgotten Man, *1883)*

Certainty we cannot achieve in human affairs, and it is for this reason that, to make the best use of what knowledge we have, we must adhere to rules.
(Friedrich A. Hayek, Competition as a Discovery Procedure, *1960)*

Pacta sunt servanda.
(Roman saying, 2nd century BC)

A deal is a deal.
(Anglo-Saxon saying, 19th century)

5.1   Overview: Rules and Enforcement

Institutions are defined throughout this book as generally known rules that apply in a community. They constrain possibly opportunistic behaviour in human interactions and always carry some sanction for breaches of the rules (North, 1990, p. 3; Ostrom, 1990, p. 51). As we said in section 2.1, rules without obligatory sanctions are useless. When sanctions are no longer applied institutions lapse. It should also be noted that institutions are man-made, not physical, constraints on human action.

We shall first elaborate on a couple of aspects of institutions to explain their character and then discuss various types of institutions that differ in how they come about and how they are enforced.

Prisoners' Dilemma

Institutions – and in particular the sanctions attached to them – allow people to make credible commitments that promises made will indeed be fulfilled. Human nature is such that self-seeking individuals will often make promises but later forget or shirk delivering on them. Our instincts play a big role in such opportunistic acts, and institutions support the control of our innate instincts in the interest of longer-term effective coordination (Hayek, 1979a, pp. 165–73; 1988, pp. 11–28). Cooperation between people thus normally requires the framework of institutions to discourage this sort of instinctual opportunism by increasing the risks of shirking and to reinforce habits of cooperation for reciprocal benefit.

The fact that when people cooperate they are often better off than when they do not cooperate has been explored by game theory under the label of 'prisoners' dilemma'. The term relates to the case of two prisoners who are not permitted to communicate (cooperate). When interrogated, each prisoner faces a dilemma in not knowing whether to remain silent, hoping that no guilt can be established, or whether to speak out with the intent of putting all responsibility on the other prisoner and claiming mitigating circumstances. Both prisoners face this dilemma, as long as they cannot cooperate with one another. Both would be better off when cooperating and making credible commitments to each other, for example promising that both will remain silent. When they cannot communicate but speak out in self-defence, they incriminate each other and are both worse off. What is at stake here can be clarified by the matrix in Figure 5.1. Such prisoners' dilemmas arise frequently when people cannot cooperate reliably. Institutions are there to enhance the chances of mutually beneficial cooperation.

Figure 5.1   The prisoners' dilemma

		Prisoner A	
		Remains silent	Speaks out
Prisoner B	Remains silent	Both go free	B is found guilty
	Speaks out	A is found guilty	Both are found guilty

An instructive example that demonstrates the advantages of cooperation based on appropriate institutions is the history of the Cold War and the strategic arms limitation agreements that followed in the 1970s and 1980s. As long as the two superpowers did not cooperate, they were tied into a costly arms race and faced the danger of a nuclear holocaust. It was increasingly realised on both sides that both would be better off with some kind of cooperation. They entered into negotiations to establish rules, monitoring procedures and sanctioned retaliations for rule violations; eventually they established credibility, making the cooperation possible that solved their prisoners' dilemma and allowed the de-escalation of the nuclear threat.

Cooperation is, however, not always desirable. Various suppliers of a product may find it beneficial to free themselves from the prisoners' dilemma of having to compete by forming a cartel that fixes high prices. But, in this instance, the prisoners' dilemma of the suppliers serves a good purpose from the standpoint of potential buyers and the community at large, just as the prisoners' dilemma serves a good purpose from the viewpoint of the interrogator. Whether to facilitate or impede cooperation by appropriate institutions thus depends on circumstances and on whose interests are included in the evaluation.

Institutions and Trust

Institutions are rules of conduct, and as such a means of channelling people's actions. They normally rule out certain actions and narrow the scope of possible reactions. Thereby they make other people's actions more predictable. They give social interaction a certain structure. American philosopher-psychologist Andy Clark has recently spoken of institutions as providing a kind of 'external scaffolding' for human choice and learning (in Drobak and Nye, 1997, pp. 269–90). Indeed, institutions facilitate predictability and prevent chaos and arbitrary behaviour. By helping to order actions, institutions establish trust and allow people to economise on the search for knowledge. Even if rule-bound behaviour is not 100 per cent certain, it can be perceived as more probable and plausible than chaos.

Institutions normally reflect what has proved useful in the past and what is needed for people to interact with others in pursuit of their individual objectives. In that respect, they are 'storehouses of knowledge' acquired by past generations. In the face of ever-present knowledge problems, institutions give people a degree of confidence that the human interactions in which they are engaged will occur as expected. This lowers the costs of information search, a difficult and risky business, as we saw in Chapter 3. The costs of transacting business with others or cooperating within an organisation are thus reduced by appropriate rules of conduct. Without trust in the wider framework, individuals would often not be able to concentrate on exploiting knowledge in their specialisation or to find knowledge in new areas, so that numerous useful actions would never take place (Hazlitt, [1964] 1988, pp. 53–61). The division of labour and knowledge would not be possible and living standards would remain low.

Humans, singly and groups, often try to cope with the knowledge problem by thinking through an overall strategy that sets a framework of rules for individual actions. Lest people be overwhelmed by *ad hoc* decisions and mal-coordination in the heat of battle, all bind themselves in their tactical day-to-day decisions by the strategy, and tactical changes are kept within that strategy. This is a practical recipe for military or business action to reduce the costs of knowledge search and coordination in the face of human ignorance and the limited resources to cope with it.

Given the cognitive and other limitations of human nature, institutions, to be effective, have to be easily knowable. To that end they should be simple and certain, and sanctions for violation should be clearly communicated and understood. This is not the case when rules proliferate and are purpose-specific, rather than abstract, or when rule systems become inherently contradictory. Nor should institutions discriminate between different people, giving some groups preferences over others. Then, institutions are less likely to be obeyed and serve their function of economising on knowledge search less well.

A related basic criterion for effective institutions brings in an intertemporal dimension: rules that change all the time are harder to know and are less effective in ordering people's actions. Rules should therefore be stable, conforming with the age-old, conservative saying that 'old laws are good laws'. The advantage of stable institutions is that people have adjusted to old institutions to the best of their advantage and have acquired a practice of following them almost instinctively. Stability therefore reduces enforcement costs, improves reliability and hence facilitates human interaction. The flipside of stability is the danger of institutional rigidity, even in the face of changing circumstances. Hence there must be some scope for adjustment. When rules are open, that is, when they apply to an indeterminate number of future cases, rigidity is less of a problem than if the rules are case-specific. But even open rules may require adaptation if new circumstances evolve.

To illustrate how appropriate rules establish trust and why that is essential to effective interaction, we can look at football rules: they lay down certain stipulations and obligatory sanctions for infringements that govern the behaviour of the players. The rules are simple and certain (no ifs and buts!), hence knowable, abstract in that they do not apply only to one specific game or player, and open-ended in that they apply to an infinite number of future games. Thanks to these qualities, the rules are able to shape the behaviour of the players, or – as institutional economists would say – are 'normative' of human behaviour, making it predictable.[1] Now imagine that these qualities were suspended. The referee would rule on every move and goal in a discretionary manner. Instead of abstract rules, he would decide case by case, giving preference to some players, possibly on the basis of expediency and changing the implicit rules all the time. The football game would at best end in conflict and total confusion, and at worst not be played. Even a deluge of directives from the referee would not be able to coordinate the players on the two sides. Likewise, civil and economic interaction without trustworthy rules soon disintegrates.

Institutions may also be categorised according to how they are framed:

(a) they may be *prescriptive*, instructing people precisely what actions to take to achieve a specific outcome, for example to move from point A to point B;

(b) they may be *proscriptive*, ruling out certain classes of unacceptable behaviour, for example not to exceed a speed limit or not to steal.

Examples of proscriptive institutions are many of the Ten Commandments which rule out certain classes of action – 'thou shalt not … '. Another example is the well-known Hippocratic oath (named after the Greek doctor Hippocrates, fifth century BC) which instructs medical practitioners *not* to harm the patient. Such proscriptive rules do not give purpose-directed commands what to do positively and leave people much scope for autonomous judgement and action.

As a result of both types of institutions, people's actions are coordinated. In the instance of prescriptions, by a visible hand and according to some leader's plan; in the case of proscriptive rules, by people voluntarily and spontaneously. As we shall see in Chapter 6, prescriptive rules are an essential part of a planned, coercive order, whereas rule-bound behaviour which is guided primarily by proscriptions is typical of spontaneous orders, such as the market economy whose rules coordinate people by an invisible hand.

We must underscore an important difference between proscriptive and prescriptive institutions. Those who prescribe actions – who give instructions and direct – will normally need much more specific knowledge than those who only rule out certain types of action. The one who prescribes the behaviour of others must be aware of the means and capabilities of the actors as well as of possible conditions for and consequences of the prescribed action. Those who rule out certain types of behaviour only need to know that certain actions are undesirable, but they leave the specific detail of the action and the evaluation of consequences to the actor. Actors thus have more freedom when guided by prohibitions of the type 'thou shalt not … '.

O Key Concepts

Institutions are widely known, man-made rules that are meant to constrain possibly opportunistic human behaviour. They always carry some kind of sanction for non-compliance. Institutions, to be effective, should be simple, certain, abstract, open and reasonably stable.

Prescriptive institutions instruct and command people positively what to do and create an order of actions which is imposed by some leader. **Proscriptive rules** leave actors much freedom in what they do, but rule out certain harmful classes of actions (negative instructions along the lines of 'thou shalt not ... ').

Prisoners' dilemma describes a situation in which two or more parties are worse off if they do not cooperate, but in which each party is tempted to go it alone since the other party or parties cannot make credible commitments. The term derives from the game-theoretical case where two prisoners are held in separate rooms and are not allowed to communicate. They are in a dilemma: should they remain silent and hope that their guilt cannot be established, but risk the other prisoner incriminating them, or should they speak out, incriminating the other and hoping for lenient treatment? The dilemma would be resolved by cooperation between the two prisoners. In other words: what is individually rational behaviour yields inferior results for the group and cooperation pays off.

A prisoners' dilemma also arises in competition between suppliers who are inclined to underbid each other in order to attract buyers. The suppliers would be better off as a group, if they did not cooperate, by forming, for example, a cartel. Here, the dilemma serves good purposes for the community. We have to conclude that cooperation is sometimes, but not always, socially desirable, and that institutions are needed to underpin such cooperation, but also to prevent it in situations where non-cooperation is to be promoted. ●

Organisations Are Not Institutions

We should draw attention to a use of the term 'institution' in everyday language which deviates from our definition. In common usage, 'institution' is frequently applied to the concept of 'organisation' (which is defined as a more or less durable combination of property rights to production factors under a leader to achieve some shared purpose, see Chapter 9). Institutional economists therefore do not call banks 'institutions', because these are business organisations. And they would not use the word 'institutionalised' for someone who has been committed to a mental hospital! Institutions are rules, organisations are players (North, 1990, p. 4).

None the less, certain institutions require organisational back-up. The rules may be embodied in organisations. Just as certain types of knowledge are implicit or embodied (built into) in capital goods, so are institutions sometimes implicit in organisational structures. An example is the family, which is an organisation that serves the various ends of its members and which embodies certain rules of conduct for mother, father and children. Certain institutions incorporate implicit knowledge and are inseparably tied to certain organisational arrangements. The importance of implicit institutions is made clear when we compare different firms in an industry. Hard-to-explain differences in productivity can often be observed between the best-practice firm and other firms in the same branch of industry and these can only be attributed to different work practices (Kreps, 1990). These implicit institutions are sometimes given fuzzy labels such as 'corporate memory' or 'organisational culture'. The fact that some institutions are built into organisations makes it hard to transfer them to other organisational environments. But the embodiment of rules also enables the owners of institutional knowhow to claim property rights in their specific institutional arrangements and to sell that proprietary knowhow by running other organisations. To give an example, some of the rules governing how to run an honest and competent stock exchange are so intimately tied to the implicit knowhow of those who run the organisation of a particular stock exchange that it is hard to imagine that such knowledge could be separated from the organisational back-up. Thus, organisations often embody institutions and are storehouses of implicit knowledge which is essential to their functioning.

The ties of implicit institutions to organisational structures become apparent when a successful company takes over another. Then, the work practices and other rules on how to operate, which were developed in the parent company, have to be foisted on to the acquired company. If the implicit institutions – and the knowhow which they embody – are not learnt there by association and cooperation, the takeover will probably fail.

O Key Concepts

Organisations are purpose-oriented, reasonably durable combinations of resources which are to some extent coordinated in a hierarchical way by a leadership. Organisations may pursue economic purposes, for example in the form of a business partnership or a share company. They may also pursue political purposes, for example in the political organisation of a local or national government, a party organisation or lobby group.

Organisations, although partly coordinated by top-down ordering, require internal rules to function effectively. Many of these rules can be implicit because they govern frequently repeated actions between the limited numbers of members of the organisation. Examples of such **institutions that are embodied in organisations** are established procedures, work practices and knowhow in routines. Such implicit institutional wisdom is often hard to transfer to other organisations and depends on association, imitation and emulation. ●

5.2   Internal Institutions

Internal and External Institutions

In Chapter 2, we touched on the distinction between internal and external institutions. To remind the reader, internal institutions were defined as rules that evolve within a group in the light of experience and external institutions as rules that are designed externally and imposed on society from above by political action. A similar distinction was made by Ludwig Lachmann (1973) to stress that many rules influencing our behaviour are the result of evolution and that communities functioned on the basis of rule-bound behaviour long before government was invented. The distinction between internal and external institutions thus relates to the genesis of the rules: how they came about. Examples for internal rules are good manners, which tell people to be punctual, and ethical standards, which are followed by the members of a community. Examples of external institutions could be the civil law or a traffic code decreed by a parliament or government authority. Of course, in practice fluid transitions between internal and external institutions are apparent.

Institutions can also be classified as to whether the sanction for non-compliance is decentralised, spontaneous social feedback (informal institutions) or through a formally organised mechanism (formal institutions). As we shall see, the distinctions between internal/external and informal/formal do not always coincide.

What matters is the degree of coercion that institutions exercise over human action. Internal institutions tend to appeal to voluntary coordination. Non-compliance with the rules is not without its consequences, but the individual decides whether or not to accept the consequences of non-compliance in specific circumstances. Coercive orders which rely heavily on external institutions and formal sanctioning, by contrast, leave the individual much less leeway to evaluate the specific situation (Radnitzky, 1997, pp. 17–76).

How Internal Institutions Evolve

Human interaction is governed by numerous internal institutions that keep evolving in the light of experience. People perpetuate internal institutions because someone discovered them and found them useful, making interaction with others possible in the first instance and easier, once these rules of conduct had spread and were widely adhered to. A good example of how such evolved institutions work is language. Humans order the sounds they are able to produce and hear into recognisable patterns called words, and words, by applying rules of grammar, into sentences. These rules have evolved over time and contain much knowledge of how to communicate. A living language has certainly not been designed by anyone. Rather, it evolves through the interaction of millions of people. Where attempts are made to design a language, such as Esperanto, the results have proved to be limited. Even where the internal institutions of language are supplemented by external rules that are policed by an authority, such as the French language by the *Académie française*, the results of such external ordering are often ineffectual or considered ridiculous. Another example of how the internal workings of society produce institutions that are designed by no one but emerge from the interaction of millions of people is the custom that people who do not tell the truth are shunned in honest society. The genesis of this habit has no doubt to do with the fact that fibbing misleads people, inflicts costs on others and destroys trust. The rule not to be opportunistic and fib is sanctioned by exclusion from social exchange, typically in a fairly informal but none the less very powerful manner. A recent example to show how internal institutions work is the new informal rule against the mass-distribution of unsolicited commercial advertising on the Internet. While it may be easy for advertisers, it would clog up the mailboxes of recipients of e-mail, a serious disadvantage. When the rule has occasionally been broken, the originators are often inundated by retaliatory mail from some of the recipients, showing them by this 'tit for tat' response what a nuisance such unsolicited communications can be. These rules have emerged internally and are sanctioned informally, because the Internet is not governed by any one central authority.

Such internal selection processes work not only generally in society but also in economic interaction. Markets function only when some basic rules are respected, for example when people are allowed to keep the profit they make in exchanges (respected property rights) and when the relevant rules are widely known and adhered to. Examples of internal economic institutions are the convention in particular markets that advertised prices are fixed, or the rule that a deal, once struck, terminates all further price negotiations. If someone tries to reopen negotiations once a deal has been struck, the sanction is not to deal with that person at all. To give a further example, work contracts operate satisfactorily for workers and employers only if institutions about many work practices are widely shared, adhered to and violations sanctioned.

An experience turns into an internal institution only when a critical mass of people accept it. Institutions may begin within a small group who benefit from sharing certain arrangements, for example the custom that credit is repaid punctually. Once the benefit of this rule becomes apparent, the rule may be adopted by more people. Successful institutions thus 'colonise' bigger and bigger groups of participants. On the other hand, institutions that are no longer found useful – such as the European and American institution that gentlemen defend their honour by duelling – lose critical mass, as other ways of sorting out attacks on one's honour are adopted. Internal institutions are thus subject to a gradual evolutionary process. They are varied, accepted or rejected (selection), and some gain critical mass. What is found to fail in changing circumstances is corrected – by 'a million little mutinies', as the Indian writer V.S. Naipaul once so aptly put it.

The importance of internal institutions in structuring social interaction, bridging the gaps between self-centred individuals and forming bonds that hold a society together, has long been recognised by philosophers and social scientists. As far back as 2500 years ago, the Chinese philosopher Confucius (551–479BC) emphasised the importance of what he called 'ritual' in creating harmonious, predictable human behaviour and in enabling many people to live together in confined areas and with limited resources. And the French social philosopher Charles de Montesquieu (1689–1755) echoed the Roman institution of unwritten laws, known as *mos maiorum*, when he highlighted the importance of *mœurs* (customs) in his treatise *De l'esprit des lois*: 'Intelligent beings may have laws of their own making, but they have some which they never made.' The Anglo-Saxon philosophers who wrote in roughly the same era, such as John Locke (1632–1704), David Hume (1711–76) and Adam Smith (1723–90), also emphasised that the institutional framework of a society must rest on evolved internal institutions. Consciously made, legislated rules, and the entire structure of politically determined institutions, had to rest on internal institutions. In modern times, the same point has been made most forcefully by Friedrich A. Hayek (1973; 1976a; 1979a, 'Epilogue', pp. 153–208).

Different Types of Internal Institutions

It is useful to distinguish four broad, though sometimes overlapping categories of internal institutions which differ in the way in which adherence is monitored and breaches are sanctioned.

1. *Conventions* are rules which are so obviously convenient that people self-enforce, by and large, out of self-interest. For example, people adhere to certain word definitions and grammatical rules because it is in their own interest to make themselves understood. Further examples of largely self-enforced conventions are tacit agreements in the market to express interest rates in terms of a percentage per annum and to quote prices in terms of money. A vegetable seller who tries to express all vegetable prices in terms of grammes of apples, which is theoretically possible, would discover pretty soon that there was little business being done! People thus adhere to conventions, because it obviously pays and because they would easily exclude themselves from interchange if they chose not to stick to the conventions.

2. *Internalised rules* are a second type of internal institution. People have learnt the rules by habituation, education and experience to a degree where the rules are normally obeyed spontaneously and without reflection (conditioned reflex, see Chapter 3). People thus have turned many rules into personal preferences and apply them fairly consistently. Such internalised (or habituated) rules constitute, for example, morality. That you should not lie and that you should pay your debts punctually are rules of conduct which people have learnt and most obey as a conditioned reflex. Internalised rules are thus both personal preferences and constraining rules. They operate as rules in the heat of battle, protecting people from instinctual, shortsighted opportunism and often saving them coordination costs and conflict. Violations of internalised rules are typically sanctioned by what we call a bad conscience (in other words, people suffer psychic costs).

These sanctions may be reinforced by reference to the transcendental or to certain symbols. For example, the ethical rule that 'you shalt not steal' has in the Mosaic tradition become a commandment whose violation displeases God (Hazlitt, 1988, pp. 342–53). As Adam Smith put it: 'Religion, even in its crudest form, gave sanction to the rules of morality long before the age of artificial reasoning and philosophy' (cited in Hayek, 1988, p. 135). In the East Asian tradition, especially in Confucianism, great attention is placed on moral education which makes young people internalise rules of interpersonal conduct. Members of society are then imbued with strongly held moral institutions which restrain them seemingly voluntarily, or at least without much reliance on formal legal rules and processes.

One benefit of internalised rules, which encourage reflexive obedience and a high degree of rule compliance, is that members of society save on coordination costs. In societies where people are spontaneously honest because they have internalised honesty, agents have lower decision-making costs and risk fewer 'accidents' than their competitors in societies where cheating is habitual and agents speculate all the time whether, in this particular instance, they will get away with cheating and what possible penalty they risk. Internalised rules that establish trustworthiness also save costs compared with a situation where trust depends on explicit, mutual contracts that have to be negotiated and monitored.

3.   *Customs and good manners* are a third type of internal institution. Violations do not automatically attract organised sanctions, but others in the community tend to supervise rule compliance informally, and violators earn a bad reputation or find themselves excluded, in the extreme even banned or ostracised[2] (Benson, 1995, pp. 94–6). Thus, children who misbehave in East Asian families are often not allowed into the house. Punishment in the West tends to rely on a different type of exclusion: badly behaved kids are 'grounded' and thereby excluded from their friends outside the home. People with bad manners tend to be lonely. Exclusion from the group can be an extremely powerful sanction. For example, an Australian Aborigine or an American Indian who was expelled from the tribe was most probably being condemned to certain death as individuals could hardly survive outside the group. Similarly, an international currency trader who loses his or her reputation for not adhering to the unwritten rules of the foreign-exchange trade is unable to pursue that profession and will soon fail to find contract partners. Other types of enforcement of such customary institutions are that misbehaving parties lose repeat business, normally a serious penalty, because much trade is not once-off but, because the search for contract partners costs considerable resources, takes place in ongoing bilateral relationships. Only in an 'end game' is there no such sanction, and many exchanges are organised as repeat games for the very purpose of retaining a sanction. Customs can also be reinforced by contract partners who offer up 'hostages', for example, a down-payment that is forfeited in the case of non-acceptance of a delivery. Another 'hostage' may be that one's reputation suffers if one sells bad products. A borderline case to the second category of internalised institutions is where one's bad conscience is reinforced by shaming, ensuring that violators face the sanction of losing face. East Asians tend to rely on this type of sanction more

heavily than Europeans, possibly because they have long been less able to rely on the formal, external enforcement of external institutions.

4. *Formalised internal rules* are a fourth type. Here, the rules have emerged with experience, but are formally monitored and enforced within the group. Communities create much law internally but then enforce it among themselves in organised ways through third parties. These may be adjudicators (people who clarify the rules and spell out possible sanctions) and arbitrators (third parties who make binding decisions on interpretation and sanctions). An example is the self-regulation of a profession. Experience may have shown that the game of soccer depends on rules which have been formalised, but these rules are only rarely enforced in the public courts. Enforcement depends instead on soccer federations who adjudicate and hand down penalties. This is done quite formally but without reliance on government which has a violence monopoly. Instead, the sports bodies rely on formal internal sanctions such as excluding offending clubs from competition. Internal rules may thus be sanctioned in formalised ways by tribunals ruling on what constitutes a breach of professional standards of behaviour. Trade and finance in most societies are based on such internal institutions which the merchants and bankers have created to facilitate their business. Thus, oriental bazaars and European markets have developed complex trading rules which are interpreted and formally enforced by community leaders or designated market arbitrators.

To cite another example for this type of internal rule, international trade relies on merchant-made laws (*lex mercatoria*) that are often enforced by professional associations and arbitrators but not by a transnational authority. Such internal institutions are often much more effective in facilitating the business than externally imposed and government-enforced laws, because self-monitoring and formal enforcement by members of the profession will be done by people with extensive knowledge specific to time, place and the profession, whereas outside judges have limited knowledge and may trigger unintended deleterious consequences through their rulings.

Informal and Formal Internal Institutions

The first three categories of internal institutions are informal, in the sense that the sanction for violations of what is socially expected is not defined and applied in an organised way, but occurs spontaneously. The fourth category of internal institution is formal in that the sanctions are spelled out and violations are met with sanctions through organised mechanisms. The distinction between formal and informal thus relates to the manner in which sanctions are applied: organised (formal) or unorganised (informal).

The first two categories of informal internal institutions tend to impose a degree of self-discipline. They are self-enforcing whether out of self-interest or to avoid a bad conscience. As a by-product, individuals behave in ways that take the interests of others into account quasi-automatically. Where these institutional control mechanisms are commonly practised, the latter two types of internal institutions, as well as formal legal and regulatory controls, are less necessary.

Spontaneous adherence to internalised institutions has consequences for individual freedom. When people are educated to control themselves and abstain from opportunistic behaviour through self-discipline, they enjoy greater freedom from formal, coercive sanctions under the rules. In a society where people can pursue their self-set purposes, effective interactions are greatly facilitated by a good measure of self-discipline and by internalised codes of conduct.

○ Key Concepts

Internal institutions can be:

- **informal**, that is, not sanctioned by formal mechanisms, namely:
  - **conventions**, that is, rules that are of obvious, immediate benefit to the persons whose behaviour they control and whose violations harm self-interest;
  - **internalised rules** whose violations are sanctioned primarily by a bad conscience;
  - **customs and manners** which are sanctioned informally by the reactions of others, for example by exclusion; or
- **formalised**, where the sanctions are implemented in an organised manner by some members of society.

To reiterate, the distinction between **internal** and **external** relates to the genesis of an institution, the distinction between **informal** and **formal** to the way in which the sanction is applied, spontaneously or in an organised manner.

Third-party enforcement occurs in the case of formal internal institutions where adjudicators or arbitrators are included in the process of enforcing institutional arrangements. This may occur, for example, when one party does not obey a trading rule and an arbitrator is called in to settle the conflict.

(Third-party enforcement also occurs in the case of external institutions where government agencies enter the fray as adjudicating and enforcing third parties.) ●

Not of Human Design

Internal institutions can be highly effective and are frequently sufficient to order even very complicated and complex situations. One remarkable modern example has already been mentioned: the governing of one of biggest networks that has ever linked humankind, the Internet. It was originally set up by the US Defense Department as a computer network with no centre or authority, so that communications between decentralised units could survive a nuclear attack on the centre. Because the facility was not fully utilised, the Internet was opened to universities and later to commercial users. As of 1997, the Internet linked an estimated 25 million users around the globe; it grows dynamically with only a very few, external, rules being imposed. Yet the traffic between users is ordered and certain internal rules have developed and are generally observed. Some of these internal rules are conventions which are of immediate usefulness to participants, such as sticking to the protocols of how e-mail addresses are written. Other rules are manners that have evolved spontaneously, such as the informal rule not to advertise commercial goods and services on the Net through unsolicited junk mail. Is it not a miracle that, by such informal means, millions of people on all continents and communicating in all the languages of the world are obeying internal institutions to make effective use of such a novel, huge network?

The internal institutions that are crucial to human interaction are not the result of human design and enforcement by an external authority. They form an important part of our civilisation, as Hayek pointed out:

> We flatter ourselves undeservedly if we represent human civilization as entirely the product of conscious reason or as the product of human design, or when we assume that it is necessarily in our power deliberately to re-create or to maintain what we have built without knowing what we were doing. Though our civilization is the result of a cumulation of individual knowledge, it is not by the explicit or conscious combination of all this knowledge in any individual brain, but by its embodiment in symbols which we use without understanding them, in habits and institutions, tools and concepts, that man in society is constantly able to profit from a body of knowledge neither he nor any other man completely possesses. Many of the greatest things man has achieved are the result not of consciously directed thought, and still less the product of a deliberately coordinated effort of many individuals, but of a process in which the individual plays a part which he can never fully understand. They are greater than any individual precisely because they

result from the combination of knowledge more extensive than a single mind can master.
(Hayek, 1979b, pp. 149–50)

Internal institutions thus contain much of the distilled, tested wisdom of our forebears. Because many of them are informal and evolve in society, they have the advantage of some flexibility. They permit experimentation and reinterpretation as and where new circumstances emerge. Therefore, internal institutions normally have the capacity to evolve further, depending on practice and acceptance. They are tested all the time in decentralised ways by members of a community. Because many participate, change tends to be gradual and slow, hence predictable. Internal institutions which have evolved from human experience therefore have the innate advantage of adjusting to changes if sufficient numbers of members of a community violate the old rule and behave according to a different pattern. Internal institutions are sometimes called 'soft institutions' because they leave some scope for variation and because the sanctions attached are at times flexible. This enhances their evolutionary capacity.

Internal institutions have the related advantage that they can be applied flexibly in slightly variable circumstances. What they sometimes lack in clarity and transparency is often compensated by the ability to tailor the precise interpretation and the sanctions to specific circumstances. When self-enforcement fails, sanctions may range from a friendly chide to a rebuke or a reproach – long before stricter sanctions, such as ostracism or formal third-party enforcement, are resorted to.

The sanctions that go along with internal institutions may also be tempered with sympathy and expressions of regret that all are fallible yet must be held to certain standards if society is to function. Internal institutions may thus be seen as part of the 'cultural cement' that holds a group together (Elster, 1989). As they evolve, internal institutions are part and parcel of the moral discourse by which institutions and shared social values are kept in tune with circumstances and experiences.

5.3 External Institutions and Protective Government

External Institutions Defined: Political Action to Design and Enforce Rules

External institutions differ from internal ones in that they are designed and imposed on a community by an agent with a political will and the power to coerce who stands above the community as such. External institutions always imply some form of top-down hierarchy, whereas internal institutions are applied horizontally among equals. The sanctions for violating external institutions are always formal and are often backed by the use of force. In many societies, governments have been given the legitimate monopoly of the use of force, for example through the police, the courts and the prison system. In turn, governments undertake efforts to control the professionals of legitimate violence by non-violent means, often expressed through formal rules and financial controls. Thus, the defining characteristic of an external rule is that the sanction is in the hands of somebody outside the community.[3]

We can distinguish various types of external institutions by their content and target:

- *external rules of conduct* are intended to constrain the actions of citizens in ways similar to internal rules. They consist of universal, prohibitive rules and are contained in the civil, commercial and criminal codes of most countries (Hayek, 1973, pp. 131–9);[4]
- a second type of external rules are *purpose-specific directives* which instruct public or private agents to bring about predetermined outcomes. Such institutions may be contained in statute law, but in many countries they are mainly to be found in by-laws based on more general enabling legislation. They place high requirements on the knowledge problem because they are prescriptive (see above);
- external institutions can also be *procedural* or *meta rules*, which target the various agents of government, instructing them how to behave and what not to do (administrative law). Many of these institutions may be aimed at keeping the rule system inherently compatible (see Chapter 6). Procedural rules can be of great importance in making the external rules of conduct effective. For example, the rules that protect citizens from police violence in general terms will require precise procedural instructions to police officers on how to carry out their duties in specific situations, reducing their information and decision-making tasks.

○ Key Concepts

External institutions are designed, imposed and enforced from above by a political authority which governs a community. External institutions are always formal in that sanctions are enforced by a predetermined authority in an organised way. External institutions often work open-ended, abstract ways; for example, private laws apply to an indeterminate number of individuals and cases. External institutions have normative effect on the behaviour of the members of society, particularly if they are in harmony with prevailing internal institutions.

Specific directives are aimed at a particular purpose or outcome, that is, they do not apply universally. An example is the rule to hand over a certain percentage of one's income to the state in the form of income tax.

Procedural rules are needed for the administration of government to facilitate the internal coordination of the various agents of government. They are contained in public law and form an important part of most bodies of laws and constitutions. Many of these procedural rules are framed in the form of laws, but, by contrast with private law, they are directed not at the citizens but at the agents of government. ●

In most communities, internal institutions order most of the conduct of members. Yet, despite the great effectiveness of internal rules in most circumstances, virtually all complex, big societies have also adopted external institutions. This is because internal institutions in complex, mass societies cannot eliminate all acts of opportunism. One reason for this is that people frequently interact with strangers they will never meet again, so that many informal sanctions (such as tit-for-tat, ostracism and damage to reputation) are ineffectual in preventing opportunistic behaviour. In such societies, there is also more likelihood of prisoners' dilemmas emerging, so that formal rules are useful to support cooperative behaviour.

External institutions have come relatively late in human history. It seems no coincidence that the invention of agriculture and animal husbandry – which necessitated respected private property rights in land, animals and the yields from them – coincided with the emergence of law givers, judges and formal government.

Although external institutions depend on political decision processes and governments, this does not mean that government owns the external institutions. Often, government agencies have only codified pre-existing law. In this context, it is interesting to note the ancient

Germanic concept of *Volksrecht*, the law which is owned by the people and only protected and nurtured by the ruler, and that a famous medieval law code, that of eleventh-century Catalonia, was called *utatges* (usages). Authority is thus guardian of external institutions, but they serve everyone in the community. External institutions may come about by formal political processes, such as constitution making and legislation; they may also come about by administrative action, for example when governments decree certain regulations on the basis of some wider, more general enabling legislation. External institutions are, in some countries, also shaped increasingly by judges, who offer new interpretations of existing laws. In the Anglo-Saxon countries, with their common law tradition, 'judge-made law' is fairly frequent.

Reasons for Rule Setting by Government

The question may be asked: What are the advantages of external government authorities in rule setting and enforcement, as compared to a strict reliance on internal rules? There are a number of advantages of collective, political rule setting and enforcement.

(a) Existing customs and conventions may be ambiguous, not spelled out clearly enough and not widely enough known. External institutions may be more easily recognisable and thereby save on the people's information cost. If internal institutions are officially codified – written down formally and pronounced in edicts – they may become more effective and sanctions can be more visibly laid down. This enhances the normative function of rules. Thus, law givers such as Hammurabi (c.1728–1866BC in Mesopotamia), Moses (who probably lived c.1225BC in Egypt and Palestine), Solon (who codified laws in Athens, 630–560BC), the *decemviri* of Rome (a committee of ten who were asked in 451BC to write down the existing law), and Ashok the Great (who died probably in 238BC in northern India) are celebrated for having codified existing internal institutions and decrees of external laws. Enhancing the institutions by formalising them and attaching formal penalties for infringements has often been effective in improving the human condition. Such law giving made it harder for people to act in a forgetful, slovenly, dishonest or negligent manner. American statesman James Madison (1751–1836) comes to mind in this context, who said as far back as 1788: 'If men were angels, no government would be necessary.'

(b) The spontaneous adjudication of internal rules by the members of the community may be haphazard and far from dispassionate and unbiased. Enforcement of internal rules may, for example, favour the rich, the popular or the beautiful. To constrain arbitrariness and bias, community leaders, with a reputation for being 'just' at stake, may be elected judges. 'Just' here means that they are even-handed in protecting people from coercion by others and treat everyone as equal before the law. Judges may then develop and make public the rules on which they adjudicate conflicts, including procedural rules of the sort that are now known as 'due process'. External rule making responds to the requirement that justice must not only be done but must be seen to be done in order to have a normative influence on behaviour.

Such adjudication does not necessarily require a government, but financing the expenses of independent judges frequently makes government funding preferable, because judges who emerge informally and who have no financial independence may fall prey to the temptations of bribery. On the other hand, the material independence of tax-funded judges has proved a weak bulwark against corrupt judges, so there will be great advantage in external institutions which facilitate the supervision of judges in the administration of justice (Benson, 1995). One external institutional device to achieve this is the existence of several layers of courts. Since judges of lower courts do not like to see their rulings overturned on appeal to higher courts, they are subject to control.

(c) When judgements have to be enforced, informal sanctions like shaming or spontaneous community action may prove unsatisfactory – just think of affective action arising out of excessive anger, such as mob rule, lynching or spontaneous expulsion from the community. Given the likelihood of thuggery on the part of some, there is an advantage in appointing 'violence professionals' (police, prison officers, the military and so on), who are licensed to inflict legitimated punishment through penalties that are accepted in the community as commensurate to the crime. The argument is that government should have the monopoly over the legitimate use of force (except in rare situations of legitimate self-defence) and that this monopoly be subjected to non-violent, institutionalised means of control by those with political power. There is of course always a certain danger that the 'violence professionals' will use their skills and equipment for their own purposes (the principal–agent problem), and therefore the agents of law enforcement must be inhibited from acting on their own account. Most communities have found that control is best exercised by turning the violence professionals into government agents and finding non-violent means of supervising them.[5]

(d) An important aspect of institutions is that they allow people to make credible contractual commitments. In certain circumstances, third parties are needed to make contractual promises credible, and government agencies can wield the weapon of formal enforcement when they become such third parties.

(e) A fourth advantage of collective over private action derives from what was discussed above as the 'prisoners' dilemma'. It has been said that cooperation, which is often advantageous, often requires reinforcing by government-backed institutions to be sufficiently credible (Buchanan, 1975; North, 1990, p. 13). Rival clans suffer from being prisoners of eternal conflict. All of them would be better off by cooperating under some external authority, such as a government. They reap, so to speak, a 'disarmament rent' by forgoing conflict (Buchanan, 1975). Commitments to such cooperation is frequently made more credible – and the peace is better conserved – if the deal which resolves the prisoners' dilemma is supported by an overarching third party, such as a ruler (Axelrod, 1984).

(f) A closely related reason for governments setting and enforcing rules is what has been called 'free-riding' (Olson, 1965). In practice, certain assets have indivisible costs or benefits. Where others cannot be easily excluded from such benefits, we have a public good. If one citizen sets up a police force that keeps internal peace in the community, fellow citizens cannot be excluded from that benefit. The first citizen has to incur high fixed costs to maintain a sufficient police force, and fellow citizens can enjoy a free ride at the expense of the initial supplier of police protection. In these circumstances, insufficient police protection will be supplied. The argument then is to nationalise the police and fund its provision by coercive taxation. This same argument applies to protecting the external peace and sovereignty of the community by a military force. Here, too, nationalisation – sharing the costs through the external organisation of government and control by external institutions – prevents free riding and leads to better provision, with the public good of protection against external aggression. (Public goods will be discussed in greater detail in section 10.1.)

(g) A further, related reason given in the literature why governments become involved in designing and imposing institutions is the 'tragedy of the commons', a situation in which members of the community, if acting in isolation, find themselves in a particular prisoners' dilemma. Members of a group exploit a common asset, for example when their cattle graze on community-owned land; as long as resources are plentiful in relation to demand, grazing land is not scarce. But as the number of users increases, for example with population growth, grazing must be rationed. Internal, informal constraints tend to be effective in rationing resource use within small communities where people know and meet each other and where spontaneous enforcement can work informally at the personal level. It has been found that informal constraints tend to work satisfactorily in groups of between fifty and seventy people (Hardin, in Henderson, 1993, pp. 88–91; Ostrom, 1990). If the group expands, information about an individual's behaviour and the informal restraints on individuals (such as damage to their reputation) are insufficient to control excessive exploitation of the commons. As a consequence, overgrazing occurs in our example, and the land deteriorates. In that situation, some authority administering external rules has an advantage: in our example, government authority could impose grazing limits. Another solution would be the division of the commons into private properties that are protected by fences.

(h) Another reason why external institutions and collective action may be preferable in certain circumstances has to do with the fact that internal institutions often work by discrimination and exclusivity. Indeed, internal institutions often have to discriminate between insiders and outsiders in order to function. Only then is the sanction of exclusion feasible. Networks of traders or financiers often build complex internal rule systems as a foundation for their business pursuits and enforce the rules by confining the network advantages to members. Examples are: the medieval European traders and bankers who managed the trade between Venice, Florence, Nuremberg, Frankfurt and Amsterdam; the famous Champagne fairs; the Arab merchants who ran the caravan trade and the bazaars; and the contemporary Chinese family networks in the Far East. Numerous people participate in these networks based on internal institutions which enable huge volumes of risky business to be conducted at low cost. But these networks can only function if the number of participants is limited and malfeasants can be excluded. Exclusivity and small size are thus essential to the functioning of the internal institutions within such networks. This may in certain circumstances pave the way for monopolies and the elimination of beneficial outsider competition. Experience indicates that the informal, internal institutions of personally networked trade and finance carry economic development only to a certain level beyond which external institutions and protective government enjoy economies of scale and ensure just, open market access to all comers (North, 1990, pp. 48–53). The infrastructures for modern, open, extended markets require sanctions other than private ones. Certain designed, formal laws and a formal judiciary then prove more effective in bringing about an open order and enabling a wider, more dynamic division of labour.

These circumstances give rise to the external imposition and enforcement of institutions by government, to what James Buchanan called the 'protective function of the state' (Buchanan, 1975). Protective government is concerned with the design, imposition, monitoring and enforcement of external institutions to facilitate effective and just conduct.[6]

It has been shown that most of the institutions which governments normally design and implement can in principle also be developed and enforced by internal non-governmental institutions (Benson, 1995; Benson, 1997 in Radnitzky, 1997, pp. 17–76). Thus, cases of fraud and violence in a sport such as soccer may be effectively controlled by the formal sports bodies who investigate incidents and enforce sanctions. However, external institutions are frequently more effective, though this is not always the case. The points listed above concerning the various reasons for government action in protecting the rules of conduct should not be read as indicating that alternatives to government action are not feasible; they only indicate that, in certain circumstances, collective action tends to have comparative advantages and allows communities to reap scale economies as compared to reliance on purely private action.

External institutions normally serve as an essential, coercive back-up to society's internal institutions. But they may also replace internal rules. If they are intended to replace *all* internal institutions of a society, problems arise – as was the case in various totalitarian regimes in the twentieth century which imposed more and more external rules at the expense of the internal workings of civil society. Monitoring and enforcement costs rose steeply, people's spontaneous motivation waned, and administrative coordination capacities were overburdened. External coordination then often leads to administrative failure. These problems are not new. They were, for example, the reason why Confucius and early Confucian scholars advocated spontaneous coordination and were extremely sceptical of 'fabricated' orders that relied on external institutions and the command from above: 'Whoever ... wants to order the state and does not rely on custom resembles a man who wants to plow without a plowshare', says the Confucian *Book of Rites* (cited by Habermann, in Radnitzky and Bouillon, 1995b, p. 75). It is not surprising that revolutionary Marxists in China who tried to replace traditional civil society with 'scientifically designed' new institutions after 1949 banned Confucianism, but ultimately failed and had to rely again increasingly on the internal institutions.

O Key Concepts

Codification of rules means that existing internal rules are formally written down in ways that make them visible and unambiguous, for example by engraving the laws on stone walls as in ancient Assyria, Egypt and India, or the formal promulgation of the laws of Israel by Moses in the form of the Ten Commandments.

Free riding refers to a situation where information or exclusion costs are such as to make it impossible to exclude others from benefiting from a good or service that someone else has provided. Thus, it may not be possible to exclude youngsters from taking a free ride on a hay wagon, and it may be too costly to exclude people from accessing the radio waves once someone else sets up a station. However, technology may change and allow measurement of use and exclusion, so that the free-rider problem disappears and private production becomes feasible.

The **tragedy of the commons** arises where commonly owned resources are used by a large number of people, each of whom can benefit by exploiting the common resource to the fullest for their own benefit. If all act like this, the tragic situation arises in which the resource is destroyed. This may be the case with fish stocks in the open seas. It has also been the case in the Sahel area of Africa, where the first Landsat photographs taken from space showed that commonly owned land was severely drought affected, whereas private, fenced-off properties conserved decent vegetation cover. The tragedy of the commons was that starvation set in and desertification took over where the land was not owned privately (Hardin, in Henderson, 1993, pp. 88–91).

Protective government is concerned with designing, imposing, monitoring and enforcing external institutions. It normally supports the internal institutions of civil society and makes the fostering of an order of actions the primary concern of public policy. ●

Two Traditions in External Rule Setting

In the European tradition of shaping external institutions, there are two strands: the Germanic/Anglo-Saxon traditions, which place great store in the common law, that is, on judges finding, developing and formatting the external rules; and the Roman legal tradition, which is reflected in designed systems of legislation such as the French *Code Napoléon*, or the German civil and commercial codes of the nineteenth and twentieth centuries. In practice, no legal system is in a pure form. Common case law has gradually been supplemented and replaced by formal, parliamentary legislation, and even the most elaborate formal law codes require judge-made case law to make them effective.

Judge-made law, which is more prevalent in the Anglo-Saxon tradition, tends to be open and adaptable. It is open to more flexible interpretation and learning and to the feedback to judgements from the judicial fraternity and the wider public, thus capturing the wisdom of more participants. But, by the same token, it lacks the cohesiveness, clarity and transparency of the designed codes of the Roman tradition.

Judge-made law is also reshaped by high courts. Members of the court are normally not elected but are, in many countries, politically appointed. Thus, the majorities of the US Supreme Court have a powerful influence on how the external rules of the United States are shaped and reinterpreted. These majorities can be greatly influenced when judges retire, so the thrust of the US legal system can change quite dramatically as compared to legal systems where the powers of the highest courts are more restricted by constitutions and black-letter law. Similar influences are also at work in other legal traditions since the incumbents of the highest courts have at least limited powers to interpret existing laws.

Judge-made law tends to undermine the division of powers between executive, legislative and judiciary, and thus the control of power in society. Another consideration is that the costs of running a common law system tend to be high, because daily practice requires the services of legal professionals and frequent adjudication by the courts, whereas many potential conflicts are avoided if transparent and comprehensive civil and commercial codes are on the books. However, in practice, formal black-letter codes also have their drawbacks. They have long lost their simplicity and logical cohesion, and experience has shown that reliance on formal legislation by parliaments often introduces rigidities in times of change. Political activists have responded to the growing complexity of social interaction by decreeing complex codes and regulations, often at the behest of special groups. This has frequently undermined the coordinative function of external institutions and has given rise to a reaffirmation of the important insight that a complex world requires simple rules (Epstein, 1995; for an argument in favour of external rules to be 'discovered' by competing judges and courts, see Cooter, 1996; Christainsen, 1989–90).

It must be concluded that external rule setting and enforcement is a complicated business and that the exclusive reliance either on codified law or on the common-law approach would fail to serve the intent of external rule setting satisfactorily. Therefore, flexible mixes that have been tested time and again are the best possible approach to an inherently intractable problem.

5.4   The Functions of Institutions

Effective Coordination and Trust

One function of institutions is to make the complex processes of human interaction more understandable and more predictable, so that coordination between different individuals occurs more readily, as we have repeatedly pointed out. In social chaos and anarchy, the division of labour is impossible because information, monitoring and enforcement problems are often insurmountable. Credible commitments cannot be made and people remain the prisoners of each others' opportunism.

In such a situation, institutions serve the key function of simplifying the cognition task by reducing the complexity of the world. By making the reactions of others more predictable and hence the world more orderly, institutions make it easier for individuals to deal with a complex, changeable world and to avoid 'cognitive overload'. When there are general, recognisable patterns of behaviour and conditions, economic agents can cope better with specifics. As institutions help people to understand the complex, confusing world around them, they protect people to a considerable extent from being confronted by unpleasant surprises and situations that they cannot handle adequately. Institutions thus help us to address our primordial fear of not being able to master life. The trust they underpin enables us to risk experiments, to be creative and entrepreneurial and to encourage others to come up with new ideas of their own (Buchanan and di Pierro, 1980).

Where institutions constrain the actions of others and rule out certain types of future eventualities, they reduce 'forward ignorance'. They make it a lot easier for people to be alert to entrepreneurial opportunities on the horizon because they create confidence about the humdrum routines of life close at hand. Thus, they confine the risks of future-orientated action. Only when human behaviour is stabilised is it possible to enhance the division of knowledge and labour which is the foundation of growing prosperity.[7]

The reduction of complexity by institutions may be non-specific. Certain general institutions may be widely appreciated because they give people psychological comfort and security: the feeling that they belong to an ordered, civilised community where coordination costs are low and risks limited, where they can feel at home. Those around can be trusted. Interaction with others is less exacting than if one lives amongst strangers or in less well-ordered communities. Institutions create bonds that appeal to a sense of belonging which most individuals find satisfying.

In other circumstances, the coordinative function of institutions is much more specific. For example, the citizens of a nation where the stability of the value of money is ensured by credible institutions can have greater confidence in saving and investing in monetary assets, as well as in financing the capital stocks essential for economic development. It has been found that the very existence of simple monetary rules tends to exert spontaneous stabilising influences on aggregate demand, as was pointed out in an article that may be considered as a classical analysis of the coordinative effect of institutions (Simons, [1936] 1948).

Institutions can enhance the effectiveness of production factors – such as labour – in meeting human wants in ways similar to other production factors, for example capital which makes labour more productive. We can therefore consider a community's institutions a valuable productive asset. We can speak of 'institutional capital'.

Protecting Domains of Individual Autonomy

A second function of institutions is to protect domains of individual autonomy from undue interference from outside, for example from others who wield power. Institutions thus protect individual freedom, one of the fundamental human values we discussed in Chapter 4. Thus, European civilisation has known the institutional concept of private autonomy since Greek and Roman times. The concept of *dominium* (domain) in Roman law, which incorporates this notion, might be loosely translated into English as 'my home is my castle': that people have a sphere of autonomy in their home which is protected by respected and enforceable institutions. Under Roman law, the master of the home had great powers within it, where he was free to act and where outside interference was inadmissible. A similar institution protects private property in many societies. Property rights protect owners from outside interference with the free uses of their assets and create a domain in which property owners are free.

The protection of liberties – spheres of individual autonomy – by institutions is never unlimited. The free pursuit of one's own purposes often affects the similar pursuits of others, so freedom must always find its limits in the freedom of others. Without such constraints, liberty would turn into license, and without appropriate constraints on freedom, society would degenerate into anarchy. We should, however, be aware that we are discussing a continuum between one extreme of totally unconstrained freedom to act autonomously and the other extreme of total domination by others. In practice, the issue is for people to enjoy as many domains of freedom as are feasible, which means having as many acceptable choices as possible. Kenneth Boulding put this idea nicely:

> Freedom is what's inside the fence
> of Morals, Money, Law, and Sense.
> And we are free, if this is wide
> (Or nothing's on the other side).
> We come to Politics (and Sin)
> When Your fine freedoms fence Me in,
> and so through Law we come to be
> Curtailing Freedom – to be free.
> (Boulding, 1959, p. 110)

We shall return to this important idea of institutions protecting and confining domains of individual freedom when discussing property rights, which establish important domains of freedom, and economic competition, which imposes controls on the uses of private property and limits what individuals may and may not do with the property they own. We shall see in section 8.4 that the entire system of capitalism depends not only on economic freedoms but also on the control of these freedoms by competition which needs to be upheld by appropriate institutions.

Averting and Resolving Conflict

A third important role of institutions is that they help to mitigate interpersonal and intergroup conflicts. Conflict between independently acting individuals is at times inevitable. When different people pursue their personal purposes, the exercise of their free will often impacts on others; and some of these impacts are unwelcome. The question then arises how conflicts can be solved in low-cost, non-violent ways, and how individual freedom to act is best constrained so as to avoid destructive conflicts. Rules of conduct, delineating spheres of autonomous action, can serve this function. At least they allow for non-violent conflict resolution, for example by providing mechanisms of adjudication if conflicts arise.

In essence, there are two fundamental ways of dealing with interpersonal conflicts:

(a) the absolute freedom of individuals (licence) is constrained in general, preventative ways by rules that limit arbitrary action and reduce the probability of conflict. Examples are the signalling of a private domain by setting up a fence, the rule for everyone to drive on the same side of the road, or the banning of emissions of noxious fumes. In all these cases, institutions serve to prevent conflicts by signalling in advance who will be in the right and who in the wrong, and hence who can expect sanctions to operate against them for breaking the rule;

(b) if conflicts have nevertheless broken out, institutions are used to adjudicate conflicts in previously agreed, and hence predictable, ways. Examples are the custom of compensating aggrieved parties for damages, or rules to settle torts under formal legal procedure, subject to known formal court procedures (Boulding, 1959, pp. 117–25; Tullock, 1992, pp. 301–26).

On Power and Choice

Potential conflicts arise not only from the freedom of individuals to act, but also when people cooperate. Individuals with wealth or charisma are able to exercise power in exchange relations. In an example to which we referred in Chapter 4, a rich person may be able to hire a poor person to do demeaning work, simply because the poor person needs the money to survive. He or she may feel that the rich employer has power, in the sense that the employment relation serves to impose another's will over one's own. This is likely to cause resentment if the poor person can perceive no alternative and therefore feels coerced and unfree. In such a situation, the poor person will sooner or later demand influence over the exercise of power, for example through worker co-management councils or the ballot box. He or she will demand a voice.

However, the power relationship exists only where there are no alternatives; in this example, where there are no alternative jobs. When many alternatives to earn money are open, people feel free and move to other employment if they feel coerced. In other words, choices among alternatives set people free. They control power even if none of the alternatives offers brilliant opportunities. Where people are in a position to vote with their feet (exit), they will not feel overpowered and will not be all that interested in exercising a political vote ('voice', as Hirschman, 1980, called the vote as a means to control power in contrast to mobility, 'exit'). Freedom of choice thus empowers people in many areas without the need for collective political guarantees of freedom. Only where individuals have no alternatives which allow them to exit and where people have little scope (or will) to adjust their aspirations in the light of past experience can they be dominated.

In societies where people have a great deal of power over others (who are then unfree), conflict is likely, with possibly costly consequences, even when strong institutions and coercive controls are in place. Where individual freedoms are safeguarded, including the freedom to move and exit, there tends to be less conflict. Institutions that ensure exit opportunities thus also limit the arbitrary use of power which infringes on other people's freedom. And people with power who submit to rules may protect themselves from the abuse of their own power in the heat of battle, so to speak. Seen from this angle, rules are the concession of the powerful to reason and social peace.

A related aspect has been pointed out by Powelson (1994, esp. pp. 4–11): a central function of appropriate institutions in long-term economic and social development is to create a power balance between different social groups, such as the nobility and the peasants, and to ensure that the lower-level groups have 'leverage', that is, they can get support from higher-level power groups. Only when power is diffused will broad-based, sustained economic development take place.

5.5   The Essential Properties of Effective Institutions

Universality

Although we touched on the issue in section 5.1, we need to ask: what are then the characteristics of institutions that are effective in coordinating individual conduct, or – as lawyers would say – have normative impact.

A first criterion is that institutions should be general. In other words, they should not be discriminatory among individuals and circumstances without a discernible reason. Generality was defined by Hayek (1973, p. 50) as 'applicable to an unknown and indeterminable number of persons and circumstances'. A second criterion is that an effective rule must be certain in a twofold sense: it must be knowable (transparent), and it must give reliable guidance as to future circumstances. The maxim of certainty thus implies that normal citizens should be able to read the institutional signals clearly, know the consequences of rule violations, and be able to rely on their relevance to their actions. The cryptic utterances of the Oracle of Delphi did not create effective institutions. Similarly, secret decrees and obscure or ephemeral legislation violate the principles of certainty. A third criterion is that institutions should be open, so as to allow actors to respond to new circumstances by innovative actions. These three criteria have been subsumed under the concept of universality (Leoni, 1961).

Universality can be safeguarded relatively easily in the case of prohibitive rules. The rule 'thou shalt not steal' is universal, giving actors great scope to make their own decisions. It applies to an unknown, open number of people and circumstances. Universality says that no one should be above the law. It thus also implies the procedural equality of all individuals, which we discussed in Chapter 4. Universality is part of what people perceive as just. A discriminatory application of rules and sanctions to people according to their status of wealth, influence, race or religion is considered unjust.

Breaches of the rule of universality tend to undermine obedience to the rule and its transparency, and hence undermine the normative, coordinative qualities of institutions. If, for example, it is the customary rule that people of a certain class of wealthy individuals are measured with a different moral yardstick from ordinary citizens, if the police can break the traffic rules with impunity, or if people apply laxer moral standards to government officials than to ordinary citizens, then spontaneous adherence to the institutions is likely to decay. The institutions then fail to fulfil the functions discussed in the previous section.

Universality is an essential formal attribute of the rule of law, a concept with a long tradition in Europe, which we shall discuss in the following chapter, after exploring the functions of systematic sets of institutions.

❖ Simple Rules for a Complex World

In the nineteenth century, great legal reforms in many countries simplified the legal rules in order to make rule compliance easier and cheaper and to reduce the costs of operating the law. Since then, the law has been made more complex, mirroring the growing complexity of society. However, epistemology and jurisprudence are increasingly demonstrating that complex rules do not work because they overtax human cognition and impose unnecessarily high compliance costs (Schuck, 1992; Epstein, 1995). Instead, lawyers propose – from an individualist position and based on the recognition of the pervasive knowledge problem – simple rules to cope with the complexity of modern life (Epstein, 1995).

Peter Schuck (1992) identified four characteristics of dysfunctional complexity in institutions:

- density, namely that institutions regulate great detail, often in a prescriptive manner;
- technicality, namely that the rules cannot be understood by ordinary citizens, but require professional experts to interpret and apply them;
- differentiation, which means that there is overlap between different bodies of law (for example local, state and national law); and
- uncertainty, which means that there are many conditional rules, so that no single question determines the legal outcome.

Richard Epstein pointed out that such a rule system imposes high compliance costs on the citizens and is costly to operate. To overcome this, he proposes simple rules, not as an exclusive, but as a dominant approach to guiding human behaviour. He writes (pp. 307–8): '[U]nder the dominant constraint of scarcity, insist that every new legal wrinkle pay its way by some improvement in the allocation of social resources.' He proposes the following simple rules:

individual autonomy, first possession, voluntary exchange, control of aggression, limited privileges for cases of necessity, and just compensation for takings of private property, with a reluctant nod toward redistribution ... The first four rules are designed to establish the basic relations between persons and their control of things, the next two are designed to prevent the coordination problems that remain in a world of strong property rights and private contracts. The entire enterprise seeks to minimize the errors arising from these two sources ...

... The protection of the rich because they are rich, or of vested interests because they are powerful, is no part of the overall plan. If people with great wealth and influence cannot continue to supply goods and services that others want and need, then they should, and will, find their own prospects diminished in a world governed by the legal principles outlined here ... This simple set of legal rules shows no favoritism. ◆

Symbols and Taboos

As we have seen, a primary function of institutions is to economise on the need for knowledge in coordinating people. To enhance their knowledge-saving quality, institutions are often made more certain by the signal of a symbol. Thus, the symbol of the red traffic light tells us quickly and certainly to stop, the symbols of uniforms and banners enhance the coordination of military action in battle, and the symbol of a banknote signals a certain value. Clearly, the symbol is a material thing (for example, a piece of nicely printed paper), but its functions depend crucially on the institutions that the symbol represents. The symbol conveniently represents and recalls complicated rules.

A similar knowledge-saving function is often attached to taboos. Instead of conveying to people the complicated knowledge that fish in certain areas of the reef are toxic at certain times of the year, Pacific islanders simply declare certain fish *tapu* (prohibited). A similar taboo has long been attached to pork in Judaism, and later Islam, because pigs in the Middle East were frequently contaminated with trichinae. Such a taboo saves people the trouble of learning the reason for the prohibition or understanding why a certain circumstance may hurt them. The purpose is to obtain unreflected obedience. This may, of course, at times restrict the adaptive capacity of a community and become a barrier to adjusting the institutions to new circumstances, a problem that we shall tackle in Chapter 12.

Symbols and taboos thus induce conditioned, often quasi-automatic responses and so serve to abbreviate the process of knowledge gathering and evaluation. They also make rule enforcement more straightforward. This does not preclude community leaders with power from sometimes abusing symbols and taboos in order to control their subordinates in self-serving ways, just as they may abuse institutions as such.

O Key Concepts

Universality of an institution means that it is general and abstract (rather than case-specific), certain (transparent and reliable) and open in the sense that it applies to an unknown number of cases. Simple rules tend to be more easily known than complicated rules and therefore tend to serve their functions better (see Leoni, 1961; Epstein, 1995). ●

5.6　The Costs of Interaction and Coordination

Coordination Costs

In most present-day societies, human cooperation has reached a truly astounding extent. Economic interaction between individuals has become extremely complex (think of the example of the pencil, see Appendix). Individuals coordinate their actions, so they are motivated to do what fulfils the aspirations of others. This requires a great deal of knowledge and causes considerable costs. Both sellers and buyers have to sacrifice other opportunities when specialising in a particular way and interacting with others by buying and selling (the opportunity costs of coordination). These coordination costs have been called 'the expenses for running the economic system' (Arrow, 1969).[8] Markets, in which individuals, teams and organisations compete, and the rule of law, which lays down anonymous, universal constraints for all players, are needed to help people to coordinate their plans and actions. These arrangements cannot be operated without considerable cost.

Thanks to better communications technology, a more effective organisation of exchange processes and, in some places, better institutions, the *unit costs* of coordinating the various specialists and property owners have probably dropped. To cite just one example: between 1930 and 1990 transatlantic telephone costs per unit dropped by an impressive 6.9 per cent per annum. But the *volume* of acts of coordination has risen enormously this century because the unprecedented economic growth this century has greatly increased through the division of labour. The snowballing of total coordination costs is part and parcel of the economic success described in Chapter 1. The volume of coordination costs in advanced economies is estimated at around half of all the costs of producing and distributing the national product (cf. North, 1992, p. 6). And it has been estimated that the share of labour dedicated to distribution and coordination in the US has gone up from 11 per cent of all work effort in the year 1900 to no less than 61 per cent in 1980 (Oi, 1990, p. 4). Much of the rapidly growing service sector in the advanced economies is concerned with the coordination of ever-more-complex production and exchange networks, and its costs are to a large extent coordination costs.

At first sight, it may seem surprising that such a large part of our economic effort should be dedicated to coordination. Yet in reality a large part of the costs of running a firm consists of costs incurred in coordinating and controlling (a) the agents who work in it, and (b) the actors with whom the firm interacts in markets. A large part of a business's total costs are for administering the internal organisation, market research, technical R&D, buying and selling, borrowing, obtaining and using legal advice, and other efforts to coordinate people. If we look at a national economy as a whole, trade and logistics, business services, finance, government administration and other segments of what has been called the 'coordination industry' take up a large and growing share of the total national product.

It is therefore surprising that the assumption of zero transaction costs is still regularly made in most standard textbooks on economics. There, the price which the buyer pays and the price which the producer obtains are, for example, assumed to be equal (the market-clearing price). In reality to arrive at the producer price transaction costs are deducted from the price that the buyer pays. Indeed, before we can even presume to speak of a market, buyers and sellers have to incur high information costs to find out whether they want to buy or sell a particular product and to find out what they need to know in order to buy or sell. Business people will tell you that their enterprises often remain competitive mainly by focusing on how to economise on coordination costs, both internally and in their dealings with suppliers and customers, not on production costs. We therefore must take coordination costs explicitly into account. Appropriate institutions can assist in economising on the costs of finding the relevant knowledge and transacting business. Communication becomes cheaper not only because of technical progress but, very importantly, also because of institutional development. When the institutions are poorly defined and activist authorities complicate the rule system, institutions can suffer from dysfunctional complexity. Coordination costs can snowball, for example, when public policy is concerned with numerous specific outcomes and induces a proliferation of prescriptive rules. Clear simple institutions can greatly cut coordination costs. A good example was the rule by the Han emperors of China 2000 years ago to standardise the axle length of carts: this enabled roads to be standardised, facilitating great cost savings in the transport industry.

Types of Coordination Costs

Figure 5.2 gives an overview of the various costs of owning and using property rights in cooperation with others. When people hold property passively (that is, without using it in transactions), they incur exclusion costs. People incur coordination costs when they put their property rights to active uses, that is, when they exchange them with someone else or combine them with other people's property rights within an organisation. When such uses are coordinated in the market place, where independent agents enter into voluntary contractual obligations and deliver on them, we speak of 'transaction costs'. These include the costs of obtaining information about what is available, under what conditions, when and where, as well as the costs of negotiating, monitoring and enforcing contracts. Transaction costs will be discussed in greater detail in section 7.3.

As an alternative, people may employ their assets by binding themselves or some of their property rights within an organisation. In this case, we call the costs of setting up and running the organisation 'organisation costs' (Figure 5.2). These will be dealt with in section 9.2.

Running institutions often requires organisational back-up by collective action, as we have seen. Governments incur agency costs in operating the external institutions for which it is responsible; these

Figure 5.2   The costs of owning and using property

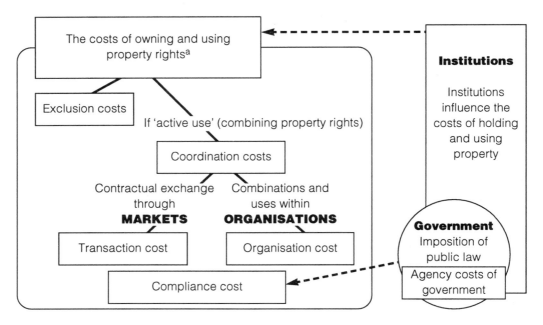

Note: [a]   Property rights = rights to dispose of and use assets.

costs are normally covered by taxation (Chapter 10). In the process, governments exercise legitimate political powers on the basis of public law mandating certain impositions on business and private citizens. In that case, coordination by collective action from above also inflicts 'compliance costs' on people who employ or hold their property. For example, citizens have to spend much time and effort on complying with tax legislation, keeping records, collecting documentation, filling in forms and hiring accountants, and they have to report to government agencies to demonstrate that they have complied with the regulations. Such compliance costs, which have to be borne by private citizens, can add considerably to the costs of transaction, organisation and exclusion. They are in addition to the agency costs of running government, which are financed through taxes and other levies.

When faced with information costs or, for that matter, other coordination costs, it is often rational for people not to be informed (we called this 'rational ignorance' in an earlier chapter). We must therefore assume that our coordination will always be with only partly informed partners, and we often misjudge reactions if we assume that others are fully informed, or indeed want to be fully informed.

In concluding this section, the point needs to be made that one man's exclusion, transaction, organisation and compliance costs are often another man's income. Those who have to bear these costs have an interest in reducing them, but those who carry out transactions or impose compliance requirements frequently have an interest in keeping these costs high. This conflict of interest plays a role in institutional reforms to reduce the costs of coordination and the agency costs of government. It explains the resistance to such reforms of many of the coordinating agents, such as government officials, lawyers and arbitrators.

O Key Concepts

Exclusion costs arise when people want to ensure that no one else makes unauthorised use of their property. The mere passive keeping of property causes such costs, for example expenses for fences, locks, night watchmen and police, share registries and patent protection.

Coordination costs arise when individuals interact with others to combine property rights which they own.

Transaction costs are the costs of employing resources when people use markets to exchange property rights. They include the costs of searching for market information, contracting, monitoring and enforcing the fulfilment of contracts.

Organisation costs arise when people try to combine their own resources with those owned by others within an organisation, such as a business firm, to pursue shared purposes. These include the costs of setting up organisations, communicating, planning, negotiating and monitoring the performance of duties within an organisation.

Compliance costs have to be incurred by private individuals and organisations whenever they are subject to the public law provisions of government. Citizens and organisations must comply with institutional constraints that arise in taxation and public regulation. This is the case, for example, when citizens have to spend resources on preparing accounts for tax declarations and when firms have to submit reports that demonstrate that they are complying with government regulations.

The **agency costs** of government refer to the resource costs of running government bodies, including the costs of monitoring what happens outside and inside government. They are typically financed by taxes, other levies and the incurring of public debt. ●

Questions for Review

- The reader should now fully understand the complete definition of what an institution is. What are the key criteria for institutions? What is behind the idea that institutions should be universal? Use examples to answer these questions.
- List the major functions that institutions can fulfil in society.
- What is the main difference between a convention, an internalised norm, a social norm and an internal rule of social organisation? What are the mechanisms by which these different internal institutions are enforced? Seek examples for each case, in particular explain how the sanctions for rule violations work in each case.
- Do you know examples of taboos in your community? Do these same taboos exist in other societies? Do they serve a rational purpose?
- How did we define:
  - — 'free riding';
  - — 'tragedy of the commons';
  - — 'prisoners' dilemma'?
  Find one or two real-life examples to illustrate each of these phenomena. Ask yourself whether the problem in these examples can be better solved by internal or external institutions.
- The American biologist turned social scientist Garrett Hardin reports that the first earth-circling Landsat satellites discovered from outer space that certain areas in the drought-stricken Sahel zone of Africa were reasonably well-conserved, whereas neighbouring stretches of land were totally denuded of vegetation. Can you, as a budding institutional economist, explain why privately utilised land was better conserved? (For more on this story, see 'The Tragedy of the Commons', in Henderson (1993, pp. 88–91).)
- List the reasons why, in certain circumstances, external institutions have advantages over purely internal institutions.
- Can you find an example where, in your community, an internal institution has been turned into (or supplemented by) an external institution? What were the reasons and the consequences?
- Can you find an example where, in your community, an external institution has been replaced by an internal institution? What were the reasons and the consequences?
- Why is the suggestion that corruption 'oils the wheels of economic growth' probably wrong?
- What do we mean by 'protective function of the state'?
- What is the principal–agent problem in government? Find an example from real political life.
- Between the end of the second world war and about 1968–71, external rules were in existence that tried to bind governments to fix the

exchange rates of national currencies (the Bretton Woods system). By the end of the 1970s, this rule system collapsed and exchange rates became flexible, that is, they were in essence determined by the supply of and the demand for each national currency. Can you guess, from your knowledge as a reader of newspapers, why international currency markets did not collapse, indeed subsequently functioned better? Can you guess what internal institutions are there to ensure that there is some element of order in the international currency trade?

- In times of war or social conflict, external institutions (including law enforcement) frequently break down. An example of this was the collapse of much of the formal administration of economic allocation in Germany after 1945. Can you imagine what informal, internal institutions took its place? Can you imagine what happens in economic life if moral fall-back rules such as personal honesty and reliability in fulfilling promises are also suspended?

- After 1989, much of the external institutional system of socialism in the former Soviet Union and its satellites collapsed, often for lack of enforcement. During preceding generations, the attempt had been made to replace completely internal institutions (and the associations of civil society that upheld them), as they challenged the state's power. Could you give an intuitive answer to whether success in eradicating internal institutions was an asset or a liability, once the process of systems transformation set in? Do you think that the emergence of Mafias (private violence professionals to enforce *some* institutions) after the collapse of the external rule system is a good or a bad thing? What are the pros and cons of Mafia enforcement?

- How are external institutions created and changed? Find examples.

- Can you explain why small groups and microsocieties (such as families or clubs) work better with internal institutions than macrosocieties such as nations? What is the mechanism of enforcement for rule violations in a family and a club? Do these same mechanisms function at the macrosocial level of the nation? If not, why not?

- List the essential properties of institutions and find practical cases from your experience to illustrate how neglect of these properties can have ill effects on the attainment of fundamental human values.

- What are the functions that institutions are meant to fulfil in a modern society?

- Define the various types of coordination costs: transaction cost, organisation cost, agency cost of government, compliance cost. Find examples from everyday life to illustrate these costs.

Notes

1. The term normative is used here in the definition commonly applied in jurisprudence: shaping human behaviour so that it conforms to a standard rule. This meaning of normative differs from the definition commonly used in economics: describing how matters should be so as to conform with a set of value judgements (for example: normative economics as opposed to positive economics).
2. Ostracism was practised in ancient Athens from 487BC as a punishment for certain misdeeds. The citizens of Athens wrote the name of a person who it was proposed to be exiled for five or ten years on broken pieces of pottery (*ostraka*); a sufficient number of *ostraka* led to exile.
3. Some authors equate what we call external institutions with formal institutions. This overlooks the existence of internal institutions which are formalised in the sense that the rules and the sanctions are applied in organised ways by a third party.
4. Private and commercial codes also contain numerous formal, prescriptive stipulations which are intended to facilitate transactions.
5. We could note in passing that a commitment of government to protect individuals does not necessarily mean that all aspects of citizen protection have to be under government control. Thus, medieval Iceland (c.930–1260) had legislation through a political organisation. Parliament laid down many rules externally, and an external judiciary interpreted the laws and decided specific court cases. Both were publicly funded. However, the enforcement of the laws and court judgements was left in private hands: people who had obtained a ruling in their favour could legitimately hire private policemen to execute the ruling (Friedman, 1979; Eggertsson, 1990, p. 311).
6. This is, of course, not the only function of modern government. Other government activities are concerned with the production of public goods and services by government agencies (for example, the provision of a judicial system), the redistribution of property rights as against the way in which they are allocated in the market place, and the raising and administering of taxes and other levies to fund the agency and other costs of government. We shall return to these in section 10.1.
7. Let us note in passing that institutions would be superfluous (a) if everyone lived in isolation, like Robinson Crusoe when he was alone on his island, or (b) if there was 'perfect knowledge'.
8. Some authors use the term 'transaction costs' to designate all coordination costs. We prefer to reserve this term to describe the costs of transacting business in markets. We also exclude transport costs (the costs of shifting products and production factors in space), because they do not have the information characteristics typical of coordination costs as defined here. But it must be acknowledged that an important cost component in the value-added in the transport services consists of information and transaction costs.

CHAPTER 6

Institutional Systems and Social Order

In this chapter, we move from the focus on individual institutions to whole systems of rules and the order that such systems can help to create. We begin by looking at what a system is and at hierarchies of rules, which range from constitutions to statute law and regulations.

To make the point that systems of more or less compatible rules have profound effects on economic life, we shall discuss two differing ways of obtaining socioeconomic order:

(a) the hierarchical or planned order which is created by some ordering hand, for example in a command economy in which collectively owned property, goods, jobs and investment funds are allocated according to someone's plan; and
(b) the spontaneous order which evolves when people follow certain shared rules, for example in a market economy where decision makers are motivated by private gain and prices emerge from competitive processes to inform them what is valued by others and what is not.

The spontaneous order is based on a vision that perceives the world as an evolving universe. Different people are motivated to pursue, of their own free will, diverse and changing self-set purposes, using their decentralised knowledge. The hierarchical order is based, by contrast, on the assumption that some political agents have both the capability to acquire and use all the knowledge needed to make relevant decisions, as well as the power to coerce the others to follow their commands. Experience has shown that hierarchical ordering does not work well in complex evolving systems, such as the modern economy, and that spontaneous self-ordering promises a better utilisation of dispersed, specialised human knowledge.

133

> We also shall see that 'culture' can be interpreted as a system of rules, which are supported by shared values.
>
> We conclude this chapter with a brief discussion of the rule of law. Its primary role is to protect individual freedom and contain conflict. It incorporates sets of rules that constrain individual behaviour, coupled with procedural rules. In many respects it supplements the economic institutions of the capitalist system, which will be discussed in Part II.

Legum servi sumus ut liberi esse possimus
[We are the servants of the law, so that we can be free].
(Tullius Cicero, 106–43BC, Roman lawyer and author)

Ubi non est ordo, ibi est confusio
[Where there is not order, there is confusion].
(Frater Lucas Bartolomeo Pacioli (1335–1520?), Treatise on Double-Entry Book-keeping, *1494)*

We have never designed our economic system. We were not intelligent enough for that.
(F.A. Hayek, The Political Order of a Free People, *1979)*

No individual is able to comprehend the world sufficiently to give practical instructions.
(Martin Heidegger, German philosopher, in an interview with the German news magazine 'Der Spiegel', conducted in 1966 and printed after his death in 1976)

Amongst the many other points of happiness and freedom, which your Majesty's subjects ... have enjoyed ... there is none which they have accounted more dear and precious than this – to be guided and governed by certain rule of law ... and not by any uncertain and arbitrary form of government.
(From the House of Commons petition to King James I, 7 July 1610)

6.1 Social Systems and Hierarchies of Rules

Man-made and Self-organising Systems

The focus in the previous chapter was on individual institutions. In reality, institutions serve their purposes not by being observed in isolation, but rather by forming constellations of mutually supportive rules. They form a system of rules that in turn influence a system of real-world phenomena. In other words, we have to investigate an order of rules which establishes an order of human actions. We have to think in terms of rule systems and economic and social systems.

By 'system' we understand a configuration of multiple, interacting elements. Systems can be quite simple, such as a clockworks. The system is man-made by a clock maker and the interaction is mechanical or electronic with regard to one attribute, the advancing of time. Other systems are more complex, containing numerous elements whose interactions are determined by numerous attributes. Influences with regard to different attributes are indicated in Figure 6.1 by arrows of different shadings. An example would be an ecological system, in which various plants and animals interact with differing characteristics in order to survive.

Complex systems are hard to plan and operate. Many of them are self-organising and self-correcting. Thus, a natural ecosystem is not run by a manager or, for that matter, has not been designed by a planner. Its coordination relies rather on the spontaneous actions and inactions of the various organisms. If we study such an ecosystem, we may discover that self-organisation depends on the various elements following certain rules or regularities which, among themselves, form a system. Complex systems may also be open, that is, they can be subject to evolution in unpredictable directions from one period to the next (Figure 6.1). Spontaneous variations of elements and characteristics occur; elements appear, mutate and disappear. These are tested and selected or rejected, and feedback ensures that the system is stabilised, so that new recognisable patterns emerge. The evolution of an ecological system over time is a good example to illustrate the interacting processes of variation, selection and stabilisation.

Another such complex, evolving system is the modern economy in which millions of individuals interact spontaneously with a great variety of different attributes and in which evolution takes place (Anderson *et al.*, 1988; Parker and Stacey, 1995). The various participants do not operate in chaos, but act systematically, taking account of a system of institutions. Therefore they display ordered patterns of interaction. The rule system that orders the actions of economic decision makers tends itself also to be subject to evolutionary change.

The limited cognitive capacity of people – as discussed in section 3.1 – often makes it necessary to spell out a number of rules whose side-effects reinforce each other. The individual rules have to be coordinated (ordered) to be effective. Thus, the institutions that protect private property have numerous consequences, one of which may be that propertied people compete with each other to find other property owners with whom they can exchange property rights. It will then be useful to spell out rules which ensure free contracting and liability for promises made in these contracts. Private property, the freedom to

Figure 6.1 Types of systems

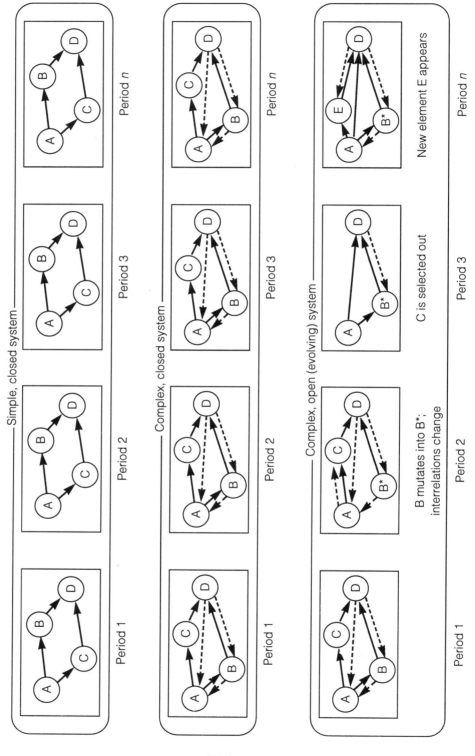

contract and liability thus form a system of mutually compatible institutions – an order of rules. If, on the other hand, people enjoy protected property rights, but are not free to contract, a contradiction arises: what use does private property have if the buying, selling or lending of property rights under contract is prohibited or severely restricted? Only when the various rules form a reasonably compatible whole will they be effective in bringing about order and controlling arbitrary, opportunistic actions that erode predictability and confidence.

Rule systems work better in ordering human actions if they form a hierarchy running from general to specific rules. General, universal rules are often abstract; they may consist of internalised moral norms (example: 'Thou shalt not steal') or general external institutions that are formally laid down in bills of rights or 'basic laws'. They tend to override more specific institutions if contradictions arise. More specific rules may, for example, explain what, in a particular walk of life, constitutes theft. Such rules may be contained in specific statute laws or by-laws. Overriding rules thus create a framework for lower-level rules. Such hierarchical rule systems are in particular typical of external institutions.

Hierarchies of external institutions tend to consist in essence of rules at three different levels: namely, constitutions at the apex, statute law in the middle and regulations at the bottom (Figure 6.2). This hierarchy constrains what private agreements can be made legally and how they are to be interpreted when doubts arise. Typically, constitutional rules are selected by processes of constitutional choice. In turn, some of the constitutional rules refer to collective decision-making that establishes laws and regulations. These govern contracts that are made at the operational, decentralised level. If doubts arise as to legality of specific low-level constraints, this will be assessed from the bottom up, that is, from the specific to the general norms.

Such hierarchies make it easier for individuals to understand the rules, because they serve to create an order among different rules and maintain consistency over time. If an authority issues a great number of rulings, decrees, edicts, *ukases* (known from the autocratic Tsarist and present-day Russian practice of ruling case by case and without reference to some consistent general standards), or *fatwas* (known from the Islamic law tradition by which different mullahs issue binding decrees to suit occurrences of the day), then there is a danger of inconsistency, arbitrariness and randomness. The rules cannot be comprehended and are therefore ineffectual in norming individual behaviour. They disorientate people and create disorder. Such a style of rule tends easily towards tyranny and discrimination and is there-

Figure 6.2 A hierarchy of external institutions

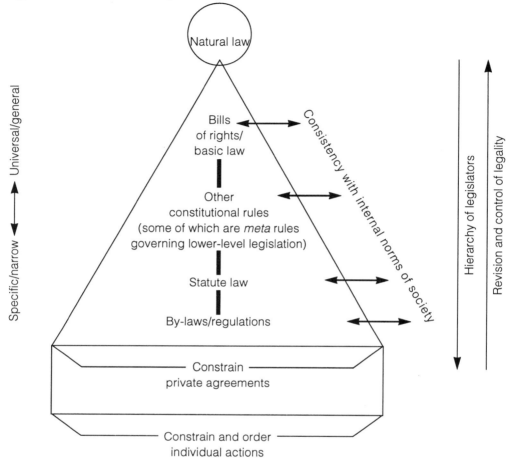

fore often perceived as unjust. All too frequently, the unsystematic proliferation of rules breeds sullen conformity and dissimulation of an individual's true thoughts and motives, a condition that is the opposite of the open competition of ideas and critical assessment of new ideas and experiments; therefore, it is not conducive to effective coordination and innovation, and hence to prosperity and freedom.

Rules systems may consist purely of internal institutions, as is the case with cultural systems (see section 6.4 below). Systems of internal rule do not normally contain many explicit hierarchical and procedural rules, but nevertheless we usually understand how conflicting rules are made compatible, for example when we accept that it is not necessary to speak the truth in certain extreme circumstances if someone's freedom or life is at stake. External institutions or mixes of internal and external rules require procedural rules to indicate how to resolve possible contradictions. Problems arise when the internal rules of a community conflict with the external rules. Then the costs of monitoring compliance with and enforcing the external rules set limits to what governments can achieve by external institutions. It has been estimated that 'government can at any one moment in time enforce at best 3 to 7 per cent of all legal norms by compulsion' if spontaneous compliance is not forthcoming (Kimminich, 1990, p. 100, our translation). External rules at all levels should therefore be reasonably consistent with the internal rules of society (some embodied in natural law) to ensure that these rules have normative influence on behaviour. In certain situations, where rules conflict, only careful moral discourse may be able to resolve the contradiction.

In hierarchies of external institutions, we observe clearer statements as to how the various rules are related to each other. Very high-level constitutional rules are often contained in bills of rights, basic laws or preambles to written constitutions; they override all other rules. They tend to be affirmed by special assemblies and often depend on special criteria of acceptance. In some legal systems, these high institutions none the less have to be compatible with natural law, which may be understood as a proxy for deeply held rules and values in the community which protect the inalienable rights of every human being. The concept of inalienable rights was already known in antiquity in Europe and was shaped into codes of fundamental liberties in the early modern era. They are now reflected in, for example, the US Bill of Rights, the European Basic Rights Charter, and the Human Rights Convention of the United Nations. Subordinate to natural law and basic laws are other constitutional rules, which tend to be more specific. They often contain procedural public-law rules which determine how rules are adopted and applied and which direct the various organs of government (*meta* rules), as distinct from rules that guide human actions. Proceeding down the hierarchy of external institutions (Figure 6.2), the hierarchy of legislators also descends, from parliaments with simple majorities, in the case of much statute law, to administrations, which pass more specific by-laws and regulations on the basis of enabling legislation. When such low-level rules are contested they are subject to revision and control of their legality in contrast to the more universal higher-level rules.

Rule Systems Assist with Cognition

Such hierarchies of institutions work as follows. Individuals conclude private contracts to cooperate. This may come under specific regulations or by-laws which constrain what the contracting parties are allowed to do and clarifies aspects of the deal which the contract does not spell out. For example, the private contract may be between an employer and a worker to establish a work relationship. The freedom to enter into such a contract may, for good or bad reasons, be constrained by regulations that prohibit work during certain hours. The contract is of course also subject to formal statute law which takes precedent over the regulation if a contradiction becomes evident. And all statutes are overridden by the higher-order rules which are contained in written or unwritten constitutions. If contradictions emerge, constitutional courts will be asked to adjudicate how a particular statute law fits in with the constitution; it may find that the statute is invalid because it contradicts a higher-order constitutional provision. Constitutional rules must in turn fit into the bill of rights and – at least in the Anglo-Saxon tradition – into natural law. Thus, it would not be a valid contract if it authorised slave labour, since slavery is deemed a violation of natural law. The higher-level institutions constitute a framework that offers stability and ensures consistency of the lower-level rules. The hierarchy represents a legal system in the sense defined above. In modern societies it tends to be complex and it evolves, reflecting changes in the real-world circumstances which the legal system orders. But the insight applies that complex rule systems are hard to comply with, so simple rules have much greater effect in ordering a complex world (see section 5.5).

To return to the example of an employment relationship: a system of rules surrounding the work contract gives employers and employees greater confidence in how future events will be sorted out under their open-ended contract. A rule system also makes it economical to write employment contracts, since many specific contingencies that might have to be stipulated by private agreement and that may not even be imaginable at the time of contracting are determined by elements in the universal institutional system, if such contingencies occur. If specific adjustments in open-ended employment contracts become necessary, they can be made with regard to specifics, whilst the overall contract continues within the stable, reliable constitutional elements of the system, so that reciprocal trust between employer and employee is safeguarded.

Hierarchies of Rules Assist with Managing Institutional Change

Since the world of private contracts is open-ended and evolves, the corresponding institutional system should also have evolutionary capacity. A key function of a systematic hierarchy of rules is to assist with the evolution in the rule system. Higher-order rules lay down what lower-level rules may and may not stipulate, even if they are changed. They ensure internal consistency in the rule system and govern procedures for rule adjustment. These *meta* rules differ from institutions that directly affect the actions of private citizens (private law) in that they instruct those who operate the external rule system (public law). *Meta* rules also promulgate known procedures for changing specific lower-order rules if necessary. Higher-order institutions thus provide a framework which confines what changes can be made and how these changes will be decided. This is essential to the predictable functioning of the institutional system over time. Rules of a higher, constitutional quality keep matters predictable when specific lower-order rules have to be adjusted to new circumstances. Institutional systems that lack such hierarchies of institutions inhibit evolutionary adjustment. They will, in the long run, probably undergo discontinuities and become uncertain.

It is not easy to keep complex institutional systems internally compatible and cohesive, that is, to maintain the order of rules. Incompatibility can be avoided when the rule makers are economical in promulgating specific, lower-level institutions and concentrate on fostering simple, general rules. A proliferation of specific, detailed legislation is hardly the sign of a competent parliament. Rather, it is an indication that the general rules are neglected at the expense of interventions to attain specific purposes. Such a style of rule setting creates insecurities for those subject to them because no one can know – let alone obey – a large multiplicity of specific lower-level rules. As rules proliferate, the system becomes dysfunctional. In such a situation, simplifying and streamlining the lower-level rules and developing new universal institutions may be a good way to making the institutional system more effective again (Epstein, 1995). Enhancing the coordinative power of institutions in this way is an important aspect of economic reforms.

O Key Concepts

A **system** is defined as a configuration of multiple elements. We speak of **complex systems** when the elements interact with regard to many relevant characteristics. If the system is open to the future, in the sense that elements or characteristics change unpredictably, we call it an **evolving system**. Then, variation, selection and self-stabilisation interact to produce new recognisable patterns. When we consider cross-connected institutions, we speak of a **rule system**. It may be ordered by experience and evolutionary learning (evolved institutional system) or by design (made, designed institutional system). The **order of rules** thus can be planned or spontaneous.

Hierarchy is a system in which status and authority are ranked vertically, with higher ranks having the right to command and order the lower ranks. In such a top-down system, order is imposed from above.

Natural law is based on the affirmation that human beings have certain inalienable rights. Aristotle wrote that every human being has certain inalienable overriding rights irrespective of where they live and what conventions and laws their community adheres to. Natural law recognises that all humans are equal in certain fundamental respects. In modern times, the concept of the natural law as a high-order legal principle has gained renewed acceptance in the light of experiences with totalitarian regimes. It is now widely accepted as the source of certain **basic** negative **liberties** (freedoms from interference by authorities and fellow humans).

Statute law is that part of the system of laws that has been adopted and written down by a formal legislative body (as distinct from common law or case law).

***Meta* rules** are procedural rules (or principles) which do not directly affect private citizens but are intended to keep the external rule system compatible. They govern how institutional changes are made, by whom they can be initiated, under what majorities they are adopted, and how conflicts over rule changes are resolved. An example of a *meta* rule is the provision that a constitutional court can review new legislation to establish whether it complies with constitutional principles. ●

6.2   Two Kinds of Social Order

Two Methods of Ordering

Human actions can, in essence, be ordered in two ways:

- directly by an outside authority which plans and implements order by instructions or directives to achieve a joint purpose (*organised or planned order*);
- indirectly and in a spontaneous and voluntary way because the various agents obey shared institutions (*spontaneous or unplanned order*).

Spontaneous ordering occurs frequently in nature. To give but two examples: when you blow into a drop of soapy water the molecules arrange themselves in a bubble, a predictable arrangement; and fertilised cells reproduce themselves spontaneously into recognisable living organisms without an outside ordering hand arranging this. We also observe much spontaneous ordering among human beings, which allows us to rely on regularities in human conduct: when people come to the beach, they often distribute themselves evenly in space so as to attain maximum privacy. And when people compete, buyers and sellers are coordinated. In all these spontaneous ordering processes, the various component parts are equals, obeying the same rules. No one acts as an authority who directs the others.

But we can also observe that much ordering is done by the visible hand of an authority. Carefully thought-out designs may guide someone to coordinate the various actors, one thinking brain may move others, like pieces on a chessboard.

The essential difference between these two kinds of ordering human actions can be illustrated by the following comparisons:

(a) the child – or the father – who plays with a toy railway by moving the levers of the electrical controls imposes an organised order on the train movements. When we watch the road traffic flows in a city from above, we also observe order. But here no one is in control, instructing drivers precisely when to accelerate, brake or turn. Instead, the observed order comes about spontaneously because people's actions are guided by prohibitive institutions, traffic rules, and the self-interest in avoiding collisions. Within these constraints, people are free to decide how and where to drive;

(b) outside our window at a new university campus, we see the coexistence of two kinds of ordering: the planners and architects laid down nicely paved paths, but much of the foot traffic takes short cuts across lawns and flower beds. Obviously, the planned order does not serve the average users, who have gradually established their own migration routes. The question then arises: should the university enforce the made order, or tolerate the spontaneous order that emerged from where people want to walk? This leads to the follow-on question: in whose interest have the walking connections been established, those of the students and academics, or those of planners who have long left the campus?

In relatively simple systems, purposive organisation and cooperation that are coordinated by top-down command can be quite effective. The more complex the coordinative task becomes, the more likely it is that spontaneous ordering has the advantage. This is so in particular when the system is open to unpredictable evolution. Thus, the production of one or several car models is planned and coordinated within a firm, but the coordination with buyers and other suppliers occurs spontaneously through market competition.

O Key Concepts

We speak of **spontaneity** in social ordering if predictable patterns emerge independently of the purposive will of actors, but rather as a by-product of individual human actions. The opposite to spontaneous is **purposive**, the wilful action to obtain a planned result from a process of interaction. ●

Human creations are often arranged along the lines of a carefully thought-out design. At least up to now, human interventions in nature proceed according to a plan, although some analysts now predict that 'nano-engineering', the spontaneous self-patterning of matter – similar to the biological ordering of matter or the growth of a crystal – will soon be feasible, so that materials and apparatuses will be created from the inside out (from gene information, so to speak), rather than according to an outside design (Drexler, 1986). Because we are so familiar with planned ordering, we find spontaneous ordering always hard to comprehend; for example, how new life evolves from a fertilised cell or how markets generate complex new products. Humans have therefore found such phenomena awe- and fear-inspiring and often assumed an ordering, visible hand to reduce the ordering process to a simpler, more comprehensible planning exercise (teleological explanation). People also probably prefer simple, visible and stable cause–effect relations and therefore feel uneasy about 'invisible hand' explanations.

The distinction between spontaneous and planned orders of actions and orders of rules (Figure 6.3) was given prominence by Friedrich Hayek, who drew on earlier writers in the Austrian school of economics, such as Carl Menger (for example, [1883] 1963, pp. 35–54). As both types of ordering actions and rules exist alongside each other, we have to learn to live with both, for example the mainly organised, planned order of the family and the firm, and the spontaneous order of the market and the open society. As we shall see below, both these coordination devices require different value systems, attitudes and modes of behaviour, so that swapping from a planned, hierarchical to an open, spontaneous order is not easy (Hayek, 1988, ch. 5).

The Planned Order and Its Limitations

The planned order presupposes, as we noted, some sort of an ordering hand, which gives the various actors positive instructions how to act. It always implies some form of design, and coordination by specific

Figure 6.3   Order of actions and order of rules

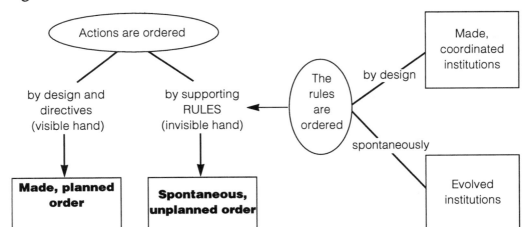

directives or *prescriptions* – such as an orchestra which follows the instructions of the composer and of its conductor, the operations of military units, or the coordination of productive activities within a factory which follow a production schedule assigning specific tasks to the various agents.

The cooperation of human action within designed, hierarchical orders places great demands:

(a) on the availability of knowledge and the capacity of those who coordinate actions to obtain relevant information;
(b) on the leaders' capability to digest, utilise and communicate such information; and
(c) on the capacity of the leaders to motivate the agents to make an effort and to monitor their performance.

When a system becomes complex and open, the cognitive limitations of the leaders to plan and implement order can easily become a bottle-neck. In complex circumstances, such as the coordination of the millions of buyers and sellers of hundreds of thousands of different goods and services, centrally planned coordination from above is bound to falter because of insuperable knowledge problems. Where central coordination is attempted nevertheless, the planners must pretend that they have the knowledge which enables them to impose an order. But in reality they are tempted to base their plans and commands on averages (the average consumer, the 'representative' firm and so on –

under the motto: 'One size fits all'). The rich diversity of knowledge and aspirations that makes up the real world is neglected to the detriment of all the diverse members of society. Following Hayek, we shall call the persistence with hierarchical ordering in the face of complexity 'constructivism'.

Planned ordering also requires that the followers who are being ordered perceive the signals and want to follow them. If the ordered community is complex and large, the signals are often distorted or lost. Despite public propaganda, moral suasion and constant 'awareness campaigns', mere commands are not obeyed when the motivation to obey is absent. Then, punishments have to be relied on for motivation. Planned orders have therefore to be accompanied by the coercive exercise of power (see section 5.4). As such, they limit freedom. That in turn places additional cognitive requirements on the rulers: they have to monitor failure to obey, before they can punish it – not an easy task when numerous people interact and many make great efforts and use considerable resources to disguise and dissimulate their true behaviour: in short, when principal–agent problems are rampant.

The limitations of hierarchical, made social orders can become critical when circumstances change and new solutions are required. Then, spontaneous experimentation and the decentralised, competitive search for solutions can have great advantages over centralised interpretation of the signals and the design of centralised responses. Central planning thus had very limited capacities to develop innovative solutions, as compared to decentralised market economies. Typically, possibly the most centrally ordered and authoritarian state in human history, the mighty Inca empire, collapsed in the 1530s because its rigid command system, coupled with cognitive weaknesses at the centre, could not adapt creatively to the challenge of a small number of Spanish conquistadores and their unheard-of weapons. Similarly, other regimes which depended heavily on central ordering, from the Persian empire under Darius, through imperial China in the nineteenth and early twentieth centuries, to the Soviet empire, ultimately failed because of the rigidities of central ordering and resulting entropy.

Often, the knowledge problem of policy makers, when they order matters top-down by prescribing specific actions, is reflected in 'unintended, unforeseen side effects'. The immediate impact of a policy intervention promotes the intended purpose, but, within a complex, open system, other effects may subsequently become dominant, so that the original intervention ultimately has perverse effects. A good example which demonstrates the knowledge problem of policy makers who want to engage in purpose-specific rules is legislation that prescribes obstacles to dismissal in order to promote job security. This may prevent some people being fired but, by making dismissal more costly, it also erects an obstacle to hiring new employees since employers may not be sure how long jobs will last. Another practical example of perverse side-effects is rent control. It may originally have been imposed to protect tenants, but, in times of cost increases, the side-effect is invariably that the provision of rented accommodation becomes unprofitable. If, in addition, it is fraught with legal compliance costs, less accommodation is made available. Housing supply becomes short, and tenants as a whole are disadvantaged.

In certain situations, designed orders and coordination by directive can be advantageous. This is one reason for the existence of firms and government organisations, which are planned orders. Where the subject matter is not overly complex, it is often more effective for authorities to coordinate and direct all agents according to a preconceived plan so that a purposeful pattern of interaction emerges. Another circumstance where hierarchical orders make sense is when people produce joint products; then, they often combine their resources more or less permanently in an organisation. Where indivisible joint products are produced or exclusive private property cannot be established, the results cannot be distributed as a direct pay-off for the individual's action and has to be allocated by command. This makes planned ordering advantageous. After all, individuals can act within a spontaneous order, such as a market, only if they expect to receive an exclusive, defined pay-off for their efforts directly and almost immediately.

The Spontaneous Order of Actions

Human limitations make it advantageous to rely on spontaneous ordering and to cultivate the devices that facilitate spontaneous order. To cite Hayek again: 'Human intelligence is quite insufficient to comprehend all the details of the complex human society, and it is the inadequacy of our reason to arrange such an order in detail which forces us to be content with abstract rules' (Hayek, 1967b, p. 88). In other words, it becomes necessary to rely on coordination by the 'invisible hand' that works through spontaneously observed rules. Adam Smith illustrated the concept of social ordering by the forces of competition by reference to the 'invisible hand', showing how people were driven by self-interest to coordinate their actions to mutual benefit. In the market process, actions are ordered by the profit–loss signal and the pursuit of selfishness which is channelled by universal institutions, but this has the unintended side-effect that an order of actions emerges on which people can rely and which provides others with material benefits and new opportunities.

The spontaneous order of actions in the market process has to give answers to the following questions:

(a) How are individuals to search for and procure knowledge that may be useful to their own individual purposes?
(b) How is this knowledge disseminated so that it may be useful to others?
(c) How are possible errors corrected in the light of feedback, so that the overall economic system is not destabilised (Streit, 1998)?

The market system does this spontaneously through the price signals that emerge in competitive processes, that expose people to incentives and controls and that convey information in the greatly simplified form of price variations. It sends participants through discovery procedures (Hayek, 1978). In Chapter 2 we defined such a process of spontaneous competitive interaction as 'catallaxy'.

Dependence on Rules of Conduct

The spontaneous order emerges in actions because individuals respond to a system of rules governing their conduct. Market activities, for example, fall into a predictable, orderly pattern because all are subject to rules: here the freedom of contract and protected property rights ensure that most market participants act in predictable ways. Normally, if the price goes up suppliers will offer more quantity and buyers will reduce the quantities they demand. Buyers and sellers make complex decisions in response to such price signals but, despite their freedom and the diversity of reasons why they respond, they can be expected to act in spontaneously coordinated ways. The market is thus not the chaos and free-for-all that ignorant observers frequently describe.

The rules that bring about a spontaneous order in the market economy must ensure that individuals are motivated to use their subjective knowledge to pursue their own purposes and are able to reliably anticipate how others will behave. In the market, this depends critically on participants being allowed to keep what they have earned (protected private property) and being confident that others will keep their promises (enforcement of contracts). The institutions that ensure this are crucial to effective order in the market process.

The advantages and disadvantages of the two kinds of ordering in dealing with complex tasks were illustrated in a telling way when, in the late 1980s, there were two major earthquakes. One occurred in Leninakan in Armenia, then in the Soviet Union. It took numerous committee meetings in distant Moscow and elsewhere to identify and plan the reconstruction effort. All this had not progressed very far when the Soviet Union collapsed.[1] The second earthquake shook San Francisco in California; within hours, glass suppliers as far afield as Chicago were loading trucks for the San Francisco market. Social critics may argue that the firms in Chicago acted out of self-interest to make a fast buck. But were the results of presumably 'unselfish' planning in any way preferable from the viewpoint of the victims of the Armenian quake?

Some Historic Philosophical Concepts of Society

Preferences for how to order social and economic life have much to do with fundamental philosophy about society and attitudes to individualism. There are two distinctly differing ways of perceiving the individual and its relation to social and economic life:

(a) one perception of society is that of an organic whole, where the whole is seen as more than the sum of its individual parts and where the whole has purposes of its own. Society is perceived somehow as an organisation or collective entity to which all belong and in which all have to serve. It is up to the leaders, however chosen, to define what is in the interest of society and what are each individual's duties towards society;

(b) an alternative perception of society, on which this book is based, differs fundamentally from the above 'organisation model' of society. It starts with a perception of human beings as self-interested, autonomous and equal individuals with limited cognitive powers and limited knowledge. Society is seen as a web of essentially voluntary interactions. In principle, all people are equal. This is not a vision of atomistic individualism, as people cooperate within certain overlapping networks and organisations and interact spontaneously by following shared institutions. Where collective action is needed, it is preferable for it to be inspired from the bottom up.

The central notion of the individual as autonomous and endowed with certain inalienable rights in Europe goes back to the Greek philosophers, such as Aristotle, and to Roman legal practice in antiquity. Individualist perceptions of society are the result of a long discourse in Europe about the individual and society. They gained renewed influence

in the late Middle Ages, for example when merchants in different jurisdictions and of different social classes had to sort out conflicts on the
basis of equality rather than on the basis of prevailing feudal law which
allotted to everyone class-specific privileges and obligations.

Perceptions of society that see it as akin to an organisation in which
the leaders order human interaction were strong in the era of the
absolutist states of Europe, when for example King Louis XIV of
France presented himself as the head of society, which was represented as the body.[2] Many eighteenth-century philosophers of the
Enlightenment attacked this concept and perceived all people to be
equal before the law. However, a collectivist notion of society was
again made popular by the French-Swiss writer-philosopher Jean
Jacques Rousseau (1712–78) who opposed individualist concepts. He
popularised the concept of a 'General Will' (*volonté générale*) which
reflects some sort of a social will that is separate from and overrides
the wishes of individuals. Mature citizens, he wrote, should voluntarily subject themselves to such a 'collective will'. To the extent to which
the 'General Will' can be understood as a system of institutions that
make living and working together feasible, there is no problem. But
where the interpretation of a 'General Will' goes beyond that, it leads
to dictatorship and wanton collectivism. Since Rousseau wrote, many
a dictator has professed his belief in the 'General Will' (invariably as
exercised by himself) and has given society a vision, a mission and a
destiny. Subsequent writers such as Auguste Comte (1798–1857), Georg
Wilhelm Friedrich Hegel (1770–1831) and Karl Marx (1818–83) depicted individual pursuits as the source of much social evil and
simplified complex historic evolution to depict predetermined historic
patterns of great societal developments.

The most prominent example of an 'organisational' concept of society
in western philosophy was Karl Marx's belief that societies run through
a preordained path of historic stages until they end up with communism – a kind of paradise on earth where scarcity is suspended. Karl
Marx thought in terms of 'iron laws of history' determining the dialec-
tic movements of society (historic determinism). In the interim stage
of socialism, it was necessary to pursue actively the objectives of
society by organising individuals into collectives (organised mass action). The collective would propel the course of history and is therefore
legitimated as a body that exists separately from its members. In case
of conflict, it has the right to override individual aspirations and to
impose its superior objectives.

This world view led to the totalitarian form of Soviet and Maoist
socialism, but is also mirrored in numerous non-totalitarian collectivist

programmes around the world which are based on the presumption that the 'right things' only happen if they are mandated by government.[3]

The opposite, individualist, world view is based on the understanding that society lacks an identity of its own which is separate from the individuals who constitute it, and that knowledge at the centre is always too limited to coordinate complex, evolving systems. Social and economic life evolves as an open system whose path is not known and cannot be predetermined by anyone. As individuals are capable of creativity, they can shape history. Hence it would be contradictory to assume anything like an 'iron law of history'.

In this perception of society, the diversity among individuals and their characteristics is considered desirable, as diversity enriches the evolutionary potential – a society's 'gene pool of ideas and capabilities', so to speak. The same applies to the coordinative institutional systems. The order of rules is seen to evolve in the light of experience and to economise on the need for knowledge search.

The two kinds of ordering are thus related to two differing visions of the world and of society. The individual's preference for one or the other hinges crucially on whether one acknowledges a constitutional knowledge problem, in particular on the part of the leaders.

O Key Concepts

Order means that repetitive events or actions fit into a discernible pattern which allows people to have confidence that the pattern of future actions, on which they may depend, can be predicted reasonably well. If the world is ordered, complexity, and hence the knowledge problem, is reduced and economic agents are better able to specialise. Institutions serve to facilitate the emergence of order.

The **order of actions** can come about when someone plans a cohesive pattern of interaction and enforces the directives, or when the agents follow shared rules in a spontaneous manner. The former leads to an **organised** or **planned order**. The latter produces a **spontaneous order**. It comes about when independent agents more or less voluntarily obey shared institutions, but otherwise are left the freedom to decide what to do. An example of a spontaneous ordering is the market economy, where stealing and cheating are prohibited by sanctioned institutions, but where participants are not instructed, for example, to produce certain goods with certain technologies.

Planned orders always presuppose a degree of hierarchy and the use of compulsion, whereas spontaneous orders emerge among equals who act voluntarily.

We speak of an **order of rules** when the various institutions form an internally cohesive, consistent set of institutions. The order of rules itself is often the result of evolution in the light of experience, but it can also be influenced by the visible, ordering hand of government (codification of formerly internal institutions; constitutional or legal reform).

Historicism (or **determinism**) is based on a view of society as a closed system whose developments follow predictable patterns, possibly to a desirable end state. An example of a historicist theory is Karl Marx's historic materialism which predicted a progression of society from feudalism, to capitalism, to socialism and to communism. Deterministic perceptions of society are contradicted by analysts (such as Karl Popper) who see society as an open system whose evolution depends essentially on the discovery of human knowledge, that is, on an essentially unpredictable, open-ended process. ●

Behavioural Syndromes of Hierarchical and Spontaneous Social Order

The two types of ordering are tied to different value systems, mental attitudes and modes of behaviour, so that switching from a planned, hierarchical order to an open, spontaneous one is not always easy. Experiences with each type of order also form and reinforce a different syndrome of human behaviour. When the members of a society are subject to a primarily hierarchical social order, they practise and learn different virtues as compared to when they act under a free, spontaneous order. These patterns become internalised and turn into social norms, which others emulate and which may then reinforce the existing order. They become part of the society's shared culture. The virtues that underpin hierarchical, closed orders prevail in societies that have little experience with open exchange and the rule of law. Here, the loyalty of the small group (the family, the clan, the village, the secret society) overrides readiness to cooperate with strangers based on abstract, universal principles.

A central element in defining the social order is openness. If members of groups believe – as the French sociologist Claude Lévi Strauss once put it – that 'the concept of humanity ceases at the borders of the tribe, of the linguistic group, sometimes even of the village', then different rules and norms will apply depending on whether basic perceptions are cosmopolitan and focused on universal human values, or whether they are tied to a tribal mentality of 'us and them'.

Table 6.1   Behavioural symptoms typical of the two kinds of social order

---

Planned, closed order: 'the guardian moral syndrome'

Shun trading	Exert prowess
Be obedient and disciplined	Adhere to tradition
Respect hierarchy	Be loyal
Take vengeance	Deceive for the sake of the task
Make rich use of leisure	Be ostentatious
Dispense largesse	Be exclusive
Show fortitude	Be fatalistic
Treasure honour	

Spontaneous, open order: 'the commercial moral syndrome'

Shun force	Come to voluntary agreements
Be honest	Collaborate easily with aliens
Compete	Respect contracts
Use initiative and enterprise	Be open to inventiveness and novelty
Be efficient	Promote comfort and convenience
Dissent for the sake of the task	Invest for productive purposes
Be industrious	Be thrifty
Be optimistic	

Source: Jacobs (1992)

American social critic Jane Jacobs (1992) made an interesting attempt to list virtues and behavioural symptoms typical of the two kinds of order (Table 6.1). She described the two sets of attitudes and virtues as 'the guardian moral syndrome', typical of closed hierarchical orders, and 'the commercial moral syndrome', typical of the open society. People who live primarily in hierarchical orders tend to focus on protecting their territory. People whose primary experience is in trade or science focus on curiosity and adapting to new, emerging circumstances.

Often, people who subscribe to the one syndrome attack the other as morally or culturally inferior. Thus, Jacobs notes the disdain for traders among 'guardian groups', such as the military, the bureaucrats and the aristocracy, and the contempt for people who preach vengeance and dwell on honour among 'commercial groups', such as merchants and researchers – people who live by trading goods and ideas. Similar systematic differences occur between people who are nationalists and live in close societies, and cosmopolitans, who think in terms of open systems. When communities are subjected to economic reforms and the fundamental institutional settings change, there is a need to change from one value syndrome to the other, but old sets of virtues often persist. This delays personal adjustment to a new order and causes difficulties in systems transformation.

The behavioural norms of the closed order can be observed, for example, among traditional East Asians, southern Italians, or people from Middle Eastern countries, who are loath to cooperate with the representatives of government authority because they are deemed to belong to another (hostile) clan and because it is automatically assumed that individuals pursue exclusively the interests of their own group. When government officials also behave as if they were representatives of a 'tribe' – and not as defenders of universal values – it is extremely hard to break with the guardian syndrome and to spread the spontaneous, open order of rules and with it the material benefits of a wider division of labour and knowledge (Klitgaard, 1995). The order of rules relies on the willingness and capability of people to distinguish between 'tribe' and open society.

O Key Concepts

The **guardian syndrome** covers a set of norms that proved to be essential for the survival of small tribes and for the defence of a given domain: sharing, loyal obedience to authority and tradition, exclusivity and defence of honour. This contrasts with the **commercial syndrome**, an alternative, inherently compatible set of virtues that make sense in an open exchange society, such as the rejection of force, openness of exchange and collaboration with strangers, inventiveness, honesty and thrift. ●

The micro society of the tribe can offer considerable comfort (Hayek, 1976a, pp. 133–5). The seeming security of the group is no doubt one of the comforts of living in a closed system. However, as the economy evolves and requires the coordination of much more complex and changing circumstances, people have to learn to interact with strangers, live in open society and acquire attitudes and virtues compatible with it. This frequently leads to what the Austrian-English philosopher Karl Popper once called the 'strain of civilisation' (Popper, 1945). It forces us to cope with the insecurities of open-ended change and great complexity. We then have to rely on abstract rules that evolve, rather than on leaders and specific rules. Many will ask whether the material gains and the freedoms of the open society are indeed worth the loss of security. This is a valid question. However, competing within the rule system of the open society also educates people to practise social virtues such as honesty, parsimony and industry. It was the hope of analysts as far back as the pre-industrial age that the spread of commercial activity would control base passions and would ultimately enhance the compliance with rules which supports civil liberties (Hirschman, 1977, pp. 56–67). To some extent at least, the limited insecurity of the market order has led to the spread of order by rules, for example in the United States, among many professional groups worldwide and more recently in several countries in East Asia where a new middle class has emerged. It now pursues a better assurance of civil liberties by contestable elections and a more rule-bound legal system and feels increasingly at home in the open order.

6.3   The Perceptions of Order Influence Public Policy

Individualism and Collectivism

There is a major divide in world views between individualism and collectivism:

(a) as noted in earlier chapters, an individualist world view sees individual motivation as the foundation of all social action and the reference point in studying social phenomena. It is acknowledged that individual actions have side-effects on others and that this requires constraining rule systems. Individualists tend to prefer a system of rules which secures domains of freedom and which allows spontaneous coordination;

(b) collectivists see society as a whole which is more than the individuals that make it up at any point in time. They presume that it is possible to identify the true and overriding interests of society and that some legitimate authority can be established to take care of those interests.

These two perceptions of society are normally coupled with some other basic preferences, such as how to conduct public policy. Although these have been noted at various points in the preceding text, it is useful to restate them:

(a) individualists prefer coordination by voluntary exchanges within a framework of rules, whereas collectivists incline to central ordering by planning and directive. Individualists appreciate that people accept responsibilities for their actions;

(b) individualists normally prefer general rules and, if possible, proscriptive rules and negative liberties. Preference is given to market processes and a containment of collective action. Collectivism relies more on prescriptions, directives and compulsion and subscribes to central planning;

(c) a third difference relates to perceptions of what a social system is: is it closed and static or open-ended and evolving? Individualists see the social system as being in the grip of unpredictable evolutionary change and accept that there is no predetermined path of development, whereas collectivists often see society as a system that goes through predictable historical patterns, following 'iron laws of history' (determinism, historicism).

Philosophical visions of society are also influenced by two fundamental attitudes among people which have little to do with individualism and collectivism: egotism and altruism. Egotism gives priority to one's own interests, altruism to those of others. Many observers have, however, identified individualism with egotism and have claimed the moral high-ground for collectivism because it supposedly aims at the interests of others (Figure 6.4). This identification is illegitimate (Popper, 1945, pp. 100–23). It is by now evident that collective group egotism can play a big role in the form of discrimination by the group against outsiders (us and them). It is also quite possible for individualists to act in altruistic ways, helping others without expecting an advantage in return.

The dichotomy between individualism and collectivism has not only been philosophical. It has been one of the major influences around the world in the twentieth century. Totalitarian collectivist movements of

Figure 6.4   Visions and attitudes

| | | Vision of society | |
		Individualism	Collectivism
Attitude to fellow human beings	Egotistic	Self-seeking individualism	Group egotism (discrimination against outsiders)
	Altruistic	Altruistic individualism (individual charity, cosmopolitanism)	Group altruism (sharing; group solidarity)

the socialist and the nationalist types mobilised much political support and overturned existing societies: first the communists in Russia; then the fascists in Italy and Germany; later communists in Eastern Europe, China and Vietnam. The observation that collectivism requires coercion has been shown to be true as many tens of millions of people have been killed and more incarcerated during the imposition of collectivist designs, and many more have died in wars triggered by collectivist regimes in this century.

Influential variants of collectivism reflect what Karl Popper described as the 'strain of civilisation' and the longing for a model society akin to a large family. Softer forms of collectivism are pursued with much less coercion: the welfare state in affluent countries and collectivist-nationalist regimes in the newly independent countries of the third world.

Individualism as a basic perception of society has, however, survived and seems to be in the ascendancy in the late twentieth century, not least because the material results of individual motivation and spontaneous ordering by market processes have proven superior. As a consequence, newly affluent middle classes are demanding individual, civil and economic rights, both as ends in themselves and as a means of maintaining and furthering their prosperity.

O Key Concepts

Individualism is a view of society that grounds explanations of economic and social phenomena in individual motivation and behaviour. It is acknowledged that individuals have differing knowledge, preferences and purposes.

Collectivism is the social theory which is diametrically opposed to individualism. It takes the group, the collective, as a being in its own right, which is subject to (collective) purposes of its own. Indeed, its purposes should override individual purposes if necessary. Collectivism was once defined (by the great British constitutional jurist Albert V. Dicey, 1835–1922) as 'government for the good of the people by experts or officials who know, or think they know, what is good for the people better than any non-official person or than the mass of the people themselves'.

Constructivism (also called **instrumentalism** or **social engineering**) denotes a habit of seeing society and policy in terms of an organisation, that is, as a cohesive hierarchy in which solutions are designed and implemented by the leaders. It is based on optimism about the feasibility of top-down problem solving and on the assumption that central actions do not lead to unforeseen side-effects. It tends to be associated with static concepts of society. ●

Two Styles of Public Policy

Obviously, these two perceptions of order imply fundamentally differing recommendations for the conduct of public policy. If one's basic philosophy is grounded in collectivism and the 'organisation model of society', one is likely to embrace comprehensive social goals, which leaders and members of society should follow, as well as a collective-hierarchical approach to ordering social life. One is likely to accept authorities which mandate and, if necessary, coerce individuals to fall in line with the planned order. Individuals who pursue their own interests in the face of social interest, as defined and interpreted by the rulers or elected governments and their agents, are depicted as egotistical. Their repression is readily accepted 'in the group's interest', 'in the national interest' or 'for reasons of state'. In societies where the organisation model of social order is widely accepted, vertical power distances tend to be great and horizontal relations between individuals weak.

Those who have the alternative individualistic perception of society tend to be rather sceptical of authoritarian top-down policies. Instead, they stress horizontal and voluntary coordination between free and equal individuals. Goals are set individually by the individuals themselves and vary from person to person. People's plans evolve and may clash with the aspirations of others. Those with this world view do not advocate a preference for anarchy; they focus on order-supporting institutions, including some institutions that are imposed externally and enforced formally by government. Public policy is seen as the activity of agents whom the citizens have appointed collectively in order to foster an order in which individuals have a good chance to attain what they aspire to. This basic philosophy gives preference to the rule of law over the rule of men (who are seen as self-interested and fallible). In essence, people are not expected to obey authorities, but to follow incentives derived from abstract rules. They cooperate with others by voluntary contract. Only where individuals break implicit and explicit agreements is it necessary for third parties, such as government agencies, to intervene. According to this perception of society, public policy is expected to concentrate on protecting the rules (protective government).

❖ Gruzino: an Early Example of Planned Order

Russia was traditionally a slovenly as well as a grotesquely inefficient country, and its reformist rulers have tended to pounce on the visible external signs of its shortcomings ...

[The most prominent reformer of the early nineteenth century was General Alexis Alexandrovich Arakcheev, who created a new, progressive order on his Gruzino estate.] Gruzino has a strong claim to be considered the first modern experiment in social engineering, an attempt to create the New Man, who, Rousseau had argued, could be born in the right conditions. The estate was 35 square kilometres and contained 2000 'souls'. The general destroyed all the old wooden buildings and put up new model villages in brick and stone. He drained the muddy roads and paved them. He dug a lake, with an island in it, on which was a temple. He built belvederes and towers, each of which equipped with a clock ... The clocks dictated [the workers'] work-, meal- and bedtimes ...

The idea was to get all peasants to work, ten hours every day of the year except Sundays. Orders, dictated by the General personally, were issued regularly, numbered and dated ... In theory, Gruzino had some of the characteristics of a miniature welfare state. There was a hospital and a school. The General got regular health reports. But the inhabitants had even less control over their lives than ordinary serfs. In an effort to raise the birthrate, lists were compiled of nubile unmarried females and widows capable of childbearing, and pressure was put on them to find partners. But the General had to approve such unions ...

... [Running Gruzino depended on] the universal reliance on savage physical punishment ... All floggings were recorded in an estate Punishment Ledger, and the General inspected the backs to see that chastisement had been thorough. Each peasant also carried, at all times, a personal punishment book, in which his or her offences were listed along with the sentence ... ◆

(*Source*: Johnson, 1991, pp. 291–3)

The Two World Views in History

A preference for spontaneous ordering, the concept of the rule of law as opposed to the rule of men, has a long tradition in western civilisation, going back at least to Solon of Athens (*c*.640–561BC). The Greek philosopher Aristotle (384–322BC) wrote: 'He who asks Law to rule is asking God and Intelligence and no others to rule; while he who asks for the rule of a human being is bringing in a wild beast; for human passions are like a wild beast and strong feelings lead astray the very best of men. In law you have the intellect without the passion' (cited in Walker, 1988, p. 93). We have already mentioned that the law of the Roman Republic knew the concept of the sovereign domain of the family, within which matters were sorted out without outside interference under the *patria potestas*, the personal discretion and control of the *pater familias*, the father of the family. He could control matters within his *dominium*: the family, the land, the assets he owned. Traditional Celtic and Germanic notions of free men reinforced Greek and Roman traditions of individual freedom and helped to give rise to the European tradition of individual freedom.

In medieval Europe, the rules that allowed the spontaneous ordering of free individuals were given clear expression in the *Magna Carta* of 1215 that is still a binding part of the constitution which shapes the government of the United Kingdom and many other Anglo-Saxon countries. It has been reaffirmed time and again, and survives to form part of the living constitutions of all common-law countries. The order of rules was also high on the agenda of the new American Republic. And it was an aspiration of the French Revolution; the revolutionary demand for *égalité* was initially understood as equality of all, including the rulers, before the law. In modern times, it is recognised that the order of rules requires not only the supremacy of the institutions, but also the formal acceptance of rules that safeguard open debate and adherence to due process in the administration of the law and other institutions (Walker, 1988, chs 1 and 2).

In the late eighteenth and the nineteenth centuries, the order of abstract rules was criticised by writers such as Hegel and Marx (as we saw), and this paved the way for major efforts to construct social orders, from totalitarian socialist and fascist attempts to less coercive attempts at 'social engineering' in the democratic societies and third world countries. Many anthropologists, psychologists and sociologists who ignored the knowledge problem, such as Margaret Mead[4], promoted these efforts because they saw human beings as a product of a culture who could be reshaped into 'new men'. They did much to promote an unjustified optimism that society as a whole could be organised along the lines of a coherent, designed order.

The feasibility of collective ordering has also been the foundation of neoclassical welfare economics and its application to public policy. To begin with, economists closed the model by assuming perfect knowledge, at least on behalf of the scientific observer. Hence, it became possible to deduce what conditions needed to be met to obtain a social optimum in the allocation of given resources, with given technologies and known consumer preferences. Next, economists could ask what mechanism would lead to the optimum – which is already known in advance by the scientific observer. The answer was 'perfect competition', and the conditions to be met were those of general equilibrium. Under these assumptions, institutions were not required to channel the choices of private decision makers. They were faced with equilibrium 'market prices', and adjustment to these prices was the only rational response open to them. The task of maximisation in this perfect competition model can be performed by a computer. Entrepreneurial talent, alertness and preparedness to incur transaction costs are then superfluous.

In this simplistic model world, it was possible to identify a plethora of cases in which competition would fail to bring about the so-called social optimum: 'market failure' was seen to abound. This, in turn, provided reasons for policy interventions. The policy maker was assumed to be able to correct 'market failures' in a perfect way, for example by taxes and subsidies. Though this model is simplistic, despite its seeming formal sophistication, it was and still is in many quarters the prevalent mode of thinking about economic policy. The verdict of a pretence of knowledge, however, applies to it all too convincingly. The whole framing of the welfare economics model, which comes inadvertently fairly close to the view of a central planner, has in reality little relevance for the policy maker who has to deal with a complex and open market system (Streit, 1992).

Although the question of individualism versus collectivism has been argued here predominantly from the standpoint of western history, we should note an important East Asian notion of ordering which has been shaped by the basic rules of Confucian morality. Predictability and coordination are achieved much more by personalised relationships than in the West. In Chinese or Malay society, for example, more reliance is placed on personal relationships and loyalties based on familiarity and ongoing contacts, so predictability is ensured by people in authority. Traditionally, it is therefore not so much the rule of impersonal law but the networking with reliable persons that ensures order (*guanxi* in Chinese society; see Redding, 1993, pp. 66–8). Accordingly, there is more reliance on personalised exchanges, where arbitrary action is constrained by unwritten rules of interpersonal relationship. On the whole, interpersonal trust rests on rules about losing face and fears of losing repeat business.[5] The order that emerges under such institutions is largely spontaneous, but the rules of conduct are often less formal and more tied to people in authority (Habermann, in Radnitzky and Bouillon, 1995b, pp. 73–96).

6.4 Rule Systems as Part of Culture

Many of the informal institutions that have evolved and are shared in a community form part of a system that is called 'culture'. Indeed, shared rules and values define a society; they are essential to social behaviour, including economic behaviour (Casson, 1993).

Culture Defined

The term 'culture' is used to mean differing things. This is bound to lead to misunderstandings if the definition is not clarified.[6] We prefer the classic definition by the English sociologist Edward Burnett Tylor (1883) who defined culture as comprising 'all capabilities and habits acquired by a man as a member of society'. It indicates nicely the tension between the individual and the social group which culture bridges. It also focuses on the fact that culture hinges on learned institutions and the values that underpin them. New-born babies have no culture. Culture therefore always has normative content. Indeed, it could be said that culture is all that is worth passing on to the next generation.

Culture in this sense consists of language (based on a rule system which governs the sounds and signs we make), ideas, values, internal and external institutions; in most definitions it also covers the tools, techniques, works of art, rituals and symbols to underpin the purely institutional side of culture. (In that wider sense, the word 'civilisation' is often preferred.) It contains many internal institutions – customs and conventions – that are acquired by practice and that are hard to spell out and transfer in a disembodied way to people who are not part of that culture. We may thus see culture as a largely implicit rule system that is underpinned by symbols and other visible reminders of its institutional content.

A shared culture underpins the division of labour, as it cuts the risks and costs of interaction. This is why fellow citizens, who share one's culture, are often appreciated: it is easier to interact with them. Those who have learned the shared culture, often without reflecting on it in their youth, feel at home amongst others of their cultural community. From the standpoint of individuals, their own culture is, subjectively, superior to other cultures, because their familiarity with their own culture's institutions saves them costs. If people move to another culture, they will often at first be tempted to conclude that the other culture is inferior because it does not produce for them the customary ease of interaction and foists additional transaction costs on them. However, the cosmopolitan knows that cultures are rule systems whose value depends on what the individual has learnt and that alternative cultures can be learnt and can function satisfactorily. They recognise that others, too, will probably also prefer their own culture. What is alien is not necessarily bad or threatening. Once this is realised, cultural superiority and self-centred missionary zeal should cease. With luck, cosmopolitans even adopt cultural concepts from other cultures. Within multicultural societies cross-fertilisation sets in. The quality of cultural institutions can only be compared by testing how in practice they help people to attain their shared fundamental values, such as freedom, peace and prosperity. It will then become clear that not all cultures are equally functional in coordinating people or coping with change. Cultural openness therefore does not mean cultural relativism and the uncritical acceptance of all cultures as equally valuable.

The role of culture is paraphrased well by Tom Sowell (1998, p. iv):

> Cultures are not museum pieces. They are the working machinery of every-day life. Unlike objects of aesthetic contemplation, working machinery is judged by how well it works, compared to the alternatives. The judgment that matters is not the judgment of the observers and theorists, but the judgment implicit in millions of individual decisions to retain or abandon particular cultural practices, decisions made by those who personally benefit or who personally pay the price of inefficiency and obsolescence. That price is not always paid in money, but may range from inconvenience to death.

Cultural Change

Culture is not a monolith but a web of (overlapping) subsystems. An individual may belong to a village culture, share the worldwide cultural conventions of a profession and also feel deeply attached to the culture of a foreign country. Nor is culture – like any single institution – immutable. Culture is a slow-moving average of individual, time-tested ideas, which is torn between the 'conservative pole', the necessity to preserve the common basis for communication, and the 'experimental pole', the necessity to prevent rigidity and atrophy in the face of changing physical, technical, economic or social circumstances. It is therefore important that cultures remain open to outside influences and maintain a capability to adjust.

Cultures normally evolve slowly; many elements are path dependent. But sometimes specific cultural traits change quite rapidly in the light of experience, either because new ideas are discovered internally or, more frequently, come from outside and are found to be superior. They are consequently imitated and gain critical mass so that they become new norms. New concepts may require systemic adaptations that are manifested in cultural change. Thus, the rulers of Europe in the fourteenth to sixteenth centuries found that merchants and manufacturers were able to migrate to countries where they found more rule-bound government and reliable institutions. This not only forced the rulers to abstain from arbitrary opportunism and provide credible rules, but also rewarded internal cultural institutions, such as honesty, punctuality and thrift. Bourgeois society and capitalism emerged when external institutions and internal cultural institutions were adapted and a new 'civic morality' spread (Weber, 1927/1995; Giersch, 1996). Similarly, cultural change accelerated in many, mainly Chinese, communities that were excluded from the traditional centre of their world and were even threatened by it after the Maoist revolution of 1949 (Redding, 1993; Jones *et al.*, 1994). What had once been a fairly conservative, atrophying cultural system mutated, under the influence of forced openness and the urgent need to acquire western technology and organisation, into a 'cultural growth asset'.[7] The changes in values and institutions were often marginal, shifting the emphasis from conservative to future- and learning-orientated interpretations of the general institutions (see section 12.2). Despite adaptations, there is a high degree of continuity in most major cultural systems. Consequently, there is no danger of mistaking someone of the Chinese or Japanese culture for a Frenchman, because the bulk of the cultural system persists strongly even if certain elements shift. The prospect of a homogeneous world culture is therefore not on the horizon.

Cultural Capital

Culture – the values and institutional system, as well as its more tangible elements – constitutes an important part of a society's human capital: that is, it has important consequences for how effectively physical resources of labour, capital and nature are converted to serve people's wants and aspirations. We therefore speak of 'cultural or social capital' (Coleman, 1990). When discussing the idea that culture has powerful economic effects on the economy, it is essential to be aware that most cultural institutions are implicit and are often embodied in organisations (Chapter 5). Indeed, cultural rules cannot often be readily made explicit and culture cannot easily be learnt from books. The rules are often embodied in 'cultural goods' and organisations which make certain cultural concepts effective (Kasper, 1994b; Weede, 1995; Giersch, 1996). Thus, the rule of law is a cultural concept. It requires complex organisational infrastructures to be effective: various types of tribunals, firms of lawyers with different professional specialisations, agreed work practices and conventions, and so on. Cultural systems can only be adopted effectively by outsiders – for example, in order to promote economic growth in hitherto less-developed countries – when the cultural rules are transferred together with the organisational structures and 'cultural goods' and are learnt by association. Cultural goods and rules therefore tend to be much harder to transfer internationally than mere machines; they require more learning of implicit skills and knowhow by practice. Such learning may possibly lead, at least temporarily, to inconsistencies between indigenous and imported institutions.

Yet the machines may prove ineffective if the cultural element needed to work them is not transferred too (Klitgaard, 1995).

As a matter of fact, the system of ideas, organisational rules and tangible assets that is often called culture ('the organisational culture of the ABC Company', 'the culture of capitalism'; Kreps, 1990) is particularly important to the production of sophisticated, modern services, such as running a stock exchange, a legal system or a complex distribution network. This is why efficient service production often proves hard to transfer to other countries and cultures, and why the influx of foreign service industries is often resisted by less-developed countries. Acquiring cultural goods, and making them work, always implies adaptations in one's own institutional system and hence in the self-evaluation of oneself and one's community.

O Key Concepts

Culture is defined here as shared values and a rule system, as well as the more tangible elements of social interaction in a community. Some of the rules may be explicit; many are implicit and informal; many are supported by symbols. Cultures tend to evolve in the light of experience, as some members of the community experiment and others try to conserve familiar, time-tested institutions.

The concept of **cultural capital** highlights the insight that certain cultural concepts, values and institutions can be of great relevance to the material wellbeing of the group which shares them. Culture is an intangible productive asset, but – if rigidly adhered to in the face of change – a traditional culture can also become a liability. ●

6.5 Social Order and Human Values: the Rule of Law

It will be useful to wind up this chapter by casting a quick glance at how institutions can be shaped under the rule of law to enhance the chances of freedom and internal peace (conflict avoidance). The 'rule of law' doctrine was developed primarily, but not exclusively, in Europe, and relates closely to the institutions of capitalism which we shall discuss in the following chapter. The basic concept that underpins the rule of law is that political power can only be exercised on the basis and within the constraints of the law and that certain substantive and procedural institutions are needed to protect civic and economic liberties from arbitrary interventions by authorities.

The legal and constitutional doctrine of the rule of law embodies many of the key concepts of ordering social and economic life that we have developed here. This doctrine is particularly entrenched in the legal philosophy of the Anglo-Saxon countries, where it has a long tradition (see the excerpt from a House of Commons petition of 1610 to King James I at the beginning of this chapter). The 'Glorious Revolution' of 1688–9 in Great Britain enshrined the basic legal controls of government power. At about the same time, John Locke (1632–1704) gave a systematic philosophical explication of freedom under the law and tied this to the division of powers, an idea taken further by Charles de Montesquieu (1689–1755). The rule of law is of course not exclusive to the Anglo-Saxon tradition. In the Roman-French tradition, the concept of legality reflects similar notions, as does the German concept of the 'law state' (*Rechtsstaat*), a doctrine of constitutionalism. In Chinese philosophy the tradition of legalism advocates similar ideas (Habermann, in Radnitzky and Bouillon, 1995b, pp. 73–96).

The doctrine of the rule of law can best be described by a number of substantial institutions which allow ordered human interaction to develop in known, certain ways and which keep the arbitrary, opportunistic rule of men at bay. The rules also contain certain procedural *meta* rules (Walker, 1988, pp. 23–42). The rule of law doctrine favours the spontaneous ordering of actions with a view to giving the best possible scope to individual liberty and to avoiding conflicts that would diminish the liberty of some (Hayek, 1960, 1973, 1976a, 1979a). It contains a number of principles:

(a) In the first instance, it is necessary to ensure that all citizens are formally protected from the arbitrary use of force by fellow citizens, which would only lead to anarchy, the opposite of order under the law. To this end, the laws must be certain, general and non-discriminatory (equal), in short, universal. The principle of universality is violated when certain persons or organisations are formally or *de facto* held to be above the law, for example when there are no sanctions for breaches of contract by trade unions, or when powerful figures get away with infringements of the law. Thus, the rule of law is based on certain stipulations of private law which order the relationships among private citizens.

(b) A second element, which follows from the first, is that the rule of law must also apply to those entrusted with political power. The actions of politicians and officials must be open to scrutiny under the law. Exempting government officials from the law for *raisons d'état* would breach the rule of law. The same holds true when administrative actions are not subject to review by judicial processes to establish whether officials obeyed the institutions, when high government officials cannot be sued by private citizens, or when governments do not have to follow the same accounting rules that they demand of private businesses. In this respect, the rule of law requires certain stipulations of public law.

(c) Like all institutions, laws of course require obligatory sanctions. But coercive sanctions must be administered by rule-bound, impartial professionals. Violations must be adjudicated by an independent judiciary and impartial tribunals which follow the rules of due process. Kangaroo courts, lynch law by private citizens, the negation of a proper hearing of evidence, and the neglect of standard procedures of proof are violations of principle of the rule of law. In this respect, the rule of law requires certain procedural rules.

(d) A further substantive requirement of the rule of law doctrine relates to the interaction between internal and external institutions. The laws must be such that they do not, on the whole, clash with the internal institutions of the community and its fundamental values, so that people are able and willing to obey the law. Where frequent infringements occur, because people's fundamental values clash with the legislation, this is a sign that the rule of law is endangered. Mere adherence to the letter of the law (legal positivism) and to the formalities of due process, but violation of widely held fundamental values and ethical rules, does not establish the rule of law. Thus, the legal formalism in Nazi Germany with regard to the rights of Jewish citizens and in the Stalinist era with regard to dissidents amounted to a clear negation of the rule of law. Likewise, if officials admit that certain actions violate natural rights but nevertheless insist on enforcing the letter of laws or regulations, they are violating the spirit of the rule of law.

(e) Finally, it is necessary for the sustained rule of law in a community for the attitude of legality to be fostered and for the citizens, by and large, to subject themselves willingly to the laws of the land, including in cases of conflict. Widespread lawlessness can make it difficult to protect individual freedom and avoid conflicts. Therefore, the rule of law requires a generally law-abiding civil society where formal judicial sanctions are supplemented by spontaneous enforcement, such as social disapproval, shaming and exclusion.

The rule of law thus is a government-supported system of institutions intended to protect civil and economic liberties and to avoid conflicts:

- by protecting citizens from the arbitrary use of power by other citizens (in the sense of the quote from Cicero at the head of this chapter);
- by obliging agents with political power to find and enforce the law; and

- by binding agents with political power to the law in dealing with private citizens and acting within government.

These substantive elements, which have been developed in jurisprudence, relate directly to the fundamentals of institutional economics and are essential to the proper functioning of the capitalist system.

O Key Concepts

The **rule of law** is a legal and constitutional concept to protect individual freedom and social peace which stipulates:

- that the people and government authorities should be ruled by the law and obey it;
- that the laws should be such that people are, on the whole, able and willing to be guided by them, more specifically, that protection from private license and anarchy is guaranteed;
- that government is placed under the law;
- that the laws are certain, general and non-discriminatory (universal);
- that the laws are generally in harmony with social values and internal institutions;
- that the law is enforced by impartial, rule-bound coercion, and adjudicated by an independent judiciary and impartial tribunals which follow due process; and
- that the law and its practice encourage an attitude of legality throughout the community. ●

Questions for Review

- What are the reasons for setting up a hierarchy of rules, for example for superimposing a constitution over statute law?
- What are the advantages and disadvantages of coordinating the economic life of a country by central planning and by competition in markets?
- In what ways is the knowledge problem responsible for the failure of socialism in designing and implementing a completely external rule system that completely replaces the internal institutions of society? What would the effects of such a revolutionary attempt be on your own society? On yourself?
- Define individualism and collectivism.
- Why is it too costly to enforce external institutions when there are no complementary internal institutions? Is it efficient to replace

your bad conscience by external rules? Under what system are you more likely to steal, shirk and lie?

- Sketch the main features of the two kinds of order and two perceptions of society by completing the table below, using appropriate and concise terms (as used in the text), following the first two completed examples:

	Hierarchical order ('Visible hand order')	Spontaneous order ('Invisible hand order')
Assumption about human knowledge:	perfect knowledge	constitutional ignorance
Knowledge	can be centralised	dispersed and variable
Humans are	....	fallible and diverse
Predominant action	....	....
Perception of social life	comparative static	....
Ideal state of the economy	....	....
Preference for	....	diversity, pragmatic improvement
Major means of coordination	prescriptive command	....
Basic philosophy	collectivism; community goals; 'steering optimism'	....
Main thrust of economic policy	setting community targets/goals, maximising goal achievement	....

- Where would you place your own society on the spectrum between reliance on hierarchical and on spontaneous ordering?
- What are the pros and cons of relying on hierarchical ordering? In what circumstances does hierarchical coordination promise advantages?
- Can you think of an instance where reliance on top-down ordering and 'tribal virtues' was inappropriate and where the order of rules and spontaneous reactions would have been a more effective coordinating mechanism?
- How do we define 'culture'? Does culture contain more than institutions?
- How do cultural traits evolve?
- Can a specific culture be marketed in another country? Can culture be transferred without transferring material goods and organisa-

tional structures in which cultural assets are embodied?
● Can you explain why cultural institutions are more important in the competitive production of services than in agricultural and manufacturing production?
● What are the key elements of the 'rule of law'?

Notes

1. In the 1990s, an American charity with links to the Mormon church built a cement plant in Armenia to assist with reconstruction.
2. The vision of society as a whole that has its own 'personality' and objectives separate from and superior to the individual goes back to Plato (427–347BC), certain group-focused Judeo-Christian visions and the long tradition of corporatism in Europe. Similar notions of collective entities exist in eastern societies, but there the notion of collective aims is more closely tied to the notion of what the ruler represents as a symbol of society as a whole.
3. Nationalism and national socialism also contended that nations have a collective destiny, which is above the individual. This has led to other variants of collectivism.
4. Margaret Mead was highly respected internationally for her views that society could be reshaped. These views were based on superficial, if not fraudulent, research in American Samoa, and pretended that stress-free societies without 'repressive' institutions that constrain 'animal instincts' were possible. It has since been proven in empirical research that Mead misread Samoan society, which is governed by strict codes of conduct, taboos and controls (Freeman, 1983).
5. Chinese ethics tends to focus on general duties in personal relationships. As the Confucian scholar and teacher Mencius (375–289BC) wrote: 'ethics [dictates] ... the principles that between father and son there is affection, between ruler and subject duty, between husband and wife distinction, between elder and junior priority, between friends faithfulness' (cited in Rozman, 1991, p. 58).
6. Culture is defined and used in the following different meanings:
   ● cultivation, ordered organic growth (main original Latin meaning, as in *agricultura*);
   ● a normatively better state or habit of mind ('cultured person', 'culture is what distinguishes your surgeon from your butcher');
   ● a high intellectual and moral state of social development (derived from the German *Kultur* which is better translated into English by the French-inspired word 'civilisation'); and
   ● a body of artistic and intellectual work (as in 'Ministry of Culture') which is better designated as 'the arts'.

7. The great pioneer of exploring cultural institutions in economic growth, the German sociologist-economist Max Weber, who coined the term 'Protestant work ethic', concluded that Chinese culture was too locked into its 'pro-conservative pole' to allow economic growth (Weber, 1951). Now, commentators speak admiringly of 'the neo-Confucian economies' and attribute their success to cultural traits (see Kasper, 1994b; also Chapter 11).

PART II

Applications

CHAPTER 7

The Institutional Foundations of Capitalism

In this chapter, we shall describe the essential elements of a capitalist system, based on property rights and the autonomy to contract. A discussion of how these economic rights are used in action will be postponed to Chapter 8, which deals with markets and competition.

The capitalist system depends on the institutions that establish and secure exclusive private property rights which can be used in voluntary exchanges based on contracts. Well-defined and protected property rights are essential to motivate people so that they undertake, of their own free will, efforts that also benefit others, often people they do not know. This is not an abstract topic of interest only to big business. It affects everyone's daily life: how to save and invest one's money, whether one's labour and skills can be employed to best advantage, and whether one can thrive with one's inspirations and resources.

Private property can only serve its functions effectively if unauthorised persons can be excluded from its use and the benefits and the costs can be attributed exclusively to the owners of the property. Where this is not possible, particular economic problems arise and political solutions may be needed to decide property use (public goods, externalities).

What is required for a capitalist system to work are institutions which allow free contracts and establish clear claims and liabilities. If contracting is unfettered, people are able to get the price information they need to interact effectively and to exploit their knowledge and other assets. We shall see that particular problems arise with relational contracts, that is, open-ended agreements to cooperate over time in circumstances in which not all eventualities can be determined beforehand. An example of this is an employment contract. Institutions are particularly important to make such relational contracts work.

Property rights are not an abstract concept which affects only big business or anonymous financial markets. They are of immediate relevance to everyone's daily life. They directly shape the job opportunities, the consumer choices, the learning incentives of everyone. Property rights are of central importance to the life opportunities of ordinary citizens, in particular those not born with silver spoons in their mouths.

We conclude this chapter with a brief discussion of money, assets which serve as a means of payment and reduce transaction costs enormously. We show that the usefulness of money depends greatly on institutions that constrain its supply.

Let a merchant begin to sell his goods on the principle of brotherly love, and I do not give him even a month before his children will be returned to beggary.
(French economist, Frédéric Bastiat, 1848)

Without the accumulation of capital the arts could not progress, and it is chiefly through their power that the civilised races have extended.
(Charles Darwin, The Descent of Man, 1871)

... in the socialist system, everything depends on the wisdom, the talents, the gifts of those people who form the supreme authority ... But the knowledge which mankind has accumulated in its long history is not acquired by everyone; we have accumulated such an enormous amount of scientific and technological knowledge over the centuries that it is humanly impossible for one individual to know all these things ... In capitalist societies, technological progress and economic progress are gained through ... people who have the gift to find new paths ... If a man has an idea, he will try to find a few people who are clever enough to realize the value of his idea. Some capitalists, who dare to look into the future, who realize the possible consequences of such an idea, will start to put it to work.
(Ludwig von Mises, Economic Policy, 1979)

The right to private ownership ... is fundamental to the autonomy and development of the person ... The modern business economy has [as] its basis human freedom exercised in the economic field ... We acknowledge the legitimate role of a profit, this means that productive factors have been properly employed and corresponding human needs have been duly satisfied.
(Pope John Paul II, Centesimus annus, 1991)

7.1 Capitalism: Property Rights and Private Autonomy

In this chapter and the next, we shall deal with capitalism, that is, the economic system that is based predominantly on private, autonomous property ownership and the spontaneous coordination of property owners by competition. The capitalist system is based on institutions that ensure respected and secure property rights and liberties of autonomous property use. Many of these institutions are the result of evolution.

We shall deal here with a pure capitalist system. For didactic reasons, we postpone to Chapter 10 the discussion of collective ownership and political activities to produce and redistribute income and wealth.

Private Property Rights

In most modern societies, individuals or organisations have autonomous rights to own and use certain assets, as long as they do not interfere with the rights of others ('private, several property'). In the case of individuals, those assets include their own bodies, skills and knowledge ('right to life' and 'right to work'). Individuals also have the right, widely respected and protected in society, to appropriate the fruit of their labour (except where there is slavery; see Engerman, in Drobak and Nye, 1997, pp. 95–120). Individuals and organisations thus have the right to enjoy the assets they own, to use them in ways they decide autonomously, to appropriate the returns from these uses and to dispose of their property as they see fit (Alchian, 1987; Alchian and Demsetz, 1973). Private ownership of an asset ensures that individuals and private groups enjoy the exclusive right to control, benefit from and divide and transfer property. This gives people confidence that the benefits of property uses, which are valued by others, can be appropriated. In turn, this motivates property owners to discover and pursue property uses which their fellows want. Violations of property rights incur sanctions which are foreshadowed by known institutional arrangements. Where these protections are deficient and where the private autonomy of property use is curtailed, property rights are less valuable. Less effort is then dedicated to offer what others value highly and to employ one's property to discover and provide even more highly valued goods and services.

We can therefore define property rights as a bundle of protected rights of individuals and organisations to hold or dispose of certain assets, for example by acquiring, using, mortgaging and transferring assets, and to appropriate the benefits from the use of these assets. This of course also covers negative returns – losses. Property rights thus entail responsibilities for the use of the property as well as benefits.

Property rights must not be confused with the physical items that are owned. A property right permits the owner to enjoy the benefits of wealth and imposes the costs which ownership entails. Property rights are therefore not physical objects but are titles and obligations which are broadly respected in society.

Private property rights always establish a relationship between defined individuals and defined assets, which can be physical goods, ideas or people's own bodies. Where these rights are well-respected and protected we speak of 'economic liberties'. It is important that the property rights relationship is universal in the sense defined in Chapter 5. Where property rights are fuzzy and uncertain, many advantageous property uses cease. For example, the ill-defined and ill-protected command over property in the former Soviet bloc led to great uncertainties and correspondingly lesser exploitation of physical and intellectual assets. The economy declined. And the growing uncertainties of land ownership originating from Aboriginal land claims in Canada and Australia has begun to lead to less investment in and use of land than previously, when the legal fiction of *terra nullius* underpinned secure land rights of those immigrants who had claimed the land.

Intellectual Property

Property rights can be attached not only to physical assets but also to identifiable bits of knowledge. As we saw in Chapter 1, modern economic growth depends greatly on improved technical and organisational knowledge. It will be produced if people can expect to appropriate the gains from their effort and risk-taking. This means that institutional arrangements have to be found which allow the owners of valuable knowledge to reap material benefits from sharing it. One such device is patent protection. Government bodies evaluate the originality and merit of distinct bits of patentable knowledge and award patent rights which allow the owners exclusive use of that knowledge.[1] In certain circumstances, this may serve as an incentive to generate and test innovative knowledge, even though the patenting procedure costs resources.

Caution and much specific technical knowledge are needed to protect intellectual property, because excessive licensing and patenting create monopoly positions that can hinder innovation (section 8.2), especially if industry and the licensing authorities collude. Therefore, the protection of 'knowledge capital' must always be of limited duration.

Capitalism

The capitalist system which is based on private property rights and their autonomous use is nowadays the most prevalent economic system in the world, although rarely in its pure form. Owners decide to offer their property, or certain uses of their property, at a certain quality, in certain amounts and at a certain price in the market. They hope to contract with buyers, who decide whether to accept the offer and who typically offer money in exchange. If buyers value what is on offer sufficiently to cover the price demanded by the suppliers, the suppliers will probably make a profit. They may even be induced to expand the quantities offered in the future. If demand falls short, suppliers are disappointed and incur a loss. In this case, they will discontinue offering that particular good or service at the original conditions of supply. In this way, buyers influence over the longer run what is being produced and supplied (consumer sovereignty).

Many institutions have developed spontaneously to order and facilitate exchange relationships and to give business partners more confidence in what to expect. Institutions make the exchange possible and develop to make exchange transactions less costly and risky, allowing markets to become more effective.

The market processes of coordination of property owners in the capitalist system will be considered in more detail in the following chapter.

7.2 Essential Characteristics of Property Rights

Excludability

The defining characteristic of private property rights is that owners have the right to exclude others from possession, active uses and benefits derived from using that property and that they are fully responsible for all the costs of property use. Excludability is the precondition of the autonomy of the owner and of the incentive mechanism through which private property rights work. Only when others can be excluded from sharing the benefits and costs that property rights assign can these benefits and costs be 'internalised', that is, have complete and direct impact on the expectations and decisions of the property owner. Then, the valuations of others about the uses of the property are signalled completely to the owner and they will have the incentive to engage in property uses that others welcome through their 'dollar votes'.

These signals and incentives are distorted when some of the benefits, or some of the costs, do not impact on the property owner. To illustrate this by a few examples:

- a land owner, who loses part of the yields of his fields to theft, will not plant and cultivate the land as intensively as a land owner who enjoys full protection of the yields;
- those who incur the costs of being vaccinated create private benefits for themselves, but also external benefits in so far as they reduce the risk of disease for others. More people would be vaccinated if somehow the external beneficiaries could be made to reward by a payment those who take the vaccination;
- a factory owner who causes costs which are only partly internalised, and which partly impact on external agents (for example, pollution of the environment), will decide to produce more than a factory owner who has to bear the full costs because he is forced to compensate the victims of pollution.

Excludability is thus important in ensuring that private property uses are steered to reflect what others want. The incentive works through the profit–loss signal, and the provision of goods and services that are wanted by others are but a by-product of that incentive (Schumpeter, 1947, p. 148).

Externalities arise when there are knowledge problems, when it is impossible or too costly to measure all costs and benefits and put them to the account of their originators. Thus, it is too costly to identify who benefits from a neighbour's vaccination and how much that benefit is valued by the neighbour. The effects of factory emissions on others may also be costly or impossible to measure and evaluate. If, however, the technique of measurement changes – for example, due to improved computer and communications technology – then excludability may become feasible and externalities may be converted into internalised benefits and costs.

When costs and benefits can, by and large, be internalised, property owners will be guided voluntarily by expected profits and losses in bilateral contracts, competing with each other in doing so, as a matter of their private choice. When major externalities exist, coordination can become much more complicated as multilateral agreements have to be negotiated. The give and take is then less clear than in bilateral exchange and the incentives to act are often fuzzy. Normally, externalities require multilateral political arrangements by which property uses and returns are established, often a complex and opaque matter. As a consequence, public or collective choice is often less effective in satisfying citizens' diverse and changing goals.

In reality, excludability is often imperfect and externalities are widespread. Many external effects are simply tolerated and do not hinder voluntary exchange activities. Often, there may be private settlements to deal with externalities; for example, when my activity adversely affects my neighbour and we agree that I compensate him. In other cases, the externalities of private action are dealt with by government agencies, for example by regulations or transfers. In some cases, external effects go beyond national boundaries and may require intergovernmental action; for example, when upstream industries along a river system in one country affect downstream users in another, as is the case along the river Rhine. Here, the Rhine Commission has settled on negotiated agreement of what is permissible and what is not. Other cases arise in environmental policy where the external effects of certain activities have worldwide impact, for example the emission of gases which affect the global atmosphere. Here, global political agreements may have to be negotiated to address the externality problem, that is, agreement between a great variety of conflicting national interests has to be reached.

Of Private, Free, Public and Common Property

We speak of private goods when all costs and benefits accrue to private owners (full excludability). Decisions about resource uses can then be left, as we saw, to voluntary, bilateral interactions that are coordinated in markets.

When excludability as to benefits or costs cannot be ensured, particular economic problems arise. We have to distinguish among a number of different categories of property, depending on whether exclusion needs to be brought about and how, and on how such goods and services are provided.

One case may be that the good in question is not scarce, that is, users need not compete with each other. We then speak of a free good (Figure 7.1). Free goods are provided by nature and may be claimed for the mere trouble of claiming. Clean water was once a free good,

Figure 7.1   Forms of property

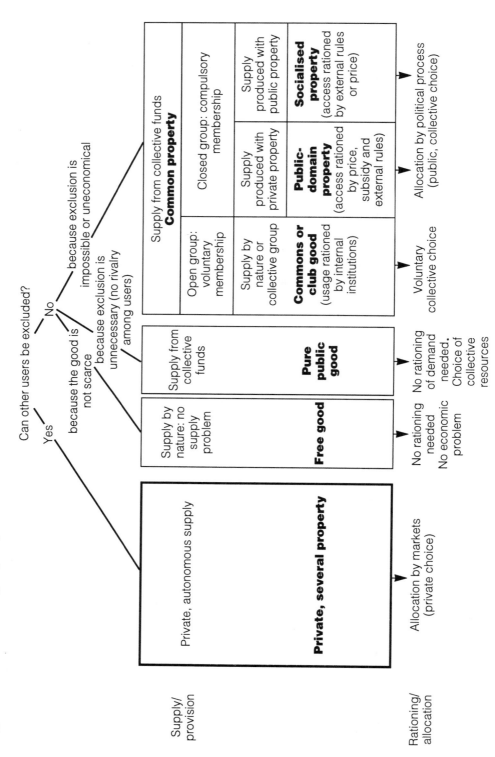

180

and still is in certain parts of the world. As more people live in an area, clean water becomes scarce and its use has to be rationed by some economic device. Likewise, parking spaces were once free in the centre of cities, and anyone could claim a free spot. As demand increased, parking became scarce and had to be rationed by price (incidentally, a process which made it rewarding to supply more parking spaces and alleviate the problem). Fish stocks in the open sea were for long free goods, but many types of fish are now scarce and exploitation rights are assigned by governments through fishing licences. It is also possible for previously exclusively owned goods to become free. For example, the junk you throw out becomes a free good; when someone retrieves it and treats it as an antique, it may become a valuable private good again. No economic problem exists with free goods, as scarcity and hence allocation problems play no role.

There are assets that can be accessed and used – at least within certain limits – without making their use impossible for others. We then speak of pure public goods (Figure 7.1). An example for such a good are radio waves: if I turn on my radio, others can continue to receive the same transmission. Here too, there is no rivalry among users. In that case, radio listeners will not be prepared to pay voluntarily. But whereas free goods are provided by nature or human generosity, a radio programme is provided at some cost. Some kind of collective action is needed to ensure its provision. Access by the public then causes no economic problems. In that respect, it is treated in a similar way as a free good. However, since pure public goods such as radio transmissions cost resources, they have opportunity costs. They would not be supplied because everyone would try to be a free rider. It would be impossible to collect a price for their supply. One solution is for collective provision, financing the costs from compulsory levies (taxes). But there are other ways of funding collective activities, for example, by raising voluntary contributions and by the sale of services, such as advertising, to finance (collective) media offerings. A collective decision therefore has to be made about what share of a community's resources should be dedicated to the provision of such public goods.

Another reason why people cannot be excluded from the use of a property by having to pay a price may be that such access rationing is impossible or uneconomical. We then speak of common or collective goods. Allocation must be done through some sort of political mechanism. We can distinguish between various types of common goods, depending on whether sharing in the costs of providing common property is voluntary or compulsory, how it is provided, and how access is rationed (Figure 7.1).

Common goods may be provided jointly by an open group in the sense that one may belong voluntarily to the group or stay away (for example, a club). Sharing in the provision of such a common good is therefore voluntary. We then speak of club goods. Non-members are excluded from access and use, but insiders can freely appropriate the benefits from such property. Where their use competes with that of others, because what one person uses is not available to others, the club must ration use. This can be done effectively by internal institutions as long as the club is small and people meet sufficiently frequently and can therefore exercise internal mutual controls over property use. When the club grows, there are increasing problems of internal information and informal control. Organisation costs rise as more formal institutions have to be implemented. On the other hand, new techniques, such as electronic cards, may facilitate measurement and allow more goods to be treated as club goods. An important historic example of club goods is the commons: land which everyone belonging to a tribe or village can use to collect timber or graze privately owned animals in the forests and meadows that make up the commons. In some parts of the world, fields are the jointly owned property of the village. They are planted on a 'first come, first served' basis by the members of the village community and access is rationed by traditional internal institutions.

Another category of property comes into existence when the supply is provided by a closed group with compulsory membership, such as a nation. Here too, we can think of assets whose use is not subject to rivalry, so that we have pure public goods (for example, the defence of the nation that is provided from compulsory tax and that benefits every citizen without diminishing the protection enjoyed by others). But where rivalry in demand use exists, it has to be rationed. This can be done in two ways (Figure 7.1):

(a) the goods or services may be produced by private owners who are subject to competitive disciplines and who are guided by the price they get. However, the access is facilitated by a political decision to provide cash or vouchers that are handed out to everyone or to selected groups (for example, school vouchers to buy private education services). Political decisions ration the amount of the access subsidy. We call these goods public-domain goods or public-access goods. Access is partially rationed by political choice. When access is subsidised, redistribution of property rights can be combined with the competitive discipline of private production (Demsetz, 1970);

(b) the goods or services may be produced in government-owned enterprises, subject to administrative controls. Rationing access to the benefits of such socialised property is by external rules that are designed in political processes.

An example of a public-domain good is a health service from which no one can be excluded and to which certain classes of citizens are given access by subsidy. Public-domain goods are supplied like private property. An example of socialised property is a hospital that is run and owned by the government, access to which is rationed by external rules, directives and waiting lists. It is often feasible to turn socialised property into public-domain goods and to reap the cost controls in production that derive from competition. In many instances since the 1980s, socialised property has been converted to public-domain property as government administrations withdraw from production (privatisation) and concentrate on providing open access. Public ownership is therefore certainly not a precondition for redistributing access rights.

We must therefore not equate 'public access' with public ownership. For this reason, we do not employ in this context the term 'public good', which can easily lead to confusion between public access and public ownership of the means of production.

Socialised property is owned by a large, closed group; its uses are authorised by politically appointed representatives. If they do not wish to bear the opprobrium of visible rationing, socialised property may be made artificially abundant and funded by compulsory levies; for example, a government may decide to make basic research results freely available to all comers, it may provide art and entertainment to all who want to enjoy it, or it may dispense medical care without rationing. This makes it necessary to expand supply and funding by increasing compulsory taxation. Because political rationing is often not very effective, the costs of such artificially created public goods snowball. If cost controls on their production are also lax, their provision may not be sustainable in the long run. One reason why socialised property may be justified is that this provides the direct control of politically controlled purse strings, for example to subject the military to civilian control.

Changes in Property Status

The property-rights treatment of certain assets changes with time and technology. When few humans lived on earth there was no scarcity of natural resources. This state of affairs is recollected in the Bible as Paradise. When more people moved into an area, resources became scarce and the institutional device of club goods was invented. Tribes excluded outsiders from the use of their property (case 1a in Figure

Figure 7.2   Changes in property arrangements: selected cases

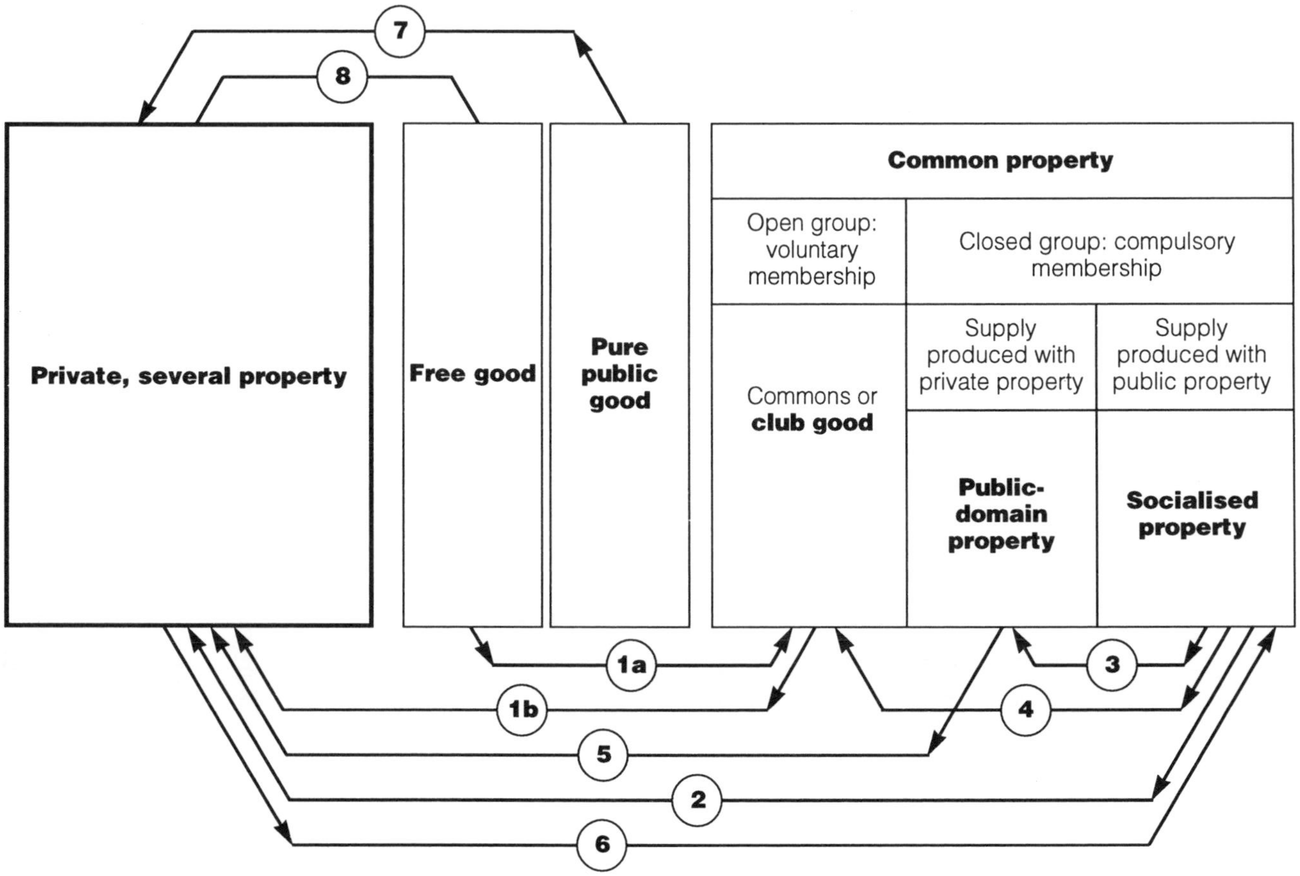

7.2). As groups grew and informal rules about rationing use began to fail, the commons was divided and fenced off, turning it into plots of private property (case 1b in Figure 7.2).

If socialised property does not function effectively, consideration may be given to breaking up big groups and making them open, so that socialised property can be treated as club property, and cheaper, less formal rationing devices become feasible (cases 3 and 4). Thus, national health services can be handed to small communities and groups who operate them exclusively for their members and ration or subsidise access. Artificially made public goods whose provision and funding is becoming too onerous on the taxpayer, can be converted into club goods or even private goods (privatisation, case 2). That may be regretted by some, because they enjoyed access to the quasi-free goods, but economic allocation may ultimately lead to more effective provision of such goods and services. This will obviate cumbersome administrative arrangements to ration use. Public domain goods may also be transferred into private ownership, in the hope either of reducing the subsidy or of reducing the costs of administering the external rules of rationing access. Thus, food vouchers may be withdrawn or certain classes of people lose free transport entitlements (case 5 in Figure 7.2). We have already seen that free goods can become private goods and vice versa (case 8), and pure public goods can become exclusive private ones, for example when public police protection is taken over by private security agencies (case 7).

When private property rights are collectivised (case 6), private, bilateral contracting is replaced by political choice, and the problems of private choice are replaced by the problems of public choice, which will be discussed in Chapter 10.

We must conclude that the property categories discussed here are not cast in concrete but depend on choice and technology, and that different societies will shape the property rights and the attendant exclusion mechanisms in differing ways.

O Key Concepts

Property rights were defined in Chapter 2 as the right to exclude others from the use of an asset and the right to use, hire out or sell the asset to others. Property rights are thus a bundle of rights: to possess an asset and hold it (passive use); to exchange it or to let others use certain aspects of it temporarily (active uses). Property rights may be attached not only to physical assets but also to intellectual property.

Excludability is the defining characteristic of property rights. It means not only that others can be excluded from the benefits of an asset, but also that the owners are exclusively responsible for the costs of asset use, as well as the costs of ensuring exclusion.

Patents are rights that guarantee the exclusive exploitation of discrete bits of valuable knowledge. They are one way of establishing **intellectual property rights**.

Private property rights are held by individuals, private associations and firms. Where the costs and benefits of property use impact directly and exclusively on the property owner, we speak of **private goods**. Where externalities become important, special problems of economic coordination arise. **Externalities** are benefits and costs of property use that do not impact on the property owner, either because monitoring is too costly or because it is altogether impossible.

Where exclusion of others from benefits is impossible or unnecessary, we speak of **common property**. Such a good may be shared in a small, voluntary group (**commons**, club property) from which outsiders are excluded, or in a large, inclusive group with compulsory membership (**socialised property**). In large groups with compulsory membership, it may often be necessary to ensure open access to the public domain. Open access to public-domain goods can be assured either by socialised production with property which is owned by a government body or by institutions that guarantee certain access conditions to the public. This can be done by certain regulations or by endowing every qualifying citizen with funds to gain access. The general public's access to privately produced **public-domain goods** tends to be through paying a price, with certain members of the public being endowed by direct cash subsidies or purpose-specific vouchers.

Free goods are assets in which no one has claimed property rights because they are not scarce. There is no economic problem with free goods. The same applies to **pure public goods**, that is, goods and services for which there is no competing demand once they are provided (for example, street lighting can be enjoyed by you without diminishing its benefit to your fellows). However, such public goods have to be provided out of collective resources.

Capitalism is defined here as an institutional system in which the means of production are held predominantly as private property and in which voluntary, private dispositions of property are coordinated in the market place.

Socialism is an economic system in which most means of production are held collectively and controlled by the political leadership or its agents. ●

Exclusion Costs

Excluding others from using one's property without authorisation causes costs to the owner. Such unauthorised uses may, for example, be theft or squatting on land. To prevent this, people incur the expenses of locks, fences, share and land-title registries and information-protection systems in computers. We call these costs exclusion costs.

High exclusion costs lower the value of property. To a considerable extent, they depend on institutional arrangements, beginning with the underlying standard of ethics that is shared in the community. If private property is spontaneously respected, private exclusion costs will be low and property values will be relatively high. If a community has invented a low-cost system of enforcing property rights, this will also benefit property values. Thus, an effective land-title registry raises land values. Where property law is enforced by collective action (legislation, police, judiciary), a large part of the exclusion costs are borne collectively, but this has considerable cost advantages for property owners over individual protection (scale economies). We know that different institutional systems have great influence on exclusion costs and property values. It is not surprising that property owners, when they have the chance, shift their property to an environment where it is highly valued and that they are prepared to contribute taxes to provide protective collective action.

Low exclusion costs are not the norm for humankind. In vast parts of the developing world, ordinary people enjoy little effective protection of their property. They are frequently subject to rackets; many experience the property risks of war and civil strife. Many are squatters, farming and dwelling on land with uneasy tenure, because government or other powerful authorities have failed to develop a land-title registry or do not enforce land titles for poor people (de Soto, 1993). Similar conditions, often underpinned by envy and anti-capitalist ideologies, persist in large parts of the former Soviet empire and in communist Asia (Chapter 13). Much could be done to reduce the costs of holding property and to enhance the value of property in these countries by more effective institutions, including a more effective organisational back-up of these institutions (by police and courts). When exclusion costs are reduced, people find it more attractive to acquire and activate property. They then help themselves out of their poverty.

In certain circumstances, such as war and internal civil strife, existing protection of private property may disintegrate. When property rights are ill-defined and poorly protected by legal means in chaotic socie-ties, people may try to define and protect them by corrupt devices. This is the origin of protection rackets of the Mafia and of self-help organisations that take the law into their own hands. Thus, the recent changes in the former Soviet Union and Vietnam have shown that institutions and their enforcement by the state are deficient, so self-organised groups who command the tools of violence set themselves up to offer 'private' property protection for a fee. Notwithstanding the propriety of this activity, it may provide a service to property owners. They may even value this service enough to pay protection money voluntarily. The danger arises that the self-appointed 'violence profes-sionals' will use their means of coercion to extract high prices for protection, or that rival gangs fight to get property owners as clients. In such a situation, collective, law-bound government can offer prop-erty owners great gains in exclusion costs (in exchange for a property tax).

Shared respect for private property may also decline when wealth distribution becomes extremely lop-sided. It then becomes necessary for property owners to incur rising exclusion costs for locks, barbed wire, fences, security guards and insurance. Certain vulnerable forms of property holding, even if potentially very useful, may then be avoided altogether. However, if collective action tries to redistribute property rights by selective interventions, this may raise exclusion costs further. If, for example, the borrower or tenant of a property is accorded increasing rights at the expense of the property owner, or the police and courts cease to prosecute violations of property rights, people's motivation to acquire property by making efforts on behalf of others will wane. Similar consequences must be expected when the penalties for failure to repay loans are not enforced: credit breaks down and scarce capital is poorly utilised. Deleterious consequences for economic growth can then be observed. These losses are often underrated because they materialise slowly, reflecting the typically slow adjustment of the internal institutions of society. It therefore takes time to break down the private property system. However, the persistence of internal institutions can also be an obstacle to economic improvements, when there is no spontaneous respect for private pro-perty and theft and fraud are widely tolerated.

O Key Concepts

Exclusion costs are incurred when owners employ resources to exclude others from owning or using the property; for example, the cost of a lock, or of a computer program that requires a password before computer files can be accessed. ●

The Divisibility and Transferability of Property Rights

To work effectively, property rights also must be divisible. Large concentrations of property can often be utilised effectively only if the property rights can be divided. Frequently, various elements of property can be used most effectively by separate people and groups. Thus, people may value real estate most highly if institutional provisions allow some people to own the property and others to use some of its benefits temporarily for a rental fee. For example, if we take the case of a forested property, some may pay an entrance fee for recreational use, while others may use the land for growing trees or to enjoy hunting animals. This divisibility allows the owners who hold title to the land to assign differentiated rights to hunt, to go for walks and to invest in growing trees. This enhances the usefulness of the property. Important institutional innovations facilitated the foundation of modern stock companies. It became possible to divide the ownership of a large company into shares which relatively small investors could buy, so that large stocks of capital for major industrial and infrastructural projects could be accumulated.

Property embraces an open-ended bundle of rights that are created and divided by demand and human creativity. Divisibility allows people with different demands and knowledge to put a particular asset to the most highly valued uses they can discover. Thanks to the institutions that establish such differentiated and divisible property rights, enterprising people without property of their own but who have creative ideas and the confidence that they could make good use of certain assets can more easily obtain the assets of others. With appropriate institutional responses, there is scope for the creation of new types of property rights which can be traded separately from the right of outright possession. Divisibility thus promotes the benefits of specialisation and knowledge search, whilst still leaving the ultimate responsibility of asset ownership with the owner.

Clearly, the gains from partitioning certain uses of property can only be reaped when the institutional arrangements are reliable enough to make this possible. Loans are only made when assets are returned as and when agreed and when debts are repaid as promised. When the institutional protection of property rights deteriorates – for example, when credit is not repaid fully because of a poor attitude to payments

– gains from property use are lost and general living standards drop. This is why institutional-legal systems are necessary to underpin the divisibility of property rights.

Another aspect of property rights is that they should be disposable (or transferable). Where tradition or other institutions prohibit the disposal of property rights, for example through trade, they tie property to the one existing owner and prevent others, who may value the property more highly because of their better knowledge and skills, from making better use of it. An interesting example to illustrate this are the inalienable property rights to certain tracts of land granted to groups of indigenous Americans and Australians. These land rights were made inalienable because the authorities wanted to protect the aboriginal owners from 'exploitation', from sale or rental at a price deemed disadvantageous to the owners. This 'protection' has, however, reduced the value of their property to the owners. It is now deeply resented by young, educated aboriginals who want to lease their land to mining companies or to sell it so that they can earn income and move to activities they find more suitable. The freezing of property transfers can also have deleterious consequences when land is made inalienable by government ownership on environmental grounds (national parks). It may be discovered subsequently that a greater variety of animal and plant species could be protected if some areas in national parks could be traded for other pieces of land with superior flora or fauna as and when such land comes on the market. After all, land resources are limited, and opportunities for nature conservation change (Wills, 1997, pp. 29–47). The best-possible use of limited resources for nature conservation can therefore frequently be enhanced by transferability, whereas inalienability – made with the best intentions and with the limited knowledge at the time – may impede conservation.

O Key Concepts

Divisibility means that property rights can be 'unbundled', mere ownership rights can be separated from rights over specific uses of an asset; for example, the title to a lake separated from the right to fish the lake or the right to swim in it.

Transferability is a quality of property rights that refers to the change in ownership, for example through sale or donation.

Inalienable property rights cannot be traded and used by others, and hence often cannot be used to the fullest potential. ●

7.3   Using Property Rights: Free Contracts and Transaction Costs

Contracts: a Deal is a Deal

As we saw in the opening section of this chapter, property can be used by its owners when they exchange some or all of the rights to the asset. In the case of private property, this is done by entering into voluntary contracts which establish a binding agreement, based on the consent of two parties:

(a) to pay an agreed price; and
(b) to hand over property rights as agreed.

Yet, even at the conclusion of complex negotiations, it is not always clear what the precise conditions of the contractual agreement are. It is therefore customary in many cultures to reiterate the agreed conditions and to mark the contract by symbolic gestures, for example, by a handshake, an exchange of signatures or a shared meal. It pays to invest in 'affirmation rituals' as part of the contract, in particular when the contract establishes a durable relation. With the lapse of time, contracting parties may be tempted to behave opportunistically, shirk duties or simply forget obligations. Cultural signals that reinforce contracts are aimed to make the mutual obligations more memorable: for example, the smoking of a pipe among North American Indians or the appearance before a *kadi* (judge) in the Middle East to affirm certain contracts. In different cultures, the appropriate institutional signals vary. What may bind a Chinese merchant may not seem sufficient to bind an American to a contract and vice versa. It is therefore a challenge for pioneers in intercultural contracts to find mutually binding signals and rituals.

In its simplest case, steps (a) and (b) above coincide with the conclusion of the contract agreement (once-off contracts, simultaneous exchange). But frequently, time elapses between the conclusion of the contract and the other two steps, as well as between steps (a) and (b). Thus, it may be agreed that delivery will be some months in the future, or that payment by instalment will extend over many months ahead. When this is the case, contracts must include provisions for credible commitments that the obligations will indeed be fulfilled. Sanctions will be provided against opportunistic non-fulfilment, and provisions have to be made for sorting out subsequent misunderstandings or disagreements among the contracting parties. A typical example of this type of contract is a loan. One side obtains the use of a physical or financial asset, that is, the owners temporarily cede a property right, and makes a credible promise to return the asset or repay the borrowed finance as agreed. To make this promise credible, specially protected forms of contract may have to be entered into, providing harsher enforcement than under general contract law, or the borrower must provide securities, such as a mortgage which the loan-giver accepts as a 'hostage'. Often, intermediaries who have a reputation to lose (such as banks) join the contracting parties as middlemen and offer more credible commitments than can the ultimate borrowers that the loans will be repaid. To make intermediaries like banks even more credible, they tend to adhere to transparent accounting rules and meet prudential requirements. These are often supervised by public authorities to add even more credibility.

Another important type of contract is very frequent in contemporary economic life: an open-ended contract which establishes a more or less permanent contractual relationship which carries mutual obligations over time but cannot regulate all eventualities that might emerge. These are called relational contracts. A typical example of an open-ended relational contract is an employment contract: provision of a wage and other emoluments in exchange for the delivery of a certain work performance.

In the face of uncertainty and given the costs of negotiating and concluding them, contracts can never enumerate and regulate all aspects of a transaction that extends over a period of time, especially relational contracts. Such contracts have to rely on universal, abstract institutions within which specific eventualities can be sorted out in reasonably predictable ways. Certain general legal principles, such as 'acting in good faith' or 'a deal is a deal', belong to this category of rules that enhance trust. In this context, we should recall that institutions are time-tested 'storehouses of knowledge' that help intending contract partners to economise on the costs of contracting and contract fulfilment and that establish the trust needed for low transaction costs.

Institutions help to convert specific aspects of contracts into standardised routines and thereby save on information and renegotiation costs. This places numerous additional opportunities to utilise property within the reach of property owners. Just imagine if there were no rules and no enforcement mechanisms to ensure the punctual repayment of debts as contracted! Many possible economic interactions would not even be attempted, and living standards would drop.

O **Key Concepts**

A **contract** is an agreement, namely the concurrence of two declarations of the will to exchange property rights. One party may wish to offer outright property ownership (sale) or the right to possess and use property for a limited time (for example, to loan or hire out); the other party may have a demand for the property or property use and typically offer an amount of money. In the case of an exchange, an agreement to sell may be based on a **once-off, simultaneous contract** or a **non-simultaneous contract**, that is, an agreement that provides for fulfilment of the contract at a subsequent point in time: physical possession may, for example, pass over the following month, and payment may be in instalments for many months after the sale.

Non-simultaneous contracts involve **credit**. In this case, particular problems of monitoring and enforcement arise. Institutional safeguards have to be found against opportunistic shirking of the contractual obligation to return the property.

Open-ended or **relational contracts** are agreements to undertake a certain performance over an indeterminate period. Not all eventualities can be foreseen, let alone regulated, by contract provisions. Relational contracts are very frequent in a complex modern economy where many economic relations are durable and repetitive and their networking is common.

Relational contracts face the contracting parties with knowledge problems; they offer some reliable structure and confidence to both sides of the agreement. But they depend on institutions to economise on information costs and allow flexibility of adjustment. Appropriate rules lay down procedures as to how unforeseen and unstipulated circumstances will be handled, so that transaction costs are limited and contract partners can have trust that the specifics of their future relationship will be sorted out in case of conflict. ●

Autonomy – Economic Liberties

High and rising standards of living thus require that people and firms are free to contract, in other words, have the greatest possible autonomy to dispose of their property rights. This maxim is not fulfilled if social customs preclude many contractual uses of property rights ('It is not done for women to work for money'; 'It is simply unacceptable for people to take up loans, mortgaging the family farm'), or if political controls deprive people of their economic autonomy (for example, in centrally planned economies). Private autonomy and the practice of disposing of physical and intellectual property in exchange for money are thus institutional preconditions of free contracting.

Private autonomy is the freedom to use property without specific interference from other citizens or government authorities. Autonomy is essential to give individuals (and private firms) the scope that allows them to explore the best uses of their property, including their knowledge. The autonomy of property owners is of course constrained by universal rules; it is, however, violated when property owners are confronted with a plethora of limitations that may derive from private power (restrictive practices of market participants) or from collective action (for example, a proliferation of specific regulations to prescribe predetermined outcomes with regard to the natural environment, human health or income distribution). Such interventions may be legitimised by political action, but they reduce individual autonomy and complicate the knowledge problem of property owners in that information and other transaction costs are increased. When such limitations of private autonomy proliferate, they tend to become contradictory and prosperity is likely to suffer. Private autonomy is the projection of individualism into property law. In collectivist regimes where there is a great tendency to impose collective goals, private property rights – even when formally in existence – will be whittled away. A great frequency and pervasiveness of prescriptive directives then eliminate private property in all but name, as well as responsibility and self-reliance.

Autonomy in using one's private property – including one's own knowledge and labour – amounts to what is sometimes described as 'economic liberties', a respected sphere of freedom of economic action. These economic freedoms in the possession and use of private property give substance to civil and political liberties. They enable citizens to defend these rights with the material means at their disposal, and to do so without prior reference to others for permission (Friedman, 1962).

Private and Political Restrictions of Private Autonomy

Private property rights can lose some of their value when their use is curtailed by the actions of other citizens, for example, when a cartel is formed to exclude other property owners from offering their property in a market. Private restrictions of property use have to do with the exercise of economic power, which we discussed in section 5.4 in connection with the analysis of how institutions can avoid conflicts. Institutions therefore should protect property rights beyond the merely formal protection of private property as such, and safeguard autonomous property uses as far as is feasible. This includes external institutions, enforced by government, against restrictive practices such as cartels and monopolies that close markets to outsiders and new-comers.

In an open, dynamically changing world, positions of economic power rarely persist for long without political patronage. Even where one or a few powerful players have closed a market, they will sooner or later face actual or potential contests with other property owners. Nowadays, in an era of low transport and transaction costs, most markets will sooner or later be contested by outsiders who then offer the free, autonomous choices of the other side of the market. Most private limitations of private autonomy depend for their durability on the support of government (Friedman, 1991).

The more durable and far-reaching restrictions on private economic autonomy therefore originate in political action. Political powers are often used to curtail the rights of property owners (economic liberties). The primary role of external institutions is to protect property rights, primarily through proscriptive, universal rules. If the principle of universality is abandoned and prescriptive, specific rules proliferate, there is a great likelihood that government will discriminate between different property owners and that property users will incur rapidly rising transaction costs. It is not the use by government of prescriptive rules (directives) *per se* that is the problem, but the frequency and density of their use.

We shall return to this problem in Chapter 8 when we discuss competition and in Chapter 10 when we deal with collective action.

O Key Concepts

Private autonomy means that the rights of property owners are free from detailed private and public limitations on how property is to be used, in other words, economic liberties are safeguarded. Autonomy can be curtailed when other property owners with power interfere with someone's property rights by arbitrary and discriminatory action. An example is private action to restrict trade, for example by excluding certain suppliers from selling in a market, thereby forming a supplier cartel. Autonomy can also be curtailed by government actions. When governments go beyond protecting the equal property rights of all and decree and enforce a great multiplicity of prescriptive directives, they erode private autonomy – and with it the proper functioning of the capitalist system. ●

Transaction Costs

When property rights are used actively, that is, when they are exchanged or combined with property rights in production factors held by others, coordination costs arise in addition to exclusion costs (compare Figure 5.1 on p. 94). When people use their property rights by contracting in markets, these costs are called transaction costs.[2] Before people know what they want and how they might trade their property rights with others, they have to obtain information, often a costly and risky process in itself (section 3.2). Next, they have to negotiate and secure contracts. This creates further resource costs (section 5.6). Finally, contract execution has to be monitored and measured and, if necessary, adjudicated and enforced. This may again be costly. The level of these transaction costs can be reduced by institutions, for example when standardised weights and measures are adopted or imposed.

Information is costly. A great deal of knowledge has to be acquired before a business transaction can even be contemplated: What goods and services exist? Who owns them? On what conditions would they be offered for sale or loan? Are variations to existing goods and services feasible? Who could make necessary variations? At what cost? What sort of persons are potential contract partners? Where can they be found? Can they be trusted to fulfil contractual obligations? What prices have to be paid? What other circumstances must be known? Once all this information has been collected, it must be evaluated. The entire effort may end with the conclusion that, after all, the intended transaction promises insufficient material advantages. In other words, the information paradox applies. As we saw, information search cannot be optimised because the value of information cannot be ascertained before it has been acquired. The way in which people typically proceed is to expend resources on information gathering until they judge from general experience that they have acquired sufficient knowledge to risk a decision. At what point their experience tells them that they are able to decide can normally not be known beforehand. And once the information costs have been incurred, they are sunk costs (Streit and Wegner, 1992). The fact that the value of information cannot be assessed before it has been acquired gives it a certain insidiousness and makes information search a risky activity, which many people resent.

Information search costs tend to be relatively low when it is possible to extrapolate from past experience or analogous cases. They are higher when new factor combinations are to be tried out (innovation). Then, costs have to be incurred to test whether products or processes are technically and commercially feasible. In all but the most favourable institutional settings, the necessary expenses on information search and other transaction costs may be prohibitive, so innovations are not even contemplated (see Chapter 8). More generally, private bilateral exchanges are complicated where information costs are high.

Once economic agents have gathered the information they consider sufficient to conclude that a certain transaction will serve their purposes, a string of further costs have to be contemplated: the costs of negotiating, concluding, monitoring and enforcing the contract. It was this type of recurrent transaction cost that British economist Ronald Coase 'discovered' for economic theory when he tried to explain why firms existed. He concluded that the costs of subcontracting certain inputs in markets can be reduced by entering into open-ended, semi-permanent hierarchical relations, in other words by combining resources to form organisations such as firms (Coase, [1937] 1952; Cheung, 1983; Demsetz, 1988). A more or less permanent organisational relation, say of an employee with a firm, saves on the costs of hiring employees on a daily basis in the market.

Transaction costs may be costly to measure and predict, because complex technical properties, timing, guarantees of contract fulfilment and provisions regarding action in cases of non-fulfilment have to be monitored, and it must be ensured that the agreed conditions are met to the satisfaction of both parties. If there is disagreement, possibly costly adjudication is required as well as contract enforcement. Given these costs, it often makes sense to enter into firm, open-ended arrangements to regulate recurrent routine interactions, such as employment contracts. Such open-ended arrangements create firms whose existence can only be explained by the existence of transaction costs.

Some authors have called these recurrent, operations-related transaction costs, which Coase first highlighted in the 1930s, 'Coasean transaction costs'.

O **Key Concepts**

Transaction costs are incurred when property rights are exchanged in market transactions (based on contracts). In the first instance, transaction costs consist of information search costs (to find a sufficient number of exchange partners, their location, product design, quality, reliability and numerous other relevant aspects prior to making a decision), as well as the costs of negotiating, concluding and monitoring the contract and the costs of possibly dealing with contract breaches. The costs of information search and preparing contracts are 'sunk' prior to transaction decisions. ●

Externalities Again: Measurement Costs and Exclusion

When private costs and benefits differ from all the costs and benefits to society (externalities), this is frequently the consequence of transaction costs. If it is too expensive to measure and assign all the consequences of private property uses to the owners, people are unable to negotiate a market price to compensate everyone for all the costs they cause and to charge them for all the benefits. Common goods also occur where users cannot readily be excluded due to the high costs of exclusion.

As measurement and information technology improves, externalities can frequently be eliminated. Private production then becomes profitable even where public production was previously seen as the only way to come to grips with an insoluble externality problem. For example, roads have long been financed from taxation, because road-usage costs were near-impossible to measure, attribute and collect, and it was near-impossible to exclude citizens from road usage. Now, it seems possible to rely on new electronic technology (transponders) to internalise the costs and benefits of certain types of road usage and create private toll roads. In these circumstances, collective action is less appropriate. Likewise, the spread of computer networking and other amenities of the communications revolution is now shifting the dividing line between market and government organisation in the direction of more coordination by markets and competitive outsourcing, and less collective action and reliance on socialised property (Barzel, 1982).

When private agents compete with each other in using common goods, they may also cause externalities among themselves. If, for example, more people use public open-access roads, they contribute to congestion which impacts on themselves and others. If the owner of the road, the government, were in a position to exclude some road users, user fees could become a rationing device. This depends again on measurement technology and the costs of exclusion. In recent years, clean air has ceased to be a free good in many areas of urban and industrial concentration. Economists have therefore proposed the principle of 'the polluter pays', namely, those who cause emissions are rationed in their polluting activities either by price (through buying auctioned pollution rights) or by regulation. This requires that pollution can be measured and attributed and that there are effective means of excluding potential polluters from contributing to the environmental problem. It also requires a value judgement as to which user of environmental assets should have priority.

What has been said about competing demand and external costs also applies *mutatis mutandis* to the case of external benefits. Where private agents used to provide capacities and amenities for others without being paid (external benefit), new measurement technology can at times enable these activities to be rewarded and hence stimulated; an example is the technology that now allows private providers to charge for the use of TV channels.

Externalities arise in two types of cases:

(a) where private property owners are not fully compensated for the costs and benefits of their activities through private exchanges, because they consider the exclusion costs for some effects of their property uses as too high (Coase, 1960);
(b) where private operators use common property and lay political claims to their share in common property.

In case (b), we can speak of externalities in the narrow sense. They take the form of external costs when private uses of common property have negative consequences for others, for example when road users have to compete for traffic space and each user adds to road congestion. They take the form of external benefits when private users alleviate the competition for common property (external benefit), for example when private reafforestation or private water conservation measures enhance the overall environment.

In all these cases, better measurement technology and lower monitoring costs – for example, thanks to new computer technology – can alleviate the problem and facilitate a resolution of the problems that always arise where externalities occur.

This probably marks a change in a long-term trend. Because of high measurement and transaction costs, certain goods and services used to be provided collectively. This led to externalities in their use (such as road congestion) as well as a lack of cost controls in production where collective provision was made by government monopolies. Advances in technology now allow the use of such goods to be measured and accounted for, and consequently externalities disappear. It is then possible to convert such goods from collective to private provision and production (privatisation). As a result, government organisations can devolve such activities (Chapter 14).

7.4   Relational Contracts, Self-enforcement and the Judiciary

We noted briefly that specific problems of contract monitoring and enforcement arise when property rights are used in open-ended, relational contracts. It cannot simply be assumed that all human beings resist the temptation to act opportunistically if they can get away with it. We saw that people are often forgetful, negligent and lazy, they shirk obligations or are inclined to cheat and lie, especially *vis-à-vis* strangers. Institutional constraints are then needed to combat these innate instinctual human tendencies and induce people to practise more reliable and predictable behaviour. There is a particular need for credible institutional constraints in the modern capitalist economy where many property uses are based on open-ended contractual relationships. They depend more than other contracts on self-enforcement mechanisms and reliable external enforcement (Axelrod, 1984; Benson, 1995).

Self-enforcing Contracts

Confidence in contract fulfilment over time derives, in the first place, from the existence of a number of self-enforcing mechanisms, which are based on internal institutions which do not require formal enforcement mechanisms:

(a) As many profitable business relations extend over a long term, the two contract partners have a reciprocal and automatic hold over each other. If one breaks the contract, the other has the option of retaliating in some way or discontinuing the business relationship altogether. 'Tit for tat' can be a powerful sanction. In the extreme and in small groups it can take the form of excluding offending parties (ostracism). It is effective when contract partners know that they depend on each other and can hold each other hostage. Then, they will be less likely to shirk and will ensure smooth execution of the contract. Over time, the experience of honesty, punctuality and reliability in trade may become an internalised institution, 'second nature'. Experience shows that such 'merchant virtues' are highly beneficial to both sides of the trade (Giersch, 1996).

(b) Another way in which contract partners may make credible commitments is to build up a reputation which they need to sell and which they can easily lose if they act opportunistically. They invest in product quality and service and advertise their services to earn a good reputation, often a costly process. The reputation becomes part of their intangible capital. If customers turn to a reputable retailer, they know that part of the price they pay is for the confidence that a contract with such a supplier will be properly executed and that possible disagreements will be settled quickly. They also know that they have a certain hold over the supplier, if they are disappointed, in that they can destroy the reputation of the supplier. In other words, they can, if necessary, hold the supplier 'hostage'. Suppliers often set themselves up to be held hostage as part of their business strategy.

Modern technology has made repeat contracts and the spread of information easier, so the reputations of opportunistic agents are more at risk. However, reputation only works as an enforcement mechanism in communities in which information is communicated and there is a modicum of shared basic values. What is necessary for the reputation mechanism to work is for the members of the community to react to the news of opportunistic behaviour in more or less the same way. If an opportunistic act – say, fraud perpetrated on a rich man – is greeted by some with approval and by others with condemnation, then the reputation mechanism is likely to fail. This is why a shared ethical and value system is an important underpinning for the enforcement of many internal institutions and crucial to low transaction costs. After all, spontaneous enforcement of internal rules tends to be cheaper than heavy reliance on external sanctions (litigation).

(c) Self-enforcement of non-simultaneous contracts can often be enhanced by the introduction of third parties. One way is to include a well-known third party as a guarantor. This role is played, for example, by banks that issue letters of credit and guarantee payment for product delivery.

(d) Enforcement is also assisted by agreement on a preselected adjudicator. Thus, chambers of commerce may be designated in a contract as adjudicators in the case of disputes over contract fulfilment. Adjudication means that an independent person or organisation is asked to look into the matter and give a verdict, but this is not binding on either party. To further enhance confidence in contract fulfilment, contracts can even provide for a stronger form of compulsory arbitration, a provision that the disputing parties will be bound by the third party's verdict.

(e) Contract enforcement in certain trading environments may depend on a third party which enters as a directly involved intermediary with its own reputation to lose: the middleman or intermediary whom we mentioned in the preceding section. Middlemen conduct back-to-back transactions on their own account. Apart from helping with information search, they fulfil the important role of offering trust in contract fulfilment. They tend to be well known and well established in their line of business and have a reputation to lose. They thus offer themselves as 'hostages' to both sides of a deal. This constitutes a credible commitment. They can thus remedy general institutional deficiencies, for example, underdeveloped legal guarantees and poor or costly judicial enforcement of the law.

The credibility of middlemen can be strengthened even further if they form an association which offers a collective guarantee of the performance of their members. Such group guarantees may derive from shared family or racial bonds (the Chinese, Jewish and Indian Marwari traders in various parts of the world), from formal professional associations (like the merchants of the Hanseatic League in northern Europe in the Middle Ages), or from mutual insurance contracts among middlemen (which was, for example, part of the beginning of Lloyd's insurance in London and which is part of bank insurance in many countries). Individual middlemen who fail to fulfil their obligations may face the penalty of ostracism: exclusion from the business network by the other middlemen who know them. If the sanction of ostracism is to work, the group has to be relatively small and mutually dependent on a network of on-going transactions (Landa, 1994).

These institutional provisions are internal to society. They work with effective sanctions that are not dependent on any government action. Most of today's trade, including world trade and international capital flows, depends on these more or less formal but internal sanctions. Such internal institutions are effective, flexible and relatively cheap to operate. Societies that cultivate these mechanisms therefore enjoy competitive advantages over societies where self-enforcement is weak.

O Key Concepts

Self-enforcing contracts provide for credible commitments. They rely on devices that ensure contract fulfilment without (costly) formal enforcement despite ever-present temptations to shirk contractual obligations. Some such devices are 'tit-for-tat', the creation of a reputation, and the provision of a security (offering 'hostages') or reliance on an intermediary to make contractual commitments more credible.

Middlemen are persons or organisations which intermediate between the ultimate buyer and seller. They have the function of reducing information costs for ultimate buyers and sellers and enhancing trust. In this way, they serve to facilitate trade in environments where impersonal institutions are not sufficient. They tend to vanish when institutions improve information flows and trust. Middlemen thus often help to remedy general institutional deficiencies, such as legal insecurity or high information costs.

An **adjudicator** or **mediator** is an independent person or organisation who passes judgement on contested aspects of contract execution, but whose recommendations are not binding.

An **arbitrator** is an independent person or organisation who passes judgement on contested aspects of contract execution and whose decision is binding on the two contracting parties. In some legal systems, the law allows appeals to public courts to challenge private arbitrators; in other systems, people can contractually bind themselves to accept the verdict of private arbitrators.

Merchant virtues, such as honesty, punctuality, a high payment morale, reliability and flexibility in conflict, are internal institutions of capitalist society that enhance confidence in contract fulfilment and hence the efficient operation of the market economy. They constitute a valuable, intangible capital asset of a community. ●

External Back-ups: the Judiciary

In many cases, the self-enforcement of contracts is supplemented by external institutions, legislation and government regulation, which rely on public enforcement organisations (the judiciary, the police, inspectors, prisons). Rulers and parliaments have tended to offer themselves as credible third parties to ensure contract fulfilment, as we saw in section 5.3. They developed formal contract law and created specialist arbitrators (commercial courts), which often enjoy scale economies (North and Thomas, 1973; Rosenberg and Birdzell, 1986). External enforcement mechanisms thus frequently enhance the confidence of contract partners. They may also reduce their information and contract negotiation costs by providing standardised conditions, for example for a real-estate sale or a work contract. However, heavy reliance on external litigation can weaken the internal institutions, which tend to be cheaper and more flexible. Litigious societies – such as the United States – tend to develop large and sophisticated networks of arbitration experts who have a self-interest in fostering disagreement and complicating conciliation: after all, they derive their incomes from it. This conflict plays an important part in the often-heard criticism of the great number of business lawyers and the cost they create for business in the United States, as compared with conditions in East Asian countries such as Japan. In East Asia, heavy reliance on internal institutions and ready recourse to simple external institutions contain the costs of doing business. For the United States, it has been estimated that (in the 1980s) 'each additional lawyer who is churned out by American law schools reduces the level of GDP by $2.5 million, a figure far greater than the present discounted value of that lawyer's earnings, substantial though they may be' (Magee *et al.*, 1989, p. 17). Irrespective of the precise methodology in arriving at this estimate, it indicates the economy-wide transaction cost advantage of an institutional system which relies primarily on spontaneous self-enforcement.

7.5   The Consequences of Capitalism

On the Early History of Property Rights

The creation of identifiable and protected property rights was one of the most important inventions of the neolithic revolution which probably began in the Middle East (northern Mesopotamia) and the Far East (north-east Thailand) some 10 000 years ago. At that time, agriculture (sowing and harvesting, rather than simply gathering) and animal husbandry were invented. Humans turned from being opportunistic exploiters of nature to cultivators and users of physical assets for production. It cannot be imagined that this important technical revolution could have taken place without the respect for and, if necessary, the protection of the exclusive use of land and animals by the owners. For all we know, property in palaeolithic hunter-gatherer societies was much more limited, if it existed at all. There is evidence that possessions were under constant challenge in those societies, much as animals may possess an item of food until a rival takes it away. The notion that 'good fences make good neighbours' was certainly not widely accepted. In the neolithic revolution, assets which had previously been under the vague control of a tribe (or the chiefs and elders in command) were now assigned more clearly to individuals or families. Once people had control of their property and its benefits, they were better motivated to make use of their assets by toiling, labouring and experimenting with them, precisely because they could have confidence that they would appropriate the rewards of their efforts and their risk taking. Private property rights are thus one of the very foundations on which human civilisation is built.

In subsequent ages, law givers have refined and codified existing property rights (Benson, 1995). Law givers often formalised and codified the already existing internal institutions in society; they did not invent property laws. In this respect, the dictum that 'law is older than legislation' applies (Hayek, 1973, p. 72). In the European tradition, it was the Athenians and the Romans who most clearly distinguished between mere possession of an asset and genuine ownership. They designed private law rules which allowed owners to retain property title while ceding possession and assigning certain rights of property use to others, for example by hiring or renting an asset. They also laid down legal rules which dealt with conflicts arising from property use and established obligations for those who harmed others by their property uses to privately compensate them (torts). And they regulated certain uses of property which might conflict with the interest of others and put in place arbitration and adjudication mechanisms to settle conflicts in a predictable and non-violent manner. Thus, a clear basis of legal rules was created so that exclusive property rights could be divided and traded by private agreement and at low cost.

The Emergence of Capitalism

For most of human history, private property has not been strictly respected. Thieves, as well as rulers and other groups with the potential for violence, have tended to impose capricious levies on property owning citizens or arbitrarily confiscated whatever assets they could grasp. This has often made it necessary for owners to hide their property even if this complicated or negated its use. After the 'Dark Ages' in Europe, private property gradually became protected more systematically by effective government action. Opportunistic rulers of the small, open European states were often confronted with an exodus of capital, propertied people and merchant-entrepreneurs from their jurisdictions. Other jurisdictions began to enhance property rights by encouraging free markets in which property rights could be traded; they protected contracts through codifying the law and setting up effective tribunals. Taxation was made orderly and subjected to the law. Jurisdictions such as Venice, Florence, Genova, and later Portugal, Nuremberg, the Netherlands and England gained from the influx of capital and enterprise, so that their revenues grew. States which gave property good institutional protection thus flourished, whereas states which did not became poorer. The successes were imitated, so the protection of property rights by governments spread through much of western Europe. The princes often resented the loss of power to mere merchants, but they had little option but to respect private property (Weber, [1927] 1995; Jones, [1981] 1987; Rosenberg and Birdzell, 1986). In the twentieth century, property rights protection has spread to many non-European economies.

❖ Max Weber on the Conditions for the Rise of Capitalism

It is appropriate to mention the conditions for the emergence of the modern capitalist business organisation – and subsequently the industrial revolution which capitalism built – identified by the pioneer of the study of the rise of capitalism, the German sociologist and economic historian Max Weber. Weber stated that business enterprises emerged as a specific type of economic organisation when the following six conditions were fulfilled:

1. Physical resources could be appropriated by organisations that were recognised as separate legal entities (in other words, the property rights of firms were respected and protected).
2. The firm was able to operate freely in markets (free entry, competition and exit were safeguarded).
3. Organisations used proper accounting methods to support rational calculus as a guide to what it should and should not do (in other words, business leaders wanted to make rational calculations, and genuine market prices made rational economic calculus possible).
4. The law and other institutions surrounding business firms became reliable and predictable (the rule of law, including commercial law, prevailed).
5. Labour was free, that is, people were free to appropriate the returns from their labour (sovereignty of the individual and free labour markets, which meant the end of slavery, indentured labour and bondage).
6. Commercialisation was possible (property rights became alienable, that is, they could be sold to others) and company capital could be financed by raising capital through the issue of joint-stock shares (creation of a share market).

Only when the appropriate institutional framework surrounding the modern capitalist business firm is ensured will business organisations be able to operate effectively. Violations of alienable property rights, lawlessness and impediments to competition do not necessarily make it impossible to create capitalist businesses, but they undermine their effectiveness in generating innovation and aggregate growth.

Weber's (historic) analysis thus highlights the interdependence between the framework of institutional conditions and the performance of economic organisations (Weber, [1927] 1995, pp. 275–8). ◆

As we mentioned in Chapter 2, the emergence of the rules that allowed the rise of capitalism was explained more recently by the British-Australian economic historian Eric Jones when he contrasted the industrial revolution in north-west Europe with the experience of China, a technically well developed country by the year AD 800, as well as other huge but closed economies in Asia. There, the rulers retained unchecked despotic and arbitrary powers to confiscate property, since capital owners and others in these huge empires were unable to emigrate to neighbouring jurisdictions. The experience of Christopher Columbus, who went from one court of Europe to another with his plan to sail west to India, could not have been replicated in China. As a matter of fact, the long-distance maritime ventures of Chinese Admiral Cheng Ho, who sailed as far as East Africa in the fifteenth century, simply stopped when the Imperial Court issued an edict to discontinue exploration.

The superior technology and organisational skills of the Chinese thus did not translate into a self-sustaining industrial revolution. China was a state ruled by a small elite which taxed the peasantry, treating it 'as its meat and fish', that is, taking as much revenue as they pleased – or managed to extract without triggering a peasant uprising (Jones *et al.*, 1994). The rulers could persist in their exploitative palaeolithic mentality and had no incentive to cultivate the common wealth. Only in periods when official confiscation was constrained and subject to some rules, such as during the Sung dynasty (960–1279), did the Chinese economy flourish. The lack of order and confidence and the practice of arbitrary official confiscation discouraged investment in industry and enterprise (Jones, [1981] 1987). This historic comparison confirms that the institutional protection of private property and its uses is essential to sustaining economic growth.

The central importance of property rights was (re)discovered by the philosopher-economists of the Scottish Enlightenment. In 1739, David Hume wrote in his *Treatise on Human Nature*: 'Property must be stable and be fixed by general rules. Though in one instance the public be the sufferer, this momentary ill is amply compensated by the steady prosecution of the rule and by the peace and order which it establishes in society' (Hume, [1739] 1965). Hume and other writers of the Enlightenment understood that exclusivity is necessary to make the system work in the interest of the maximum number of people. They also focused on the basic economic freedoms of autonomous property use and castigated public monopolies and political protections of private privilege. Reflecting these considerations, the US Constitution protected property explicitly against arbitrary confiscation. These protections were later emulated in many other constitutions around the world – at least in the wording, though not necessarily in the spirit.

Community Consequences of Property Rights

Historical experience has shown, time and again, that private property and autonomy have on balance a number of distinct advantages that transcend the individual. Admittedly, property owners act in their self-interest, but by those very actions they produce results that benefit others. In the real world, economic systems based on private property rights and private autonomy in disposing of property are never 'pure'. They do not work 'perfectly'. But a solid case can be made for a system based largely on widely distributed property rights and the individual autonomy to use and dispose of them as the individual sees fit (economic freedom), which tends to have a number of (unintended) beneficial consequences for the community.

Arguably the two most important consequences of a properly working capitalist system are that it helps to control individual actors, including those with power, and that it gives everyone incentives to make active use of property and knowledge – including by stimulating the creation and testing of valuable information. Respect for and protection of property rights is beneficial in that it channels entrepreneurship, human energy, creativity and rivalry into constructive and peaceful directions. War or theft only divert enterprising spirits into zero- or negative-sum games, whereas the protection of private property rights facilitates numerous positive-sum games (Tullock, 1967; Baumol, 1990). These positive-sum games add up to overall economic growth and make it easier for members of society to realise their own aspirations.

As we noted, a second important consequence of private property rights is that they give material substance to individual freedom. When government agents show an inclination to limit individual freedoms, private property protection often serves as their most potent bulwark (Mises, [1920] 1994; Friedman, 1962, ch. 1; Seldon, 1990, chs 7 and 8). In societies which are made up of 'citizens of property', the people strive to buttress their economic liberties by democratic and legal constraints on the rulers. As long as people are in control of their material resources, they enjoy considerable autonomy to proceed freely in civil and political affairs. The interaction between private property and freedom was evident in Europe and North America over the last two centuries and was well understood by the early protagonists of individual liberties. This connection has now become equally evident in a growing number of capitalist countries in East Asia where the rising middle class demands the rule of law and democracy as well as economic liberties and economic autonomy (recent examples are Korea, Taiwan and Thailand, with a number of neighbouring countries beginning to follow the same path: see Chapter 14; Scully, 1991, 1992; Gwartney and Lawson, 1997).[4]

A third welcome community consequence of the institutions that guarantee private property is that owners are normally induced to economise on resources. People tend to conserve valuable assets if they are allowed to own them and to appropriate the benefits for themselves and their heirs. When people own assets, they control depletion and make the best long-term use of the scarce resources they own. The fundamental fact that ownership encourages careful stewardship was already known to the Greek philosopher Aristotle (384–322BC) who wrote: 'What is common to many is taken least care of, for all men have greater regard for what is their own than what they possess in common with others' (cited in Gwartney, 1991, p. 67). Empirical studies that we already referred to have shown that, in modern mass societies, conservation of assets, including of natural resources, is greatly assisted by clearly defined property rights. In small, traditional communities, internal institutions that are applied informally often suffice to conserve commonly owned property, such as natural resources, at least as long as population pressures on existing resources are not high (Ostrom, 1990). But in big communities private property often seems better suited to conservation.

Wise stewardship of scarce natural resources can thus be promoted by permitting private owners to claim exclusive property rights to these natural assets, where this is feasible. Successes in nature conservation through this procedure can be observed in numerous privately owned conservation areas in several continents. Depleting fish stocks, once they have been turned into the exclusive property of private owners, for example, have increased because the owners could use the offspring as a return on what is now their property (Anderson, in Block, 1990, pp. 147–50; Anderson and Leal, 1997; Wills, 1997). This point was demonstrated in a cogent manner in Zimbabwe after property rights in (endangered) African elephants were assigned to local villagers. That led quickly to an end to poaching and a big increase in elephant numbers (Insert).

In many instances, conservation has a better chance when property rights in natural resources are made tradeable, so that people who wish to make long-term investments in material resources can get access and have a better chance of reaping long-term material rewards (Gwartney, 1991).

❖ Property Rights and Nature Conservation: African Elephants

While elephant populations have declined throughout most of Africa, the conservation policies of some southern African countries have been ... successful ... In 1900, Zimbabwe's number of elephants was estimated approximately 5000. Today it is estimated to be 43 000.

'Wildlife is a continual source of danger to rural populations ... During certain months of the growing season, villagers have to spend valuable time protecting their crops against marauding wildlife. If a villager's maize field is destroyed by an elephant, he will not be compensated. If a family is unfortunate enough to experience such a disaster, it may well face starvation. Under such conditions, it is not surprising that poaching flourishes ...

... in 1989, local Zimbabweans were [made] responsible for reporting ... poachers. [Institutional changes were introduced that gave] local people ... [the right to] manage the wildlife in their area ... [The programme] gave landholders the responsibility for the conservation and use of wild animals on their lands. Some predicted that this would result in the widespread destruction of wild animals. Instead, the opposite has occurred.

The effects [of this institutional innovation] ... were felt much more slowly on communal lands ... [But in 1989], the Government gave the district councils ... the right to manage their own resources. The main objective ... is the strictly controlled use of wildlife to create income ... [Now] local people are once again benefiting from their wildlife ... They are receiving cash dividends from the proceeds of wildlife management and being compensated if their crops are damaged ... Meat is distributed at cost price ... The main source of income at present is from safari hunting ... Before the ban [on ivory trade] ivory from the shoot was also sold by the communities.

... [Local] support for the scheme is ... strong ... new skills and techniques acquired by locals enable them to carry out some of the more fundamental management tasks ... the project now looks as if it may offer real long-term hope for the ecological and economic future of these communities. ◆

(Source: A. Bradstock, 'Community is Key to Conservation', Geographic Magazine, December 1990, p. 17)

While private property can often promote conservation goals, this mechanism leaves the decisions about this to unorganised private actors. If private owners, for reasons of their own, decide to prefer short-term exploitation, this may inflict long-term (intertemporal) external costs. Thus, monoculture or concentrations of tourism developments may well cause long-term damage which nature cannot regenerate and subsequent generations cannot repair. In these cases, public policy may have to step in, but this presupposes that policy makers know better – and have the motivation to attain outcomes that attain (someone's) nature conservation goals better – than the decentralised judgements of various, self-interested resource owners.

The importance of private property in the conservation of nature has also been evidenced by the track record of the socialist countries of eastern Europe and East Asia. The politicians and bureaucrats entrusted with the stewardship of collectively owned natural resources obviously perceived no direct incentive to conserve, whereas they could expect political and career rewards for resource depletion and environmental degradation in order to meet production targets. Since the natural assets belonged to no one in particular, no one defended them against excessive exploitation.

A further important consequence of widely held private property is that it tends to enhance peace and harmony in society by preventing or defusing material conflicts. When people have no property to lose, they engage more readily in confrontation and destructive conflict, whereas propertied people risk much if they tolerate a chaotic society. When property is owned widely and the owners have acquired the habit of cultivating what is theirs by long-term investment and learning, then the majority have an interest in keeping the peace, internationally and internally. Popular notions that capitalists are war mongers may have some historic foundation in regimes where property was held by the few who hoped to gain from armaments or conquest. But it does not apply to nations where property rights are widely distributed.

It must not be concluded that dispersed private property is a panacea for all human problems; it draws on the knowledge and motivation of many people and can achieve community consequences that the majority of citizens find beneficial.

7.6   Institutions Which Secure the Services of Money

Money and the Division of Labour

Money is a device that saves enormously on transaction costs. It is therefore of great importance to the division of labour and the functioning of the exchange economy. It serves as a general means of exchange. This also implies that it can serve as a unit in which assets, liabilities and transactions are measured and accounted for and as a store of value. The functions of money are tied to physical money tokens, which come in many different shapes and forms: cowrie shells, bits of metal, pieces of paper, a debit entry in a bank's accounts. However, money fulfils its functions only if its creation and use are constrained so that the stability of its value in terms of a basket of goods is secured (controlled money supply). In the case of money tokens that were taken from nature and were monetised (outside money, such as gold), natural availability controlled the supply. In the case of money that is based on credit (inside money), the control of supply depends on institutional constraints on the provision of central bank money (a form of outside money). The importance of stable money has long been realised by economists – indeed, the study of money, and what it takes to make it function properly, was one of the earliest concerns of institutional economics.

To explain the importance of money, we have to start by considering multiple, bilateral barter, that is, a system in which a person can trade items of property only by finding exchange partners who want some of those specific assets and by being willing to exchange for specific assets that others hold. This creates an enormous information problem as soon as the trading community covers more than a few property owners and commodities. Most of the transactions that we carry out would be prohibitively expensive. Barter also causes storage costs. These costs reduce the gains from trade and therefore limit the division of labour. R.W. Clower (1969, p. 25), in his analysis of money makes the point with a colourful example quoted from British economist Stanley Jevons (1835–82). Apparently, in the nineteenth century a certain Mademoiselle Zélie, a celebrated singer from Paris on a world-wide tour, entertained the Polynesian natives in the Society Islands with her arias, in exchange for which they gave her pigs, fowl, coconuts and fruit. As Mademoiselle could not consume the payment herself and found the information costs of identifying the demand for pigs, fowl and fruit in the local market overwhelming, she had to store the proceeds from her concert, but that made it necessary to feed the fruit to the animals ...

Once a widely accepted intermediate means of exchange – money – is introduced into a barter system, the information, storage and other transaction costs are greatly reduced. It is possible to shift from direct exchanges to indirect exchanges through the intermediation of money. The gains from the division of labour are greatly enhanced. This economises on transaction costs by splitting a direct, bilateral barter transaction into two separate transactions with money serving as an intermediate medium of exchange (indirect exchange). If necessary, money can also serve as a temporary intermediary as a store of value (Brunner and Meltzer, 1971; Eggertson, 1990, pp. 231–44).

In a world of perfect information with zero transaction costs, as assumed by simple neoclassical economics, there is no need for money (Eggertson, 1990, pp. 232–7). Everyone would know all possible barter partners. It is only the knowledge problem that makes money a useful, indeed a crucial, institution in facilitating the division of labour. Similarly, the need for financial intermediation (by banks, insurance companies, money markets and the like) can only be understood if we do not assume 'perfect knowledge'.[5]

Price Level Stability

It is also essential that the value of money – in terms of a representative basket of goods and services – does not fluctuate unpredictably. If institutions are in place that create firm expectations of a stable value of money, then business lenders can concentrate on producing and marketing their products, on innovating production methods and saving costs. They will interpret movements in individual prices in factor and product markets as signals that scarcities are changing and will adjust their plans accordingly. They will, for example, trust that a factor price increase is signalling to them that they should economise on that particular production factor; and that a product price increase is signalling that buyers want more of that particular product, so they should think about expanding supply. In other words, if institutions safeguard price-level stability, the 'radio traffic' of price signals sends clear messages. If, on the other hand, the institutions fail to secure stable money and people experience erratic variations of the price level, then producers cannot understand clearly the price variations they are observing: is a price increase just part of general inflation, or is there a new sales opportunity? The radio traffic is, so to speak, overlaid by static. Communication and coordination become more difficult and less reliable. Producers now become distracted from their core business and have to make guesses about inflation, a task for which they are ill prepared. They may divert scarce time and resources from their speciality into asset speculation. In the longer term, inflation therefore always undermines economic growth, destroys jobs and redistributes income and wealth from net savers to the (often well-connected and more affluent) net borrowers (Friedman and Friedman, 1980). Consequently, the end result of poor monetary institutions will be a lesser provision of goods and services and therefore a poorer economic outcome for the community at large.

Limits to Money Supply

The most fundamental quality of money, if it is to fulfil its role effectively, is that its supply is limited and is seen to be limited and that it does not fluctuate unpredictably over time.[6] Only then will all members of the public readily accept effectively valueless money tokens in exchange for their work effort or their property rights. The only reason why money is accepted to settle claims is that everyone assumes that everyone else also accepts money. When this assumption proves wrong, for example in times of inflation, money tends to be replaced quickly or at least loses some of its functions.

Outside money supply is, as we have already noted, limited when a material which cannot be readily multiplied by human effort is used as the token of money. Thus, cowrie shells were money in the mountains of Papua-New Guinea but not in communities along the coast. And rare metals, such as gold and silver, were turned into money. Money can also be created inside a community, for example when members of society create credits that are monetised. This means that the users of these credits (inside money) have to trust that they can be turned into outside money at any time, for example central-bank money. As long as the creditors keep their reputation for converting these monetised credits into outside money, the credit chain holds. But such trust depends on institutions: if the issuers of paper (or fiat) money break the rules and supply excessive amounts of money, then the services of money as a unit of account, store of value and means of payment deteriorate and, in the extreme, disappear (see box).

❖ The Disappearance of the Cook Island Dollar

The small South Pacific Island territory of the Cook Islands (1995: 18 000 inhabitants), a former colony of New Zealand, issued its own currency at a par with the New Zealand dollar. However, in 1994 when the Cook Islands government, after a phase of profligate spending, appeared to issue excessive supplies of the currency to cover government deficits, the two locally operating commercial banks refused to accept Cook Island dollars as payments into savings accounts or for transfer overseas. Depositors had to produce New Zealand dollars for these purposes.

The Cook Island currency disappeared promptly from circulation. The government slid into a budget crisis and near-bankruptcy, since the deficits could no longer be covered by supplying its own money, and foreign aid donors refused to bail them out. ◆

(Source: The Australian, *13 March 1996, p. 11)*

Numerous rulers have found it advantageous to enter the business of supplying money and imbuing it with their authority. King Croesus of Lydia in Asia Minor (sixth century BC) is reputed to have invented gold coins: pieces of metal certified by his stamp to be of standard quality and weight. This reduced the transaction costs of payments (better information by standardisation). Like many other rulers, the Ming Emperors of China issued money. Their innovation during the 'Great War period' (1368–98) was to imprint pieces of silk and paper with the unmistakable warning: 'He who imitates the Emperor's money will be executed'. Nowadays, governments have created central banks which issue money and are meant to control its supply to prevent its volume growing at an inflationary rate.

The institutional constraints on the opportunistic expansion of money supply have frequently been weak. Opportunistic kings and other agents of government diluted the gold and silver value of coins by adding cheaper metals in order to finance their expenditure more easily, and the first experiment with paper money by the Ming Emperor ended in destructive run-away inflation and subsequent economic decline.

It is therefore a priority for public policy to create – directly or indirectly – effective institutional constraints that prevent the inflationary expansion of money supply in order to control the obviously massive temptations to do otherwise. In the case of credit-based money, now the prevalent form of money around the world, there are essentially two institutional mechanisms:

(a) Those licensed to print money are subject to transparent rules and are made independent of the vote-seeking agents of government and parliamentarians who are subject to the usual temptations of political opportunism. An outstanding example of this is the German central bank, which was made independent of detailed government directives in the 1950s and which is committed by legislation to a policy of stable money. In another case, that of New Zealand, the central bank is subject to clear-cut general instructions. The Reserve Bank of New Zealand Act assigns only two roles to the central bank, namely (a) to operate money supply so as to keep consumer price inflation within limits that are stipulated by periodic contracts between the government and the central bank governor (at the time of writing 0–3 per cent), and (b) to supervise the commercial banks so that they comply with certain standards of prudential behaviour and reporting.

(b) Those who issue money are subject to open competition with other money issuers. If one central bank expands the quantity of its money too rapidly, alert investors will shift their portfolios out of this money into other moneys. This disciplines money suppliers who fail to stick to the rule of supplying stable money. In the case of competing central banks, the institutional framework that ensures competitive discipline consists of the free convertibility of the currency and freely floating exchange rates. Exchange rate movements quickly signal the judgements of alert financial markets and have immediate controlling feedback into the conduct of the central bank.

Whether the former or the latter institutions are more effective in securing the services of stable money depends on the costs of monitoring differing moneys and of shifting between different monetary assets, as well as the likelihood of central banks obeying their institutional constraints (even under political pressure). In practice, the free convertibility of most major national currencies nowadays combines the constitutional with the competitive constraints (variants (a) and (b) above).

O Key Concepts

By enabling direct exchange (barter) to be converted into indirect exchanges, **money** saves information (transaction) costs and thereby enhances the gains from the division of labour, making many transactions and property uses rewarding. Money serves as a means of exchange (or payment) by being a unit of account to express values and ultimately also by being a store of value over time.

Money can only perform its functions if its supply is credibly limited. In the case of paper money, this requires institutions that prevent the opportunistic expansion of the money supply. In addition, money suppliers can be exposed to competitive control. Such competition requires convertibility and flexible exchange rates.

We have to distinguish the functions of money from the token or symbol to which it is attached. **Money tokens** may consist of physical items, such as gold, cowrie shells, or money bills issued by a central bank with a monopoly to issue legal tender. These come from outside the private community (**outside money**) and the liabilities of reputable organisations, such as merchant banks, which gain currency (**inside money**).

Monetary stability is important to **credit**, the loaning of property for a fee. Credit is transacted in **capital markets** between savers (people who plan to accumulate positive net monetary assets) and borrowers (who plan to accumulate negative net monetary assets, typically for the purpose of investment in capital goods). In these markets, **financial intermediaries** operate to convey information, for example by creating a reputation and offering that reputation to give savers the confidence to part with their assets in exchange for the payment of interest as a user fee. ●

Rules versus Authorities in Controlling Money Supply

The supply of money by a central bank can be steered by rules or by trusted authorities (Simons, [1936] 1948). A money supply rule might stipulate that the money volume can only be expanded each year by the projected rate of real economic growth plus the rate of unavoidable inflation. A central bank that consistently adheres to this rule would probably stabilise the expansion path of national monetary demand: at times of fast demand expansion, market interest rates rise, a circumstance that curbs the demand for money. At times of demand expansion slower than the money supply growth, interest rates drop and stimulate money demand. Simons and many other economists prefer such rule-bound behaviour to trusting a discretionary central bank authority which judges circumstances from time to time and acts according to its forecasts and judgements. He pointed out that authorities may commit forecasting errors and may be subject to political directives and opportunism, so that adherence to a rule seemed, on balance, preferable in the conduct of monetary policy. However, economists who are in the habit of assuming perfect knowledge tend to argue for discretionary monetary policy. In recent decades, the discussion of 'rules versus authorities' in controlling money supply has received great attention, and many monetary authorities have adopted policies which tie monetary expansion to the growth of the national economy or some similar measure.

To sum up, money only fulfils its functions properly if its supply is subject to constraints, either physical or institutional. In practice, they have unfortunately been honoured more in violation rather than in adherence.

Questions for Review

- Explain how property rights probably came into existence early in human history.
- Define 'private good', 'pure public good', 'free good', 'club good', 'public domain good' and 'socialised property'. Find an example of each category from your daily experience.
- Are you familiar with a case where property is held in common by a club or similar open group of people? Do members use it as if it were their own? If there are opportunistic club members, how does the club encourage or enforce responsible use of the property?
- If children fight over toys, does it make sense to allot to each of them specific toys as their personal property? Why?
- If you were deprived of the property rights in your labour (in other words, if you were a slave), would you work harder, or loaf? By what means could you be induced to put in more effort?
- When Brazil proposed to abolish slavery, the slave owners argued that this would ruin Brazilian agriculture and reduce the national product. Would you have agreed with this prediction (which turned out to be wrong)? If not, how would you have argued? Can you explain why labour productivity in Brazilian agriculture rose after the suppression of slavery?

- Imagine that you are an adviser to the leader of the ruling party in a poor country. If you were asked how government revenue could be enhanced in a sustainable way, would you advise protecting property and fostering markets? If the leader argued that this reduces political powers: what would your reply be?
- Think of a country where there is widespread violation of property rights, because the government is ineffectual and because administrators do not believe in private property for ideological reasons (as is the case in Russia and other ex-communist states). Can you imagine the emergence of internal institutions and private organisations to protect private property? If so, what institutional arrangements would you predict would come about spontaneously?
- Why did China, despite advanced technology and the beginnings of a factory system in the eighth to tenth centuries, not develop a sustained industrial revolution?
- List the consequences of well-protected property rights for the community. Compare this with the alternative of heavy reliance on socialised property.
- Why is the protection of intellectual property rights conducive to economic growth?
- In Figure 7.2, we gave examples of selected changes in property status. Please think of other practical examples of the various cases.
- What would you say to people who argue that private property in natural assets should be abolished in the interest of nature conservation? How many chicken (or elephants, or guppies, or trees) would there be in your country if private property in chicken (or elephants, or guppies, or trees) were prohibited? Is private property sufficient to ensure nature conservation?
- Does widespread private property ownership in your country make people more or less free of arbitrary political rule? Think of international or historical comparisons when giving an answer.
- Is widespread private property likely to promote peace, internally and externally? Illustrate your answer with historical examples.
- Define 'relational contract' and give examples.
- Define self-enforcement of contracts and give examples of self-enforcement.
- List the pros and cons of supplementing internal sanctions with formal external sanctions for non-compliance with agreed contract conditions.
- Give several examples of search goods and experience goods. Which category increases faster relatively when the economy modernises? What consequences does that have for the marketing conduct of business?
- What are the services of money to society?

- How are these services ensured in the case of 'special money' (such as gold) and in the case of 'credit-base money'?
- What are the mechanisms by which one contract partner has confidence that the other party will comply with contract conditions?
- How do banks make 'credible commitments' to depositors?
- Have you ever reflected on your trust in institutions when you work hard to gain income, forgo immediate gratification by saving and then turn your hard-earned savings over to someone who gives you a piece of paper or a mere entry in an electronic data register? If you have ever been so trusting, on what institutions did you rely?
- Return to the start of this chapter and test whether you now agree with the two statements on capitalism by Darwin and the Pope.

Notes

1. Official protection for the exclusive exploitation of knowledge, such as patents, tend to be unwieldy and costly to obtain. To appropriate the gains from new ideas, innovators dedicate much effort to embodying knowledge in devices that inhibit imitation. For example, new knowledge is built into mechanical or electronic contraptions that imitators cannot easily construct; or companies which own intellectual knowledge refuse to hand out licences, which might enable imitation later on, and instead insist on producing using that knowledge in their own plants.
2. As we shall see in Chapter 9, similar coordination costs arise when people interact economically within organisations. We shall call these costs 'organisation costs'.
3. The reader may ask why middlemen, who fulfil such an important function in filling institutional gaps and in wealth-creation, are so frequently despised and persecuted (Sowell, 1994, pp. 46–59). Their cultural or ethnic peculiarities seem an insufficient explanation. Rather, many middlemen have created monopolies and enticed national government leaders into closing off markets on their behalf, often exchanging licences for lucrative kickbacks. This does not always protect middlemen from subsequent persecution by those same government leaders. The way to reduce the cost of middlemen is to enhance the institutional infrastructure, fostering the institutions of a relatively impersonal market order, which is accessible to all, thus reducing the relative advantages of middlemen.
4. This is not to say that only electoral democracy is capable of protecting private property and autonomy. Some autocratic rulers have given effective protection to economic freedoms, including security of property rights from confiscation. The case of colonial Hong Kong comes to mind, where private property has been well protected (under British law and in a wide-open economy), with all the growth benefits that follow from this. But without electoral control, such protection is normally fragile, in particular when the rulers have the power to close the national economy (tariff protection, controls on capital flows and migration).
5. Social critics of the financial industry tend to assume (implicitly) perfect knowledge, and then of course fail to understand the information function of money and financial intermediation between savers and investors.
6. Tokens of money should have other useful attributes, namely that they are portable, homogeneous, recognisable, divisible and indestructible (Clower, 1969, pp. 12–14).

CHAPTER 8

The Dynamics of Competition

The focus of this chapter is on capitalism in action, namely on competition, the dynamic processes of interaction in markets among buyers and sellers. Economic competition is a process that induces rival sellers (as well as rival buyers) to incur costs to search for and test new knowledge. Buyers and sellers enter into contracts to exchange property rights with each other, setting prices which coordinate and inform others. The competitive process among property owners also controls inevitable errors through the loss signal.

As long as buyers are alert and incur transaction costs to inform themselves, the economic rivalry among suppliers stimulates product and process innovation. We shall highlight the role of the enterprising supplier and the role of institutions supporting pioneers who test innovative ideas in the hope of a profit. We shall also show that political intervention in competitive processes undercuts competitive rivalry and eases the need to incur the costs of innovation.

Finally, we move beyond competition in a single market and look at the intensity of competition in entire economic systems. We shall find that competing entrepreneurs in one industry often create the conditions for commercial success in others, so that clusters of competing entrepreneurs help each other to innovate and be profitable. Competitive economies have considerable economic and non-economic advantages; property owners are, time and again, challenged to employ their assets and search for knowledge, so that power is controlled and economic progress is pursued. It will therefore be argued that economic competition deserves promotion and protection.

The monopolizer engrosseth to himself what should be free for all men ...
the monopolist that taketh away a man's trade, taketh away his life ... all
monopolies concerning trade and traffique are against the liberty and
freedom.
(*British lawyer Sir Edward Coke (1552–1634), cited in Walker, 1988, pp. 111–12*)

The very industriousness of commercial life ... eats away at grinding drudg-
ery. Commercial life creates novel and enterprising ways of evading it, not
only on assembly lines and in mills but in homes, too, and on farms.
(*Jane Jacobs*, Systems of Survival, *1992*)

Capitalism is by nature a form or method of economic change and ...
never ... can be stationary ... The fundamental impulse that sets and keeps
the capitalist engine in motion comes from the new consumers' goods, the
new methods of production or transportation, the markets, the new forms
of industrial organisation that capitalist enterprise creates.
(*Joseph A. Schumpeter*, Capitalism, Socialism and Democracy, *1942*)

8.1   Competition: Rivalry and Choice

Competition as a Discovery Procedure

Private property rights are exchanged by voluntary contracts to put
them to active uses. Thus, a capital owner may have to acquire capital
goods, labour services, the services of knowledgeable, skilled experts
and raw materials in order to start producing. What uses owners can
envisage for their property depends on their knowledge, which is, as
we saw in Chapter 3, constitutionally limited: individuals have 'sideways uncertainty' about what others are doing and 'forward
uncertainty' about what will happen in the future. As circumstances
change, the stock of knowledge which they acquired in the past de-
preciates. Acquiring new, more up-to-date knowledge is costly and
risky, as we have learnt, because people have only limited capacity to
collect information and to digest it to produce new knowledge through
processes of reflection. Moreover, the process is liable to errors: what
people perceive may be wrong, they may wrongly extrapolate from
their knowledge of the past, they may predict certain consequences of
their actions wrongly, and they may face unforeseen difficulties in
implementing their decisions to use their physical assets, labour and
knowledge.

This raises three important questions, namely:

● How can constitutional ignorance be reduced?
● How can useful knowledge be dispersed?
● How can knowledge use be controlled to ensure that errors are not
  perpetuated and the system is not destabilised?

The point we shall make in this chapter is that the competitive use of property rights by individual buyers and sellers promises the best solutions to these problems which humankind has yet discovered; certainly better solutions than central planning and someone's plans imposed by a visible hand.

Economic competition is a dynamic-evolutionary process of human interaction in which people are motivated to pursue their self-interest because they are able to internalise the costs and benefits of property use. In the process, they benefit others as a by-product of the pursuit of their own self-interest. This interaction takes place in markets, the meeting grounds of buyers and sellers of closely substitutable goods and services (Figure 8.1). The process of interaction and exchange, in which people discover and test new knowledge, is sometimes called *catallaxis*. Whereas economics often focuses on scarcity and economising, *catallaxis* stresses the dynamic discovery procedures: how people discover new wants and new means to satisfy them.

Typically, there are fewer buyers than sellers. The sellers rival each other to position themselves advantageously for potential exchanges with the buyers and they incur transaction costs to do so. Likewise, buyers vie with other buyers to be well positioned for contracts with suppliers, and they incur costs to inform and position themselves so that they can strike an advantageous deal. The sellers will try to substitute better goods than those that other sellers are offering, and entrepreneurial buyers will also try to gain a competitive position that enables them to attract a choice of offers from sellers. The buyers and the sellers thus rival each other to acquire knowledge about better substitutes and exchange partners. The alternative is what has been described as 'nightcap competition': the cosy continuation of the way in which suppliers have always made and marketed goods and in which buyers accept what happens to be on offer out of an aversion to incurring information costs.

New information and new knowledge do not come cost-free to rival sellers and buyers. The intensity of rivalry among potential participants on both sides of the market depends on their readiness to incur transaction costs, which – as we saw – have the insidious quality of having to be sunk before there is a known probability of a return.[1] The preparedness to incur information costs will in turn depend not only on the curiosity, creativity, boldness, acquisitive urge and readiness to incur risks of the various competitors, but also on the institutions within which they operate (Kirzner, 1973, 1997). If the institutions in a community make information search relatively cheap and establish trust so that people can afford to cope with less explicit information,

Figure 8.1   The market: a meeting place

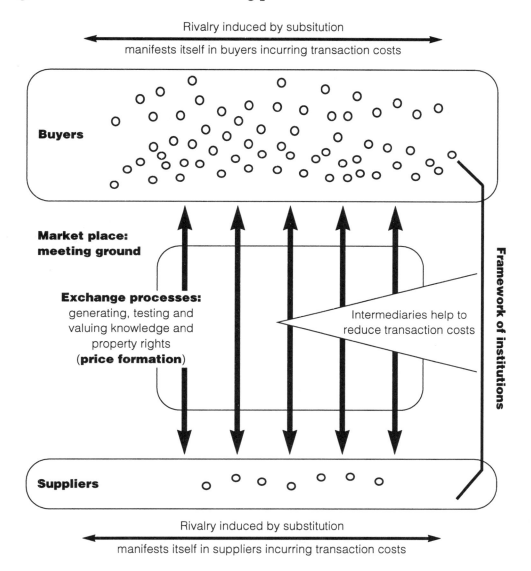

the information search will be intense. On the other hand, if institutions are poor and fuzzy, so that information and transaction costs are high, buyers and sellers will not invest much in information search. They will, correspondingly, discover less useful knowledge and will in the aggregate probably achieve less economic growth.

What matters here in particular is the capacity and preparedness to make surprising discoveries: finding knowledge of which the discoverer had no inkling prior to the discovery – not just the capacity to search for second-hand information on matters about which people had some prior knowledge (section 3.1). Israel Kirzner (1997, p. 72), in a survey article on Austrian economics, put it well when he wrote:

> Without knowing what to look for, without deploying any deliberate search technique, the entrepreneur is at all times scanning the horizon, as it were, ready to make discoveries. Each such discovery will be accompanied by a sense of surprise (at one's earlier unaccountable ignorance). An entrepreneurial attitude is one which is always ready to be surprised, always ready to take the steps needed to profit by such surprises. The notion of discovery [is] ... midway between that of the deliberately produced information in standard search theory, and that of sheer windfall gain generated by pure chance.

The knowledge search by alert and interested buyers is essential to the supply of innovative products in a market. Buyers have to invest time and effort to find out what is new and have to vie with each other to find the special deals and the novelties. If potential buyers of computer software were to make do with what they have and not search for new, improved programs, advances in software programming would soon slow down. Therefore, the keenness of the buyers – whether or not they devour the computer magazines and search the Internet for new programmes – is essential to driving suppliers to invest in improvements of knowledge. This explains why innovative markets require a demanding clientele and why sophisticated, active demand is so useful to successful industries (Porter, 1990).

When there are no near-substitutes, hence no rivalry on one side of the market, we speak of monopoly (single seller) or monopsony (single buyer). People who lack rivals have no incentive to incur information costs, and knowledge search flags. However, in an evolving economy buyers and sellers can never be sure that they will hold such a position for long. For example, buyers may find new substitutes in other countries and import them; or suppliers in another industry may invent close substitutes for what a monopolist has been offering. Thus, the railway monopolies of the nineteenth century, which to some contemporary observers seemed to spell the end of capitalism at the time, discovered that new rivals emerged in the form of motor cars and trucks. This shows that most monopolies are contestable. And this is what forces single sellers to engage in knowledge search, just in case. Thus market power is often controlled by potential, not only by actual, rivalry.

These processes of rivalry on both sides of the market are closely related to the exchanges between buyers and sellers across the market. They sort out conditions of contract and conclude deals in a continual process in which people vote with their money on the basis of their diverse, changing, subjective knowledge, expressing their own preferences and valuations (Figure 8.1). Once buyers or sellers have acquired sufficient knowledge about products, exchange partners, qualities and other conditions of exchange, and have put personal values on what they know, they will select a contract partner and try to strike a deal. In the process, personal knowledge about alternatives (substitutes) will be important in negotiating the deal, in particular the price. The price communicates new knowledge, albeit in coded form, to others, expressing also the valuations of other participants in the economic game. For many decisions, the coded price signal will be sufficient to convey the needed information; indeed, more detailed knowledge about what is behind a price change might only overtax people's cognitive capacities. Suppliers will be content to know that a higher price is better, and buyers will prefer a lower price and act accordingly.

The rivalry on both sides of the market place and the core exchange process between the two sides takes place all the time and simultaneously in an evolutionary web of numerous concurrent actions and reactions. Competition has, therefore, to be understood as a process in which useful knowledge is sought, tested and affirmed; in which, so to speak, individuals dedicate resources to peering into the fog of ignorance. It does not operate without errors but, as in all evolutionary processes, errors can be corrected if necessary. In this way, the competitive process is a discovery procedure – not one that will ever produce 'perfect knowledge', given the constitutional forward and sideways lack of knowledge, but one that will reduce ignorance to manageable levels for market participants.

We should remind ourselves here of what was said about information search and decision making: paradoxically, we can never assess 'rationally' how much information cost we should expend; we can only incur information costs up to a certain extent, and stop incurring search costs when experience indicates that we probably know enough to make a decision. We can try to arrive at a decision when ignorance is reduced to manageable levels (bounded rationality).

It should be evident that people only expend transaction costs on searching for knowledge so as to stay ahead of their rival suppliers (or buyers, as the case may be). On the other hand, people on the other side of the market will welcome the rivalry on the opposite side because that gives them more and better choices. To vary an old saying, what is good for General Motors – the saving of transaction costs when there is little producer rivalry – is therefore bad for the car-buying public of the world. Buyers and sellers always have opposite interests in the competitive game.

The Functions of Competition

We can now return to the three questions raised earlier in this section.

Reduction of Ignorance: A system of private property rights motivates people to search for rewarding uses of their assets. It allows them to keep the rewards, thereby inducing rivalry among suppliers (or competing buyers) who respond competitively to search for new knowledge which they can use to improve their position. In that way, competition is a process in which many are engaged all the time in costly and risky information search – not a comfortable situation for those involved but one that is good for the freedom of choice of the other side of the market and for the wealth of nations. Where and how people search for knowledge differs from individual to individual, as subjective experience and inclination dictate. A great variety of search methods will be employed. The broad base of the search effort and the multiplicity of search methods promise more advances in useful knowledge than the alternatives, such as delegating only a few specialists to find new information.

Dispersal of Knowledge: The second question relates to how tested, useful knowledge is made accessible to others. In a competitive economy, successes in the market place become known. Profitable suppliers attract imitators, and successful buyers are often emulated by their neighbours. Moreover, the price signal spreads coded information about what the other side of the market wants and what one's rivals can offer. A price change can be recognised quickly and will trigger appropriate action to enhance property value. This spreads information quickly to interrelated markets.

Thus, very few people needed to understand the full reasons for the petroleum shortages of 1974–5 and the early 1980s, whether it was a war in the Middle East, rapidly growing transport demand, the exhaustion of oil wells or actions of the OPEC oil cartel. Whatever the complex, hard-to-decipher reasons, the oil price shot up. Drivers in New York and London reduced their demand immediately and began to think about switching from gas guzzlers to petrol misers. Industries around the world adjusted their energy use patterns. But the chain of price information went further: in thousands of laboratories, people began to incur search costs to find oil-economising technologies, such as fuel-efficient engines, electronic controls, weight saving, replacing

oil with other energy sources and so on. The price impulse also rip-
pled through to energy suppliers, spreading outwards like the waves
from a stone thrown into a pond: the drilling of new oil and gas wells
was speeded up; new technologies were tried out to extract oil from
continental shelves and other difficult locations; new coal fields were
opened, and research into coal liquefaction was started. Extraction
and refining methods were enhanced in hundreds of different locations.

These and many other reactions eventually overcame the oil crises,
thanks to a myriad of costly search efforts both on the supply and the
demand side. The competitive system 'radioed' the necessary signals
through the simple, easily perceived price signal and quickly dispersed the knowledge that oil was in short supply. The signal gave
incentives to property owners, who acted in self-interest and did so
with urgency, hoping to beat their rivals. No other system could have
spread the knowledge as effectively and quickly as the price mechanism in competitive markets and no other system could have mobilised
so much follow-up knowledge search.

Control of Errors: When people commit errors in a competitive system,
they soon learn from the reactions of the other side of the market and
from how they are beaten by their rivals. They learn that they are not
using their property rights to the best benefit of others and hence their
own benefit: they incur the 'reprimand of red ink', making a loss. In
an institutional system that ensures private property rights, they are
responsible for that loss and are therefore likely to correct their error.
If property is held collectively, economic agents can go on throwing
good money after bad, arguing why they should persist ('voice').
When they are deserted by exchange partners in markets ('exit'), they
have to make corrections quickly and search pragmatically for rem-
edies. As a consequence, the competitive system has built-in,
spontaneous self-controls. Errors usually remain limited because they
can be exploited by competitors who know better.

This system of knowledge search through competitive market processes has been given the name 'catallaxy', as we learnt in section 8.1:
the interaction between buyers and sellers to find out what ideas are
useful. The system, and its capacity to generate knowledge and prosperity, was well understood by the philosopher-economists of the
eighteenth century, such as Adam Ferguson and Adam Smith. They
also stressed the need for rules of the competitive game to ensure that
competitive rivalry remained intense and that property owners were
challenged time and again to expose their assets to the challenges of

competition. Protection from competition – for example, monopolies, political privileges and tariffs – were seen by the founding fathers of economics as great impediments to the search-and-dissemination process of knowledge, and hence to progress.

The essence of the competitive process, as set out here, was lost when economists made the assumption of 'perfect knowledge' one hundred years later (Mahovec, 1998). This assumption allowed them to construct the elegant, simple, comparative-static models of neoclassical economics.[2] The phenomenon of competition, which deals with an evolutionary process of decentralised knowledge search, cannot be grasped by the static neoclassical analysis of supply and demand based on the assumption that knowledge is known. The concepts of transaction costs, which is a consequence of ignorance, and institutions to economise on transaction costs cannot be analysed meaningfully unless we consider competition as a discovery procedure of knowledge which no one has. Only when we see competition in the context of human ignorance and as part of a complex, evolving system can we comprehend what important functions it serves: to cite Hayek, competition is a 'procedure for the discovery of such facts, as without resort to it, would not be known to anyone, at least would not be utilised' (Hayek, 1978, p. 179).

Competition can therefore not be depicted merely by snapshots; for example, by counting the number of competitors and saying that monopoly (one seller) or oligopoly (a few sellers) is inferior to atomistic competition (countless sellers), as is done in neoclassical textbooks. Comparative-static economic models are as unsuited to capturing the essence of competition as the comparison between two still photos: the runners in the starting blocks and on the finishing line. It takes a film to depict the full drama of a footrace or of any other sort of competition.

O Key Concepts

The **market** place is a meeting ground between people who want to buy and sell, offering or demanding property rights in exchange for other property rights. Typically, suppliers offer goods and services in exchange for money, and people exchange goods and services indirectly through money, as opposed to the direct exchange which occurs when people barter.

Competition is the evolutionary process of interaction between buyers and sellers in markets: buyers compete among themselves to obtain relevant knowledge of where and what to buy, what new products to try out and how to get advantageous deals; sellers rival other suppliers of close substitutes to place themselves in an advantageous position *vis-à-vis* potential buyers by exploring new knowledge on product variations and production processes, on organisation, communication and selling methods, and on possible exchange partners. At the same time, exchange processes between buyers and sellers take place across the market. These convey information: whether deals are profitable (and might be imitated) or whether losses are made, so that errors can be corrected by the search for alternatives. Actual and potential exchanges trigger rivalry on both sides of the market. The entire process of competition creates strong incentives to search for and test useful knowledge because the competitors risk their own private property and are responsible for their actions and their errors. The intensity of competition depends on the propensity of both sides of the market to incur transaction costs and on the institutions that protect competition.

The concept of **catallaxis** derives from the Greek *katallatein*, which means to exchange and thereby turn an enemy into a friend. It relates to mutual interaction and accommodation, as distinct from imposition. Catallaxy evokes the image of processes in which new demands, new production methods and new products are discovered. This contrasts with 'economising', which relates to the maximisation of utility or profit with given demands, given production technologies and given types of products. What matters to economic growth is the catallactic capability of society. The concept was revived in modern economics by Ludwig von Mises (1949, ch. xiv) and has gained growing acceptance with the spread of evolutionary economics.

Monopoly is a situation in a market where there is only one supplier. Because a single supplier faces no rivalry from others who might offer buyers more advantageous substitutes, the monopolist does not have to incur transaction costs in the search for new knowledge and in offering better and cheaper products. However, many single suppliers have in reality to fear competitive challenges from potential substitutes unless the market is closed by government intervention. As a consequence, they will behave competitively, that is, engage in information search against potential contests by outsiders. ●

Dharma: the Principle of Non-competition

The concept of competition can be explored a little further by reference to its opposite, non-competition: not being alert, not making an effort to gain advantage and knowledge. In traditional Hindu philosophy, non-competition is made an ideal, *dharma*. The word derives from the Sanskrit word *dhar*: to carry, to bear, and is often translated as 'unquestioningly obeyed custom, duty, making a virtue of the fatalistic acceptance of how things are'. The concept is often used to describe the submissive acceptance of their fate by the members of a caste and the unquestioning acceptance of the knowledge of the forefathers. *Dharma* must be contrasted with the attitude 'I can make a difference', which is typical of western and Far Eastern individualism and with the attitude of sceptical curiosity. People whose behaviour is ruled by the principle of *dharma* can of course be controlled more easily, but they are also less likely to explore new ways or the means to better their own circumstances and, with it, those of others. Competitive attitudes in economic life are necessary for catallactic or dynamic efficiency, the capability of people to discover and test ideas, to generate economic improvements (Chapter 2; Cordato, in Boettke, 1994, pp. 131–6; Kirzner, ibid., pp. 103–10).

Living under the principle of *dharma* may be more comfortable than under the dictate of competition, because people unthinkingly follow established rules, whether this hurts them materially or not. They do not have to put up with the transaction costs of knowledge search. When established institutions regulate every detail of life, information and search costs are low. Power hierarchies remain intact. The disciples of *dharma* accept existing institutions, irrespective of their consequences. This is the hallmark of a conservative, unfree society and a stagnant economy. Economic growth and a free society, in which conflicts are minimised, require occasional institutional innovations: the challenge and testing of old rules and their reaffirmation or adaptation in the light of new circumstances. Competition therefore depends not only on given rules that make human interaction predictable, but also on the adaptation of rules when circumstances merit this in the eyes of (most of) the participants.

Search Goods – Experience Goods: Who Bears Transaction Costs?

Sellers often adjust the institutions of markets so as to reduce the effective transaction costs to the buyers, including their information costs. An important case was pointed out by Phillip Nelson (1970) when he introduced the distinction between 'experience goods' and 'search goods'. The quality of some goods and services can be evaluated readily by inspection prior to a purchase, for example, a dress on a rack or fruit in a produce market. Buyers can search for the quality they desire with little expense on information costs (search goods). But in many instances the quality of goods and services can only be established by the experience of using or consuming them (experience goods). When product qualities are variable, buyers of experience goods often incur high information costs in measuring quality prior to the purchase. Some examples of such experience goods are tinned fruit, motor cars, tourist packages and open-heart surgery.

Where buyers can easily search for the desired quality (and may even enjoy the experience of shopping around), market conventions tend to leave the information search costs to the buyers (Barzel, 1982). However, those costs are normally shifted to the suppliers in the case of experience goods. Suppliers find it useful to bear the costs (and to incorporate them in their prices) of standardising the quality and giving buyers credible commitments of quality, for example through advertised brand names, setting up chains of outlets, or franchising. One way in which suppliers can signal the quality of the experience goods they offer is to acquire a reputation for quality, a costly and time-consuming exercise which saves buyers the costs of much information search. Customers are therefore prepared to pay a quality premium in the form of a higher price to avoid disappointing experiences. They can assume that it would be irrational for producers with a good reputation and for owners of known brands to sell rubbish, because this would quickly become known and destroy the benefits of a good reputation. Many techniques aimed at cutting the information costs of buyers of experience goods amount to standardising and averaging, even if buyers have subjective preferences for differing product qualities. What might be an exciting tourist package for you may bore me to death! None the less, many intending travellers are loath to incur higher information costs; they therefore opt for the standardised package.

Another way in which suppliers can compete by reducing the transaction costs of the buyers of experience goods is to offer catalogues, free samples and other trial experiences. Thus, nightclubs may offer customers free entry for the first five minutes, and pay TV channels let you watch the first ten minutes of a movie before you pay.

The costs of transacting business are sometimes shifted between sellers and buyers in response to changing competitive conditions. When the rivalry between sellers is intense, they incur a large share of the transaction costs to ensure that deals can be struck with buyers. When supplies become scarce, buyers shoulder a larger share of the transaction costs. Such a shift in market power from a buyers' to a sellers' market, which is reflected in who bears what share of the transaction costs, can, for example, be observed in the hotel market: in the low season, when hotels have a low occupancy rate, they advertise, drum up business by staging special events and offer free bottles of champagne. In the high season, customers have to ring around to find a hotel room and accept being put on waiting lists. Similarly, the incidence of who bears the transaction costs fluctuates in the course of the business cycle. Indeed, much of the profitability of boom times results from businesses saving on transaction costs and customers shouldering them because sellers' markets prevail.

It should be noted in this context that neoclassical economists and their followers who assume 'perfect knowledge' frequently castigate advertising as an abuse of the capitalist system and argue for controls on advertising expenditure. However, advertising makes sense if one starts with the realistic assumption of competition as a process of knowledge search and accepts that buyers have to bear considerable information costs, so that they welcome advertised information. Moreover, those who propose to control advertising (other than to ban fraudulent or deceptive advertising) imply that it is possible to determine what information is objectively useful to the buyers. This completely overlooks the subjective nature of all perception and all knowledge acquisition.

O Key Concepts

Search goods are products whose (variable) quality the buyers can establish readily, at low information cost and prior to the purchase decision (for example, fruit in a market). By contrast, the quality of **experience goods** can only be measured by using the product, that is, after purchase. To avoid buyers having to bear high or insurmountable information costs, competing suppliers develop devices to give prior assurance (such as brand names, reputable sellers, samples, the employment of a middleman).

Buyers' market conditions exist when sellers compete intensely with each other in searching for purchase opportunities and therefore hold a relatively weak bargaining position. This is reflected in the sellers incurring a large share of the transaction costs. **Sellers' markets** are those in which the sellers hold a relatively strong position and do not have to incur many transaction costs, because it is the buyers who are prepared to shoulder these costs in order to find a deal. The shift from buyers' to sellers' market conditions can consequently have a great impact on the profitability of a business. ●

Intermediation

Information problems, particularly in experience goods markets, can also be reduced by trading through middlemen, who are better known to buyers than the producers, who want to continue doing business with the buyers and who can offer credible guarantees of quality (section 7.4). This is the case, for example, in the markets for housing, second-hand cars, horses and tourist services, where intermediary agents are common. The middlemen have experience in assessing quality and enjoy scale economies in measuring product quality; they also have a reputation to lose if they pass on bad products. The once-off final buyer knows this and therefore trusts the advice of the middleman, whose livelihood depends on a good reputation. Thus, we shop in a department store because we trust its image and because we buy many products there, and we avoid direct marketing from producers with whom we might deal only once.

Other devices of intermediation which save on transaction costs are franchising and the creation of brand names. In both cases, buyers of experience goods prefer to pay more in exchange for the services of a known intermediary – even if the actual product is made by someone unknown, as long as the product has the middleman's stamp of approval.

Middlemen help buyers and sellers to economise on their respective transaction costs. Their services cost resources, but their fees are only resented by people who assume perfect knowledge.

In traditional societies, competition relies heavily on personalised trade and credit, on personal ties with people with whom there is an ongoing economic relationship and who keep their contractual promises because they benefit from that ongoing relationship. Such personalised economic ties are reinforced by personal friendship, sometimes even by adoption or marriage. However, as external institutions and third-party enforcement by government bodies improves, open competition and exchanges among strangers becomes possible. This is now happening in many third world countries which are enhancing the institutions of the market economy: people now deal not so much according to who they know, but according to what is offered.

Market institutions are often developed by entrepreneurs to minimise the effective information costs to the other side of the market. Frequently, the competition is won by suppliers who concentrate on lowering their and their customers' transaction costs, rather than their production costs, particularly in markets for services (see box).

❖ An Innovation to Reduce Transaction Costs: Micro Loan Banking

In less-developed countries, many people have the knowledge to operate small businesses more profitably if only they had access to capital and credit. However, the fixed costs of assessing credit risks and of administering enforcement mechanisms in institutionally fuzzy environments severely restrict the availability of credit to small borrowers. Credit is therefore available only on a personal basis, to people with a good reputation and large asset backing (personalised credit). Small, asset-poor borrowers can only go to money lenders, where they face forbiddingly high interest rates because institutional deficiencies lead to high loan monitoring costs and costly enforcement in the case of default.

These problems were tackled in an imaginative and effective way by the Grameen Bank of Bangladesh. The bank was founded by a US-trained economist, Dr Muhammad Yunus, who understood the institutional deficiencies and addressed them in the following way. Small operators and vendors could obtain small loans if their loan application was guaranteed by a circle of from five to ten persons. This enabled them to start up small businesses, for example to operate a cellular phone for rent in the village. When the first borrower from a borrowers' circle had duly repaid the loan, other members qualified for credit. The risk-assessment costs, as well the enforcement costs, are thus borne not by the bank, but by the borrowers' circle. Members act responsibly, because they themselves have a keen self-interest in establishing their creditworthiness. If there is a default, the entire circle is in default and is no longer creditworthy.

The organisation of borrowers' circles also serves as an important information exchange and turns a once-off loan contract into an open-ended, ongoing game (offering 'hostages'). Borrowers learn how to keep accounts and what to do to repay on time. Thrift is thus learnt in a community-support setting. Many borrowers have also become micro-shareholders in the Grameen Bank.

The Grameen Bank has a very low default rate, and most borrowers are women, an extraordinary circumstance in a Muslim country. By reducing the information, monitoring and enforcement costs through the formation of borrowers' circles, the Bank has been successful where less innovative enterprises have failed. It is the case of an enterprise that thrives through institutional innovation. ◆

(Source: Fuglesang and Chandler, 1987*)*

On the other hand, as the division of labour evolves and becomes more complex, there are new demands for intermediation and new types of middlemen to cater to it. An example of this is the modern credit-card organisation which allows buyers to acquire goods and services on credit without having first to build up a reputation with the shop in order to negotiate credit terms. A second example is the enormous rise of financial intermediation in global financial markets. International payment transactions may appear quite impersonal to the outside observer, but in reality this extended market network is supported by much personalised intermediation which reduces risks and transaction costs. International payments depend on chains of intermediaries who have frequent contact and mutually guarantee contract fulfilment.

Thus, a personalised microcosm of relationships thrives within the extended order of competitive markets, as individual traders normally deal with partners whom they know and trust and who will return a favour, if needed.

8.2   Competition from the Suppliers' Perspective

What has been said so far about competition and knowledge search applies to both sides of the market, supply and demand. To gain more specific insights into how the capitalist system works, we now turn to the rivalry between suppliers of goods and services for the favours of buyers.

Price and Non-price Competition

Suppliers rival for the attention of buyers by employing a number of different means:

(a) price variations (price competition);
(b) product innovation: the product may be improved in the hope of attracting more loyal – price-insensitive – buyers; to this end suppliers incur research and development costs;
(c) advertising (and the creation of brand names) for a particular product is a way for a supplier to position himself in the market; this causes transaction costs;
(d) sales organisation: distribution channels are developed in the hope of beating other suppliers and attracting loyal buyers (for example, new logistics networks, wholesale outlets, own retail shops, mail order trade), again at a cost;
(e) financial assistance is extended to buyers, for example through credit or instalment payment;
(f) after-sales services – such as ongoing advice on product use, guarantees of speedy repairs and spare parts supplies – can also serve to bind buyers to one specific supplier because this cuts their information and other transaction costs when using the product; for technically complex or hard-to-use and hard-to-repair products and services, which are typical of many modern markets, after-sales service has become a very important tool of competition. The necessary arrangements on the part of the sellers can be costly, but they are made in the hope to beat other rivalling sellers;
(g) sellers may also seek to gain advantage through lobbying for political restrictions on competition, which again costs resources, but may none the less be advantageous from the standpoint of sellers.

Cases (a) to (f) constitute economic competition, efforts by suppliers to attract the interest of voluntary buyers. In that category, we distinguish between price competition (case (a)) and non-price competition (cases (b)–(f), see Figure 8.2). In contrast to economic competition, lobbying in the political arena (case (g)) seeks intervention to compel

**Figure 8.2   Instruments of competitive action from the suppliers'
perspective**

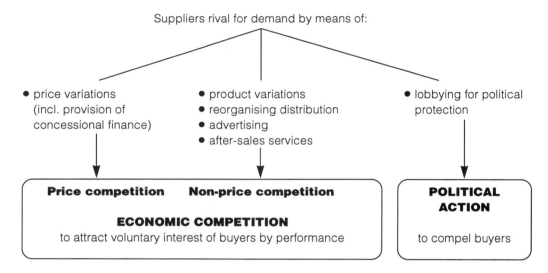

Note: The definitions focus on the competition amongst suppliers for buyers. Competition also exists among buyers for supplies, and these definitions can be adjusted *mutatis mutandis*.

or restrict buyers. In this latter case suppliers collude with government agents to gain economic advantage by influencing the external institutions which govern their markets to introduce elements of compulsion or restriction, instead of competing for the favour of the other side of the market. Thus, economic competition covers the rivalry among suppliers to attract buyers through better performance. What is good performance is judged by the buyers. This arrangement is in the interest of the buyers. Lobbying is competition for political favours and for political protection that allows sellers to offer buyers less choice.[3]

In most markets, a few suppliers who know each other vie for the favour of the buyers. This is much more common than markets with numerous anonymous suppliers (in other words, oligopolistic, not atomistic, competition is the norm). Many modern markets for industrial goods and services are, moreover, typified by experience goods, open-ended relational contracts and long-term demand–supply relationships between business partners who know each other, rather than once-off purchases amongst anonymous agents.

Each individual supplier usually has a notion of the reactions of potential buyers to possible variations in their offer prices as well as of the rivals' capabilities to react to price variations. From past experience, a supplier can often conjecture by how much the demand for his or her products is likely to drop if the price were raised a little or vice versa. Given the transaction costs of searching for new suppliers, buyers will react only slightly to small price variations. But the quantity a supplier can expect to sell varies by a disproportionately wide margin in response to a large price variation. Buyer loyalty thus tends to be limited. Each competitor therefore enjoys a 'market niche' (a section of relatively price-inelastic demand, to put it in the terminology of economic theory). Each seller has, at any moment in time, a mental image of the demand curve, which has a 'double kink' in it (Blandy *et al.*, 1985, pp. 47–60; Figure 8.2).

Competing suppliers typically operate in circumstances of limited knowledge amidst complex, dynamic changes and with considerable fixed costs. Therefore, they prefer to operate within a market niche where price increases lead to only small quantity reductions in demand. If unexpected cost increases occur and force suppliers to increase their prices, turnover does not drop much, so that (possibly high) fixed overhead costs do not have to be distributed over a much reduced sales volume. After all, this would drive up unit costs and prices even more, leading to further expected losses of sales. Suppliers therefore have a great incentive to widen and secure their market niche and to stay within it.

The market niche – the limited preference of buyers for a particular supplier – is cultivated by the tools of non-price competition (cases (b)–(f) above). Suppliers incur transaction costs to gain such a position, but their rivals will employ the same tools to the best of their knowledge and ability to compress the first supplier's market niche. This leads to a continual tug of war and to considerable insecurity of suppliers about their market niches, persuading them to incur new transaction costs. If, for example, a car producer has gained a fairly secure market niche because of the introduction of a well-received new model (product innovation), competitors will not rest until they can also offer improved models even if that forces them to incur high search costs. This compresses the first supplier's market niche again (Figure 8.3). Competition is thus an ongoing process of rivalry which exerts an unrelenting discipline, from which there is little respite. In the process, valuable new productive knowledge emerges, but the effort is costly and often uncomfortable to suppliers.

The results of non-price competition are of genuine value to buyers, who welcome product variations or assistance in reducing their own transaction costs. Buyers will only be attracted to contracts if they are convinced by the good performance of the seller.

Figure 8.3   A supplier's competitive position: a snapshot of a dynamic process

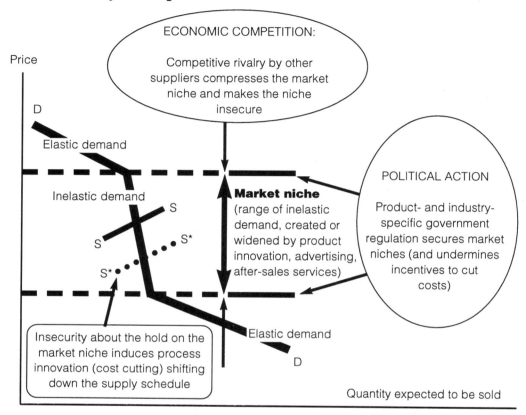

Price and non-price competition exerts an unrelenting discipline on all competing producers. As long as buyers remain alert and are prepared to incur transaction costs to find out what is on offer and what serves them best, competition is the source of unceasing pressures on suppliers to search for knowledge and quality. As we saw, this creates various costs. Competition may also be seen by suppliers as the reason for disappointing results. Therefore it is understandable that they often try to organise themselves to reduce their rivalry by private agreement or to obtain political protection from competitive pressures (rent-seeking). For times immemorial, this has occurred not only in product markets, but also in markets of production factors such as labour. Once political intervention occurs, buyers need not be offered as wide a choice as before. They are impeded from initiating as much rivalry among the sellers as before by using the 'exit option' (substitution). As a consequence, sellers are under less pressure to perform and can save on the transaction costs of rivalry. As we shall see shortly, rent-seeking therefore has profoundly deleterious consequences for innovation and the economic welfare of buyers.

Product and Process Innovation

The competing attempts of buyers to improve their position drive suppliers to innovate products, often by incremental, adaptive steps to find better substitutes for what others produce, but sometimes by discontinuous improvements. These steps shape the evolution of an industry, for example the aircraft from the contraption of the Wright brothers to the modern jumbo jet. Buyers may value the new products sufficiently to justify the transaction costs which the innovating supplier has incurred, who then earns a (probably temporary) 'pioneer profit' (Schumpeter, 1961). Yet this success often eludes innovating pioneers, and they incur losses instead. Probably most new products which are launched each year in affluent economies fail to make a profit and are not accepted sufficiently by the ultimate arbiters of product innovation, the buyers. What survives in the basket of goods and services that are produced is thus ultimately decided by buyers ('consumer sovereignty'). But buyers do not choose from an unlimited range of possibilities, only from what suppliers offer in the hope that it will be profitable. Rivalry and buyer choices thus interact to drive product innovation.

Competition also drives process innovation. Because the width and durability of their imagined market niche is never precisely known to suppliers and, in any event, is always open to dynamic challenges from rivals, suppliers face constant pressures to control their costs (Figure 8.3). They will try out new production processes or find cheaper inputs and adjust organisational arrangements: they will engage in process innovation. In other words, insecurity about the loyalty of buyers and the readiness of buyers to inform themselves of new offers from rival suppliers are essential to keeping producers in 'creative unease', forcing them to incur information costs with uncertain returns.

Unease about future sales and profits induces cost control, and also the control of organisation costs, which are easily driven up by agent opportunism in big firms, as we saw in section 3.4. Only the disciplining pressures of competition which endanger the market niche will mobilise energies to cut back unnecessary activities. Without rivalry among suppliers and active buyers, it is virtually impossible for firms to keep a check on their costs.

For the past 200 years the competitive market process has been powerful in driving process and product innovations and thereby raising productivity and living standards. It has indeed been the major driving force of the evolution of useful knowledge and of economic progress

(Schumpeter, 1961; Clark, 1962; Hayek, 1978; 1988). The innovative performance of suppliers depends in large measure on whether buyers are willing and able to incur transaction costs, so pioneer profits remain a temporary phenomenon.

O Key Concepts

Rivalry among suppliers is conducted by means of price variation as well as by **non-price competition** (product differentiation, varying distribution channels, advertising and after-sales services). Apart from these forms of **economic competition**, competitors may form alliances to lobby for political interventions that 'protect' them from the need to rival each other by economic means (**rent-seeking**).

A **market niche** is a conjecture in the mind of suppliers that they can expect small quantity responses to small price variations around the existing market price and disproportionately large variations in the quantities demanded if the price is varied by a considerable margin. It reflects limited knowledge and transaction costs on the part of the buyers, and is reinforced by instruments of non-price rivalry amongst suppliers as well as political interventions.

Innovation is the practical application of new knowledge resulting in new combinations of property rights, for example to create a new product or to implement a new (cost-saving) production process. Persons or teams who risk innovations and organise the many resources and ideas necessary for an innovation are called economic **entrepreneurs**. Entrepreneurship seeks to overcome existing constraints by new combinations of property rights and the exploration and testing of the search for either new knowledge or hitherto untapped existing knowledge from new sources.

Product innovation is carried out by producers who vary existing products or launch altogether new products as a means of securing a market niche, hoping to reap a pioneer profit.

Process innovation is motivated by uncertainty about the extent of the market niche and the wish to lower production costs by implementing new production processes. Frequently, product and process innovation are connected in practice.

A **'pioneer profit'** (Joseph Schumpeter) is reaped by an innovator who meets with the approval of buyers so that they pay prices that exceed the costs of the novelty. The pioneer profit tends to be temporary, because successful innovations are either imitated or challenged by further innovations which competing suppliers introduce to take away market share. This in turn tends to trigger efforts to implement further innovations in the hope of earning renewed, albeit again temporary, pioneer profits, keeping the process of dynamic rivalry alive and driving forward the innovative search for and use of knowledge. ●

A Partial View: Scientific Discovery, Inventions and Technical Innovations

The knowledge for which market participants search may consist of technical knowledge that can be described explicitly and conveyed to others for evaluation (a discrete invention). Such technical knowledge may sometimes derive from scientific discovery, the result of scientific research. When scientific discoveries are tested for their technical feasibility and are developed by engineers and applied scientists into laboratory models, we call this activity 'applied research and development'. The result is an invention (a discrete idea about how to use or manipulate nature). But inventions as such are not necessarily useful to members of society. They also have to be tested for their commercial feasibility, that is, whether they are sufficiently valued by buyers to be profitable. This is often a much more complex task than establishing mere technical feasibility. Whether a product or service will be commercially viable is the province of entrepreneurial judgement about whether the product will be bought and at what price. The correctness of entrepreneurial hunches will then be discovered in the competitive process.

Technical changes that move from scientific discovery to invention and innovation are described by the 'linear model of innovation'. For example, such a path was followed by nuclear energy and space satellites. However, relatively few innovations come about in this way: more often, innovations derive from the adaptive development of existing products and concepts, from responses to conjectures of market demand, from capital replacement, and from the imitation of successful rivals, that is, from 'reverse engineering' which leads to the diffusion of technology. Innovations are often adaptive and piecemeal. Frequently, we also observe important emergent innovations which owe nothing to science, for example the invention of the railway in the nineteenth century by George Stephenson, an untutored engineering tinkerer who lacked theoretical knowledge of physics and mechanics. Like some other inventors with connections to the English mining industry, he mounted existing steam engines on a cart and prevented the cart from sinking into the mud by placing it on iron rails and then went on to improve the new device (Johnson, 1991, pp. 580–3).

Knowledge which ensures high and advancing living standards in the capitalist system therefore often consists not of grand scientific or technical ideas, but of dispersed, petty knowhow about conditions that vary in space and time. If suppliers wish to produce something as commonplace as a quality pencil or a computer diskette, they need – apart from the discrete technical description of the product (the invention) – much practical commercial knowhow on how to obtain the raw materials and power supplies, where best to buy components of precisely what shape, quality and form, how to train the skills needed for production or where to hire skilled workers, how to organise the logistics of the distribution system, how to find out who can best assist with advertising to inform potential buyers, how to finance the cost of setting up production, where to acquire land or buildings, how to link the production unit to transport and distribution systems, how to set up communications networks, how to set up marketing and after-sales services, and many other specific practicalities. The entrepreneurial task is to marshal the necessary knowhow to solve each of these interlocking problems. Most of the necessary information is costly to get and has often to be found by time- and resource-consuming trial and error (Hayek, 1945; Rosenberg, 1988).

Innovating suppliers will be influenced in their knowledge search: (a) by how well existing institutions help them to find and test the new information; (b) by the intensity of rivalry with other suppliers; and (c) by the anticipated responses of potential buyers. Intensive competition tends to induce more innovation. Once market niches are perceived to be secure, the innovative drive is likely to lose momentum. Different institutional systems therefore differ enormously as to their innovative capacity. Although entrepreneurs are always present in a society, the institutions channel their energies either into innovative economic performance or into other, non-productive outlets for their energies, for example military, political or sporting rivalry (Baumol, 1990). Entrepreneurial people sometimes even migrate to institutional environments which are more conducive to using their knowledge in economic competition. Thus, backward regions and, to an even greater extent, developing countries often lose their brightest technical and economic innovators because the institutional framework there does not give innovators the necessary business confidence, whereas developed market economies do.

O Key Concepts

A **scientific discovery** is a new insight into how nature works. Sometimes this gives rise to an **invention**, that is, a discrete addition to knowledge about how use can be made of nature in a technically feasible way. But only when an invention is commercially (economically) feasible will it be turned into an innovation. **Technical feasibility** is proven when the invention works under laboratory conditions. **Commercial feasibility** is tested in the market place where the receipts from buyers are assessed against the costs of the producers: is the innovation profitable?

The progression from scientific discovery, the result of scientific research, to an invention, the result of technical development, to innovation, the result of a profit calculation by the producer, is called the **linear model of innovation**. An example of this is the progression from the discovery of atom splitting, to the invention of the test reactor, to the innovation of nuclear energy generation. More important are other forms of innovation, particularly creative responses to feedback from the market and imitation of successful rivals.

The **diffusion of technology** occurs when technical processes and products are imitated in the hope of a better market position.

Entrepreneurs are people on the alert for opportunities who overcome the constraints to exploiting new knowledge. More specifically, the term relates to producers who go beyond the bounds of existing knowledge and combine production factors (property rights) in novel ways. Entrepreneurs may find out that they pioneer property uses which meet with the approval (the cash votes) of sufficient numbers of buyers; then they make a profit. They may also incur a loss which conveys the knowledge that that particular property use does not meet with sufficient approval from the clients. ●

A Panoramic View of Technical and Organisational Progress

Technical change always requires organisational changes and adjustments throughout the economic system. Thus, a new product can only be marketed if the necessary organisational dispositions for its production and distribution are made. What is necessary is not always known, and indeed may cause higher transaction costs than the technical side of the innovation. The demand for new products is not known because buyers cannot know about the new product; they may not even be curious to find out about it. When the technical invention of bonding carbon particles to paper by means of light to produce photocopying was made, the major task was to induce potential buyers to discover that they had a demand for photocopying (Mueller, 1996).

If sellers and buyers in an economy are generally on the alert and prepared to incur transaction costs to discover new opportunities, the entire market system will be competitive. Indeed, the existence of some competitive operators generates the opportunities for other suppliers to compete successfully. This often enhances the competitive attitudes in yet other markets. An example of how innovative, competitive enterprise led to 'virtuous circles' of economic progress was the railways boom of the nineteenth century. Enterprising mechanical engineers overcame obstacles of technical feasibility to build faster and more reliable railway engines, but they depended on – and created opportunities for – civil engineers who devised and laid the tracks. Both interacted with steel producers and bankers whose contributions were essential in revolutionising transport. The steel producers could apply the then new technology of the Bessemer process in steel making, and the bankers benefited from the rise of a prosperous middle class who were eager to find investment opportunities for their capital. This induced the organisational innovation of joint-stock company laws and organisational changes in banking. In the mutual interaction of entrepreneurs in these diverse industries, a whole cluster of competing suppliers created opportunities and technical and commercial solutions for each other. Over time, this widened markets as transport costs fell, and gave rise to numerous new activities in areas as far apart from each other as new wheat production in the American Midwest, tourism in the Alps and the opening up of Canada and Siberia. Austrian-American economist Joseph Schumpeter (1883–1950), who analysed this phenomenon of development, spoke of the 'swarm-like appearance of entrepreneurs' who create, by their competitive interaction, 'new possibilities more advantageous from the private economic standpoint' for each other (Schumpeter, 1961, p. 214). A similar competitive process is currently taking place in clusters of computer-related industries: because competing manufacturers have driven down the cost of microchips and enhanced their quality, computer assemblers, software developers, telecommunications firms, teachers of computer skills, developers of knowledge, computer graphics artists, e-mail marketeers and distance-education experts, whose products can be carried on computer networks, interact in a cluster of dynamic development. They are all mutually dependent for their commercial success on the readiness of each part of the cluster to incur search costs and on innovative entrepreneurs in new fields joining in. They also depend on rapidly changing demands that avid buyers are discovering in the process.

In a similar vein, competitive product markets depend on competition in factor markets for labour and capital. And in turn factor markets will only be competitive if the products which capital and labour help to produce are exposed to product market competition. The economic effects of competition thus depend on the competitive interaction of all elements of the market system. As long as the institutions fail to discourage opportunism according to the maxim 'rip off and let rip off', it is very difficult for individual competitors to succeed. This highlights the importance of a consistent institutional set which facilitates knowledge search and reduces the risks of opportunism among business partners and on the part of governments.

The interactions of buyers and sellers in response to new ideas can often take a long time. Thus, the Crusaders of the European Middle Ages brought back – among many ideas – the knowledge of Arabic numerals, including the concept of zero. This gradually enabled merchants to calculate assets, expenses and revenues more easily and facilitated double-entry bookkeeping. This, in turn, helped the emergence of big trading houses and the reorganisation of European distance trade and had many impacts on the division of labour. Of course, numerous other conditions were needed to favour this historical sequence of events, a complex web of changes in knowledge, physical capital and technical expertise. It is interesting to reflect why the invention of gunpowder in China led only to the innovations of fireworks and rockets, whereas the Europeans, with their traditions of rivalry in war and commerce, soon used the original invention for guns and cannons, in mining and road construction and to obtain more solid building materials – each setting off further long-term chains of innovative effort.

8.3   Restrictions of Economic Competition

Private Restrictions of Competition

The free exercise of property rights which leads to competition in the exchange process can be inhibited by the restrictive business practices of others who try to avoid or mitigate competitive pressures. Where economic agents can exert economic or political power, they may use it to defend their market niche by artificial impediments. This strengthens their hand in contract negotiations and reduces the (cost-controlling) unease with which they normally have to live. A case in point is the formation of a cartel, an agreement among sellers to supply only with uniform conditions of sale. At first glance, this could be seen as a legitimate use of the freedom of contract; but such a cartel agreement interferes with the freedom of buyers. Their freedom of choice amongst sellers is made meaningless by the joint action of the sellers. As the freedom of choice and contract is a quality worth promoting and protecting, sellers must be denied the freedom to cartelise by a rule that prohibits cartels.

It is essential to growth, freedom and the control of power that the private restriction of competition is ruled out. Private business practices which hinder competition can be the result of horizontal and vertical concentrations of businesses: buying up former rivals (mergers) or integrating suppliers or buyers into the same business organisations. The empirical evidence shows that merged organisations are frequently hampered by a progressive rise of their internal organisation costs, that internal rule coordination becomes increasingly difficult and that the adaptive capacity of mega organisations is reduced by the growth of internal administration. This can be explained by principal–agent problems in big organisations which are not subject to competitive discipline. Seeing matters from this angle, a case could be made that it is up to those who have merged to internalise all the benefits and costs of such action. None the less, there may be cases where it is worth investigating whether a particular takeover infringes the freedom of other property users to contract freely. But such an investigation always poses serious knowledge problems, as well as creating problems of legal definition: what is the size of a merger that will come under prior or subsequent investigation?

As we have mentioned, private restriction of competition can also result from agreements among firms to cooperate instead of competing (collusion), from the readiness of powerful firms to defeat rivals by underselling them so that they are squeezed out of the business, to coercive or fraudulent treatment of rivals or contract partners. In such situations, competition may need to be protected, in the first instance by rules which create sanctions against force and fraud. Institutions should be framed to rule on which private restrictions of competition are not permissible and which actions require the action of an arbiter because they may represent a misuse of market power. In many countries, the rules are laid down in trade practices legislation and require the supervision of undue market power by specialist competition agencies. However, this often fails to produce the desired results because these agencies are easily captured by the supervised firms and because those in charge of such agencies suffer from intractable knowledge problems, as well as the policy handicaps inherent in enforcing specific outcomes. (For a thorough assessment of competition policy, see Armentano, 1991.) The alternative to surveillance of competition by authorities are simple rules that proscribe private restrictions of competition combined with sanctions. Possible infringements of competition, which are not ruled out by proscriptions, are then left to the controlling discipline of open markets, that is, to potential competition. This, of course, requires that governments abstain from all actions to close markets artificially or to favour incumbent competitors.

A case where there is no rivalry, which has long played a role in the economic literature, is 'natural monopoly': a situation where property rights are established in a unique asset, one with no close substitutes. However, such cases are extremely rare, because potential rivals of the monopolist will seek to find close substitutes. In an evolving world, rivals will invest heavily in substitutes if a 'natural monopolist' reaps high returns, and experience shows that few natural monopolies have ever been durable, unless protected by political authority (Friedman, 1991). One reason for this is that monopolies normally occur in a defined geographic area, so high profits attract out-of-area competitors. With the secular decline in transport and communication costs, such out-of-area rivals have become increasingly common.

Political Restrictions of Competition

Frequently, the free disposition of private property rights is restricted by political intervention. As we saw earlier in this chapter, suppliers, or organised supplier interests, try to obtain political intervention that softens the competitive pressures on them and secures their market niches more permanently than can be done by economic competition. This enables them to save costs and therefore is worth the expense to obtain political favours (rent-seeking). Political agents respond – often willingly out of agent opportunism – by regulating markets and restricting market access. Some of these interventions may be justifiable in that they enhance the knowledge-creating capacity of competition, for example when government stipulates standardised weights and measures. However, in most instances, regulations exclude or hinder potential rivals, increase the compliance costs of market participants and limit the freedom of contract. Specific rules which stipulate certain outcomes are, as such, not a problem, but their proliferation quickly overtaxes most entrepreneurs' cognitive capacity, and so hinder the use of knowledge.

To suppliers, government restrictions of competitive action are often welcome substitutes for private restrictions (Stigler, 1971a). Supplier lobbies and government agents often present themselves as promoting some worthy health or safety purpose or as a means of redistributing income. Government intervention in the complex, open market system, however, tend to have unforeseen and unwelcome consequences, simply because the intervening authorities cannot foresee all the consequences. We only need to recall the example of maximum house rentals and asymmetric contract conditions that are intended to benefit low-income tenants, which, sooner or later, inhibit house building and work to the detriment of tenants, especially those on low incomes.

A typical and frequently used example of a market intervention to benefit some suppliers is the tariff. The short-term impact of a new tariff is to raise the price of imported goods, thus easing the competitive pressure on producers of import substitutes. This reallocates property rights from the many dispersed and unorganised buyers, as well as foreigners, to the few organised domestic producers. Tariffs are often justified with the argument that producer profitability enhanced by import substitution raises investment and therefore enhances domestic industry employment and incomes, or that they 'buy time' for ailing industries to adjust, helping to conserve jobs. The worldwide evidence on import substitution, however, supports the conclusion that these advantages are, at best, temporary. Over the long run, market interventions create an industrial, politicised rentier class and ease the competitive pressures for innovation, so that protected industries end up and remain as high-cost, unenterprising laggards (Papageorgiou et al., 1991).

In electoral democracies, rent-seeking producers are able to appeal to politicians who themselves have to compete for re-election, party finance or promotion (and who are often imbued with the guardian instincts). Rival suppliers thus develop a strong demand for political efforts to 'fortify' their market niches (see box). When agents of the government issue licences to producers or impose tariffs to exclude additional rivals from entering the market, this assists in converting active economic rivalry among suppliers into cartels or monopolies.

Parliamentarians, bureaucrats and other political agents have strong incentives to supply favours which protect client producer groups. By legislating, regulating or passing judicial judgements to reduce the intensity of rivalry among suppliers in a market, holders of political power can prove their own importance to the few suppliers and their workers in that industry, each of whom may gain a considerable advantage. Political entrepreneurs who seek rewards from redistributing property rights by recourse to political power therefore respond willingly because patronage increases their 'territory' and influence (Stigler, 1971a). Few political leaders are therefore wedded to a strategy of 'no favours all around', that is, to a policy of non-discrimination between particular firms or industries.

Intervening government officials and parliamentarians may share in the profits that they allocate to regulated industries (through collecting licence fees; assistance with party funding; political support or lucrative positions for retired bureaucrats and politicians; or through outright corruption).

The disadvantage of interventions that tamper with competition tends to be small for each of the thousands of buyers in the same market. Consequently, an intervention may go unnoticed or, if noticed, is not worth the expense of lobbying against. It is rational for buyers to remain ignorant and not to engage in political action to counter the supplier lobbies and political favouritism. After all, the fixed political transaction costs of interventions tend to be high. This is why interventions in competitive processes tend to be supplier-biased and to the detriment of the many ill-organised buyers.

The capitalist market economy therefore needs institutional constraints on competition for political favours. The constraints should be on suppliers, who have strong incentives to escape the relentless economic-competitive bind, and on political agents, who benefit at elections from competition (Olson, 1965; Buchanan and Tullock, 1962; Tullock, 1967; Stigler, 1971a; Buchanan et al., 1980; Tollison, 1982).

Another form of political intervention in the free private dispositions of property rights in many countries is judicial activism. In some countries, judges, whose traditional function has been to protect citizens under a transparent, cohesive system of law, have become activist creators of new interpretations of the law aimed at obtaining certain specific outcomes, often on behalf of organised interest groups. Given a constructivist bent in legal training and an absence of checks – such as election to office or the discipline of having to raise the finance to implement the outcome of decisions – in many countries judges have taken powers to remake the law and to hamper free competition on the basis of universal property rights. Courts then become the preferred battle ground for circumventing economic competition and for benefiting from political competition. In these circumstances, it is particularly important that the principles of competition and protected private property rights are given protected, high legal status.

When those in control of the external institutional framework side with the interests of the few influential suppliers, they divert the pursuit of market niches by entrepreneurs from active economic rivalry and innovation into rent-seeking, and they act against the citizen-principals whose agents they are. Once the rules fail to prevent political and bureaucratic operators from intervening, the commitment to knowledge search wanes and the pace of innovation slackens. Cost controls in business are then likely to become lax. Economic growth decelerates.

It is therefore important for the growth of useful knowledge – as well as for equity of opportunity – that rules are in place which force parliamentarians, bureaucrats and judges to support a constitutional principle of competition. Protecting the rules of competition should therefore be one of the central tasks of public policy.

❖ Rent Seeking, Illustrated by Two Historic Cases

I

William Fairbairn, one of the best-known engineering pioneers of the industrial revolution in England, wrote in his *Useful Information for Engineers* (1860) about his youth, when the Engineer Mechanics Union objected to his legal entitlement to enter his chosen trade:

> When I first entered London, a young man from the country had no chance whatever of success in consequence of trade unions and guilds. I had no difficulty in finding employment, but before I could begin work, I had to run the gauntlet of the trade societies ... [After having tried in vain to be accepted as a member of the Union], I was ultimately declared illegitimate and sent to seek my fortune elsewhere ... [There were three competing unions] to exclude all those who could not assert their claims to work in London and other corporate towns. Laws of a most arbitrary character were enforced, and they were governed by cliques of self-appointed officers, who never failed to take care of their own interests.

Fairbairn was forced to move and seek work with the Dublin inventors of a revolutionary nail-making machine: 'The Dublin iron-manufacture was ruined ... not through any local disadvantages, but solely by the prohibitory regulations enforced by the workmen of the Trade Unions' (Johnson, 1991, p. 574).

II

An early case in which initial privileges granted to an organised group led to growing rent-seeking, including by violent means, occurred in the United Kingdom after the Napoleonic Wars:

> Trade unions, which had long existed in Britain, were given special privileges through several Acts of Parliament in 1824. Prior to this legislation, the urging of workers to strike had been punishable under the conspiracy provisions of the Common Law and specific statute laws. Now, unions were legalised and awarded a privilege – the right to break contracts – denied to any one else ... The two bills went through Parliament almost without debate, the general assumption being that they would help to produce industrial peace.

> Never was an illusion more ill-founded. The consequence of lifting legal penalties produced the first real wave of organised strikes ... [In 1825], there were strikes among the spinners and weavers of Scotland, among the textile workers of Lancashire and among the colliers in ... the coal fields ... [A strike] halted London seagoing traffic – something which had never happened before in the port's existence, which went back to Roman times ...

> Moreover, some of the most destructive and frightening aspects of modern trade unionism at its worst made their instant appearance ... There were widespread demands for the introduction of the closed or union shop; for restrictions on entry, especially for apprentices, and the introduction of new machinery; for the dismissal of unpopular (efficient) foremen; and for

limitations of every kind on recruitment of new labour. In short, most unions immediately produced long shopping lists of requirements, each of which tended to lower productivity, raise manufacturers' costs or restrict the employer's right to run his business. All were backed by the threat of strikes.

What was particularly alarming were the harsh and often brutal efforts by union leaders and militants to compel their fellow workmen, whether they liked it or not, to back these demands. New union rules, now lawful, not only enforced a wide range of restrictive practices but introduced entry fees, forced levies on wages, and inter-union action, or what are now called secondary boycotts … The new activity of 'picketing', often violent, began outside workplaces … There was a good deal of terrorism, … a union passed a sentence of death on four men … , one of whom was actually murdered. (ibid., pp. 868–9) ◆

8.4   The Competitive System

The Benefits of a Competitive Economy

It may be useful to look beyond competition in individual markets and to review the wider, societal benefits of competition in the use of property rights.

A high degree of competitiveness throughout an economic system has a number of important benefits for the community at large:

(a) As we now know, intensive rivalry encourages the incurring of information costs and fosters the discovery of valued knowledge and hence overall economic growth. Competitive economies therefore tend to cope well with the need for structural change in response to inevitable shifts in demand, technical opportunities, resource supplies, income levels or other circumstances. Competitive economies are characterised by flexible responses to changed conditions, including a high degree of responsiveness of the owners of production factors to changes in relative prices, that is, a high degree of factor mobility. Market rivals continually explore variations of what they have been doing, and exchange partners select what they prefer. What succeeds is expanded, what fails to find favour is discontinued or varied, so that errors are corrected. The resulting structural changes will force some market participants to adjust their expectations downward: their skills may no longer be needed, they incur losses of capital, or the technology they own may become worthless. However, competitive, flexible and fast-growing economies offer resource owners new opportunities. If, for example, growth is fast and labour markets are free, a high share of the labour force is likely to be employed. Individual workers who lose their jobs then have a better chance of finding new employment soon. By contrast, uncompetitive economies with rigid prices and little factor mobility tend to grow slowly, so people who have lost their jobs tend to be out of work more or less permanently, suffering because of structural adjustments. Such experiences then often inspire more widespread resistance to structural change.

(b) Another important benefit of intensely competitive systems is that economic power is controlled. Monopolies and market niches are temporary and limited, so that property rights are not too concentrated. Competition challenges property owners time and again to validate their assets and to search for new ways to test whether their assets are still valued by the other side of the market (revealed preferences). As rivals strive to discover new alternatives to attract contracts from the other side of the market, old property rights may lose their market value – what Joseph Schumpeter aptly called 'creative destruction' – and other items of property may rise in value. The game is an evolutionary one, in which social and economic positions are not sacrosanct but are open to ceaseless challenges.

(c) Another benefit of a high intensity of competition relates to income distribution. In competitive economic systems, income distribution tends to be in flux. The pioneer profits of property owners and the incomes of workers wax and wane as market fortunes change. The fairly durable differences in incomes and wealth observed in advanced economies normally have much to do with political intervention and anti-competitive regulations (Friedman, 1962, pp. 119–32). For instance, restrictions in the labour market and controls of house rents often cement unintended inequalities, which public redistribution policies subsequently try to mitigate. It is worth noting in this context that several of the most competitive new industrial societies of East Asia – such as Taiwan – also have a very even income distribution, although none of them has implemented redistributive welfare policies (Riedel, 1988, pp. 18–21).

(d) At a wider societal level, economic competition ensures that industrial power brokers will be cautious in using their wealth to buy undue political influence. As long as economic competition is lively and widespread, 'monopoly capitalism' is kept at bay. Ordinary citizens thus have a better chance of escaping the consequences of attempted political discrimination (Friedman, 1962, pp. 119–32).

(e) A further consequence of a competitive economy is that agents on both sides of the market can choose with whom to contract. They are able to 'exit' from previous contractual binds and situations where they are exploited by powerful counterparts. This not only controls power, but also promotes freedom at large. Private autonomy becomes effective when people are free to choose.

(f) On a closely related plain, inevitable conflicts between buyers and sellers are defused when the 'exit option' exists. Conflicts in competitive economies tend to be handled in decentralised, anonymous ways. People accept changed market prices and adjust to them. By contrast, conflicts are often allowed to build up in non-competitive systems and lead to a confrontational recourse to the 'voice option'. Conflicts are then emotionalised and politicised by political entrepreneurs who hope to rally conflicting parties behind their cause. Seen in this light, economic competition tends to serve social peace and stability by pulverising and defusing unavoidable economic and social conflicts.

(g) Last but not least, competitive economies also tend to absorb external shocks better, and business cycles are smoothed by spontaneous, flexible price and quantity responses. If monetary policies are conducted in a stable, predictable manner, they tend to be met with stronger stabilising responses in competitive systems, whereas economic systems that are dominated by rigid monopolies and oligopolies may require major doses of discretionary countercyclical policy to correct boom–bust cycles. Where wages and work practices are rigid, cyclical demand fluctuations are reflected in big profit fluctuations. This is likely to set off further, destabilising fluctuations in investments. Flexible wages and competitive work practices in labour markets, by contrast, act as a buffer which averts cumulative instability. Some may argue that labour should not act as a shock absorber. However, it may also be asked whether greater job security and stability of employment are not more valuable to workers than a constant wage. These considerations apply more generally: competitive markets are conducive to overall spontaneous self-stabilisation and hence economic security.

The Autonomous, Competitive Use of Property Rights: a Constitutional Principle

These advantages of the competitive use of property rights – of what might be called the 'constitution of capitalism' – are easily undermined by political action that is driven by political rivalry. It is therefore desirable to attach a high moral value to protecting the free use of private property in competition. Property rights protection and free contracting should be elevated to principles with a high constitutional status, into overriding, universal institutions which govern the making and implementation of lower-level rules and which cannot be overturned by simple court judgements, simple parliamentary majorities or mere administrative action to suit specific cases. If the basic institutions of a competitive economy enjoy high legal protection, this establishes trust in a self-controlling, self-organising economic system in which policy interventions are used sparingly and in which ordinary citizens can thrive.

In Chapter 10, we shall return to this idea when discussing the style and content of public policy. First, however, it seems necessary to turn to economic organisations such as business firms.

Questions for Review

- Describe competition in general and economic competition in particular.
- In what ways does rivalry between sellers benefit buyers?
- What is the difference between price and non-price competition?
- Try to find a definition of 'competition' in a standard first-year economics textbook of your choice. Does this definition square with what is said in this chapter?
- In what ways are buyers who are prepared to incur transaction costs essential to the liveliness and effectiveness of competition?
- In what ways do you compete as a buyer in the market for food? Who are your rivals?
- With what tools of non-price competition do business firms typically compete?
- What transaction costs do sellers of goods incur to position themselves advantageously for the attention of buyers?
- How does active rivalry among sellers affect the prevalence of attitudes of (a) bounded rationality and (b) creative-entrepreneurial rationality in a society? Make sure you express your answer in language understandable to the layman.
- Define what is meant by 'innovation'. What is the criterion for the 'commercial feasibility test'?
- What is meant by 'pioneer profit', and why can it be expected to be temporary as long as there is no protection by political intervention?
- Think of the technical progress of the motor car since the first sputtering cars appeared on European and American roads a hundred years ago, and pinpoint the institutions that motivated the process of competition and innovation over time.
- Can you guess why the car industry in centrally planned economies achieved much less technical progress?
- What is the difference between 'process innovation' and 'product innovation'?

- What are the effects of political intervention on a specific market in your country? In what ways does political activism shape the institutions of a community? How does this affect economic growth?
- Can you think of historical examples, other than the two given in the text (railway boom and computer-communications revolution), of clusters of competitive producers in a number of industries lifting themselves to commercial success by mutual, responsive interaction?
- List the societal benefits of a competitive economy. Can you also think of drawbacks? How do you personally value the balance between the benefits and costs of being competitive?
- At what levels does competition control power? How does that relate to the fundamental value of individual freedom?

Notes

1. This conception of the competitive process owes much to what has been termed 'German market process theory' (for a survey, see Kerber, in Boettke, 1994, pp. 500–7; Streit and Wegner, 1992).
2. For a discussion of different approaches to model the competitive process, see M. Addleson, 'Competition', in Boettke, 1994, pp. 96–102; and Kirzner (1985).
3. It should be noted in passing that most neoclassical textbooks ignore non-price competition, which tends to be much more important in most markets for complex products and services. Standard textbook analysis also proceeds on the assumption that no transaction costs intervene between the two sides of the market.

CHAPTER 9

Economic Organisations

The reader will become familiar with the possibly surprising insight that teams, firms and other economic organisations are created primarily to save on the costs of frequent or risky market transactions. To economise on such transaction costs, people commit production factors in more or less enduring, cooperative, purpose-orientated arrangements which are called organisations.

What matters in deciding whether a firm should do an operation in-house, keeping it under its organisational control, or subcontract in the market is the ratio between (a) the organisation costs of coordinating processes within the company and (b) the transaction costs of using markets to buy the necessary inputs. Where markets function poorly and are costly to use – or do not function at all, as was the case in the socialist countries – there is a tendency to integrate as many activities as possible within the organisation. In market economies, advances in computing, communications and institutional design in recent decades have led to growing specialisation (devolution, subcontracting, and networking).

Particular problems arise in organisations as people cooperate on the basis of open-ended, incompletely defined relational agreements. The owners of specific assets, such as large chunks of capital, may often fear being 'held up' by the owners of complementary production factors, for example by suppliers of vital material inputs or by skilled labour.

Many modern organisations, such as joint-stock companies, are managed by agents (company directors) – rather than the owners of the capital who are the principals. This gives rise to the 'principal–agent problem', the danger that the agents may not act in the principals' interest. The problem is confined by internal rules of corporate governance, external laws and regulations and – very importantly – effective markets for products, capital and managers which surround corporate organisations in a capitalist economy. We shall also see that different forms of private economic organisation – for example, clubs, mutual societies, family companies and stock companies – have differing likelihoods of performing effectively in the owners' interest, because different incentive structures and sanctions apply.

A leader is best when people barely know that he exists ... A good leader talks little. When his work is done, his aim fulfilled, they will all say: 'We did this ourselves'.
(Lao Zi, Dao de ching, *6th century* BC)

The directors of ... companies ... , being managers rather of other people's money than their own, it cannot well be expected that they should watch over it with the same anxious vigilance with which partners in a private copartnery frequently watch over their own. Like the stewards of a rich man, they are apt to consider attention to small matters as not for their master's honour, and very easily give themselves a dispensation from having it. Negligence and profusion, therefore, must always prevail, more or less, in the management of the affairs of such a company.
(Adam Smith, The Wealth of Nations, *[1776] 1931, p. 229)*

We have witnessed in modern business the submergence of the individual within the organization, and yet the increase to an extraordinary degree of the power of the individual, of the individual who happens to control the organization.
(Woodrow Wilson, 31 August 1910)

To some extent every organization must rely also on rules and not only on specific commands ... it is possible to make use of knowledge which nobody possesses as a whole, ... [an] organization will determine by commands only the function to be performed by each member, the purposes to be achieved, and certain general aspects of the methods to be employed, and will leave the detail to be decided by the individuals on the basis of their respective knowledge and skills.
(Friedrich Hayek, Rules and Order, *1973, pp. 48–9)*

9.1   Economic Organisations: Definition and Purposes

Up to this point, the reader may have gained the impression that we focus excessively on individuals pursuing their economic and other interests independently by competing, all on their own, in the market place. But of course individuals often cooperate in organisations and submit the property rights they own to control by the leader, or leaders, of organisations on a more or less permanent basis. As a matter of fact, organisations often provide humans who are 'social animals' with the stimulus of their fellows' company. Organisations, such as family enterprises or large corporations, provide individuals with a social framework in which they can thrive and validate their thoughts and actions with others.

Much division of labour to produce what we need to survive has therefore always taken place in reasonably durable organisational relationships, such as the family group, a tribe, cooperative ventures or business partnerships and teams. In all of these, productive activities and rewards are coordinated at least partly by leader(s) who command and control from the top down. The spontaneous form of coordinating the division of labour – through market exchanges – certainly seems a much more recent innovation in human history, as compared with the hierarchical organisation of economic life in hunting packs and cooperation within families and tribes. Only when technology and the number of participants in the division of labour reached a stage of considerable complexity were market exchanges invented to complement organisational forms of human coordination. There was then a need for what Hayek called an 'extended order' in markets under the universal rule of law. As we saw, this permitted a much more complex division of labour and higher living standards than was possible within self-sufficient organisations. But this does not mean that organised coordination is not highly effective in many circumstances, nor that competitors in markets should not be organised in teams. Common sense (and game theory) show that cooperation is frequently of mutual advantage in coordinating people; indeed, that it often yields more desirable results for participants than rivalry (Axelrod, 1984; North, 1990, pp. 12–16; section 5.1).

A Definition of Organisations

We define organisations as more or less durable, planned arrangements to pool productive resources in order to pursue one or several shared purposes. These resources are coordinated within some kind of hierarchical order by a mix of institutions and commands. Performance is monitored and controlled if it falls short of the set goals. Organisations are based on a set of rules, a constitution which derives either from voluntary contracts or from political authority (Vanberg, 1992). Examples of private voluntary organisations are cooperatives, clubs and business firms. An example of the creation of an organisation by political authority is an administrative body. In most communities, organisations are entitled to act legally as independent units (corporate actors); they can sign contracts on their own behalf (firms: from *firma*, Latin for signature). Organisations normally cover complex interactions that cannot be spelled out and negotiated completely (relational contracts).

The mere juxtaposition of resources, where the property owners retain completely independent rights of disposition and are not subject to any directives, does not constitute an organisation, even if all resource owners share a common interest. Thus, the gathering of spectators at a football match, who share the purpose of being entertained, does not make an organisation. Only when economic agents pool some of their resources and abandon part of their rights to use these resources independently do they form an organisation which becomes a 'collective actor' (Coleman, 1990). This would be the case, for example, when certain spectators form a club, promise to pay membership contributions, and subject themselves to shared rules that are monitored by a committee of the club. In this chapter, we shall deal only with private economic organisations which are based on voluntary contractual commitments, leaving political organisations to the following chapter. Economic organisations serve the purpose of mobilising and exploiting resources for a material purpose. Organisations allow individual collaborators to combine the production factors they own and to operate them conjointly in an ordered, predictable setting. Organisations create an environment in which individuals are able to interact closely with others and which economises on information search and coordination costs. The other members of the organisation and the hierarchical order in which individuals are placed are familiar to them, as are many of the organisation's internal rules and routines. Part of the task of organisational leadership is to save on information requirements by designing and realising a plan and informing the various collaborators of their role in it, as well as fostering implicit and explicit institutions which steer the interaction of the members of the organisation.

As long as organised teams are exposed to external competition, which forces them to adjust to outside changes and challenges, the organisational order is unlikely to rigidify and become an obstacle to the exploitation of new opportunities (section 8.1). Economic organisations may therefore be seen as social arrangements which facilitate information flows, serve the acquisition, testing and exploitation of knowledge and satisfy aspirations for social stimulation and interaction.

O Key Concepts

Organisations were defined in Chapter 2 as purposive and reasonably durable arrangements of productive resources which are coordinated to some extent in a hierarchical order by a leader (or leaders). Typically, the relations and obligations are incompletely defined.

Economic organisations may, for example, be production firms that have chosen the pursuit of profitability as their objective and that operate between input and output markets, requiring voluntary cooperation through contracts with people who do not belong to the organisation. **Political organisations** are created by political will and may then be able to compel others to interact with them. ●

Economic organisations take many forms. Probably the best known example is the incorporated firm, which nowadays tends to be a fairly durable arrangement to pursue an open-ended purpose, such as making a profit. But temporary economic organisations are also quite common. For example, they may be set up for the sole purpose of building a bridge or developing a piece of land; they are disbanded after the completion of the task. Other forms of open-ended voluntary economic organisation are family firms, trade associations, clubs, co-operatives, trade unions, trusts and mutual benefit societies. What they have in common is that they bundle some resources together with the aim of pursuing a shared purpose and give themselves some constitutional structure, for example the statutes fixing the duties of the chairman and secretary.

The defining questions for any economic organisation are: Who keeps the residual profit or bears a possible loss? How are profits and losses distributed if more than one partner owns the organisation? Follow-up questions are: Who controls the organisation's operations, both short- and long-term? How do owners control the managers, if ownership and management control are separated?

A great variety of legal forms have been developed to address the problems of voluntary economic associations. Owner-managed firms and partnerships may provide for total, unlimited liability of the owners. Alternatively, liability for contractual obligations may be limited by statute to the organisation's capital (limited liability company). Some economic organisations may be non-profit, dispersing possible surpluses through lower prices, additional services or higher rewards to the production factors they employ. Other organisations may pool limited resources of a great many partners in pursuit of a shared financial aim, such as insurance against certain risks, or joint saving and investment (mutual societies, *kongxi* societies in Chinese communities, trusts). Yet others pool not only capital, but also the rights to the owners' labour, knowledge and land in order to pursue a specific purpose (cooperatives). Some organisations are set up under traditional and private law; others are heavily regulated under specific statute laws and formally supervised by government authorities.

Transaction Costs and Organisations

It is conceivable that a producer may buy all the inputs he or she needs in the market place. Theoretically, each day's labour could be hired in the labour market, all capital could be borrowed on a periodic basis, each quantity of input could be bought separately, and all items of output could be offered and sold in the open market. But – as Ronald Coase ([1937] 1952) discovered in the 1930s (see section 7.4) – such a way of marshalling productive resources would involve extremely high transaction costs. Relying exclusively on one-off contracts would create enormous information costs; in each instance, new contracts would have to be negotiated, monitored and enforced. This is why repetitive production is normally coordinated within organisations called firms: they combine key resources more or less permanently by entering into relational contracts and operate in pursuit of a shared purpose (or purposes). Such more or less permanent arrangements, which create 'durable coalitions of property rights', may reduce the freedom of individuals to dispose of their property rights at each point in time, but because the commitments to the organisation reduce coordination costs, they enhance the value of the property rights.[1] The desire for complete independence and freedom from all commitments therefore tends to come at a price in terms of effectiveness in attaining one's goals and one's income (Milgrom and Roberts, 1992).

Asset Specificity

Oliver Williamson (1985) drew attention to a related aspect of the existence of firms: owners of capital, knowledge and other resources are often obliged by technical reasons to commit their resources irreversibly and for a long time to specific forms (asset specificity). The owners of financial capital thus commit their assets to specific capital goods, just as putty is 'committed' to a fixed form when it is baked to form vessels. The owners of a company who have invested their capital in buildings and equipment cannot readily switch out of those investments. They also acquire valuable specific knowledge which they can use only if they remain in specific operations (human capital specificity). These investments will only pay the expected returns if the specific assets can be operated undisturbed for a long time. However, the owners of other, complementary resources, such as skilled labour, may want to exploit the inflexibility of the capital owners and holders of specific knowledge by 'holding up' operations and extorting higher pay. This is a case of people having and exploiting power because their counterparts have no scope for substitution or evasion (exit, see section 5.4). Wherever such power constellations are prevalent and are not ruled out credibly by internal and external institutions, there is a motive for binding the owners of complementary resources into an organisation. In many cases, this may even be the precondition for a specific investment to go ahead. Thus, capital owners may only invest in an aluminium smelter or a steel plant if they can secure input flows by securing direct organisational control over the sources of power and raw materials. In such cases, the motive for combining property rights in an organisation is risk-avoidance, in other words, the wish to reduce uncertainty and to economise on information costs by creating a more credible organised order.

The need to deal with asset specificity is predicated on three interlocking conditions (Williamson, 1985):

(a) people have limited information, limited aspirations, and consequently act with bounded rationality;
(b) people are opportunistic, unless prevented by institutions;
(c) some people hold assets of pronounced specificity.

In these conditions, gaps in what relational contracts stipulate may be exploited by opportunistic individuals to the detriment of the owners of specific assets, who do not have rewarding alternatives available from changing the uses of their assets.

The test of whether these assumptions always apply depends also on wider social circumstances and traditions. Frequently, opportunism is controlled by external institutions (the law) and by internal institutions of the community at large (morals, customs). In many communities, people who interact take a long-term view and do not play opportunistic end games. They understand that their prosperity depends on mutual, ongoing and rule-bound interaction as well as on trust and good faith (Flew, in Radnitzky, 1997, pp. 107–24). Neither is it clear whether the leaders of organisations can always anticipate the future costs and benefits of buying inputs in markets as compared to tying these input supplies within their organisations. The ever-present knowledge problem complicates such an assessment because the cost ratio changes due to technical and institutional evolution.

Conclusions from the Williamson model for the conduct of public policy – namely, that vertical integration should be tolerated in the interest of overall efficiency – therefore seem based on dubious foundations, not least the notion that the overall effects of alternative arrangements can ever be known.[2]

O Key Concepts

The **putty-clay concept of capital formation** refers to the fact that people save monetary assets (often called capital) which can be used in numerous alternative forms. Like putty, it is fungible. But the act of investment into specific capital goods locks capital into a fixed form (so to speak, it bakes the clay). The costs of converting out of specific capital goods are often high, so capital owners become vulnerable to the exercise of power by the owners of complementary and supposedly more fungible production factors.

Asset specificity is a condition of a productive asset – such as an item of capital equipment or a body of specialised knowledge – which does not allow it to be switched to alternative uses. The proprietors of specific assets cannot exit and are therefore open to abuses of power, namely the hold-up of operations by complementary production factors. Thus, aircraft owners depend on pilots to make a profit and may be forced by a pilot strike to make increased salary payments. This explains why owners of specific assets have a keen interest in binding complementary inputs providers in organisations (or in obtaining strong institutional controls). ●

Hierarchy and Leadership

The definition of an organisation invariably contains the constitutional element of having a unifying purpose or set of purposes (goals). The goals may be set autonomously by the leaders or arise from consultation and participative decision making among the members. In this respect, organisational coordination always differs from the coordination of independent agents in the market place. In markets, no goals are set *ex ante* and from the outside for participants; self-motivated people are coordinated by the evolutionary market process of trial and error. Organisational behaviour is coordinated to pursue at least to some extent one or several preset goals.

The definition of private economic organisations also contains the element of durability over time: there is a durable pooling of property rights to capital, labour, knowhow and land (Vanberg, 1992). The early joint-stock companies of Renaissance Europe were set up for a limited time by merchants who pooled capital and, maybe, their own knowledge and labour. Rights to complementary resources were bought in the market; for example, sailors were hired and trade goods were bought. Like time-limited ventures in real-estate development nowadays, they entered into incompletely defined contracts for the purpose of exploiting a specific trading venture, such as bringing a shipload of spices from the East. After the voyage, they shared the profits (or losses) as agreed in the company's constitution and dissolved the share company. Many of the early share companies thus lasted only for the duration of a specific venture. Nowadays, most economic organisations are intended to be permanent.

The concept of organisation also contains the notion of coordinated action under a plan that assigns specific tasks. This requires some decision about who has ultimate powers to plan, command and control at least some aspects of the organisation's activities and implies some kind of hierarchy. The hierarchical aspect may be pronounced (strong subordination, complex multilevel organisation) or weak (much self-responsibility of team members, flat organisation). In any case, not all aspects of an organisation's activity can be planned and commanded, so rules have an important part in organisation-internal coordination. When discussing organisations, therefore, a distinction should again be made between directives (or instructions, commands, prescriptions) that order affairs by assigning specific tasks, targets and functions to agents, and general rules of conduct that assist spontaneous ordering (Vanberg, 1992, pp. 244–5; also see section 5.1). The pooling of resources under common control must be based on a constitution (a set of general rules about how to proceed and how to change rules) to bind the individual resource owners to form the organisation (ibid., pp. 239–41).

General rules invite collaborators to make independent judgements and initiatives in the organisation, whereas prescriptions are based on authority and subordination. The organisation-internal rules are normally bound by the constitution of the organisation and steer the use of pooled resources and the distribution of the joint product between the various owners who have contributed their resources. Where rules do not bind the leaders in charge of organisation, there is scope for arbitrary decisions. If not exercised with care, this may destroy order in the minds of the members of the organisation and undermine their productivity and loyalty.

Whether the hierarchical command elements in a business organisation are pronounced or weak has a great impact on its performance and flexibility (see section 9.3 below). Heavy reliance on hierarchical commands may stress cohesion and tight coordination, but it often conflicts with the limits of knowledge on the part of the leaders and of cognition on the part of the subordinates. Command structures often require costly control, measurement and monitoring. Heavy reliance on command may also undermine the motivation and creativity of the members of the organisation to perform. These problems tend to weigh more heavily in a complex, changeable world, so that de-emphasising hierarchy and command in the mix of the means of internal ordering frequently confers competitive advantages. Business leaders who have to manage rapid change often discover that control is more effective when exercised through universal rules that give collaborators and subteams general guidelines. Beyond this, they trust their collaborators to further the company's shared purpose. Modern business organisations therefore often emphasise training in judgemental skills and try to motivate collaborators by imbuing them with the 'business culture', that is, the general goals and rules of the organisation (Kreps, 1990). They promote flat hierarchies, teamwork and performance-derived rewards for successful internal competition. This style of management is nowadays often seen as more appropriate than hierarchies, pyramid-climbing, obedience to commands and reliance on close controls.

Economic organisations (firms) tend to be structured, coordinated and led by the owners of the production factor which is the bottleneck to growth. They tend to design the organisation, coopt rights to other resources and control the use of all production factors. What constitutes a bottleneck factor to economic growth has varied with time and circumstance. If security of life, limb and property is the bottleneck to economic growth because basic institutions are deficient, economic organisations tend to be led by the providers of security. This was frequently the case under feudalism in Europe and is now the case in parts of the third world and post-communist Russia. Once community-wide institutions safeguard security of life and property, as was done after the Middle Ages in Europe, capital tends to become the bottleneck to growth, so the capital owners typically control economic organisations and hire the other resources (capitalism). In industries where labour is the bottleneck to the expansion of business – be it because labour is scarce or because artificial constraints limit labour supply – labour representatives typically control economic organisations (worker codetermination).

Recently a few new ventures are being run by the owners of scarce knowledge, who borrow capital and hire labour; for example, some gifted fashion and computer software designers have created their own business organisations, and some film ventures and theatres are run by famous stars. Where deficient institutions make market access the bottleneck to business expansion, it is typically the operators with market access, such as the people who are able to obtain licences through political connections, who organise businesses.[3]

○ Key Concepts

Authority is the right and the power to enforce obedience, that is, to compel subordinates to follow instructions. Authority may be comprehensive (and allow arbitrary decisions) or be limited by institutions to specific circumstances (rule-bound behaviour).

Directives are detailed, prescriptive instructions for concrete actions. Directives leave no scope for free, self-responsible decision. Directives tend to downplay trust in subordinates and their judgement, and require much knowledge from those who direct.

A **pooling of resources** (property rights) occurs when market transaction costs are expected to be higher than the organisation costs to combine production factors. ●

9.2   Organisation Costs, Relational Contracts and Hold-up Risks

When people are coordinated within organisations this creates organisation costs, just as coordination in markets causes transaction costs (section 7.4). As we have already indicated, organisation costs may often be less than the transaction costs for coordinating similar activities through markets because organisations provide a firmer order to the various agents and many intraorganisational transactions are repetitive routines, offering the opportunity of reaping scale economies.

In principle, business organisers incur the fixed (and, once incurred, sunk) costs of finding information when they plan and set up an organisation, and recurrent costs when they run the organisation: communicating with collaborators, (re)negotiating assignments and deals, monitoring the performance of the various agents, and having to exercise sanctions against under-performing members of the organisation.

Organisation Costs and Leadership

The art of leadership of an organisation has much to do with keeping the internal organisation costs low. It has a lot to do with (a) gaining correct information on all aspects of the organisation's activities, and

(b) making that information compatible. It also has a lot to do with avoiding conflicts and disagreements amongst collaborators and sorting out possible conflicts. An understanding of shared objectives and, as mentioned, outside competitive pressures can greatly facilitate the leadership task. If leaders stick to transparent rules in their own actions and abstain from arbitrary decisions, they will build up a reputation for trustworthiness. Followers will then identify their leader with a predictable internal order. Such an image economises on the need to incur information costs. It becomes a valuable capital asset that saves organisation costs (Milgrom and Roberts, 1992, pp. 89–99). Trust is especially valuable when routine operations cannot be continued because the organisation has to undergo structural change. Then, it is doubly important that all those who are to be coordinated have an understanding of the shared strategic purpose (the overriding goals) that goes beyond tactical specifics. Napoleon referred to this aspect of leadership when he demanded that every soldier should 'carry a marshal's baton in his knapsack'.

The mix of reliance on directives and universal rules has a great impact on the costs of running organisations. The mix that is possible depends, however, on the quality of the team. The better educated, trained and motivated the various collaborators are, the more will shared rules serve to create a competitive advantage over organisations that rely heavily on case-by-case commands. The relative advantage of a style of management which emphasises rule coordination also increases with the complexity of the productive tasks. For example, mass production of a standard industrial product on the assembly line may well be coordinated most cheaply by relying on a fixed plan, on commands and close supervision. This style of management became known as *Taylorism*, after the American engineer who became probably the world's first modern 'management guru,' Frederick Winslow Taylor (1856–1915).

By contrast, piecework and quick changes in markets require complex, changeable responses by motivated skilled staff who act responsibly within firm-internal institutions. When products and services have to be tailormade, reliance on commands and close monitoring would only erode the motivation of collaborators to perform spontaneously and to share information with the top. In organisations that rely heavily on rule coordination, it may sometimes even pay to give members of the team scope to commit errors or to risk their own experiments because that may well unearth useful new information. The comments in the preceding chapter about rule-protected domains of freedom and innovation in markets also apply to the internal use of information in organisations.

The knowledge problem is thus a central challenge for all organisations. The art of leadership has much to do with handling this problem. If there were perfect knowledge, there would be little need for management. This is one of the reasons why much management teaching and many business administration courses have turned away from models of neoclassical economics which assume perfect knowledge: if the assumption of perfect knowledge were true, management would be virtually superfluous (Dahmén *et al.*, 1994).

Integration and Out-sourcing

Much coordination of production factors can be done alternatively *ex ante* and *ex post*. Organisations rely more on *ex ante* planning than is the case in coordination through the market process. The leaders of organisations therefore have to evaluate regularly what to coordinate as an integral part of the organisation and what should be left to subcontracting. A general rule is to compare the expected transaction costs in markets with the expected organisation costs. This ratio is a function, amongst others, of the quality of market institutions and of technology. Where market institutions are poor and create high transaction costs, for example because of poor regulation, legislation and jurisdiction, a tendency to integrate many activities under organisational control may be observed. A high degree of vertical integration is, for example, typical of heavily controlled economies where markets for many inputs are not allowed to develop and where genuine prices are not formed, so that much valuable information is never communicated. By contrast, well-functioning market economies give rise to many specialised subcontractors to whom producers can delegate specific tasks, not least in information gathering. Thus, the financial industry has developed specialised subcontractors to the big savings and investment banks who deal with foreign-exchange risks, overnight money, forward markets, options, insurance, legal issues and many other specialised aspects of the capital market. Another example is building contractors who rely on specialist markets to sell them electricity and water networks, advice on statics and waste treatment, advice on colour schemes and building security, amongst others.

The relative costs of organising and contracting are also affected by technology. For a considerable time, the spread of mainframe computers favoured big organisations. In the 1960s and 1970s computers came as big, indivisible packages that could handle large volumes of standardised information, so big corporations and big government had competitive advantages. This created an incentive to integrate more and more activities into the framework of big organisations. But from the late 1970s, technology changed to decentralised, flexible computing power, user-friendly software and low-cost, user-friendly communications. This gave small operators the tools to better exploit their decentralised, highly specialised knowhow and skills. Contracting out frequently became the cheaper option, as distributed computer networks lowered transaction costs and cheaper telecommunications allowed frequent, intensive communications between client and provider of inputs. It is no coincidence that this has given rise to numerous new market niches and to increased outsourcing and networking. Thus, the car industry increasingly used subcontractors to develop and produce specialised car components and concentrated on assembling them. Computer links permitted 'just-in-time' delivery and intense sharing of technical expertise among independent businesses (networking, productive alliances). Entirely new markets emerged to support big organisations with inputs and specialised information. 'Concentration on the core business' became the slogan in business organisations. This was often accompanied by flatter, less complex, less hierarchical internal management structures and a trend towards encouraging competition amongst fairly autonomous teams within the same firm. In government organisations, that same shift in the cost ratio has favoured out-sourcing and privatisation (Drucker, 1993; Naisbitt, 1994; Bickenbach and Soltwedel, 1995; Siebert, 1995).

The shift to more reliance on market coordination puts a premium on reliable institutions and low transaction costs. These form social capital that can make an economy internationally more competitive than economies with fuzzy, costly institutional environments. The increased interest in institutional economics, to which we referred in Chapter 1, has much to do with this shift, as does the need to reduce transaction costs by appropriate public policies and fostering appropriate business ethics.

Explicit and Implicit Relational Contracts

One-off contracts are relatively less important in modern complex economies than open-ended or relational contracts. As we saw in section 7.4, circumstances will change over time, so it is impossible to cover all contingencies completely by explicit stipulations in the contract. Relational contracts therefore often contain implicit understandings of give and take and of implicit sanctions. Implicit internal contracts establish institutions that make up the 'company culture' or the 'team spirit', they keep internal information and coordination costs low and guarantee scope for independent decision making for those who act within this rule structure. This is important for motivation and creativity, for shifting the organisation from mere set-goal compliance and satisficing ('Don't ask me, I only work here!') to creative-entrepreneurial behaviour. Hierarchical controls may conflict with reliance on implicit relational contracts – control maniacs destroy motivation. Explicit and implicit relational contracts establish only a certain measure of predictability and contain clauses that deal in a universal, non-specific way with contingencies (for example, an agreement to seek an independent arbitrator in case of conflict). Ongoing relations depend heavily on institutions to establish a measure of confidence for both sides of the agreement.

Relational contracts between the owners of property rights in different production factors make the owners and their assets part of the organisation. The bind is reinforced by sanctions for deficient or incomplete fulfilment of relational contracts, which can consist of pre-agreed penalties (for example, exclusion from profit sharing, payment of penalties for late delivery, or loss of influence over management decisions), exclusion from the organisation and hence from future benefits or sanctions under external law.

O Key Concepts

Organisation costs are the resource costs of planning, establishing and running an organisation. They include fixed, sunk costs of information search and design and variable costs of operation. The latter contain the costs of monitoring the performance of collaborators according to their contractual obligations, the notification of shortcomings and adjudication of intraorganisational conflicts, and, if necessary, the enforcement of agreed performance standards.

Implicit relational contracts are mutual understandings of give-and-take between the members of an organisation or a team. They cover open-ended internal institutional arrangements that channel many of the vertical exchange relationships between the owners, the leaders and the collaborators in an organisation, as well as some of the horizontal exchanges between collaborators and teams. ●

9.3   Ownership and Control: the Principal–Agent Problem in Business

The defining criterion of any economic organisation is the answer to the question: Who gets the profit, once all contractually agreed expenses have been deducted from the receipts, and who bears losses?

We call those to whom this applies the principals. The question then is: Do the risk-bearing principals have effective and direct control over the organisation and its detailed operation? This is the central issue of corporate governance in any organisation. It arises whenever the principals of the organisation do not manage all activities themselves, and in particular in joint-stock companies where the owners have delegated the control of daily business to executive managers who act as their agents. The manager-agents are of course much closer to the action and are normally much better informed about the organisation than the principals.

Agent Opportunism

In this situation, there is a danger that the agents may act opportunistically in their own self-interest and neglect the interest of the principals (section 3.4). They may try to shirk risks and hide behind cumbersome committees instead of taking decisions, preferring the quiet life, although taking risks and deciding expediently would probably enhance the profits earned by the principals. They may create unnecessary subordinate positions to justify promotion to a supervisory position. They may enjoy high on-the-job consumption (use of business facilities and company property for personal purposes, splendid offices, prestigious company premises, frequent enjoyable conferences and unnecessary business trips; excessive investment in equipment which is subsequently underutilised; acquisition of information and skills on the job are then marketed elsewhere; preparation of reports that no one reads; frequent staff lunches, and the like). They may tolerate avoidable costs although these expenses do not serve to promote the ultimate purposes of the organisation. And they may readily settle for higher wage claims and accept costly settlements in court cases, because fighting a strike or defending a challenge in court is uncomfortable and risky to management. A frequent manifestation of agent opportunism is satisficing, adjusting performance standards to lesser outcomes in the past, rather than pursuing excellence in achieving set goals or risking creative-entrepreneurial action to overcome obstacles (section 3.4).

Some forms of agent opportunism are against the law (for example, fraud), other forms may only be against general standards of behaviour such as honesty and punctuality. In all cases, it may be difficult and costly for the owners to detect and prove.

The principal–agent problem can arise as soon as the owners hire others. Even owner-managers have the problem of monitoring the performance of their employees and enforcing their compliance with the organisation's objectives. It is therefore a focal task of management to prevent or contain such opportunism by obtaining sufficient information about the performance of collaborators, for example, by appropriate incentives and mixes of command and organisation-internal rules. (For a good survey of the principal–agent problem in business, see Arrow, 1985.)

The principal–agent problem has been analysed in particular detail for joint-stock companies where the control of day-to-day operations – indeed, of major strategic choices – is left to managers. The principals, the shareholders, are not directly involved in the running of the organisation. Executive managers tend to be much better informed and more closely involved, so they may act in their own interest to the detriment of the interests of the less well informed principals (Berle and Means, 1932). For example, the managers of a joint-stock company may arrange business so that they run only a small risk of being fired or enjoy high on-the-job consumption. At the same time, they tolerate low profits, which is presumably against the principals' interests. The separation of ownership and control thus has the potential to create high information and organisation costs. The problem is compounded by the fact that shareholders – and small investors in particular – have insufficient incentives to incur the high information cost necessary to find out whether managers are acting responsibly in their interest.

Is the Principal–Agent Problem the Achilles Heel of Capitalism?

Some analysts who observed the growth and spread of the modern corporation considered the principal–agent problem to be the Achilles heel of the capitalist system, predicting increasingly poor usage of capital by risk-shirking managers and growing resistance to cost controls which benefit the principals but may hurt some of the agents (Berle and Means, 1932). Some observers came to the conclusion that only strong legal and regulatory intervention in corporate governance could overcome the principal–agent problem (Galbraith, 1967). Others saw unsurmountable knowledge and enforcement problems for public corporate-watchdog agencies (Demsetz, 1982, 1983, 1988, [1982] 1989). These latter observers also feared that the judgement of managers in risk-taking and innovation would suffer when corporate governance is heavily regimented, since many management decisions are, by their very nature, beyond the analysis of lawyers, bureaucrats and others, who are the wiser only with hindsight. Given the knowledge problem, there are real dangers of regulatory failure in the close supervision of corporate governance.

However, management-run corporations in most advanced capitalist countries have not performed systematically worse than owner-managed firms, so the principal–agent problem in corporate governance is obviously less severe than originally thought. Indeed, experience has shown that there are a number of powerful checks on the agent opportunism of corporate managers (Jensen and Meckling, 1976, esp. pp. 308–9; Jensen and Ruback, 1983; Jensen, 1983):

(a) modern business organisations have designed a number of effective company-internal institutions to contain manager opportunism and have created incentives for managers to act in the owners' interest: regular internal and external audits to ensure openness and accountability, imposition of budget controls, shareholder meetings and audit committees which work for the shareholders, incentive pay, part-remuneration of managers in company stock, and job tenure dependent on performance. These devices create what have been called 'bonding costs' (Jensen and Ruback, 1983, p. 325), but they tend to be less than the costs incurred when managers are poor and self-seeking;

(b) competitive capital markets tend to evaluate the performance of share companies regularly, with freely traded shares allowing owners to exit or enter at low cost and share prices reflecting these evaluations almost daily. Moreover, financial institutions assess management teams professionally as a client service to shareholders, in particular when companies try to raise new finance, which tends to uncover manager opportunism sooner or later;

(c) new, specialised information markets – professional analysts for large and small investors – and the business press also reduce monitoring costs for the principals, as long as corporations are required by law to report regularly and completely on their business (accountability);

(d) there are competitive markets for managers and management teams. These tend to reward agents who have earned a reputation for honest, effective management with promotion and higher salaries. These markets are often supported by specialist information markets and agencies, for example in the form of corporate head-hunting agencies;

(e) markets for the corporate control of going concerns exist in most capitalist economies: when incumbent management teams obviously perform below market standards, new owners will come in with (friendly or hostile) takeover bids and merger proposals, and will install new management teams who are expected to be more effective. Managers may also attempt buy-outs to realign control and ownership. Takeover battles can be costly, but they tend to enhance ownership control and reduce potential losses due to self-seeking management;[4]

(f) product markets also reflect the performance of management teams. As long as product markets are not monopolised, management teams which act opportunistically will sooner or later lose market share and this will signal the opportunism of the managers. Product-market competition complements the competition in the capital and the manager markets in ensuring that the interests of the principals are safeguarded.

Competition and the rules which ensure transparent information enhance shareholder control simply by being a potential threat to and discipline on opportunistically inclined managers. The unrelenting pressure of rivalry for market share (discussed in Chapter 8) thus serves to empower the owners of companies and reduces their monitoring costs. Costly direct controls and sanctions of opportunistic managers then need to be exercised but rarely. The principal–agent problems in joint-stock companies tend to become virulent only when managers obtain political protection against the various contests for their position, for example when parliaments legislate to impede take-over bids or control foreign investment.

In the economics literature, the consequences of the principals' knowledge problem concerning the actions of opportunistic agents have sometimes been discussed under the label of X-inefficiency. Leibenstein (1966) contended that business organisations, which had market power and were not exposed to vigorous competition, tended to operate less effectively in pursuit of their principals' objectives and tended not to innovate as much as firms that were exposed to active market rivalry. The extensive work on X-inefficiency thus underpins the general message from this section, namely that competitive (product and factor) markets surrounding a firm ensure that the principals' interests in stock companies are pursued – and not the opportunistic goals of the agents. Competitive markets are thus in the interest of the capital owners, though not necessarily in the interest of company managers and workers.

O Key Concepts

The **principal–agent problem**, which was defined in section 3.4, is seen by some to be particularly pronounced in **joint-stock companies** where managers control the business operations and shareholding principals are often far removed from business activities. Experience has shown that competition exercises strong spontaneous checks on manager opportunism: share markets constantly evaluate company performance, markets for managers reward with higher salaries those who act in the interest of the principals, and takeover bids exert control over opportunistic managers.

On-the-job consumption is prevalent in business organisations that enjoy market power and are shielded from vigorous competition in a market niche (see Chapter 8). On-the-job consumption – like other aspects of the principal–agent problem – is curbed by exposure to intense competition. It also occurs in the management of government agencies (Chapter 10).

X-inefficiency describes the phenomenon of weakened cost controls, reduced risk taking, and on-the-job consumption that can be found in corporations which have fairly secure market niches and are not exposed to competition in product and factor markets. ●

Organisational Design: Styles of Management

Experience in firms shows that a very effective way of structuring economic cooperation is the competition of organised teams (profit centres, 'enterprises within enterprises'). Teams are bound by implicit, relational contracts that require the delivery (and trust in the delivery) of certain mutually agreed levels of performance between the leaders and the team members; for example, pay for predefined work performance. Within the team, information and coordination costs can be kept low because the interaction within teams tends to be intensive and repetitive. Individual team members can be confident of a certain ordered division of labour and are informed of the knowledge and skills of other team members. They follow a leader who coordinates some activities.

The order in which members of a business team operate with confidence is always a mix of top-down, designed order and of bottom-up, spontaneous order. The traditional approach of 'scientific management' (Taylorism) was to rely heavily on the top-down (command) end of the spectrum, whereas the flexible pursuit of changing opportunities by creative, entrepreneurial firms requires a management style much closer to the bottom-up (rule-coordinated) end of the spectrum. When surrounded by competitive markets, teams and firms are, in any event, disciplined by competitive outside challenges from other teams. Outside competition enhances the leader's coordinative influence, as it is based on the understanding that 'we are all in the same boat'. External competitive challenges ensure that internal infighting and insubordination are quickly sorted out and that information feedback is enhanced.

Organisational design can differentiate between top-down command and participative management to cope with different types of tasks (Table 9.1). Thus, a company's big strategy may be driven by a cohesive, designed plan, whereas the tactical decisions in implementing the strategy may be left to decentralised initiative within certain universal rules. Organisations may need more coordinated, top-down management when they find themselves in a crisis, whereas participative management, which fosters evolutionary creativity, may be appropriate for times of steady business.

The approach to organisational design which is appropriate depends on the framework in which the organisation operates and the quality of the workers. When industrial mass production was developed to cater to stable markets with the help of standardised production technologies and when many workers were unskilled in industrial work, 'scientific management' was developed. It relied on good planning and effective control. In a steady state, this approach to organisation can reap scale economies and achieve regular product standards even with low-skilled workers because the production process is broken up into many small, repetitive steps. However, in recent decades markets have become more changeable and specialised. Many outputs no longer consist of standard mass products, but are demanded and sold in flexible, customised job lots. This is so particularly in service industries, where frequently each job is customised and sometimes even designed in close consultation with the customer. In dynamic markets, perpetual adjustment and innovation are required (Bickenbach and Soltwedel, 1995; Vickery and Wurzburg, 1996). In these circumstances, there is great advantage in participative management, which gives collaborators or subteams much scope for decision making and mobilising the creative-entrepreneurial potential. Participative team organisation relies on implicit relational contracts and general material motivation for performance (Table 9.1). This approach to organisational behaviour is certainly suited to emphasising creative rationality on the part of all members of the organisation (section 3.2).

Business organisations which want to compete successfully in dynamically changing, highly specialised markets will focus on the demands of their diverse customers, rather than on the internal requirements of rigid production processes. They will stress performance by the whole team over individual performance and will create incentives for performance rather than reward mere attendance or effort. This requires organisation-internal rules that cope with divisions of interest. It also requires the defeat of inward-looking attitudes which only lead to the monopolisation of information.

Table 9.1   Organisational behaviour: scientific versus participative management

	Scientific management (Taylorism)	Participative management
Main area of application	Industrial mass production; control of standardised product quality; scale economies	Market-oriented job lots; service industries; flexible, spontaneous adjustment; made-to-measure production; economies of scope
Organisational design	Multistage hierarchy; separate specialised steps in production process; big firms (vertical and horizontal integration of activities)	Flat structures; teams; stress on creativity; integrated processes and functions; concentration on the core business; interfirm networking; subcontracting; joint development by groups of firms
Mode of operation and control	Hierarchical control, vertical communication; top-down quality control; penalties for under-performance ('sticks')	Scope for decision making and self-control of quality; reliance on self-motivation and spontaneous horizontal communication, backed by incentives ('carrots') and sanctions ('sticks')
Main motivational principle	Command and control, design of detailed work plan; authority based on position, avoidance of penalties by subordinates	Incentives through implicit contracts; shared general goals; penalties for gross malfunction/opportunism and differentiated pay incentives for goal attainment; multiskilling
Focus of leaders	Good planning; close supervision; ensure obedience and compliance	Consultation of all staff; shared enterprise culture; training to enhance the productive and creative potential and the responsiveness to new information of all staff
Ideal conditions	Stable, predictable environment, low skills and low motivation of workers, mass production	Variable, diverse markets: highly skilled and motivated collaborators; complex production processes

Such a style of participative management will foster organisation-wide cooperation. Reliance on team support is likely to cost networking time, but it saves on control and monitoring costs such as too much internal reporting, long hierarchical decision channels and enforcement of commands. It will also economise on the information cost of the leaders of the organisation. If one of the key problems of leadership is to obtain and digest necessary information, then leaders have to be ready to listen and, at times, be prepared to withhold criticism and sanctions. Above all, an 'advance payment' of trust in subordinates is needed when they carry out their own experiments and act on their own knowledge and judgement. The need for information and coordination can be reduced by encouraging subordinates to take a degree of proprietary interest in their own team or operation, for example by materially rewarding performance at the team level (salary premiums for measured success; see box), by encouraging interteam competition, and by keeping agents in jobs long enough to identify with them.

❖ A Case of Participative Management

In June 1996, the American clothing manufacturer and distributor Levi Strauss & Co. promised to distribute $750 million in bonuses among all its 75 000 employees worldwide on condition that the company met a sales-growth target of 2.1 per cent per annum to the year 2001.

This 'global success sharing plan' is based on the company's avowed opinion that 'motivated employees are our source of innovation and competitive advantage'. It has the characteristic of a simple-to-understand, general target and shuns prescriptions and detailed controls, relying instead on implicit, open-ended understandings (institutions) between employer and employees. The incentive scheme relies on the creativity and cooperation of workers and work teams to come up with their own creative solutions to promote the company's overall sales objective, and it makes the bonus payments clearly conditional on measurable performance. ◆

(Source: Press reports, June 1996)

Management Style and Societal Institutions

The style of management and the preferred type of organisational behaviour depend not only on the diversity and dynamism of individual markets in which firms operate, but also on the wider institutional framework. Thus, participative management, which is based on trust, is less likely to succeed if the internal institutions of society do not encourage honesty. Similarly, a heavily regulated labour market may make it impossible to offer the material incentives that motivate collaborators to align their own purposes with those of the firm. Legislation or judicial interpretations of the law may also make it difficult for supervisors to discriminate between those collaborators who perform and those who do not when they reward performance, because that judgement may not be capable of being 'proven' to the satisfaction of a court. This indicates that labour market deregulation and the confinement of governments to protecting individual liberties is an essential precondition for successful participative human-resource management. A similar complementarity between the wider institutional context and the internal constitution of the organisation also exists with regard to internal sanctions for breaches of implicit contracts and the responsiveness of collaborators to incentives to perform and learn. These complementarities between organisation-internal management and the external institutions of a society explain why multinationals often have to make adjustments to their organisational behaviour when they move to new locations in other countries, and why institutional reforms to enhance a country's competitiveness require time to gain full impact: business cultures react only slowly to new societal institutions. Leaders then have to rethink their philosophy of leadership and workers have to adjust their routines and practices to remain successful.

There are also important international differences. It is no coincidence that participative styles of management have been greatly inspired by Japanese and other East Asian experiences. In these 'neo-Confucian societies', there is much reliance on informal, implicit institutions that encourage self-control of opportunistic instincts. Thus, team competition and non-prescriptive management could draw on general cultural characteristics, whereas societies with strongly individualistic, self-seeking cultures, such as those of Latin America, probably require more reliance on top-down control and stronger sanctions against agent opportunism. When management analysts now speak of a 'global competition of workplace cultures', they normally refer to the ease or difficulty with which flexible, low-cost organisational designs can be implemented in different societies as well as the ease or difficulty of motivating collaborators in loyally supporting a business's purpose.

O Key Concepts

Organisational behaviour refers to the vertical and horizontal interaction of the members of an organisation and the institutions which structure that interaction. It is an important part of the leadership of an organisation to ensure that agents, who are bound to pursue their own purposes, indeed act in the interest of the self-set goals of the organisation, for example by designing incentive pay structures, stipulating performance, skill development and pay in explicit contractual terms, fostering informal institutions and shared values.

Scientific management is the term applied to the teachings of F.W. Taylor, who developed the principles of how industrial work processes should be planned, controlled and broken up, so as to obtain standard quality and economies of scale. These methods often led to a many-layered management hierarchy, complex approval and monitoring processes ('control mania'), but also high attainment levels of set objectives. They are suited to the world of 'end–means rationality' (section 3.2).

Participative management describes a style of organisational behaviour that is fairly decentralised and not very prescriptive, leaving scope for decentralised decision making by collaborators and subteams, relying on incentives within a network of often implicit, open-ended contracts and on the cultivation of the creative-entrepreneurial potential of collaborators. This style of management is better suited to a competitive, dynamically changing environment, as well as tailormade job-lot production to cater to specialised market niches. It is suited to promote an entrepreneurial rationale. ●

Business Organisation and Profitability

How well the principal–agent problem is controlled under various organisational arrangements has great import for the return on capital invested. The question has been asked whether various types of business organisation – owner-managed firms, partnerships, cooperatives, mutuals and share companies – are equally effective in employing investment capital, controlling costs and making a profit. Or do differing internal control mechanisms produce systematically differing results? This is primarily an empirical question. However, what we know about human nature and institutions suggests that the rules which coordinate the internal dealings of an organisation are of great relevance to performance and the achievement of the organisation's purposes.

Owner-managed firms, partnerships, cooperatives, mutual societies, trusts and non-profit organisations may have some advantages over large corporations: easier direct information exchange and monitoring by the owners – as well as the spontaneous enforcement of directives and agreed rules – will result in lower internal organisation costs. Collaborators and appointed managers may be prevented from acting opportunistically in their own interests when the boss is directly involved and is familiar with the daily business. This explains the strength and resilience of many family firms.

We noted that openness for capital owners – the ease of exiting if they are displeased with the management – is an important lever to control manager opportunism and cost levels. Partnerships, mutual societies and trusts are less open to new capital owners joining and old ones disassociating themselves from the venture, than are joint-stock companies. Here, 'exit' and 'entry' through share transactions on the stock exchange are feasible at low transaction cost. The resulting openness of joint-stock companies signals manager performance. This suggests that the managers of joint-stock companies face stronger incentives to perform according to the principals' stated objectives than economic organisations whose capital cannot be so easily traded. In small firms, direct internal information flows may be sufficient to control the principal–agent problem, but if organisations grow in size and complexity, a growing knowledge problem on the part of the principals and greater opportunities for self-seeking agents could be anticipated. Then, indirect signals through the share and other markets must be relied upon to keep a check on the manager-agents. Based on this logic, particular principal–agent problems could be expected in non-profit organisations where surpluses are left in the organisation until profit is dispersed by one means or another. The incentive to control costs effectively is then correspondingly weak.

Available empirical evidence indeed suggests that this is correct. Small companies can be run effectively when few owners directly supervise the manager(s). If enterprises grow and more owners join, it becomes difficult to form a joint view amongst the various owners, and each individual owner may not have a sufficient personal stake to incur the considerable costs of constantly monitoring managers, so managers are often able to 'highjack' organisations. The evidence, at least for the United States, indicates that joint-stock companies tend to attain better results in comparable activities than mutual societies or non-profit organisations. In particular, the evidence suggests that managers of joint-stock companies are, on balance, inclined to take more profitable investment decisions (Fama and Jensen, 1985). The gradual conversion into listed share companies of many family enterprises, partnerships, trusts and mutual societies which have grown in size also suggests that the advantages of indirect evaluations through the open share and other markets give owner-principals advantages. Openness (owners buying and selling shares) and competitive surroundings tend to enhance company performance and serve innovation.

In winding up, we may say that teams and organisations, which combine goal-setting and coordinative directives from above and rule-guided coordination within competitive checks from without, are in the best position to tackle ever-present knowledge problems. Besides, the reliance on rules that give collaborators spheres of freedom and self-responsibility pays off because it motivates people to give their best. A welcome by-product of a participative, rule-based management style is, incidentally, that working life, which takes up the larger part of the waking hours of many people, then tends to contribute more to human fulfilment and satisfaction.

We conclude by saying that the general insights from institutional economics can shed much light also on organisation science and help organisations to exploit knowledge and other resources.

Questions for Review

- Human action can be coordinated in markets and organisations: what are the defining characteristics of an 'organisation'?
- Which of the following are organisations, as defined here, and which not:
  - an agricultural cooperative;
  - a football club;
  - a sports team;
  - the stalls in a market place;
  - a gathering of onlookers around an accident in the street;
  - that same gathering, after they have voted to get together to help the victim;
  - a public utility;
  - a group of students who go on an excursion;
  - a franchising agreement (for example, to sell hamburgers under the McDonald label)?

  Give reasons for each of your answers.
- Which of the following coordinative devices are (a) prescriptions (directives), and (b) proscriptions (institutions):
  - 'drive on the left-hand side of the road';
  - 'buy sufficient raw materials for the plant';
  - 'always speak the truth';
  - 'when you deal with Mr X, fulfil the contract scrupulously';
  - 'deliver on time';
  - 'do not deliver the next consignment to the ABC company'.

  (NB: Always ask yourself whether the instruction is directed at persons who have a specific responsibility to obey (but no one else) or whether it is an abstract, universal rule directed at an undefined number of unspecified people concerning general categories of actions.)

- Who are agents and who principals in business organisations:
  - the shareholders;
  - the private proprietor of a small shop;
  - the hired chief executive officer (CEO);
  - the director of finance;
  - the treasurer of a club;
  - the members of a mutual society (such as an automobile association).
- List a number of different types of economic organisations and establish in each case who bears the risk of losses and gets a profit.
- Give a series of examples for the opportunism of corporate managers which is at the expense of the owners.
- What is 'on-the-job consumption'? Give examples that you have observed in an organisation that you know.
- Write down the attributes of good leadership that we gave in the text and explain – with reference to what we learnt about human behaviour in Chapter 3 – why these attributes create well-led organisations. Try to match the attributes of good leadership with their opposites and judge, for an organisation you know, where on the spectrum you would rate their leaders.
- Many successful mutual societies around the world, such as savings and insurance societies, have been transformed into open share companies. Can you guess the reasons why this might be the case, thinking of the incentives to control costs and expand the market?
- If the security of life, limb and property remains a major long-term problem in a country like Russia, who will organise economic ventures and hire rights to other complementary production factors: the owners of capital, the security providers (such as the Mafia or local bureaucratic over-lords), or technical experts?
- Can you think of a recent example where an organisation found that the ratio of organisation to transaction costs had shifted so that a previously integrated operation was subcontracted? Or vice versa?
- Can you make an estimate of the share of all organisation costs in total costs in a business firm you are familiar with? How has the spread of computers affected (a) the unit cost of organisation, (b) the volume of acts of coordination, and (c) the volume of all organisation costs [(a) × (b) = (c)]?
- What can the leaders of a business do to ensure cohesion and quick response to new challenges? Why do military organisations tend to rely more on command than, say, business firms?
- If we consider the family as an economic organisation, what mix of directive- and rule-guided behaviour seems appropriate? Should that mix change with the age and maturity of children? If so, why? If the family provides the comfort of order to its members, what purpose does that serve in your own experience?

- Define 'asset specificity'. Give an example of a fixed asset which your family owns which depends for its usefulness on complementary inputs. Have you been 'held up' by the providers of the complementary input? If not, why not? If yes, could you think of an arrangement where this risk could be reduced or eliminated?
- Does the principal–agent problem exist in a workplace with which you are familiar? How is the potential opportunism of collaborators controlled there?
- List the mechanisms which control the agent opportunism of managers of joint-stock companies in your country. Do you know of instances in which these mechanisms failed? What went amiss?
- Do company managers in your country face close legal and regulatory supervision? If so, how does that affect their willingness to take risks? How does that affect the readiness or otherwise of gifted people to become managing company directors?
- Does the regulation of corporate governance by an official corporate watchdog seem superfluous to you in the light of what you learnt in this chapter? If so, why? If not, why not?

Notes

1. The obverse question of why markets exist can be answered with reference to the increasing complexity of the coordination task as organisations grow. The exponential rise in organisation costs draws a line to the growth of organisations and brings markets into play.
2. We owe these points to an article by Daniel Kiwit, 'Zur Leistungsfähigkeit neoklassisch orientierter Transaktionskostenansätze', Ordo, vol. 45 (1994), 105–36.
3. Since the right to organise business confers material and non-material benefits, the owners of different production factors tend to engage in collective, political action to shape the external institutions that enhance their chances to set up organisations or hamper the opportunities of the owners of rival production factors to do so. Such collective action may of course undermine overall economic growth and, with it, the chance for all production factors to earn high returns.
4. Takeovers may not always enhance knowledge. Where takeover merchants engage in the sheer 'conquest of territory', for example by highly leveraged buy-outs which saddle companies with high debts, they may promote a management culture that lives by the virtues of tribal conquest and not the virtues of the commercial-innovative culture described in Chapter 6. Managers of taken-over firms may then concentrate on more takeovers and on liquidating bundles of assets, rather than competition by performance in serving demand. Such a shift will, however, sooner or later run its course. Companies that adhere exclusively to the tribal conquest strategy will frequently go bankrupt and leave unpaid 'junk bond' debts in their wake, as was the case, for example, in the United States takeover flurry during the 1980s.

CHAPTER 10

Collective Action: Public Policy

Apart from a protective role (discussed in Chapters 5 and 7), governments also take on productive and redistributive functions. Over time, productive and redistributional functions have been expanded in most advanced economies, raising the government share in the national product.

There are particular problems with collective decision making as compared to a situation in which private property rights are disposed of on the basis of voluntary, bilateral contracts. We shall discuss systematic reasons why outcomes of collective action are often less likely to meet individual aspirations than as market solutions.

There is the danger of pervasive principal–agent problems in government. Political agents (rulers, parliamentarians, administrators) often pursue their own purposes, even at the expense of the average citizen, the principal in collective action. In government, competition is normally absent – and with it the constraints that agents in business are normally facing. Where possible, it therefore pays to reduce the functions of government by corporatising, deregulating and privatising. Where this is not feasible, attempts can be made to control political agents by other means, for example by constitutional rules, hierarchical controls, the separation of powers and periodic electoral control. Yet, such controls constrain government agents only imperfectly. To be more effective in promoting the interests of the citizen-principal, these controls have to be complemented wherever possible by openness to competition with other governments and by openly accessible information (free press, accountability).

Policy makers who wish to foster the self-organising properties of the market system will be cautious when intervening in specific economic processes and outcomes. They will then also feel better protected from being captured by particular rent-seeking interests.

The chapter ends with a brief discussion of the attributes of economic and political constitutions which support discovery and information search and which keep property rights open to the ceaseless challenges of competition, thereby safeguarding freedom and prosperity.

The state is a potential resource or threat to every industry in the society. With its power, to take or give money, the state can and does selectively help or hurt a vast number of industries.
(G. Stigler, 'The Theory of Economic Regulation', 1971, p. 3)

The objective of the Constitution was to define the islands of government powers within the ocean of individual rights.
(William A. Niskanen, in J.D. Gwartney and R.E. Wagner (eds), Public Choice and Constitutional Economics, 1988)

The government is not a cow that is fed in Heaven and can be milked on Earth.
(Ludwig Erhard, German Minister of Economics, 1957)

The State [has a role] in the economic sector. Economic activity, especially the activity of the market economy, cannot be conducted in an institutional, juridical and political vacuum. On the contrary it presupposes sure guarantees of individual freedom and private property, as well as a stable currency and efficient public services. Hence the principal task of the state is to guarantee this security, so that those who work and produce can enjoy the fruits of their labours and thus feel encouraged to work efficiently and honestly.
(Pope John Paul II, Centesimus annus, 1991)

This chapter deals with collective action and public policy, that is, collective economic choices and the political coordination of entire communities. Such action has to rely often on top-down directives and legitimated coercion. The authority for this is derived from a political mandate which gives authorised persons defined powers to coerce all those who live or operate in a jurisdiction. Political authority places a coercive bind on individuals which differs fundamentally from the power of the leadership of private organisations. These are based on voluntary contracts; members can exit relatively easily if perceived advantages and disadvantages change. By contrast, people normally have to rely on voice to influence political choices.

The government's authority to mandate collective action may be derived from the transcendental ('by the grace of God', 'the Mandate of

Heaven'), from inheritance, or from once-off or periodic elections under some constitutional rule. Public authority normally needs to be legitimated by the support of private citizens who will assess whether it assists them in the pursuit of their fundamental objectives overall. Collective action should normally do so in ways that are predictable and commensurate with the cognitive and coordinative limitations of the citizens.

10.1   Public versus Private Choice

Complexities of Public Choice

When we discussed the various forms of property in Chapter 7, we identified certain types of property whose uses cannot be made exclusive, that is, whose costs and benefits cannot be internalised so that these assets cannot be allocated by private competitors in voluntary, bilateral contracts. They were:

(a) free goods, where no rationing and hence no economic choices are needed;
(b) pure public goods, where demand does not need to be rationed as no rivalry among users occurs, but where the total supply has to be decided by collective choice as their provision costs resources;
(c) common property, in particular in groups with compulsory membership (public-domain property and socialised property).

Categories (b) and (c) require collective choices which are determined by some sort of centralised political process. We noted briefly in section 7.2 that this created difficulties in allocation and knowledge search as compared to private choices. We now have to elaborate on this:

(a) When others cannot be excluded from property uses, more than two contracting parties have to agree. Since collective decisions involve more participants, with their own changing opportunity costs and varied purposes, clear-cut decisions are harder to arrive at. The transaction costs of decision making tend to be higher than in private, bilateral choice.
(b) As individual preferences have to be amalgamated and averaged, collective decisions are unlikely to match the diversity of individual aspirations as well as diverse private choices. 'One size fits all' expresses this phenomenon. The experiences after the end of collectivism in the formerly centrally planned economies certainly show how much people appreciate the choice of their own diverse cloth-

ing, hair styles, careers, cars and lifestyles. With hindsight, the mandatory wearing of Mao uniforms may have brought technical gains of mass production but great losses of individual satisfaction.

(c) Give and take are clearly related in reciprocal and equivalent private exchange, so decision makers have complete feedback from their decisions. By contrast, collective choice involves multilateral give and take where the benefits are normally indirect and non-mutual and decision makers get no immediate feedback. The collective choice of a community may, for example, be to build a bypass road around their town. This will affect taxpayers who have to fund the road-building costs and it affects the inhabitants differentially. Some may discover that they benefit from less traffic noise, others that their businesses suffer. Because it is a 'package deal' and the costs and benefits are diffused and non-equivalent, the decision on a bypass road has to be forced on the community by appropriate rules after the majority has decided. The temptation would otherwise be to opt out of paying and to free ride on the benefits. Where costs and benefits are not equivalent – as is the case in private, self-responsible decisions – there are the temptations of 'moral hazard', the dangers of a 'tragedy of the commons' and high monitoring and enforcement costs (sections 3.4, 5.3 and 7.2).

(d) A further problem of public choice, which had already troubled the Oxford mathematician Charles Dodgeson, better known under his *nom de plume* Lewis Carroll, in his book *Alice's Adventures in Wonderland* back in 1865, relates to what Kenneth Arrow (1951) called 'the impossibility theorem' in an analysis that earned him a Nobel Prize in Economics. He showed that a mix of individual preferences cannot be aggregated by a voting procedure in ways that ensure that the choice which individuals prefer will also be chosen by collective decision. He showed that inconsistencies arise which prevent the aggregation of individual preferences without contradiction and conflict. The 'collective will' can only be expressed imperfectly, as compared to the method of decentralised, diverse individual 'dollar votes'.

(e) Except in very small groups, collective choices have to be made by representatives. They may be self-appointed or elected. They amalgamate individual preferences to arrive at feasible decisions. Collective choices by representatives require three basic arrangements:

(i)   rules and procedures for collective voting have to be agreed. For example, the rule may be to act unanimously (which imposes very high negotiation costs) or to act on a two-thirds or a 51 per cent majority. These rules and procedures also have to lay down how votes are to be taken, and what matters the representatives are empowered to decide;

(ii)   because there is no direct reciprocity between give and take, as in the bilateral exchange of private property, the 'give' has to be determined by political choice, for example by setting tax rates. Incentives are considerable for individuals to reduce their contributions (but to free ride on the benefits), so that monitoring and enforcement become necessary and corresponding agency costs have to be incurred. In smaller collectives (local government, clubs), participants may be able to observe a measure of correspondence between 'give' (tax) and 'take' (benefit from collective action). In that case, the agency costs may be relatively small. But in big collectives, such as nations, and in collectives where individuals feel powerless and disenfranchised, solidarity is weak. Monitoring and enforcement costs then soar correspondingly;

(iii)   the third arrangement lays down how collectively generated benefits are distributed, on what criteria citizens can access those common-property goods when they rival with each other. This requires political power and leads to principal–agent problems of its own.

(f) As we saw in earlier chapters, the use of political power creates principal–agent problems: how can the citizen-principals ensure that their agents, once appointed, indeed do their bidding? The problems multiply, as we shall see shortly, when the political system is populated by party organisations, organised interest groups and self-seeking bureaucracies which may all pursue ends of their own. A related problem of collective choice arises in multistage majoritarian decision making: if general decisions are made on bundles of collective choices, such as party programmes, and specific decisions are later made by particularly concerned persons within the elected party or committee, it is possible that only 51 per cent of 51 per cent (that is, 26 per cent) of the votes of the principals determine the decision. Then, the majority feel disenfranchised. Constellations are realistically imaginable where even small minorities with a keen interest in a particular public choice make the decision, so that it is possible to speak of the 'exploitation of the majority by avid minorities'.

(g) In a complex society, the information costs of citizens who want to be aware of all public choices are extremely high. They will prefer to stay 'rationally ignorant'. If citizens want to give their individual preferences political weight, they would, moreover, have to incur high organisation costs, often for modest gain. It therefore is often rational for principals to remain inactive and to tolerate collective choices that disadvantage them to a degree (Downs, 1957a, b). Whilst such rational ignorance is understandable, it nevertheless contributes to an erosion of solidarity with the group and a feeling of disenfranchisement and insecurity, in particular when a large share of decisions on property use are subject to collective choice. Then, reforms that seek to decollectivise economic decisions (privatisation or conversion to club goods of socialised property, see section 7.2) can be a way of enhancing spontaneous community cohesion, voluntary rule adherence and confidence.

Democracy, Political Parties, Bureaucracies and Interest Groups

Much of what has been said in this book about public policy has at least implicitly related to democracy, that is, to that version of collective decision making which controls agents by periodic elections, the division of powers and the rule of law. Modern democracy is based on the recognition of certain inalienable basic rights of individuals which override other rules (section 6.1) and on the ultimate sovereignty of the people in giving its collective representatives temporary powers.

In its traditional version, the modern model of democracy was first developed in England, in a long process in which Parliament defended the 'people's law' against that of the kings. The process culminated in the affirmation of the Bill of Rights in 1688 during the Glorious Revolution. The original model of democracy did not incorporate certain important elements that are observed in modern public-choice processes: namely, political parties that bind elected members to a collective programme; bureaucracies that have the expertise and hard-to-get information to dominate complex choices; and organised and well-funded interest groups. These elements have a major influence on public choices, often to the disadvantage of the individual citizen. From the standpoint of an individualistic world view, these phenomena often augment the disadvantages of public over private choice.

Political agents are, in most democracies, organised in a few political parties that engage in political competition for the periodic vote. Given the high information costs of voters, they will offer crude, general programmes. Where there are two parties or blocks of parties, they will focus their rivalry on the median voter, the floating voter. The bulk of voters who are committed or who shy away from incurring the transaction costs of making fresh voting decisions each time can be neglected. As a consequence, most political programmes focus not on the bulk of the principals, all the voters, but only on the decisive, floating minorities. This tends to distort political action to the detriment of the 'silent majority'.

Political parties demand group solidarity and are able to enforce it by influencing candidate selection or re-election, as well as by expulsion of renegades from the party. The running of political parties nowadays requires massive funds to cover agency costs and advertising. The political interest is to get re-elected and gain the majority in parliament and dominance over the administration. Fund raising and the re-election motive may often lead to collective actions which are to the detriment of the citizens.

The problem is aggravated by organised interest groups which normally represent concentrated supplier interests and which are free to organise under the freedom of association, a basic right. As we have seen in sections 8.2 and 8.3, suppliers often try to 'fortify' their market niches and escape from costly rivalry among themselves by seeking political restrictions of competition after they have organised themselves into lobby groups. The advantage of obtaining political intervention tends to be massive for the few suppliers, whereas the disadvantage to buyers is thinly spread and hence not worth the high fixed costs of counter-lobbying.

Privileged producer groups will find it advantageous to invest a share of their gains from intervention in lobbying and bribing parties and bureaucracies, as well as in 're-educating' the public into thinking that the intervention is in the national interest. The interplay of supplier lobbies and political parties nowadays greatly influences public choices. It continually creates political motives to intervene in private property right uses (Hayek, 1979a, pp. 17–50). The scope of what is decided in an economy by the second-best mechanism of public choice, with its potential for arbitrary decisions and rule erosion, is expanded and the scope of private choice is correspondingly reduced.

In addition to supplier groups, modern democracies are also typified by social lobbies which argue for a great deal of transfer payments to those they represent. These social interest groups mobilise voters to object to budget cuts, although they are frequently organised by the providers of government welfare services and in that respect represent another producer lobby.

The public-choice bias in modern states is also increased by another group, which did not figure in the traditional model of democratic government: the bureaucracy. Public servants have often a self-interest in regulating markets so that free private choices are overshadowed or replaced by public choices. They create specific institutions because such institutions confer power and influence on them. The observation that someone's transaction costs are often someone else's income applies. This leads to a bureaucratic deformation of the institutions and a displacement of internal institutions.

Bureaucracies often enjoy information advantage. They cannot be effectively controlled by elected politicians, who are loath to incur the information costs. There is a tendency, given the complexity of modern economic life, for parliaments to create a framework of enabling legislation which allows bureaucratic experts to write the specific rules in the form of regulations. Where this tendency is strong, the rules proliferate and change frequently; the domain of free private choice is correspondingly curbed. The deluge of black-letter legislation and ordinances in all advanced countries, most of which originate in a self-centred bureaucracy, is testimony to that tendency (Bernholz, 1982).

As parties, lobby groups and bureaucratic interests are not part of the original model of democracy, they are rarely mentioned in constitutions and are even more rarely constrained by explicit rules of collective action.[1] We shall have to elaborate on how political competition works in a world with political parties, lobbies and bureaucratic interests and how that has led to demands for political controls of these groups. But first, we turn to the basic functions of government: protection, provision of public goods and redistribution of incomes and wealth.

O Key Concepts

Public choice relates to decisions on the uses of property rights which are not made by individuals. Whereas individuals are aware that they have to shoulder the full costs and also enjoy the full benefits when they enter into contracts over property uses, decisions that involve a multiplicity of people agreeing on the choice are normally less well informed. They are also less well placed to influence decisions. Public choices have to be made, however, where costs and benefits cannot be fully internalised (where externalities exist). But they are often extended to areas that can be left to private choice. Because public choice involves no reciprocal give and take, but only non-mutual benefits, it can easily lead to free riding, moral hazard, the tragedy of the commons and agent opportunism. In any event, public choice therefore requires coercion.

Rational ignorance may explain why voters and market participants do not incur the information costs necessary to be better informed. In many instances, they know that the gains from acting on additional information are nil or negligible. Rational ignorance is, for example, part of the constellation that facilitates rent seeking by organised supplier groups, but dissuades the many disorganised buyers from engaging in lobbying against political rent creation.

The **median voter** in electoral democracies designates the floating voter group which two contending political parties need in order to gain a 51 per cent majority and, with that, dominance of the legislature and frequently also the executive. ●

10.2   The Functions of Government

When discussing external institutions in Chapter 5, we said that protecting and backing the institutions of society was one of the major functions of government. The protective function of government facilitates order and gives individuals and private firms and associations confidence by making their coordinative tasks easier in the face of ignorance ('order policy'). We also saw that the protective task may at times require the use of legitimate force (law courts, police, military) to prevent free riding and principal–agent opportunism and to enforce the rules if necessary.

O Key Concepts

Government is an organisation (top-down, hierarchical order) which pursues certain collective aims and is politically authorised to exercise power, within certain rules, over its jurisdiction.

The **functions of governments** typically are: (a) to protect the freedoms of the citizens; (b) to produce public goods; and (c) to redistribute property rights. To carry out these functions, it incurs agency costs and has to raise taxes to administer and finance material resources to meet these costs. ●

Over time, the size of government and the share of the nation's resources that government agents command have risen considerably. Government spending as a percentage of the gross domestic product in what are now the big five industrialised economies – the US, Japan, Germany, France and the United Kingdom – used to average about 10 per cent around 1870 (Tanzi and Schuknecht, 1995); this average rose to about 25 per cent in the mid-1930s, and over 40 per cent in the mid-1990s. As of 1995, the share of government expenditure in overall demand was 54 per cent in the European Union, 39 per cent in the non-European Anglo-Saxon countries, and 27 per cent in the East Asian manufacturing countries (other than China) (World Economic Forum, 1996, p. 21). While the trend has been towards bigger government, collective decision making has occasionally been cut back, most notably in Germany and Japan after the second world war, frequently only to be pushed up again later.

The Protective Function

The protection of order and the rule of law by collective action has a long tradition. Its origins probably go back at least to when permanently settled villages, towns and cities came under some kind of leadership. Kings, high priests and judges emerged in these communities to adjudicate disputes and to enshrine or lay down principles according to which disputes amongst members of the community would be resolved or avoided (external institutions). This role of a third-party adjudicator may at first have been given to respected and experienced elders or priests, but later there were formal, constitutional arrangements to set up rulers (Benson, 1995). The concepts of collective action, political power and government were thus born: certain actions were taken on behalf of the community, and certain officials and official organisations were accorded authority and coercive powers over ordinary citizens and citizen associations. In all these cases, constitutional arrangements had to decide the fundamentals of collective action: how to appoint representatives and how to allocate the costs and the benefits of collective action (see section 10.1 above).

The most obvious protective function of government is to prevent the coercion of some citizens by others. It has been argued that the takeover of the protective function by government amounts to a kind of (hypothetical) 'disarmament treaty' amongst all citizens (Buchanan, 1975). If we had anarchy, if coercion were only confined by the 'violence potential' of other parties and if all citizens had to defend their property against others, this would be extremely costly (high exclusion and enforcement costs). They would prevent much beneficial division of labour and hinder prosperity. It is therefore expedient to employ an agent who is given the task of preserving the peace. To be effective, the agent must be given powers to coerce. At the same time, it has to be ensured that the agent – the government – does not use its powers against the principals, that is, the citizens. Others have made the point that the role of government is to protect spheres of individual freedom (Hayek, 1960).

How can governments keep the peace and protect freedom? The answer lies primarily with institutions: it is necessary to establish and enforce a system of rules that apply to all citizens equally (rule of law) and which prevent them from pursuing their purposes by force, deception or other forms of thuggery. Protection is thus closely related to the preservation of individual freedom. Without such institutional constraints, liberty would become licence and order chaos. In modern states, many of the rules which governments are asked to enforce under its protective function are formally laid down in the penal and the civil codes. In addition, protection also refers to the prevention of external threats; namely, the defence of the present and future freedom (security) of the citizens against coercion from the outside.

The Limits of Protection

A considerable part of the protective function of government is implemented through regulations, for example to protect health and safety. Such regulations are often economically justified because they deal with externalities. Thus, the untrammelled use of a specific private asset in an industry may endanger the safety of the workers. Ways to protect them are to regulate the uses of industrial assets and to prescribe safety rules. Externalities also occur with regard to the environment and health. A purpose of public health regulations is to reduce information and other transaction costs. Thus, one presumes that a government-certified pharmaceutical can be taken safely within stipulated limits — without the need to undertake one's own research into the consequences of taking that product. Or a rule that limits driving speeds in certain locations prevents costly 'discovery procedures' in the form of accidents. However, the ultimate regulatory purpose must always be kept in mind, namely that the institutions serve the citizen. In many countries, numerous health, safety and environmental regulations are now being adopted that do not stand up to this test. Their proliferation raises transaction costs and undermines the coordination and control function of competitive markets. The problem is not the existence of such specific interventions as such, but their high incidence and frequency. Therefore, each such regulation needs to be assessed as to its likely costs and benefits on the overall system.

The costs of regulations, including the compliance costs imposed on citizens (see below), need always to be taken into account when deciding whether governments should become active in regulating to protect citizens from certain risks. The attitude that no cost is too high if we protect certain purposes – such as human lives, the health of children, or national grandeur – is often held, in particular by people who support particular causes. But the average citizen has to bear the opportunity cost of regulations and tends to pursue a great variety of purposes.

The total-system costs of regulation are frequently not assessed when private self-constraint is replaced by collective regulation, at least if the compliance costs are widely distributed or not immediately evident. Thus, when it comes to health, safety or environmental protection, parliaments have sometimes decreed regulations that impose exorbitant compliance and other costs, typically in response to pressures from single-issue groups, whose members do not bear the costs of regulation. It must be asked, for example, whether US safety regulations made sense when they caused a cost for one life saved of $168 million when benzene waste standards were tightened in 1990, or of $920 million per one life saved when new drinking water standards were decreed in 1991, let alone the cost for saving an additional life in listing hazardous wastes in wood preservation in 1990 of no less than $5700 billion (Breyer, 1995; Viscusi, 1993; for an illustration, see box). The requirement to weigh the long-term social benefits against the long-term social costs of each regulation of course also applies to environmental conservation.

These figures illustrate a trend in the protective function of government in favour of an emphasis on security at the expense of fostering the coordination and control capacity of the competitive system and hence prosperity. When no account is taken of these costs, alternatives to public regulation are not considered and the interest of the average citizen, which is to put scarce resources to the most beneficial uses, is neglected. If the prevention of one premature death costs billions of dollars, it is likely that these resources used in another way – for example, by producing dialysis equipment – could save or extend numerous lives. If parliaments and bureaucracies yield to such tunnel visions of safety, they allow the costs of protective regulations to cumulate and curtail people's freedom to experiment and decide for themselves. The result is poor growth, ultimately greater risks to human lives and safety and a spreading feeling of being disenfranchised.

❖ Protecting Canadians from Camembert and Roquefort Cheeses

Health Canada, in all its collective wisdom, recently proposed an amendment to the Food and Drug Regulations that would have prohibited the production and sale of raw cheeses. This amendment would have outlawed about 90 varieties of raw-milk cheeses, including Camembert and Roquefort. The proposed regulation appeared to be based on links between unpasteurized cheeses with outbreaks of *listeria*, *salmonella* and *E. coli* ...

The regulators at Health Canada obviously wanted to create a safer world. Since 1971, 14 outbreaks of disease believed to have been caused by the consumption of raw-milk cheeses were reported *world-wide* [emphasis in original]. These outbreaks resulted in 57 deaths.

What Health Canada regulators set out to do was, by and large, more destructive than useful. They appeared to have very little regard for the practical consequences of the proposed amendment ... Given the relatively low level of risk associated with non-pasteurized cheese and the extremely low level of risk in Canada, eliminating a whole industry seems a rather drastic course of action ... .Regulating the minimal risks raises the cost of the things we buy. In this case, ... it would have destroyed a new and thriving industry and the livelihood of many. Legislation such as this suggests that Canadians are incapable of understanding and assessing risks. Indeed, it seems that the government has taken upon itself to act as a parent. ◆

(Source: K. Morrison and L. Miljan, 'Cheese, Politics, and Human Health: How the Media Failed to Critique Recent Government Policy', On Balance, *vol. 9, no. 5, May 1996; cited in* Fraser Forum, *September 1996, p. 38)*

Note: This particular recommendation of a scientific panel was ultimately not enacted.

The proliferation of specific protective regulations overburdens the cognitive capacities of economic agents and undermines the order which decision makers need to compete with confidence. Hence, regulations should be streamlined if government is to be effective again in its protective function. However, administrators may of course have self-interest in complex regulations.

The protective function of government has increasingly been supplemented by two other functions: the provision of public goods and the redistribution of starting opportunities, income and wealth.[2] Obviously, these functions create agency costs which have to be funded by tax collection or borrowing, and the material resources of government have to be administered, which creates additional agency costs.

The Productive Function

A case can be made for the government providing citizens with access to certain goods. We saw that pure public goods are goods and services from whose use it is very costly, if not impossible, to exclude those who have not paid for them and which, once provided, are not scarce because there is no rivalry in demand within certain limits (section 7.2). As private owners would in this case have to tolerate free riding by those who do not contribute to the cost of procurement and maintenance of these goods, there is a *prima facie* argument for public provision and funding by compulsory taxation. In this situation, private owners cannot properly exercise their property rights, including the right to exclude others. This presents an institutional shortcoming. One classic example is street lighting: if one member of society were to finance street lighting in order to enjoy its advantages, others could freely access the amenity. Another classic example of such a natural public good is defence against aggression from the outside: if one member of society were to provide a defence force, all the fellow citizens would get the benefit of protection and would not be excluded. The larger the gap between the costs and the benefits that can be exclusively appropriated, the smaller is the incentive to procure such a good. The possibility of free riding – the impossibility of exclusion – prevents the emergence of a market for such goods. Public goods would be undersupplied, as compared to private goods whose costs and benefits can be fully internalised by individuals. Pure public goods are extreme cases where provision by government has marked and positive external effects.

As we saw in Chapter 7, it may become possible to capture and internalise the positive externalities, for example by new electronic devices to measure or to exclude property uses. We noted that what is or is not a public good may change.

A general case for the provision of common goods thus exists, but this gives rise to the problems which were discussed in section 10.1 above. Governments may even respond mainly to the preferences of specific, organised groups when deciding what goods to provide and how to spread the costs among the citizenry. Thus, problems of hidden redistribution easily arise. They can be contained to some extent by fiscal decentralisation (fiscal federalism, see section 12.5) and when some citizens and capital are able to move to the jurisdiction which comes closest to providing the desired mix of public goods and other locational qualities. This is because the mobility of taxpayers and production factors among jurisdictions (openness) exerts some control on governments that want to redistribute costs and benefits in the provision and financing of public goods.

Access to goods from whose use others cannot be easily excluded, but for which there are rival demands, can be rationed by external rules and government directives. Whether they are produced by socialised property or by private competitors is a secondary consideration. What matters is the *provision* of goods and services from public resources.[3] It certainly is not necessarily for access that those goods and services are *produced* with socialised property. However, for a number of reasons, governments choose to organise and fund production by employing publicly owned property:

(a) Where large indivisibilities are presumed to transcend the financial capacity and organisational capability of individuals and private partnerships, or where sizeable scale economies are perceived to exist, rulers have often taken it upon themselves to mandate the design of work, its financing and implementation. This was frequently so – as in early Egypt or China – in the case of irrigation and drainage works, but also in the provision of infrastructure. The same rationale has been relied on more recently to turn space exploration into a government activity. In this context, it is often argued that large-scale ventures constitute 'natural monopolies' and that it is desirable for such monopolies to come under direct political control. In reality, however, such monopolies have frequently come into existence because government authorities erected barriers to competition, or failed to reduce the transaction costs of competing (Friedman, 1991). Once these operations were turned into government-owned monopolies they became high-cost operations. Nowadays, however, large-scale and internationally open capital markets are able to finance such big ventures, as long as user fees can be charged (excludability). With improved measurement technology, the case for many traditional public monopolies now falls by the wayside.

(b) One reason for providing certain services by public monopoly is that it gives more direct control to political authorities. Thus, non-violent control by professionals such as police and military forces, as well as law courts, seems a valid argument for public ownership of the resources. The costs of competition among these professionals would, after all, be excessive (think of Cambodia and Bosnia). Therefore these services are provided in most countries by public monopoly enterprises. Control problems also exist when these services are produced by public monopolies (police corruption, military coups, corrupt tribunals), but internal organisational command and financial controls by political authorities are often considered preferable.

(c) Governments have often claimed exclusive production rights to certain types of mining and trade as convenient sources of revenue (for example, salt or alcohol monopolies). When promising new technologies offer themselves as revenue raisers, governments have often taken over the ownership of these activities (for example, the public ownership of rail and telegraph systems in the nineteenth century when these technologies were new). Likewise, many governments have nationalised the oil and gas industry as a means of getting easy access to revenues. In these cases, other arguments for public production could probably also be adduced, but the interest in monopoly revenue no doubt often plays the key role.[4]

(d) State-operated production is often also used as a politically easy way of facilitating redistribution (see below).

Providing Access to Public Domain Goods

Where these considerations are not dominant (such as in education and health services), the provision of goods from the public budget may be done indirectly: public funds are used to acquire goods and services and the government acts as a quality controller, not the producer.

This requires elaboration in a number of respects:

(a) The question of how the provision of these goods and services is funded needs, as we have noted, to be kept apart from the question of whether these goods and services should be produced with government-owned (socialised) means of production. If it seems politically desirable to provide citizens with certain goods and services out of public budgets, private production and subsidised access will often be less costly and will offer citizens more choice. The argument that public production saves on transaction costs and eliminates the duplication of competitive private supplies assumes prior knowledge of outcomes and overlooks the potential of competition to uncover process and product innovations. In any event, public production is always fraught with the long-term dangers of unchecked agent opportunism and a reduced likelihood of innovation (see section 10.3).

(b) The issue of public ownership and control should also be considered separately from the issue of public monopolies. Even where government organisations engage in productive activities, there may be a case for competition among different public agencies (for example, between different publicly owned but corporatised power plants, hospitals and universities) and for competition with private suppliers (for example, allowing private telephone companies, trains, buses or airlines to compete with public-sector providers of these same services). Thanks to the drop in measurement and communications costs, there are now few 'natural monopolies' where competition is technically not feasible. Few existing monopolies survive long unless they are backed up by political intervention (Friedman, 1991).

(c) A third important issue in the socialised production of public goods is accountability, that is, full and transparent information on all the costs of and returns from the use of public property, as well as subjecting government-owned producers to firm budget constraints. Accountability is enhanced when public production ventures are corporatised, that is, their activities are administratively separated from the budget covering general government business. It is not always easy to enforce a hard budget constraint and withhold budget subsidies from loss-making public enterprises. However, if competitive pressures and the accountability of public office holders are weak, public servants become self-serving (high salaries, overstaffing, excessive on-the-job consumption). Where lax practices have become entrenched, moves to control the private appropriation of public property tend to be fiercely resisted. This has become evident in the course of many privatisation projects around the world (Chapter 14).

(d) Production by government agencies creates 'political firms': firms to which state ownership gives not only economic influence in markets, but also direct political influence over policy making (Alessi, 1980, 1982). Since no interested individuals have a direct claim on the residual profit of public-sector operations (nor are directly liable for the losses) and ownership rights cannot normally be transferred (except by privatisation), it is likely that 'political firms' will not be as closely monitored by the principals as private companies. After all, monitoring is a costly procedure. The managers of public enterprises therefore are exposed to incentive structures quite different from those applying to the leaders of private economic organisations (Chapter 9). It may, for example, be found that the monitoring of leave applications in public operations costs two or three times as much administration time than in private industry, or that the management of a comparable volume of bill payments costs five times as much operation time and higher-cost employees to carry it out than in private industry. Indeed, monitoring can be particularly expensive when special public-sector accounting practices apply or public-enterprise accounts are not publicised because the operations of political firms are secret (defence, intelligence agencies). In any event, the outputs of publicly owned firms are often difficult to measure.

Alessi reviewed much evidence from private and public production of comparable goods and services. He showed that political firms indeed have a poorer economic performance than comparable private producers (Alessi, 1980). The higher costs of carrying out and monitoring comparable tasks under public-sector conditions may, for example, be the consequence of the need for more intensive supervision and less reliance on self-responsibility. When the relentless discipline imposed by genuinely competitive markets is lacking, the discipline of administrative controls often proves comparatively weak and costs are high.

Reforming Socialised Production

The principles of business accounting should be applied to public production ventures to provide quality information about them which allows government leaders to check on principal–agent problems. This means that it is not only recurrent outlays and revenues (in the budget) that should be estimated and made public, but also the impact of each such activity on the government's assets and liabilities (accrual accounting). Each year, the activities of the public-sector corporations should be recorded in independently audited public-sector balance sheets and the effects on the government's net wealth made transparent. Few governments around the world, however, produce the information that they demand of private corporations. Public-sector production sometimes seems advantageous for the sole reason that not all costs and revenues are taken into account and are clearly separated out from general government business. This allows for hidden transfers. When publicly owned ventures have transparent accounts, they are shielded to some degree from the day-to-day political intervention which tends to disrupt production planning and opens the door to political rent-seeking.

Reforms may alleviate the problems with public production. For example, socialised production can be devolved to competing low-level governments, turning socialised property into a kind of club goods (Foldvary, 1994, pp. 62–78, 86–112), or it can be privatised with assurances that access to the goods and services will remain in the public domain. In addition, accounting systems can be reformed to match best-practice private firms. Modern management techniques of motivation and monitoring may help to extract efficiency dividends for the taxpayer. To this end, managers must be given clear, measurable output targets by their political masters, but they have to be made responsible for choosing the methods by which the outputs are to be produced and how the necessary inputs are acquired. Such a responsibility system will only work when public-sector managers have limited tenure and are paid for performance: an arrangement that differs fundamentally from the traditional public-service approach with lifelong tenure. Where such reforms are not feasible, the production of goods and services should be taken out of the public sector and privatised so that the disciplines of competitive private business apply.

We shall return to these issues in Chapters 13 and 14, when we discuss privatisation, the transformation of socialist economies and the reform of mixed economies.

O Key Concepts

Common property was defined in Chapter 7. These goods are, as we saw, 'institutionally deficient' in that many of the benefits cannot be exclusively 'internalised' (captured), since third parties cannot be excluded from using such goods. Where demand needs to be rationed, this may be done through transfer to clubs (or local government), through subsidised access to privately produced, public-domain goods or socialised property.

Public provision refers to governmental administrative arrangements that make goods and services available to citizens or certain classes of citizens, either through public funding (cash handouts, tax remission), purpose-specific vouchers (such as for food or education), or *in specie* distribution (for example, of blankets after a catastrophe). Public provision does not necessitate **public production** of these goods and services in publicly owned enterprises. Public access does not require or justify public ownership and monopoly production.

Political firms are publicly owned production agencies. They tend to have access to subsidies out of tax revenue, hence face a softer budget constraint than private companies, which can go broke more easily. The managers of political firms also tend to have indirect political influence on how governments shape the rules governing them.

Accountability relates to standards of reporting the costs and benefits of actions to the principals of an organisation, normally both the recurrent flows (income and loss statement, budget) and the effects on their stocks of assets and liabilities (balance sheet). Accountability also implies sanctions against breaches of the standards, that is, agents are held accountable and are not given subsidies out of general budgets (no **soft and fuzzy budget constraints**).

Accrual accounting is the practice of deducting recurrent expenses from the net capital position and adding benefits (receipts) to that position by constructing a balance sheet of assets and liabilities. It shows the debt and asset position, including the unfunded obligations of new political initiatives. This furnishes quality information for political decision makers. Nowadays, most national governments can only guess whether they operate with net liabilities (are broke) or own net capital assets, and whether new initiatives will enhance or prejudice the nation's public wealth.

Privatisation is an act of transferring publicly owned property rights to private owners (the opposite of socialisation or nationalisation), whereas **corporatisation** refers to acts of reorganising publicly owned assets and organisations so that they constitute an entity separate from the general core business of government. The leaders of corporatised, publicly owned organisations are made clearly accountable to the principals and have to face clear-cut budget constraints without recourse to budget subsidies. ●

The Redistribution of Property Rights

A third function of government in many countries is the redistribution of incomes and wealth; that is, the confiscation of the property rights of some and their reallocation to others. This is based on concepts of 'social justice', which in the Judeo-Christian tradition, as well as in Islam, probably have stronger historic roots than in other civilisations. In Europe, rulers have long used public revenues to assist 'the waifs and widows', and public organisations – such as communal poor houses – have attended to the basic needs of the destitute. Based on this tradition, social reformers, such as the Fabian socialists in Britain and the former British colonies, the social democrats in continental Europe and a strand of the Democratic Party in the United States, have often claimed the moral high ground. In the process, security and justice have been equated with the conservation of certain social and economic positions in the face of change and with outcome equality in the distribution of incomes and wealth (section 6.3). The advocates of redistribution by government also base their case on an optimism about the practical feasibility of their redistribution programmes, de-emphasising problems of cognition, rational ignorance, moral hazard and the self-interest of political agents. On the basis of these popular philosophies, collective resources have been taken to serve as an insurer of last resort against the risks of life. That role is typically left to the family in other cultures, such as in East Asia.

Redistribution can be attempted by two categories of policy instrument:

(a) one is to attenuate or even neutralise the outcomes of the competitive game by using the government's coercive right to tax and hand out transfer payments;

(b) the other is to alter the functioning of markets by directly intervening with the competitive base which is founded on private property rights, by influencing the accumulation of financial, physical and human capital and by intervening with the freedom to conclude contracts (Figure 10.1).

The redistribution of property rights which are the outcome of market processes can rely on the coercive power of the state to raise taxes and transfers that are decided in political processes. Examples are a progressive income tax that does not treat all money earned equally, but takes the size of the income flow of the property owner into account; and a tax on certain categories of spending which exempts other types of spending. Transfers may consist of outright cash payments, but can also consist, for example, of real resource transfers. Thus, government

Figure 10.1   Instruments of redistribution policy

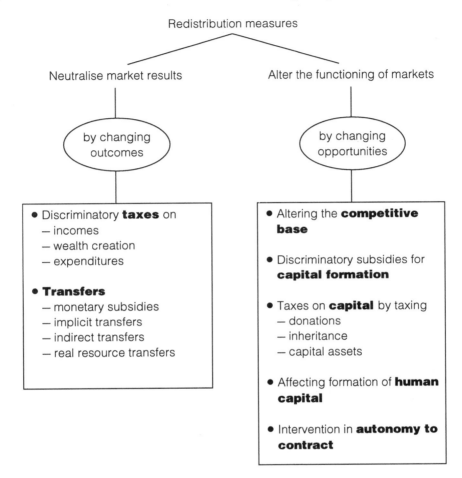

and parliament may decide to provide more government-owned in-frastructure to regions where the average income is low or where critical votes can be won.

The second category of redistribution instruments aims at altering the starting opportunities before people engage in competitive uses of their property rights in markets (Figure 10.1). Examples are measures to assist certain groups with the formation of physical or human capi-tal. Government may fund access to education, which turns education into a public-domain good (as discussed in sections 7.2 and 10.1), so as to redistribute the chances of young citizens to compete subse-quently in the labour market. Opportunities to compete may also be altered by direct intervention in the private autonomy to contract, for example when legislators give one side of the market asymmetric privileges in contracts to work or to rent housing, such as prohibitions on dismissing workers for non-performance or on evicting tenants after non-payment of rent.

Another example for the second type of redistribution policy is tariff protection, which we have touched upon already in connection with our discussion of rent-seeking in Chapter 8. Foreign producers and domestic buyers see the value of their property diminished by artificial tariff barriers to selling across national borders, whereas domestic producers see the value of their property increased because their opportunity to sell at a higher price has been improved by political action. Such redistributive interventions have unintended longer-term consequences for the supply of the regulated product; for example, notoriously high costs and poor incentives to innovate in tariff-protected industries. Another case of well-intentioned intervention is rent control; but that discourages investment in housing and is likely to create housing shortages. The short- and long-run consequences of this form of redistribution policy are intransparent and complicated by unexpected and unwanted side-effects. For this reason alone, it seems preferable that redistribution policy should rely on the more transparent means of taxation and transfer through the budget, a method that is subject to more explicit parliamentary and public control than is administrative intervention in markets.

How much redistribution is attempted in a society is of course for the voters to decide. Here, we can only point to the unintended consequences of such policies which are commonly observed and discuss ideas which may help to contain the unintended side-effects of pervasive redistribution by government. We shall return to the consequences of such policies when we discuss the failures of the welfare state in section 10.4 below.

O Key Concepts

Fabian socialism and **social democracy** split from totalitarian socialism, which aimed at the violent overthrow of the 'bourgeois order', in the late nineteenth century. In perpetuating pre-Marxist philosophical traditions, social democrats were for most of the twentieth century critical of private property and advocated the gradual nationalisation of land, housing and a great variety of industrial assets, as well as banking and many other services. They also advocated 'corrective intervention' in the market, so that people could have more equal incomes. They nationalised the provision and production of health and education services, as well as provision for old-age and of housing, and more generally replaced the private provision of welfare by public welfare.

Social democrats tend to have great faith in the capability of political leaders and political processes to bring about outcomes to meet politically prede-termined goals (**optimism about political feasibility** of programmes). ●

Agency Costs: Taxing and Administration

The agents of collective action – the rulers and their administrative assistants – have to expend resources to fulfil their functions. These are called the agency costs of government. They must be met, nor-mally by the compulsory levying of taxes. Taxation and the administration of public moneys in turn cause further agency costs.

The organisation of the administrative business of government and its funding is the subject of fiscal studies. Although institutional econom-ics has numerous applications in the running of political organisations, most of that discussion must remain outside the framework of this book. However, we should note that institutions can have a major impact (a) on the size of government, and (b) on how high the agency costs are for attaining a given set of government objectives.

The size of government, and with it the agency and tax costs, can be reduced if socialised property can be turned into club goods – devolv-ing the tasks of government to small, self-organising and self-monitoring groups – or if it can be privatised and public-domain services be sub-contracted and provided from public funds – separating production from provision. This makes the government's business more feasible because government agents can then concentrate on planning, direct-ing, monitoring and correcting the core activities (section 7.2).

The Core Functions of Government

If we ask what functions really need to be carried out by government, we must address fundamental value judgements. These have played a major role in the public debate on the size and reform of government in recent years. One such normative answer was given by Milton Friedman (1962, p. 34):

> A government which maintained law and order, defined property rights, served as a means whereby we could modify property rights and other rules of the economic game, adjudicated disputes about the interpretation of rules, enforced contracts, promoted competition, provided a monetary framework, engaged in activities to counter technical monopolies and to overcome neighbourhood effects widely regarded as sufficiently impor-tant to justify government intervention, and which supplemented private

charity and the private family in protecting the irresponsible, whether madman or child – such a government would clearly have important functions to perform. The consistent liberal is not an anarchist.

A similar position was taken by the reformist former New Zealand Treasurer, Ruth Richardson (see box), in which she argued for a reduction of the functions of government to a core. This is premised on a perception of government which sees the citizens as the principals who periodically elect politicians as their agents. Some of these agents form the board of directors (the cabinet), which lays down general guidelines and clearly spells out objectives against which the performance of bureaucrat-managers and their government departments can be measured. Clear and simple targets as well as performance-based pay coupled with limited tenure for the top managers will create incentives to perform and control agent opportunism in public administration. The elected directors (ministers) should not get involved in managing how government services are produced or how the necessary inputs are acquired. This is the task of expert managers, the administrative heads of government departments and their assistants. Over time, contracts with the top managers of government business could stipulate an efficiency dividend, and international benchmarking should assist with reducing the costs of meeting the stipulated targets. Changing the rule set could thus create incentives to reduce the agency costs of government.

Once the functions of government are laid down and the best 'production technology of public services' has been identified, input costs can be estimated. Then, the politically elected board of directors can decide how public expenditure is to be funded, taking into account assessments of (independently audited) public assets and liabilities, time-tested principles of financial prudence and intergenerational justice. It is important that all elected politicians have access to proper financial information, including the government's balance sheet. Simple, broad-based taxes would impose low compliance and monitoring costs (see below), freeing their energies for proper economic pursuits. Such a tax regime would also keep the agency costs of tax collection relatively low.

❖ Small Government in Action

(Excerpts from an interview with Ruth Richardson, reformer and former New Zealand finance minister)

We should start with asking the fundamental question: what should the state do? We should 'de-invent' government in many areas. The state definitively has a role in protecting the rule of law; in addition a minimal role in ensuring income sufficiency as discussed. It must be funded to that extent ... The state's role is to establish the rules, to be the steward who ensures that citizens get quality, and to fund pupil or patient choice. If you ask the people they still think that the state should be the referee as well as the player! We know the state is bankrupt as a business operator, but most still think it can produce quality health and education services! ... By reducing the role of the state, government spending will automatically shrink. Governments should not produce, for they cannot create wealth. They can only protect a climate in which private citizens can assess freely what enhances their wealth ... Regulation has to be general and light-handed. Governments should for example come in only as referees where a market becomes uncontestable. The state has a legitimate role to blow the whistle when monopolies undermine competition ...

... [Reform] is about doing away with political privileges for organised groups. When you redesign taxation, you begin by thinking afresh about the role of government and therefore the expenditure demands that taxpayers can legitimately be expected to fund. Next you make sure that you get the most efficient way of obtaining the desired results from collective action. You organise the business of public administration by creating incentives to be as effective as possible. The citizens have every right to ask that the administration is run competently and efficiently. Modern management methods need to be applied to financial and human-resource management. Ministers should contract for the production of specified outputs and leave the chief executives of the government departments the responsibility for organising the inputs and production processes, as they see fit. Over time, the politicians should extract an efficiency dividend. In New Zealand, this performance-based management approach has yielded enormous fiscal savings, income tax reductions and freedom from foreign debt.

Once one knows what has to be funded from taxes, one must ensure that this is done with the least distorting tax system one can design. People must chase market opportunities and must not be diverted from solid business reasons by artificial tax reasons. Therefore, the tax system must be broad-based with low rates of tax. I would probably favour a mix of income and value-added tax – a flat 15 per cent income tax, 20 per cent maximum, with a negative income tax at the low end, and a comprehensive 10 per cent value-added tax. If tax rates go higher, they become distortive.

A broad-based, low-rate tax regime would induce governments and households to save; it would lower the cost of capital. We would gain much voluntary compliance and an enormous saving on transaction costs ... Such an intelligent tax regime would – in the interest of fairness and credibility – have to be coupled with strong sanctions and draconian penalties for tax cheats. There is no scope for forging and forgetting – just as it is false, self-defeating generosity to forgive violence or offences against the laws of ethics and crime. ◆

(Source: W. Kasper, 'Responsibility and Reform: a Conversation with Ruth Richardson', Policy, vol. 12, no. 3, (1996), pp. 25–31)

Historically, the agency costs of a purely protective state were small in times of peace – of the order of one-tenth of a community's income. But, as we have seen, modern states make a massively bigger claim on private production and incomes, due to the subsidisation of production and, above all, (potentially limitless) redistribution. In the process, the number of government employees has increased enormously and with it the agency costs of government. Frequently, a growing government sector is a purpose of government action in its own right; for example, when government is expanded in the hope of ensuring more jobs or when agents expect better promotion opportunities if they can hire more subordinates.

Compliance Costs

Collective action not only imposes resource costs that citizens bear by paying tax and other compulsory levies, but also compliance costs. These are the resource expenses that private citizens and organisations have to incur when they obey government laws and regulations (external institutions). For example, taxpayers have to keep records they otherwise would not, have to fill in forms for the government, have to carry out their activities in ways different from how they would otherwise do. They may have to desist from certain activities and engage in others involuntarily, sometimes at great cost. Citizens and businesses are often obliged to hire staff to cope with the paperwork. In most countries, government has given rise to an entire 'compliance industry' of tax agents, government-relations experts, lawyers and lobby groups.

The compliance costs caused by governments vary considerably between jurisdictions. Often, the streamlining of administrative practices and, gradually, of legislative and regulatory systems can be achieved without much loss in regulatory purpose. Certain health or safety outcomes can be achieved in various ways, but with massive savings in compliance costs (Chapter 14). Different national tax systems also impose greatly differing levels of compliance costs. For example, income and corporate tax regimes that contain numerous exemptions and stipulations for the purpose of redistribution tend to be more costly to comply with (in terms of paperwork, use of specialist tax consultants and litigation) than exemption-free, low income tax regimes or low general indirect taxes (see box above). Compliance costs are also driven up by frequent changes in the procedural administrative instructions which are intended to fine-tune or re-engineer legislation and regulations. Finally, it should be noted that many compliance costs are fixed costs, so that small enterprises face relatively higher cost obstacles than large corporations, which can better afford to run specialist legal and government relations departments. Compliance costs are therefore an obstacle to outsider competition, job creation and innovation by small start-up firms.

O **Key Concepts**

Redistribution is a process inspired by notions of 'social justice' and based on political powers to reallocate property rights among citizens and organisations, either by taxing and subsidising or by intervening in the free play of market forces; for example, by rental controls that lower the value of houses to owners and enhance the position of tenants; or food price controls that enrich consumers and make agriculturalists poorer.

When redistributive policy measures intervene in specific market processes or aim at specific outcomes, the consequences of such interventions are typically underrated. Markets work through self-coordination by exchange and self-control by competition. These spontaneous ordering forces in the complex economic system are disturbed or incapacitated by specific policy manipulations, and unintended side-effects emerge which, in turn, frequently call for further interventions.

Compliance costs are incurred by private citizens and firms who have to obey mandatory collective action; for example, when tax payers have to prepare cumbersome paperwork or firms have to monitor and report certain activities, such as smoke emission, or the content of private contracts which they have concluded. The design of government administration and legislation has great impact on the level of compliance costs, and constant re-engineering and fine-tuning of administrative rules tends to drive up these costs. ●

10.3   A Liberal Model of Public Policy: Order Policy

Order Policy versus Process Intervention

Three threads which run through this book underpin the maxim that the central function of public policy should be to support and enhance social and economic order ('order policy'). They are:

(a) that people's cognitive abilities are limited, so an order which allows the uncovering of recognisable patterns enhances the division of labour and hence living standards, as well as giving people known spheres of freedom;

(b) that freedom of individual action (autonomy) is a precondition for competition, the most powerful discovery procedure and the most effective control device known to human kind;

(c) that it is normal for people to have asymmetric information and to yield to the temptation to act opportunistically (principal–agent problem). This makes it necessary to establish binding commitments and to enforce rules.

If public policy is guided by a commitment to enhancing order, then individual freedoms are likely to be more secure, economic coordination is likely to be more effective and discrimination and rent-seeking are more likely to be kept at bay. Such a style of policy focuses on cultivating the institutions and their organisational back-up. The approach is to emphasise the need for competition and secure property rights, and to de-emphasise policies aimed at directly influencing specific processes and outcomes. A style of public policy that relies on arbitrary *ad hoc* decisions can easily run into problems of cognitive overload, both amongst those subjected to it and amongst government agents. The likely consequences of such a result-orientated, instrumentalist style of policy will be apathy amongst the public and confusion and malcoordination in public policy.

This basic philosophy was first advocated in a consistent and detailed manner by the German *ordo* liberal school. Economists and lawyers at the University of Freiburg, most notably Walter Eucken and Franz Böhm, analysed the dire failures of democracy in the Weimar Republic which gave rise to totalitarian National Socialism. Writing during the 1930s to 1950s, they came to the conclusion that electoral democracy had failed to foster a non-discriminatory and sufficiently competitive order. Instead, organised pressure groups and the politicians who did their bidding had engaged in widespread opportunistic rent-seeking (Kasper and Streit, 1993). The *ordo* liberals went back to the basic tenets of the Scottish Enlightenment, which recognised that the protection of property rights, freedom of contract and the rule of law were essential to the functioning of a capitalist economy. The Freiburg circle of lawyers and economists focused on the essential control and incentive functions of a competitive system and added further considerations to the basic principles of the Scottish Enlightenment to adjust the policy prescription to the modern industrial age. They acknowledged that there were now concentrations of industrial and union power, that modern electoral democracy with universal suffrage created major temptations for political intervention, and that organised pressure groups had great influence on parliaments and public policy. They became known as the Freiburg School or German *ordo* liberal school.[5]

The fundamental advice to public policy makers was to distinguish between (a) making the protective function the focus of government, particularly by fostering and setting institutions conducive to a competitive economic system, and (b) intervening in specific economic and social processes and outcomes (Eucken, [1940] 1992). The former – the *ordo* liberals said – was to have precedence over the latter. Government should concentrate on using its coercive powers to promote and defend competition as a public good. The freedom of contract, the *ordo* liberals concluded, must not be interpreted to encompass the freedom to form cartels and close markets to new entrants, because contracts to close off markets would curtail the freedom of others, including the freedom of choice of buyers. They also found that public policy often introduces disturbances which destabilise expectations and hence are counterproductive. The hand of public policy on external institutions should therefore be steady. Political activism in pursuit of specific outcomes was seen as disorientating and destabilising. Their reservations about intervening in economic processes led them to be critical of the conscious discretionary policy, advocated in the 1940s and 1950s by the Keynesians, of using budgetary and monetary policies to counter cyclical swings in aggregate demand. Instead, they preferred basically stable institutions and steady public policies to enhance the inherent self-stabilisation of the system. They feared that pump priming and the manipulation of aggregate demand would gradually erode market signals and change patterns of private behaviour. In that respect, they anticipated the criticism of the 'rational expectations school', but placed it in the wide methodological context of market conformity.

Market Conformity

The focal concern of the *ordo* liberals was with competition – not so much in single markets but throughout the entire competitive system. Competitive systems deserved to be defended and shored up, they taught, because they have essential knowledge-generating and controlling functions which alternative, collective systems cannot match in the context of a modern complex economy. They therefore stipulated that all measures of public policy should 'market conform', which is to say they should not undermine the pervasive role of competition. Each measure of policy, as well as the overall design of collective action, should be evaluated according to whether it affected competitiveness. Thus, redistribution measures of the sort discussed in section 10.1 above found little favour with the *ordo* liberals unless they enhanced the starting positions of competitors in ways that would not distort competitive signals. Institutions that are universal and apply to all are preferable to specific directives and discriminatory process interventions.

The Constitutive Principles of *Ordo* Policy

The basic principles that constitute the essence of such a policy are:

- private property;
- freedom of contract;
- liability for one's commitments and actions;
- open markets (freedom of entry and exit);
- monetary stability (inflation-free money);
- steadiness of economic policy.

These principles should be given overriding, constitutional status and made the guiding stars of public policy, the *ordo* liberals said. These principles constitute a strong, consistent support of the free-market order that permits the unfolding of effective coordination, the use of knowledge by creative entrepreneurship and the control of economic power (sections 8.1 and 8.4). If public policy is guided by these simple, constitutive principles, it does not foster untrammelled *laissez-faire* but protects individual rights and effective cooperation within a knowledge-saving framework of institutions. This type of policy also binds the rulers to follow the principle of non-discrimination, ensuring 'no favours all round'.

An important insight of the *ordo* approach, which Walter Eucken stressed, is that these principles should apply in equal measure to all interdependent markets (Kasper and Streit, 1993). If the 'suborder' of institutions in the labour market, for example, is incompatible with the 'suborder' in product markets, this is likely to cause costly contradictions, for example distorted relative prices. Regulated labour markets alongside freely competitive product markets would make production unprofitable. Job destruction would follow. This might sooner or later require the deregulation of labour markets or the suppression of untrammelled competition in product markets. The compatibility of suborders is also important in areas that border on economic life. Thus an incentive-destroying social welfare system or a legal order that erodes property rights tend to clash with a competitive economic order. Only a compatible mosaic of 'suborders' is stable and efficient. This fundamental insight relates to the plea for an order of rules which we discussed in Chapter 6.

Adhering to such a style of public policy precludes legislative and regulatory activism. It also requires tolerance of some outcomes that certain groups of society may not like. Above all, it requires caution with redistributional policies and counsels that observed unequal outcomes in income and wealth can best be analysed and addressed in the context of ongoing evolution. Relatively poor individuals may, however, need assistance by gaining better starting chances, rather than by handouts.

However, the hope of the *ordo* liberals that the mere commitment to 'order policy' protects governments in the heat of political battles and public controversies from readily yielding to redistribution-seeking pressure groups and from being held responsible for everything has not been borne out. Mere commitment to the above catalogue of guiding principles did not protect German parliaments and executive administrators from the errors of activist macroeconomic stabilisation policy and the favouritism to interest groups when they were facing elections. The politico-economic processes that were later described as 'rent-seeking' proved too powerful in electoral democracies with established interest groups to fend off violations of *ordo* principles by simply tying the hands of politicians.

The members of the Freiburg School preceded the public-choice economists to some extent in diagnosing rent-seeking and political favouritism as the influences that impair the proper functioning of the market system. Yet, beyond stating the general principles, the Freiburg School had little to offer by way of practical antidotes for what is nowadays called the 'institutional sclerosis of the market system' in parliamentary democracies (Streit, 1992; Kasper and Streit, 1993). The critical observer half a century later, however, has to admit that substantive reforms to block the 'rent-seeking drive' from within are still not very likely. Whatever incentives there are nowadays to reform seem to derive primarily from the pressures of institutional competition with other jurisdictions (Chapter 12).

Ordo Policy and Coordination

Assuming for the moment that hand-tying could be made effective, *ordo* policy could make communities more governable and the job of governance more feasible in real-world conditions of limited knowledge. Adherence to a relatively simple set of principles could help the agents of government to resist the temptation to promise a plethora of specific outcomes which are far beyond their capability to deliver. But it would also facilitate the coordination of collective action. The various agencies of government would, by adhering to these principles, remain reasonably coordinated in what they undertake, so that one agency does not have to correct, or compensate for, the unintended side-effects of other agencies' actions (interagency coordination). The principles would also assist in keeping policies consistent over time, thus fostering a predictable pattern of policies (intertemporal coordination). Beyond that, adherence to these few guiding principles – instead of frequent interventions in specific processes – would before long lead private agents to predict the rules of the policy game and induce them to react more predictably (private–public coordination). Policy, by being more predictable, would then become more credible and more effective.

Order policy requires policy makers to be blind to the specific outcomes of rule-guided behaviour. Adhering to a policy of supporting the known institutional system and desisting from 'outcome engineering' will sometimes lead to unpopular results. Policy makers who then place the specific outcome over and above the maintenance of the rule, trigger hard-to-foresee side-effects and undermine the general, easy-to-perceive institutional system. They raise coordination costs. Process intervention, for example in the form of 'knee-jerk legislation' in response to undesirable singular events, may earn short-term popular acclaim, but it violates the non-discrimination rule and over the longer run destroys confidence. Order policy therefore demands political backbone and a good understanding of how human interaction is coordinated over the long term. This probably exceeds what politicians in electoral democracies (and other systems) can deliver.

A design of public policy which, first of all, aims to foster a simple order of actions and order of rules has been demanded for many years by economists and other social scientists with a preference for individual liberty and economic growth.

O Key Concepts

Ordo **policy** focuses on internal and external institutions and their organisational back-up as a framework for economic processes, with the intent of facilitating the emergence of order in the mind of the citizens. It places the maintenance of a clearly understood, transparent system of policy rules above interventions in economic processes. The maintenance of competition is seen as a public good whose promotion and preservation has priority over and above providing stabilisation over time or the redistribution of incomes.

The **constitutive principles** of *ordo* policy are:

- private property;
- freedom of contract;
- liability for one's commitment and actions;
- open markets (freedom of entry and exit);
- monetary stability (inflation-free money);

● steadiness of economic policy.

If elevated to constitutional principles that govern public policy, these principles can serve to coordinate government activity between agencies and over time and to create private expectations that make their attainment easier and the pursuit of rent-seeking harder.

The **compatibility of suborders** is a feature of policy design which pays attention to the interdependence of institutional frameworks of interdependent markets. This requires not only that product and factor markets are subject to similar freedoms to compete, but also that social, economic and legal policies are compatible. An institutional system that consists of compatible suborders of rules is effective in the sense that the various institutions mutually support each other and can be more easily deciphered.

When we speak of the **coordination of policy**, we have to think of making public policy actions compatible (a) amongst various agencies of government, (b) over time, and (c) between the public policy makers and private individuals, organisations and associations who are subjected to public policy. ●

10.4 Failures of the Welfare State

The Consequences of Redistribution

It has been argued in economics and public policy for most of the twentieth century that market processes fail to produce a distribution of incomes and wealth which correspond to certain normative precepts. This has given rise to the argument that government should intervene to 'correct the market' to ensure a distribution of property rights different from that which the competitive process generates. Real-world income and wealth distribution is distorted by restrictions of market rivalry by powerful private and public interests. This normally leads to further concentrations of power. The choice then is to enhance the competitive process or to intervene politically to redistribute. Most of the time, most electoral democracies have gone the second route, but in the process have often entrenched power positions and undermined the intensity of competition. This was also true when the design of *ordo* liberalism was applied to postwar Germany: over time, interventions to redistribute property rights destroyed the political commitment to protect the competitive order (Giersch *et al.*, 1992). Under the pressures of electoral politics, organised interest groups and powerful bureaucracies, the commitment to protect the constitution of capitalism crumbled.

As of the 1990s, the commitment in many western democracies to redistribution policy by numerous 'corrective' interventions has come under increasing scrutiny, as such interventions tend to have unforeseen side-effects; for example, the coordinative capacity of the system and incentives to bear risks and produce are eroded over the longer run.

Since politicians can derive gain from redistributing incomes and wealth, there are great incentives, as we have seen, to expand the redistributional function of government. The opportunistic rivalry among competing political parties for the popular vote and popular and interest-group pressures have led to a burgeoning of the redistributive function. In the western 'welfare democracies', redistribution has therefore grown enormously in importance and impact during the second half of the twentieth century. This expansion has caused a considerable number of problems for public policy:

(a) Most political programmes of redistribution have not worked. Even where redistribution policies have been massive, poverty and income inequalities persist, or even increase.

(b) Public provision to cope with more and more private contingencies has led to 'moral hazard' among welfare recipients and a spreading claims mentality: individuals and families no longer feel obligated to make sufficient provision of their own for sickness, accident and old age, and they no longer avoid risks to their health or security. This is documented by the drop in the private savings rate in virtually all welfare states. However, collective risk provision is invariably less well tailored to diverse individual requirements by reason of the obvious limitations to knowledge at the centre. Instead, risk coverage is provided for the 'average consumer' according to the motto 'one size fits all'. The shift to socialised provision therefore leads to a poorer coverage of individual risks. At the same time, people learn to rely on claiming hand-outs and blame their misfortunes on insufficient hand-outs, rather than relying on their own effort and blaming themselves if they have insufficient means. The growing transfers through taxation and subsidy have consequently not produced the promised results in terms of a more even distribution of economic opportunity and the eradication of poverty.

(c) In the long term, the socialisation of charity tends to reduce solidarity with the poor and hence voluntary giving. Voluntary giving, combined with some personal supervision and advice to the indigent recipient, has increasingly been replaced by an impersonal compulsory tax-subsidy apparatus. Affluent people conclude that they already pay enough taxes and that anonymous welfare recipients receive sufficient support. Therefore they give less to

voluntary charitable organisations. Moreover, charitable organisations often neglect the difficult business of genuine fund-raising
from private citizens and concentrate on lobbying for a part of the
tax cake. They then become little more than extensions of the
public welfare machinery.

(d) A corollary of this is group polarisation between recipients of welfare and preferential programmes and those who have to fund the
expense, with the dangers of political backlash (heightened tension,
mob violence and so on; Sowell, 1990, p. 174). Redistribution policy
is based on the (false) premise that inequality is injustice (Flew,
1989) and serves to politicise and emotionalise economic life. What
used to be the outcome of anonymous market processes which
simply had to be accepted has now become the political responsibility of government. The problem now tends to be addressed by
political processes of public posturing and lobbying, whereas before
attempts were made to address it by self-help, increased resource-
fulness and effort. In the shift from self-responsibility to reliance on
government agencies, social harmony is lost. Related to this is another impact of the welfare state on the constitutional control of
state powers: many objectives of welfare policy cannot be achieved
by general laws and therefore require open-ended legislation and
the delegation of powers to public authorities. As a consequence, a
growing part of the administration escapes parliamentary and judicial scrutiny (Ratnapala, 1990, pp. 8–18). This can easily pave the
way for what Hayek calls 'the miscarriage of the democratic ideal':
the weakening of the principle that government should be subjected to the constitution (Hayek, 1979a, pp. 98–104).

(e) The intergenerational effects of public redistribution have changed
individual habits and long-term life plans, so many young citizens now behave in ways that minimise the risks and costs of tax
confiscation and maximise the chances of obtaining welfare services. This is evident in Sweden, for example, which has been
converted into a collective 'people's home' (*folkshjem*) where shirking by the younger generation has become widespread (Karlsson,
1995; Lindbeck, 1995). As a result, growth of the tax base from
which public welfare can be funded has been reduced.

(f) The public provision of welfare resources has favoured the emergence of public-sector monopolies in the production of health,
old-age and other services. The consequence is less choice, a lack
of competitive cost control, an appropriation of rents by organised
groups of service providers, and waning motivation to experiment and innovate.

(g) Where redistributive interventions (and consequently tax and regulatory burdens) are massive, black markets develop. People who
find that the visible hand inflicts injustices and inefficiencies on

them and deprives them of their freedom opt out of the law and into a domain of lesser security, where their transactions depend solely on internal institutions and self-enforcement. Frequently that works, but it may also give rise to thuggery and crime and outcomes that are inferior to those obtainable with collectively protected property rights.

(h) The combination of lower productivity in providing welfare services through the public sector, an eroded tax base and a greater preparedness to claim welfare has led to severe fiscal problems in virtually all welfare democracies. In western Europe, governments are spending on average 54 per cent of gross domestic product, (marginal) income tax rates are high, but governments nevertheless accumulate further deficits, so welfare states face mounting public debts (World Economic Forum, 1996, p. 23). Faced with a slowing down or even a reversal of population growth and the general ageing of the population — changes that are not independent of past redistribution policies — public policy makers are compelled to respond by tightening or rescinding promised welfare provisions. This leads to unforeseen changes in the lives of people who had banked on the sustainability of public welfare, and to spreading insecurity and distrust.

(i) The demand for 'social justice' is the mirror image of positive freedom. Its pursuit underpins the notion that there are 'freedoms to claim something', such as funds to protect from penury and ill health – a limitless task. Parliaments in electoral democracies are therefore subject to an endless creep of claims for more collective action, and become increasingly liable to disappoint the electorate and curtail personal liberty.

(j) Redistribution is often claimed to flow from the rich to the deserving poor. In reality, this is often not the case. Those with political power or those well enough organised use their authority to have governments reallocate property from individuals and groups with little or no power. The empirical evidence in countries with strong redistribution policies is that benefits have gone disproportionately to the more fortunate, not to the poor (Sowell, 1990, p. 174). In electoral democracies, this process has spread particularly in circumstances where the property rights of the majority can be diminished by small, almost imperceptible margins. The (fixed) information and transaction costs of each member of the majority are too high to seek a change by political intervention, whereas the few recipients of substantial, concentrated benefits of intervention have good reason to organise and lobby public policy makers for more such redistributions. This constellation is particularly frequent in markets where a few suppliers (with an interest in high prices) face countless buyers (with an interest in low prices and good quality). As a consequence, public redistribution policy tends to be governed by a 'supplier bias', in particular if conditions have been undisturbed for a long time, so that vested interests and political alliances have had the time to become well entrenched (Olson, 1982).

(k) Preferential programmes which are considered temporary not only persist but are expanded for political reasons, even if they turn out to be economic failures.

(l) In electoral democracies, parliaments and governments tend to vie for the vote of the median voter, that is, the middle class. Many public welfare handouts are therefore aimed at winning the electoral support of the middle class, which in turn forms the biggest class of tax payers. What may be intended as redistribution thus only turns out to be what Anthony de Jasay aptly called 'churning': giving and taking from the same people (de Jasay, 1985). Churning creates considerable agency costs (or, seen from the angle of the 'churners', considerable incomes).

(m) The growing redistribution by government tends to run into serious macroeconomic problems: fiscal deficits, rising public indebtedness, often also foreign debts, erosion of private saving, tax-payer revolts and the undermining of the country's international competitive position. Eventually, these issues make policy adjustments unavoidable and inflict adjustment burdens on individuals who had trusted in the permanence of public welfare provision.

(n) A more fundamental problem caused by the welfare state is, as we briefly noted earlier, that it is in direct conflict with the rule of law and the protective function of government. If the central function of government is to protect individual freedom and – correspondingly – private property without discrimination between citizens, then this clashes with the reallocation of private property by collective action. Redistribution undermines market signals which guide economic agents and offer incentives to act. The redistributive state makes it impossible for people to internalise all the gains from using their property, labour and knowledge. The constitution of capitalism then becomes fuzzy, and order is undermined. The likely consequences are less individual effort, risk-taking and innovation. In addition, many citizens will perceive a sense of injustice if their earnings are taken away by public fiat. Spreading disaffection with the political process may, sooner or later, outweigh the gains in communal loyalty and support for the government which derive from engineering a greater equality of outcomes. Cynicism and falling support for the political process can then undermine the legitimacy of political authority, the stability of the regime and long-term expectations of a reliable order.

(o) Another fundamental problem with redistribution policy derives from the static vision of society on which such policies are based. Economists who take the complexity and openness of the economic system seriously are aware that the observed income distribution among groups or individuals at any point in time is only a snapshot from the 'film of social life', so to speak. In reality, there are ongoing dynamic changes in relative positions of wealth and incomes, as well as in the size of the cake. Kirzner (1997, p. 25) derided what he called 'the "given-pie" framework for distribution of economic justice' in the context of discussing the negative effects of redistribution policies on the entrepreneurial discovery potential. Income and wealth distribution is rarely static for long. People who are relatively poor this year may be affluent a decade down the track, and hugely profitable corporations may have disappeared in a generation from now (only consider how few of today's Fortune 500 companies existed back in 1950). It is natural in an economy with private old-age provision that young people are relatively poor and people on the threshold of retirement relatively asset-rich. Should redistribution policy intervene to make old and young people more 'equal'? Who would bear the consequences? Should redistribution policy intervene on behalf of those who are for the time being relatively poor and thereby undermine their incentives to enhance their economic position by personal effort?

These many difficulties and contradictions have taken time to become virulent – and economists have taken time to diagnose that welfarism is based on a comparative-static world view based on *ceteris paribus* assumptions, whereas evolutionary reality reveals many unintended side-effects. This became increasingly evident as the welfare state was expanded further and further in the 1970s and 1980s. Side-effects have cumulated, leading to seemingly unmanageable problems such as unemployment and public-sector deficits, pointing to the conclusion that the welfare state is not sustainable (Lindbeck, 1995; Karlsson, 1995).

Nevertheless, there is always likely to be a majority of voters in the democratic welfare states with affluent economies who favour some degree of redistribution by collective action. Voters expect governments to alleviate cases of poverty and extreme bad luck (for example, after a natural calamity). Observers who are critical of the size of the welfare state and who recognise the dangers for liberty and formal justice from the growing redistributive function of government may, nevertheless, see government action as a last line of defence against poverty, once self-responsibility and voluntary private assistance have been exhausted (Green, 1996). In the final analysis, social policy has to be analysed in terms of personal wellbeing. This is not solely or even predominantly determined by what is in the individual's purse. People also want the freedom to take control of their lives; and they are often alienated by policies which treat them as inert creatures whom an anonymous state provides with socially engineered satisfactions (Richardson, 1995, p. 207).

Income Distribution and Competition

The observation that 'the rich are getting richer and the poor are getting poorer' can be heard frequently in the mature industrial countries. If this is true, is it despite the growing redistributive efforts of government or because of them? The question seems justified as we observe that property rights are frequently redistributed from the unorganised poor to the better organised rich. Many market interventions benefit the affluent. If governments intervened less in markets, established positions of wealth and power would be more readily challenged and pioneer profits would be more quickly dispersed (section 8.4). It is also likely that free labour markets provide for high employment, arguably the best welfare policy. When general access to education and similar measures that ensure the equality of starting opportunities are combined with a comprehensive competitive order, vertical mobility is enhanced and gross income inequalities are then unlikely to survive.

Evidence is available to support this point of view: competition and even income distribution are a common feature of many of the new industrial countries of East Asia. They pursue very limited public welfare policies. Responsibility for material welfare resides with the family, which explains high savings rates and small government budgets. Yet, despite – or should we say: because of – the lack of public welfare policy, measured income and wealth differences are surprisingly low, and certainly lower than in OECD countries (Riedel, 1988, pp. 18–21; Fields, 1984). Indeed, fast-growing, competitive Taiwan had the most even income distribution of a sample of 34 developing countries, with Singapore, South Korea and Hong Kong not far behind (Riedel, 1988, p. 20). In the dynamic societies of East Asia, the poor frequently do not belong to a 'class' of poor people for long, but move instead to higher income echelons.

In the light of what has been said, it may be asked why public welfare provision has been expanded to the degree observed in the old industrial countries. The answer probably has a lot to do with the mistaken application to large industrial societies of the small-group model of tribal solidarity (section 6.2). It also probably has a lot to do with mistaken conclusions from the historic experience of the 'Great Depression' of the 1930s, when a massive drop in demand and employment, accompanied by a politically engineered disruption in the international division of labour, created pockets of poverty and gave rise to demands that government give the people 'a new deal'.

10.5   Political Action and Rent Creation

Principal–Agent Opportunism in Government

The problems of collective action are not caused by the knowledge problem and unwarranted optimism about the feasibility of collective action alone. Throughout history, another critical problem with political power has been that the agents of government – whether hereditary rulers, elected parliamentarians, ministers or appointed government officials – have been tempted to act in their own self-interest. In other words, the principal–agent problem applies to political and administrative organisations, as insider agents (bureaucrats, politicians) are better informed than their principals, the outsider citizens. However, in contrast to business, where agent-managers are disciplined by competition, the principal–agent problem in government lacks these automatic checks. This makes for a greater imbalance in information and, consequently, greater opportunities for agent opportunism.

The principal–agent problem surfaces at all levels of collective action. It frequently arises from collusion between organised interest groups and government agencies. In most political systems, there is a political market for intervention and discriminatory variations to the universal institutions of government: many producers seek regulation of their industry to mitigate the ceaseless rigours of competition (section 8.2). On the supply side of the political market for intervention, the politicians, bureaucrats and judges engage in rent-creation. This has benefits for politicians and bureaucrats: they gain influence with powerful groups, as well as political and material support, whether for the party or personally for the interventionist. Political intervention normally also confers the satisfaction of being a guardian and living by the guardian virtues of caring for one's fellows (section 6.2).

The alliance between rent-creators and rent-seekers who act against the interest of the citizen-principals can be documented for many epochs and nations and is found at all levels of collective action. Thus, Queen Elizabeth I of England, Louis IV of France and other mercantilist monarchs granted well-connected traders monopoly rights to trade with certain parts of the world, for example India and America. In exchange, they shared the monopoly gains in the form of funds for the nation's and their personal treasuries. More recently, protection from international competition through tariffs and quotas has created rents for domestic agriculture and industry, as well as kick-back advantages for protectionist governments. In the process, the institutional emphasis has shifted from a commercial positive-sum mentality to the mentality of redistributive political guardianship and economic stagnation (Thurow, 1980).

Modern parliamentary democracies are dominated by voting alliances which are frequently beholden to interest groups. Then, discriminatory preferments are handed out by parliamentary majorities to their client groups. Majorities are often formed on the basis of other handouts being awarded to various interest groups. This phenomenon has been called 'log rolling' in the United States. It follows the strict political rationale of parliamentarians who want to be re-elected. To achieve this objective they have to buy off pressure groups which will give them political and financial support, and this can only be achieved by giving their consent to other politicians who represent and want to favour other pressure groups. Log rolling has become a way of life in many parliaments and has contributed greatly to the rise of political redistribution and rent seeking – but also to widespread disillusionment with democracy and cynicism about the political process. In the extreme, this may lead to the refusal of the wider public to defend democracy when it is attacked by totalitarian enemies. The Weimar Republic in Germany in the 1920s and early 1930s was dominated by ruthless special interest group representatives and was not defended by the people when the totalitarian onslaught came (Kasper and Streit, 1993).

Where government agents are involved in rent creation, they redistribute income and life opportunities, and politicise and emotionalise public life. The example of successful rent-seeking coalitions induces emulation by other groups. Once the general presumption that everyone has to compete in markets (as opposed to competing for political favours) is dispensed with, capital owners and organised labour coalesce to demand political preferment in more and more industries. Favoured industries then easily become prey to organised labour monopolies. Protected industries become unprofitable and clamour for more protection. Officials then raise the intensity of their intervention to avert political criticism and to safeguard their own political and material gains. Good money is thrown after bad. A spiral of interventionism eventually destroys the spontaneous forces of market-driven initiative and growth.

○ Key Concepts

Rent creation is a political activity by parliamentarians and bureaucrats to allocate 'rents', that is, incomes that are not obtained by competitive effort in the market. They derive from political privilege for private supporters or organised groups of supporters of political elites. Typically, political intervention redistributes property rights from the unorganised many to the organised few, who are then able to share their rents with the intervening agents of government. It is the mirror image of rent-seeking, which we defined in section 8.3.

Vested interest groups are politically active associations of agents who have a shared interest in obtaining political intervention that favours their income position and gives them influence over political processes.

The **political 'market'** is a process in which demand comes from producers who demand political intervention to redistribute property rights, and suppliers are agents of government who intervene in free competition on behalf of vested interests. According to this simplistic analogy with economic markets, the demand side tends to pay a price in the form of outright payments to and political support of the suppliers of market interventions (parliamentarians, politicians, bureaucrats, judges). ●

10.6   Controlling the Political Agents: Authority, Rules, Openness

Over the centuries, a large number of policy devices have been invented to control the intractable problem of agent opportunism in collective action and to enhance the chances that public policy meets – as best it can – the aspirations of citizens:

(a) The highest government leaders are made the guardians of sustainable, non-discriminatory institutions. This of course requires that the leader – the monarch, the president – is informed of the actions of her or his subordinates and that provisions of administrative law are adhered to and enforced. In the case of a modern mass society, this is a rather naive assumption since rulers have cognitive limits too. Administrators can be expected to collude in covering up breaches of proper administrative principles, and judges sometimes collude with the executive power. Indeed, the authority of the ruler by itself has proved a fallible safeguard of citizen interests. Many observers since Confucius and Plato have therefore suggested that future rulers should be imbued with the highest moral standards, so that these would later be practised in their oversight of the administration and the enforcement of the external institutions.

Relying on education poses the problem of who is to do the educating – and in whose interest – against the temptations of power.

(b) The device of a constitution which subjects the rulers, elected politicians and officials to general constraining rules became popular in modern times in Europe, and now increasingly worldwide. One important constitutional device – which was made popular by French philosopher Charles de Montesquieu (1689–1755) and was enshrined in the American Constitution – is to separate the powers of government between the legislative (rule making), the executive (rule-bound implementation) and the judiciary (adjudication of conflicts), and to lay down a system of checks and balances between the holders of these three types of authority over collective action (for one example of how this can work effectively in practice, see box). However, the principle of the separation of powers is frequently undermined, for example when judges make the law or when the executive creates rules by regulation (Ratnapala, 1990, ch. 6). The division of powers is undermined in particular in those many democracies where the majority in parliament forms the executive, as is the case under the modern 'Westminster system': 51 per cent of the seats, which may at times be obtained on a minority of the votes, confers temporary powers to legislate as well as to execute policies. Then, effective controls on the exercise of power are weakened and the legislative process becomes deformed by the dominance of the executive and the bureaucracy (Hayek, 1979a; Bernholz, 1982). This easily creates an atmosphere in which arbitrary uses of powers go unchecked and the political competition for votes leads to a growing redistribution of property rights.

❖ A Swiss Case: Controlling the Agents of Government

Swiss democracy is based on a division of powers which often seems to the outsider fuzzy and clannish. However, the system is given backbone by the instrument of the citizen-initiated referendum (that is, not the politician-initiated referendum typical of many other countries); 100 000 voters are, for example, able to initiate a referendum to alter the written federal constitution.

This method was used after the emergency of the second world war, when the government was reluctant to cede plenary powers obtained during the war. A small group of French Swiss agitated for a quick and complete return to direct democracy by the insertion of a clause in the constitution that guarantees that the federal government cannot abuse its emergency powers. A popular vote on 11 September 1949 liquidated the central government's wartime powers; by contrast many other democracies were permanently saddled with some authoritarian legacies of the war. More generally, Swiss referendums have typically thrown out government initiatives and countermanded administrative projects.

One telling episode of effective parliamentary control, which served yet again to caution the Swiss Federal parliamentarians, ministers and the bureaucracy that the 'sovereign', the Swiss people, will not tolerate misleading information and overspending, occurred in the wake of the purchase of a new jet fighter aircraft for the military in the early 1960s. The episode became known as the 'Mirage affair'. The military high command proposed to buy French-made Mirage jets, and the cabinet and the two chambers of parliament approved the expense of SFr870 million. Cost overruns (and possibly initial underestimates of the costs) made it necessary to ask parliament to raise the authorisation to SFr1350 million (a 55 per cent increase). This led to the threat of a citizen initiative to throw out the entire project. Various public inquiries were set up. They revealed that bureaucrats had trusted they would later be able to mobilise support for the supplement and that military experts had demanded numerous costly upgrades in the aircraft's technical specifications. Essentially, a different one was being bought from that authorised by parliament. Cost controls had been lax, leaders were kept partly in the dark, and the Military Department proceeded despite being well aware of the unauthorised cost increases. Had this process not been stopped, the total-systems expense would have risen further, to some SFr2000 million. In the face of the threat of a citizen initiative, it was decided to nearly halve the number of jet fighters that the military were permitted to acquire (from 100 to 57) and to put a strict ceiling of SFr1750 million on the entire project.

The very existence of recourse to a citizen-initiated referendum thus induced parliamentarians to assert their control over administrative spending. The normally considerable powers of Cabinet and government departments were reined in. The Swiss parliament reasserted its right to control the administration directly. It is hard to imagine such decisive action to control government on behalf of the people if the ultimate backstop of a citizen-initiated referendum had not been available. ◆

(Source: Based on W. Martin and P. Béguin 1980, Histoire de la Suisse, *pp. 350–3)*

(c) Another form of dividing the powers of collective action, which has served many affluent and stable nations well, is the division of the powers of governance by constitutional arrangement to create several autonomous levels of government; say, local, state and national governments (federalism). When much collective action is decided and implemented at local level, information and control of government by the principals, the citizens, is easier. Then, government agencies also have to compete. They will do so by searching for different administrative solutions, a method of discovering relevant administrative knowledge (section 12.3). In addition, central and state governments can control each other, as long as each has independent taxation powers.

(d) Many nations also try to control agent opportunism in legislatures by dividing the legislative power in a bicameral system; in federations this is normally attempted by matching a directly elected first chamber of parliament with a controlling second chamber that represents regional interests. However, second chambers have come to be dominated by party discipline and bloc voting on party lines, just as first chambers have, so this offers weak controls over political opportunism.

(e) In the face of failure to check effectively the concentration of political powers, proposals have been made to devise further constitutional checks against opportunistic behaviour by temporary parliamentary majorities. One such proposal is to establish a separate chamber responsible only for setting the framework rules, as against passing enabling ('purpose') legislation (Hayek, 1979a, pp. 177–9; 1960; 1979a, pp. 147–65) advocated the creation of a Legislative Assembly whose task it is to pass laws to legitimise the collective coercion of citizens. He advocated the election of members according to age cohorts, so as to ensure representation that is independent, as far as possible, of party discipline and of the other chamber, the governing assembly. Its scope of action would be limited by the rules that the legislative assembly has passed. Its role would be to appoint the executive and to determine the extent to which public goods are supplied and how they are financed. This arrangement might give teeth to the basic principle that elected parliaments are there to serve the average citizen. In the past, elected parliaments were the protectors of citizens' rights against the rulers, for example in eighteenth-century England and in Switzerland. It seems doubtful, however, whether party machines can be prevented from dominating both chambers of such a parliament in ways similar to today's multichamber parliaments.

(f) The growing complexity of public policy makes it increasingly difficult for the concerned citizen to keep informed of government actions – a fundamental precondition for controlling agent opportunism in government. Governments have therefore sometimes been obliged by parliaments to provide better, systematic information; for example, by sticking to agreed, transparent standards of accountability, annual budget plans and reviews, reporting to elected parliaments, and scrutiny of the accounts by an independent expert agency such as an auditor-general. An independent press and review of government activities by expert scrutineers, such as academic researchers, credit-rating agencies or international agencies, further enhance accountability and control opportunism in office.

(g) Another constitutional control of agent opportunism in government is the periodic exposure of at least some government agents to review by the electorate, whether the leaders of the administration (democracy) or other officials in the executive and judiciary (election of city officials or judges). This certainly makes the leadership of government contestable, but whether it controls agent opportunism depends on correct information and citizen involvement.

(h) In many constitutional settings, electoral contests between political parties have become 'auctions' of discriminatory, redistributional measures that appeal to median voters. Many observers therefore advocate constitutional rules which constrain political opportunism and limit the sovereignty of elected parliaments to engage in discriminatory intervention (Hayek, 1960; Buchanan, 1987, 1991; Brennan and Buchanan, [1980] 1985; McKenzie, 1984). The rules that may be imposed on governments can relate to the procedure and the results of collective choice. Examples of procedural constraints are the prescription of big majorities, or even unanimity, when raising taxes or public expenditures, so that minorities are protected. Certain revenues may also be tied to certain expenditure purposes (equivalence) and automatic sunset clauses may be imposed on collective actions. Rules that prescribe the results of collective action may demand a balanced budget or limit the government's debt. It is also possible to limit the growth rate of the budget or the level of certain spending programmes. Thus, higher-level rules may lay down maximum tax rates, as was done by 'Proposition 13' in California in 1978 when the state property tax was formally limited to 1 per cent of property value. Another such result-orientated constraint would be an institution that forces governments to correct income tax collection for inflation or to tie public expenditure to absolute or relative maxima, such as a certain percentage of the national income. A related procedural constraint to control executive powers are term limits, which are meant to prevent elected politicians from losing contact with the principals, to make it harder for rent-creating coalitions to form and to avert the sterility of life-long careers in politics.

O Key Concepts

The **control of political opportunism** has to rely on a multiplicity of devices, for example, the moral education of leaders, constitutional constraints such as the division of powers and citizen-initiated referendums, the assurance of free information flows, the practice of accountability of office holders, electoral democracy, a general commitment to high standards in public life and the openness of jurisdictions to competition with other jurisdictions.

The **separation of powers** is a constitutional device first made popular by French philosopher Charles Montesquieu (1689–1755). It demands the separation of the legislative, the executive and the judicial power as a means to control political power.

Citizen-initiated referenda allow the citizenry to overrule appointments and government actions which they do not like. They differ from politician-initiated referendums, which are common in many countries, in that the initiative for a vote on a particular measure comes from the people and their associations, and not from the top down. ●

(i) Another control device is the citizen-initiated referendum, whereby the principals are given a tool to vary or throw out government initiatives they do not like.

(j) One device to control opportunistic agents of government, which is preferred in some North American jurisdictions, is the recall (or impeachment) of elected representatives: if an elected parliamentarian, judge or administrator behaves in ways unacceptable to the vast majority of the citizenry, they have the right to recall that person through a renewed vote at any time during the tenure of office. Such a procedure is of course costly and will therefore be rarely used; but the mere possibility will act to moderate agent opportunism and may also induce the electorate to incur the information costs necessary for good government. Related to this provision is the possibility of the indictment of officials by courts or committees when specific misdemeanours can be proven.

(k) General social conditions can give teeth to citizen control. Effective controls of government powers benefit from a reasonably advanced level of education, which makes citizens economically and politically literate, and of affluence, which enables citizens to bear the information and monitoring costs needed for decent democratic government. This has been facilitated by the rise of a broad middle class: citizens of property who have a stake in a stable and growing economy. The freedom of association is also an important condition because it allows like-minded citizens to organise in order to control officials. While general social conditions are reasonably favourable to the control of government agents in the affluent democracies of the West, they often remain unfulfilled aspirations elsewhere. Citizens who do not have much private property of their own and are narrowly educated can be easily dominated by totalitarian regimes who suppress free association and an independent electorate. However, when economic growth leads to the emergence of an educated middle class, as has been the case in many of the smaller advanced East Asian countries, demands for free association and the effective electoral and judicial control of the rulers become more widespread.

(l) Arguably the most powerful control of agent opportunism in government nowadays is the openness of jurisdictions to trade and factor flows. History has taught us – as is discussed elsewhere in this book – the importance of openness. The exit challenge – the relocation of production capacities and emigration – to exploitative political power brokers has become stronger as the transaction costs of moving have declined. Moreover, freer information flows are now making interjurisdictional comparisons easier. Where government agents are self-seeking, demand high taxes and offer poor services and infrastructures, the economy and the revenue base are likely to shrink nowadays. Becoming the mayor of a ghost town or the leader of a state with capital flight is bound to give strong feedback to administrators, similar to the effective control of agent opportunism of managers in competing joint-stock companies (section 9.3). Over the long term, the new openness is therefore likely to constrain the principal–agent problem in government and to empower the citizen – a point to which we shall return in the chapter on international economic relations (section 12.3).

We have to conclude that no single device is effective enough on its own to control the principal–agent problem in government. At times, all the above devices will be needed to contain the problem. Even that may sometimes fail to protect the citizens from the deleterious consequences of political opportunism. Like a mother's job, the defence of freedom and the rule of law is never quite done.

10.7   Political and Economic Constitutions

The principles and institutions discussed here under the heading of constraints on collective action are high-order, universal constraints on public policy that serve to check the uses and abuses of political power. They are intended to limit collective authority, safeguard individual domains of liberty and constrain agent opportunism and rent-seeking. In other words, these principles and institutions are designed to limit the political power to discriminate. They have often been elevated to form part of political and economic constitutions: namely, overriding principles that will stand even in the face of evolutionary change.

Constitutions, as we saw in section 6.1, contain high-level institutions that cannot be changed as easily as lower-level rules and that therefore give a framework of continuity and predictability to the inevitable adjustments of lower-level institutions. Constitutions contain affirmations of basic inalienable individual rights that should not be negated by lower-level rules or the use of force by private citizens or government authorities. Individualist constitutions include the protection of private property because it lends material substance to individual autonomy. The constitutions of individualist communities also assert the sovereignty of the citizens in selecting their representatives, who determine collective action. Constitutions also contain provisions for the division of powers although, as we saw, these are nowadays often rather illusory.

Constitutionalism which binds those in charge of collective action to certain constraints depends for its effectiveness on electoral democracy, the prevalence of the rule of law, and the openness of the economy and the society to outside competition between governments and economic agents (Figure 10.2). These conditions form a web of mutually supportive suborders that underpin individual liberties.

Figure 10.2 **Constitutionalism: a web of mutually supportive institutional systems**

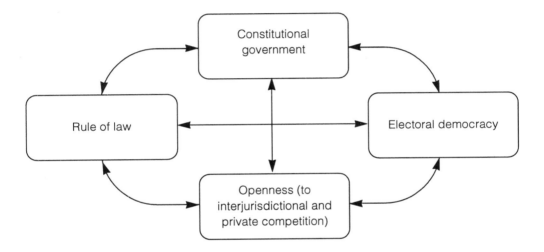

Constitutional Economics: Choice Among Rules

In this context the following questions may be asked: What are the economic effects of alternative sets of constitutional rules? Which constitutional rules serve individuals in coordinating their economic activities, given their limited knowledge? Specifically, which constitutional conditions serve best to ensure competition and innovation? The first question falls into the category of positive economics (positive constitutional economics); the others belong to normative constitutional economics. In general, the focus on constitutional economics has moved attention from the issue of choice *within* given rules to the choice *between* alternative rules (Voigt, 1997; Buchanan, 1991).

As we saw in Chapter 7, the constitution of a capitalist market economy requires the protection of private property rights and autonomy to enter freely into contracts, as well as formal equality before the law.

This implies the protection of private autonomy and full responsibility for one's contractual obligations, as well as the freedom of information, speech, occupation and movement.

In this context we should recall that 'constitution' is defined as a set of fundamental, high-level principles and recognised precedents according to which a community or an organisation are to be governed, and according to which existing lower-level rules may be altered (section 6.1). Constitutional rules should be universal, that is, general, open-ended and abstract (not case-specific) and reasonably predictable.

On Contractarianism

The concept of a constitution based on the concept of a 'collective will' has been attacked by public-choice theorists (Downs, 1957a, 1957b; Buchanan and Tullock, 1962; Buchanan, 1975, 1978, 1987, 1991; McKenzie, 1984). They have also drawn attention to the likelihood and danger of opportunism by self-seeking agents of government, including in electoral democracies. The public-choice school began by perceiving society as unstructured, an anarchy in which individuals live in a state of 'war of all against all'. It saw a constitution as a general contract that would enhance life conditions for all, a notion first made popular by the British philosopher Thomas Hobbes (1588–1679). Public-choice theory took up the notion of Swedish economist Knut Wicksell (1851–1926) that a constitutional contract requires unanimous acceptance to ensure that no members of society are worse off. At least hypothetically, a consensus of this kind should be conceivable in relation to specific constitutional rules. The contractarian school of constitutional economics, which pursues this line of argument, perceives the members of society as being in a prisoners' dilemma which can be ended by a contract of all. This leads to a 'disarmament' of harmful opportunism. The constitutional contract then gives the state a protective function.

The contractarian concept of the constitution, however, seems at variance with historic reality. Communities did not originally live in anarchy, but developed internal institutions and organisational support structures long before formal government ever came about. Contractarianism also implies that some observers, who design the constitutional rules, somehow have superior knowledge about which constitutional rules are optimal. The contractarian model of constitutional economics may also be criticised on the grounds that even the highest-ranked agents of government have a self-interest in breaking constitutional rules. Such breaches would require regression to an even higher authority than the leaders of the national government to enforce rule compliance. But such an authority does not exist. Ultimately the critique of collectively based constitutions by the public-choice school is based on efficiency: do constitutional arrangements enable private citizens to attain their purposes better?

An alternative critique of collectivist constitutions comes from Hayek (1960), who considered the protection of individual liberty to be the ultimate function and normative test of constitution. His position is based on an evolutionary world view and on giving a high priority to civil and economic liberties. He advocates a constitution of liberty based on constitutionally bound behaviour. This approach does not require the fiction of a unanimous contract.

Given the fundamental logical problems of the contractarian concept of a constitution, another school of thought has begun to develop from the Hayekian position. It sees a constitution as a bundle of pre-existing conventions. Constitutions do not exist to solve prisoners' dilemmas of anarchy among isolationist individuals. They cannot be reconstructed as a contract among the many. Rather, it makes more sense to perceive humans as 'social animals' who develop social ties from birth. Many of these ties are consolidated into internal institutions. This and shared fundamental values form the foundation for higher-level institutions, including constitutional rules. Culture precedes a constitution. Admittedly, constitutions need not necessarily be based on shared values and principles as analysed in this book. But constitutions do not require explicit, or at least tacit, agreement by millions of citizens. Indeed, they can even function when imposed by a minority, as was the case in colonial Hong Kong. A further indication that the contractarian theory of the constitution is misguided derives from the fact that many constitutional provisions lack the explicit, formal sanctions typical of contracts but instead rely on spontaneous compliance (self-enforcement).

Is Hand-tying Possible?

From a functional viewpoint, the main function of political and economic constitutions is to tie the hands of policy makers when, in the heat of battle, they are tempted to abandon principles. Constitutional provisions are then made to rule out arbitrary rent-seeking and disorder-creating decisions in the conduct of day-to-day public policy. Certain constitutional provisions – such as the independence of the central bank, or a balanced-budget rule – can serve to prevent short-sighted and costly political opportunism, in ways similar to the tying of Ulysses to the mast of his ship in Homer's tale lest he be lured by the Sirens. However, many democrats are of the view that the parliamentary majority of the day is absolutely sovereign and should not be subject to any constraints. This interpretation is commonly accepted in Westminster-style democracies: absolute power rests with the elected parliament. Those who reject the hand-tying of legislatures open the way for parliamentary majorities to pass erratic and inconsistent legislation which undermines order. Only when we understand the importance of order will we favour safeguards against the opportunism of parliamentary majorities.

Rigid 'hand-tying', if successful, creates problems when conditions change and rule adjustments are necessary. To alleviate this problem, rules governing the method of rule changes can be laid down and constitutional amendments can be made dependent on prescribed majorities in ballots.

A more fundamental problem with 'hand-tying' is that constitutional provisions are very difficult to enforce if those in government violate them: after all, they control political power, have enormous financial resources and the monopoly over the use of legitimate force. When parliaments and governments are bent on breaking constitutional limitations, the constitution may serve only as a reference point for castigating parliamentary or governmental opportunism. We must therefore conclude that constitutions on their own are only a weak bulwark against political attacks on individual liberties.

O Key Concepts

A **constitution** is a set of high-level institutions which circumscribe what lower-level institutions may or may not stipulate, who governs, and set down '*meta* rules' that form general principles for the shaping and adjustment of the more specific external institutions.

The analysis of the economic consequences of different types of constitutions is the subject of the new discipline of **constitutional economics**. Whereas we usually study human **choices within given institutions**, constitutional economics is concerned with alternative rule sets and **choices between rules**.

As in public-choice theory (the economic analysis of political choices, see Chapter 2), from which it derives, the basic premise of constitutional economics is that it is individuals who act in their own interest, not classes or groups of people. The constitutional-economics approach therefore is focused on the rules that channel individual choices and appeal to individual values.

We speak of **positive constitutional economics** when we analyse the emergence of constitutions and the observed or hypothesised outcomes of alternative rules, and of **normative constitutional economics** when the quest is for the rule sets that enable the members of the community to achieve certain purposes better and more effectively.

Contractarianism is based on the fiction that a society's constitution is derived from, or can be hypothetically conceived as, a social contract of all, on the assumption that the pre-constitutional state is anarchy in which all are in the bind of opportunistic, selfish behaviour.

Hand-tying relates to constitutional arrangements and agreements which are intended to preclude short-sighted, opportunistic decisions by agents of political power. An example would be a constitutional stipulation that obliges governments not to raise budget expenditures by more than 3 per cent each year, or the formal promise by parliament to forgo their right to change certain laws. ●

Formal constitutional provisions can, at best, serve as a limited constraint to control agent opportunism in public policy. Constitutional provisions need to be supplemented by the many other devices which we discussed earlier in this chapter (free press, accountability, federalism, openness to trade and factor flows, and so on). The control of political power in the interest of the freedom and prosperity of the citizen-principals is bound to remain a never-ending and challenging task for any community. This is an evolutionary problem, not one that can be solved once and for all by some panacea.

The Dual Pretence of Knowledge and Feasibility

Many government activities are still being justified by the argument that they address 'market failure'. This argument is based on the comparison between complex, imperfect reality and a reference system of 'perfect competition', which does not exist. The comparison is therefore invalid. Harold Demsetz (1969, p. 160) aptly labelled this the 'nirvana approach' to public policy. The model of 'perfect competition' has little bearing on the evolutionary market processes that are observed in reality. Above all, it ignores the knowledge problem (section 3.1) and the role of institutions in tackling that problem. Instead, its protagonists simply assume that government knows best and that government agents are benevolent. As explained earlier in this chapter, government does have an important role to play, but in discussing public policy allowance must be made for lack of knowledge in government and the possibility of government failure. It cannot be automatically assumed that collective action is driven by noble altruism, as we have already seen. Nor can it be assumed that costly solutions, which private agents have evaluated and rejected, will be less costly when implemented by government. The only effect of handing knotty problems to collective action may be that this frees the individual from rationally calculating all resource costs and benefits. The cumulative, long-term neglect of proper cost benefit calculations, however, only undermines the chances of achieving the material and non-material aspirations of the people.

Public policies always have unintended side-effects which those in charge of public action programmes can frequently not foresee or comprehend. After the side-effects appear, 'corrections' then trigger further intervention. Modern mass societies are so complex and evolve so unpredictably that only relatively general and simple government programmes can be comprehended by those in charge: the minister and the top administrators. Complex intervention programmes invariably get enmeshed in unpredictable contradictions. Coordinating the policies of different government agencies to achieve a great variety of goals then becomes a task that no one can fully understand and carry out. Public policies are often also ineffectual because the citizens fail to pay 'perfect attention'.

Analysts who have not thought through the knowledge problem are often overly optimistic about what discretionary collective action can achieve. They advocate or engineer elaborate government programmes to achieve numerous specific aims. They believe that an increasingly complex community has to be ordered by increasingly complex legislation and regulation – and are bewildered if disorder, confusion and apathy result. By contrast, the analyst who is imbued with the notion of the knowledge problem, who knows about the dangers of cognitive overload and understands the function of universal, abstract institutions in ordering complex situations, will advocate modest government and stress the need for government agents to be always mindful of order. He or she will advocate simple rules for our complex world (Epstein, 1995), and will perceive the goals of ambitious public guardians as based on the pretence of knowledge and on an unwarranted optimism of what it is feasible to achieve by public action.

Questions for Review

- List the reasons why collective choice is likely to realise the aspirations of individuals less well than private choice. Find examples for each reason from public life in your community.

- What are the apical functions of government?
- Would you argue for reducing the speed limit in built-up areas to 10 km/h, if that saved human lives? If not, why not?
- Why do governments engage directly in the production of goods and services? Do you know of publicly produced goods and services in your country that are produced and distributed privately in other countries?
- Is there a case to justify the operation of government-owned trains that run on government-owned tracks, when private trucks run on publicly owned roads and pay for the access?
- What are the advantages and drawbacks of an intensive political commitment to redistributing income and wealth?
- Give an example from your country where redistributive action has benefited the organised rich and hurt the unorganised poor? How has that case affected the career of politicians and administrators who create and carry out the redistributive action?
- Are you aware of judge-made laws that increase the redistribution of property rights and that are subsequently found to have deleterious side-effects which the judges did not foresee?
- What is the level of taxation and other obligatory government levies as a percentage of your country's national product? What was it one generation ago?
- Give an example of a compliance cost which has been imposed on you by a government agency.
- What are the interests of parliamentarians and industry leaders in the regulation of their industry? How does a regulation, such as the licensing of a limited number of taxis in a town, affect the income positions of (a) taxi owners, (b) regulators of the taxi industry, and (c) customers? Who has the most concentrated interest in regulation?
- Can you imagine how programme cost overruns are dealt with in your country? Compare this to the 'Mirage case' in Switzerland. Do you think that the threat of a citizen-initiated referendum to overrule such a project would strengthen the hand of the tax-paying principals?
- In what ways are agents of collective action (parliamentarians, ministers, bureaucrats, judges) typically controlled so that they serve the citizen-principals in your community? If you know of a principal–agent problem in your local government, what mechanism of control has failed? What would you advocate to avert a recurrence of such an event?
- If you know of a specific case of police corruption in your or another country, what are the effects on the attainment of fundamental human values?
- What was the main argument for stating that the main purpose of public policy should be to enhance order?

- List the constitutive principles of 'order policy' and give arguments, based on your knowledge of institutional economics, which justify that these concepts are given the status of universal principles for the conduct of public policy.
- Find cases from public policy in your country in which parliaments and politicians violated the constitutional principles of 'order policy'. Why were the principles violated in each case? How did each case affect the predictability of conditions under which individuals and firms operate?
- In what ways does the pursuit of productive and redistributive functions conflict with the order-protecting function of public policy? Give examples from the recent policy experience in your country where the protective function has been subordinated to the production and redistribution activities of government agencies.
- What purposes are served by a constitution? Does it contain only the written document that is often spelled with a capital C or other rules and conventions that are not spelled out so formally?
- Where did the constitution stand in the hierarchy of rules that we discussed in section 5.1?
- Outline the contractarian approach to constitutions and list the logical difficulties with that approach which we discussed in the text.

Notes

1. Some constitutions make explicit mention of political parties (for example, that of the Federal Republic of Germany), thus raising their status further relative to the individual citizen-voter.
2. It has also been argued that the maintenance of stability over time of specific indicators, in specific markets or the overall national economy, is also a function of government. However, lags in cognition, difficulties in reacting promptly and political conflicts about stabilising interventions have made this a controversial assignment for governments. In any case, the single most important aspect of stabilisation, namely the provision of stable money, can be subsumed under the protective function.
3. The public-finance literature often erroneously equates the provision of access to certain goods and services with the in-house production of these goods and services. This has led to the term 'productive function of government'. We have reluctantly retained this term in this book to remain consistent with other authors (such as Buchaan, 1975). 'Provision function' might, however, be a more appropriate term.
4. Sources of easy revenues, which are often beyond the scrutiny of elected parliaments, tend over the long run to open the way for the appropriation of these revenues by organised groups, such as the employees of public enterprises. Instead of contributing to general revenue, the proceeds from public production are frequently used to fund high salaries, sinecures for officials, overstaffing and high on-the-job consumption (opportunistic rent-seeking by agents of government). These abuses are now reasons why public opinion in many countries favours the privatisation of government-owned enterprises (Chapters 13 and 14).
5. *Ordo* is the Latin word to describe that state of society in which free Roman men could feel free and prosper. Eucken – like the other German *ordo* liberals – used the word *Ordnung* (order) throughout his writings whenever he argued for *ordo* policy. However, the translator of the first of Eucken's books, T.W. Hutchinson, avoided

the word 'order' and used the word 'system' which has less of a normative conno-
tation and fails to convey the full meaning of order as used in this book. Eucken's
second central book on *ordo* policy (*Grundsätze der Wirtschaftspolitik* [Foundations
of Economic Policy], first published 1952), though much reprinted in German, has
as yet not been published in an English translation.

CHAPTER 11

The International Dimension

This chapter looks at the problems peculiar to international trade and the movement of capital, knowhow and firms across national borders. Such exchanges have to deal with the particular risk that the contractual obligations of defaulting contract partners cannot be readily enforced in foreign jurisdictions. Various institutional and organisational arrangements have been developed by the international business community to tackle this problem. International trade and finance are based on effective and complex institutions which fall outside the umbrella of national institutions.

Openness gives the subjects of national jurisdictions the exit option. This weakens the power of governments. It is sometimes perceived as an affront to the rulers. Powerful national interest groups who clamour for protection from international competitors often induce governments to interfere with international trade, capital flows, migration and technological exchanges. This reduces competition, diminishes the institutional underpinnings of a non-discriminatory order based on private property and abridges the property rights of foreigners and nationals. It is also a source of international conflict. It is therefore useful to constrain the scope for opportunistic national interventions in international exchanges. This is done, for example, under the World Trade Order (WTO) and OECD codes on foreign investment.

Finally, we shall discuss the international monetary order from an institutional angle. It has changed over the past century from the gold standard to fixed parities and then to more or less flexible exchange rates. We shall discuss the rules that allow international merchants and financiers to cope with the existence of different currencies and differing national monetary policies.

If a foreign country can supply us with a commodity cheaper than we ourselves can make it, better buy it off them with some part of the produce of our own industry.

In the home trade ... [the merchant] can know better the character and situation of the persons whom he trusts, and if he should happen to be deceived, he knows better the laws of the country from which he must seek redress.
(*Adam Smith*, The Wealth of Nations, *1776*)

To the Honorable Members of the Chamber of Deputies:
Gentlemen: We are suffering from the ruinous competition of a foreign rival who apparently works under conditions far superior to our own for the production of light that he is flooding the domestic market with it at an incredibly low price. From the moment he appears, our sales cease, all the consumers turn to him, and a branch of French industry whose ramifications are innumerable is all at once reduced to complete stagnation. This rival, which is none other than the sun, is waging war on us. We ask you to be so good as to pass a law requiring the closing of all windows ... and outside shutters through which the sun is wont to enter houses to the detriment of the fair industries with which, we are proud to say, we have endowed the country ...
(*Frédéric Bastiat, 'Letter from the Manufacturers of Candles, Tapers, Lanterns, ... and Generally Everything Connected with Lighting', Le Libre Échange, 1846*)

11.1 The Growing Significance of the International Dimension

Engines of Growth

International trade, investment and payments has fairly consistently outgrown the growth of national economies. Thus, world output (in current prices) went up more than eightfold between 1972 and 1995, whereas world exports increased thirteen-fold, direct international investments nearly twenty-fold and international financial flows by a stunning fifty times. In many countries, international trade and direct investments have been the most important vehicles for transferring useful knowledge to local producers and buyers. Many of the concepts and ideas that make high living standards possible can be learnt most easily by experiencing imported models which demonstrate their usefulness, whether that relates to an imported product that someone begins to use or to technical and organisational methods that foreign subsidiaries and immigrants practise. Frequently, the transfer of such knowledge to new locations will also require adaptation and learning on the part of the trader and foreign investor.

The process of intensifying international exchanges of goods and services and the growing international migration of production factors is now given the label 'globalisation'. Its ramifications today reach a very large share of the world population. Never in the history of mankind have so many people gained access to modern and changing forms of production, exchange and consumption. The process has much to do with the unprecedented acceleration of global economic growth, to which we referred in section 1.2. It would not be imaginable without the unprecedented development of an institutional framework that facilitates cross-border transactions. Advances in these institutions, coupled with technical progress in communications, transport and travel, have been powerful engines of economic growth and have increased the relative importance of the international dimension of national economies. This has also had great impact on the capacity – or otherwise – of domestic policies to affect developments within national jurisdictions. Where the exit option is available, the political power over economic life is limited. Where economic and social networks go beyond national borders, the nation state loses a considerable part of its clout. The new openness has had feedback into the evolution of internal and external national institutions of most nations. At times, this has been resented by those who experience the loss of their power. They then try to 'protect' their influence by impeding international trade and payments.

The Drop in Exit Costs

Since the 1960s, the competition among distant locations and national jurisdictions for mobile production factors, such as capital, has greatly intensified. In part this is due to advances in technology. In the second half of the twentieth century, containerisation, roll-on/roll-off ships, pipelines and jumbo jets have saved transport costs in innovative ways. But advances in transport technology pale in comparison to the revolutionary advances in communications ('the transportation of ideas'). The fax, satellite communication, fibre cables, computing and data compression, e-mail, microwave transmission and widely available portable video cameras have brought down the costs of long-distance communication by phenomenal margins. People are better informed about living and working conditions in distant places and civilisations.

There have been secular declines in the costs of international shipping and port handling (–0.4 per cent per annum from 1950 to 1990) and passenger air travel (–2.5 per cent); the costs of intercontinental telephone and similar communications fell even faster in recent decades, thanks to the steep decline in computing costs and the advances in reorganising the communications business on a competitive footing.

Between 1975 and 1995 the cost of mainframe information processing fell by no less than 37 per cent per annum, and telephone costs, if measured by the price of a transatlantic call, fell by an average 8.3 per cent per annum between 1930 and 1996 (Kasper, 1993, p. 84; *The Economist*, 18 October 1997, p. 99). Moreover, at least the producers and traders in the core countries of the world trading system (the OECD and capitalist East Asia) can now rely on established, fairly standardised trading practices, shared procedures of insurance and conflict resolution, and a body of globally orientated executives who share a common set of internal institutions on how to do business. The risk of disruption of trade and foreign investment by war and blatant anti-foreigner discrimination among the OECD and the new industrial countries has dwindled compared to historical standards. Nevertheless, the costs of doing business internationally differ greatly from country to country due to differences in government policies and the culture of internal institutions and values. As investors find that the costs of investing in different locations vary by great margins, the international division of labour has become intense. For example, cotton fibres are grown in Australia, crudely processed in China, chemically treated in Japan, spun and dyed in Thailand, woven in the United States and tailored into garments in Mauritius – all this for the German market. Nowadays, a motor car is no longer made from components that are produced by one single western nation, as a quick glance under the bonnet of any vehicle will reveal. The 'value-adding chain' of modern industrial products is distributed across many locations and nations. Increasingly, local and national institutions are becoming a key cost factor that determines what is produced where – not surprisingly, because coordination costs account often for half of all costs and because these are greatly influenced by prevailing institutions.

The ease of international communication has created an altogether new phenomenon, namely the long-distance trade in services which could previously only be produced near the buyers. Many services are now internationally transportable. This has great impact because services are the dominant sector in the world economy, accounting for some two-thirds of world production. Up to the 1980s, few activities such as organisation, planning, controlling, administering, advising, servicing, teaching and designing had been traded internationally. But as of the 1990s, overnight airline bookings for American customers may be done by a clerk in Ireland, letters dictated in New York can be typed in Jamaica and remitted back on-line, daily accounts for firms in New Zealand are processed on-line in Manila, and sections of the major Singapore newspaper are written in Sydney. When criminal interference by the Chinese Triads and cost levels created problems for the Hong Kong betting industry, it relocated the settling of bets to Australia. And joint textbook chapters can be edited in cyberspace between Australia and Germany. Before long, ATMs and Internet connections will give individuals a choice among overseas banks and among offshore insurance companies for their life, health and cars.[1]

Locational Choice

The number of potential locations for production has thus multiplied for many types of enterprises. Indeed, production plants, through which many manufactured goods pass, often belong to the same multinational company. As a matter of fact, some 33 per cent of world trade in the early 1990s was between subsidiaries of the same multinational corporation, and a further third of world trade had a multinational corporation as one of the two contract partners (United Nations, 1995, p. 193). Different plants in the same 'value-adding chain' are thus located in different places and countries to ensure the highest possible expected profit. The expected profit is defined as the difference between the expected selling price and the (weighted) sum of expected unit costs of production, transport and distribution, multiplied by the expected volume of sales:

$$\text{Profit} = (\text{price} - \text{unit costs}) \times \text{sales}$$

$$= \left(\text{price} - \frac{\sum \text{factor prices} \times w}{\sum \text{factor productivities} \times w} \right) \times \text{sales}$$

where w designates the weights of the various production inputs.[2]

This definition may look simple, but – even for one location – it is often extremely difficult to collect and assess the relevant knowledge about changing prices, the many input markets, production techniques, logistics and distribution networks, the costs of using the public-domain infrastructures, the laws, regulations and customs that affect production, productivity and products, labour, investment and commercial transactions, the political risks and many more aspects on which profit expectations are based.

The information and entrepreneurial assessment problems multiply when different locations in different countries are evaluated and compared, particularly when little empirical experience has yet been gathered with regard to some of the new industry locations. Locational choice therefore requires real entrepreneurial talent. The attractiveness of different locations to mobile production factors – capital, technical knowledge, high expertise, and bundles of these factors which are organised in firms – is thus shaped by expectations of the relative movement of all factors affecting profitability.

Despite the enormous difficulties of assessing the complex and changing data, businesses are all the time incurring these transaction costs to make international locational decisions. It can be safely assumed that the owners and managers of internationally immobile production factors – key among which are nowadays normally labour, government and land – are critical in determining the levels of unit costs in a location. Location-specific coordination costs and institutions are often critical for competitiveness (Kasper, 1994a; see box).

O Key Concepts

Profitability measures a business organisation's expected excess of receipts over expenses, often expressed as a percentage of a business's capital. When the difference is negative, the business expects a loss. Per unit of sales, profitability is the difference between the sales price and the unit costs of production and distribution.

The **competitiveness** of a location relates to the expected profitability of specific economic activities in that location as compared to alternative locations. Competitiveness thus varies between different activities. It is greatly influenced by the availability and cost of factor supplies, as well as the institutions that facilitate the combination of production factors. When all components of relative profitability are taken into account and the focus is on what influences the long-term movement of mobile production factors, we often speak of 'attractiveness'. ●

Institutions and International Competitiveness

If a location loses its cost competitiveness, production facilities tend to move elsewhere. We then observe locational innovation, driven by entrepreneurs. This has become easier because many firms now have direct experience of conditions in many nations and much manufacturing is now lightweight and hence more easily relocated and its products more easily transported to distant markets. Many a production unit can be quickly moved elsewhere – sometimes it can be packed into just a few containers.

In the production of most sophisticated modern services, such as banking, insurance, planning and logistics, the quality of human capital and institutions is of even greater importance than in manufacturing or agriculture. Many services are tailored to customer requirements and change all the time, so there is a premium on an institutional environment that facilitates quick innovative response and low-cost coordination.

The costs of taxation and compliance with government policies as well as the quality of government-provided services and infrastructures also matter greatly to the attractiveness of a jurisdiction to service providers. Financial intermediaries, for example, depend crucially on staff who share cultural traditions of honesty, reliability and caution, as well as on the external institutions of financial regulation, fiduciary oversight and accountability. What also matters greatly is credible, unbiased enforcement of the law. Jurisdictions which offer business-friendly customs, conventions, laws and regulations and facilitate lower transaction costs and a reliable competitive order will attract international producers who cater to global markets (Kasper, 1994a). Jurisdictions that fail on this score are, by contrast, likely to experience an increasing outmigration of industries such as component assembly, research and development, finance, entertainment, accounting and legal advice, planning and logistics services and so on.

❖ Factors that Shape International Competitiveness

The owners of those production factors that are in a position to move among locations and nations tend to assess the costs of the immobile or less mobile production factors in making their locational choices. Nowadays, capital, technical and organisational knowledge, high skills, and bundles of these factors – called firms – as well as raw materials tend to be internationally mobile. Labour, land and legal, political and administrative systems tend to be the internationally immobile inputs, whose costs determine the international attractiveness or otherwise of a location or nation. Institutions in turn determine the capacity of the owners of the various factors to interact, creating economic growth. They are therefore important in determining the relative transaction costs of production and innovation.

Against this background, various research organisations measure international competitiveness, for example the Swiss-based World Economic Forum, in whose 1996 annual report Harvard economists Jeffrey Sachs and Andrew Warner wrote:

> international competitiveness means the ability of a nation's economy to make rapid and sustained gains in living standards ... The Competitiveness Index attempts to summarize in a single quantitative index the structural characteristics of an economy ... that are likely to determine the economy's prospects for medium-term growth ... One of the key assumptions of this study is that certain kinds of structural characteristics can be measured with standard

published data, while other kinds ... are better measured by opinion surveys ... The survey data come from 2000 business executives in the 49 countries considered in this report.

In the end eight clusters of characteristics are settled upon ... :

- openness of the economy to international trade and finance;
- role of the government budget and regulation;
- development of financial markets;
- quality of infrastructure;
- quality of technology;
- quality of business management;
- labor market flexibility;
- quality of judicial and political institutions ...

Judicial and political institutions measure, however, imperfectly, the extent to which legal and political systems provide for low 'transaction costs' in writing and defending contracts and in protecting property rights. The expectation is that an honest and efficient judiciary and a political system that respects private property rights, are important factors in producing economic growth in complex, market-based economies ...

... Differences in economic growth attributed to differences in competitiveness are sizeable. According to the slope of the line linking competitiveness and growth, the difference in medium-term growth due to differences in competitiveness between the most and the least competitive countries in the sample, is on the order of 8.1 percentage points per year ...

Does the index help to explain cross-country patterns of economic growth ... ? The answer is a resounding yes: competitiveness matters ... The bottom line on competitiveness is that national economic policies make a profound difference to economic growth in the medium term. Open markets, lean government spending, low tax rates, flexible labor markets, an effective judiciary and stable political system, all contribute ...

... Infrastructure, management and technology also contribute, though measurement is much harder and effects are much more elusive. These basic facts are becoming increasingly appreciated: indeed, they are helping to orient market reforms ... the quest for national competitiveness can be an important stimulus for much needed policy reforms in many economies around the world. ◆

(World Economic Forum, 1996, pp. 8–13)

On the Supply of and Demand for Protectionism

Free international trade and factor flows are often blamed for the need to adjust and consequently are the object of political action to displace economic competition. Political entrepreneurs can hope to gain influence and political advantage by discriminating against foreign suppliers and investors who do not have a vote. Domestic buyers, who would benefit from unhindered international trade competition, often remain 'rationally ignorant' about the effect of such unequal treatment imposed on them.

The point can be illustrated by the example of a car tariff that protects domestic car manufacturers. Let us assume a medium-sized country with, say, five local car producers and a tariff that raises car prices by, say, $3000 on average. If we assume that the price rise does not reduce the volume of 750 000 cars sold a year, the redistributional benefit (rent) to the average national car producer is:

$$(\$3000 \times 750\,000)/5 = \$450 \text{ million per annum.}^3$$

By contrast, each car buyer may buy a new car only every eight years – in particular, when tariffs make cars expensive – so that the disadvantage from the car tariff to each buyer is:

$$\$3000/8 = \$375 \text{ per annum.}$$

Instead of joining a car buyers' lobby organisation, it is probably rational for households to swallow the disadvantage and concentrate on recouping the political redistribution loss in markets where they have supplier power, for example by joining a union to extract higher wages.

It is understandable, given the high costs of organising a lobby group, that car producers have a keen interest in tariffs and a high capacity to invest some of the rents that the tariff confers into political lobbying so as to perpetuate or further increase the car tariff. The usual asymmetry in markets thus plays into the hands of political entrepreneurs who wish to discriminate against foreign competitors and transfer property rights from poor, ill-organised people to rich, well-organised groups. Similar political motives for redistributing property rights sometimes come to bear when foreign producers (multinationals) wish to set up production facilities in a country and politicians try to lure them by guaranteeing them a protected domestic market (Streit and Voigt, 1993, pp. 54–8).

The political economy of protection is straightforward. Import-competing interest groups lobby for protection and political parties are willing to grant protection as long as they believe that providing privileges to some groups will improve their chances of being re-elected. Opposition parties are willing to take up pleas for protection because they are trying to win support in order to become elected. Potential domestic interest groups who might lobby for free trade – for example, consumers, producers who use imported inputs, exporters who bear the burden of costly inputs, wholesalers and retailers who rely heavily on imported goods – tend to have more difficulty in rallying support. Industry groups that lobby for protection therefore tend to have few members, and offer members selective incentives (cf. box).

❖ Indonesia's 'National Car'

The national car program, launched in February 1996 through a Presidential decree, gives [the firm] Timor Putra exclusive exemption from hefty tariffs and luxury sales taxes, and the right to import 46 000 cars from joint-venture partner Kia Motors Corp. of Korea, for three years until their plant in Indonesia is operational ... Even though the cars are from Korea, they carry the national car brandname, 'Timor'.

This has enabled the 1600 cc 'Timor' sedan to easily undercut its competitors, with the car selling for around ... half the price of comparable Japanese vehicles ... While it has enjoyed a huge price advantage, sales of the 'Timor' have fallen well below expectations.

Timor Putra is controlled and managed by Mr Hutomo Mandala Putra, the youngest son of General Suharto, the President of Indonesia. He is a businessman with little experience in the car industry.

Several months ago Mr Hutomo asked the Government for a US$1.3 billion line of credit to enable local production of the car to go ahead. After being instructed by President Suharto to coordinate the loan package, the Governor of Bank Indonesia ... has initiated a US$690 million credit facility ...

... Indonesian government departments must now buy the ... car in a move to boost the vehicle's flagging sales. Minister for National Planning, Ginanjar Kartasasmita, confirmed after a Cabinet Meeting ... that the 'Timor' would become the standard car for all government agencies purchasing sedans for official use ...

... The Government's national car policy has been strongly condemned by Japan, the US and the European Union as a flagrant breach of international trade rules. Japan and the EU have both approached the World Trade Organisation seeking an arbitration panel to hear their complaints. [In May 1997], Indonesia blocked an EU request to set up a dispute settlement panel to determine whether Jakarta's national car project breaks WTO rules. Diplomats expect the EU and Japan to bring their complaints before the WTO again ... Indonesia cannot block a second request ... but said it would strongly contest the case. If Indonesia loses, it would have to end the offending program and compensate the complainant states or risk sanctions against its exports.

In the wake of the East Asian currency crisis in the second half of 1997, during which the Indonesian government sought assistance from the International Monetary Fund, the Indonesian government undertook to submit to an investigation of the 'National Car' deal by the World Trade Organisation, as well as to tighten and enforce national credit policies and in early 1998

Indonesia appears to have abandoned the project altogether as a response to the collapse of its international credit and its currency. ◆

(Source: Various press reports in The Australian *between January 1997 and February 1998)*

Lobby groups are easier to organise if they can win the support of government as a regulatory agency. It will then be possible to exert pressure or even coerce individuals to join the group because of the support of government. Lobby groups, once set up by a government intervention, therefore work to perpetuate the intervention.

The preparedness of politicians to supply protection to an industry is determined by the shared values of a society (for example, popular views on cosmopolitanism versus nationalism, or preferences for security and welfare redistribution), prevailing institutional arrangements (for example, whether officials have great discretionary powers to intervene or are bound by legal principles that protect private autonomy), and economic circumstances (such as unemployment or increases in import penetration). It also depends on the perceptions of politicians about the potential costs of breaking the free-trade rule, such as fear of foreign retaliation and formal proceedings under WTO rules: internationally agreed institutions bind governments to some extent not to provide opportunistic protection measures. They can play a role in stemming protectionism at least in the case of smaller economies (Odell, 1990). The binding power of WTO rules is, however, weakened by a proliferation of escape clauses which weaken its normative power. Moreover, the possibilities of enforcing WTO rules are very limited.

The Challenge of Openness

International trade and factor flows exert pressures, as we noted, that challenge established political power constellations. Power brokers therefore have the incentive to resist globalisation (see box). In an open environment, political attempts to create rents by the discriminatory reallocation of property rights and for the sake of political convenience are harder to uphold. Globally mobile investors are frequently not part of established national 'old boy networks' and entrenched political cliques. They may have learnt that political favours can be costly for them in the long run, as political 'entrepreneurs' extract returns for political favours granted. Therefore, experienced internationally mobile investors are nowadays no longer easily attracted by specific protection and handouts. They normally prefer a clear set of abstract, universal rules that preclude political favouritism and treat nationals and outsiders equally (Giersch, 1993).

❖ China: a Case Study in Political Control and the New International Mobility of Information

Excerpts from a press agency report

Unnerved Chinese leaders ... are scrambling to defend against a threat they can't and don't understand – the Internet.

... Seven months after it was allowed into the country, the Internet is looming as the most unwieldy and revolutionary threat yet to the Communist government's obsessive control over information.

It is estimated that more than 100 000 people in China – mostly the so-called intelligentsia – already have access to uncensored news from around the world on the Internet. In turn, grassroots information the government wants kept in China is leaking out. While the Internet is still seen as essential in China's modernisation, leaders right up to Premier Li and President Jian are on alert and moving to patch up dangers they see the system posing against stability.

... [A] new State Council committee is understood to have demanded that all registered Internet subscribers re-register and sign a pledge not to engage in destabilising activities. Future subscribers would have to sign the same pledge. But this is one battle against freedom of information nobody expects the government to win.

Efforts to restrict capacity can easily be circumvented, and while material transmitted on the Net can be monitored, it cannot be stopped.

The ramifications of the Internet on China's future cannot be underestimated ...

[A] western source says: The Government really doesn't understand the Net. Li Peng and Jian Zemin are always talking about it with foreign businessmen, asking questions about how to control it ... In terms of a totalitarian regime keeping tight control, they have something to worry about.

... The Internet won't create a consciousness, but it may, in the end, exacerbate it ... The conflicting argument is that if this regime doesn't succeed economically – and the country can't modernise without the Internet – they're also doomed. In that sense, the Government is damned if it does and damned if it doesn't. There's no effective way to censor the Net. That's why it's known as the final blow in over-running national boundaries.

In the course of 1996, it was reported that the Chinese government authorised the acquisition of Internet connections by private citizens, but ensured that all international traffic went through two government-controlled gateways which filtered out certain communications. It was also reported that back-street shops were selling devices which allowed Chinese Internet subscribers to bypass the gateways and plug directly into the Hong Kong network. ◆

(Source: AAP Report, 29 January 1996, and subsequent press reports)

11.2   The Institutional Framework of International Exchanges

The Peculiarities of Crossing Borders: Bridging Gaps in Space and Between Institutional Systems

When people trade products (property rights), this normally entails transport costs because producers and customers operate in different locations. In addition, they incur transaction costs. Likewise, mobility costs have to be borne when production factors are moved in space. These costs are low in the case of financial capital because it travels by wire. Bulky capital goods cost more to move. Moving knowledge causes greatly varying costs (relative to the market value of that knowledge), and the relocation of people tends to cause considerable expense. The costs of transport and factor mobility, which we might call 'space bridging costs', occur in interregional as well as in international transactions. Taken by themselves, they do not create a systematic difference between cross-border and interregional transactions (Kasper, 1993).

However, peculiar costs and risks arise when trade or factor flows cross national borders. The two contracting parties do not transact under the umbrella of a shared institutional framework and the same jurisdiction. National rule enforcement ends at the border, so there are specific risks in international contracts. If one party defaults on delivering on a contractual promise, the means of coercing it or obtaining redress for damages are less straightforward than when both parties operate under the same jurisdiction. Sometimes, extraterritorial parties have diminished or no rights under the customs and laws of specific countries (discrimination against foreigners).

Differing customs, conventions, work practices, design standards, laws and regulations cause specific 'international institution-bridging costs' – higher transaction costs of contracting across borders. In extreme cases, there may be international enforcement failure. We can thus conclude that international transactions often take place within greater uncertainty and higher transaction costs.

O Key Concepts

Space-bridging costs arise whenever an economic transaction is between contract partners who are in two different locations. They may consist of *transport costs* to shift physical products, *communications costs* to move information, and *mobility costs* to move production factors; for example, when people migrate, a factory is moved to a different place or financial capital is transferred.

International institution-bridging costs arise when the institutional orders of various countries differ, so people who trade or move production factors between different countries incur costs that do not arise within the same nation. In particular, transaction costs and risks arise when contractual obligations have to be enforced in foreign countries.

The risk of **international enforcement failure** arises when private contracting parties have no or lesser access to the enforcement mechanisms in foreign countries or are ignorant of what enforcement mechanisms are available to them. It may be extraordinarily costly to seek tort damages or contract fulfilment in another country because the judiciary, police and informal enforcement mechanisms behave differently from those with which one is familiar at home. ●

If we take an international trade contract as an example, higher information costs need to be incurred to identify contract partners, product specifications may vary from the standards in the home market, as do the essential attributes of foreign contract partners. Thus, their creditworthiness, solvency and payment morale may differ from the standards with which one is familiar. However, it is not necessarily always true nowadays that international transactions are more difficult and costly than national ones. Traders in New York may have lower transaction costs if they buy or sell in London than if they trade with someone in Wichita. Moreover, the communications revolution and intensification of distance trade has slashed important components of transaction costs.

Additional costs also arise when production factors move across national borders. But again, this does not always mean that the costs of international mobility are higher than in the case of national relocation. For example, academics in China may have more information and share more cultural traits with their professional colleagues in America than with Chinese villagers, so they may find it less costly to move internationally than within the country, within a professional network rather than outside it. Private networks often overlap national borders. Borders therefore constitute less clear-cut lines of division than a summary analysis might suggest. None the less, it must be recognised that peculiar cost categories occur in border-crossing transactions.

One cost that frequently arises in international transactions relates to different languages. This causes translation costs and possible misunderstandings. Interlanguage communication involves not only vocabulary and grammar but a host of cultural concepts and habits which may differ between nations. To the extent that trading communities develop a shared *lingua franca* they reduce the translation costs. This was the case, for example, with Greek and Latin in antiquity, 'trader doggerel' in the Middle Ages in Europe, Arabic throughout the Middle East, 'bazaar Malay' in South East Asia, and English on a global scale today. Sometimes, specific groups whose members reside in different countries share the same language and culture, such as Jews in Europe or certain Chinese communities in the Far East, and this gives them a cost advantage which they exploit to become middlemen.

There may be extra transaction costs in international contract negotiations because tacit institutions differ between countries and cultures and the differences may need to be made explicit and dealt with during contract negotiations. The internal and external institutions in different countries may be incompatible and require additional contract clauses to override the differences. It may take much specific and hard-to-learn knowhow to cope with these aspects of international business, and additional transaction costs may have to be borne.

Arguably the most thorny problems peculiar to international transactions arise with the enforcement of contracts, in both trade and finance. A defaulting party cannot be coerced through recourse to shared national jurisdictions operating under the same law. The judiciary or the police, even if their services are readily available to citizens of foreign countries, may operate under quite different rules and administrative practices, as people who trade and invest in some developing countries can readily attest.

Another cost peculiar to international transactions arises from the existence of different currencies. Receipts or expenditures have to be converted in the foreign exchange market, which is not cost-free. Traders and investors often incur foreign exchange risks, as deferred payments may eventually be converted at a rate of exchange different from that expected. These problems and their institutional solutions are discussed in section 11.3 below.

Institutions which Facilitate International Transactions

Since there are these additional transaction costs in border-crossing trade and factor flows, it may well be asked why international trade has been growing about twice as fast as world production and why international investment and migration are burgeoning. Indeed, how do people manage without overarching common enforcement agencies based on external government powers (Curzon and Price, in Radnitzky, 1996)? One explanation could be that international trade and finance respond to higher profit incentives than are available in national transactions, possibly because relative factor prices differ greatly or because international trade, investment and migration exploit profitable transfers of knowledge, which has been tested in one country, to a market of a larger international scale. As international trade and investment grow, extraordinary profit margins are, however, whittled away so that profits are in reality not systematically higher than in domestic trade.

The answers to the puzzle lie with institutional economics: a rich variety of individual arrangements has been developed spontaneously to economise on the peculiar costs of international trade and factor movements. In reality, international exchanges occur not in a vacuum, but within a sophisticated spontaneous order (ibid.; Streit 1996; Streit and Mangels, 1996). These institutions allow people to risk their fortunes in dealings with partners in far-distant countries whom they have never met. This is frequently even done without written contracts, simply based on trust in the informal institutions of a particular professional network and enforcement mechanisms which owe nothing to government back-up.

International Private Law

One approach to dealing with the uncertainties and enforcement problems of extraterritoriality is to take recourse to international private law, that is, to laws created in specific jurisdictions to deal with international transactions. It contains legal principles that determine which state's private law is to be applied in specific circumstances. As such, it is the law of a specific country which tries to reduce the scope for collision between conflicting legal norms. International private law thus may reduce conflicts. But considerable uncertainties remain: How will national tribunals interpret certain rules? Will tribunals be able to cope with foreign laws, or reinterpret foreign law in the light of domestic judicial traditions? At times, related matters may be interpreted on the basis of either domestic or foreign norms. Moreover, what if foreign private laws collide with overriding domestic legal principles? Then, the national interest in public order may be taken to justify decisions to override foreign laws and the ruling of international private law.

Despite these fundamental difficulties, a uniform code governing international commodity transactions was ratified under United Nations auspices in 1980 in Vienna. By and large, it codifies trading customs. The Vienna convention is now recognised in some 40 jurisdictions. None the less, the application of the Vienna convention does not necessarily create the certainty of effective institutions because it depends on national courts that operate within differing judicial conventions. The outcome of law cases is far from predictable. Contracting parties tend to agree to accept the norms of a third country, so as not to give one party an asymmetric advantage over the other, but this increases the information costs for both contracting parties and leads to 'forum shopping' by the more powerful contracting party.

We must thus conclude that international private law does not create legal certainty and often increases transaction costs. It is therefore not surprising that very few trade conflicts are litigated by government courts on the basis of international private law (Streit and Mangels, 1996).

The New *Lex Mercatoria*

The alternative to the formal, official judiciary processes on the basis of external rules is private arbitration on the basis of internal rules. This is, indeed, how most conflicts in international trade contracts are adjudicated and settled. It is reported that some 90 per cent of all international transactions provide for some form of private arbitration and that, where necessary, some 90 per cent of decisions by arbitrators are accepted voluntarily and without further recourse to public courts (Streit and Mangels, 1996, p. 24). The institutional set on which this is based has become known as the 'new *lex mercatoria*', echoing the legal principles that European international traders developed in the Middle Ages and thereafter to facilitate their business (Law Merchant). The medieval Law Merchant was based on certain legal principles, such as equality before the law, which was a path-breaking deviation from the feudal class law prevailing at the time. It covered certain customs of trade that were adjudicated by arbitrators who were part of the merchant profession. It was internal law, which was at times formalised but which was enforced without recourse to officials with public power.[4]

The contemporary Law Merchant is likewise a set of internal, formal or informal, institutions (section 5.2). They consist in the first place of trading customs that are generally recognised by all participants in a given branch of trade and that are generally expected to be observed. Many of these customs bind the contracting parties tacitly; some have been codified to enhance transparency; and they typically apply to specific industries to suit highly specialised circumstances.

The internal institutions that underpin international transactions also consist of standardised contracts, contract clauses and general conditions of business. These greatly reduce the costs of contract negotiation and monitoring. Examples are standardised letters of credit in international trade and standardised insurance coverage for certain transactions that have been laid down by international chambers of commerce. International traders in machinery and equipment often agree to standardised and highly elaborate conditions concerning the delivery and installation of the equipment to save on contract negotiation costs and to cover possible conflict during the execution of such contracts.

Another type of transaction-cost saving institution deals with international trade clauses which apply to contracts across a wide variety of specialised trades, the so-called International Commercial Terms (Incoterms). These institutions have been codified by the international chambers of commerce to stipulate each contracting party's rights and obligations; for example, 'free on board' (f.o.b.) and 'cost, insurance and freight' (c.i.f.). These terms are now used worldwide and across all industries and serve to simplify contracting and contract monitoring. Likewise, certain general legal principles are typically assumed to apply to international contracts, such as the rule of *rebus sic stantibus* (that conditions are accepted as found at the time of contract) and an understanding of the principle of 'common honesty and decency' in reporting information to contract partners. These principles constitute a kind of general institutional safety net for people who normally operate in much more explicit national legal and cultural traditions and who cannot negotiate complete contracts that regulate all eventualities.

International Arbitration

These institutions confine the actions of international merchants and financiers. Where conflicts about specific actions or rule interpretations arise, most international operators appeal to international arbitration tribunals. This demonstrates a number of interesting institutional principles.

Specific arbitrators may be agreed on in the contract. Where this has not been stipulated, the parties may appeal to arbitrators by subsequent agreement. Arbitration tribunals are normally private and are run by chambers of commerce, for example, in Zurich, London, Stockholm and Paris. There is an American Arbitration Association and international chambers of commerce also provide arbitration services. These organisations typically make their arbitration rules known and provide arbitration and related administrative services. They tend to give clout to trading customs, clarify the internal institutions of international trade and create confidence when contracting parties leave the umbrella of external national institutions.

Private arbitrators are often known for their expertise in specific branches of trade and investment and earn the trust of contracting parties by their specialist knowledge. They have to compete with others who offer similar arbitration services. When contracting parties agree on a certain arbitrator, they keep expediency and the quality of arbitration services in mind. The arbitrators apply their own rules (in contrast to government courts under international private law, which apply laws made by others) and have a keen interest in keeping their services predictable and simple. If they fail, the business moves elsewhere.

Arbitrators have to earn a reputation for expediting matters and keeping procedures simple. They apply prevailing trade customs and legal principles, that is, the law created by the private merchants and financiers themselves. They negotiate in confidence and pursue settlements that do not damage the reputations of their clients. Arbitrators tend to work towards preserving the commercial connection and facilitating trade. Since international arbitration nowadays is big business, governments have abstained from interfering with it for fear of losing the industry.

Adherence to Arbitration Judgements

The judgements of arbitrators are usually adhered to in 90 per cent of cases, as noted above. Why is this so? The answer lies with the mechanisms of enforcement of internal institutions that we discussed in sections 5.2 and 7.4: if one of the contracting parties in an international trade deal were to appeal to a national court to overturn a private arbitration outcome, it would face uncertainty about the final outcome, long delays, considerable costs and the risk that its reputation would be damaged. And if a government court were to award damages, then the litigant would still face uncertainties about how the other party, resident outside the jurisdiction, could be forced to pay.

The incentives to accept the judgement of private arbitrators and to get on with the business are therefore considerable. Moreover, since arbitrators tend to be specialised in specific industries and have an interest in remaining in the business, they are fairly likely to shape judgements that are acceptable to the trade. Even if a specific arbitration deal is not welcome, most traders will recognise their long-term interest in the security of the rules. After all, they are frequently engaged in an open-ended sequence of deals that is to their reciprocal advantage. Cooperative behaviour therefore normally pays off. Where there are one-off deals (end games), traders may make mutual commitments (hostages) that guarantee an honest and proper execution of the contract. In all of this, they will think of their reputations, fearing that in their specialised branch of trade they may in future be seen by others as a less desirable contract partner. At the time of rapid and intense international communications by fax and e-mail, reputations can be quickly destroyed, at least among those who share similar values and basic norms.

It is important to note in this context that modern international trade is typically not conducted among anonymous partners and in one-off deals. Business partners are bound by more or less durable networks, although they always have the exit option and pursue their exchanges voluntarily. Networks of traders with highly specific knowledge and shared business practices conduct trade in the many technically and organisationally complex areas of international exchange. Much of the relevant information could never be completely fixed in contracts, and the open-ended nature of contracts forces people to rely on institutions. Thus, reputation, trust and other self-enforcing institutional mechanisms are crucial to making savings on knowledge-gathering costs and thus beating the competition.

○ Key Concepts

Law Merchant (or the **Custom of Merchants**, Latin: *lex mercatoria*) emerged in Europe during the twelfth to fifteenth centuries as a body of unwritten laws that were to be implemented by merchants for merchants and in avoidance of local rulers and courts. Its purpose was to establish known rules that facilitated the exchange of commodities and credit across the borders of different jurisdictions to reduce transaction costs. The Custom of Merchants introduced the concept of all being equal before the law. The Custom of Merchants, which ruled over groups who moved between jurisdictions, was central to establishing individual economic liberties even over and above the rights of the rulers.

The **new *lex mercatoria*** is a system of internal institutions which govern international trade and payments and which contain self-enforcing mechanisms, as well as relying on private arbitration. The customs of international merchants and financiers are sometimes codified and formalised. They tend to be specific to particular industries or branches of trade. In many areas, merchant customs have replaced national and international private law, because they operate more expediently, flexibly and – in the ultimate analysis – with lower transaction costs. ●

International Intermediaries

Intermediaries also enter the game. International banks, for example, issue letters of credit. They have an interest in being perceived as cooperative and supportive.

Specialist international trading organisations frequently do not confine themselves to merely conveying information but become active middlemen, undertaking back-to-back trade deals on their own account, cutting the costs of contract negotiation and monitoring and reducing the perceived risks of default. When there is no ready recourse to a national judiciary, it may be preferable to deal with a known specialist in international trade who has a reputation to lose and is bound by high sunk costs. Sometimes, international trading houses, banks and government agencies are also involved in two-way trade, so they present themselves as even more credible 'hostages' or guarantors of contract execution (section 7.4); examples are trade or credit guarantees by government agencies, and the minority participation of well-known companies in international ventures. Joint ventures of partners from two countries reduce the perceived risks of enforcement failure in foreign countries. On similar grounds, multinational companies are often able to reduce their transaction costs because they are established in various countries. They are credible trade partners because they have international reputations to lose. They have overcome part of the problem of extraterritoriality by internalising it within their own network of subsidiaries.

It is no coincidence that international trade has frequently been taken over by middlemen networks when there is a lack of shared institutions. Networks of middlemen then have advantages in lower transaction and enforcement costs, as we saw in section 7.4. Such international networks become even more credible when the middlemen are bound by specific cultural and family ties which set them apart from the wider communities in which they trade or give loans: the Jews throughout medieval Europe, German merchants in eastern

Europe, Arab traders in the Middle East, ethnic groups such as the Marvari from India in East Africa, specific Chinese ethnic groups in East Asia and elsewhere (Sowell, 1994, pp. 46–59; Landa, 1994). They are often not confined to trade but may become dominant foreign investors (Germans in post-medieval eastern Europe, Chinese in South East Asia).

The understanding that relational trade and investment contracts with foreigners may involve steep enforcement risks and therefore depend on personal trust in shared internal institutions is particularly well developed in the overseas Chinese community, probably on the basis of long and painful experience. It is virtually impossible for strangers to strike a major business deal quickly with a Chinese family enterprise. Before this can be done, it is necessary to establish and nurture a personal relationship, often on the basis of non-commercial interchanges (Ch'ng, 1993). The often-told story about Hong Kong shipping magnate Y.K. Pao is typical: when approached by Aristotle Onassis, the Greek shipping tycoon, about a joint business strategy at their first business meeting and with no preliminaries, Mr Pao rejected such a potentially rewarding deal out of hand, because it was simply not done to enter into deals with strangers, especially those from foreign countries (ibid., p. 47).

To sum up: international trade and finance are carried out in a social context of shared institutions that offer reasonably clear, transparent rules which are understood as stable and reasonably enforceable. Trading associations often codify emerging trade practices and give them a sufficient degree of certainty. Traders have a choice of rule systems. This induces competition among arbitrators and rule sets. Autonomously evolved law (trade customs) thus not only keeps made law and external judiciary processes at bay, but often replaces them, because it is cheaper and works more expeditiously.

Trade and investment among business people in different nations thus operate within well-developed frameworks of internal institutions which the traders and investors have created for themselves. Normally, personal contacts, reputations and the threat of exclusion are important in facilitating trade-supporting institutions. International business is therefore in reality a far cry from the notion of anonymous, impersonal contracting that is frequently implied in traditional textbooks on international trade and finance.

❖ International Business Must Bridge Cultural Gaps

Differences in the internal and external institutions require international businessmen to adapt their *modus operandi*. This is probably nowhere more true than between westerners, who have grown up with a tradition of impartial, universal rules and the rule of law, and the Chinese, who have operated under deficient or non-existent general institutions, legal and court systems and who have learnt to rely on long-lasting personal relationships as the essential institutional foundation for contract enforcement.

This point is made evident in the following excerpts from an article in *The Economist*:

... many foreign firms have failed to grasp what networking in Asia is really about.

Most western multinationals setting up in Asia have formed some sort of joint venture or alliance with a local firm – principally as a way of acquiring local influence and knowledge ...

... The most common complaint of western businessmen throughout the region is that local partners often turn out to have an agenda of their own. Usually the local partner is less interested in building up brands or expanding market share than in extracting short-term profits in order to invest in new ... ventures.

... Western and eastern firms have a different approach towards relationships ... western firms ... first ... decide which businesses or projects it is interested in, and then seeks to cultivate the necessary connections. Asian companies believe that the relationships come first, and that investment opportunities flow from them ...

... This philosophy has deep roots ... local firms were established by migrant Chinese ... they built up networks in which extended families and clans did business only with one another in order to reduce risk ... This web of connections, or *guanxi*, still sits at the heart of most overseas-Chinese groups.

... Rather than move towards this system, most western firms seem to shrink ever further away from it. Sometimes they ... associate networking with bribery ... the current trend for moving executives every three or four years may tie in well with ideas about being a 'multicultural multinational'. But it means that business relationships are institutional rather than personal ...

... [One leading western businessman] argues that western firms should treat networking in Asia as a form of protection. It will take years until Asian markets become as transparent as those in the West; years too until the necessary rules and regulations are written and enforced. In the meantime *guanxi* is often the safest or only form of commercial security ...

... In the long term, business methods in Asia will probably come to resemble more closely those in the West. Already some of Asia's sprawling conglomerates are reaching the limits of the ability of their founding families to manage them. ◆

(Source: The Economist, *29 March 1997, pp. 73–4)*

Financial Intermediation

An extreme – well-nigh awe-inspiring – case of spontaneous rule compliance can be found in international money markets. Participants in global currency markets have developed sophisticated arrangements that allow international buyers and sellers to transact huge volumes of business virtually without any written documentation, and this at great speed with low transaction costs and a minimal number of mishaps. The *daily* turnover in global currency markets in 1992 was estimated at a staggering US$880 billion, growing at a trend rate of between 25 per cent and 30 per cent annually (*The Economist*, 7 October 1995, p. 6). Among other things, these sophisticated markets allow international businessmen to cover exchange rate risks, for example by engaging in currency futures markets. They generate valuable information (Streit, 1984). Currency markets rotate ceaselessly around the globe, operate with small profit margins, and cover tens of thousands of independent participants who never meet personally but deal only by telephone and e-mail.

International currency markets function smoothly without a central authority that might sanction defaulters. World currency traders have developed a spontaneous institutional infrastructure that is highly effective. It has been adapted to rapidly changing technologies and rapid market expansion, particularly since the major currencies were floated in the late 1960s and early 1970s. The institutions of international currency exchange have been strong enough to withstand major oil shocks, wars, government defaults and the demise of totalitarian socialism – all without a major panic or breakdown in the market network. Occasionally, governments have intervened with the goal of stabilising exchange rate movements. But these actions have normally proved to be more destabilising than confidence-building, and markets have weathered political convulsions.

How can the miracle of global currency markets happen on a daily basis? The key institutional enforcement is the sanction of ostracism (exclusion). If a currency trader violates the unwritten rules of the trade, for example, by refusing to fulfil a contract or bear a share of the loss incurred in a misunderstanding, he or she will soon find that no one accepts their offers. Reputation is essential, and repeated opportunism destroys reputations and entails virtual exclusion. Informal information networks around the globe are incredibly efficient and sanctions can be very swift. This is essential to allow currency traders to transact their risky business at low transaction cost, to rely on punctual delivery from business partners in far-away countries, and to do so without costly, legal documentation.

Governments and Extra-territoriality

In some cases, international commerce and finance have benefited from cost- and risk-reducing government involvement. When hegemonial powers established themselves, they often used their supremacy to enforce certain institutions in dealings beyond their borders. This is why empires were often perceived as good for trade and prosperity. The *Pax Romana* spread beyond the vast borders of the Roman empire and projected certain Roman institutions where traders from the empire dealt with outsiders. The *Pax Mongolica* after the conquests of Chinggis Khan (1155(?)–1227), whose empire soon crumbled, was strong enough to back up institutions that made the Silk Road trade between China and Europe possible for two centuries. The Aztecs projected their power far beyond their borders in present-day Mexico to back certain informal mercantile institutions. And the *Pax Britannica* and the *Pax Americana* gave institutional infrastructures to trade and investment far beyond their immediate sphere of military influence. Although the wealth-creating benefits of secure, shared institutions were usually enormous, the opening-up of closed national markets by such regimes was also often unpopular because the imperial power challenged established local institutions and power structures.

Finally, something needs to be said about institutional arrangements which facilitate the international movement of production factors. The fixed costs of such relocations are often high and have to be sunk before it is discovered whether relocation has been worthwhile (in other words, living or working in another country is an 'experience good', as defined in section 7.4). The information problems are considerable in a border-crossing business relationship that may last many years into the future. To overcome these peculiar costs, host governments have long granted immigrants and foreign investors cost-saving privileges. As far back as the twelfth century German merchants and craftsmen were granted special privileges, including the right to their own law courts, if they settled in Norway. Later, similar privileges were extended by East European rulers to attract German and Dutch knowhow and people: extra-territoriality, guarantees of protection of their own customs and practices, tax-exempt status, grants of free land. Similar devices were employed in medieval China to induce northern people to migrate south (Rozman, 1991, pp. 68–83) and by the Ottoman sultans to attract Jewish and western knowhow and capital to Istanbul.

From there it is but a short step to present-day efforts to attract foreign capital and enterprise to new industrial countries in the face of the handicap of the high costs of mobility and across the 'international institutional discontinuity'. For example, the provision of free land, industrial land and infrastructures, tax exemptions, 'pioneer status', free-trade and free-enterprise zones (which reduce information and compliance costs in institutionally deficient countries) and official participation in joint ventures are used as devices to reduce, or compensate for, such transaction costs. In many cases, such measures have been employed widely in East Asia since 1960. Initially information costs about producing in the Far East were high. They came down as the pioneers in new industrial locations demonstrated how the previously unknown institutional framework of East Asia worked and as internal and external institutions were enhanced in response to the demands of mobile capital and enterprise. Once the new industrial countries had established a reputation as attractive institutional conditions, Asian governments and workers could demand higher taxes and wages. In a similar vein, many southern hemisphere governments, such as those of Australia and Argentina, long assisted migrants by subsidising their transport and settlement costs. Once international migrants could observe the demonstrated success of the migrants in the new countries, the subsidy could be reduced. Settlement gradually became more convenient for new migrants. The adjustment costs to becoming productive in the new country dropped, thanks to institutional adjustments in these immigrant societies, which reduced the institutional gap that migrants had to overcome.

Not an Institutional Vacuum

Diverse historical evidence shows that the essentially 'government-free sphere' of private international transactions has been far from an 'institutional vacuum'. Time and again, people who wanted to trade and invest beyond the boundaries of their own jurisdiction went about developing a great variety of institutional arrangements and networks that made international transactions less risky and more profitable. It is worth noting that the solutions which evolved were frequently not dissimilar to those internal institutions that can be observed in national economic life in areas where governments are reluctant to intervene.

11.3   Policy Issues: International Economic Order

Trade Policy: Discrimination and Most Favoured Nation Clause

Governments and other political agents often intervene in international economic relations for the same reasons that motivate domestic interventions: initially, it is promised that interventions enhance transparency, open access to international trade and finance, limit free-riding and make the institutions more credible. But sooner or later government interventions in international trade and payments close markets in order to cater to organised domestic client groups and to protect the government's own position from competition with foreign jurisdictions (as we saw in section 11.1). Frequently, interventions to reduce the openness of a national economy are the consequence of domestic redistribution policy.

Throughout history, international merchants and investors have also organised to seek political protection, using the argument that they are facing high risks or have to invest big lumps of capital in international ventures. Mercantilism in post-medieval Europe had much to do with the fact that rulers could gain revenue by licensing and protecting selected groups of merchants. Thus, Queen Elizabeth I gave the East India Company a licence with exclusive rights to trade with India and took a royal share in the resulting monopoly rents. The Dutch United East India Company (VOIC) opened up most of what is now Indonesia under a similar deal, and the Hudson Bay Company did the same in Canada. Nor was the granting and protection of international trading monopolies an exclusive European invention; the Japanese government licensed a few of their traders to deal with the Portuguese and the Dutch, and the Chinese emperor licensed a limited number of *hongs* in Guangdong to deal with westerners. In these cases, isolationism was probably a primary motive, but the cut in the trading profits that went into government coffers was not unwelcome.

As we saw in section 11.1, frequent instances of rent-seeking and rent-creation in foreign trade and investment can be found. Domestic suppliers, whose interests are concentrated and easy to organise, seek intervention in international competition, and the rulers oblige, receiving fees, undercover payments, influence and protection from interjurisdictional competitors. This allows political transfers of property rights that are not possible in an open economy and enhances the domestic sway of political operators. In closed economies, a culture of redistribution and interventionism can grow and uncompetitive practices become entrenched. Once such a state of affairs is reached, capital flight and the emigration of citizens are seen as affronts to the rulers and their client groups. The fundamental fact that free trade and a high degree of factor mobility are important conditions for a better division of labour and for the diffusion, discovery and use of productive knowledge around the globe is then easily overlooked.

The World Trade Organisation

The agents of government frequently find themselves in a conflict between interests in free international exchanges and particular national interests in protection. Given this conflict, there is a case for fostering a free international economic order by multilateral agreements that ban protectionism and political rivalry in discriminating against outsiders. In other words, there is a case for an international truce in discrimination against foreigners. Such inter-government agreements are likely to promote growth opportunities and overcome governments' reluctance to liberalise trade unilaterally. Such a multilateral agreement was adopted among western governments in the late 1940s when they signed the General Agreement on Tariffs and Trade (GATT), which has now been converted into the wider World Trade Organisation (WTO). The central institution of the GATT and WTO is the most favoured nation (MFN) clause. It stipulates that a trading 'concession' – in the sense of removing man-made obstacles to trade – made to one country must be extended to all others in the club. In other words, it enshrines the principle of non-discrimination in international trade. Since the 1960s, a growing number of governments has also agreed to treat foreign investors as the equals of national investors. Certain risk-reducing conventions that protect foreign investors have also been put in place, for example under OECD auspices.

In these cases, governments stake their international reputation and act as middlemen (Streit and Voigt, 1993). Commitments to free international exchanges often become more credible when governments enter the game of international give and take. Such international government-to-government agreements are not enforceable outside a government's own jurisdiction, since there is no access to a higher-level enforcer. At best, there are the sanctions of collective international moral suasion and collective retaliation (trade bans). Yet the limits to extraterritorial sanctions from rule breaches have become clear, time and again. In the case of the GATT, at least the big players could flout the agreed rules of the international exchange with impunity. Free trade rules work only if the big players want free trade and if the national public supports free trade. But frequently, influential domestic political alliances between industry lobbies, political parties and government bureaucracies are able to subvert commitments to free trade.

In these circumstances, the formal international trading order as well as treaty commitments not to discriminate against foreign investors are only a weak institution constraining interventionist governments, at least nowadays.[5] Violations may trigger coalitions of foreign countries to castigate a nation's protectionist behaviour. But there are no formal means of compelling national governments except the sanctions of ostracism, which are employed only rarely and hardly ever against the big international players.

Economic Integration:
Free Trade Areas, Customs Unions and Economic Blocs

The developments in trade, transport, communications and finance increasingly transcend the borders of the nation state. Cross-border transactions increase and weave national or regional markets more closely together. This process is called 'economic integration from below', and is driven by the spontaneous action of autonomous private agents (Kasper, 1970; Streit and Mussler, 1994). Part of this type of integration is the emergence of internal institutions to save transaction costs, as described above. Integration can also be driven from above by the adoption of shared external rules and policies based on government-to-government agreement and detailed top-down directives.

An example of how bottom-up, spontaneous integration can be facilitated is the GATT and its successor, the WTO, which we have just discussed. Other examples are free trade areas, customs unions and economic unions. When several jurisdictions join in a free trade area, they agree to remove all artificial barriers to trade across their joint borders (removal of tariffs and quotas). This enables greater economic integration from below, that is, voluntary market integration by autonomous private decision makers. The nations in free trade areas retain their individual border controls *vis-à-vis* third countries, for example their individual tariff regimes. If tariffs differ greatly, traders will export from that part of the free trade area which meets the lowest trade barriers and will import from third countries through low-tariff borders. This may divert international trade (and customs revenue) and may be controlled by secondary regulations, for example by stipulating local-content rules so international trade has to originate where the bulk of the product or service has been produced.

The monitoring and enforcement costs of such arrangements are considerable.

One way to obviate these institutional problems is to create a customs union, a multi-jurisdiction alliance that has a common set of external trade regulations, in particular a common tariff, with free trade within the customs union. When customs unions are tied together internally through intensive trade links, interjurisdictional competition tends to increase as entrepreneurs make locational choices on the basis of competitiveness factors, including government and cultural institutions, wage differentials, land prices and proximity to markets (see section 11.1 above). Government agents, as well as established private operators, who find themselves exposed to such competitive pressures then often argue for economic union, which is a customs union in which all production factors, such as labour, can move about freely. An example for such an economic union is the European Union which was established in 1957 among six member states. In the early years, integration from above and below was, by and large, complementary. The Treaty of Rome provided for an unimpeded flow of trade and production factors within the Community and banned national distortions of competition, whether by private or public action. The integration from above, as contained in the treaty rules, paved the way for the integration in the markets below. However, some of the treaty rules of 1957 implied a quite different kind of integration from above. For example, rules were introduced to establish a Common Agricultural Policy, and these rules were highly specific and interventionist. Over time, the Community obtained further scope for such interventions, so that integration from above relied on specific interventions rather than on paving the way for competition (Streit and Mussler, 1994).

When there are close economic ties between countries, international cooperation may also extend into areas beyond trade and finance. National governments may agree to fix certain rules concerning economic competition and enforce them in their own territories, or they may follow social welfare and income redistribution policies that are laid down by international agreements. In some instances, such cooperation is justified by genuine externalities, for example when the environmental impact of certain activities falls outside the countries in which these activities take place. In many other instances, integration relies on top-down directives, as has become increasingly the case in the European Union. Such 'integration from above' may at times be the expression of the wish to limit interjurisdictional competition by forming a cartel of national governments. When this approach is successful and national governments are no longer allowed to compete with each other to providing rival administrative solutions, nation states become increasingly constrained in their autonomy. When this is not successful and governments are induced to compete with each other, the classical nation state – a creation of the nineteenth century – is also undermined and its borders become unclear.

The feedback from the increasingly open economy which empowers private autonomy in trade and the location of economic activities on the development of external institutions can be powerful, as we saw repeatedly when we touched on the emergence of the institutions of capitalism in the small open states of Europe. In the following chapter, in which we shall discuss the evolution of institutions over time, the international dimension will play a central role.

O Key Concepts

The **most favoured nation (MFN) clause** is the embodiment in international trade conventions of the principle of non-discrimination. It says that a freedom granted by a specific government to the nationals of one foreign country must automatically be extended to the nationals of all countries that participate in such an international agreement, in other words that governments forgo the right to discriminate among foreigners from different countries which are part of the club. The best known enshrinement of the MFN clause is in the General Agreement on Tariffs and Trade (GATT).

Economic integration relates to intensified interaction between market participants in different local or national markets. We speak of 'economic integration from below' when interregional or international exchanges intensify as a result of growing trade; this normally goes along with the development of internal institutions to facilitate these exchanges. By contrast, 'integration from above' relates to the setting or changing of external institutions through political processes. An example where this process now dominates is the European Union, which has since the late 1950s developed external institutions to remove barriers to trade and factor movements within the Union, and to create rule sets that are shared throughout the EU area, but it has increasingly developed interventions that directly prescribe certain conduct for the citizens of all member countries.

A **free trade area** covers a multiplicity of jurisdictions between which there are no obstacles to cross-border trade; various jurisdictions may have differential trade obstacles *vis-à-vis* third countries. A **customs union** is a free trade area which has a common external set of trade obstacles, for example a common tariff. An **economic union** embraces a customs union but also allows free factor movements throughout, as well as harmonising the economic policies of the component jurisdictions. ●

International Monetary Orders:
Gold Standard, Political Standard and Flexible Exchange Rates

One peculiarity of international, rather than interregional, transactions is that the two contract partners often calculate their gains in different currencies. This leads to conversion costs (which are nowadays minor) and exchange rate risks. Monetary assets are nowadays based on national currencies and are underpinned by monetary policies of state central banks and finance ministries. As a consequence, international monetary transactions are of concern to government agencies. There are certain rule sets under which national authorities conduct their international monetary policies which establish an international monetary order. The rules may, for example, establish a gold standard or the presently prevailing system of flexible exchange rates. These rules have differing impacts on the conduct of national monetary policy.

The gold standard laid down the following rules of the game: each national currency that participated in it before the first world war was defined in terms of a certain quantity of fine gold (fixed exchange rate between national bank notes and gold). This definition was considered irrevocable, although breaches occurred. Central banks undertook to convert national bank notes into gold at the fixed rate (free convertibility). National central banks, which lost public trust (and were asked to convert their bank notes into gold), were forced to contract the money volume as people withdrew gold and shipped it abroad. When the money volume shrank, factor and product prices were expected to drop. This would make the producers internationally more competitive again, raising exports and enabling stronger competition between domestic producers and imports. The gold redeemed from the central bank would be transferred to a more trusted central bank of another country, triggering an expansion of that country's money supply and a rise in prices. This, it was assumed, would impact on the external balance and contribute to correcting international imbalances and price level divergences. It was assumed that prices would respond flexibly to changes in the national money volume, so that recessions and unemployment would at best be temporary. If prices were sticky, then deeper recessions and more unemployment would occur (Lutz, [1935] 1963).

Under this system of rules, central banks and governments had little sovereign control over the money volume, let alone domestic price levels (and possibly employment levels). The rules of the game thus essentially deprived governments of influence on the macroeconomy.

The advantage of that institutional arrangement was that exchange rates between two currencies were each tied to gold and therefore were fixed and predictable. International currency conversion was cheap and easy – an important consideration at a time before computers and international telephones. Another advantage was that the 'gold mechanism' effectively tied the hands of governments that wanted to pursue inflationary policies.

A variation on the gold standard is the currency board regime. Here, domestic financial discipline (limitations on money supply and controls of bank lending practices) is enforced by an institutional arrangement under which the central bank credibly commits itself to redeem local currency for a foreign currency at a fixed rate of exchange, and to supply local money only in exchange for a given amount of foreign currency. This means that the central bank cannot extend credit, for example to the local government, and that local monetary conditions have to stay in line with those in the reference currency. Flexibility of demand management is given up under those rules for the credibility of the means of payment (International Monetary Fund, 1997, pp. 78–94). Smaller economies have opted for such an institutional arrangement, for example Brunei since 1967, Hong Kong after 1983 (although the monetary authority attempts some independent monetary manipulation), and more recently transition economies with no tradition of domestic money supply control, such as Estonia.

In the eyes of people who wanted governments to influence prices and employment, a lack of flexibility in influencing national money supply was the main disadvantage of a system of rigid exchange rates. Tying the hands of domestic money supply policy through the gold standard broke down at the outset of the first world war. After failed attempts to resurrect the gold standard in the 1920s, the global recession after 1929 saw its abandonment. A successor regime – namely the Bretton Woods system – was set up in 1944 to fix parities among national currencies. It also allowed parity changes in certain circumstances. The institutions governing the system worked during the 1950s and early 1960s as long as most international capital flows were strictly controlled. As currencies became fully convertible and national monetary policies diverged in the late 1960s/early 1970s, the Bretton Woods rule system had to be abandoned since national governments were not willing to abandon their monetary sovereignty.

The place of the Bretton Woods system was taken by new institutions: the free formation of the price of a currency (in terms of another) in response to supply and demand in the market of that currency. The floating exchange-rate system gave national monetary authorities the sovereignty to inflate and deflate, but they had to face the highly visible depreciation or appreciation of their currency as well as the trade and employment consequences of currency fluctuations. These new institutions eliminated the contradiction between a fixed exchange rate and independence in monetary conduct. The new institutions gave national governments and central banks control over, but also responsibility for, the price level. Monetary authorities wishing to pursue the objective of stable money were no longer confronted with inflationary capital inflows and the pull of external prices (imported inflation), and monetary authorities pursuing lax policies soon got the feedback of domestic inflation and a depreciating currency value. Since the move towards flexible exchange rates, it has been found repeatedly that monetary authorities which want to return, for whatever reasons, to fixed or predetermined exchange rates introduce an institutional incompatibility and are sooner or later forced to abandon official attempts to fix currency rates. The latest such attempt goes further: namely, the plan to introduce one common currency in the European Union, but with the retention of national fiscal and other macroeconomic policies.

Under a flexible rate regime, the movement of the exchange rate conveys powerful and visible signals that often, but not always, feed back into the conduct of domestic monetary policy. If monetary authorities respond to a currency depreciation by tightening (and to an appreciation by loosening) domestic monetary policy, the exchange rate is likely to be fairly stable over time. If all monetary authorities do this, the system *de facto* functions in ways similar to the gold standard, and exchange rates remain fairly predictable.

Competing Moneys

The flexibility of exchange rates makes it clearer that national currencies are in competition with each other. National authorities cannot act with unconstrained monetary sovereignty, for depreciating monetary assets tend to be deserted.[6] In the extreme, poorly managed moneys disappear. Thus, international monetary authorities are subject to assessment by investors and traders in currency markets. They have to conduct themselves in ways that attract and maintain demand for their assets. This is a powerful, though not always welcome, constraint on opportunistic national monetary conduct.

It has been argued that the private production of competing monetised assets is desirable because competition amongst providers of monetised assets produces and selects new ideas about how best to provide the public with money (Hayek, 1976b). The competition would discipline the producers of money. The ground rules would probably ensure that stable moneys (in terms of a basket of products) would gain wide acceptance from the public. Inflationary moneys would not be held in portfolios, so they would ultimately disappear. This would lead to competition among producers of monetary assets to supply quality assets. A problem with such a system is that it imposes relatively high information and other transaction costs on the public. Holders of different types of money would have to keep themselves informed about whether their assets were safe. Users of money might not accept certain types of cash if they had doubts (or at least they might ask for a discount).

This goes back to a point we made in section 6.3, namely that money, to be useful, depends on credible institutions. The relevant rules may be designed and imposed from above, as national monetary authorities do now, or money may be provided competitively and the requisite rules evolve in the process of competition between various monetary assets. What is preferable depends on the empirical observation of where the public's information and other transaction costs are lowest. In reality, government-made money and the spontaneous order of competitive private moneys need not be mutually exclusive. A particular government-designed money nowadays has no monopoly in the eyes of the citizens, given free convertibility into other currencies. National central banks that issue inflationary moneys tend to lose clients to the better-run central banks of other countries. Thus, many payments in inflationary countries such as Russia or Vietnam are made in US dollars, and savings are made by storing greenbacks in mattresses. Citizens thus have choices as to what moneys serve them best as a means of payment, store of value and unit of account. What therefore matters most to the interest of citizens is the rule of free convertibility, which gives them a choice, empowers them and constrains the issuers of money, whether they are public or private.

O Key Concepts

The **gold standard** is a set of rules that is based on the definition of each national money in terms of a fixed quantity of gold. This institution established fixed exchange rates between various national currencies (or moneys) and subjected national central banks and national governments to the rule that they had to defend the gold parity even at the expense of failing to pursue national price-level stability and employment objectives.

The **exchange rate** is a price ratio of the value of one currency in terms of another. When you read that the exchange rate of the Deutschmark in New York is $1.50, this means that US$1 can be exchanged for DM1.50.

A system of **flexible exchange rates** is a regime in which the price of a foreign currency is determined by the interplay of supply of that currency (by exporters and foreigners who want to bring foreign capital in) and demand (by importers and people who want to export capital). Flexible exchange rates allow national monetary and general economic policies to differ from one jurisdiction to the other (monetary sovereignty). However, exchange rate movements signal important information to policy makers and the public and tend to have powerful educational feedback into policy making. Hence, they constrain the monetary sovereignty of national authorities. ●

11.4   On Strengthening the Open Economic Order

Political groups are likely to strike back when the 'affront of openness' undermines their power. In particular, they need intervention in international exchanges to back up the political reallocation of property rights. To disguise and justify border controls, they may argue that poorer countries engage in 'social dumping', undercutting domestic wage levels or operating with lower levels of tax. In a similar vein, they may try to obtain protection on the grounds that foreign competitors are not burdened with environmental imposts which they have to bear, so they require trade protection of the high domestic standards of environmental protection (environmental dumping). These arguments are now evident in the debate in the mature industrial economies about deindustrialisation, in which it is argued that domestic industries migrate to low-wage locations, creating structural unemployment. Restraints on capital outflows are demanded to restore high domestic employment, irrespective of the cost level of domestic labour. The same intent to defend political power is evident when environmentalists demand trade protection as capital, enterprises and jobs vote with their feet for locations that are less heavily regulated on environmental grounds. More generally, particular interest groups who lose clout in the open economy tend to appeal to popular feelings of nationalism to contain the 'affront of openness'. In Japan and many East Asian countries, lobby groups have also tried to exert political pressures against open trade and free capital flows in order to remain politically influential. As of the mid-1990s, however, the closure of national markets is rarely feasible. Technology has changed, and many capital owners and enterprises are internationally mobile. This is why those who wish to avoid being disciplined by openness are now increasingly resorting to economic bloc formation: the European Union, a

North American Free Trade Area, and efforts to create an East Asian economic caucus promise political operators at least a degree of political primacy over economic life.

But the battle for openness is not fought in a static world. The transport cost and communications revolution is moving on. It is making it harder to organise and keep together protectionist coalitions: in the era of the Internet, it is now virtually impossible to stop the free flow of capital and ideas through global networks. This is why the essentially open international economic order has a chance of survival.

Sovereign nations cannot coerce each other to fulfil international treaty obligations (short of the use of military force). It may therefore pay to enhance the self-fulfilling qualities of treaties that keep national economies open. To this end, Jan Tumlir, the long-time chief economist of GATT, proposed to enhance economic openness by introducing 'self-executing treaty provisions'. He argued for giving affected citizens actionable legal rights against governments which violate openness and the principle of non-discrimination against foreigners (Tumlir, 1979, pp. 71–83). Private citizens and foreigners would under this proposal be given the legal right to take government agencies to court in private tort actions if border controls diminished their property rights. This rule would give teeth to the principle of equality between nationals and foreigners. The concept is applied within the European Union in certain circumstances, but not, however, *vis-à-vis* third countries. It fits well with an era in which technological development increasingly mitigates against the concept of national boundaries and strengthens cosmopolitan concepts and modes of behaviour.

In the next chapter, we turn to a very important reason why the battle for openness is important, namely that international competition augments the evolutionary potential for enhancing national rule systems.

Questions for Review

- What differences in institutions apply between selling in another region of your country and selling abroad? What additional information and other costs arise?
- Do you know of middlemen in international trade, say between raw material producers and the industrial users of those raw materials? What is the role of these middlemen from an institutional standpoint? What happens when middlemen in international trade are suppressed, as has happened in numerous developing countries?

- Why do we get 'international enforcement failure'?
- Since there is no supranational authority to help international traders enforce contracts in other countries, what types of 'hostages' can international traders invent to ensure fulfilment of international trade contracts?
- What are the advantages of internal institutions in international exchanges (including arbitration by private autonomous persons or bodies) over external institutions, including international private law?
- What institutions and enforcement mechanisms are there to ensure that international currency traders fulfil their telephone contracts with far-distant counterparts? Does that explain why you, as a private citizen, cannot trade currency or commodity futures with New York, Sydney or Johannesburg?
- What is the role of the principle of non-discrimination in international trade? Why should governments not discriminate against foreign producers?
- What happened under the institutional framework of the gold standard when a country experienced rapid inflation? How was such inflation brought under control again? Highlight the various rules of the game that had to be obeyed to ensure an automatic return to price stability.
- If a national government creates inflation in an economy with a flexible exchange rate, what happens? Are there automatic controls that ensure a return to price stability?
- Are you in favour of your national government having a monopoly over the issue of the national currency, or would you prefer various big banks and trading houses to issue money (by incurring special debts)? Give reasons for and against each position.
- If international trade, investments and payments benefit from further reductions in transport and communications costs, do you predict that we shall have better or worse government in the sense that it helps or hinders private citizens to attain their objectives? Support your answer with a well-reasoned argument.

Notes

1. Some services are of course unlikely ever to become footloose (think of haircuts) and will continue to be produced where the demand is located.
2. The weights w reflect the importance of the various cost factors. These will differ between the various economic activities. Therefore, different locations are of different attractiveness to specific economic activities.
3. If the assumption that higher prices do not reduce the volume of sales is dropped, reduced sales, higher unit costs of production and hence a lesser rent accruing to car manufacturers can be expected. However, this does not alter the basic logic of the argument.

4. Many conventions and rules to facilitate international trade and investment evolved even prior to the emergence of modern nation states in Europe (*lex mercatorum* or the Custom of Merchants) and in the Islamic world (Rosenberg and Birdzell, 1986). The privately developed Custom of Merchants first established the legal principle of contracts between equals and equality before the law, everyone having legal autonomy. This important principle was pioneered by commerce and not by rulers or legal philosophers (Jacobs, 1992, pp. 38–40). The *lex mercatoria* enabled the rise of a system that was the result of human action, but was not designed by anyone.
5. We write 'nowadays' because the option of military compulsion (gun-boat diplomacy, military incursion after trade violations or the confiscation of foreign owned assets) is ruled out.
6. In reality, the issue is complicated by variable nominal interest rates and expectations about future rate movements.

CHAPTER 12

The Evolution of Institutions

So far, we have considered institutions as being unchangeable. Indeed, we have worked on the assumption that institutions are better known and hence more effective in norming human behaviour when they remain unchanged. But circumstances change, so existing rules may have to be adapted as well.

We begin with some historical reminiscences which illustrate how and why institutions have changed over the long term and how collectivist and individualist philosophies have influenced the evolution of rule systems.

We then observe how the internal institutions and the underlying values of a community evolve, not haphazardly, but normally on a path of gradual evolution within a system of *meta* rules that give change a measure of predictability and continuity.

By contrast, the external institutions (set up through legislation, regulation, judicial rulings) are changed by political action, sometimes abruptly. At other times, political action may lead to institutional rigidity and sclerosis. External rules are not always changed in the direction of greater freedom for individuals in pursuit of their own purposes. Openness has, however, favoured the adaptation of external institutions in that direction.

In the late twentieth century, the impact of openness has been advanced greatly by what has become known as globalisation, intensifying international trade and worldwide factor mobility. National cultures and external institutions are now exposed to competition with other cultures and institutional systems. Rule systems form important competitive assets in the competition between producers, traders and investors in different jurisdictions; but they can also constitute severe competitive liabilities.

Institutional competition can also take place at subnational levels within federations when local communities and state governments compete with each other to attract investors by shaping business-friendly institutions.

Finally, we discuss the role of the constitutional principle of freedom in setting a framework for institutional evolution. Freedom helps individuals to realise their aspirations and to discover what others want. It also hampers the political interplay of parties and pressure groups that tend to rigidify the institutional system.

Παντα ρει
[All is in flux].
(*Ancient Greek proverb*)

It is an error to imagine that evolution signifies a constant tendency to perfection. That process undoubtedly involves a constant remodelling of the organism in adaptation to new conditions; but it depends on the nature of those conditions whether the direction of those modifications shall be upward or downward.
(*T.H. Huxley*, The Struggle for Existence in Human Society, *1888*)

Capitalists have the tendency to move towards those countries in which there is plenty of labor available and in which labor is reasonable. And by the fact that they bring capital into these countries, they bring about a trend toward higher wages.
(*Ludwig von Mises*, Economic Policy, *1979*)

Institutions gain much of their normative power over human behaviour from their immutability. But when circumstances change, immutable rule sets may create harm and require adjustment. After all, institutions are not ends in themselves, as conservatives sometimes think: they are only means to pursuing fundamental values, such as freedom, prosperity and peace. We therefore have to explore how and why institutions change, and how predictability (order) can be safeguarded in the process.

12.1 Historic Reminiscences: the Long View on Institutional Change

The 'European Miracle'

Habsburg emperor Charles V (1500–58), whose court bragged that, in his empire, the sun never set, once complained bitterly that the Jewish bankers and merchants, who had been advancing him money but were now fleeing from the Inquisition, were by this act 'pointing the crossbows at the very heart of my power'.

Two and a half centuries later, German poet-playwright and historian Friedrich Schiller, who was at the time considering the offer of a chair in history at the University of Jena, wrote in 1781 to a friend about the university: 'The governance of the Academy, because it is divided among the four Dukes of Saxony, makes this a fairly free and safe republic in which suppression is not easy. The professors at Jena are almost independent people and need not worry about any of the princes' (our translation). He referred to the fact that the university came under the joint rule of four independent princes and expected that their rivalry would ensure sufficient protection of his freedom.

These two apparently unrelated snippets from European history neatly bracket the great historical transition from the medieval system of feudal rule to the emergence of the values and institutions which made the industrial revolution possible. The two historical references also highlight the consequences of the interjurisdictional mobility of capital and of gifted, enterprising people for the evolution of the institutions of capitalism.

The fundamental influence on Europe's social history was its geographic diversity, which in turn favoured the emergence of many small states with independent rulers. These rulers contended not only through war but increasingly also through interjurisdictional competition to attract productive capital and skilled, knowledgeable people. The small size and openness of the European economies, which made interjurisdictional factor mobility possible, created the conditions for an evolutionary process that acted in two ways.

First, faced with interjurisdictional differences in rule systems, some of the owners of capital, knowledge and enterprises decided to move to those locations where the immobile production factors – above all, land, unskilled people and the institutional infrastructure – promised them a good rate of return as well as the security and freedom to work and live. In some cases, the primary motive was the search for secure living conditions. Thus, religious repression in the Habsburg empire, and later in France, caused Jews and Huguenots to move to domains where they enjoyed better guarantees of their religious, civil and economic liberties. In other cases, the main motive was the search for economic gain. Some rulers had an interest in enhancing the tax base of their realm. At least the small states could not obtain sufficient revenue from taxing the land, but had to rely on distance trade. They began to offer credible guarantees of economic and civil liberties to attract merchants and manufacturers (Jones, [1981] 1987; Findlay, 1992). At the same time, the internal institutions of different European societies differed. Some places, where the 'commercial secondary virtues' were cultivated, had a locational advantage. The experience soon showed that the guarantee of property rights and individual autonomy, as well as rule-bound government, did much to attract mobile resources. Civil and economic freedom also mobilised domestic economic entrepreneurship; instead of being drawn into political rivalry at court, gifted people in jurisdictions with these freedoms increasingly turned to economic entrepreneurship in trade, finance and production. They often combined their property and labour with newly attracted immigrants and incoming capital. Economic growth in enterprise-friendly jurisdictions – such as Venice, Genoa, Florence, Antwerp, Nuremberg, the Netherlands, England and Prussia – demonstrated the material rewards of the rule-bound behaviour of the rulers, whereas absolutist, arbitrary monarchies ruling over larger, more closed areas – such as Spain, Russia and Austria – began to lag behind in economic development (Weber, [1927] 1995; Jones, [1981] 1987; Giersch, 1993). Thus, economic entrepreneurs voted with their feet: they exited and engaged in what we might call 'locational substitution'. This caused divergence in productivity, innovative activity, living standards and the economic base of political power.

Second, it also challenged the political system to respond to and enter into political competition. Political rivalry set in motion processes of institutional development. Faced with the exit option of mobile capital and skilled people, the rulers felt constrained from taking opportunistic, arbitrary action (control function of exit) and learnt that it paid to foster certain institutions, such as secure property rights, individual autonomy and unlicenced investment, as well as liberties in general. The rulers' purpose was to retain and augment power, but the byproduct was that they were educated to act on behalf of the citizens. At the same time, the resident population learnt to adopt rules conducive to trade and innovation. The feedback from material success or failure thus set off learning processes that reshaped internal and external institutions. Merchants cultivated civic virtues, such as punctuality, honesty and urbane manners, and the political regime was eventually converted from feudal and, later, absolutist reign into constitutional monarchies and electoral democracies. In this long-term process, governments lost their power to control private pursuits, some administrations remodelled themselves into support organisations for economic development, and modern capitalism became possible.

When emperor Charles lived, the rulers of Europe were perceived as ruling with great powers by the grace of God, though somehow in theory bound by notions of Christian morality and natural law. Two and a half centuries later, when Friedrich Schiller was writing, governments were increasingly considered as subject to the forces of interjurisdictional competition, which limited their absolute powers. They were expected, at least by the leading spirits of the times, to respect individual, inviolable spheres of freedom.

By Schiller's time in the late eighteenth century, the understanding and the practice of the institutions essential to the spontaneous order of capitalism and economic growth were most advanced in Britain. There, the writers of the Scottish Enlightenment (Chapter 1) had highlighted the necessary institutional conditions for a market order after the 'Glorious Revolution' of 1688 had brought formal recognition of individual autonomy and property rights. As we saw in Chapter 11, Adam Smith had a good understanding of interjurisdictional competition. We may conclude, with German sociologist Erich Weede, that 'European disunity has been our good luck' (Weede, 1996, p. 6).

An offshoot of these developments in Europe was the constitution of the newly formed United States which was framed by people who were aware of the power of the exit option. It was shaped in an explicit debate about institutions that support 'the pursuit of happiness'. The US constitution, with its clear statement of the legal-constitutional rules of a free society, became an inspiration and a model for subsequent reformers in numerous countries around the world.

From Individualism to Collective Design:
from Open to Closed Systems

The concepts of rule-bound, limited government and of the inalienable basic rights of the individual captured people's imagination when Schiller wrote shortly after the American and before the French Revolution. And, as his letter indicates, it was understood that intergovernment rivalry was an effective way of guaranteeing these institutions. In the eighteenth century, many European intellectuals highlighted the institutions which are crucial to freedom and prosperity. It was also accepted that institutional systems could be shaped by conscious design, as the French Revolution was soon to demonstrate.

Admittedly, philosophers ever since Plato (427–347BC) had speculated about Utopian visions of an ideal society and its governance; but they never bothered about designing or describing in detail how such a society might actually work. The institutions were not discussed. The notion of a concerted, active change in a nation's constitutional design was a novel development in the late eighteenth century. In the following century, philosophers such as Georg Friedrich Wilhelm Hegel (1770–1838), Claude Henri de Saint Simon (1760–1825) and Karl Marx (1818–83) tried to design entire, collectivist ideologies of the nationalist and socialist *genre* to overturn the inherited, spontaneously grown social order. But, again, they failed to think through the institutional details, if they bothered to address such mundane practicalities at all. When collectivist conceptions were put into practice in the twentieth century, first in the Russian revolution (1917–23), then by the Fascist-nationalist attempts at redesigning society in Italy, Germany and elsewhere, the problems of institutional design to coordinate the complex economic system turned out to be overwhelming. It is no coincidence that these regimes tried to reduce the complexity of the economic coordination task, for example by closing the economy to international trade and investment and by reducing the number of goods that were to be produced. Later, in the construction of new regimes in the third world after colonial rule ended in the second half of the twentieth century, collectivist development strategies went in a similar direction, closing national economies and suppressing the rich diversity of markets.

Inevitably, the revolutionary overthrow of evolved institutional systems and their replacement with consciously designed rule systems was disruptive. When the inherited order is smashed abruptly, people are disorientated; coordination of their activities becomes difficult. In the totalitarian revolutions of the twentieth century, many internal institutions were replaced by designed, external institutions which subsequently failed. After the Russian revolution, Vladimir Lenin (1870–1924) and his fellow revolutionaries faced the difficult task of having to invent new institutional mechanisms to coordinate economic life, after deciding to replace private property, markets and many other institutions of tsarist Russia. Karl Marx's writings had ill prepared the revolutionaries. Lenin adopted the model of German war mobilisation which he had observed during the first world war. It was based on extraordinary, temporary government powers over the allocation of resources, including labour. The German system had focused on the sole objective of supplying the military effort (Johnson, 1983, pp. 89–95). By the 1990s at the very latest, we knew the deleterious effects of the overthrow of the inherited order in Russia by that newly designed communist regime and of the closing of the economy to international influences (section 13.2). But we are now also learning that the recent institutional disintegration in the former centrally planned economies – deficient as their institutions were when compared to those of capitalism – can have deleterious effects, too.

Collectivist orders were also designed and imposed by the Fascist regimes of the 1930s and 1940s. Many of the internal institutions of civil society were suppressed by external rules that were implemented by government-mandated organisations. Although these attempts failed during the second world war, they subsequently inspired imitations in the third world, from Argentina to Indonesia, where leaders sought to engineer change by designing national ideologies and imposing a new order of their own making. To make this easier they closed the economy in the name of nationalism.

Return to the Open Order

The experiences with 'scientifically developed' rule systems, which were designed on the basis of collectivist ideologies to repress many of the internal institutions and organisations of civil society, led to a better understanding of the merits of capitalism and openness in coordinating modern economies and facilitating institutional evolution to keep pace with ongoing changes. They also focused attention on the need for an interplay of internal and external institutions in maintaining functioning socioeconomic order in the face of on-going technical, demographic, social and economic changes. Indeed, modern Austrian economics and philosophy developed from the debate of economists with the protagonists of central planning (Hayek, 1937, 1944; Mises, [1920] 1994, 1949); and modern philosophers such as Karl Popper gained much impetus for their study of individualism and collectivism from actual experience with totalitarian collectivism and closed regimes.

Worldwide experience with economic growth in open, market-coordinated economies since the 1960s has demonstrated the advantages of autonomy, secure private property rights and the coordinative power of competitive markets, with governments concentrating on protecting that order and abstaining from discriminatory process interventions. Regimes that kept their economies closed to international trade and factor movements tended to grow more slowly (Sachs and Warner, 1995; Gwartney and Lawson, 1997). The closed economies were less exposed to challenges to reform their institutional set-up; they gained less experience in adapting traditional institutions. None the less, the economic success of neighbouring countries, which had created the conditions to attract capital, enterprise, knowledge and which demonstrated the benefits of economic reform, exerted a powerful educational influence. Demonstrated success enhanced the chances of institutional reforms in laggard countries. A telling example is an episode in Malaysia in the 1970s and early 1980s, when the Malay-dominated government embarked on a major income redistribution scheme to promote the poorer Malays at the expense of the more affluent Chinese Malaysians and foreign investors. The government curbed the autonomy and property rights of foreign and Chinese-Malaysian investors. Private investment soon stalled despite big, oil-and-gas financed public spending, whereas neighbouring economies with a less discriminatory regime continued to prosper. This brought about a pragmatic reorientation of Malaysian policies: discriminatory controls were mitigated or undone; public funds were divested from industry; infrastructures were privatised. The Malaysian economy then resumed rapid growth. Similar cases of neighbourhood rivalry have spread economic liberalisation to other parts of the third world, even to communist countries like China, where now well over half of all output is produced by private enterprise, Vietnam and quasi-feudalist countries in Latin America. There, oligarchies had ruled until they experienced economic difficulties in the 1980s and 1990s. As a result of such interjurisdictional competition, reforms to move the external institutions in the direction of a capitalist system have now become a worldwide phenomenon (Scobie and Lim, 1992; Gwartney and Lawson, 1997). We shall return to this topic in Chapters 13 and 14.

Globalisation: Changing the Political Game

Towards the end of the twentieth century, globalisation has brought a fundamental change to the political game plan of nations (Chapter 11). Smaller cost differentials now trigger 'arbitrage' by private agents who are aware of conditions in different countries, so feedback into national policies and institutions is more immediate and interjurisdictional differences are less likely to persist. Institutions which influence the (growing share of) transaction costs are now subject to institutional competition amongst nations.

The effects of globalisation on national institutional systems are often resented by those who used to have unquestioned political power and who gained political preferments as long as economies were less open. In countries that are losing competitive position and facing a net outflow of mobile capital, people and enterprises, this is seen as an affront (Chapter 11). It will be argued that employment needs to be defended against cheap foreign competitors and that globalisation lowers the chances of holding on to highly skilled jobs (deskilling). Defensive rhetoric may serve to postpone the challenge of openness, as it does, for example, when European agriculture is protected to the detriment of European consumers and non-European producers, when third world countries maintain tariffs and quotas on imported manufactures, or when service industries enrol the help of their governments to impede foreign competitors. Such interventions violate the principle of non-discrimination (and in many countries also fail the test of legitimacy). Sooner or later, the likelihood of an outside challenge to the institutions increases (Giersch, 1993, pp. 121–34).

Despite such resistance, globalisation has – in recent decades and on the whole – been a major force in driving the evolution of national institutions in the direction of less political reallocation of property rights and more freedom to compete. Political and economic freedom has been enhanced by creative political entrepreneurs in politics, government administration and industry associations, which have emulated rules that demonstrate their worth in facilitating economic success elsewhere. A big factor has probably been the experience of the 1930s, when spreading political discrimination was the key to deepening the recession into the Great Depression and, ultimately, into the calamity of global war. This gave rise, as we saw in the preceding chapter, to the principle of non-discrimination amongst nations, enshrined in the 'most favoured nation' (MFN) clause in the General Agreement on Tariffs and Trade (GATT) and now in the World Trade Organisation (WTO). Equally importantly, economic success greatly contributed to the defeat of discriminatory policies. As a result of easier exit, there has been much improvement in the economic and other institutions around the world from the standpoint of freedom and prosperity.

12.2 Internal Institutions: Evolution within Cultural Values and *Meta* Rules

Spontaneous Self-organisation: Internal Institutions

The internal institutions of society evolve within certain higher-level rules in the light of chance and experience: what works well for individuals and organisations is adopted and emulated; what does not is discontinued. This is a process of decentralised trial and error to cope with our ignorance about the many side-effects of rule changes on complex social interaction (Parker and Stacey, 1995). The process of adjustment is informed by the knowledge, wisdom and rationality of the many, as far as this can be called rational given the inescapable limits of human knowledge. Internal institutions such as conventions and customs have, as we saw in section 5.2, an automatic problem-solving, coordinative capability even if a specific circumstance might suggest otherwise: people stick to them unthinkingly and others rely on this. Only if experience shows repeatedly that the old customs and conventions yield poor results and cause people to miss opportunities will the pressure of expediency induce an adaptation of internal institutions.

In Chapter 5, we touched briefly on the process of evolution of internal institutions by innovation and variation, by acceptance and rejection (selection), and by some gaining critical mass, so that they become accepted community standards with normative force. This evolutionary and pragmatic view of institutions differs from the conservative stance that always defends known, old rules for their own sake.[1]

Acceptance of internal institutions is normally informal because they are not rigidly enforced (soft institutions). Consequently, internal institutions offer scope for further experimentation and evolutionary change. An established custom or convention will in certain circumstances be violated by some players. They accept the risk of sanctions because they feel that breaking the rule none the less confers advantages. If they are proved wrong, they will return to rule compliance; if they are right, others will sooner or later see the advantage too, and imitate the new behaviour. If sufficient numbers emulate this, a critical mass will develop and so – eventually – new internal institutions evolve.

Decentralised experimentation with breaches of established internal institutions form a large part of cultural evolution. Thus, internal rules defining what constitutes acceptable behaviour are occasionally violated, either in discussion or in deed. For example, someone found it too pompous to end letters with the formula 'your obedient servant' and replaced it by 'yours sincerely', and someone else changed the greeting 'good morning' to 'hi'. This may have attracted the conservative response of (slight) social disapproval, but then the new convention spread.[2]

Another example of evolutionary change to internal rules was observed in the smaller new industrial countries of East Asia (Hofheins and Bond, 1988): they shifted to future-orientated values and deemphasised the traditional rules of hierarchical submission, because this was widely seen as advantageous in the new world-competitive atmosphere of the 1950s and 1960s in the East Asian market economies that were increasingly exposed to world-market influences. Some members of society who broke the old rules were materially successful, so the accepted internal institutions soon changed across the board at a time when most people were desperate for material success. This process often created personal conflict, some confusion and malcoordination, though much less than the pervasive disruptions of the social order after the communist revolution in China and Vietnam, which were enforced in the name of modernisation. In the final analysis, the capitalist East Asian societies adjusted the internal rule systems and turned their adapted neo-Confucian rules into an asset in international competitiveness. Thus, institutional evolution is propelled by those 'million little mutinies' and the evaluation of these 'little mutinies' by numerous other people. In the process, much considered wisdom is incorporated into the institutional system.

Inertia: Path Dependency

Normally, a community's shared fundamental value system and its *meta* rules are reasonably stable. This makes for fairly steady institutional evolution; after all, new institutions impose learning costs and may lead to malcoordination in the transition phase. This is often an argument for sticking with tradition. New rules therefore fail to obtain the critical mass of voluntary followers to make them sufficiently generally accepted in the community. The acceptance of new rules is also often hindered by fears that these innovations may clash with other rules. Traditional rule systems tend to contain many complementarities which make for cohesive networks, and people have adjusted their complex interactions to make the best use of the prevailing rules. The dictum that 'old rules are good rules' has considerable weight, because widespread, quasi-automatic rule compliance reduces coordination costs. Consequently, there is path dependency in institutional change, and institutional systems rest to a considerable measure on inertia. They normally evolve slowly along a fairly steady path. Evolutionary adjustments, rather than convulsive shifts, are essential for the information-economising basic function of institutions.

There are situations in which communities fail to attain their fundamental values by big margins because the rule system is totally out of sync with new conditions (as in the case of postwar East Asia). Then, fairly rapid institutional change may occur if the old rules are widely recognised as the cause of poor performance. The disruptions of war and the threats of invasion in smaller East Asian countries created conditions in which a critical mass for new rule interpretations was reached quickly. The new export orientation and the information revolution soon ensured that adherence to new rules produced material success in the 'neo-Confucian societies'. Yet, despite the pervasive 'cultural revolution' in the new industrial countries of East Asia, it is amazing how continuous the adherence to traditional rules has nevertheless been: no one would therefore confuse present-day Japanese or Hong Kong society with European or American society despite shared technologies and the trappings of a global consumer society. In many instances, the lower-level norms were adjusted, but within a framework of time-tested higher-level rules and values. This led to an evolutionary path, not a revolution. And where totalitarian attempts at changing the rule system by external intervention were made, such as in China, Vietnam and Cambodia, the long-term results turned out to follow a more predictable path than the revolutionaries would ever have expected.

Institutional Evolution

The emergence of internal institutions and their evolutionary changes are driven by dispersed entrepreneurial discoveries: people and organisations discover advantage in violating established internal rules and get away with it. They assess the pros and cons of possible sanctions. But because the sanctions are often 'soft', some people gamble fairly readily on experimenting with moving outside the accepted rules. They may hope that they will be able to explain their rule violations to the people affected and to obtain acceptance or at least toleration of their experimentation. Thus, sons and daughters of a certain age tend to violate the family's institutions, for example on obedience to parental authority. They may hope to gain an advantage and may explain to parents why they broke the rule. Whether such experiments lead to new institutions depends on whether the new practices are transmitted to others and accepted, so that they gain the critical mass needed for new institutions to emerge. Such experimentation is not conflict-free, but the conflicts tend to be sorted out at the decentralised, personal level where good information, empathy and solidarity are brought to bear.

The process by which internal rules change has the characteristics of all decentralised order: there is decentralised experimentation with breaches of existing rules (institutional innovation); there are decentralised, spontaneous selection processes in which innovations are accepted until they gain critical mass to become new standards or are rejected; and these processes are normally conducted within *meta* rules that tend to keep evolution on a continuous path and reasonably predictable. The rule system remains ordered (order of rules), so that it retains its capacity to influence the order of actions (Chapter 6). Such evolution captures the wisdom and judgement of the many and yields a set of institutions that owes much to past experience, but that is not completely rigid in the face of changed circumstances.

How internal institutions are adapted often makes the difference between successful and failing multicultural societies. As is the case in the United States or Australia, where the implicit knowledge and the embodied rules of various cultures merge or are adjusted to form a new, more or less shared institutional set, creative cross-fertilisation is triggered and knowledge is put to constructive use. But where the pre-existing implicit institutions of a host society are rigidly defended and where each group perseveres obstinately with its own institutions, integration is difficult and costly social conflicts may arise (Sowell, 1994, 1996, 1998).

Which challenges to internal rules gain critical mass, so that they are readily accepted, and which are widely rejected depends in part on how experimental variations relate to people's fundamental values. We saw in Chapter 4 that these values inform the institutions and often serve as overriding priorities against which institutional arrangements are judged. As these values are deeply and firmly held, they underpin continuity and cohesiveness in the internal institutions. This makes for path dependency. Communities that share a high degree of clear and common understanding of fundamental values manage a more predictable, orderly evolution of their institutions than societies whose members share few values. Shared values thus serve as a filter and as the cohesive cement for the evolving internal rules of society.

Some Internal *Meta* Rules: Tolerance, Humour and Free Speech

Given the importance of cultural change to the continued wellbeing of a community that is faced with changing circumstances, the decentralised processes of testing and re-evaluating institutions deserve protection. Informal internal *meta* rules which enhance the evolutionary capacity of internal rule systems are important here: for example, a measure of tolerance of experimentation; the rule that conflicts can be eased by a sense of humour; and a commitment to free speech. Societies which are too conservative to tolerate experimentation and are doctrinaire in rejecting any deviation from established internal rules tend to lose out when material or technical conditions change. When conflicts arise and internal institutions fail to handle them, the practice of a humorous escape may serve as a social safety valve and a way of economising on interpersonal transaction costs. Another *meta* rule in an evolving system of internal institutions that can reduce conflict and transaction costs is the rule that argument should be depersonalised: play the ball and not the person. In a society in which *ad hominem* arguments typically lose out to factual debate, there is more likelihood of peaceful, problem-orientated evolution than in a society where personal slurs gain popular acclaim.

Societies in which the free expression of one's ideas is considered a punishable crime forgo the relatively cost-free exploration of alternatives by discourse. Open discourse – including the expression of outrageous deviant opinions about accepted rules – is a useful part of how communities cope with change. An open discussion of alternative solutions costs fewer resources than either trial and error by implementing and maybe later rejecting institutions or unresolved, simmering conflicts. Free discussion – and the virtue of listening to dissidents – is a means of keeping the process of cultural evolution open to all the members of the community and hence open to all available experience, knowledge and wisdom. The institution of free speech fits in with the 'commercial entrepreneurial syndrome' discussed in section 5.5 as it is the engine of non-violent institutional evolution. It therefore deserves to be protected.

Thus, even internal rule systems contain *meta* rules that facilitate adjustment when necessary but that at the same time keep institutional change on a predictable path.

12.3 Changing the External Institutions: Political Entrepreneurship

Political Action: Rigidity, Convulsion and Orderly Adjustment

External institutions are designed and enforced from the top down on the basis of constitutions by authorities with political power. Changes in the external institutions therefore require political action. External rule changes depend on collective decisions which are more difficult to bring about than voluntary decisions, as we saw in section 10.1. External rules may therefore sometimes be fairly rigid, even when circumstances have changed. When changes are made, they occur in – sometimes convulsive – steps. They are inevitably caught in a fundamental conflict between the maxim of predictability embodied in existing institutions and the need to cope with changing circumstances, including changing internal institutions which may lead to inconsistencies in the rule system. This conflict is exacerbated as changes in external institutions often affect the distribution of incomes and economic opportunities. It touches on the very foundations of institutional arrangements. After all, institutions are like good wine: they improve with age, at least for some time! But sometimes they have to be changed, even if this disrupts the smooth coordination of human actions.

When external institutions are adapted to address changed circumstances, this is normally less disruptive than rule changes which reflect political opportunism. Unfortunately, modern mass democracies with changing coalitions of organised interest groups and a commitment to social welfare generate much opportunistic, often ephemeral legislation ('knee jerk legislation'). This may conflict with the internal rule system in contradictory and excessively intrusive ways. In other contexts, political opportunism may produce institutional rigidity and sclerosis. Vested interests defend the existing rules against adjustment, even if changed circumstances call for such adjustments which would be advantageous for the community as a whole. Indeed, external institutions can become so rigid that they prejudice material progress and other fundamental human aspirations. Numerous historic experiences bear witness to this: the Byzantine empire, for example, was unable to adjust its institutions of governance to rise to the Turkish challenge; the China of the Ming and Ching dynasties rigidified its external institutions in the face of outside challenges; and big corporations and associations, such as the Pan American airline or the British coal miners' union during the 1980s, rigidly adhered to time-tested institutions which exceeded their use-by date. Business organisations which suffer from ossification of their rules tend to go bankrupt. In communities where outside challenges fail to trigger necessary reforms of the external institutions, material decline and conflict follow.

In other instances, outside challenges may trigger reforms of external institutions that would otherwise not be feasible. That helps to rejuvenate them, as in the case of globalisation that we discussed.

Overcoming External Institutional Constraints

Various agents are part of the processes by which external institutions are changed:

(a) Economic organisations, led by entrepreneurs or a team of enterprising leaders, and individuals, who pursue their self-set objectives, normally operate within given and accepted constraints, be they of a technical, economic or institutional nature. One possible mode of behaviour is to pursue self-set objectives to the maximum within these constraints, another is to adjust objectives in the light of past experience (adaptive, bounded rationality). Existing constraints frequently have disadvantages for organisations and individuals, but the constraints are nevertheless accepted, since altering them is perceived to be too costly, if not impossible.

(b) Another course of action is to tackle the constraints head-on to overcome them in creative, entrepreneurial ways (Chapter 8). Once constraints are recognised as harmful, entrepreneurial creativity may lead to organising cheaper or new factor supplies, saving costs through process innovation, streamlining the organisation, product innovation, or moving to a more competitive location. In all these cases, the creative effort aims at innovation in the sense of a 'new factor combination' as defined by Joseph A. Schumpeter (1883–1950) (Schumpeter, 1961). This same sort of entrepreneurial creativity may also be directed against costly institutional constraints: individuals and organisations may on occasion refuse to accept existing institutions, challenging them head-on, either in court or by disobedience, even risking sanctions. Technical innovations may sometimes require institutional innovation as well. For example, new forms of production, transport, communication and consumption may necessitate adjustments in the definition of property rights or in business and work practices. Thus, the railway building boom of the nineteenth century brought not only technical changes, but also new institutions governing share and bond markets (Rosenberg and Birdzell, 1986). So far, the process is essentially identical for changing the internal and the external institutions.

(c) When external institutions are to be altered, individuals and organisations must become involved in the political process by raising their 'voice'. They may try to exert direct influence on policy matters, but this is relatively rare in modern mass societies because of very high fixed costs. For many citizens, it remains rational to ignore or tolerate existing external institutions (rational ignorance). However, where the costs imposed by existing external institutions are sufficient to be perceived as important, people may form organised interest groups to exercise their political voice. In most modern societies, political constitutions are meant to facilitate orderly external rule changes by offering formal channels of change, such as legal challenges and parliamentary votes. If political operators recognise the signals, the laws are changed through elected legislatures subject to general higher-level constitutional constraints and possible review by the courts. In many countries, the judiciary has become another agency for changing the rules, as judges interpret the law in innovative ways.

(d) The mechanisms for changing external institutions are populated by political agents. They of course pursue their own objectives (Downs, 1957a, 1957b; Buchanan *et al.*, 1980; Bernholz, 1966) and are subject to the usual cognitive limitations. 'Political entrepreneurs' may be politicians, bureaucrats and leaders of private associations and clubs, such as industry organisations, trade unions and other special-interest lobbies. They promise to alter existing institutions in exchange for influence, payment and other rewards. They act as middlemen who have insider knowledge of political change processes and organisations. Political entrepreneurs drive a large part of the process of public policy in modern states. They have a personal interest in changing or conserving certain external rules, reflecting their own aspirations, and this may often go in the direction of more reliance on collective mechanisms and less on spontaneous self-organisation. In parliamentary democracies, some will try to convince others and will seek allies in exchange for support for other political deals (political trade-offs, log-rolling).

Private Acceptance and Legitimacy

Not all external institutional innovations will be in the interest of private citizens. It is possible, for example, for the agents of the political process to err and institute rules that later turn out to damage wealth creation. More probably, political motivations lead to rule changes that complicate effective economic coordination. If the system is open and the various political agents are on the alert for growth opportunities, there is a likelihood that errors will be corrected and obstacles to economic growth removed proactively, that is, before outside challenges force rule changes. But this is not often the case.

If the proposed change of an external rule is to be adopted in a parliamentary democracy, the change has in the first place to be privately accepted by sufficient numbers of people and private organisations, either because they expect benefits from it or because they tolerate the change because its negative impacts are imperceptible. A second test: acceptance of a rule, by itself, does not guarantee that this rule is conducive to economic growth. Thus, tariff protection may be retained with popular consent if it is perceived to confer benefits on a sufficient number of members of the community and its negative impacts are imperceptible. This happens when the beneficiaries of protection – the capital owners and the workers in the protected industry – are well organised and united and those burdened with the consequences of protection are rationally ignorant, given the information and organisation costs of lobbying for a tariff reduction. The tariff will stay in place. Rent-seeking and the impairment of the catallactic capability of the economy continue. If reforms of the external rules are wanted, private acceptance of the changes must be achieved first.

If external rules are to be changed so as to enhance the capacity of market participants to generate prosperity, then the rules have to become less discriminatory. If external rules confer privileges on some, and this is recognised by those affected, then the general commitment to using one's assets by incurring exploration costs is weakened. As we saw when discussing rent-seeking in Chapter 8, the political motivation is often to create rents rather than to introduce changes in external institutions that curb rent-seeking. When the shapers of collective action persist with discriminatory external rules, economic stagnation or decline becomes more likely.

Sooner or later this will probably induce political entrepreneurs again to seek political gain from reforming the external institutions. Political entrepreneurs, possibly of a new generation or from a new political grouping, will then see a chance to gain political support by promoting reforms that break the cycle of stagnation and institutional rigidity. They may even seek to forge political majorities for comprehensive constitutional change (see the case of long-stagnant New Zealand in the early 1980s, section 14.1). Such attempts may, of course, be rejected time and again by entrenched interest groups, self-seeking parliamentarians and bureaucrats who trust that they can rely on a lack of interest among the public. This would reinforce the process of institutional sclerosis and relative economic decline. Powerful groups and entrenched majorities, who find the proposed reforms privately unacceptable, may simply not accept the constitutional principle of competition. This may then trigger widespread cynicism, if not internal political and sectarian conflict, which undermines prosperity further and hinders the evolution of institutions that make for non-discrimination and openness.

Sooner or later, communities with such a poor economic performance will be confronted by another type of agent of institutional change: outside challengers, leaders of other polities who have the potential to intervene politically or militarily to take advantage of the apparent economic weakness of the community in question. They may threaten force or actually use it to have their way. One possibility then is for the outside challenger to impose a change in external institutions. Examples are the takeover of a country by a colonial power and the imposition of the victors' will after a lost war. This was the case in Germany and Japan after the second world war, when the establishment of a democracy and a market economy was in the vital interests of the United States once the Cold War had begun. Entrenched rent-seeking coalitions are then simply disbanded (Olson, 1982, pp. 76–80, 130–1). Another possibility is for the outside challenger to become a player in the internal political process, initiating changes within existing constitutional arrangements. This is the case, for example, when international bodies such as the International Monetary Fund or the World Bank intervene in debtor countries, when foreign agricultural exporters lobby the European Union to abandon agricultural protectionism, or when governments engage in direct political pressure on other governments to reduce trade barriers. Such outside challenges (or even threats thereof) depend to a considerable degree on a country's openness to foreign trade, ideas and factor flows.

12.4   Outside Challenges: Institutional Competition

Inertia and Change

The evolution of internal and external institutions is driven not only by passive responses to international trade and factor flows, but also by active institutional adjustments to compete better for market share and for mobile production factors. Globalisation has led to 'institutional (or systems) competition'. Institutional systems now influence cost levels to such an extent that they are important elements in international competition. Consequently, governments compete more or less directly with each other.

Although globalisation is now giving real bite to international institutional competition, the concept is not new. Unsurprisingly, Adam Smith referred to the basic interplay between mobile and immobile production factors and the evolutionary effect of factor mobility in his *Wealth of Nations* in 1776, when he analysed the expected reactions to differences in the taxation of capital:

> Land is a subject which cannot be removed; whereas stock easily may ... The proprietor of stock is properly a citizen of the world, and is not necessarily attached to any particular country. He would be apt to abandon the country in which he was exposed to vexatious inquisition, in order to be assessed to a burdensome tax, and would remove his stock to some other country where he could either carry on his business, or enjoy his fortune more at ease. By removing his stock, he would put an end to all the industry which it had maintained in the country which he left. Stock cultivates land; stock employs labour. A tax which tended to drive away stock from any particular country, would so far tend to dry up every source of revenue, both to the sovereign and to the society. Not only the profit of the stock, but the rent of the land, and the wages of labour, would necessarily be more or less diminished by its removal.
> (Smith, [1776] 1970–1, vol. 2, pp. 330–1)

One of the first social scientists in the twentieth century to describe the relevance of institutional evolution was Max Weber ([1927] 1995).[3] More recently these same issues have been analysed by, among others, Douglass North (North and Thomas, 1973, 1977; North, 1981, 1993), Eric Jones ([1981] 1987, 1988, 1994), Nathan Rosenberg and L.E. Birdzell (1986) and Erich Weede (1990, 1995, 1996).

Openness can be a powerful antidote to rent-seeking. When formerly closed political and economic systems are opened, institutions have to be changed and power groups lose their grip. A clear-cut historical case was the opening up of Japan by American naval intervention in 1854 which led to the overturn of the shogunate in 1867 and paved the way for modernisation in the Meiji Revolution. The institutional transformation was not without conflict and far from deeply entrenched. In the 1930s and early 1940s, the Japanese fell prey to inward-looking isolationism and aggressive power groups. American intervention after 1945 in a way opened Japan up a second time, and this again triggered pervasive institutional reforms in Japan as well as an unpredicted rise in prosperity.

Openness has not been a one-way street in the history of humankind. However, lower transport, communications and transaction costs in cross-border trade and factor flows have, on the whole, promoted openness and undercut the tendency to lobbying and rigidification. Openness serves as a powerful incentive to incur information costs and places a premium on universal rules, for example a straightforward private property system.[4]

Figure 12.1 summarises the interactions of economic and political processes when institutional systems compete. Lower transport and transaction costs make it easier for traders and factor owners to opt out of other institutional systems. They also are likely to become more aware of alternative institutional conditions in different countries.

When owners of internationally mobile factors relocate across borders, they inevitably make a choice between institutional systems. They may even expect differences in profitability as a direct consequence of differences in the institutions in other countries, as long as they recognise and properly interpret the effects of differing institutions. Then, institutional choice becomes an option in economic competition. The option is affected by the openness of the economy, and this depends on the freedoms to trade, move and convert currencies, as well as the *meta* rules that secure these freedoms. Economic agents who make such a choice do so individually in exercising an 'exit' option.

Such economic 'exits' send out signals to those in the political process, either the electorate and organised interest groups or directly to political agents. It is, however, not certain that these signals are properly recognised and interpreted. Political agents in 'sclerotic' jurisdictions, who have no experience of responding entrepreneurially to change and who are self-centred, may not have the ability to adjust; indeed, they will have a limited capacity to read the signals. Nor may organised interest groups and the electorate at large recognise the need for change (Figure 12.1). Their vote (voice) will only have effect if it is exercised by a group of sufficient size; and it may or may not favour institutional adjustment, depending on how the voters are influenced by vocal rent-seeking groups, and a tribal-guardian mentality prevails. As we noted above, parliamentarians and bureaucrats in alliance with rent-seeking lobbies are therefore often able to entrench discriminatory external rules, obstruct openness and hinder the evolution of competition-supporting rules. In most countries and for most of the time, this has indeed been the normal condition of humankind and governance. Spreading freedom and the impacts of globalisation are, for most nations, still a novel experience, achieved only during the second half of the twentieth century (Gwartney and Lawson, 1997). It is therefore not surprising that tribal xenophobic instincts often still prevail in the face of economic exit options.

Only when a majority of voters supports change, even in the face of interest-group resistance, or when organised groups discover merit in

Figure 12.1   Institutional competition: basic interactions of economic and political processes

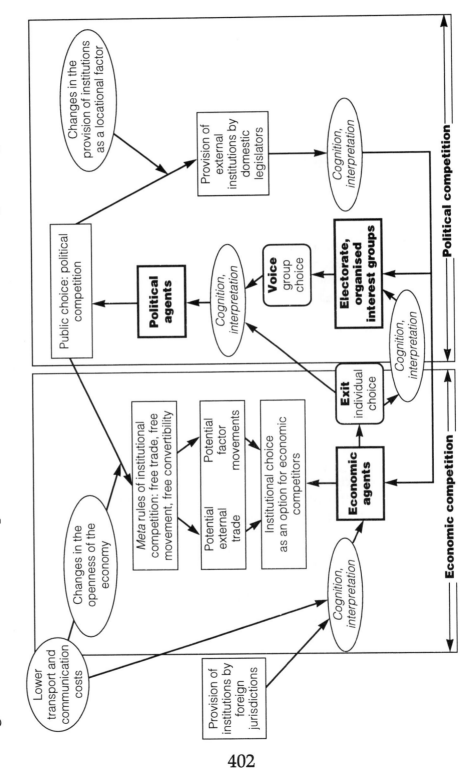

openness will institutional innovation begin. If it does, governments begin to compete with other governments (interjurisdictional competition).[5] Much therefore depends on the capacity of governments and the public to recognise the importance of the 'exit signals' and to draw from them the conclusions that they must supply institutions which constitute an attractive locational factor, even in the face of pressure group resistance and inward-looking tribal instincts.

We shall add further substance to the complex interactions depicted in Figure 12.1 when we discuss the transformation of economic systems and the institutional reform of mixed economies in Chapters 13 and 14.

O Key Concepts

Institutional competition (or 'systems competition') is a term that highlights the importance of internal and external rule sets to national cost levels and hence international competitiveness. With globalisation – intensified trade and greater factor mobility – there is more immediate feedback to high-cost institutional systems and, with it, the need to adjust those systems, not only passively but possibly even pro-actively.

Political entrepreneurs are people and agencies who seek political advantage from implementing or hindering institutional change. Political entrepreneurs are often 'young Turks' who see that existing institutions and power structures prevent them gaining political influence and who therefore enrol support to gain more 'voice' for a platform of institutional change. ●

Institutional Competition: Economic, Industrial and Political-administrative Creativity

Institutional competition is a process that mobilises creativity in several areas of human pursuit:

(a) Technical and organisational changes and the opening of economic systems have made it possible for competitors to engage in international locational substitution. This mobilises technical, organisational and economic creativity.
(b) The mobility of factors and trade in goods and services exerts a disciplining control on local institutions, both the internal practices and conventions and the shaping and implementation of external institutions, which we have just discussed. This contributes to the control of principal–agent problems and triggers

institutional creativity. Over time, openness delivers feedback into the evolution of internal and external institutions, stimulating on-going institutional discoveries:

(i)   it promotes entrepreneurship in industry associations and other groups of civil society who work to discover and test improved business standards, work practices, enforcement procedures and the like to expedite productivity growth;

(ii) it promotes political-administrative and judicial entrepreneurship in government administrations in creative, proactive ways to expedite productivity growth and enhance competitiveness.

As long as people have the freedom to make their own choices, openness tends on the whole to stimulate greater innovation in the various walks of life which are interdependent.

12.5   Competitive Federalism

Trade and Factor Mobility Within Countries

Within a nation, federal-state constitutions can be designed to capture some of the advantages of interjurisdictional competition within the country. Federalism is a way to exploit the rivalry among (state and local) political organisations in the interest of discovering preferred administrative solutions and institutions.

If people and producers have the opportunity to move between independent subnational jurisdictions, then legislators and administrators are compelled to compete. The exit option gives them feedback from the citizen-principal.[6] When public policy is less concentrated in the hands of the centralised government, there is a better chance to control rent-seeking, pressure groups and agent opportunism.

Subsidiarity

There is an advantage from the viewpoint of citizens and enterprise in favouring the principle of subsidiarity, that is, that each task of collective action should always be placed at the lowest possible level of government. Numerous tasks of governance can be decentralised and provided by competing authorities. Competing state or local governments may for example carry out, finance or regulate the provision of public welfare, the maintenance of many infrastructures and the bulk of education and health services. In certain cases, there are advantages in centralising government tasks, for example when common institutions, such as uniform commercial codes and traffic laws, allow great savings in transaction costs, or when there are advantages of scale and scope, such as in military defence. Because institutional evolution and the discovery of new administrative solutions can benefit from experiments in competing state or local governments, the normative principle of subsidiarity might therefore be turned into a high-level constitutional principle and exemptions should be made only when they can be explicitly justified.

Adherents of centralised government frequently object to subsidiarity with the argument that it is necessary to secure national cohesion and unity by promoting equal income and employment opportunities and equal outcomes across the various regions and provinces and by guaranteeing the uniform provision of public goods to all citizens, irrespective of where they live and which politicians they voted into office. However, the worldwide record of equalising regional policy is hardly more convincing than the record of social welfare equalisation, not least because it weakens spontaneous, self-correcting responses to regional income differentials. Ailing regions that have easy access to central government aid may refuse to offer lower wage levels which would attract new investors. Moreover, the uniform, centralised provision of public goods may go against different regional preferences and priorities. Because public policy makers are more remote from the citizens, centralisation fosters principal–agent opportunism as well as moral hazard on the part of the voting public. Federal diversity in policy making allows voter choice and the style of governance to make a difference to the provision of public goods. Then, citizens will take more interest in cultivating local and regional economic development.

To give content and substance to the principle of subsidiarity, competitive federal systems should adopt three general institutional devices (Kasper, 1996b):

(a) federations should adhere to the rule of origin which stipulates that products which are produced legally in one part of the federation are automatically legal for sale throughout; in other words, discrimination between different locations of production is ruled out;

(b) federal constitutions should assign the various tasks of governance exclusively to one particular level of government: they should rule out overlap and duplication of tasks, which only confuses voters about who is responsible for delivering. Exclusivity reduces the scope for shirking by politicians and administrators;

(c) federations should stick to the principle of fiscal equivalence, banning the vertical transfer of public funds and forcing each administration to finance the tasks for which it is responsible or which it has chosen to tackle with the taxes, fees and debts which it raises itself. This limits redistributional transfers and imposes fiscal responsibility on the various competing administrations.

Competitive Federalism

We may call such a system 'competitive federalism'. It allows 'clients' to vote with their feet, but inevitably it operates with some friction and creates some resource costs – as all competitive systems do. But it is likely that state and local rivalry will generate outcomes that citizens find superior to those provided by the one centralised administration. Competitive federalism empowers the citizens and fosters those innovations in public policy which citizens really want. It is no more than an application of the power-controlling devices of competition that induce governments to incur information and transaction costs so as to attract citizens and investors. The evolutionary feedback from interjurisdictional entrepreneurship in local and state administrations is also likely to strengthen the international competitiveness and attractiveness of nations. Seen in this light, it seems no coincidence that many of the prospering democracies of long standing have federal constitutions (Switzerland, the US, Canada and Australia, amongst others) and that regional communities in many other countries have been trying to affirm their collective identities by demanding devolution of government functions (for example, in Spain, Britain, South Africa, Russia, the People's Republic of China). Channelling regional identity into constructive administrative-institutional rivalry seems preferable to smothering such aspirations by centralisation and risking political confrontation amongst regions.

O Key Concepts

The **principle of subsidiarity** relates to the division of the tasks of government among various levels of government (for example, local, provincial and national government). It stipulates that a task of governance should always be carried out at the lowest possible level. It is violated by the needless centralisation of tasks. Subsidiarity needs to be given substance by the rule of origin (which rules out impediments to free trade throughout the nation), the exclusive assignment of tasks to specific levels of government, and fiscal equivalence (the requirement for each government to be responsible for financing its own tasks). ●

12.6   The Constitution of Freedom as a Framework for Evolution

Freedom and Competition

Our analysis of institutional evolution highlights again a point made repeatedly in this book: institutions evolve and are changed to meet what people demand, as long as individuals have freedom of choice. Where economic liberties are curtailed, established groups use their power to entrench institutions that serve their particular interests. Indeed, powerful groups strive to curtail equality before the law and liberty in order to shore up their particular positions. They are often successful for considerable periods of time. When a system that is dominated by powerful groups is opened up to spontaneous or forced outside challenges, institutional systems come under pressure to reform. It then depends on whether freedom of action can be guaranteed, so that all individuals can express their preferences, or whether powerful groups can obtain preferment, which curtails individual economic freedom.

This highlights the essential role of an overriding commitment to freedom in controlling power concentrations and hold-ups by politically well-connected groups. Where freedom is made a constitutional principle, individuals can experiment with alternatives, can by their example invite others to emulate them and may generate a critical mass of followers to establish new institutions. In the case of external institutions, which require political processes for institutional change, freedom is a constitutional foundation for marshalling the political will for institutional change if that change is widely desired. The combination of party monopolies and organised interest groups, including bureaucratic interests, makes it harder for individual aspirations and outsiders to challenge rule systems which curb individual liberties. In modern democracies, it is particularly important for the evolutionary potential of the system to protect the freedom of exit (free international trade, migration and capital flows) and freedoms of association, information, and so on, as guarantees against institutional sclerosis and rigidification.

The role of freedom is thus key to the evolutionary capacity of institutions and their wide-ranging consequences. Freedom should therefore be enshrined in an overriding constitutional principle that has high protection.

Questions for Review

- What is the difference between evolution and revolution? (Check a good encyclopedia.)
- Why did emperor Charles V feel threatened by the international mobility of Jewish merchants and bankers?
- Which of the production factors discussed in Chapter 1 are nowadays typically internationally mobile and which internationally immobile?
- What was meant by 'two-way relationship between institutional evolution and factor mobility'? Can you give examples from your experience to illustrate how these mechanisms work?
- Why must institutions evolve over time?
- What effect did the Russian and the Chinese Revolutions have on the inherited economic order? How does revolution affect coordination and individual living standards?
- Why are tolerant behaviour and free speech important to institutional evolution?
- Why is the 'syndrome of commercial virtues' more attuned to institutional evolution than the 'guardian syndrome'?
- What motivates political entrepreneurs?
- What was meant by 'private acceptance test' and 'constitutional test' in external institutional change?
- Define competitiveness. How do the various elements cited from the World Competitiveness Report relate to that definition?
- Explain why political authorities are likely to become support agencies for internationally competing producers when capital and enterprise are highly mobile among jurisdictions.
- Why do existing political interest groups and power brokers who wish to reallocate property rights enjoy an advantage in a closed economy as compared to in an open economy?
- In what ways does the Internet undermine the power of central authorities in China? Why do these authorities nevertheless permit the spread of the Internet in the People's Republic?
- What cases do you know from the press that point to a growing assertion of regional political interests in specific countries?
- Why do governments tend to centralise the tasks of governance? What is the role of the redistributional functions of government in this context?
- What purposes are served by 'fiscal equivalence'?
- Does the 'rule of origin' apply in your country without exception? What are the exceptions, if any, and do they seem justified to you?
- What is the advantage of proactive creative institutional change as against reactive, reluctant adjustment of the institutions to new conditions?

Notes

1. In the last chapter of his *Constitution of Liberty*, entitled 'Why I Am Not a Conservative', Hayek showed that a clear dividing line runs between conservatives and liberals (or libertarians in American terminology). Liberals always ask what is better. Sometimes, they find that new institutions serve human interests better, whereas conservatives always defend the old institutions and are fond of established authorities (Hayek, 1960).

2. Cultural evolution, of course, goes beyond the institutional system. Cultural content is subject to ongoing evolutionary processes of innovation, imitation, selection and rejection. An example would be when what was considered good music and painting under then-existing cultural conventions was overturned by artistic innovators such as Ludwig van Beethoven or Gustav Mahler or the Impressionist painters of France. Their breach of cultural conventions earned them the hostility of the established academies and a conservative public, but they gradually made a sufficient number of converts to establish new cultural standards.

   In a similar vein, the economics profession has adopted the shared conventions that have been labelled the 'neoclassical paradigm'. This has facilitated interaction amongst professional economists. When alternative conventions which, for example, demand the explicit consideration of institutions and reject the tacit assumption of 'perfect knowledge', are being tried out, the established schools of thought and the adherents of the conventional paradigm are challenged. Their reactions may be inspired by a habitual conservative refusal to contemplate new conventions, which are perceived as unwelcome complications, that only hinder coordination and the exchange of ideas among scholars. The intellectual challenge to the established paradigm may also induce attempts to defend acquired intellectual capital against potential depreciation. Hence, protagonists of the neoclassical paradigm may resist change, for example by rejecting publication of unconventional articles in journals or vetoing the career promotion of deviants. Changes in economic thinking are gradually promoted by attempts to integrate plausible parts of the alternative institutional-economics paradigm into the dominant school of thought, building hybrid models (Furubotn, 1994). If these turn out to be inherently inconsistent or fail to explain important real-world phenomena, further incentives to reconsider the mainstream paradigm will be felt. Only in the light of experience will the many participants in economic discourse evaluate, in gradual and decentralised ways, whether the change of widespread conventional assumptions is acceptable and useful.

3. Long before Weber focused on institutional evolution, British analysts wrote about it. Scottish philosopher-historian Adam Ferguson (1723–1816), with his *Essay on the History of Civil Society* (1767), and English historian Edward Gibbon (1737–94), who wrote the celebrated *Decline and Fall of the Roman Empire*, deserve to be remembered as pioneers in the analysis of institutional evolution.

4. Openness to international challenges is not the only competition faced by sclerotic institutions: people may opt out of shared external institutions if they find them disadvantageous and will operate black markets. The shadow economy depends on internal rules and its spread can be interpreted as a competition between official formal and spontaneous informal rules.

5. American economist Paul Krugman (1994, p. 34) attacked the notion that countries compete: "Countries do not compete with each other as corporations do.' In so far he was correct. But, like other neoclassical economists who habitually assume zero transactioncosts and therefore overlook institutions, he was blind to the supply of collectively produced institutions by governments as a means of cutting cost levels and attracting mobile productive factors.

6. In many countries, whether federal or otherwise, the free mobility of goods and production factors throughout the national territory is not guaranteed, for example because there are internal border controls or because regulations hinder interregional trade. Such countries forgo important gains from the division of labour, both comparative-static specialisation gains and dynamic gains from more intense competition among suppliers and regulators.

CHAPTER 13

Alternative Economic Systems and Systems Transformation

The purpose of this chapter is to demonstrate how well the institutional economics approach is suited to analysing some of the most exciting economic issues of our time: Why has there been faster growth in capitalist economies than under regimes with central planning and socialised ownership of capital? Why did socialism and central planning collapse in the Soviet sphere – so unexpectedly to most observers? What do the formerly socialist countries have to do now to transform their economies?

We begin by reviewing briefly the economic performance of the socialist regimes, whose main instruments to motivate producers were planning and coercion. When comparing the performance of these economies with capitalist market economies, we find that socialism falls far short of capitalism on innovative performance. The defunct experiment with central planning starkly demonstrates just how many institutional and organisational problems pop up when spontaneous market coordination and voluntary initiatives are suppressed.

The chapter concludes with a brief review of the problems which need to be tackled when a thorough transformation of the economic system is attempted – a complex task. Paradoxically, collective action is needed to undo the dominance of collective action. The main lesson from the recent experiences in the transformation economies seems to be that governments, because of their limited capacity to initiate and coordinate human actions, have to keep their institutional designs simple. They must concentrate on fostering and protecting the basic rules of the game. Attempts at combining the protective function of government with more than minimal redistribution (a strategy that has been called the 'Third Way') only promote agent opportunism and hinder the emergence of effective internal institutions.

The distinguishing feature of communism is ... the abolition of bourgeois property ... modern bourgeois property is the final and most complete expression of the system of producing and appropriating products that is based on class antagonism, on the exploitation of the many by the few. In this sense, the theory of Communists may be summed up in the single phrase: Abolition of private property ... The Communists ... openly declare that their ends can be attained only by the forcible overthrow of all existing social conditions.
(Karl Marx and Friedrich Engels, The Communist Manifesto, 1872, cited from the English edition of 1888)

As the self-styled 'progressives' see things, the alternative is: 'automatic forces' or 'conscious planning'. It is obvious, they go on saying, that to rely on automatic processes is sheer stupidity. No reasonable man can seriously recommend doing nothing and letting things go without interference through purposive action. A plan ... is incomparably superior to the absence of planning ... The truth is that the choice is not between a dead mechanism and a rigid automatism on the one hand and conscious planning on the other. The alternative is not: plan or no plan. The question is: whose planning? Should each member of society plan for himself or should paternal government alone plan for all? Laissez faire ... means: let individuals choose how they want to cooperate in the social division of labor and let them determine what the entrepreneurs should produce ... and do not force the common man to yield to a dictator.
(Ludwig von Mises, 'Laissez Faire or Dictatorship', in Planning for Freedom, *1952, pp. 44–9)*

They pretend to pay us, we pretend to work!
(Warsaw cabaret in the 1980s, describing the socialist system)

The Soviet leaders' attempt to reform the system is not inspired by some noble recognition that the system is unjust and poorly regarded abroad, but by strict necessity.
(Milovan Djilas, former Yugoslav Communist Party member, in Encounter, *1988)*

[Describing how communism imploded]: 'They had ... stuck posters on the pedestal demanding free elections, democracy, the end of one-party rule, dialogue, freedom of expression and information, the dismantling of the People's Militia, solidarity with the students, a general strike and the resignation of the government. Only a few days ago no one would have dared voice a single one of those demands, let alone write them down and post them in the centre of the city. ... the present regime's time had simply come without its even noticing.
(Ivan Klima, Waiting for the Dark, Waiting for the Light, *1990, p. 134)*

13.1 The Economic Performance of Alternative Systems

Convergence Failed to Materialise

From the 1950s to the 1980s, a 'convergence hypothesis' was popular. It predicted that the institutions of the centrally planned, socialist 'second world' would converge with those in the capitalist 'first world'. Some economic and political liberalisation in the East and spreading regulation of the free exercise of property rights and a growing socialisation of economic activity in the West would bring about this outcome (see, for example, Tinbergen, [1961] 1965). A related hypothesis was that the centrally planned economies were catching up with the productivity levels of the 'first world', whilst the capitalist economies were experiencing a slowdown in economic growth, at least after the oil crisis of 1973 (Chapter 1). Both hypotheses were wrong. We can now reassess the economic performance of the socialist planning system as compared to the capitalist system on the basis of much better information.

After the fall of the Berlin Wall in November 1989, many of the published statistics on living standards in communist countries – based on totally different measurement conventions from those used internationally – turned out to bear little correlation with actual conditions. Statisticians in communist countries systematically confused plans with actual achievements. Moreover, the price system of these economies bore no relation whatever to real scarcity prices, so any direct comparison with the capitalist economies was distorted to an unknown extent (see section 13.2 below):

> [The widely quoted income data from UN and CIA sources] were false ... income per-capita in Hungary and Yugoslavia ... in 1988 reached half the level of Greece ... Poland's income per capita ... only matches half the level of Portugal ... It is not true that living conditions in the rich former socialist countries ... were on a par with less advanced nations of Western Europe. Moreover, environmental damages were ignored, medical facilities were inappropriate, housing was poor and social security insufficient. (Siebert, 1991, p. 5)

Statistics published by the World Bank since 1989 compare incomes based on assumptions that come closer to reality, although they are admittedly still questionable (World Bank, 1997). The World Bank estimates markedly lowered income levels for the former central-plan economies relative to non-socialist economies, compared to what has previously been assumed. The income decline in the former central-plan economies since the mid-1980s has been massive (Figure 13.1). It has indeed frequently been more than capitalist western societies experienced in the 1930s during the Great Depression. Virtually all successor states of the Soviet Union and its allies are now in the range of lower middle-income countries, in the same category as the more affluent African and the poorer Latin American nations, and some are now rated by the World Bank among the world's poorest (Figure 13.1). Growth rates were typically negative after the demise of communist regimes in 1989, but the statistics of economic decline may, in

Figure 13.1   The road from socialism: living standards and transformation costs

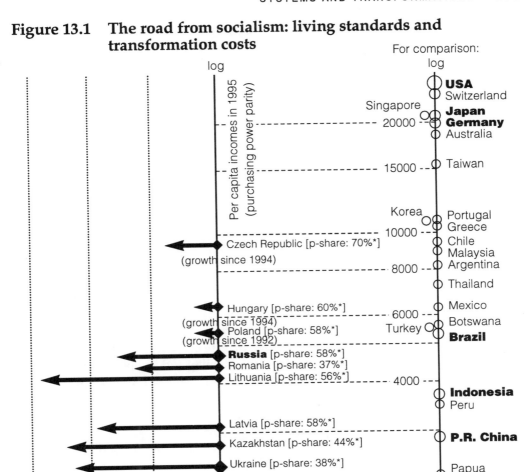

Notes: 1. Estimates of per capita incomes (plotted on the vertical axis) are measured at purchasing power parities in 1995 international US dollars, which seems to be the best basis for international comparisons over a wide income range. On the horizontal axis are depicted rates of change in per capita incomes, but because of statistical limitations it was necessary to use GNP per capita measured at exchange rates, a different and less satisfactory measure of living standards. Note that these data are estimated differently from the long-term income data used in Figure 1.1. 2. *The p-share is private sector output as a percentage of GDP in 1995.

Sources: *World Bank Atlas 1996* (except Taiwan data, which are from national statistics); International Monetary Fund, *World Economic Outlook*, May 1997.

part, reflect the artificial exaggeration of earlier living standards and productivity levels, as well as an under-recording of new, decentralised activities, in particular in services which have been developing rapidly since 1989. As of the mid-1990s, the decline appears to have ended, as fewer productive capacities from the socialist era are 'dying' and many new, market-orientated capacities are being 'born' and are growing.

Comparisons of Growth

It is instructive to compare past growth performance as far as is possible. Although some of the following numbers are crude approximations, comparisons of aggregate per capita statistics indicate massive divergences in economic performance between different economic systems when direct comparisons can be made:

(a) Starting roughly from the same (low) level of incomes after the war, West Germans had reached one of the highest income levels in 1988 by fostering order, private property, competition, constitutional government, economic stability and an open economy during the 1950s and 1960s (see Chapter 14). After 40 years of development under a different system of coordination, the average incomes of East Germans were probably only 40 per cent of those of their western compatriots.

(b) An even bigger difference is evident from a comparison of the increasingly market-orientated Taiwan and communist China. Although the Taiwanese started from a somewhat higher base in the early 1950s, their measured living standards are now some 4.5 to 8 times higher than average living standards in the People's Republic (Figure 13.1). And free-trading Hong Kong citizens reached developed country status within 45 years, with average living standards probably some ten times those in China, despite a big influx of destitute refugees and a total lack of natural resources.

(c) As of 1994, the 36 million overseas Chinese were producing about as much as the 1000 million Chinese operating under the institutions of the People's Republic (Tanzer, 1994, pp. 144–5).

(d) On all available indications, South Koreans, who started from a poorer industry base than the communist North and had to cope with a totally war-ravaged country in the 1950s, are now at least ten times better off materially than their compatriots who live under totalitarian socialism (The Economist, 22 February 1997, p. 33).

(e) Two decades after the end of the Vietnam war, communist Vietnam is still among the poorest nations on earth, whereas neighbouring Thailand and Malaysia – with similar resource endowments and living standards in the 1930s, but open capitalist market economies – have affluent, fast-growing economies. Measured material living standards there appear to be some 20 times those of socialist Vietnam.

Such comparisons indicate only rough orders of magnitude. They do not fully describe the economic condition in the various socioeconomic systems. It has long been accepted in the communist countries that consumers – at least those without access to specific party privileges – had to make sacrifices for 'socialist construction' which would benefit future generations. Rationing of consumer goods was mostly done by queuing, a procedure with high transaction costs for the ordinary citizen, especially women and the aged. Less well known were the increasing shortfalls in across-the-board innovation, net investment and maintenance of the capital stock – the very assets that will benefit future generations. Also, military hardware and its supports deteriorated badly, and this turned out to be one of the reasons why the Soviet elite began to doubt central planning and reliance on coercive means. With hindsight, it is now evident that the international rivalry was lost resoundingly by centrally planned regimes, on social policy and on moral grounds as well. Access for average citizens to education, health and old-age services was poorer than in the West or the newly industrialised countries of East Asia. The destruction of environmental amenities far exceeded anything that democratic societies tolerated. Supervision and control of average citizens and dissidents were pervasive. Consequently, there was widespread cynicism and indifference to what was happening beyond the narrow circle of family and friends. Top-down coercion also encouraged indifference, subservience, shirking, duplicity and careerism, as well as ruthless rent-seeking by Communist Party agents. Freedom of speech, information, travel, career choice and association were denied to ordinary citizens for the sake of maintaining the command economy and the privileges of the leading agents of the regime. These failures explain the speed with which the socialist order collapsed once matters began to unravel in the late 1980s.

O Key Concepts

Socialism is a system of economic institutions in which the property rights to the means of production are predominantly held by agencies of the state. How these property rights (including labour) are used and allocated is determined by agents of government at central, provincial or local level. To facilitate top-down control, the means of production of many internal institutions of civil society have to be replaced by externally designed, predominantly prescriptive institutions, and central planning substituted for spontaneous coordination in markets.

Communism was a Utopian state of affairs which Karl Marx and other communists imagined for a future when the state would wither away and no property rights in the means of production would be assigned to anyone. It was assumed that society would become so productive and affluent that it would be possible for all to consume according to their needs and work according to their capacity and inclination. In that sense of the word, there has never been – and will never be – a communist country, but only socialist regimes that designated themselves 'communist'.

Transformation means 'to be changed or change from one state or regime to another'. In the present context, the term relates to the change of institutions, from predominant collective ownership of productive resources and control of their use by government or party agents, to predominantly private ownership and use according to the decentralised decisions of individuals and private groups.

Convergence was a theory, prevalent from the 1950s to the 1980s, which predicted that the capitalist and the socialist economic systems would gradually but inevitably become the same. Reforms in western capitalist economies and the collapse of socialism in the Soviet orbit proved this theory wrong. ●

13.2   Socialism in Retrospect

Soviet-style Socialism

It seems worth recording, at least briefly, how the problems of economic coordination and use of knowledge were solved in the socialist countries once the constitution of capitalism and the civil society had been abolished. The institutions were revolutionised with brute force in Russia in the confusion of the war year 1917, when V.I. Lenin (1870–1924) invited deserted soldiers and workers, with the slogan 'Loot the looters!', to expropriate all public and private property. He also tried to do away with most traditional institutions of civil society, attempting to replace them with a simpler set of rules. The leaders of the Russian Revolution soon faced the task of having to design some system of economic coordination once they had suppressed the internal and external institutions of tsarist Russia (which had often been arbitrary and deficient). Lenin adopted to the institutions of 'wartime socialism' which he had observed in Germany during the first world war (Johnson, 1983). Government committees were given the task of deciding what the newly nationalised industries should produce in what quantities and qualities, and how these products should be distributed:

> [Collective ownership] will be our salvation ... [it] is something centralised, calculated, controlled and socialised ... [We will achieve] the organisation of accounting control of large enterprises, the transformation of the whole of the state economic mechanism into a single huge machine, into an economic organism that will work in such a way as to enable hundreds of millions of people to be guided by a single plan.
> *(Lenin, 1918, cited in Pipes, 1990, pp. 680–1)*

This was accompanied by a conscious attempt to destroy the institution of money through fostering inflation; the index of consumer prices rose from 100 in 1917 to 85 858 000 in 1923 (ibid., p. 671). In terms of an analogy with computing, it could be said that this amounted to removing the time-tested operating system and other software from the computer of society and imposing a much more primitive new software system. Not surprisingly, the performance of the hardware – the productivity of visible, physical capital, people and their skills – dropped.

There was widespread resistance to the pervasive change of all the known civil and legal institutions – which may have been deficient, unclear and contradictory – and the suppression of all those associations, such as private clubs, parties, churches, cooperatives, which make up civil society. Russians clung to that part of social interaction which was not beholden to the central government. The revolutionary changes therefore had to be enforced by the 'Red Terror' during an extended civil war. Meanwhile, production dwindled. In 1920, coal output was at 27 per cent of the prewar level, iron production only 2.4 per cent, and cotton yarn output 5.1 per cent, for example. It has been estimated that the productivity of the average industrial worker in 1923 was only 30 per cent of the already low level of 1917. Employment fell by half (all these figures are quoted from ibid., pp. 671–97).

In the face of massive administrative failures, the revolutionaries felt compelled to readmit some market mechanisms (New Economic Policy). They embarked on a less ambitious system of central planning, at least temporarily. Altogether, the transformation process was extremely costly, as coordination problems multiplied and the consequences of the liquidation of the known institutional system accumulated. The drive to abolish private property in agriculture (collectivisation) by force during the 1930s led to reductions in production and an estimated 6 million deaths, mainly due to centrally orchestrated starvation.

In the 1930s, the Soviet central planning system was improved and more strictly enforced. This contributed to a rise in productivity and living standards (from very low levels). The system operated on a cycle of five-year plans in which the political elite laid down quantitative objectives for the production of those goods that were considered of particular political or military importance. These objectives (targets) had to be fulfilled, and non-fulfilment often incurred penalties.

Although the planning system went through many permutations, its general *modus operandi* remained: the plans were broken down into annual plans for various industries which were under the command of specific ministries. These normally operated regional offices. The planning process typically began with the managers of production plants signalling current production capacities and wishes for additional investment. Planning authorities then consolidated this information and tried to square planned productive capacities with the mandated political targets which reflected collective demand. All planning was done in terms of quantities of output (material balances). This required information about quantities of input requirements based on a knowledge of production functions. To keep the process manageable, millions of different products and product qualities had to be aggregated into classes of goods. The diversity of inputs quickly becomes an unmanageable problem; for example, when there are plans to build an airliner consisting of 500 000 different components but plan bureaucrats are only conditioned to think in 'tons of aircraft components'. Since targets were set in terms of quantities of output, plant managers often had an incentive to produce heavy output with little concern for quality. The information requirements at the centre, even to replicate last year's production, were thus enormous. Input–output relationships had to be simplified, different qualities to meet specialised purposes often had to be averaged and much product differentiation had to be eliminated. The information generating and processing mechanism of the market was thus replaced by a coordination system which worked much more poorly (Winiecki, 1988).

This economic system was exported after the second world war to the countries of eastern Europe which the Soviet army had occupied, as well as to China after 1949, where it was soon found to be deficient and was abandoned. India and other third world countries emulated Soviet-style planning, but none with any lasting success.

The Knowledge Problem – Once Again

An evaluation of the costs and benefits of alternative products and production methods was simply not possible under socialist economic calculation. There were no market prices to communicate scarcity and allow individuals and organisations to assess their opportunity costs as a basis for economising. This led to efforts from the 1960s onwards to reform the system, and in particular to attach a scarcity price to capital.

Since the profit incentive of privately owned capital was abolished, the Soviet revolutionaries also had to invent a new instrument of economic motivation. Self-interest was replaced by command and enforcement through threats and penalties. Propaganda stressed the achievements of high performers, but in practice people had to be coerced by threats and punishments to fulfil set targets. If managers had obtained low, easily met production targets, they were careful not to surpass them for fear that the target would be raised in the next plan period. Thus, it is reported that tramways in Lublin in Poland ran every month to meet the targeted number of trips. Towards the end of the month, when sufficient trips had been made according to the monthly plan, the tramway ceased operations for a few days, until the new monthly plan began. In many other cases, production was lax for most of the plan period until, towards the end, the pace of production was forced to meet the plan target, often with deleterious consequences for workplace safety and product quality, which brought no reward to the producers. The socialist institutions encouraged compliance with the simple command but discouraged individual initiative and working to the level of capability.

The information and incentive deficiencies of the command economy became even more acute when changes in production structures were required, for example to cope with product innovation. Plant managers may have known of possible product improvements but they had no incentive to enhance the product. Indeed, they faced plan bureaucracies who had strong disincentives to endorse any change, as a new product requires numerous, complex adjustments throughout the economy (only think of the story of the pencil, in the Appendix). Moreover, new products may or may not work to the requirements of the users. In a command system, plant managers and higher administrators receive no reward (other than praise and a medal) for initiating a new product. But they face the danger of a reprimand, demotion or trial before a tribunal if the new product fails to work. The incentives to innovate are thus not commensurate with risks, whether in the case of product innovation or cost control by process innovation.

During the final period of the Soviet system, incentive schemes were developed to encourage applied research and innovation in politically selected priority areas. These incentives were similar to those commonly used by non-socialist governments to promote research and technical development. In western countries, these methods have often led to rent-seeking and principal–agent problems, despite the fact that they face the ultimate control of the market. These problems probably pale into insignificance compared to what happened in the socialist economies. The absence of a workable system of scarcity prices and competitive control of opportunism made the Soviet R&D incentives very ineffective. Rent-seeking and agent opportunism were even more of a handicap in the socialist system because competition as a discovery procedure was systematically suppressed, and government agents knew even less which 'winners' to pick for the preferential spending of R&D funds.

Managers in a system of socialised capital ownership and central planning were not surrounded by the same stringent budget constraints as those faced by their counterparts who manage privately owned assets and have to compete. The 'soft budget constraints' of the socialist system were reflected, for example, in weak pressures to operate at a profit, in the coverage of deficits from the government's budget, in the possibility to negotiate non-payment of taxes and the possibility for well-connected managers to obtain easy credit. The incentives and the information content of capitalism were thus lost and replaced by unclear rules and the arbitrary rule of influential political operators.

The problems with making better use of existing knowledge and with developing and testing new knowledge in the complex division of labour in a modern centrally planned economy had already been diagnosed in the 1920s by Ludwig von Mises ([1920] 1994); they were further analysed by Friedrich von Hayek ([1935] 1948, 1937, 1940, 1945). Both these Austrian economists showed that the information mechanism of competitive markets based on freedom of contract and the incentive mechanism of private property rights could not be done away with without enormous losses of dynamic efficiency. Economic calculation and proper incentives to incur risks are simply impossible in a socialist system.

The Failure of 'Market Socialism'

This basic institutional economics argument provoked a Polish socialist economist, Oskar Lange (1904–65), and other socialists who worked in the West in the 1930s and 1940s to demonstrate that the information role of market prices could be incorporated into a socialist system. They tried to show that market pricing could be made compatible with the abolition of private property (Lange and Taylor, [1939] 1964). They designed an institutional system – called 'market socialism' – which made provision for government-appointed but semi-autonomous plant managers. Their task was to plan production in response to prices according to certain specified rules, so as to maximise profits. The managers should be able to buy and sell in product and labour markets which were assumed to operate as if there were 'perfect competition' (with prices reflecting marginal cost). It was argued that such managers would meet demand more effectively than if they worked to meet quantitative plan targets. They would enhance productivity by following the profit maximisation rule, even when capital ownership was socialised. This system was to make the socialist maxim of collective capital ownership compatible with the market mechanism. But the fundamental incentive problem remains as long as the rewards for successful management cannot be privately appropriated. Innovations could not be incorporated in the model and no premium for successful innovation was foreseen.

The protagonists of 'market socialism' argued that premiums should be paid out of a plant's profit to the managers and workers as an incentive to perform and innovate. This can have motivational effects up to a point, at least if consumer goods are made available. But what if successful people want to accumulate their premiums and want to convert them into savings (store them over time)? They are not permitted to invest in productive assets, as that would violate the central maxim of socialism. The incentive to perform is therefore eroded as long as private people cannot acquire ownership of the means of production.

The price–profit system that Oskar Lange designed cannot remotely overcome the knowledge problem in a complex modern economy with millions of goods of different quality and ongoing evolution. Socialist managers are severely handicapped – compared to autonomous firms in a market economy – when they want to exploit their local knowledge, and central planners can never hope to match price changes with the ceaseless evolution of a complex economic system (Wohlgemuth, 1997, pp. 4–6).

It simply goes against the grain of any economic reasoning to separate decisions on the current allocation of resources from intertemporal allocation between consumption and capital formation; nor does it make sense to decide on the distribution of income as if it were separate from processes of allocation and production. Such efforts to compartmentalise the economic problem are bound to fail. Economists have long known that 'everything depends on everything else', that all economic choices are interdependent. No meaningful system of signalling scarcities and controlling the allocation of scarce resources is feasible when this interdependence is systematically disrupted (Winiecki, 1988; Streit, 1992).[1]

The 'market socialist model' played a role in reforming centrally planned systems after the second world war. Predictably, it failed to match the motivational and coordinative power of capitalist institutions. In Yugoslavia, and later in other 'reform communist' regimes, some semblance of market socialism, with profit incentives to managers and workers, was introduced. Often, the property rights in a plant's means of production were in effect turned over to the collective ownership of the workers at that plant. Within centrally mandated guidelines and subject to the delivery of mandated outputs to the state, the workers were allowed to vote how profits should be used: whether for upgrading and expanding the capital stock, for collective benefits, such as better company housing and factory-run health clinics, or for more holidays and higher wages. Almost invariably the workers voted for higher wages, that is, they wanted to appropriate the gains from their efforts. In practice, they increased their wages at the expense of upgrading or even maintaining the capital stock which in effect belonged to no one. The 'Yugoslav model' thus led to the running-down of the capital stock and poor economic performance due to underinvestment (Pejovich, 1966; Prychitko, 1991; Burkett, in Bornstein, [1965] 1989, pp. 234–58).

The Evolution of Socialism in China

In the late 1970s, the 'Yugoslav model' was also being emulated in China. The strict Soviet-style planning model which China adopted after the revolution in 1949 had been pragmatically jettisoned in the late 1950s because of its patent failures. Mao Zedong instigated continuous revolution in the 1960s and early 1970s to prevent opportunistic agents of party and government entrenching their power and to stay in control himself. Mao also aspired to create a new, selfless man who would be motivated solely by solidarity with the community. But the continual upset of any semblance of order had dire consequences for living standards, personal security and freedom (see box).

❖ The Rule of Men: an Insider's View

I thought of China as one huge family and believed we needed a head. Chairman Mao was the chief [p. 127].

It was not until the Great Leap Forward, when millions of Chinese began dying during the famine, that I became aware of how much Mao resembled the ruthless emperors he so admired. Mao knew that people were dying by the millions. He did not care [p. 125].

The individual was merely a tiny cog in a large and complex machine. If the cog performed its functions well, it could be of use to the machine. At the slightest complaint, the smallest deviation from the norm, the cog could be thrown aside [p. 65].

... the country's scientists and intellectuals had never recovered [from the purges of 1957], ... hundreds of thousands had been fired, demoted, or sent to do labor reform. A pall of depression continued to hang over the intellectual community. Even those who had not suffered direct political persecution existed in a perpetual state of fear, afraid to speak out, [and] forced to attend so many political meetings that their capacity to work had suffered [p. 389].

The awful poverty afflicting Chinese villagers and the injustice of the type of class struggle I was witnessing [during the Cultural Revolution] ... depressed me. After sixteen years of revolution, it seemed to me that China had not progressed at all. The standard of living was terrible. The government was cruel. Life for the disenfranchised was harsh. However bad life may have been under the Guomindang, hard work and good luck had always brought rewards. Poor people with talent had a chance to rise to the top. ... Change for the better was always a hope [p. 429].

As the Cultural Revolution turned first against this enemy and then against that, as the Communist party was decimated ... the people of China became fed up, disgusted. They were coming to see the political campaigns for what they really were – naked high-level power struggles that had little to do with them [p. 578].

I write this book ... for everyone who cherishes freedom. I want it to serve as a reminder of the terrible consequences of Mao's dictatorship and of how good and talented people living under his regime were forced to violate their consciences and sacrifice their ideals in order to survive [p. 638]. ◆

(Source: Li Zhisui, The Private Life of Chairman Mao, 1994)

Note: Dr Li served during Mao Zedong's last 22 years as his personal physician. He wrote this autobiographical book after moving to the US in 1988.

Mao's successors tried market socialist experiments in the late 1970s but – as elsewhere where variants of the 'Yugoslav model' were tried out – workers and plant managers voted for high pay-outs (on-the-job consumption, higher wages) and neglected to reinvest in the capital stock. This is not surprising as the capital stock had no champion, whereas workers and directors had the motivation to appropriate profits for their own personal enjoyment. The various failed reforms of socialism led Deng Xiaoping to make the remark that he did not care whether the cat was red (collectively owned) or black (privately owned), as long as it caught the mice. By the late 1980s, China had a fairly liberalised economy where allocational decisions on about 60 per cent of all goods and services are undertaken by private individuals and firms (a bigger share than, for example, in Germany). The economy is increasingly open to the world market, but party commissars and officials often try to extract rents from producers. What remains of the state industry sector tends to incur heavy losses. These are compensated for by budget subsidies, which puts a heavy burden on the emerging private sector and fuels inflationary ways of covering budget deficits. It has led to a decline in real living standards among those in the state sector. Workers and pensioners of state enterprises now experience marked drops in living standards compared with those who work in private enterprises. In 1997, the party – under a new principle of 'seizing the large and releasing the small' – decided to sell off or close numerous small, loss-making state-owned enterprises and to concentrate on keeping about 1000 large ones in socialised ownership (International Monetary Fund, 1997, pp. 119–27).

Privatisation of the Communes

The biggest *de facto* privatisation of collectively held property ever attempted occurred in the late 1970s and early 1980s when the Chinese authorities conducted a decollectivisation of agriculture. The land and capital used in Chinese agriculture had been taken out of private ownership in the 1950s. All collectively owned land was aggregated into huge 'people's communes' in the late 1950s and early 1960s. Tens, if not hundreds, of thousands of rural workers were coordinated under a command structure and instructed by the political leaders of the communal organisation what to plant, when to plant and harvest, as well as all the other details of their daily work. In the second half of the 1950s, orders were issued by Beijing Centre to accelerate rice production and build up rural industries in a campaign named the 'Great Leap Forward'. Because the party had set a target to overtake Britain in iron and steel production, small-scale furnaces were set up in backyards all over China. Frequently, knives and iron bedsteads were converted into inferior metal – to meet production targets for new knives and iron bedsteads. Forests were destroyed to fuel the exercise. The centrally steered campaign of the 'Great Leap Forward' to collectivise agriculture created great confusion and malcoordination, from which massive famine resulted.

Some 30 million Chinese are estimated to have starved to death as a consequence of this experiment in 'social engineering' (Becker, 1996), repeating and outdoing the consequences of forced collectivisation in the Soviet Union during the 1930s. In the early 1960s, Chinese agriculture recovered, but food distribution was soon seriously disrupted again by the 'Cultural Revolution', another centralised political campaign that caused massive disruption to production, exchange and people's daily lives.

By the late 1970s, after Mao's death, there were food riots in the inland province of Sichuan in western China. Provincial party leaders knew of no solution other than to disband the communes and allot land to farmers. Families were not given clear legal property rights, but there was a firm understanding that 'household units' (families) would be able to till the allocated land in the future more or less as they saw fit, and that they could pass the land on to their children and sell it. They were permitted to sell their produce freely in private markets once officially claimed plan quotas had been delivered to the government for a fixed (low) price. Produce delivered under plan quotas was channelled into the state trading system to supply the cities with low-cost bulk food.

The results of the Sichuan reforms were dramatic. Food supplies went up by 50 per cent within two years and a much greater variety of fresh food became available (Kasper, 1981). Even fresh fruit reappeared in the cities. Farmers once more found it rewarding to harvest and transport peaches to urban markets, whereas they had previously fed the fruit to pigs or distilled brandy for their own consumption because the plan had not set a target for peaches. The central planning system simply had not been able to make provision for the expedient distribution of fruit which spoiled quickly. Instead, effort was concentrated on durable foodstuffs which could be more easily handled through central planning and distribution.

The positive experiences with reform in Sichuan soon spread the new concepts to all peasants as well as to part of manufacturing throughout China. The commune system, which had been a much-reported rural innovation, vanished quickly and with little comment from western economists. The biggest ever system transformation, affecting over 500 million rural Chinese, was achieved without great problems and ushered in a decade of very rapid increases in rural living standards.[2]

As of the mid-1990s, the state's role in the economy has been greatly reduced, and the dynamic non-state sector now generates two-thirds of the national product. The economy is increasingly open to trade and foreign investment and macroeconomic management has passed to a considerable extent to an increasingly independent central bank.

These institutional changes have gone along with spectacular economic growth (1979–97: 9.4 per cent per annum, a fivefold rise in gross domestic product). The improved institutions have not only mobilised much capital investment but have also substantially contributed to the improved productivity of capital, labour and skills (International Monetary Fund, 1997, p. 123), underlining the crucial importance of appropriate institutions to economic growth (section 1.3).

Whither after Socialism?

China still has a large state-owned sector which obtains quasi-automatic budget subsidies, as long as the managers in charge are well-connected. As of the mid-1990s, some 100 million workers are employed in the ailing state enterprise sector. Half the 100 000 state firms operate at a loss and another 30 000 barely break even. Segments of state industry are now allowed to whither away. In 1997, when the government decided to privatise or devolve many state-owned enterprises, it sent out strong signals that a growing part of the economy would be subject to market signals and strict budget constraints. The Communist Party leadership also decided to subject the residual state sector to the institutional disciplines of *de facto* capitalism by corporatising it, strictly separating ownership from management. These moves no doubt have much to do with the apparent successes of the capitalist system elsewhere in East Asia and the fast economic growth in China's private industries and in the (fairly) free enterprise zones within China. In these special economic zones, the Chinese leadership conducted pragmatic experiments with different non-communist institutions, allowing private property, stock markets and freedom from *dirigiste* regulation of factor and product markets (International Monetary Fund, 1997, pp. 119–27). This was a pragmatic way to find out what worked best to enhance productivity and innovation.

Although China's emerging market system is not well supported by a protective state and consistent, stable institutions, important institutional changes are taking place, albeit often in unclear and indirect ways. Private entrepreneurs often have to rely on personal networks and the business acumen of self-interested officials. And managers of many public firms, in particular in the coastal provinces, are faced with openness to world market competition and tightened budget constraints. Local authorities, which control many public enterprises, now have to cultivate their revenue base; they cannot afford to maintain poorly run firms, so they impose 'hard budget constraints' on the managers of the collective enterprises they own. By contrast, provinces in the interior depended for longer on fiscal transfers from the centre and therefore operated their enterprises with less stringent budget constraints. At the same time, operators in these provinces were isolated from most world market pressures. As a consequence of these institutional differences, less modernisation occurred and costs were less closely controlled (Raiser, 1997). However, as of the 1990s, increasingly interjurisdictional rivalry can be seen. In many instances, this seems to offer a reasonably effective, though uneven, protection of the emerging new economic order in China (see box).

In parts of China as well as in parts of the Vietnamese economy, socialist rhetoric no longer has any great effect on actual institutions. However, politically powerful members of the Communist Party often lay corrupt claim to property rights when they observe economic successes. Often people with political clout alter the rules arbitrarily and extort payments from successful private enterprises. The socialist system has thus been eroded, but few universal capitalist institutions are in place. Property rights are ill-defined; credible commitments are difficult to make; market contracts can often not be enforced; laws and regulations are often intransparent and arbitrary. It is why much exchange and credit is personalised and conducted among well-connected people. This is not dissimilar to the situation in Europe before the rule of law was asserted by a rising merchant class and the bourgeoisie. After the Middle Ages, when Europeans reached the limits of interpersonal exchange and credit, they demanded firm government institutions to protect their market exchanges; in other words, they demanded the extended order of the rule of law and genuine markets for protected property rights.

❖ China's Second Revolution: Institutional Reform

From a press article about the legacy of Deng Xiaoping

[During the Deng era, 1978–92] China's per capita income ... roughly quadrupled ... the benefits were spread widely throughout the population ... China stabilized internally ... and achieved rapid technological advance ...

... in the mid-1970s, Chinese people could not choose their own haircuts, their own clothes, or their own jobs. They were watched every minute through neighbourhood associations. They went to endless political education classes and were grilled ceaselessly on their political beliefs ...

Today, the people of China choose their colorful clothes and stylish haircuts. They increasingly move around the country and change jobs according to their own wishes. They hear not just their leaders' opinions, but also those of foreigners – through the radio, the TV, and direct contact with foreigners ... The Chinese of today have diverse opinions which they express vigorously, including personal opinions highly critical of the government ...

In the 1990s, the Chinese government has acknowledged the right of the people to sue the government and the Party. However ... inadequate the implementation ... the emergence of a right to sue the government in formerly totalitarian China ... is a milestone in the global development of human rights ... recent years have seen ... limitations on the rights of police to hold prisoners indefinitely without charge, of limitations on the Ministry of Justice's control over lawyers, and on respect for the concept of the rule of law ... And China now has roughly four million competitively elected local officials ... .

As trade, tourism and television opened the country, people's minds were liberated. As China's economy changed from one where 100% of the working people were employed by the government to one where fewer than 20% were, the government lost one of its principal levers of totalitarian control ... As business reached ... [large] scale ... businesses demanded the assurance of institutionalized law. As the regime sought scientific progress ... [it] had to acknowledge the legitimacy of open debate in a large number of areas ... China ... sent ... its ... elite students [overseas], ... no totalitarian thought controls could possibly survive that decision.

Determined to achieve his economic goals [Deng] ... reluctantly conceded unintended freedoms in area after area. ◆

(William H. Overholt, 'One Man's Legacy for One Billion', Asian Wall Street Journal, 26 February 1997)

The Israeli Kibbutz System

Another experiment in doing away with private property rights and creating a 'new, selfless man' (and woman) deserves at least passing reference: the kibbutz system in Israel. Starting in 1909, inspired socialists set up communities of volunteers on rural land, which often needed development. The ownership of all land and other resources was kept in collective hands. Normally, production was organised by command and ordered in a hierarchical, planned way, but with worker co-determination. Consumption was also organised by central allocation and often delivered in common facilities such as canteens and clubs. As long as kibbutz workers were idealistic, lifestyle alternatives limited and the size of the kibbutz remained small, the system offered sufficient motivation to be productive. But soon voluntarism had to be supplemented by moral suasion and means of coercion. Individuals were discontented with communal consumption, and wished instead to pursue their own diverse private purposes. As people grew older and started families, many opted out into the alternative free market system. Consequently, the contribution of the kibbutz experiment to the Israeli economy has declined in relative importance.

O Key Concepts

Civil society consists of the individuals and the free associations and organisations that individuals form, as well as the internal institutions that govern their interaction. It is that part of society that is independent of the political power of government. Totalitarian regimes have tried to replace these pluralist networks by external institutions and by organisations that depend on government. Part of the recovery from socialism is the renewed cultivation of civil society.

The **central plan** was a central compilation of production plans for individual products and groups of products. It set obligatory output targets (**quotas**) for selected types of products and production units. The various production plans and resource uses were made compatible with each other *ex ante*, that is, coordination took place before the production period began. In the Soviet Union, central plans were drawn up on a four- or five-year cycle, with more specific annual or quarterly plans, which were often also regionally disaggregated. The main coordination task was in the hands of the Central Plan Office.

The **New Economic Policy** (NEP) was adopted in 1921 in the Soviet Union after the initial experiment in abolishing property rights had led to economic collapse. The NEP made some allowance for private initiative and markets, for example permitting farmers to sell output over and above the plan quota in free markets and allowing the government to grant licences to foreign-owned private industrial enterprises. The NEP led to a recovery in the war- and socialisation-ravaged economy. However, in 1927–8 the NEP was abolished in favour of more comprehensive control of economic activities.

The **Mises–Lange debate** was one of the great classical controversies about institutional systems. Ludwig von Mises had shown in the 1920s what enormous difficulties socialist calculation had to face. He deduced from his analysis that it was humanly impossible to centrally plan widespread, across-the-board production, consumption and capital accumulation, let alone innovation. Von Mises and Hayek asserted the superiority of the decentralised market system and the private holding of property rights in the means of production, and in so doing gained new insights into coordination in complex systems, thus advancing Austrian economics.

Oskar Lange tried to show in the 1930s how the benefits of a system of market prices in accordance with the model of 'perfect competition' could be incorporated into a system of collective ownership of the means of production (called **market socialism**). As von Mises and Hayek had predicted, the Lange model, when it inspired reforms of communist economies, failed to secure satisfactory outcomes in current production and failed to offer incentives for capital accumulation and innovation. Managers of government firms often behaved opportunistically because they faced soft budget constraints, that is, they could obtain resources from the government when their spending exceeded their receipts. No solution was found for allocating resources intertemporally, that is, between current spending and saving. The approach was bound to fail because it had no means of coping with the general interdependency of all economic decisions.

The **Third Way** is advocated by some observers (for example, democratic socialists) to permit the private ownership of many means of production, but combined with comprehensive controls on the use of these property rights for collectively determined purposes. What was said in Chapter 10 about the incompatibility of protective government and pervasive redistribution of property rights applies to the concept of the Third Way. ●

13.3   Transforming Socialist Economies

The Collapse of Soviet-style Socialism

Whereas the *de facto* transformation of centrally planned socialism in Asia (except in North Korea) has followed a pragmatic path, the socialist system in the former Soviet bloc collapsed spectacularly in 1989 under the cumulative burden of its failures, which economic analysts such as von Mises and Hayek had long predicted.[3] In the 1950s and 1960s there had been popular uprisings against the imposed centralised order. The use of force, with the Red Army as the ultimate backstop, had prevented the abandonment of socialist institutions. Gradually, after the 1970s, economic growth slowed down and social indicators, such as mortality rates, even pointed to an absolute deterioration in living standards. While the imposed order had been more strictly – often brutally – enforced in the era of Jossif Stalin, the Soviet dictator from 1924 to 1953, enforcement was gradually relaxed after his death. Consequently, economic performance slackened. Despite strict controls on international travel and information flows, the citizens in communist countries also became increasingly aware of the amenities of life and the freedom that people in the capitalist market economies were enjoying, due not least to the spread of new communications technologies.

In the 1980s, the leadership of several socialist countries attempted economic reforms of the system. The intention was not primarily to liberate 'the masses', but to overcome the increasingly obvious failures of the Leninist system. Reform failed consistently to deliver across-the-board economic growth and technical innovation, while the capitalist West and the new industrial countries were forging ahead with a great variety of innovations. In the end, socialism simply imploded. It left behind an uncompetitive structure of production, a worn-out, poorly maintained capital stock, run-down housing and health-care facilities, a badly damaged environment and, last but not least, poor skills and a people insufficiently motivated to be responsible for themselves. The failures of socialist central planning which became obvious left even ardent western critics of socialism surprised.

By 1989, it was clear to most citizens of the unravelling Soviet empire that the system of central planning and political coercion had to be abolished. But it was not so clear to most of them what new institutions would be needed and how the necessary institutional changes should be initiated. Many intellectuals and citizens wanted to retain widespread public welfare provision (subsidised access to publicly owned housing, kindergartens, health services and so on) and to control private property rights through strict regulation. Considerable reservations about the capitalist system were widely held. This led many to advocate a 'Third Way', an untidy amalgam of individual political liberties and economic controls, based on a Utopian vision of an ideal society and pretended knowledge of how such a society should be designed and ordered. Governments were henceforth to be led by non-coercive, well-meaning leaders. The commercial disciplines of capitalism, though unfamiliar, were often rejected as morally inferior to a 'tribal morality' that appealed to love, solidarity and voluntary sharing. Many of these observers would reject what has been said in this book about motivation (section 2.3) and the values of the individualistic commercial order (section 3.3 and Chapter 6).

Few East European observers had the clarity of vision of the then Czechoslovak Finance Minister, later Czech Prime Minister, Václav Klaus, who dismissed this school of thought with the remark that 'the Third Way is the fastest road to the Third World', as he saw that such a poorly defined system would not create the incentives for unlearning habits of helplessness, for productive effort and for better mobilisation of resources.

The Essentials of Transformation

The transformation of the socialist economic system is a most complex task in which many interactive changes have to take place in ways that no single mind can fully comprehend. From the standpoint of institutional economics, the transformation process has at least a known and well-founded objective, namely the basic conditions of a capitalist order, as summarised in Table 13.1:

(a) Private citizens must claim their civil, economic and political liberties, including the right to sell their own labour and skills freely, to own property, to associate, to seek information, to speak out and to move about. The resumption of free contracts and property ownership implies that responsibility for material and spiritual wellbeing must be reprivatised, too.

(b) Producer organisations, which previously had to obey directives from the central plan bureaucracy, must be made autonomous and self-responsible. The owners and the managers have to relearn how to be responsible for their profits as well as their losses; in other words, they must learn to make decisions under strict budget constraints. For this reason, firms need to be turned into independent legal entities which have the freedom to contract, including being fully liable for contracts entered into. This requires back-up by company law and a commercial code, as well as the administrative and judicial organisation and knowhow to support these laws. Judges and commercial lawyers have to be trained.

(c) The role of government had to be rethought from the foundations up. The maxim for its existence is not some notion of national grandeur or presumed 'iron laws of history', but service to the principals, the citizens. After the collapse of communism, the principle of rule-bound, constitutional and limited government needs to be recognised in theory and entrenched in practice. Strong institutional controls and accountability are required to control deeply rooted agent opportunism. The rule of law has to be imposed on all government agents. As long as government agencies act on the assumption that they do not have to pay their bills and that they are above the law, this essential requirement is violated.[4] Given regional and sectarian tensions in many formerly centralised communist countries, multilevel government with a strong commitment to subsidiarity and competitive federalism will confer distinct advantages (section 12.4).

Transformation requires a strong commitment to the protective function of government, not least to draw a line below the socialist past, when citizens' freedoms and the institutions of civil society

Table 13.1   Checklist of essentials for systems transformation to a market economy

Area of reform	Institutional goals	Organisational support
Private citizens	Civil, economic and political liberties; establishing private responsibility	Civil and economic law; private property and autonomy; civil courts and police subject to the rule of law
Firms	As above; autonomy in decision making; freedom of contract; liability	Corporatisation; privatisation; commercial code; courts; standards of accounting; capital markets, labour markets; banking legislation and prudential supervision
Government	Protection of the rule of law (rule-bound, limited constitutional government); control of agent opportunism; subsidiarity	Definition of the essential tasks of government in a constitution; reduction in the size of government; phasing out subsidies; administrative law; budget reform and establishment of a system of effective tax collection; assistance with (soft and hard) infrastructures, privatisation; independent central bank with the task of pursuing monetary stability; devolution of tasks to local and regional governments; independent judiciary
	Redistribution	Measures to establish equality of opportunity; minimal social safety net; provision of access to, but not necessarily production of, public services
International economic relations	Opening the economy	Freedom of movement; liberalisation of trade; currency convertibility; flexible exchange rates (membership of WTO, IMF and other international bodies that cultivate rules of open international interaction)

were poorly protected. None the less, it can be argued that older citizens contributed during their working lives to the collective economic effort and now depend on the government for old-age support and other basic services. It must be acknowledged that they have acquired some property claim on the socialised capital stock. A minimum social safety net may also have to be created to ensure minimum standards of equity of outcomes, at least for the very young, the old and the ill. It can be accepted that this is an investment in social stability, even if it creates conflicts with formal justice, freedom and incentives (section 10.1).

(d) Given the powerful influence of international competition and factor mobility, the transformation process and the imposition of strict budget constraints will need the stimulus of openness in order to develop the necessary momentum. The freedom to travel abroad, to become informed of how people operate elsewhere and to trade internationally helps to convey much-needed knowledge to people who lived for one or two generations under a different set of institutions. Likewise, international investment and payments must be liberalised to open up opportunities of a better international division of labour, to transfer productive and business knowhow and to exert competitive stimuli. Currency controls need to be abolished, so that the exchange rate can reflect world market prices. Domestic markets will then be informed by world price information.

In some post-communist countries, these essential institutional changes have been made more quickly and consistently than in others, often in the face of popular resentment and electoral backlash. In others, the essentials have been implemented spasmodically and incompletely, so the institutions are now at least in part contradictory and decision makers still operate with institutions that make for fuzzy market signals (soft budget constraints; Raiser, 1997). Moreover, reforms have sometimes moved on a zigzag course, disorientating private coordination, hampering private initiative and harming living standards.

A New Role for Government

Paradoxically, these minimum institutional objectives for the transformation of a socialist economy cannot be realised without collective action. Government power is needed to undo government powers. The institutional arrangements listed in Table 13.1 also require organisational support from private associations and business organisations. Government has to legislate and enforce a code of civil and commercial laws, presumably anchored in a new constitution. Courts and police have to be educated to administer the new law, and the various agencies of government have to be supervised and made accountable. This is a major task from the starting point of a totalitarian police state. Businesses that were previously government-owned need to be corporatised, that is, taken out of the undifferentiated state sector and made accountable against strict budget constraints. And most of them need to be privatised: the titles of ownership, which were held collectively, must somehow be allocated separately to individual owners. One way to effect this important institutional change is to give vouchers to all citizens with which they can acquire state assets of their choice at auction, from the housing stock to shares in large companies and public-domain utilities that own and run infrastructures.

Government leaders in the formerly communist countries face a knowledge problem when they want to privatise: no one knows what the government owns and how much it is worth. One way to begin privatisation is the method that became known in the Czech Republic as 'strawberry picking'. Teams of agents swarm out and pick promising state-owned objects that are being sold off. No one knows how many such objects there are, as more and more privatisation objects are being picked and sold off. No one knows how fast the prices paid at auctions will be amortised, if at all, since so many variables of commercial success remain unknown. However, people (re)learn the institutions of markets and property ownership, and government agencies develop administrative skills to protect the emerging order. Thus, the conditions for commercial success are gradually being created. Governments also have to decree a commercial code and clear bankruptcy laws which give substance to freedom of contract. Also, a coherent judicial system, various public registries (land title, shares and so on) and expert supervisory bodies (bank supervision, commercial standards arbitration) are needed to run private ownership at low transaction costs and with a low risk of fraud. While the implementation of accounting standards and practices of economic calculation is a private matter, governments can do much to assist to reduce the information costs and to speed up learning processes.

It is not strictly necessary for the institutions that underpin factor and product markets to be set up by collective action. Considering the actual track record of governments in general and noting that the institutions underpinning the market economy in the West are largely the result of long evolutionary processes, one may be sceptical about collective action to establish capitalism (de Jasay, 1995). The degree of scepticism may vary from country to country, according to historical experience, shared values and norms (Voigt, 1993). In principle, a protective state can make a major contribution to fostering and supporting the internal institutions of a newly developing market economy. It can do much to limit the disproportionately high information and transaction costs during transformation. Well-targeted, consistent and limited collective action can provide some fixed points from which new rules can crystallise. In the extreme case of total system transformation, government probably has scale economies in creating that 'gossamer veil' of essential institutions that we mentioned in Chapter 1. This seems particularly urgent in the case of credit and banking and in providing the supervision of prudential norms to avoid bank collapses and commercial fraud. Delays in the emergence of financial order are costly, because money and credit depend on credible institutions and are of central importance to a well-functioning market economy.

The first task in the transformation to a capitalist system is probably to demobilise the huge bureaucracies that exerted enormous power under socialism, a task similar to the disbanding of armies after a war. This is necessary not only to cut back government cost to the private economy, but also to overcome the resistance of organised bureaucratic pressure groups with a stake in continued pervasive intervention. Another way of cutting public expenditure is to phase out quickly all subsidies to producers. It also seems necessary to introduce standards of accountability in government similar to those in business, preferably by introducing not only income–expenditure budgets but also, in view of the major changes in public assets and liabilities, government balance sheets that show independently assessed assets, liabilities and future contingencies. Such information is useful to determine which actions are useful and which create losses. The proceeds of privatisation must certainly not be considered as revenues available for funding new recurrent expenditures, because privatisation is only a rearrangement of property rights. A major aim is to define the tasks of minimal government and how they will be administered and to design effective, broad-based taxes to finance these tasks. When tax collection falls far short of public spending, this is a major case of government failure.

It is open to debate whether transformation governments should provide all the hard infrastructures, given the very limited capabilities of the new administrations and their lack of experience in economic calculation and coordination. Since new electronic measurement technology is now available, there is an argument for private producers, that is, the owners of newly privatised utilities or competing new investors in public-domain infrastructures, to leap-frog into the competitive provision of public-domain services such as electric power, water, roads, mass transport and communications.

A central collective task in creating a new post-socialist order is to guarantee stable money (Sachs, 1995). When so many variables change, as is inevitably the case during transformation, it is essential that market prices are signalled as clearly as possible to reflect changing scarcities and opportunities. Relative price changes should therefore not be overlaid with hard-to-interpret inflation disturbances. During transformation, individuals and firms have an information problem that far surpasses what people normally face. The task of providing stable money requires the creation of a two-tier banking system: the first tier comprising a central bank which oversees the fiduciary standards of commercial banks and is itself aloof from the second-tier private banking business. A strong and independent central bank therefore is a necessary institutional and organisational reform. In any event, citizens should have access to alternative foreign moneys (free convertibility) and should be able to quote prices in foreign currencies. If their administrative capacities are limited, governments may of course explicitly forgo the role of central banking. Indeed, foreign money could be allowed to circulate. With some restrictions, this is now the case in Russia and Vietnam, where poor monetary management has caused high rates of inflation. Alternatively, transformation governments may set up a currency board system or allow several trusted domestic commercial banks to supply their own bank notes in competition with foreign moneys.

Changing Perceptions and Expectations

These are daunting tasks, and they demand much of inexperienced parliamentarians, political leaders and administrators. Their enormity makes it necessary for parliaments and governments to concentrate on the universal essential rules and a few simple organisations (as summarised in Table 13.1 above). Economising on people's necessary coordination work and information gathering is an essential precondition for success. That means that governments abstain from specific intervention and redistribution policies. Only then will property rights and effective markets emerge and a new order be spontaneously discerned by more and more people. This will occur only if there is no interference with market signals and property rights; indeed, if they are expressly protected from interference by parliamentarians and administrators.

As we noted, openness is a precondition for attracting foreign capital, knowledge and firms to the transition economies and compensating for structural rigidities in the domestic economy. Openness is essential, given typically low propensities to save and the underdeveloped capital markets. It may also help to overcome resistance when people are exposed to competition and privileges are withdrawn. When growing numbers of workers gain income from companies to which foreigners contribute knowhow, capital and export market access, this becomes a valuable antidote to xenophobia. Governments faced with the complex task of institutional transformation also need access to international bodies which cultivate rules of non-discriminatory behaviour and help to transfer knowledge about collective management, such as the World Trade Organisation (WTO), the International Monetary Fund (IMF), and the Organisation for Economic Cooperation and Development (OECD).

Transformation inevitably creates a great discontinuity of expectations. It invalidates the former, familiar means of coordination. The old institutions – ineffectual though they may have been compared to a market system – are taken away, but a new system of institutions does not develop overnight. What may survive of the old institutions is the shadow economy with its adaptability and self-organising capabilities. Black markets and informal, if not illegal, exchanges formed an important part of all socialist systems. Unfortunately, the shadow economy also displays some unpleasant, at times criminal, features. They will persist as long as the internal institutions are weak and the rule of law is not backed effectively by governments. In a positive sense, the shadow economy can serve as a means for the 'transformation from below' (Naishul, 1993). 'Spontaneous privatisation' (the hijacking of government-owned assets) may help to speed the process of transformation, although this violates principles of justice and equity and helps to entrench old power elites. However, since the rules change and are uncertain, it is quite possible that black markets will become more competitive and gradually turn into valuable 'white markets' which are training grounds for entrepreneurs and the use of property rights (Shleiffer, 1995; Jefferson and Rawski, 1995). It is also possible that criminal operators may discover the advantages of a 'truce' on violence and fraud and begin to enforce proper institutions in their dealings.

Once a centrally planned regime is beyond repair and has been suspended, temporary losses of output and employment seem unavoidable. The speed with which the new system of spontaneous coordination can put down roots and yield superior results depends on the clarity, consistency and speed of the institutional reforms. An important point is whether the transformation should be done in one 'big bang' or gradually. Experiences with the evolution of existing economic systems offer little guidance on this question. Arguments for gradualism are that learning is normally gradual and that change is easier to absorb constructively if it is evolutionary. But once the old system is totally discredited, there is an advantage in moving quickly to the new rules and in ensuring that change occurs on all fronts. Slow reform only leaves time for old and new rent-seeking coalitions to form and build up resistance to further change. Slow reform also makes for distortions of relative prices, as some sectors are freed up and others still lag behind. The incompatibility of suborders is always the source of instability and loss of effectiveness in coordination.

There is therefore considerable strategic advantage in moving quickly, consistently and completely to new rules (big bang), even if that destabilises expectations over the short run and if there is political resistance. Arguably, the voice of old interest groups will be heard less in response to a consistent and proactive reform package than with hesitant or reluctant gradualism. The new institutions will be learnt and adopted more expediently if they are simple, universal and largely proscriptive. To make such a clean and sweeping transition requires a government willing and capable of doing it, which in turn requires a new political system that is sufficiently consolidated and popularly supported. As we shall see below, this condition has not been fulfilled in a considerable number of formerly socialist countries. In that case, it becomes simply impossible to steer a consistent course of transformation. The costs of transformation will be correspondingly higher and longer lasting.

Transition is bound to cause real costs, as many skills and capital stocks which were built up under central planning prove to be of little value once consumer preferences count and world market prices are applied. Indeed, once world market prices are applied to inputs and outputs, it will often become apparent that producers were previously engaged in value destruction rather than value adding. Thus, Polish producers of orchids discovered that they were incurring much higher energy and other resource costs than they could earn from their orchids in export markets, once they had to pay market prices for energy, labour and the use of hothouses. In a world competitive economy, structures of distribution and trade have to be reworked, and socialist factories, which were fairly autarchic, will have to spin off marginal support operations to make the best of their core assets. Discovering profitable lines of production poses a major knowledge problem during institutional transformation: indeed, the entire transformation problem can be seen ultimately as a major knowledge problem. From this it follows that nothing should be done which impedes discovery procedures and learning during the transition.

In the first half-decade after the collapse of communism, the economic order in all the formerly planned socialist economies moved in the direction set out in Table 13.1, but typically in haphazard ways, with reversals and often massive rent-seeking by the organised groups which had power in the former regimes.

Political Problems

In essence, the problems of transformation are not dissimilar to the problems of reforming the institutions of mixed economies and mature democracies (which will be discussed in the next chapter). However, the resistance to change is likely to be disproportionately greater when the entire rule system is to be transformed. More deeply entrenched and more massive privileges have to be taken away from well-organised groups – the *nomenklatura*, the managers of the military-industrial complex and privileged groups of workers, as well as the general bureaucracy. These privileges have to be withdrawn to make room for individual freedom and self-responsibility. The system of state-provided social security also needs to be reshaped, slimmed down and better targeted. This is not an easy task for political reformers in a new, insecure democratic setting.

The withdrawal of privileges and cuts in the public provision of social security are felt immediately whereas the benefits take time to materialise. They are widely and thinly spread. Gains can therefore not be easily attributed to specific reforms measures. It is not easy for individuals to realise that risk-taking and self-responsibility are nothing but the reverse side of freedom and that material security in that situation conflicts with freedom (Chapter 4).

In the inevitable disorientation of transformation, it is easy to lose sight of the fact that the price for a perceived sense of security was serfdom, fear, low living standards with little consumer choice, and unsustainable degradation of the natural environment. It may often be difficult for the population to conclude from the collapse of socialism that the system was, after all, not able to guarantee material security. Popular misapprehensions, the shock of the system's collapse and the inevitable changes in policy make it easy for populist interest groups to gather support against reforms and for a return to collectivism. This paves the way for election reversals and time inconsistencies in the reform strategy, which in turn increases people's cognitive burdens when the institutions give little assistance to perception, and when it is very difficult for entrepreneurs to discover avenues to prosperity.

Any reversal in the reform process makes it much harder for citizens to discern the emerging order. It imposes massive costs in terms of disorientation and economic burdens. All transformation economies therefore have registered declines in living standards. Government leaders and parliamentarians failed to set up minimum institutional support for market institutions. Indeed, they often added to the confusion, for example, by allowing inflation to run out of control. As prices were freed, it was therefore often not clear to individuals and potential producers whether observed price rises signalled a scarcity and an opportunity to produce, or whether it was part of the unpredictable general inflation. In the chaos of transition, many voters understandably began to hanker after the old familiar order.

What was said about basic attitudes under the rubric of the commercial and the guardian syndromes in section 6.2 also has a bearing on systems transformation. Marxism was an extension of tribal morality to macro society. It had immediate popular appeal. Loyalty, obedience, sharing and authority are virtues that were preached in socialist societies which were structured as hierarchical organisations. By contrast, the virtues of the commercial world – not sharing, but accumulating, competing, questioning authority and the like – can only take root after long and regular practice. They contain knowhow that cannot easily be made explicit and needs to be acquired through practice. It is therefore not surprising that the internal institutions of a free, open society do not emerge spontaneously and that many people lament the passing of collectively engineered social cohesion. It will take time and constant practice to acquire the internal institutions and the commercial ethics which ensure that an individualist economic system functions effectively and that populist political entrepreneurs cannot gain political support by advocating a return to the failed, old system or the pursuit of a 'Third Way'.

O Key Concepts

Privatisation is the assignment of previously collective property rights to specific private owners. This can be done by a number of different mechanisms:

- restitution of property rights to previous private owners, in some cases after possibly complicated and drawn-out processes of proving previous legal title; where specific restitution is found too costly in terms of transaction costs, previous owners may receive monetary compensation which they can use to buy new property titles;
- outright sale to domestic and foreign buyers, either to a new individual owner or a newly formed group of share owners;

- exchange of specific property titles for vouchers that have previously been distributed to citizens (**voucher privatisation**);
- donation of collective property to current managers or other classes of people, for example, assigning property title to apartments and houses to those who happen to live in them; and
- theft of collective property by people with the influence and power to do so ('spontaneous privatisation'), possibly gradually, as managers or others begin to behave as if the property were their own so that they eventually obtain legal title to it.

A **two-tier banking system** consists of a central bank that supplies money, and commercial trading banks which the central bank or a specialised agency supervises (accounting standards, standards of precaution and honesty). Such a two-tier system differs from the socialist financial system in which banks were simply government cash-transaction agencies and instruments to control the execution of the central plan, and did not have autonomy to do business.

The **'big bang' theory** of transformation advocates fast, concerted change in institutions to the essential elements of capitalism, on the grounds that **gradual transformation** would lead to incompatibilities and the emergence of organised resistance to transformation. ●

Some Country-specific Experiences

The above statements become clearer when we look at a few country-specific experiences. There have been considerable differences in the speed, consistency and content of systems change. A good indicator of transformation to date is probably the rate with which new private firms have been formed (Table 13.2).

Of the sovereign transition countries, it was probably the Czech Republic which initally managed to come closest to the list of minimum conditions laid out in Table 13.1, with Poland not far behind. In the Czech Republic, privatisation by vouchers and a concentration on the basics allowed people relatively soon after the 'Velvet Revolution' to discern the outlines of a new order: a 'market economy without adjectives', as Prime Minister Václav Klaus called it. The new order could be understood sooner than in other transition societies because it was relatively simple and consistent. By focusing on the essentials and targeting redistribution on groups such as pensioners, government agencies were better able to manage what its leaders had promised to deliver. By contrast, government leaders elsewhere often made ambitious, unrealistic promises, then people became disappointed and the government found itself bogged down in contradictions. Even in the

Table 13.2   New enterprises formed per 1000 inhabitants, 1989–95

Czech Republic	68.4
Hungary	50.7
Slovenia	36.3
Slovakia	35.0
Bulgaria	34.3
Poland	27.6
Estonia	19.7
Romania	16.0
Lithuania	15.4
Albania	12.1
Latvia	9.9

Source: Eurostat, quoted from *The Economist*, 9 November 1996, p. 144.

Czech Republic, it proved impossible to institute price-level stability and to police active competition in many product and capital markets. Openness was limited, for example, in banking and financial markets. After a few years, there was an electoral backlash possibly because the costs of transformation were widely felt, whereas the gains were coming in only gradually and imperfectly. After the initial shock of the systems transformation, the pursuit of 'social justice' became more prevalent again in most ex-socialist countries, a factor that created political obstacles to the gradual transformation process.

Developing a capitalist economy and the institutions on which markets are based proved difficult. Thus, many of the newly private banks and other financial intermediaries in the Czech Republic operated in opportunistic ways, exploiting the deficient standards of fiduciary supervision and the lack of international competition in financial markets. Several banks went bankrupt and depositors lost money. While this may be interpreted as part of a learning process, it might also be argued that the inexperienced depositors could have been saved transaction costs by external institutions and stricter enforcement of those rules. In any event, the experiences, which led to a visible depreciation of the Czech currency in 1997, led to the belated provision of more explicit regulations and mandatory fiduciary standards. International feedback was here too an important transmission mechanism that worked towards institutional development.

Another leading country in the transformation process is Poland. Having been a pioneer in undoing some socialist institutions during the 1980s and having a large residue of private agriculture, Poland, after the fall of the Berlin Wall, did not forge ahead as fast as its southern neighbours. Managers continued to operate under soft budget constraints. But gradually, Polish governments implemented systemic changes in the institutions governing labour, financial, capital and product markets, coupled with trade and currency liberalisation. Bit by bit, government-owned industries were privatised, inflation was gradually wound back, budget deficits and public debt were cut back. Foreign investments were attracted, partly no doubt also because of low wage rates. As a result, foreign trade was reorientated towards the OECD countries, and economic growth resumed strongly in the 1990s (from 1994 to 1997, it averaged 6 per cent per annum in real terms).

In other transformation societies, a less clearly defined 'transformation journey' has been followed. There have been more process interventions, turnarounds and inconsistencies, and hence less order. Parliaments have often been the battlegrounds for retrospective ideological disputes and massive rent-seeking. The institutions of property rights and free markets often lack legal and judicial backup, and internal institutions are grossly violated by criminal groups who appropriate wealth and use violence without effective sanctions. Nevertheless, a semblance of a new order has begun to emerge during the 1990s in most transformation economies and the decline is giving way to new growth. Understandably, the contraction has been deepest where law and order are most brutally violated and least protected, namely in the former Yugoslavia and parts of the former Soviet Union. In large parts of Russia, there is little tradition of the rule of law – in contradistinction to the Czech Republic or Hungary – so that the task of institution building is much harder. Consequently, losses in the division of labour and knowledge were greatest after the end of central planning, since only very rudimentary coordination systems were left in place (see box).

❖ Some of the Economic Consequences of the Demise of the Soviet System

An object lesson in just what the costs of the demise of a system of known institutions can inflict in terms of losses in effective coordination – and hence in output and investment – is the harsh experience of Russia after the collapse of communism, central planning and compulsion. Although that system had been failing, its termination without the bare rudiments of shared, predictable ordering devices has led to a decline in Russian living standards which exceeds that of the Great Depression in the West during the 1930s.

In the early 1990s, deficient and unsystematic institutions emerged: it is said that most constitutions drawn up for federal states and regions break the terms of the Federation Treaty of 1992. The presidential office issues a steady stream of arbitrary *ukases* with unknown impacts and of uncertain durability. In the early 1990s, inflation was allowed to run to a peak of 2500 per cent per annum, but has since been wound down. Contracted payments are not made and defaulters cannot be forced to pay. Markets do not exist, so, for example, half of all food is produced in little family plots, and 40 per cent of industry output is bartered. In a climate of thuggery and lawlessness, the internal institutions are weak and unreliable. The managers are not accountable to owners and refuse to pay taxes, partly because the tax laws are complex and uncertain. Big firms, banks and warring clans can obtain political favours that prevent competition. There is hardly any foreign investment and massive capital flight, with Russians holding foreign portfolios that exceed Mexican foreign holdings (see *The Economist*, 17 July 1997, Survey Russia).

As Figure 13.2 shows, gross domestic product shrank by 40 per cent in the first six years after the collapse of communism, industrial output by 50 per cent and gross investment by no less

Figure 13.2   The economic consequences of the collapse of the Soviet order

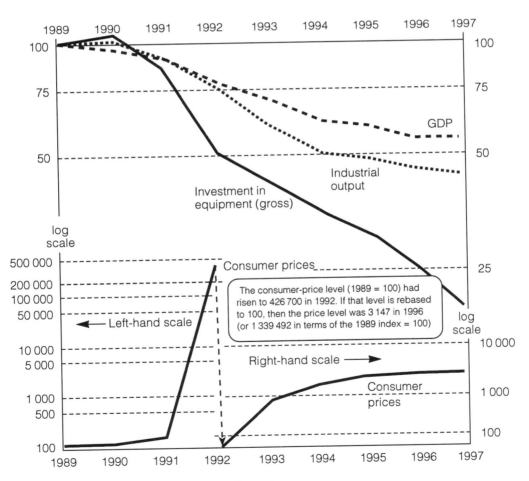

Source: Goskomstat Rossii (Russian Statistics Bureau).

than 70 per cent. The loss of effective coordination was greatly accentuated by the destruction of the monetary system. The process had begun with the arbitrary confiscation of old bank notes by the State Bank in the dying days of the Soviet Union. It was propelled further by public deficit finance through the printing press. In 1992, inflation peaked, and cumulative inflation between 1989 and 1995 was over 1 million per cent (or some 360 per cent per annum).

As of 1997, some 20 per cent of the population are living below subsistence level, but that share is slowly declining. In some places, institutions are becoming clearer, as capital owners insist on exerting influence on firms, as contract partners discover the advantages of trust and reliability, and as voters insist on selecting new officials. Inflation has come down and the massive contraction in real gross domestic product seems to have ended (see ibid.). The evolution of certain, universal institutions will take time in Russia, and the experience promises to become an object lesson on institutional economics. ◆

In East Germany, transition was greatly facilitated when tested external institutions were 'parachuted in' by the immediate extension of the German federal constitution and of civil, criminal and commercial law supported by a massive organisational effort. Between 1990 and the end of 1994, a specially created temporary government agency privatised some 38 000 enterprises and real estate titles, discovering in the process that the markets valued many items much less than the politicians and their bureaucratic expert advisers had originally assumed. West Germans bought 85 per cent of the property, but many plants and farms proved to be unviable. The privatisation of the east German economy cost some DM343 billion, including job maintenance schemes, but fetched only DM68 billion in the market place. Massive tax-funded subsidies buffered the coordination losses of the systems change. In the period 1991–5, an estimated US$440 billion were transferred from west to east, that is, some $26 000 for every inhabitant in the east. In 1995, the transfer burden on the West German gross domestic product was 5 per cent.[5] On top of this, the European Union transferred considerable funds to east Germany. In the process, the redistributive function of the German government was greatly increased and the government share in the gross domestic product of the united Germany rose to nearly 58 per cent by 1995.

Old institutions had to be unlearnt by the east Germans and new ones learnt, including the values underpinning a self-reliant, individual, capitalist order. This took time and practice. To most, the system change, though welcome, had come as a shock. Expectations were destabilised. This gave way to the gradual realisation by many that the new institutional reality could be deciphered and used to the individual's advantage. The ready availability of massive public subsidies and reliance on welfare redistribution, however, probably complicated and delayed the necessary learning processes. Neither was the adjustment of existing assets and skills to world market conditions helped by Germany's corporatist labour-market constitution. The western trade unions established themselves quickly in the east. Restrictive west German product-market regulations and the quick introduction of a common currency further undercut the adjustment capability of the east. These conditions facilitated a rapid rise in wage rates, when labour productivity still suffered from the costs of socialist malcoordination and underinvestment. After unification, east German labour-unit costs in most branches of industry were probably 50 per cent higher than in the west. By 1993, the labour cost disadvantage of the east had narrowed to about one-third and has stayed there. It should be noted that labour costs in eastern Germany are very much higher than in neighbouring transformation economies. In 1994, wages and on-costs in eastern Germany were some seven times the average labour costs in Hungary, Poland and the Czech Republic. Since the competitive advantage of better external institutions and infrastructures in eastern Germany could not compensate for these massive handicaps, numerous existing capital stocks and jobs were lost.

Great opportunities were, on the whole, missed which would have demonstrated in the east how effectively a deregulated market system can work to create jobs and how beneficial a competitive private supply of energy, transport, health, telecommunications and other infrastructural services can be. The political reluctance to pursue a genuinely competitive strategy can be readily explained by pressures from vested interests in the west who did not want to see new low-cost competitors in the German market and interests in the east who wanted quick income rises and greatly overestimated the world market value of their skills and assets. Unification was based on a 'social justice strategy' whose effect was to destroy existing capital and jobs and to delay the restructuring and modernisation of eastern Germany.

Losses from the breakdown of the old division of labour were also evident in the substantial decline in international trade. The Soviet bloc countries had planned their trade under the Comecon organisation which disappeared in the general collapse. Importers realised they could frequently obtain better products from world markets or they simply ran out of funds to buy imports. And Comecon exporters of some commodities – oil, gas and other raw materials – realised that they could obtain much higher prices by selling in open world markets. Consequently, a large part of the former intra-Comecon trade disappeared. Similar losses of continuity and established specialisation advantages were also incurred when the Soviet Union fell apart and the newly independent countries in its territory tried to substitute imports by local production. Alternative trade links, and accepted institutions and organisations to support them, took time to evolve, particularly since the transition was accompanied by runaway inflation and great political and judicial uncertainty.

Despite opportunities at the start that were far better than in most former command economies, a quick transfer of the basic institutions and massive material aid, east German living standards are lagging far behind those of western Germany. As of 1996, average per capita standards in the east are barely half those in the west, and the speed with which the gap is closing has decelerated sharply during the mid-1990s.

If transition experiences to date teach us anything, it is the crucial importance of simple, universal institutions, order and coordination. Those regimes which have replaced the pervasive, prescriptive interventions of totalitarian socialism with pervasive, prescriptive interventions of nationalist statism and the arbitrary rule of men have failed to turn the economic and civic decay around or have managed little improvement in economic conditions. But the regimes which concentrated on a few general rules, made way for individual initiative within a framework of simple, certain institutions, and relied on rule-bound behaviour appear to have weathered the transformation. Some six to eight years after the end of central planning and socialism, they are on the road to sustained economic growth. The transition experience teaches us once more that high living standards, indeed the very survival of the people, are critically dependent on the division of labour and the use of knowledge, and that this hinges on appropriate institutions.

Questions for Review

- The reader should check the historical background to the collapse of communist regimes by referring to a recent encyclopedia, almanac or history book.
- Imagine you lived in an economy, in which most of the familiar rules have changed or disappeared. What would you require to set up and run a small business? How do you hire labour? Where do you get the capital from, and how can you make a credible commitment to repay? How do you carry out your business calculations to assess future profits and losses? Who helps you with accounting? Who tells you what your tax burdens are? How do you find the

market for what you want to produce? Who can help you with guessing the prices at which you will be able to sell?

- To what extent do the institutions and their organisational backup in your country deviate from those sketched in Table 13.1?
- Imagine that someone wanted to abolish the institutions of capitalist coordination in your country (private property, free markets, money and so on). What would have to be put in its place so that the division of labour did not collapse completely?
- If you found our thumbnail sketch of 'market socialism' (as proposed by Oskar Lange) too cryptic, read about it in a book on the Soviet system (such as Gregory and Stuart, 1981). Then discuss how market incentives to perform are brought to bear on factory managers and workers. What can managers and workers do with the bonuses they earn, if they are not allowed to acquire capital? Does this limitation erode their incentive to perform? If so, why? Why is it unlikely that the central-plan bureaucrats could ever set prices that match relative scarcities and technical opportunities to produce?
- How did the commune system of planned, collectivised agriculture in China disappear? What did farmers do when they were again allowed to grow what they chose and to sell on their own account? How did that affect the living standards of townspeople?
- What does Figure 13.1 tell you about the consequences of undoing the socialist order? Can you explain why per capita incomes declined less in Hungary, Poland and the Czech Republic than in the successor states of the USSR?
- What minimal functions should government promise to fulfil when a socialist central planning system is discontinued? What happens if governments fail to do this?
- What happens to social interaction and the emergence of internal institutions when the process of reform is reversed?
- When you study this chapter, update your knowledge about the transformation process from newspaper reports and other sources. Has anything emerged that is not in line with what has been said in this chapter?

Notes

1. This, incidentally, also holds true of recent versions of market socialism (Roemer, 1994) which fail to address the well-established critique in the tradition of Mises and Hayek, despite explicit claims to the contrary (Wohlgemuth, 1997).
2. The income position of Chinese peasants improved partly because they were able to sell output privately at high prices in free markets while continuing to obtain many inputs (such as fertilisers and electricity) at regulated, low prices.
3. For a thorough assessment of the formative phase of Soviet socialism, which was

already showing all the features of its ultimate collapse when judged by the analyses of von Mises and Hayek, see Boettke, 1990.

4. In Russia, for example, wages to the tune of 26 per cent of monthly GDP and industry receivables to the tune of nearly 120 per cent of monthly GDP were reported to be in arrears in mid-1997 (*The Economist*, 12 July 1997, Survey of Russia, pp. 5 and 11).

5. Source: *Annual Report of the German Council of Economic Advisers (Sachverständigenrat), 1995–6*, Stuttgart: Kohlhammer, p. 151.

CHAPTER 14

Reforming the Mixed Economies

The purpose of this final chapter is to explore how the institutions of mixed economies can be reformed in the interests of greater freedom and prosperity. During much of the twentieth century, the institutional systems of most affluent economies gradually drifted from a market orientation to a regime where private property is heavily interfered with, markets are pervasively regulated and market outcomes are continually 'corrected'. What may have begun as an economic constitution that safeguarded a confidence-inspiring order based on private autonomy has in the process been changed into a system that is less predictable, adaptive and capable of innovation. As a consequence, social and political conflicts have increased and citizens have become cynical about government. Also economic growth and job creation have flagged.

To reverse these tendencies and to cope with the increasing competition from less regulated and more dynamic new industrial countries, widespread efforts have been made since the late 1970s to reform the economic institutions in many of the mixed economies: recasting the role of government, privatising government-owned production assets, liberalising markets for products, labour and capital, and reshaping public welfare provision.

Similar fundamental points about cultivating the economic constitution, as well as the complementary political constitution, are also being raised in developing and new industrial countries. *Dirigiste* import substitution policies, direct government involvement in investment and industry and the shackling of economic liberties have turned out to be counterproductive to economic development. We shall discuss what developing countries have to do to shape their institutions so that an extended market order is cultivated, privilege and corruption are made less likely and equitable opportunities for material advancement are made available.

It is wrong to see the existing state as an all-knowing, all-powerful guardian of all economic activity. But it is also incorrect to accept the existing state which is corrupted by interest groups as irreversibly given and consequently to despair of mastering the problem of building a proper political-economic order. The interdependency of the political and the economic orders forces us to tackle both at the same time. Both are parts of the same integral order. Without a competitive order, there will be no government capable of acting, and without such a government there will be no competitive order.
(Walter Eucken, Grundsätze der Wirtschaftspolitik, *1952; our translation)*

Macrea's Rule: Once it is clear we are doing something silly, let's stop it.
(Norman Macrea, former deputy editor of The Economist*)*

Today we resort to more and more administrative controls and receive less and less in exchange. That unhappy state of affairs means that there is an enormous and welcome political opportunity for any political party which understands that, by doing less, government will achieve more.
(Richard Epstein, Simple Rules for a Complex World, *1995)*

In the politics of reform you have to go for the first-best. You get only one shot at reform, so you have to keep it simple and clear. There are no second chances at reform. Second-best reforms ... only yield 4th or 5th best results. You become a double loser, (a) because you deny yourself the full yield of the reform, and (b) because you suffer an enduring loss of credibility, when piecemeal half-measures don't work. Reform gets a bad name.
(Ruth Richardson, reformist New Zealand Finance Minister, 1996)

14.1   Economic Liberties and Prosperity

In Pursuit of Economic Freedom

Since the late 1970s, renewed attention has been focused in affluent and poor countries alike on civil, political and economic liberties and institutions. Many observers and policy makers have concluded that arbitrary political action is playing too much of a role in the economy. In principle, private property is protected in most countries. But in practice property rights are often undermined by manifold collective actions. The collapse of centrally planned economies and totalitarian socialism focused renewed interest on the institutional foundations of capitalism and the spontaneous ordering of economic life. As a consequence, the dividing line between the spheres of central coordination and spontaneous ordering has again been critically re-evaluated. Many countries which have embarked on reforming the rules of the game support more spontaneous coordination. Opening up national economies, the deregulation of markets and the privatisation of formerly collectively owned and managed assets have been the focal points of these reforms.

The reforms of institutions in mixed economies have certain aspects in common with the transformation of the formerly socialist economies, but in many other respects they differ. Economic reform implies a shift on the margin, so that the reformed institutions can appeal to patterns of behaviour with which people are reasonably familiar. Voluntary coordination and rule-bound behaviour are better understood in the mixed economies of rich and poor countries than in economies where coercion and plan have long been the dominant instruments of economic coordination.

In many respects, the reforms of the 1980s and 1990s are reminiscent of the pervasive institutional reforms which were implemented in Britain after the Napoleonic wars and which triggered the Victorian era of unprecedented innovation and spreading prosperity (see insert below).

❖ Britain: An Historic Precedent for Institutional Reform

In the early nineteenth century, British law makers and political leaders reacted to the insights of liberal philosopher-economists and the monumental changes of the Industrial Revolution which had begun a generation earlier. They gave institutional substance to liberal philosophies, as propounded, for example, by Adam Smith, and made a major effort to streamline and simplify laws and regulations, cutting taxes and reforming foreign trade. The thorough depoliticisation of economic life was greatly helped by the conversion from mercantilism to liberalism of many traders and industrialists. They actively lobbied through numerous petitions for simpler institutions and greater security of economic liberties.

Sir Robert Peel (1788–1850), after becoming Home Secretary, made an effort to enforce laws which were on the statute books but which had previously not been enforced consistently, for example, on work in factories. He pushed through legislation to limit child labour (1819) and created the London Metropolitan Police (1829):

> He thought that there were far too many laws and statutory crimes ... he was determined to reduce the number of statutory ... crimes ... He transformed the judges ... from potential enemies of reform to active friends ... In March 1825 his Juries Regulation Bill consolidated 85 statutes [followed by further legal streamlining] ... Finally, in 1830, he consolidated 120 forgery statutes into one. This programme reduced 398 criminal statutes into 9 and involved reforms in over 90 per cent of the cases that came before the courts.
> (Johnson, 1991, pp. 864–7)

As tax revenue rose in the prosperity of the 1820s, the British government introduced across-the-board cuts of taxes and import duties, abolishing petty taxes (for example, on windows, vehicles, horses, servants, imported wool, the coal trade). As internal duties, quotas and bounties were removed, Britain's domestic market became a nationwide free trade area. The Chancellor of the Exchequer who presided over the tax and duty reductions, Fred Robinson (Viscount Goderich), earned himself the popular nickname 'Prosperity Robinson' (ibid., pp. 878–9) – at least until a speculative crash in 1825–6.

Later, when he was British Prime Minister, Peel gave effect to free trade ideas, first reducing the protective corn tariffs (1842) and in 1846 abolishing the Corn Laws. A conservative inclined to object to populist agitation, Peel opposed demands for continued protection from vocal agricultural interests in Parliament, insisting that he had 'the courage to do that which in our conscience we may believe to be just and right, disregarding all the clamour with which these demands may be accompanied' (quoted in ibid., p. 903). Free trade made food and other consumer goods cheaper for workers. This marked the defining victory of free trade in general. Peel also rejected subsidies and other direct government interventions to support ailing industries as 'quackery' (ibid., p. 902). However, his free trade policy eventually cost Peel the premiership.

The institutional reforms of the Victorian era combined a streamlining, simplification and liberalisation of the law with more effective enforcement of the rules. These institutional reforms paved the way for an unprecedented outburst of industrial creativity and prosperity which made Britain the first industrialised country and began the process of sustained long-term economic growth.[1] What had been the luxuries of the rich became the ordinary amenities and comforts of the middle class and soon of the workers. Penury and starvation disappeared in Britain, and the fight for mere survival gave way to widespread aspirations to higher living standards. ◆

Towards the end of the twentieth century, renewed interest in reforming economic institutions had much to do with international comparisons. Institutional systems that allow for more freedom and focus on the universal rules of property rights have delivered rapid advances in living standards. They have ensured international competitiveness and attractiveness most effectively. It has also been found that regimes which followed the interventionist economic policy fashions of the 1950s and 1960s fared disappointingly; hierarchical ordering by activist, result-orientated, discretionary public policies often caused disorientation. Governing markets in selective ways and constant interference in economic processes failed to protect domestic industries, to foster import substitution, to turn government agencies into development leaders or to pick 'industrial winners'. Forced savings and public borrowing often failed as a means of increasing the capital stock. By contrast, economic growth was vigorous in institutional settings which encouraged open international competition and secured the private control of savings and investments, limiting government involvement in specific industries, and which concentrated instead on monetary stability – in short, in regimes that fostered an open, competitive economic order. Over time, it became evident that among rich and poor nations alike there was an advantage in fostering property rights and private autonomy.

Measuring Economic Liberties

Research was undertaken in the early 1990s to establish whether the perceived link between economic growth and institutions that safeguard economic liberties is systematic. Researchers constructed an index of economic liberties (Gwartney and Lawson, 1997). The index covers internationally comparable information on:

- monetary stability;
- the regulatory order, that is, the direct involvement of governments in spending and production, price and quantitative controls on markets, the freedom to enter into and exit from markets, and the freedom of capital markets;
- the size of government and the redistributive function of government; and
- the openness to international competition in trade and freedom of capital movements.

For each country, this information is weighted – with implied relative valuations suggested by knowledgeable economists – to form an index which is meant to reflect the institutional makeup of a country's economy, as far as statistical shortcomings permit. The 1997 index, which measures economic freedom as of the mid-1990s, was compiled for 115 nations. Its components were rated on a scale from completely controlled (0) to autonomous individual decision making (10). The index was then compared with income levels and economic growth rates. Figure 14.1 gives a summary of the findings: if countries are grouped according to the 1997 ratings on economic freedom into five quintiles from highest economic to least economic freedom (from 1 to 5), it can be seen that income levels as well as medium-term economic growth (from 1985 to 1996) are clearly and strongly correlated with economic liberties (Gwartney and Lawson, 1997, p. 34). Even taking into account that this exercise implies value judgements, it offers empirical confirmation of the views which we have developed throughout this book: economic freedom – safeguarded by simple, universal institutions – enhances economic growth; complex, prescriptive regulatory systems and big government hinder it.

A look at the economic freedom ratings of individual countries reveals that some of the developed nations and many of the fast-growing developing countries, in particular in the Asia-Pacific region, rate in the top ten: Hong Kong, Singapore, New Zealand, the United States, Mauritius, Switzerland, Britain, Thailand, Costa Rica, Malaysia, Philippines, and Australia (the latter four are rated equal tenth; ibid., p. 27).[2] Statistical association does not of course prove causation, but the observed association is in accordance with the analytical reasoning in this book.

Figure 14.1   Economic liberties and prosperity

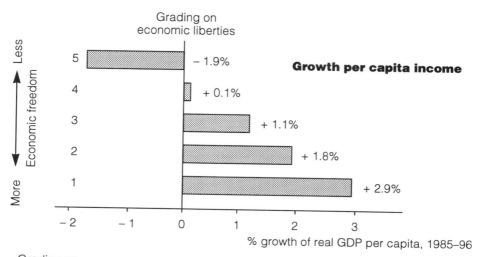

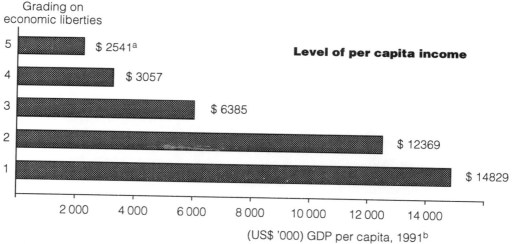

Notes:
a   The per capita income data are updates of the Penn World Tables, converted to US$ by the purchasing power parity method.
b   Average per capita income for each quintile rating on economic freedom.

Source: Gwartney and Lawson (1997, p. 34)

14.2   Economic Development: the Role of Institutional Change

Top-down Development Strategies

After attaining independence, many developing countries embarked on centrally designed and mandated economic development strategies, most of which were inspired by constructivist visions and attempted 'social engineering'. The new leaders, and their advisers, frequently opted for modernisation strategies that depended greatly on political guidance and collective action and that were coordinated under centrally mandated development plans which set 'national targets'. Often, attempts were made to replace poorly defined, internal institutions and existing cultural traditions with external institutions. Often, traditional internal institutions clashed with the new laws, regulations and ideologies; the clash led to contradictions and a diminution of the existing economic order (Bates, 1990). Often, centrally designed schemes failed to function as expected because the administrative apparatus to implement them was lacking and the new external institutions were not supported by internal institutions. The enforcement of central schemes was costly. Moreover, the problems of development were too complex and intricate to be comprehensible to anyone at the centre. As a result, private incentives to modernise were destroyed, and knowledgeable elites in established private businesses were suppressed. The political elites in many developing countries acted out of an arrogant pretence of knowledge, treating 'their' nations as if they were simple organisations. This had a destructive effect on economic welfare and other fundamental human aspirations. A typical, though extreme, case of this collectivist approach is Algeria (see box).

❖ Algeria: a Case Study in Imposing a New Order

To see if economic freedom matters to living conditions and economic growth, look at the country with the lowest ranking on economic freedom. This has consistently been Algeria (Gwartney and Lawson, 1995, p. 27).

Algeria is one of many former colonies in which the new leadership, after gaining independence, set out to impose a new order in the interest of national development and self-sufficiency. As of the mid-1990s, Algeria is at the bottom of the economic freedom rankings (115th out of 115 countries; ibid., p. 270). What does such a state of economic institutions mean in practice?

After an acrimonious war against the French, Algeria became independent in 1962 under the leadership of the National Liberation Front (FLN). In a pattern fairly typical of decolonialisation at the time, the new leaders had a new constitution accepted by a popular referendum and established a 'socialist-Islamic' one-party state. The many residents of French origin, who owned valuable skills, were 'encouraged' to leave and there was a wave of reprisals against Algerians, often the best educated, who had collaborated with the French. The governing politbureau of the FLN proceeded to introduce socialist central planning and nationalised much of the agricultural land, all the manufacturing and mining and the oil and gas sectors, as well as all foreign trade and the banks. A state monopoly was set up to buy and distribute agricultural produce. The government made the development of heavy industry a priority.

The new military government introduced strict press censorship and developed the elaborate surveillance techniques of a police state with technical aid from Soviet bloc countries. The leadership was repeatedly purged by sending some of the leaders into exile and murdering them. Algeria became a central player in the OPEC oil cartel and in the so-called 'Non-aligned Movement', an essentially anti-western association of third world countries. The economy, despite big gas and oil reserves being tapped, developed slowly and inadequately, given the very high birth rates. Private investment, which was still about 60 per cent of total capital formation in the early years after independence, dwindled to little more than 5 per cent in the late 1970s (Bennoune, 1988, p. 174). Unemployment was high, and urban migration aggravated local unemployment problems. Many Algerians therefore emigrated to Europe.

Gradually, officials and well-connected businessmen were granted more scope to transact profitable business on their own account. Income inequalities then increased, since these opportunities were not open to the average Algerian. Economic liberalisation was uneven and haphazard; enforcement of the rules depended on personal connections with the bureaucracy.

In 1988, violent riots broke out, triggered by increases in official food prices. They were at first repressed, but a fundamentalist Islamic movement agitated violently to organise further resistance until free elections were promised in 1991. In the first round of these elections, the fundamentalist party FIS won a big majority, triggering fears of a dramatic change in political and economic institutions and possible further losses of civil liberties. The military suspended the elections. Their leader was murdered by fundamentalists in 1992, and from 1992 to 1997 about 100 000 murders were reported, including the terrorist killings of liberal academics, journalists and foreign technical personnel. In 1995 and 1997, there were further elections which gave the new, formerly military leader a measure of legitimacy.

By the mid-1990s, Algeria (1995: 28 million inhabitants), the owner of the world's biggest gas fields and with ready markets for energy and agricultural produce in nearby Europe, had a per capita income only in the lower middle-income group (US$5300 at purchasing power parity). From 1985 to 1995, per capita income fell by 2.4 per cent per annum, or one-fifth overall. Inflation ran at about 25 per cent per annum, or nearly 600 per cent over ten years. Investment had dwindled since 1980 and illiteracy remained relatively high. A very small percentage of women are in the workforce. Data on government finances are not available. Foreign reserves are fairly thin, despite massive remittances from émigré workers and aid transfers from foreign governments. Foreign debt is high.

The Algerian case illustrates the interaction between a closed economy, absolute power, institutional rigidification, gross violations not only of economic but basic civil liberties, and long-term economic growth. It shows that property rights and competition are not only a matter of concern to big banks and anonymous company boards, but that they pervasively affect the daily lives, opportunities and wellbeing of ordinary people. ◆

(Sources: H.C. Metz, Algeria: A Country Study, *1990; M. Bennoune*, The Making of Contemporary Algeria, *1988; World Bank*, World Development Reports, *various)*

The 'constructivist impulse', based on the notion that an elite knows best what it takes to raise the level of economic development, was often combined with increases in the ownership of socialised assets, either because property inherited from colonial times was transferred into government ownership or because new factories and infrastructures were set up as government-owned enterprises.

The need to couple economic development with the development of a rule system that facilitates a modern division of labour and the effective signalling of emerging opportunities and scarcities was not fully appreciated by foreign advisers and international bureaucracies. Reflecting the prevailing neoclassical assumptions, the community of development advisers, as represented for example by the World Bank, neglected the institutional perspective. At best, economists began to argue for the opening up of national economies and for macroeconomic stability from the 1960s onwards (see, for example, Krueger, 1994).

In the 1950s and early 1960s, central development plans were typically drawn up to promote industrialisation. In many newly independent countries, capital assets were nationalised and the growth of government-owned enterprises was artificially promoted. Information about supply and demand conditions in the outside world was often suppressed, as public export monopolies were created and import protection programmes introduced. Import licensing and tariffs were implemented to generate high profits for privileged domestic producers, often 'political firms'. But a side-effect of import substitution was that rent-seeking politicians, business administrators, bureaucratic supervisors and organised labour were able to appropriate the profits. Import substitution was normally done piecemeal and in response to political pressures. There was much artificial preferment for the owners of capital and much diminution of the opportunities of farmers and workers. The various protection measures piled unintended consequences on various industries as the chaos in 'effective rates of protection' revealed when these rates could be calculated[3] (Krueger, 1997). Comparative advantage and knowledge transfer by international trade were grossly neglected. Production costs were driven up. Political preferment allowed firms to shirk innovation and cost control. Constructivist drives for development frequently went along with massive but ineffectual public spending and large public budget deficits. Resulting high levels of public and foreign debt fed into an inflationary expansion of the money supply.

The priorities and methods of development policy from the 1950s to the 1970s as described in this thumbnail sketch were far from uniform. Latin American countries started with higher levels of development but also more deeply entrenched interest groups, such as landholders or the military. These groups often took hold of the central political controls to create rents. Little was done to foster the rule of law and protect the universal institutions of a genuinely competitive order where these had existed before. Instead, politics was seen as the instrument for seeking gain from redistributional discrimination (Borner *et al.*, 1992). Inflation tended to advantage the rich, well-connected borrowers and disadvantage the poor. In South Asia and many African countries, development also depended on five-year plans and heavy interventions. In many respects, East Asian developing countries deviated increasingly from the predominant fashions in development in the 1960s and 1970s.

More Market-driven versus More Planned Development Strategies

While the above summary seems on the whole an appropriate characterisation of development policy in the less developed countries in the 1950s, 1960s and 1970s, great variations could be observed within the amorphous third world. Some regimes relied more than others on constructivist development strategies and on state ownership of the means of production. In the meantime, the evidence shows that more market-reliant economic regimes attained faster economic growth, less inflation and a more even income distribution than the more interventionist-constructivist countries (World Bank, *World Development Reports* 1979 and 1996; Gwartney and Lawson, 1997). This conclusion is also suggested when looking at roughly comparable pairs of countries that differed with regard to their institution set. While many factors influence actual growth rates and many shortcomings exist in statistical measurement, the following variations cannot be explained without reference to systematic differences in institutions:

- India adopted fairly detailed trade controls and central planning after independence in 1948. In the 1960s, its *dirigiste* style of economic development was reinforced with experiments in the state ownership of industry. Pakistan, by contrast, pursued a less interventionist strategy, and indeed freed markets and prices. India's real growth rate in the 1960s was 3 per cent per annum, a little above the population growth rate, whereas Pakistan managed 5–6 per cent per annum. India's inflation averaged in that period 5.5 per cent annually, whereas Pakistan's freer markets averaged an inflation rate of around 2 per cent.

- In East Africa, Kenya adopted a more market-orientated set of institutions, whereas neighbouring Tanzania engaged in pervasive economic interventionism, coupled with socialist development, and trade controls. Kenya's economic growth per capita in the 1970s averaged 2.4 per cent, more than double Tanzania's 1.1 per cent annual rate.
- In West Africa, Ghana implemented socialist-*dirigiste* concepts, suppressing markets and private enterprise, whereas neighbouring Ivory Coast relied more on markets and private enterprise. In the 1970s, Ghanaians suffered a 2.6 per cent annual decline in living standards, whereas the citizens of Ivory Coast managed a 1.5 per cent increase in their per capita incomes annually.
- In Asia, the former British colony of Sri Lanka shifted in the 1960s to central price fixing, investment controls and much socialist capital formation, whereas similarly endowed Malaya (later Malaysia) pursued a policy of openness to trade and investment and reliance on markets. Malaysia overcame a communist emergency, thanks not least to the rule of law that gave access to economic opportunities. The growth rate in per capita income averaged about 4.5 per cent (1960–75), coupled with minimal inflation (Kasper, 1974). By contrast, Sri Lanka's economic interventions became more and more detailed and allowed increasing discrimination on racial grounds. As a consequence, per capita incomes grew by about 2 per cent in real terms (1960–75) and then decelerated. Racial tensions exploded into a protracted and bloody civil war, and inflation steadily accelerated despite mandated price controls.[4]

The list of country comparisons could be extended without affecting the general conclusion, namely that reliance on the institutions that secure private property, private autonomy and openness went along with faster growth. It may be asked whether these differences in economic performance are due to market institutions causing faster growth, or whether only fast-growing countries can afford economic freedom. The economic theories developed here should leave little doubt that the causation runs mainly from institution set to economic performance.

Admittedly, the above comparisons rely in the first instance on indirect evidence, inferring the growth consequences of market orientation which are brought about by differences in institutional frameworks.

Direct evidence of the impact of institutions on growth in developing countries is still scarce and hardly systematic. However, studies such as de Soto's (1990) analysis of the informal economy of Peru drew attention to the central importance of institutional change for development. Similarly, some cross-country evidence has been prepared recently which shows how institutional arrangements can help or hinder economic development (Borner *et al.*, 1992; Brunetti *et al.*, 1997).

Institutional awareness is also penetrating the policy advice emerging from international organisations. Economic reforms since the 1980s have been strongly influenced by what has been dubbed the 'Washington consensus', namely monetary stabilisation, structural adjustment and trade liberalisation (Edwards, 1995, pp. 58–70; World Bank, 1993, various). It was pointed out that the control of budgets and money supplies, financial development, deregulation of domestic trade, privatisation and the move to a lean state required thorough institutional reform. Yet all too often it was assumed that systematic institutional change would somehow result from the mere implementation of concrete policy proposals. And the proposals themselves were based on neoclassical micro- and macroeconomics. Only gradually have international organisations begun to consider that the problems of institutional change must be solved first (see, for example, Klitgaard, 1995).

The importance of institutional change to economic development can be demonstrated by the fast-growing East Asian countries that re-shaped institutions in order to rely increasingly on individual initiative and openness, and by the East Asian institutional crisis of 1997–8 which has much to do with institutional backsliding and reluctance in institutional reform.

O Key Concepts

Development plans are drawn up by bureaucracies and governments to predetermine economic and industrial changes over four, five or twenty years into the future and to identify the need for certain political actions in order to ensure that the planned developments will take place.

Where such plans were used as indicative, broad-brush exercises to identify needs for long-term infrastructure investment or to assist in budget forecasts, they may have fulfilled a useful information role. Where they were made obligatory and seen as a replacement of coordination by markets, they tended to run into the difficulties of central planning for complex, dynamic development.

Import substitution is a policy of protecting domestic producers (capital owners and workers) from international competition by tariffs and import quotas. The primary intent is to secure markets for initially non-world-competitive local producers and thus enable them to learn how to produce. It is also intended to create investment, jobs and tax revenue at the expense of foreigners. Import substitution tends to work by redistributing incomes and wealth from buyers, who now have to pay higher prices, to domestic producers and governments. In the process, import substitution also encourages rent-seeking by domestic workers and capital owners in the protected industries. By making market niches longer lasting, it reduces competitive stimuli to control costs and to innovate. Over the long term, import substitution therefore detracts from economic development. ●

The East Asian Model

In East Asia, where the second world war and the Chinese communist revolution had led to cataclysmic turmoil, the 1950s' fashion of top-down development policy, in particular import substitution policies, was not emulated widely or for long. But there were exceptions, most notably in the communist countries, Sukarno's Indonesia, South Vietnam and the Philippines. The governments of the normally resource-poor, densely populated countries of East Asia decided instead to rely mainly on export orientation and, more importantly, on attracting foreign enterprises (Kasper, 1994a; World Bank, 1993). This fundamental decision had much to do with insecurity (perceived threats from the Soviet and Chinese military, communist insurgencies, wars) and the insight that economic prosperity would be the real source of strength in defence against aggression and domestic subversion. Growth through openness required respect for life and property by government; indeed, the active protection of the property rights of the internationally mobile resources that were to be attracted. As governments in the Asia-Pacific region learnt how to deal with the owners of mobile resources, they engaged in legal and regulatory reform and enhanced their protective role. For example, foreign exchange and capital markets were freed, the prudential supervision of banks was enhanced, and industrial operating and building codes were clarified in most of these countries. While numerous exceptions and lapses in enforcement can probably be cited, the general trend in government activity has been to strengthen and clarify the universal rules necessary to underpin the extended order of the market. In the more advanced Asian economies, it now largely matters less than a generation ago whom you know than what you know. In this context it is worth recalling that the survey of economic liberties, which we quoted in section 14.1, lists many of the countries in the Asia-Pacific region among the top nations.

The fundamental decision in favour of openness had several gradual but important institutional consequences:

(a) Knowledge from the outside world was more freely available and impacted directly and pervasively. World market prices, as well as direct feedback from sophisticated buyers, guided much of the development effort.

(b) Policy makers were soon exposed to the learning process that we described in section 12.4: they frequently went all out to attract foreign capital, skilled people and enterprises, and they did so in pragmatic-evolutionary ways. Political leaders enhanced the attractiveness of their countries by focusing on low-cost supplies of local labour, land and government services, and on ways to raise productivity. In the process, they developed reasonably consistent and reliably enforced institutions. Complex, discriminatory political preferments were increasingly found to fail, whereas 'getting the fundamentals right' proved a good way to attract foreign investors and avoid unintended side-effects. There were exceptions to this: most notably in strongly nationalist, constructivist Korea during the 1960s and 1970s; during a xenophobic phase in the People's Republic of China prior to 1979; and in Vietnam. But the opening-up strategies led to economic success, and the successful economies were, on the whole, emulated sooner or later. This was even true of China after 1979 and unified Vietnam after the mid-1980s. Domestic lobby groups found it hard to organise themselves in the wide-open, competitive economic climate, even where these lobbies were based on ideological foundations and organisational structures, such as Communist Party membership. And governments relied on an arm's-length approach to private business interests that emulated the Confucian teacher–pupil relationship, which helps to keep the rules fairly universal (Kasper, 1994a). This is not to say that corrupt practices did not occur or that massive rents were not created and shared by government officials. But on the whole such practices were seen to be prejudicial to international competitiveness and growth (Mauro, 1995).

(c) By contrast with less open economies in other parts of the third world, the governments of the export-orientated East Asian countries conducted monetary and fiscal policies to safeguard stability and international competitiveness (World Bank, 1993).

(d) Partly for reasons of tradition and partly because the wish to be internationally competitive was a high priority, East Asian governments did not engage in much redistribution through the tax–welfare mechanism. Rather, they concentrated on getting the basic rules right, promoting growth and competition. This, as we have already noted, led frequently to a remarkably high degree of income equality. Governments fostered those external institutions that complemented the traditional internal institutions, instead of trying to replace them (except in the communist countries). Awareness of culture as a potential institutional asset was widespread. In addition, governments of the capitalist export-orientated economies engaged in some productive pursuits, but normally to a lesser extent than in South Asia or Latin America.

(e) Fast world-market-driven economic growth ensured that expanding businesses had sooner or later to compete for qualified workers. This is reflected, for example, in the fact that economies with rising export shares in national production averaged a real-wage growth of 3 per cent per annum from 1970 to 1990, whereas inward-looking economies (with falling export to GNP ratios) averaged a decline of real wages (World Bank, 1995). This supports the contention that competitive markets are conducive to spreading the fruit of economic growth around and do so more effectively than constructivist public redistribution policies.

(f) As the East Asian economies developed, many governments discovered that the provision of infrastructure services was an important factor in international competitiveness and that they had only limited administrative capabilities to run complex modern infrastructures, such as telecommunications, ports and urban transport systems. Since the 1980s, many of existing public production ventures have been privatised, and private competition among public-sector firms has been encouraged. The north–south motorway in west Malaysia, for example, is a private road; telecommunications is open to competition and is largely privately owned throughout the region; new infrastructure investments are frequently financed by private consortia. Even communist China now has private motorways. Governments have laid the legislative and regulatory basis for the provision of public domain goods, not by accumulating socialised property but by private production. In that respect, East Asian countries leap-frogged ahead of old industrial countries, with institutions that ensure competitive supply, quality control and open access to the public.

When development first took off in East Asia, political leaders often involved themselves directly in fostering new industries. As in mercantilist Europe 200 years ago, it often mattered whom you knew if you wanted to gain access to trade, mineral leases, credit and other resources. Personalised exchange and credit thus mattered a lot in the early period of development, because the universal economic institutions were poorly developed and enforced. On personal connections guaranteed contract fulfilment. Frequently, middlemen served the purposes of transmitting information and of lowering transaction costs, important functions in a less developed and rapidly changing economy. Had modernisation depended solely on the markets, the transaction costs might have been forbiddingly high, constituting a barrier to economic take-off. However, as the East Asian economies have modernised, economic interaction has become more complex and more closely integrated with the rapidly changing, competitive global economy. Limits to what can be achieved by personalised exchange and credit and without the institutions that ensure property rights and private autonomy have therefore become obvious in the 1990s. Big investments to finance large, world-market-orientated factories and to set up big transport and communications networks typically proved beyond the reach of personalised credit. Nor could complex technologies be handled by the institutional mechanisms of personalised exchange which had proved so effective for developing simple trade and processing. The need for the impersonal open institutions of the extended market order became obvious. Further economic development now requires that the institutional apparatus of capitalism – the extended order of markets and the rule of law – are developed and further improved. A key part of development policy now is to lend support to more reliable institutions and more sophisticated enforcement in the better developed parts of East Asia (Kasper, 1994b).

The need for further institutional development and a more consistent enforcement of the institutions on which a market order is based became obvious in 1997 when, after a decade of unprecedented growth and in the wake of credit expansion and cost increases, a currency and credit crisis hit many East Asian economies. The 'affront of openness' was acutely felt by long-established political power elites when global markets signalled – once again – that the economic and political institutions had to be reformed or better enforced in order to enhance international competitiveness.

Openness and Internal Change

The East Asian experience since the 1960s of having to compete in world markets and setting up modern economic structures within little more than a generation has had profound and lasting effects on the internal institutions of East Asian societies, as noted in earlier chapters. Civic virtues such as hard work, frugality, punctuality, honesty and reliability – which often derive from traditional culture – have been sharpened by the experience of economic competition and have gained more weight. As the economies became more complex and more 'experience goods' were produced, East Asian manufacturers quickly discovered the importance of a good reputation, learning to supply good quality and delivering reliably on their contractual obligations. They developed brand names, whereas they had initially competed only on price. They also learnt habits of searching system-atically for innovations. They learnt to keep transaction costs low and benefited themselves from this. However, these preferences, as well as the organisational infrastructures for modernisation, appear to be more readily acquired in concrete activities, such as manufacturing, mining and agriculture, than in abstract, sophisticated services, such as finance or logistics, which rely on more abstract and complex institutional systems (Kasper, 1994b). None the less, centres such as Singapore and Hong Kong have cultivated the requisite institutions and consequently managed to expand service production rapidly as well.

The contrast in institutional achievement between the increasingly open, market-reliant societies of East Asia and the still partly control-led economies in countries such as Vietnam, Cambodia and China is now considerable. Whereas the former countries rank high in eco-nomic liberties,[5] the institutional uncertainty in the one-party states poses a serious obstacle to major, long-term investments. Partly for ideological reasons, private property is ill-protected and commercial law is still uncertain. The structures of governance are often unclear, with overlapping authorities (party, local, regional, provincial and central governments) engaged in decreeing laws and regulations, of-ten with the aim of extracting legal as well as corrupt levies. Investors who are prepared to pay off officials to secure a semblance of security for their operations have relocated to the 'institutionally vague and unclear' economies on the grounds of low costs, market potential and the hope of institutional improvement. They reap the competitive advantages of cheap labour and land. To date, long-term, reliable commitments to learning and fixed capital formation are often de-feated by political 'hold-up risks'. None the less, China, which currently ranks a poor eighty-first on fundamental economic liberties (Gwartney and Lawson, 1997), has begun to ensure better defined economic insti-tutions (The Economist, 13 January 1996, p. 21). The need for proper commercial and company laws and their consistent enforcement is increasingly recognised.

In developing countries, too, the disciplinary feedback from interjurisdictional factor mobility is often considered an affront to national sovereignty and is resented by established political leaders, as became clear – yet again – in the wake of the 1997 currency crisis in East Asia. Some may try to use xenophobic sentiment to shore up their political positions and to depict rent-seeking policies as being in the national interest; others may stress the superiority of autocratic policies in obtaining economic progress as compared to the decadent western democracies. A degree of personal autocracy was certainly part of the East Asian development equation (World Bank, 1993; Kasper, 1994a), but in open economies that is tempered by the feedback from trade and capital flows as long as the autocrats are prepared to put economic prosperity first. As the middle class has grown and new economic entrepreneurs want open access to markets, and as a young generation, who have grown up without the extreme penury experienced by their parents' generation, begin to demand political as well as economic liberties, there is a growing demand for universal economic and political liberties. The new, educated middle class in Korea, Taiwan, Thailand, Singapore, Hong Kong and Indonesia favour greater political liberties to shore up their economic freedoms. Many of its members are less tolerant than their parents of political and bureaucratic autocracy for the sake of economic advancement. The rapid integration into global information networks adds to this tendency.

During the 1990s, rapid economic development and growing globalisation required changes in the external institutions which many political regimes in East Asian countries were unable or unwilling to make. Economic success often seemed to signal that further institutional innovations were not necessary. While the East Asian countries had engaged in more institutional reforms than other third world countries, institutional evolution had not kept pace with the rapid economic development and the requirements of globalisation. Indeed, there were more frequent rule violations by a rising 'crony capitalism' and new rent-seeking alliances between politicians and newly formed interest groups, by more interventionist policies and by flagging controls of corruption. At first, they did not appear to inflict economic harm. Autocratic elites in government began to assert 'Asian values' and to reject foreign warnings. Institutional backsliding and a certain arrogance borne of evident success widened the lag of institutional evolution behind economic progress (Kasper, 1994b). Institutional shortcomings did not matter all that much, as long as low costs attracted manufacturing exporters, but they became more of a handicap when land and labour became more costly. Institutional deficiencies also had more of a negative impact in the service sector, such as banking, where imbalances were allowed to accumulate without the check of enforced institutions.

When foreign and local capital owners finally reacted to the institutional backlogs with the 'exit option' during the economic slowdown of 1997, the market signals hit suddenly and painfully. The political agents found themselves overtaxed. The challenge now is to overcome the political inertia and to reform the external institutions (Kasper, 1998). This challenge from world markets was often resented by established power brokers, and interest groups often rallied to mobilise tribal-nationalist sentiment. The mechanisms and problems outlined in section 12.3 became acutely evident. The resolution of the 1997–8 crisis in the various countries will depend on how well and how fast political entrepreneurship is mobilised to make the institutions more universal and to sanction rule violations irrespective of the political power of the violators.

The Spread of Reforms

Elsewhere in the third world, liberalisation and privatisation have also gained momentum in the 1980s and 1990s (Scobie and Lim, 1992; Scully, 1992). The worldwide tendency has been towards institutions that protect the autonomous use of private property rights and the free exploration and exchange of human knowledge, despite many reversals. There is, however, nothing automatic about the drift towards more liberal political and economic institutions, despite the openness of the communications era. The institutional arrangements of a community are tied to deep-seated, fundamental values, and cultural rules have a habit of changing only slowly. The mere reform of external institutions will not make much change if the internal institutions and belief systems do not adjust too. This is a lesson of history which has had to be learnt in many historical episodes, for example, in tsarist Russia where top-down reformers, such as Peter the Great (1682–1725) and Alexander I (1801–1825), had little lasting effect. To date, it is mainly the north-west European countries and Japan, where there were institutions that diffused power, that have managed to create economic and political constitutions which favour economic growth (Powelson, 1994, pp. 327–41). The signs for sustained growth look hopeful elsewhere in East Asia, but the test of whether appropriate constitutions will be firmly established is yet to be passed.

The search for an order-creating economic constitution will be decisive in how the large part of humanity who live in the third world will succeed in attaining a materially more satisfactory and a freer life. For many individuals, it will be a matter of survival.

14.3   Reforming the Mature Economies

The Erosion of the Economic Constitution

The unprecedented experience with high, sustained economic growth after 1945 gave rise to the widespread assumption in the old industrial economies that economic growth could be taken for granted (section 1.2). Many made the tacit assumption that a decline in living standards – which had often occurred earlier in history – could now be categorically ruled out (Kahn, 1979). Much political and popular attention therefore turned from the pursuit of prosperity to redistribution, risk avoidance by increasingly detailed regulation, the protection of past socioeconomic positions, the conservation of nature and past cultural achievements, and a great variety of other particular causes – regardless of the unknowable consequences for economic growth. In the process, the institutional foundations on which growth was based have been allowed to decay (Niskanen, in Gwartney and Wagner, 1988). As a result, all the old industrial countries now have mixed economies where spontaneous market signals are mixed with signs from the visible hand of government. Economic motives are often overlaid by political motives, including those of opportunistic agents of government, political parties and bureaucratic and industrial lobbies.

In electoral democracies, compulsion and political rent-seeking have spread mostly because of the redistributional urge of parliaments, judges and specific government agencies, who are supported by particular-interest advocates. As Joseph Schumpeter (1947) had foreseen, political entrepreneurs are often elected to office because they promise to hand out economic privileges to their supporters, disregarding the fundamental institutions that underpin capitalist civilisation. The lessons of a few success stories, such as the fundamental reform of the economic (and political) constitution of West Germany after the second world war, were disregarded. Even in Germany, growth was gradually taken for granted and the 'order policy' of the immediate postwar era gave way to much parliamentary activism and redistributional rent seeking (see box). Throughout the developed world, elected parliamentarians adopted increasingly intricate specific interventions. Thereby they have, often unwittingly, weakened the universal, abstract rule system and have curbed individual liberties. This may have ensured for them office, stature and re-election, but it undermined economic order, often in gradual and almost imperceptible ways, and eroded dynamic efficiency.

❖ West Germany: from Institutional Reform to Sclerosis

I The economic 'non-miracle'

In 1945, at the end of the second world war, Germany was divided in four military occupation zones and reduced in size. The economy reached a nadir. The Western Allies did much to impose a capitalist constitution on the western zones and to promote political protagonists of private property rights and competition. In 1948, they handed a considerable degree of sovereignty back to German political leaders. The western occupation zones became the Federal Republic of Germany under a constitution which safeguarded basic civil and political liberties and ensured property rights, freedom of contract and limited, accountable government. The Russian zone became a separate unitary communist state onto which Soviet-style central planning and collectivisation were foisted. (This regime would collapse in 1989–90.)

In the West, the Economics Minister of the first federal government, Ludwig Erhard, made use of favourable political circumstances and – with skill and luck – implemented market-orientated reforms, which the Western Allies favoured. He and his collaborators were strongly influenced by the teachings of the Freiburg school of *ordo* liberalism (section 10.4) and by similar, liberal views taught at the University of Cologne. Monetary reform had been implemented to wipe out the inflated paper values of assets and liabilities left behind by the inflationary policies of the Nazi regime. A fairly independent central bank was set up to ensure the supply of stable money, since many Germans feared a repetition of the destructive consequences of runaway inflation that had occurred in 1919–21 in the wake of the first world war. Much emphasis was placed on fostering the basic institutions of protected private property rights and free competition in markets (reinforced later by antitrust legislation). The government abolished most wartime regulations and normally desisted from intervening in specific processes. There was little macroeconomic policy along the lines of the then fashionable Keynesian school. Instead, the government created a stable framework of universal rules to give people confidence after the cataclysmic experience of the war (Kasper and Streit, 1993; Giersch *et al.*, 1992).

During the 1950s and early 1960s, the Federal Republic was a leader in liberalising international trade and payments and in European integration. The government encouraged capital formation and saving, but also guaranteed certain minimal income levels to those out of work or in old age. In the late 1950s, the government privatised ownership of some publicly owned enterprises. The mix of fostering the institutions of capitalism with a measure of tax-funded social welfare was given the label 'social market economy'.

The results of these institutional reforms were impressive: between 1950 and 1960, real output more than doubled (growth of 8.8 per cent per annum over the decade). Total employment went from 20 million to 25 million. The number of unemployed fell from 1.9 million to 300 000 despite a massive influx of prisoners of war and refugees from the east. Labour productivity rose by an average of 5.7 per cent per annum and income per worker by 4.9 per cent per annum (see table below). The currency was stable and had to be revalued upwards in the early 1960s. West Germany was a leader among OECD countries in introducing the free convertibility of its currency.

Foreign economists, who were at the time under the spell of Keynesianism and had a habit of disregarding institutions, dubbed the quick emergence of the war-torn economy the 'German economic miracle' – and miracles do not have to be explained. The postwar German economic

track record does not, however, appear a miracle to economists who understand the importance of simple, transparent and reasonably stable institutions as well as limited government
and a central bank committed to the pursuit of price-level stability.

	Productivity: growth of income/ person in active labour force (% p.a. at constant prices)	Income: growth of total income (% p.a.)	Socialised sector: government share in full-capacity GNP (selected years, % share)	
1950–60	4.9	8.2	1955:	30.3
1960–73	4.1	4.4	1965:	37.2
1973–80	2.2	2.2	1977:	47.2
1980–95	0.9	1.7	1987:	45.3
1995	—	—	1995:	57.6[a]

Notes:
1950–89: West Germany; from 1990: all of Germany.
[a] All of Germany, including the one-off effect due to the takeover of East Germany.

II   From growth to sclerosis

The economic momentum of the 1950s and early 1960s did not last. In part, this was to be
expected. Gradually, the economy reached full employment and industry caught up with international technical standards, so that the growth process could no longer draw on unutilised
resources and rely on catching up with technology levels abroad. But to a considerable extent,
the slowdown from the 1950s to the 1990s (see table) had to do with institutional changes.
Parliament became again a forum for privilege distribution, as industries and groups organised
themselves into 'rent-seeking coalitions' (Olson, 1982; Chapter 4) and people took the fundamental economic constitution for granted. The political commitment to a 'social market economy'
opened the door for the growing redistribution of property rights, often to the electorally strong
middle class and to well-organised groups.[6] As the redistributional function of government
expanded and a considerable involvement of government with production demanded ongoing
subsidies, parliaments and governments became increasingly involved with specific outcome-
orientated interventions. Tax and regulatory burdens on producers were raised. The policy
focus on the competitive legal-institutional order was diluted.

The decay of the rule system led to what was called 'sclerosis' and a weakening of Germany's
international competitive position. As well-meaning parliamentarians were piling new legal
obligations on employers, driving up the on-costs and constraining enterprise with more and
more health, safety and environmental prescriptions, Germany lost its attractiveness as a
location for foreign investors, and capital and enterprises moved out.

Thanks to the high levels of affluence reached within a generation and the embedding of the
German economy in the regulated European Union, the gradual loss of international competitiveness could be ignored for some time. Learning processes and political-institutional innovation
could be delayed. The major enterprise of taking over the failing former communist East
Germany after 1989 raised the share of public spending on the national product, which was
estimated at 57.6 per cent in 1995 (source: OECD), and for economic freedom Germany was

rated a modest twenty-fifth out of 115 countries in the study by Gwartney and Lawson (1997, pp. 98–9). ◆

(Sources: Erhard, 1960; Kasper and Streit, 1993; Wolter, in Harberger, 1984; Giersch et al., 1992; and German Council of Economic Advisers, Annual Reports, various)

The old industrial countries came from the 1960s under competitive challenge from the growing ranks of new industrial countries. These benefited from the transport and communications revolution and kept their economies open. Progressive moves under GATT auspices to liberalise international trade since 1945, as well as the evolution of internal institutions to facilitate economic coordination, enhanced worldwide competition. The new industrial countries, which provide little public welfare, are increasingly winning the interjurisdictional contest for globally mobile enterprises and capital. This in turn enhances their 'social capital', their reputation as good locations for industry and their own innovative capabilities. In some old industrial countries, this has renewed an interest in 'repairing' the capitalist system by privatising and deregulating, streamlining existing regulations, reforming taxation and public welfare, and rethinking the role of government (Scobie and Lim, 1992). Openness and international competition are the reasons why the capitalist civilisation has as yet not come to an end and why it shows a new capacity to regenerate itself by such economic reforms.

Microeconomic (Institutional) Reform

The specifics of institutional reform vary from country to country, given the differences in national systems; yet surprising fundamental parallels emerged among the OECD countries in the 1980s:

(a) Government-owned agencies producing goods and services were widely subjected to scrutiny. Many government-owned enterprises were privatised. Where socialised property was returned, companies were often at least corporatised, exposed to private competition and subjected to detailed comparisons with world best practice (bench-marking). Private mail delivery agencies, for example, are now allowed to erode many of the public postal monopolies, and there is new competition for public transport and communications monopolies. Moreover, technical changes have helped to erode public monopolies, for example, in communications or power supply. In many instances, publicly owned enterprises were set aside from the general budget and given clear-cut corporate objectives. Admittedly, it remains to be seen whether firm budget constraints and protection from day-to-day political interference will be upheld.

(b) The redistributional function of government has also come under renewed scrutiny. It is now widely understood that direct intervention in markets for political and redistributional motives often failed to achieve the expected goals. Indeed, interpersonal wealth and income differences were often exacerbated by policy interventions (for example, in labour and housing markets), penalising the poor and assisting the wealthy. Consequently, many redistributive regulations were abandoned in at least some of the old industrial economies. As globally mobile enterprises gained political influence, new political entrepreneurs saw careers in deregulation and in streamlining the remaining regulations with a view to cutting the transaction and compliance costs.

(c) The redistributional use of taxes and subsidies also came in for much criticism in virtually all the old industrial democracies, as individual attitudes to working and saving gradually adapted to the expansion of public welfare, and as ageing populations placed additional pressures on welfare budgets. Public welfare was increasingly seen as an impediment to international competitiveness, although political action in response to these insights has varied widely between countries.

(d) In a number of developed countries, the protective function of government was again emphasised by the political right and the left (see section 10.5).

In no OECD country was the swing in public policy more dramatic and pronounced than in New Zealand, which had long been an economy strongly influenced by Fabian ideals of constructivism and egalitarianism (see box). In the decade from 1984 to 1994, New Zealand moved from being the most heavily regulated 'mixed economy' in OECD to the one with the best-secured economic liberties. Indicators such as growth, job creation, inflation control, international competitiveness and external balances are responding favourably to the new economic order (see box). The fact that these dramatic reforms were implemented in New Zealand seems no coincidence, because this small economy is more of a 'frontline state' than most other OECD countries in the interjurisdictional competition with the new industrial countries of East Asia.

❖ New Zealand: a Case Study in Comprehensive Institutional Reform

New Zealand (1995: 3.5 million inhabitants; per capita income at purchasing power: US$ 14 500, or 63 per cent of US income levels) had the most heavily regulated economy in OECD in the early 1980s; as of the mid-1990s, the country has the least regulated economy. It therefore serves as a telling case study of (a) how the institutions in mature mixed economies can be liberalised, and (b) what effects such reforms are likely to have.

I From affluence to sclerosis

New Zealand soon reached high living standards in the nineteenth century thanks to rich natural resources, skilled immigrant labour and tested imported British institutions. Early in the twentieth century, political preference was given to a package of industrial and labour-market regulations at home and protection against international competition. The aim was to create an egalitarian, secure society. After the second world war, public welfare provision was made more comprehensive; domestic labour and capital markets could be tightly controlled thanks to internal institutions of obedience and cooperation; imports were licensed and foreign exchange was rationed. New Zealanders created the prototype of inward-looking, protectionist policies and interventionist, redistributive 'social justice' policies.

In the 1960s and 1970s, New Zealand living standards started to slip behind those of other OECD countries, as industries failed to raise productivity and the share of government in economic activity rose. For most of the 1970s, per capita GDP rose by about 0.2 per cent per annum. The national government tried massive Keynesian demand stimulation by developing big projects. Its main consequence was an unmanageable debt crisis. What had been a harmonious, secure society began to show symptoms of social decay and tensions, including strikes organised by compulsory and privileged unions who demanded higher wages than were awarded by the centrally administered, parastatal wage arbitration system. Many young New Zealanders emigrated in search of a less boring and more promising environment elsewhere.

II Partial reform produces incompatible suborders

In 1984, the interventionist conservative government lost the election and a Labour government came in, putting reformist Finance Minister Roger Douglas at the economic helm. He drew on a small team of reform-minded officials and business leaders and quickly pushed through the liberalisation of capital and foreign exchange markets. All price controls were discontinued and most subsidies were abolished. Many government activities were corporatised or privatised, and the tax regime was simplified and shifted from progressive direct taxes to flat taxes on the sale of goods and services. International trade was freed more gradually. At the same time, labour markets were re-regulated (reintroduction of compulsory unionism) and social welfare was 'quarantined' to protect ordinary New Zealanders from the effects of deregulation. The Reserve Bank of New Zealand was made independent of day-to-day political directives; its role was to produce inflation-free money. In managing 'the business of government', traditions of civil service tenure and control were replaced by performance pay and contracts for the top managers. By 1988, when Roger Douglas was sacked and the Labour government took a 'tea break in reform', the institutional game plan had been fundamentally and irreversibly changed.

The reforms of 1984–7 changed the economic order from heavy reliance on planned, centrally mandated coordination to market institutions, but with important exceptions (labour, social welfare and hence budget policy). The reforms gave New Zealand an inconsistent rule system, with the result that many relative prices were distorted, a wage explosion occurred and profitability in many businesses was squeezed. Interest rates soared (up to 40 per cent per annum for business loans). Inflation gradually came down from the two-digit range, but many businesses closed down or were reduced in size. Unemployment began to climb (to over 11 per cent in the early 1990s). The reforms had begun with several 'big bangs' but then petered out. All this made the future less predictable and introduced inconsistencies among suborders.

III   A consistent institutional system

In late 1990, a conservative government was elected amidst a deep recession. The Nationals – inspired by Ruth Richardson, who later became their first Finance Minister, and other young political entrepreneurs – had, with a lag, followed the conversion to free-market principles. It now proposed to complete the economic reform agenda. Central wage fixing was abolished and employment contracts were subject to normal contract law. Targeting welfare on those in need and curbing welfare payments allowed government expenditures to be cut. When the economy and tax revenues began to grow fast (1992–5: about 5 per cent per annum), direct tax rates were reduced and public debts were repaid.

The process of fiscal reform was assisted by the introduction of accrual accounting: like businesses, government departments had to document not only the annual flows of receipts and expenditures, but also the independently audited value of their assets and liabilities. It emerged that the New Zealand government had many unfunded liabilities – in business terms, it was bankrupt. Privatisation of government-owned enterprises was resumed. The policy was increasingly acceptable to the citizens as the quality of service from and prices for public-domain services showed demonstrable improvements. For example, NZ Rail, after being sold, reduced its workforce from 23 000 to fewer than 5000 and at the same time more than doubled its transport volume. The proceeds from privatisation were used predominantly to mend the public sector's balance sheet. After the 1993 election, which the National government won with a reduced majority, the key reformer, Ruth Richardson, was sacked; but by then the central institutions of the least regulated economy in OECD were firmly established.

The second reform wave made the various suborders reasonably consistent again and cata-pulted New Zealand into the top three countries on economic liberties in 1995, up from a very poor forty-fourth ranking in 1975 (Gwartney and Lawson, 1997, pp. 140–1). It ushered in a strong economic upturn and a dramatic improvement in New Zealand's international competi-tiveness and attractiveness. Between 1987 and 1994, the core part of government had shed 4000 civil servants, and the privatised production enterprises had saved another 37 000 em-ployees. The government-owned enterprise sector shrank from 12 per cent of annual production in the early 1980s to about 5 per cent in the mid-1990s. Yet overall employment rose strongly.

Rethinking government

Functions of government	Reform action
Protective	Rules streamlined and liberalised (deregulation); protection of monetary stability; protection of freedom of contract for labour
Productive	(Most) privatised; remainder declared 'core business' and corporatised; set targets; enhanced accountability
Redistributive (a) by intervention:	Terminated by deregulation
(b) by transfers:	Targeted transfers, with reduced eligibility
Fiscal/administrative	Budget balance; tax reform; Fiscal Reponsibility Act

By 1995, the public budget had a surplus of 3 per cent of GDP despite tax cuts. Government credit ratings improved. The deregulation of labour markets was followed by modest real-wage growth, strong employment growth and dramatic drops in unemployment, including among the weaker segments of the workforce, such as young people, women and Maoris, a development probably aided by the dampening of welfare incentives not to work. The NZ currency appreciated and capital costs came down. Private investment was strong, and the workforce pursued skill upgrading and innovation. Surveys showed great satisfaction with working life, remuneration and job security.

The key institutional reforms were made explicit in major items of legislation, namely the Reserve Bank of New Zealand Act of 1989, which credibly committed the independent central bank to a maximum consumer price inflation of 2 per cent per annum; the Employment Contracts Act of 1991, which freed labour markets; and the Fiscal Responsibility Act of 1994 which tied the hands of future governments on deficit finance and reductions in accountability.

The second wave of reform made the economic institutions consistent across the board. Overall, the reforms reprivatised responsibility to some degree, and emphasised private initiative and spontaneous coordination. The three major functions of government were thoroughly re-evaluated. The protective function (and little else) was declared the 'core business' of government and reorganised so as to make government agents more accountable. The productive function of government was first corporatised and then gradually it was largely privatised (exceptions are education and health). The distributive function of government was targeted a little more on helping poor citizens through transfer payments. Virtually all redistributive market interventions – such as job regulations, price and quantity controls – were abolished.

In the wake of electoral reforms, the economic reforms came to an end in the mid-1990s and there has been limited back-sliding from economic rationalism to political and rent-seeking imperatives. ◆

(Sources: Kasper (1996), where the interested reader can find a detailed list of literature on the New Zealand case. See also the autobiographical accounts by two politicians: Richardson, 1995, and Prebble, 1996)

Privatisation

The transfer of property rights from collective ownership (at different levels of government) to private ownership has been driven mainly by the intention to control agent opportunism and to make 'hard' budget constraints credible to the managers and workers in formerly government-owned enterprises. By allowing for a genuine threat of bankruptcy, agent opportunism is curbed. As we saw in Chapter 8, managers in firms that are surrounded by competitive markets have to control their inclinations to act opportunistically and have to explore ceaselessly what the customers want. But we saw in Chapter 11 that similar competitive pressures have been lacking in the public sector. Administrative disciplines are often comparatively weak and ineffectual and the supplier is often in a monopoly situation, so the incentive to meet the customer's aspirations is comparatively weak. Therefore, the transfer of an operation from public monopoly to private competition promises gains in cost control, innovative capability and effectiveness.

Fiscal motives also play a role in privatisation. Governments hope to gain scope for debt repayment and for new budgetary initiatives from the receipts of asset sales. They also want to reduce political responsibility for loss-making, underperforming public enterprises, for inadequate service to the public and for high infrastructure costs that prejudice international competitiveness. In many countries, the problems of publicly owned enterprises have increased over time, as access to fiscal subsidies and protection from the discipline of competition gradually encouraged the emergence of rent-seeking alliances; for example, when labour unions aggressively pursue higher wages, easy work practices and overstaffing.

The privatisation wave gathered speed during the 1980s, led by the Thatcher government in the United Kingdom. In the 1990s, privatisation became a worldwide phenomenon. Numerous state-owned enterprises in telecommunications, banking, energy, mining and basic industries have been sold or otherwise privatised. Between 1985 and 1995, state-owned assets worth an estimated US$535 billion were sold to private owners (O'Leary, 1995). Governments such as those of France, Britain, Australia, Japan and Italy have transferred substantial assets to private ownership, in each of these cases over $4 billion in 1992–6 (OECD estimates, reported in *The Economist*, 22 March 1997, p. 123).

Once it has been decided to privatise government-owned enterprises, several practical issues arise. Different solutions have been found in different experiments with privatisation:

(a) How should publicly owned assets be valued before they are sold to buyers who will make their own valuations of future earnings from these assets? Some assets have been privatised for relatively low prices because it was hoped that subsequent share price increases would give the initial buyers of the shares a windfall profit – and the government a political gain. At times, provisions were made for a preferential sale of shares to employees or small savers. This has been justified with arguments about the benefits of 'popular capitalism', that is, a widespread holding of stakes in the capital stock. The main argument against low selling prices for government-owned assets rests on the view that public budgets should receive the maximum value possible from asset sales, so that public debt and tax burdens can be alleviated as much as possible.

(b) The argument is often made that the public already own collectively held assets, so these assets cannot be sold to it again. Instead, tradable shares to all privatised assets should simply be distributed or auctioned off against vouchers that are distributed free of charge to all citizens (voucher privatisation). This argument carries less weight when the debts were incurred against future tax payments and other revenues which a future generation has to bear. When the proceeds of the sale of socialised assets are used to retire public debts, the 'collective mortgage' on future generations is reduced. Outright asset sales are also more readily feasible in economies with high savings and well-developed capital markets, in contrast to formerly communist countries, where privatisation has been a relatively much bigger task than in the mixed economies.[7]

(c) In some instances, the argument has been made against privatisation that essential protective functions of government cannot be safeguarded once certain assets are privately owned. For example, national airlines should remain nationalised for defence reasons. However, most nations have laws that allow the diversion of privately owned property to collective purposes in cases such as a national emergency. The same purpose can be served by a 'golden share' which government retains and which gives it a majority vote in certain clearly defined situations, such as a state of war.

(d) A frequent argument against privatisation is that government loses a tool to achieve redistributional equity. However, equitable access to certain services, such as education, housing or health, does not depend on the public production of these services (sections 10.1 and 10.5). Indeed, if competing health, education and housing providers offer a greater range of choices and produce them at lower cost, then economically weak groups benefit.

(e) As we mentioned in the preceding chapter, privatisation is often coupled with the task of exposing an existing monopoly to competition. Simply converting a publicly owned monopoly into a privately owned monopoly may not be desirable on grounds of equity, efficiency, justice and freedom. Indeed, one classic argument for governments taking control of private property was the public control of private monopolies. Thus, privatisation should promote competition wherever possible. This can be done, above all, by removing all legal and regulatory impediments to the emergence of potential private rivals and by facilitating arrangements that allow exclusion (control of free-riding). In many instances, technical progress has facilitated competitive supply where this was not possible in an earlier age. Thus, the radio spectrum can now be split more finely, so competing radio, television and communications networks are feasible, and the fixed costs of entering a freed telecommunications market have plummeted thanks to new technology when simultaneously users can be excluded by coding the signals and the use of decoders. It is now possible to privatise electrical power generation and to trade in competitive bids from private suppliers to a shared power grid, just as competing private train operators can share a publicly owned rail system.

There is now a fairly broad variety of experiences with privatisation, most of which are positive from the viewpoint of individual customers; some are negative, especially where public monopolies were simply converted into private monopolies (*World Bank, World Development Report 1996*, p. 49). Much of the resistance to privatisation – and the debate about its merits after the event – has focused on distributional consequences. Frequently, the fiercest opposition to privatisation has come from employee organisations who have lost privileges, such as high on-the-job consumption, overstaffing and protection from innovation – in other words, the rents typically obtained by opportunistic agents who are not subject to effective controls by the principals. Privatisation has indeed often been accompanied by job losses, reflecting earlier overstaffing. Privatisation has also been costly to the former public or new private owners in cases where high contractual retirement payouts were secured by the employees of the public monopoly companies. In some cases, the market value of public corporations, net of their high pension liabilities, has been negative. To stop the burden of further losses, such companies had to be given away, at times to the staff.

The experience to date indicates that on the whole corporatisation tends to offer one-off performance stimuli, but that exposure to the permanent disciplines of private ownership confers continuing incentives to control costs and enhance service and performance. Privatisation has also made the task of governing easier, since cabinets and political leaders with limited decision capabilities are now able to concentrate on fewer problems in overseeing collective action.

O Key Concepts

Corporatisation is the conversion of a publicly owned production facility to a separate, discrete, accountable public enterprise that is given a specific function. A corporatised public enterprise has to show how its net assets perform and can normally not gain automatic access to tax subsidies if it makes a loss (hard budget constraint). Corporatisation is often the precursor of privatisation.

Privatisation is the transfer of property rights from collective to private own-ership and of the right to manage the property from collective to autonomous private decision making. ●

Deregulation

Legal-regulatory systems have evolved over time as parliaments and administrations tried to refine their protective functions and to pursue redistribution (section 10.1). Proscriptive, universal institutions have been increasingly replaced by prescriptive, specific regulations, often at the behest of organised pressure groups. In the process, new exter-nal institutions often clashed with traditional internal institutions and have become inherently contradictory and costly to comply with. No one could foresee the many side-effects of these institutional changes. Pervasive interventionism, as well as discriminatory taxes and social security charges, have induced private operators to transfer into the 'informal sector' (black markets, the shadow economy) and has alien-ated the population from governance – a danger to the stability of a political regime and the welfare state (Streit, 1984).

As political doubts about the merits of redistributional intervention increased and international systems competition heated up in the 1980s and 1990s, deregulation was put on the agenda by political entrepre-neurs in industry associations, lobby groups, public administrations and parliaments. The ensuing institutional innovations varied, depending on existing regulations, the intensity of international competition and the cohesion or otherwise of the organised rent-seek-ing coalitions.

Yet over and above the peculiarities of specific national circumstances, a number of common, fundamental issues emerged in the deregula-tion debate around the world:

(a) Should regulatory reform follow a pattern of piecemeal tactics, introducing change where the problems are pressing or political opportunities for pragmatic changes arise? Or should reform be based on a cohesive strategy and be implemented in a radical 'big bang'? Most reformist political entrepreneurs – given the stric-tures of parliamentary majorities, electoral and interest-group dynamics and complex vote-seeking alliances – opted for 'piece-meal re-engineering' to move in the general direction of freer markets. This pragmatic procedure at times introduced contradic-tions between 'suborders', for example between newly freed product markets and still-regulated labour markets (see the box on New Zealand, pp. 474–7). Such inconsistencies in suborders were bound to distort relative prices: for example, squeezing profits and hence destroying jobs and specific capital values. The costs of institutional reform can certainly be lessened if it impacts on all major markets simultaneously and evenly. Where this maxim had to be violated for political-tactical reasons, the apparent costs may subsequently demonstrate the need to complete the reform agenda (as was the case in New Zealand) or help to undo the reforms because they are perceived as too costly. When reforms are over-turned by political entrepreneurs who appeal to particular interests in the status quo, this tends to be costly because it confuses order and greatly increases information costs. On the balance of prob-abilities, therefore, speed and momentum to overcome political and social resistance and to enhance across-the-board consistency of institutional change is preferable in most circumstances. On the other hand, reforms cannot be started with the notion of a known 'reform agenda', a finite list of actions to go through. When a list of deregulatory measures is implemented, the reformers suffer from a knowledge problem: what complementary measures will become necessary to ensure that the reforms of the first hour meet expectations. 'Big bang' reforms are therefore likely to lead to the discovery of further reform requirements, as the consequences of the 'big bang' become known.

(b) The above point is tied closely to the discussion of how to se-quence reforms. The question of whether factor markets should be freed before product markets, or capital before labour markets, is frequently discussed in the academic literature. Whatever the arguments for the ideal speed and sequence of reforms, this de-bate is developed on the wholly unrealistic assumption of perfect knowledge on the part of the observer. The point was made by leading New Zealand reformer Roger Douglas and approvingly quoted by Czech transformer Václav Klaus who wrote:

> I was struck by the identical reasoning by former New Zealand Finance Minister Roger Douglas (now Sir Roger) who states: A great deal of technical debate has been aired worldwide about the optimum sequencing of structural reform, and the alleged sequencing errors of governments … Armchair theorists postu-late the desirability of tackling the labour market or the tradeable goods market before embarking, for example, on the deregula-tion of sectors such as finance. At a purely analytical level the debate is entertaining, but no clear-cut messages emerge. Moreo-ver, from my point of view as a practitioner, the question is irrelevant. Before you can plan your perfect move in the perfect

way at the perfect time, the situation has already changed. Instead of a perfect result, you will have a missed opportunity.

Some decisions take full effect the date they are made. Others take two to five years' hard work before they can be fully implemented. Perfect sequencing is just not achievable. If a window of opportunity opens up for a decision or action that makes sense in the medium term, use it before the window closes!

(Klaus, 1991, pp. 9, 13)

(c) Normally, economic reforms extend to international economic relations. Openness has proved to be an essential ingredient in the sustained reform of domestic institutions (Papageorgiou *et al.*, 1991). Within closed systems, the incentives to carry out genuine reforms in the face of resolute rent-seeking are weak. The prompt feedback from threatening losses in international competitiveness therefore seems essential to keep the reforming momentum alive.

(d) Reforms of labour-market institutions are politically difficult because they directly affect the majority of the electorate. When this leads to regulatory hold-up, unemployment results. Moreover, the price signals from competitive labour markets are often blunted by redistributional policies, such as unemployment payments which nearly equate earnings from work, high and progressive income taxes, minimum wage legislation, and the disbursement of subsidies to families. In many OECD countries, people have learnt habits of helplessness and are confronted by disincentives to seek work, because the sum total of 'benefits' received for not working often exceeds the market wage net of taxes and other costs of working (section 10.4). In particular, reformers have to tackle the difficult issue of material disincentives for the transition from public welfare to work, since net incomes sometimes drop when people accept low-paid work. These problems arise in particular when governments rely heavily on income taxes and tax rates progress steeply.

(e) The outcomes of microeconomic reforms are normally closely tied to the restoration of the basic macroeconomic conditions, most particularly stable money and fiscal discipline to ensure sustainable levels of public debt. The creep of redistributionary activism has, in many affluent democracies, exceeded the tolerated limits of taxation, leading to 'taxpayer revolts'. As a consequence, public debt levels have crept up. Virtually all OECD governments are now much more highly indebted than they were a generation ago, often more than is prudently compatible with prospective tax receipts.

(f) Budget reforms are closely tied to a re-examination of the various functions of government. Many observers want to lay down constitutional rules to force governments to balance the budget, to impose debt limits, to enhance accountability and to decentralise government powers along the lines of competitive federalism, as discussed in Chapter 12. While the 'hand-tying' of elected parliaments has had only limited success, given the politico-economic forces that favour rent-seeking, the view is gaining currency among independent observers in many industrial countries that 'absolute power also corrupts parliaments and elected governments absolutely'. To give 'hand-tying' a somewhat better chance, the provision of transparent information and clear accountability (accrual accounting) could be mandated.

(g) In most developed countries, budget reform has to extend to tax reform. Because direct taxes cause disincentives to work, to save and to pursue international competitiveness, (progressive) income, profit and wealth taxes have in many countries had to be deemphasised in favour of (flat) indirect taxes. The argument that progressive income taxes would bring about a more equal distribution of incomes has proved to be incorrect, since lobbying and parliamentary changes to tax laws have produced numerous specific exemptions. As a consequence, the incidence of progressive income taxes is often lower on the rich than on the middle-income earners. The shift to indirect taxes affects income and wealth distribution and raises much political 'voice' from those who expect to lose as well as from those who expect to gain. When taxation is less distortive, enterprises and individuals can base their decisions more on their economic expectations and their own preferences, and less on considerations of how to minimise tax burdens.

(h) Regulatory reforms have often been stalled by political stalemate. Parliamentary and cabinet coalitions may be unstable, upper and lower houses of parliament may be at loggerheads, and the executive and parliament may hold each other in check. These problems are aggravated when the political leadership focuses on mere tactics, or yields to organised interest groups. As interjurisdictional competition heats up, it may well become apparent that certain social value systems, constitutions and institutional systems are less capable of evolutionary reform. The price of a nation's given institutional system may well be continued stagnation and relative decline (section 12.3). From a long-term historic perspective of the rise and decline of civilisations, this is not a novel discovery.

O Key Concepts

Deregulation is an act of removing selective legislative and regulatory constraints on the free use of property rights, facilitating coordination by market forces.

Streamlining is an exercise in which multiple related (and often contradictory) controls of markets are simplified on the understanding that certain political purposes (such as health or environmental protection) can be achieved more simply and with reduced compliance costs.

'Big bang' is a strategy of institutional reform which tries to achieve all the changes which are considered necessary simultaneously and quickly. This contrasts with gradualism, which is a strategy of piecemeal and stepwise change of the institutions.

Hand-tying relates to the laying down of rules that restrain future parliaments or governments from taking certain opportunistic actions. It is based on the notion that, in the heat of battle, costly or discriminatory decisions may be taken which, in a calmer moment, would be seen as harmful – similar to the request of Odysseus to be tied to the mast before he sailed past the Sirens. In practice, elected governments and parliaments have been loath to be tied down, either by election promises or formal acts of legislation and constitutional rules. ●

Reaffirming a Constitution of Capitalism?

Although not all the old industrial countries have embarked on comprehensive reform, some institutions have been reformed in all 'mixed economies' since the 1970s. In the postwar period, the reforms in Germany and Japan were the exceptions to the then-prevailing worldwide trend away from capitalism. However, since the late 1970s, the trend has gone in the opposite direction. Political entrepreneurs now see gain from undoing *dirigiste* controls and liberalising the uses of property rights. The reforms have, however, been piecemeal and have not been entrenched, so they can be easily undone. And many of the politically more difficult reforms – such as of social welfare – have been left undone.

Therefore, observers have called for the formal, legislated entrenchment of the reforms and the stipulation of cohesive constitutional rules that could avert the future opportunism of parliaments and administrations, that would give the individual reforms cohesion and that would enhance their coordinative impact. This means that explicit general rules of constitutional quality should be adopted to safeguard private property rights and to limit the powers of elected parliamentary majorities or activist judges to interfere with autonomous property uses. Many written constitutions, such as those of the US and Germany, contain explicit protections of private property. Yet in practice the free use of property rights suffers increasing interference. When high courts have to adjudicate on whether the principle of private property is violated by new legislation, they normally cannot do so merely by methods of formal justice. Judicial processes cannot cope with the complex economic issues and the political trade-offs involved. In any event, much deregulation will be needed to reach that level of economic autonomy that the citizens of the United States or Britain enjoyed last century, or that is *de facto* now practised in many parts of the new industrial countries.

In any event, it seems probable that the constitution of capitalism has a chance to gain ground against political controls and collective rent-seeking as long as openness and interjurisdictional competition put a check on the pursuits of political agents. Continuing reductions in transport and communications costs are likely to stimulate that process further.

When interventionism is found to raise compliance costs to intolerable levels and weaken international competitiveness, demands for reform frequently spread. They are then inspired by attitudes similar to those reported from a meeting of the French finance minister, Jean-Baptiste Colbert (1619–83) with the merchant Thomas LeGendre. When Colbert benevolently inquired what the government might do for LeGendre's business, he exclaimed '*Laissez-nous faire!* [Just leave us alone!]'.

The reader of this book will in the future no doubt have the opportunity to test the veracity of the dictum that 'the price of freedom is eternal vigilance' and that fostering the right institutions is a job that is never quite done.

Questions for Review

- How do you rate the economic institutions in the country in which you live on a scale between:

  (a) a high degree of economic freedom protected from private and public interference by minimal, transparent and reliably enforced rules; and
  (b) precarious economic freedoms because the laws are poorly enforced?

Does the rate of growth in per capita incomes over the past ten or twenty years correlate with your judgement in the way suggested in this and preceding chapters?

- Can you think of societies that have poor political and civic liberties but great economic freedom? And vice versa?
- What is the difference between 'personalised credit' and an impersonal credit market? Do industrial entrepreneurs in your country depend on personalised credit? Is it easy for small entrepreneurs to get access to credit, or do they need 'connections'? How was impersonal credit made available to small operators in Bangladesh (see box on pp. 233–4)?
- Can a politically well-connected businessman (say, the president's cousin) in your country go bankrupt? To what extent does the answer reveal how well private property rights are protected? Could you take the president's/king's/party chairman's son to court over an unpaid debt in your country?
- From what was said about Algeria in the box on pp. 457–9, what is, in your opinion, the connection between the treatment of private property rights after independence and political confrontation and the rise of fundamentalism a generation later? What would you advise Algerians to do in the present situation?
- How has international competition affected the evolution of informal, internal institutions in the capitalist societies of East Asia?
- Do you expect corruption of government officials to enhance or diminish the international competitiveness of an open economy? Give reasons for your reply.
- What are the arguments in favour of exposing public sector monopolies (for example, in education, health care, transport, power supply and communications) to private competition? What are the arguments against this? Does the balance of arguments for and against vary between industries?
- Would you expect producers (the managers, the unions, the individual workers) in public monopoly firms to be for or against their exposure to competition?
- In the text we said that public monopolies encourage 'on-the-job consumption'. How does this manifest itself in practice?
- What are the arguments in favour of privatisation of government-owned production enterprises?
- What are the arguments against privatising the protective functions of government? Should governments rely on private police forces and armies? If not, why not?
- What do you expect to happen to the commitment to massive redistribution in the old industrial countries if the governments of new industrial countries continue to treat old-age and health provision as private responsibilities? Will the owners of mobile enterprises,

capital and high-level knowledge 'vote with their feet' in favour of low tax/low welfare locations?

- Do you know of privatisation projects in your country? How were these projects managed with regard to the critical issues of privatisation discussed in this chapter?

- Try to discuss the arguments for rapid deregulation in your country in the light of what you have learnt from this book.

- Why did two of the boldest reformers of recent times, Václav Klaus of the Czech Republic and Roger Douglas of New Zealand, deride elaborate academic theories of sequencing in economic reform?

- Why is the institution of macroeconomic stability important to economic growth and the development of new industries? What do unforeseen fluctuations in inflation do to long-term plans to invest and innovate?

- Are the government's budget-making processes in your country transparent? Are public accounts bound by the same rules of estimating revenues, expenditures, assets and liabilities that govern business accounting in your country?

- What are the reasons for the assertion that 'the price of freedom is eternal vigilance'?

Notes

1. Peel's era, however, also marked the beginnings of legislation which gave trade unions special privileges, a development that was later to undermine Britain's competitive order and the rule of law (as we saw in section 8.1).
2. A noteworthy exception to the general rule that freedom and growth go along with each other is the People's Republic of China, ranked eighty-first out of 115 countries, but growing at an average rate of 7.8 per cent (1980–96). However, China's economic freedom rating has been going up steadily from 1975 to the mid-1990s. In the light of what was said in the preceding chapter, it is also interesting to see which of the regimes that shed totalitarian socialism have now attained the *relatively* best institutional guarantees of individual economic freedom. Those were Estonia (fifty-second place), Lithuania (fifty-fifth), the Czech Republic (sixty-second) and Hungary (sixty-third), with the other regimes in the former Soviet orbit trailing amongst African countries (which tended to have both poor economic performance and few economic liberties).
3. Effective rates of protection are based on estimates that try to take into account the impact of protection on the costs and receipts of an industry.
4. There were racial riots in Malaysia in 1969, but this remained a one-off event, as people of different races interacted by and large under the institutions of free markets, which are 'racially blind'. By contrast, the *dirigiste* economic policies of Sri Lanka were given a racial edge, so racial problems blew up in long-lasting open conflict. This comparison highlights the important insight that cooperation in markets tends to erode racial differences and prejudices, whereas political action often exploits these differences and aggravates them (Rabushka, 1974).
5. As of 1995, for rankings among the top twenty on economic freedom Hong Kong is first, Singapore second, Thailand eighth, Malaysia equal tenth, Taiwan sixteenth, Japan and South Korea equal eighteenth (Gwartney and Lawson, 1997, p. 27). China ranks eighty-first.
6. There is an uncanny parallel between the German reforms of the 1950s and the British reforms of the 1820s–1840s (see Chapter 8): in both cases the reform of the economic institutions laid the foundations for an outburst of innovation and pros-

perity. But paradoxically, the reformers also laid the basis of rules that violate competitive principles: the granting of legal privileges to organised labour in the case of nineteenth-century Britain (Chapter 8) and political social-welfare provision in 1950s Germany. Both these exceptions from the competitive imperative planted the seed for the growth of vested interests which eventually overturned competition-supporting institutions and the economic benefits these had conferred.

7. One has to treat privatisation in formerly socialist plan economies differently from privatisation in mixed economies. In socialist countries, government debt was, as a rule, part of a financial system whose purpose was to control the execution of the plan. Government debt can therefore be compared with the book-keeping entries in an unconsolidated balance sheet of a multistage firm, in this case the state, bank and public enterprises. The capital stock, which was built up by collective action but was under the control of the state, can be seen as 'belonging' to the population as a whole (as well as to foreign savers who gave socialist countries loans). In these circumstances, voucher privatisation is a way of allocating parts of the collective capital stock to private owners. By contrast, voluntary savers in a mixed economy who invested in government bonds in a market decision with the knowledge that their savings would be invested in a public sector project, can expect that the public debt will be retired when that project is privatised.

APPENDIX

I, Pencil

*Leonard E. Read**

I am a lead pencil – the ordinary wooden pencil familiar to all boys and girls and adults who can read and write. (My official name is 'Mongol 482'. My many ingredients are assembled, fabricated and finished by Eberhard Faber Pencil Company, Wilkes-Barre, Pennsylvania.)

Writing is both by vocation and my avocation; that's all I do.

You may wonder why I should write a genealogy. Well, to begin with, my story is interesting. And, next, I am a mystery – more so than a tree or a sunset or even a flash of lightning. But, sadly, I am taken for granted by those who use me, as if I were a mere incident and without background. This supercilious attitude relegates me to the level of the commonplace. This is a species of the grievous error in which mankind cannot too long persist without peril. For, as a wise man, G.K. Chesterton, observed, 'We are perishing for want of wonder, not for want of wonders.'

I, Pencil, simple though I appear to be, merit your wonder and awe, a claim I shall attempt to prove. In fact, if you can understand me – no, that's too much to ask of anyone – if you can become aware of the miraculousness that I symbolize, you can help save the freedom mankind is so unhappily losing. I have a profound lesson to teach. And I can teach this lesson better than can an automobile or an airplane or a mechanical dishwasher because – well, because I am seemingly so simple.

Simple? Yet, not a single person on the face of this earth knows how to make me. This sounds fantastic, doesn't it? Especially when you realize that there are about one and one-half billion my kind produced in the US each year.

Pick me up and look me over. What do you see? Not much meets the eye – there's some wood, lacquer, the printed labeling, graphite lead, a bit of metal, and an eraser.

Innumerable Antecedents

Just as you cannot trace your family tree back very far, so is it impossible for me to name and explain all my antecedents. But I would like to suggest enough of them to impress upon you the richness and complexity of my background.

My family tree begins with what in fact is a tree, a cedar of straight grain that grows in Northern California and Oregon. Now contemplate all the saws and trucks and rope

---

* First published in 1958. Reprinted with the kind permission of the Foundation for Economic Education in New York who hold the copyright.

and the countless other gear used in harvesting and carting the cedar logs to the railroad siding. Think of all the persons and the numberless skills that went into their fabrication: the mining of ore, the making of steel and its refinement into saws, axes, motors; the growing of hemp and bringing it through all the stages to heavy and strong rope; the logging camps with their beds and mess halls, the cookery and the raising of all the foods. Why, untold thousands of persons had a hand in every cup of coffee the loggers drink!

The logs are shipped to a mill in San Leandro, California. Can you imagine the individuals who make flat cars and rails and railroad engines and who construct and install the communication systems incidental thereto? These legions are among my antecedents.

Consider the millwork in San Leandro. The cedar logs are cut into small, pencil-length slats less than one-fourth of an inch in thickness. These are kiln-dried and then tinted for the same reason women put rouge on their faces. People prefer that I look pretty, not a pallid white. The slats are waxed and kiln-dried again. How many skills went into the making of the tint and kilns, into supplying the heat, the light and power, the belts, motors, and all the other things a mill requires? Are sweepers in the mill among my ancestors? Yes, and also included are the men who poured the concrete for the dam of a Pacific Gas & Electric Company hydroplant which supplies the mill's power. And don't overlook the ancestors present and distant who have a hand in transporting sixty carloads of slats across the nation from California to Wilkes-Barre.

Complicated Machinery

Once in the pencil factory – $4 000 000 in machinery and building, all capital accumulated by thrifty and saving parents of mine – each slat is given eight grooves by a complex machine, after which another machine lays leads in every other slat, applies glue, and places another slat atop – a lead sandwich, so to speak. Seven brothers and I are mechanically carved from this 'wood-clinched' sandwich.

My 'lead' itself – it contains no lead at all – is complex. The graphite is mined in Ceylon. Consider the miners and those who make their many tools and the makers of the paper sacks in which the graphite is shipped and those who make the string that ties the sacks and those who put them aboard ships and those who make the ships. Even the lighthouse keepers along the way assisted in my birth – and the harbor pilots.

The graphite is mixed with clay from Mississippi in which ammonium hydroxide is used in the refining process. Then wetting agents are added such as sulfonated tallow – animal fats chemically reacted with sulfuric acid. After passing through numerous machines, the mixture finally appears as endless extrusions – as from a sausage grinder – cut to size, dried, and baked for several hours at 1850 degrees Fahrenheit. To increase their strength and smoothness the leads are then treated with a hot mixture which includes candililla wax from Mexico, paraffin wax and hydrogenated natural fats.

My cedar receives six coats of lacquer. Do you know all of the ingredients of lacquer? Who would think that the growers of castor beans and the refiners of castor oils are a part of it? They are. Why, even the processes by which the lacquer is made a beautiful yellow involves the skills of more persons than one can enumerate!

Observe the labeling. That's a film formed by applying heat to carbon black mixed with resins. How do you make resins and what, pray, is carbon black?

My bit of metal – the ferrule – is brass. Think of all the persons who mine zinc and copper and those who have the skills to make shiny sheet brass from these products of nature. Those black rings on my ferrule are black nickel. What is black nickel and how is it applied? The complete story of why the center of my ferrule has no black nickel on it would take pages to explain.

Then there's my crowning glory, inelegantly referred to in the trade as 'the plug', the part man uses to erase the errors he makes with me. An ingredient called 'factice' is what does the erasing. It is a rubber-like product made by reacting rape seed oil from the Dutch East Indies with sulfur chloride. Rubber, contrary to the common notion, is only for binding purposes. Then, too, there are numerous vulcanizing and accelerating agents. The pumice comes from Italy; and the pigment which gives 'the plug' its color is cadmium sulfide.

Vast Web of Knowhow

Does anyone wish to challenge my earlier assertion that no single person on the face of this earth knows how to make me?

Actually, millions of human beings have had a hand in my creation, no one of whom even knows more than a very few of the others. Now, you may say that I go too far in relating the picker of a coffee berry in far-off Brazil and food growers elsewhere to my creation; that this is an extreme position. I shall stand by my claim. There isn't a single person in all these millions, including the president of the pencil company, who contributes more than a tiny, infinitesimal bit of knowhow. From the standpoint of knowhow the only difference between the miner of graphite in Ceylon and the logger in Oregon is in the type of knowhow. Neither the miner nor the logger can be dispensed with, any more than the chemist at the factory or the worker in the oil field – paraffin being a byproduct of petroleum.

Here is an astounding fact: Neither the worker in the oil field nor the chemist nor the digger of graphite or clay nor anyone who mans or makes the ships or trains or trucks nor the one who runs the machine that does the knurling on my bit of metal nor the president of the company performs his singular task because he wants *me*. Each one wants me less, perhaps, than does a child in the first grade. Indeed, there are some among this vast multitude who never saw a pencil nor would they know how to use one. Their motivation is other than me. Perhaps it is something like this: Each of these millions sees that he can thus exchange his tiny knowhow for the goods and services he needs or wants. I may or may not be among these items.

No Human Master-mind

There is a fact still more astounding: The absence of a master-mind, of anyone dictating or forcibly directing these countless actions that bring me into being. No trace of such a person can be found. Instead, we find the Scottish economist and moral philosopher Adam Smith's famous 'Invisible Hand' at work in the marketplace. This is the mystery to which I earlier referred.

It has been said that 'only God can make a tree'. Why do we agree with this? Isn't it because we realize that we ourselves could not make one? Indeed, can we even describe a tree? We cannot, except in superficial terms. We can say, for instance, that a certain molecular configuration manifests itself as a tree. But what mind is there among men that could even record, let alone direct, the constant change of molecules that transpire in the life span of a tree? Such a feat is utterly unthinkable!

I, Pencil, am a complex combination of miracles; a tree, zinc, copper, graphite, and so on. But to these miracles which manifest themselves in Nature an even more extraordinary miracle has been added: the configuration of creative human energies – millions of tiny bits of knowhow configurating naturally and spontaneously in response to human necessity and desire and in the absence of any human master-minding! Since only God can make a tree, I insist that only God could make me. Man can no more direct millions of bits of knowhow so as to bring a pencil into being than he can put molecules together to create a tree.

That's what I meant when I wrote earlier, 'If you can become aware of the miraculousness which I symbolize, you can help save the freedom mankind is so unhappily losing.' For, if one is aware that these bits of knowhow will naturally, yes, automatically, arrange themselves into creative and productive patterns in response to human necessity and demand – that is, in the absence of governmental or any other coercive master-minding – then one will possess an absolutely essential ingredient for freedom: a faith in free men. Freedom is impossible without this faith.

Once government has had a monopoly on a creative activity – the delivery of the mail, for instance – most individuals will believe that the mail could not be efficiently delivered by men acting freely. And here is the reason: Each one acknowledges that he himself doesn't know how to do all the things involved in mail delivery. He also recognizes that no other individual could. These assumptions are correct. No individual possesses enough knowhow to perform a nation's mail delivery any more than any individual possesses enough knowhow to make a pencil. In the absence of a faith in free men – unaware that millions of tiny kinds of knowhow would naturally and miraculously form and cooperate to satisfy this necessity – the individual cannot help but reach the erroneous conclusion that the mail can be delivered only by governmental master-minding.

Testimony Galore

If I, Pencil, were the only item that could offer testimony on what men can accomplish when free to try, then those with little faith would have a fair case. However, there is testimony galore; it's all about us on every hand. Mail delivery is exceedingly simple when compared, for instance, to the making of an automobile or a calculating machine or a grain combine or a milling machine, or to tens of thousands of other things.

Delivery? Why, in this age where men have been left free to try, they deliver the human voice around the world in less than one second; they deliver an event visually and in motion to any person's home when it is happening; they deliver 150 passengers from Seattle to Baltimore in less than four hours; they deliver gas from Texas to one's range or furnace in New York at unbelievably low rates and without subsidy; they deliver each four pounds of oil from the Persian Gulf to our Eastern Seaboard – halfway around the world – for less money than the government charges for delivering a one-ounce letter across the street![1]

Leave Men be Free

The lesson I have to teach is this: Leave all creative energies uninhibited. Merely organize society to act in harmony with this lesson. Let society's legal apparatus remove all obstacles the best it can. Permit creative knowhow to freely flow. Have faith that free men will respond to the 'Invisible Hand'. This faith will be confirmed. I, Pencil, seemingly simple though I am, offer the miracle of my creation as testimony that this is a practical faith, as practical as the sun, the rain, a cedar tree, and the good earth.

Notes

1.   Ed.: Some things have changed since this essay was first published in 1958!

Bibliography

Abramovitz, M. (1979), 'Rapid Growth Potential and its Realization: the Experience of the Capitalist Economies in Post-war Period', in: E. Malinvaud and R.O.C. Matthews (eds), *Economic Growth and Resources*, vol. 1, London and New York: St Martin's Press, 1–50.

Alchian, A. (1987), 'Property Rights', in J. Eatwell, M. Milgate and P. Newman (eds), *The New Palgrave: A Dictionary of Economics*, London: Macmillan, and New York: Stockton Press, 1031–4.

Alchian, A. and H. Demsetz (1972), 'Production, Information Costs, and Economic Organisation', *American Economic Review*, vol. 62, 777–95.

Alchian, A. and H. Demsetz (1973), 'The Property Rights Paradigm', *Journal of Economic History*, vol. 33, 16–27.

Alessi, L. de (1969), 'Implications of Property Rights for Government Investment Choices', *American Economic Review*, vol. 59, 16–63.

Alessi, L. de (1980), 'A Review of Property Rights: a Review of the Evidence', *Research in Law and Economics*, vol. 2, 1–47.

Alessi, L. de (1982), 'On the Nature and Consequences of Private and Public Enterprise', *Minnesota Law Review*, vol. 67, 191–209.

Alessi, L. de (1983), 'Property Rights, Transaction Costs, and X-efficiency: an Essay in Economic Theory', *American Economic Review*, vol. 73:1, 64–81.

Alessi, L. de (1995), 'Institutions, Competition, and Individual Welfare', in N. Karlsson (ed.), *Can the Present Problems of Mature Welfare States Such as Sweden be Solved?*, Stockholm: City University Press, 76–87.

Alston, L.J., T. Eggertsson and D.C. North (1996), *Empirical Studies in Institutional Change*, Cambridge: Cambridge University Press.

Anderson, P.W., K.J. Arrow and D. Pines (1988), *The Economy as an Evolving, Complex System*, Redwood: Addison-Wesley.

Anderson, T.L. and D.R. Leal (1991), *Free Market Environmentalism*, San Francisco: Pacific Research Institute for Public Policy.

Anderson, T.L. and D.R. Leal (1997), *Enviro-capitalists: Doing Good While Doing Well*, Lanham, MD: Rowman-Littlefield.

Armentano, D.T. (1991), *Antitrust and Monopoly: Anatomy of a Policy Failure*, 2nd edn, New York and London: Holmes & Meier.

Arndt, H.W. (1978), *The Rise and Fall of Economic Growth*, Melbourne: Longman Cheshire.

Arrow, K.J. (1951), *Social Choice and Individual Values*, New York: John Wiley.

Arrow, K.J. ([1962] 1971), 'Economic Welfare and the Allocation of Resources for Invention', in D.M. Lamberton (ed.), *Economics of Information and Knowledge*, Harmondsworth, Middx: Penguin, 141–60.

Arrow, K.J. (1969), 'The Organization of Economic Activity: Issues Pertinent to the Choice of Market versus Non-market Allocation', in Joint Economic Committee (91st US Congress, 1st session), *The Analysis and Evaluation of Public Expenditure*, vol. 1, Washington, DC: Congressional Printing Office, 59–73.

Arrow, K.J. (1985), 'The Economics of Agency', in J.W. Pratt and R.J. Zeckhauser (eds), *Principals and Agents: The Structure of Business*, Boston, MA: Harvard Business Books, 31–57.

Arthur, W.B. (1995), 'Complexity in Economic and Financial Markets', *Complexity*, vol. 1:1, 20–5, reprinted in Drobak and Nye (eds) (1997), *The Frontiers of the New Institutional Economics*, San Diego: Academic Press, 291–304.

Axelrod, R. (1984), *The Evolution of Cooperation*, New York: Basic Books.

Banks, G. and J. Tumlir (1986), *Economic Policy and the Adjustment Problem*, London: Gower.

Barro, R.J. and X. Sala-I-Martin (1995), *Economic Growth*, New York: McGraw-Hill.

Barzel, Y. (1982), 'Measurement Cost and the Organization of Markets', *Journal of Law and Economics*, vol. 25, 27–48.

Barzel, Y. (1989), *Economic Analysis of Property Rights*, Cambridge: Cambridge University Press.

Bates, R. (1990), 'Macropolitical Economy in the Field of Development', in J. Alt and K. Shepsle (eds), *Perspectives on Positive Political Economy*, Cambridge: Cambridge University Press, 31–54.

Baumol, W.J. ([1952] 1965), *Welfare Economics and the Theory of the State*, London: Bell.

Baumol, W.J. (1990), 'Entrepreneurship: Productive, Unproductive and Destructive', *Journal of Political Economy*, vol. 98, 893–921.

Becker, G. (1964), *Human Capital*, New York: National Bureau of Economic Research.

Becker, J. (1996), *Hungry Ghosts: China's Secret Famine*, London: John Murray.

Beckerman, W. (1974), *In Defence of Economic Growth*, London: J. Cape.

Benegas-Lynch, A. Hijo (1997), 'Towards a Theory of Auto-government', in G. Radnitzky (ed.) (1997), *Values and the Social Order*, Vol. 3: *Voluntary versus Coercive Orders*, Aldershot, UK and Brookfield, US: Avebury, 113–172

Bennoune, M. (1988), *The Making of Contemporary Algeria*, Cambridge and New York: Cambridge University Press.

Benson, B.L. (1988), 'The Spontaneous Evolution of Commercial Law', *Southern Economic Journal*, vol. 55, 655–61.

Benson, B.L. (1995), 'The Evolution of Values and Institutions in a Free Society: Underpinnings of a Market Economy', in G. Radnitzky and H. Bouillon (eds), *Values and Social Order*, vol. 1: *Values and Society*, Aldershot, UK, and Brookfield, US: Avebury, 87–126.

Berger, P. (1987), *The Capitalist Revolution*, Aldershot, UK: Wildwood House, and New York: Basic Books.

Berle, A.A. and G. C. Means (1932), *The Modern Corporation and Private Property*, New York: Macmillan.

Bernholz, P. (1966), 'Economic Policies in a Democracy', *Kyklos*, vol. 19, 48–80.

Bernholz, P. (1982), 'Expanding Welfare State, Democracy and Free Market Economy: Are They Compatible?', *Journal of Institutional and Theoretical Economics*, vol. 138, 583–98.

Bernholz, P. (1995), 'Efficiency, Political-economic Organization and International Competition between States', in G. Radnitzky and H. Bouillon (eds), *Values and Social Order*, vol. 2: *Society and Order*, Aldershot, UK, and Brookfield, US: Avebury, 157–203.

Bickenbach, F. and R. Soltwedel (1995), *Leadership and Business Organization: Findings from a Survey of Corporate Executives*, Gütersloh: Bertelsmann Foundation.

Bish, R. (1987), 'Federalism: a Market Economic Perspective', *Cato Journal*, vol. 5 (Fall), 377–97.

Blandy, R., P. Dawkins, K. Gannicott, P. Kain, W. Kasper and R. Kriegler (1985), *Structured Chaos: The Process of Productivity Advance*, Oxford and New York: Oxford University Press.

Block, W. (ed.) (1990), *Economics and the Environment: A Reconciliation*, Vancouver: Fraser Institute.

Boettke, P. (1990), *The Political Economy of Soviet Socialism: The Formative Years, 1918–1928*, Dordrecht, London and Boston: Kluwer.

Boettke, P. (ed.) (1994), *The Elgar Companion to Austrian Economics*, Aldershot, UK, and Brookfield, US: Edward Elgar.

Borner, S., A. Brunetti and B. Weber (1992), *Institutional Obstacles to Latin American Growth*, San Francisco: International Center for Economic Growth.

Bornstein, M. ([1965] 1989), *Comparative Economic Systems: Models and Cases*, 6th edn, Homewood, IL: Irwin.

Bouillon, H. (ed.) (1996), *Libertarians and Liberalism: Essays in Honour of Gerard Radnitzky*, Aldershot, UK, and Brookfield, US: Avebury.

Boulding, K.E. ([1956] 1997), *The Image: Knowledge in Life and Society*, 11th edn, Ann Arbor, MI: University of Michigan Press.

Boulding, K.E. (1959), *Principles of Economic Policy*, London: Staples Press.

Boulding, K.E. ([1962] 1968), 'Knowledge as a Commodity', in *Beyond Economics: Essays on Society, Religion, and Ethics*, Ann Arbor, MI: University of Michigan Press, 141–50.

Boulding, K.E. (1969), 'Economics as a Moral Science', *American Economic Review*, vol. 59, 1–12.

Brandel, F. (1981–4), *Civilization and Capitalism, 15th–18th Century*, 3 vols., London: Collins.

Brennan, G. and J.M. Buchanan ([1980] 1985), *The Power to Tax: Analytical Foundations of a Fiscal Constitution*, Cambridge and New York: Cambridge University Press.

Brennan, G. and J.M. Buchanan (1985), *The Reason of Rules: Constitutional Political Economy*, Cambridge and New York: Cambridge University Press.

Breyer, S. (1995), *Breaking the Vicious Circle; Toward Effective Risk Regulation*, new edn, Cambridge, MA: Harvard University Press.

Brunner, K. (1978), 'Reflections on the Political Economy of Government: the Persistent Growth of Government', *Schweizerische Zeitschrift für Volkswirtschaft und Statistik*, vol. 114, 649–80.

Brunner, K. (1985), 'The Limits of Economic Policy', *Schweizerische Zeitschrift für Volkswirtschaft und Statistik*, vol. 121, 213–36.

Brunner, K. and A. Meltzer (1971), 'The Uses of Money: Money in the Theory of the Exchange Economy', *American Economic Review*, vol. 61 (Dec.), 784–805.

Brunetti, A., G. Kisunko and B. Weder (1997), *Institutional Obstacles to Doing Business: Region-by-Region*

Results from a Worldwide Survey of the Private Sector, Washington, DC: World Bank.

Buchanan, J.M. (1965), 'An Economic Theory of Clubs', *Economica*, vol. 32, 1–14.

Buchanan, J.M. (1969), *Cost and Choice: An Inquiry in Economic Theory*, Chicago: University of Chicago Press.

Buchanan, J.M. (1975), *The Limits of Liberty: Between Anarchy and Leviathan*, Chicago: University of Chicago Press.

Buchanan, J.M. (1978), 'From Private Preferences to Public Philosophy: The Development of Public Choice', in Institute of Economic Affairs, *The Economics of Politics*, London: Institute of Economic Affairs, 3–20.

Buchanan, J.M. (1987), 'The Constitution of Economic Policy', *American Economic Review*, vol. 77, 243–50.

Buchanan, J. M. (1991), *Constitutional Economics*, Oxford, and Cambridge, MA: Basil Blackwell.

Buchanan, J.M. and A. di Pierro (1980), 'Cognition, Choice, and Entrepreneurship', *Southern Economic Journal*, vol. 46, 693–701.

Buchanan, J.M. and G. Tullock (1962), *The Calculus of Consent: Logical Foundations of Constitutional Democracy*, Ann Arbor, MI: University of Michigan Press.

Buchanan, J.M., R.D. Tollison and G. Tullock (eds) (1980), *Toward a Theory of the Rent-seeking Society*, College Station, TX: Texas A&M University Press.

Bush, P. (1987), 'The Theory of Institutional Change', *Journal of Economic Issues*, vol. 21, 1075–116.

Casson, M. (1993), 'Cultural Determinants of Economic Performance', *Journal of Comparative Economics*, vol. 17, 418–42.

Chenery, H.B. and M. Syrquin (1975), *Patterns of Development, 1950–70*, London: Oxford University Press, for the World Bank.

Chenery, H.B., S. Robinson and M. Syrquin (1986), *Industrialization and Growth: A Comparative Study*, New York: Oxford University Press, for the World Bank.

Cheung, S. (1983), 'The Contractual Nature of the Firm', *Journal of Law and Economics*, vol. 26, 1–21.

Ch'ng, D. (1993), *The Overseas Chinese Entrepreneurs in East Asia: Background, Business Practices and International Networks*, Melbourne: Committee for the Economic Development of Australia (CEDA).

Christainsen, G.B. (1989–90), 'Law as a Discovery Procedure', *Cato Journal*, vol. 9, 497–530.

Clark, J.M. (1962), *Competition as a Dynamic Process*, Washington, DC: Brookings Institution.

Clower, R.W. (ed.) (1969), *Monetary Theory: Selected Readings*, Harmondsworth, Middx: Penguin.

Coase, R.H. ([1937] 1952), 'The Nature of the Firm', in G.S. Stigler and K.E. Boulding (eds), *Readings in Price Theory*, Homewood, IL: Irwin, 331–52.

Coase, R.H. (1960), 'The Problem of Social Cost', *Journal of Law and Economics*, vol. 3, 1–44.

Coase, R.H. (1988), 'The Nature of the Firm: Origin, Meaning, Influence', *Journal of Law, Economics and Organization*, vol. 4:1, 3–47.

Coleman, J.S. (1990), *Foundations of Social Theory*, Cambridge, MA: Belknap Press of Harvard University Press.

Cooter, R.D. (1996), 'Decentralised Law for a Complex Economy: the Structural Approach to Adjudicating the New Law Merchant', *University of Pennsylvania Law Review*, no. 144, 1643–96.

Cooter, R.D. and T. Ulen (1997), *Law and Economics*, 2nd edn, New York: Addison-Wesley.

Cordato, R.E. (1994), 'Efficiency', in P. Boettke (ed.) *The Elgar Companion to Austrian Economics*, Aldershot, UK, and Brookfield, US: Edward Elgar, 131–7.

Coughlin, C.C., A.K. Chrystal and G.E. Wood (1988), 'Protectionist Trade Policies: a Survey of Theory, Evidence and Rationale', *Federal Reserve Bank of St Louis Review*, vol. 70:1, 12–29.

Curzon-Price, V. (1997), 'International Commerce as an Instance of Non-coerced Social Order', in Radnitzky (ed) (1997), *op. cit.*, 425–38.

Cyert, R.M. and J.G. March (1992), *A Behavioral Theory of the Firm*, 2nd edn, Cambridge, MA: Blackwell Business.

Dahlmann, C.J. (1979), 'The Problem of Externality', *Journal of Law and Economics*, vol. 22, 141–62.

Dahmén, E., L. Hannah and I.M. Kirzner (eds) (1994), *The Dynamics of Entrepreneurship*, Crawford Lectures, no. 5, Institute of Economic Research, Malmø: Lund University.

Dean, J.W. (1981), 'The Dissolution of the Keynesian Consensus', in D. Bell and I. Kristol (eds) *The Crisis in Economic Theory*, New York: Basic Books, 19–34.

Demsetz, H. (1964), 'The Exchange and Enforcement of Property Rights', *Journal of Law and Economics*, vol. 7, 11–26.

Demsetz, H. (1967), 'Toward a Theory of Property Rights', *American Economic Review*, vol. 57, 347–59.

Demsetz, H. (1969), 'Information and Efficiency: Another Viewpoint', *Journal of Law and Economics*, vol. 13, 1–22.

Demsetz, H. (1970), 'The Private Production of Public Goods', *Journal of Law and Economics*, vol. 13, 293–306.

Demsetz, H. (1982), *Economic, Political and Legal Dimensions of Competition*, Amsterdam and New York: North-Holland.

Demsetz, H. ([1982] 1989), *Efficiency, Competition and Policy: The Organisation of Economic Activity*, Oxford and New York: Basil Blackwell.

Demsetz, H. (1983), 'The Structure of Ownership

and the Theory of the Firm', *Journal of Law and Economics*, vol. 26, 375–93.

Demsetz, H. (1988), 'The Theory of the Firm Revisited', *Journal of Law, Economics and Organization*, vol. 4:1, 141–61.

Denison, E.F. (1967), *Why Growth Rates Differ?*, Washington, DC: Brookings Institution.

Department of Foreign Affairs, East Asia Analytical Unit, Australia (1995), *The Overseas Chinese*, Canberra: Australian Government Publishing Service.

Doti, J. and D.R. Lee (1991), *The Market Economy: A Reader*, Los Angeles: Roxbury Publications.

Downs, A. (1957a), *An Economic Theory of Democracy*, New York: Harper & Row.

Downs, A. (1957b), 'An Economic Theory of Political Action in a Democracy', in E. J. Hamilton (ed.), *Landmarks in Political Economy*, vol. 2, Chicago: University of Chicago Press, 559–82.

Drexler, K.E. (1986), *Engines of Creation: The Coming Era of Nanotechnology*, New York: Doubleday.

Drobak, J.N. and J.V.C. Nye (eds) (1997), *The Frontiers of the New Institutional Economics*, San Diego: Academic Press.

Drucker, P.F. (1993), *Post-capitalist Society*, New York: Harper Business.

Eatwell, J., M. Milgate and P. Newman (eds) (1987), *The New Palgrave: A Dictionary of Economics*, London: Macmillan, and New York: Stockton Press.

Edwards, C. (1995), *Crises and Reforms in Latin America*, Oxford and New York: Oxford University Press.

Eggertsson, T. (1990), *Economic Behavior and Institutions*, Cambridge: Cambridge University Press.

Eggertsson, T. (1997), *The Old Theory of Economic Policy and the New Institutionalism*, Discussion Paper, Max-Planck Institute for Research into Economic Systems, Jena: MPI for Research into Economic Systems.

Elster, J. (1989), *The Cement of Society: A Study of Social Order*, Cambridge and New York: Cambridge University Press.

Epstein, R. (1995), *Simple Rules for a Complex World*, Cambridge, MA: Harvard University Press.

Erhard, L. (1960), *Prosperity through Competition*, 3rd edn, London: Thames & Hudson.

Eucken, W. ([1940] 1992), *The Foundations of Economics: History and Theory in the Analysis of Economic Reality*, New York and Heidelberg, Springer; first German edn, 1940.

Fama, E.F. and M.C. Jensen (1985), 'Organizational Costs and Investment Decisions', *Journal of Financial Economics*, vol. 14:1, 101–19.

Fels, G. (1972), 'The Choice of Industry Mix in the Division of Labour Between Developed and Developing Countries', *Weltwirtschaftliches Archiv*, vol. 108, 49–66.

Fields, G.S. (1984), 'Employment Income Distribution, and Economic Growth in Seven Small Open Economies', *Economic Journal*, vol. 94, 74–83.

Findlay, R. (1992), 'The Roots of Divergence: Western Economic History in Comparative Perspective', *American Economic Review*, vol. 82 (May), 158–61.

Flew, A. (1989), *Equality in Liberty and Justice*, London and New York: Routledge.

Foldvary, F. (1994), *Public Goods and Private Communities*, Aldershot, UK, and Brookfield, US: Edward Elgar.

Freeman, D. (1983), *Margaret Mead and Samoa: The Making and Unmaking of an Anthropological Myth*, Canberra: Australian National University Press.

Freeman, R. and B. Berelson (1974), 'The Human Population', *Scientific American* (Sept.), 32–49.

Friedman, D. (1979), 'Private Creation and Enforcement of Law: a Historical Case', *Journal of Legal Studies*, vol. 8:2, 399–415.

Friedman, M. (1962), *Capitalism and Freedom*, Chicago and London: University of Chicago Press.

Friedman, M. (1991), 'The Sources of Monopoly', in J.L. Doti and D.R. Lee (eds), *The Market Economy: A Reader*, Los Angeles: Roxburg Publications, 103–6.

Friedman, M. and R. Friedman (1980), *Free to Choose: A Personal Statement*, Harmondsworth, Middx: Pelican Books.

Fuglesang, A. and D. Chandler (1987), *Participation as Process: What We Can Learn from Grameen Bank, Bangladesh*, Oslo: Ministry of Development Co-operation, NORAD.

Fuller, L. (1977), *The Morality of Law*, New Haven, CT: Yale University Press.

Furubotn, E. (1994), *Future Development of the New Institutional Economics: Extension of the Neoclassical Model or New Construct?*, Lectiones Jenenses, Jena: Max Planck Institute for Research into Economic Systems.

Furubotn, E. and S. Pejovich (1972), 'Property Rights and Economic Theory: a Survey of Recent Literature', *Journal of Economic Literature*, vol. 10, 1137–62.

Furubotn, E. and R. Richter (eds) (1991), *The New Institutional Economics*, College Station, TX: Texas A&M University Press.

Galbraith, J.K. (1967), *The New Industrial State*, Boston, MA: Houghton Mifflin.

Gates, W.H. with N. Myhrvold and P. Rinearson (1995), *The Road Ahead*, New York and London: Viking-Penguin.

Gerken, J. (ed.) (1995), *Competition among Institutions*, London: St Martin's Press.

Gibbon, E. ([1776–88] 1996), *The History of the Decline and Fall of the Roman Empire*, London: Random House.

Giersch, H. (ed.) (1980), *Towards an Explanation of Economic Growth*, Tübingen: Mohr-Siebeck.

Giersch, H. (1989), *The Ethics of Economic Freedom*, Sydney: Centre for Independent Studies.

Giersch, H. (1993), *Openness for Prosperity*, Cambridge, MA: MIT Press.

Giersch, H. (1996), 'Economic Morality as a Competitive Asset', in A. Hamlin, H. Giersch and A. Norton, *Markets, Morals and Community*, Sydney: Centre for Independent Studies, 19–42.

Giersch, H., K.H. Paqué and H. Schmieding (1992), *The Fading German Miracle*, Cambridge and New York: Cambridge University Press.

Graham, A. and A. Seldon (1990), *Government and Economics in the Postwar World*, London: Routledge.

Green, D.G. (1996), *From Welfare State to Civil Society*, Wellington, NZ: NZ Business Roundtable.

Gregory, P.R. and R.C. Stuart (1981), *Soviet Economic Structure and Performance*, 2nd edn, New York: Harper & Row.

Gwartney, J.D. (1991), 'Private Property, Freedom and the West', in J.L. Doti and D.R. Lee (eds), *The Market Economy: A Reader*, Los Angeles: Roxburg Publications, 62–76.

Gwartney, J. and R. Lawson (1997), *Economic Freedom of the World 1997: Annual Report*, Vancouver: Fraser Institute.

Gwartney, J.D. and R.E. Wagner (eds) (1988), *Public Choice and Constitutional Economics*, Greenwich, CT: JAI Press.

Hahn, F.H. and R.C.O. Matthews (1969), 'The Theory of Economic Growth: a Survey', in Royal Economic Society and American Economic Association, *Surveys of Economic Theory*, vol. II, London: Macmillan, 1–124.

Harberger, A. (1984), *World Economic Growth*, San Francisco: Institute for Contemporary Studies.

Hardin, G. (1968), 'The Tragedy of the Commons', *Science*, no. 162, 1243–8.

Hardin, G. (1993), 'The Tragedy of the Commons', in D. Henderson (ed.), *The Fortune Encyclopedia of Economics*, New York: Time Warner Books, 88–91.

Harper, D.A. (1996), *Entrepreneurship and the Market Process: An Inquiry into the Growth of Knowledge*, London and Florence: Routledge.

Harrison, L.E. (1992), *Who Prospers? How Cultural Values Shape Economic and Political Success*, New York: Basic Books.

Hayek, F.A. ([1935] 1948), 'The Nature and History of the Problem', in F.A. Hayek, *Individualism and Economic Order*, 2 vols, Chicago: University of Chicago Press, vol. 1, 1–40.

Hayek, F.A. (1937), 'Economics and Knowledge', *Economica*, vol. 4, 33–54.

Hayek, F.A. (1940), 'Socialist Calculation: the Competitive "Solution"', *Economica*, vol. 7, 125–49.

Hayek, F.A. (1944), *The Road to Serfdom*, Chicago: University of Chicago Press.

Hayek, F.A. (1945), 'The Use of Knowledge in Society', *American Economic Review*, vol. 35, 519–30.

Hayek, F.A. (1960), *The Constitution of Liberty*, London: Routledge & Kegan Paul.

Hayek, F.A. (1967a), 'Notes on the Evolution of Systems of Rules of Conduct', in F.A. Hayek, *Studies in Philosophy, Politics and Economics*, London: Routledge & Kegan Paul, 66–81.

Hayek, F.A. (1967b), 'Kinds of Rationalism', in F.A. Hayek, *Studies in Philosophy, Politics and Economics*, London: Routledge & Kegan Paul, 82–95.

Hayek, F.A. (1973), *Law, Legislation and Liberty*, vol. 1: *Rules and Order*, Chicago and London: University of Chicago Press.

Hayek, F.A. (1976a), *Law, Legislation and Liberty*, vol. 2: *The Mirage of Social Justice*, Chicago and London: University of Chicago Press.

Hayek, F.A. (1976b), *Denationalization of Money: An Analysis of the Theory and Practice of Concurrent Currencies*, London: Institute of Economic Affairs.

Hayek, F.A. (1978), 'Competition as a Discovery Procedure', in F.A. Hayek, *New Studies in Philosophy, Politics, Economics and the History of Ideas*, London: Routledge & Kegan Paul, 179–90.

Hayek, F.A. (1979a), *Law, Legislation and Liberty*, vol. 3: *The Political Order of a Free People*, Chicago and London: University of Chicago Press.

Hayek, F.A. (1979b), *Counter Revolution of Science: Studies on the Abuse of Reason*, 2nd edn, Indianapolis: Liberty Press.

Hayek, F.A. (1988), *The Fatal Conceit: The Errors of Socialism*, London: Routledge, and Chicago: University of Chicago Press.

Hazlitt, H. ([1964] 1988), *The Foundations of Morality*, Lanham, MD: University Press of America.

Henderson, D. (ed.) (1993), *The Fortune Encyclopedia of Economics*, New York: Time Warner Books.

Hirschman, A.O. ([1970] 1980), *Exit, Voice and Loyalty: Responses to Decline in Firms, Organizations, and States*, Cambridge, MA: Harvard University Press.

Hirschman, A.O. (1977), *The Passions and the Interests: Political Arguments for Capitalism before its Triumph*, Princeton, NJ: Princeton University Press.

Hobbes, J.T. ([1651] 1962), *Leviathan*, London: Collins.

Hodgson, G.M. (1988), *Economics and Institutions: A Manifesto for a Modern Institutional Economics*, Philadephia: University of Pennsylvania Press, and Cambridge: Polity Press.

Hodgson, G.M. (1989), 'Institutional Economic Theory: the Old versus the New', *Review of Political Economy*, vol. 1:3, 249–69.

Hodgson, G.M., W.J. Samuels and M.R. Tool (eds) (1994), *The Elgar Companion to Institutional and Evolutionary Economics*, 2 vols, Aldershot, UK and Brookfield, US: Edward Elgar.

Hofstede, H. and M.H. Bond (1988), 'The Confucius

Connection: From Cultural Roots to Economic Growth', *Organizational Dynamics*, vol. 16 (Spring), 5–21.

Hogarth, R.M. and M.W. Reder (eds) (1986), 'The Behavioral Foundations of Economic Theory', *Journal of Business*, vol. 59:4 (special issue), S.181–S.224.

Hume, D. ([1739] 1965), 'A Treatise of Human Nature', in D. Hume, *The Philosophical Works of David Hume*, ed. T.H. Green and T.H. Grose, Oxford: Clarendon Press.

Hutchison,T.W. (1981), 'On the Aims and Methods of Economic Theorizing', in T.W. Hutchison, *The Politics and Philosophy of Economics: Marxians, Keynesians and Austrians*, New York: New York University Press, 266–307.

International Monetary Fund (1997), *World Economic Outlook*, October 1997, Washington, DC: IMF.

Jacobs, J. (1992), *Systems of Survival: A Dialogue on the Moral Foundations of Commerce and Politics*, New York: Random House.

James, J.J. and M. Thomas (eds) (1994), *Capitalism in Context*, Chicago and London: University of Chicago Press.

Jasay, A. de (1985), *The State*, Oxford and New York: Basil Blackwell.

Jasay, A. de (1995), *Conventions: Some Thoughts on the Economics of Ordered Anarchy*, Lectiones Jenenses, Jena: Max Planck Institute for Research into Economic Systems.

Jefferson, G.H. and T.G. Rawski (1995), 'How Industrial Reform Worked in China: the Role of Innovation, Competition and Property Rights', in World Bank, *Proceedings of the World Bank Annual Conference on Development Economics, 1994*, supplement to *World Bank Economic Review*, Washington, DC: World Bank, 129–70.

Jensen, M.C. (1983), 'Organization Theory and Methodology', *Accounting Review*, vol. 58, 319–39.

Jensen, M.C. and W. Meckling (1976), 'Theory of the Firm: Managerial Behavior, Agency Costs, and Capital Structure', *Journal of Financial Economics*, vol. 3, 305–60.

Jensen, M.C. and R.S. Ruback (1983), 'The Market for Corporate Control: the Scientific Evidence', *Journal of Financial Economics*, vol. 11:1–4, 5–50.

Johnson, P. (1983), *A History of the Modern World, from 1917 to the 1980s*, London: Weidenfeld & Nicolson.

Johnson, P. (1991), *The Birth of the Modern World Society, 1815–1830*, London: Weidenfeld & Nicolson.

Jones, E.L. ([1981] 1987), *The European Miracle: Environments, Economies, and Geopolitics in the History of Europe and Asia*, 2nd edn, Cambridge, Melbourne and New York: Cambridge University Press.

Jones, E.L. (1988), *Growth Recurring: Economic Change in World History*, Oxford: Clarendon Press.

Jones, E.L. (1994), 'Patterns of Growth in History', in J.J. James and M. Thomas (eds), *Capitalism in Context*, Chicago and London: University of Chicago Press, 115–28.

Jones, E.L. (1995), 'Culture and its Relationship to Economic Change', *Journal of Institutional and Theoretical Economics*, vol. 151:2, 269–85.

Jones, E.L., L. Frost and C. White (1994), *Coming Full Circle: An Economic History of the Pacific Rim*, Melbourne: Oxford University Press.

Kahn, H. (1979), *World Economic Development: 1979 and Beyond*, London: Croom Helm, and Boulder, CO: Westview Press.

Karlsson, N. (ed.) (1995), *Can the Present Problems of Mature Welfare States Such as Sweden be Solved?*, Stockholm: City University Press.

Kasper, W. (1970), 'European Integration and Greater Flexibility of Exchange Rates', in H.N. Halm (ed.), *Approaches to Greater Flexibility of Exchange Rates: The Bürgenstock Papers*, Princeton, NJ: Princeton University Press, 385–8.

Kasper, W. (1974), *Malaysia: A Case Study in Successful Economic Development*, Washington, DC: American Enterprise Institute.

Kasper, W. (1981), 'The Sichuan Experiment', *Australian Journal of Chinese Affairs*, no. 7, 163–72.

Kasper, W. (1982), *Australian Political Economy*, Melbourne: Macmillan.

Kasper, W. (1993), 'Spatial Economics', in D. Henderson (ed.), *The Fortune Encyclopedia of Economics*, New York: Time Warner Books, 82–5.

Kasper, W. (1994a), *Global Competition, Institutions, and the East Asian Ascendancy*, San Francisco: International Center for Economic Growth.

Kasper, W. (1994b), 'The East Asian Challenge', in H. Hughes, W. Kasper and J. McLeod, *Australia's Asian Challenge*, Sydney: Centre for Independent Studies, 19–33.

Kasper, W. (1995a), *Competitive Federalism*, Perth: Institute of Public Affairs, States' Policy Unit.

Kasper, W. (1996b), *Free to Work: The New Zealand Employment Contracts Act*, Sydney and Wellington, NZ: Centre for Independent Studies.

Kasper, W. (1997), 'Competitive Federalism for the Era of Globalization', in G. Radnitzky (ed.), *Values and the Social Order*, Vol. 3: *Voluntary versus Coercive Orders*, Aldershot, UK and Brookfield, US: Avebury, 477–502.

Kasper, W. (1998), 'Transitions and Institutional Innovation', *Malaysian Journal of Economic Studies* (July), 54–65.

Kasper, W. and M.E. Streit (1993), *Lessons from the Freiburg School: The Institutional Foundations of Freedom and Prosperity*, Sydney: Centre for Independent Studies.

Khalil, E.L. (1995), 'Organizations versus Institutions', *Journal of Justitutional and Theoretical Economics*, vol. 151: 3, pp. 445–66.

Kilby, P. (ed.) (1971), *Entrepreneurship and Economic Development*, New York: Free Press.

Kimminich, O. (1990), 'Institutionen in der Rechtsordnung', in E. Pankoke (ed.), *Institutionen und Technische Zivilisation*, Berlin: Duncker & Humblot, 90–118.

Kirzner, I.M. (1960), *The Economic Point of View*, Kansas City: Sheed & Ward.

Kirzner, I.M. (1963), *Market Theory and the Price System*, Princeton, NJ: Van Nostrand.

Kirzner, I.M. (1973), *Competition and Entrepreneurship*, Chicago: University of Chicago Press.

Kirzner, I.M. (1985), *Discovery and the Capitalist Process*, Chicago: University of Chicago Press.

Kirzner, I.M. (1986), 'Roundaboutness, Opportunity and Austrian Economics', in M.J. Anderson (ed.), *The Unfinished Agenda: Essays on the Political Economy of Government Policy in Honour of Arthur Seldon*, London: Institute of Economic Affairs, 93–103.

Kirzner, I.M. (1992), *The Meaning of the Market Process: Essays in the Development of Modern Austrian Economics*, London and New York: Routledge.

Kirzner, I.M. (ed.), (1994), *Classics in Austrian Economics: A Sampling in the History of a Tradition*, 3 vols, London: W. Pickering.

Kirzner, I.M. (1997), 'Entrepreneurial Discovery and the Competitive Market Process: an Austrian Approach', *Journal of Economic Literature*, vol. 35:1, 60–85.

Kiwit, D. (1996), 'Path Dependence in Technological and Institutional Change: Some Criticisms and Suggestions', *Journal des économistes et des études humaines*, vol. 7:1, 69–83.

Klaus, V. (1991), *Dismantling Socialism: A Preliminary Report*, Sydney: Centre for Independent Studies.

Klaus, V. (1997), *Renaissance*, Washington, DC: Cato Institute.

Kliemt, H. (1993), 'On Justifying a Minimum Welfare State', *Constitutional Political Economy*, vol. 4, 159–72.

Klitgaard, R. (1995), *Institutional Adjustment and Adjusting to Institutions*, World Bank Discussion Paper no. 303, Washington, DC: World Bank.

Kreps, D. (1990), 'Corporate Culture and Economic Theory', in J.E. Alt and K.A. Shepsle (eds), *Perspectives on Positive Political Economy*, Cambridge and New York: Cambridge University Press, 90–143.

Krueger, A.O. (1994), *Political Economy of Policy Reform in Developing Countries*, Cambridge, MA: MIT Press.

Krueger, A.O. (1997), 'Trade Policy and Economic Development: How We Learn', *American Economic Review*, vol. 87:1, 1–22.

Krugman, P. (1994), 'Competitiveness – A Dangerous Drug', *Foreign Affairs* (March/April), 60–85.

Kukathas, C. (1990), *Hayek and Modern Liberalism*, Oxford: Clarendon Press.

Kukathas, C., D.W. Lovell and W. Maley (1991), *The Transition from Socialism: State and Civil Society in the USSR*, Melbourne: Longman Cheshire.

Lachmann, L. ([1943] 1977), 'The Role of Expectations in Economics as a Social Science', in L. Lachmann, *Capital, Expectations, and the Market Process: Essays on the Theory of the Market Economy*, ed. with an introduction by W.E. Grinder, Kansas City: Sheed & Andrews, 655–80.

Lachmann, L. (1973), *The Legacy of Max Weber*, Berkeley, CA: Glendessary Press.

Lal, D. (1995), 'Eco Fundamentalism', paper delivered at the Mont Pèlerin Society's Regional Meeting, Cape Town, South Africa, mimeo.

Landa, J.T. (1994), *Trust, Ethnicity, and Identity: Beyond the New Institutional Economics of Ethnic Trading Networks, Contract Law, and Gift-exchange*, Ann Arbor, MI: University of Michigan Press.

Lange, O.R. and F.M. Taylor ([1939] 1964), *On the Economic Theory of Socialism*, New York: McGraw-Hill.

Langlois, R.N. (ed.) (1986), *Economics as a Process: Essays in the New Institutional Economics*, Cambridge and New York: Cambridge University Press.

Lavoie, D. (ed.) (1994), *Expectations and the Meaning of Institutions: Essays in Economics by L. Lachmann*, London and New York: Routledge.

Leakey, R. (1994), *The Origin of Humankind*, London: Weidenfeld & Nicolson.

Leibenstein, H. (1966), 'Allocative and X-efficiency', *American Economic Review*, vol. 76 (June), 392–415.

Leibenstein, H. (1984), 'On the Economics of Conventions and Institutions: an Exploratory Essay', *Journal of Institutional and Theoretical Economics*, vol. 140, 74–86.

Leoni, B. (1961), *Freedom and the Law*, Princeton, NJ: Van Nostrand.

Lindbeck, A. (1995), 'Welfare State Disincentives with Endogenous Habits and Norms', *Scandinavian Journal of Economics*, no. 97:4, 477–94.

Lutz, F.A. ([1935] 1963), 'Goldwährung und Wirtschaftsordnung' [Gold Standard and Economic Order], *Weltwirtschaftliches Archiv*, vol. 41, 224–36; reprinted in an edited English translation in H.G. Grubel (ed.), *World Monetary Reform*, Stanford, CA: Stanford University Press, 1963, 320–8.

Machlup, F. (1981–4), *Knowledge: Its Creation, Distribution and Economic Significance*, 3 vols, Princeton, NJ: Princeton University Press.

Maddison, A. (1991), *Dynamic Forces in Capitalist Development*, Oxford: Oxford University Press.

Maddison, A. (1995a), *Monitoring the World Economy, 1820–1992*, Paris: OECD Development Centre.

Maddison, A. (1995b), *Explaining the Economic Performance of Nations: Essays in Time and Space*, Cheltenham, UK and Brookfield, US: Edward Elgar.

Magee, S., W.A. Brock and L. Young (1989), 'The Invisible Foot and the Fate of Nations: Lawyers as Negative Externalities', in S. Magee *et al.* (eds), *Black Hole Tariffs and Endogenous Policy Theory: Political Economy in General Equilibrium*, Cambridge and New York: Cambridge University Press.

Mahovec, F.M. (1998), 'Paradigm Lost: The Walrasian Destruction of the Classical Conception of Markets', in G. Eliasiou, C. Green (eds), *Microfoundations of Economic Growth – A Schumpeterian Perspective*, Ann Arbor: University of Michigan Press, 29–56.

Mäki, U., B. Gustafsson, and C. Knudsen (eds) (1993), *Rationality, Institutions and Economic Methodology*, London and New York: Routledge.

Martin, W. and P. Béguin (1980), *Histoire de la Suisse, avec une suite (L'histoire récente)*, 8th edn, Lausanne: Payot.

Mathews, R.C.O. (1986), 'The Economics of Institutions and the Sources of Economic Growth', *Economic Journal*, vol. 96 (Dec.), 903–18.

Mauro, P. (1995), 'Growth and Corruption', *Quarterly Journal of Economics*, vol. 104:3, 681–712.

Mayhew, A. (1987), 'Culture: Core Concept under Attack', *Journal of Economic Issues*, vol. 21:2, 587–603.

McKenzie, R.B. (ed.) (1984), *Constitutional Economics: Containing the Economic Powers of Government*, Lexington: Lexington Books.

Meadows, D.H., D.L. Meadows, R. Randers and W.W. Behrens III (1972), *The Limits to Growth*, New York: Universe Books.

Menger, C. ([1883] 1963), *Problems of Economics and Sociology*, Urbana, IL: University of Illinois Press.

Menger, C. (1985), *Investigations into the Method of the Social Sciences*, New York: New York University Press; original German edition published 1883.

Metcalfe, S. (1989), 'Evolution and Economic Change', in A. Silberston (ed.), *Technology and Economic Progress*, London: Macmillan.

Metz, H.C. (ed.) (1994), *Algeria: A Country Study*, 5th edn, Washington, DC: US Library of Congress, Federal Research Division.

Milgrom, P.R. and J. Roberts (1992), *Economics, Organisations and Management*, Englewood Cliffs, NJ: Prentice-Hall.

Mises, L. von ([1920] 1994), 'Economic Calculation in the Socialist Commonwealth', reprinted in I.M. Kirzner (ed.), *Classics in Austrian Economics: A Sampling in the History of a Tradition*, London: W. Pickering, vol. 3, 3–30.

Mises, L. von (1949), *Human Action: A Treatise on Economics*, Edinburgh: W. Hodge; reprinted Chicago: Contemporary Books, 1978.

Mises, L. von (1978), *Liberalism*, Kansas City: Sheed & Ward.

Mises, L. von (1983), *Bureaucracy*, Cedar Falls: Center for Futures Education.

Mitchell, W.C. and R.T. Simmons (1994), *Beyond Politics: Markets, Welfare, and the Failure of Bureaucracy*, Boulder, CO: Westview Press.

Mueller, D.C. (1996), *On the Decline of Nations*, Lectiones Jenenses, Jena: Max Planck Institute for Research into Economic Systems.

Naisbitt, J. (1994), *Global Paradox: The Bigger the World Economy, the More Powerful its Smallest Players*, New York: William Morrow.

Naishul, V. (1993), 'Liberalism, Customary Rights and Economic Reforms', *Communist Economies and Economic Transformation*, vol. 5, 29–44.

Nelson, R.R. (1970), 'Information and Consumer Behavior', *Journal of Political Economy*, vol. 78:2, 311–29.

Nelson, R.R. (1990), 'Capitalism as an Engine of Progress', *Research Policy*, vol. 19:3, 193–214.

Nelson, R.R. (1995), 'Recent Evolutionary Theorizing about Economic Change', *Journal of Economic Literature*, vol. 33:1, 48–90.

Nelson, R.R. and S.G. Winter (1982), *An Evolutionary Theory of Economic Change*, Cambridge, MA: Belknap Press of Harvard University Press.

Nishiyama, C. and K.R. Leube (eds) (1984), *The Essence of Hayek*, Stanford, CA: Hoover Institutions Press.

Niskanen, W.A. (1971), *Bureaucracy and Representative Government*, Chicago: Aldine, Atherton.

North, D.C. (1981), *Structure and Change in Economic History*, New York: W.W. Norton.

North, D.C. (1990), *Institutions, Institutional Change and Economic Performance*, Cambridge and New York: Cambridge University Press.

North, D.C. (1992), *Transaction Costs, Institutions, and Economic Performance*, San Francisco: International Center for Economic Growth.

North, D.C. (1993), 'Institutions and Economic Performance', in U. Mäki, B. Gustafsson and C. Knudsen (eds), *Rationality, Institutions and Economic Methodology*, London and New York: Routledge, 242–63.

North, D.C. (1994), 'The Evolution of Efficient Markets', in J.J. James and M. Thomas (eds), *Capitalism in Context*, Chicago and London: University of Chicago Press, 257–64.

North, D.C. and R.P. Thomas (1973), *The Rise of the Western World: A New Economic History*, Cambridge: Cambridge University Press.

North, D.C. and R. P. Thomas (1977), 'The First Economic Revolution', *Economic History Review*, vol. 30, 2nd series, no. 2, 229–41.

Odell, J. (1990), 'Understanding International Trade Policies: an Emerging Synthesis', *World Politics*, vol. 453, 139–67.

O'Driscoll, G.P. Jr and M.J. Rizzo (1985), *The Economics of Time and Ignorance*, New York: Columbia University Press.

Oi, W.Y. (1990), 'Productivity in the Distributive Trades', paper presented to the Economic and Legal Organization Workshop, University of Rochester, mimeo.

O'Leary, J. (ed.) (1995), *Privatization 1995*, Los Angeles: Reason Foundation.

Olson, M. (1965), *The Logic of Collective Action: Public Goods and the Theory of Groups*, New York: Schocken Books.

Olson, M. (1982), *The Rise and Decline of Nations: Economic Growth, Stagflation and Social Rigidities*, New Haven, CT, and London: Yale University Press.

Olson, M. (1993), 'Dictatorship, Democracy and Development', *American Political Science Review*, vol. 87:3, 567–76.

Olson, M. (1996), 'Big Bills Left on the Sidewalk: Why Some Nations are Rich, and Others Poor', *Journal of Economic Perspectives*, vol. 10, 3–24.

Ordeshook, P. (1992), 'Constitutional Stability', *Constitutional Political Economy*, vol. 3:2, 137–75.

Ostrom, E. (1990), *Governing the Commons: The Evolution of Institutions for Collective Action*, Cambridge and New York: Cambridge University Press.

Papageorgiou, D., A.M. Choksi and M. Michaely (1991), *Liberalizing Foreign Trade*, Oxford and Cambridge, MA: Basil Blackwell.

Parker, D. and R. Stacey (1995), *Chaos, Management and Economics: The Implications of Non-linear Thinking*, London: Institute of Economic Affairs.

Peacock, A. (1978), 'The Economics of Bureaucracy: an Inside View', in Institute of Economic Affairs, *The Economics of Politics*, London: Institute of Economic Affairs, 117–28.

Pejovich, S. (1966), *The Market-planned Economy of Yugoslavia*, Minneapolis: University of Minnesota Press.

Pejovich, S. (1995), *Economic Analysis of Institutions and Systems*, Dordrecht and Boston, MA: Kluwer Academic.

Petersmann, E.V. (1986), 'Trade Policy as a Constitutional Problem: On the Domestic Policy Functions of International Trade Rules', *Außenwirtschaft*, vol. 41, 243–77.

Pethig, R. and U. Schlieper (eds) (1987), *Efficiency, Institutions and Economics Policy*, Berlin and New York: Springer.

Pipes, R. (1990), *The Russian Revolution, 1899–1919*, London: Collins Harvill, and New York: Vintage Books.

Polanyi, M. (1966), *The Tacit Dimension*, New York: Doubleday.

Popper, K.R. ([1945] 1974), *The Open Society and its Enemies*, 2 vols, London: Routledge & Kegan Paul.

Popper, K.R. (1959), *The Logic of Scientific Discovery*, London: Hutchinson.

Porter, M.E. (1990), *The Competitive Advantage of Nation*, London: Macmillan, and New York: Free Press.

Porter, P. and G. Scully (1995), 'Institutional Technology and Economic Growth', *Public Choice*, vol. 82, 17–36.

Powelson, J.P. (1994), *Centuries of Economic Endeavor*, Ann Arbor, MI: University of Michigan Press.

Prebble, R. (1996), *I Have Been Thinking*, Auckland: Bay Press.

Prychitko, D.L. (1991), *Marxism and Workers' Self-management: The Essential Tension*, Westport, CT: Greenwood.

Putnam, R.D. (1994), *Making Democracy Work*, Princeton, NJ: Princeton University Press.

Rabushka, A. (1974), *A Theory of Racial Harmony*, Columbia, SC: University of South Carolina Press.

Radnitzky, G. (1987), 'An Economic Theory of the Rise of Civilisation and its Policy Implications: Hayek's Account Generalised', *Ordo*, vol. 38, 47–90.

Radnitzky, G. (ed.) (1997), *Values and the Social Order*, Vol. 3: *Voluntary versus Coercive Orders*, Aldershot, UK, and Brookfield, US: Avebury.

Radnitzky, G. and H. Bouillon (eds) (1995a), *Values and the Social Order*, Vol. 1: *Values and Society*, Aldershot, UK, and Brookfield, US: Avebury.

Radnitzky, G. and H. Bouillon (eds) (1995b), *Values and the Social Order*, Vol. 2: *Society and Order*, Aldershot, UK, and Brookfield, US: Avebury.

Raiser, M. (1997), *Soft Budget Constraints and the Fate of Economic Reforms in Transition Economies and Developing Countries*, Tübingen: Mohr-Siebeck.

Ratnapala, S. (1990), *Welfare State or Constitutional State?*, Sydney: Centre for Independent Studies.

Redding, S.G. (1993), *The Spirit of Chinese Capitalism*, Berlin: Walter de Gruyter.

Rheinstein, M. (1954), *Max Weber on Law in Economy and Society*, Cambridge, MA: Harvard University Press.

Richardson, R. (1995), *Making a Difference*, Christchurch, NZ: Shoal Bay Press.

Richter, R. and W. Furubotn (1997), *Institutions and Economic Theory: An Introduction to and Assessment of the New Institutional Economics*, Ann Arbor, MI: University of Michigan Press.

Riedel, J. (1988), 'Economic Development in East Asia: Doing What Comes Naturally', in H. Hughes (ed.), *Achieving Industrialization in East Asia*, Melbourne: Cambridge University Press, 1–38.

Robbin, L.R. (1976), *Political Economy, Past and Present: A Review of Leading Theories of Economic Policy*, London: Macmillan.

Robertson, P. (1993), 'Innovation, Corporate Organisation and Industry Policy', *Prometheus*, vol. II:2, 271–87.

Rockwell, L.H. (ed.) (1988), *The Free Market Reader*, Burlingame, CA: Ludwig von Mises Institute.

Roemer, J.E. (1994), *A Future for Socialism*, Cambridge, MA: Harvard University Press.

Röpke, W. (1948), *Civitas Humana: A Humane Order of Society*, London: W. Hodge.

Rosenberg, N. (1988), 'Technological Change under Capitalism and Socialism', in A. Anderson and D.L. Bark (eds), *Thinking about America*, Stanford, CA: Hoover Institution Press, 193–202.

Rosenberg, N. and L.E. Birdzell (1986), *How the West Grew Rich: The Economic Transformation of the Industrial World*, New York: Basic Books.

Rostow, W.W. (1978), *The World Economy: History and Prospect*, London: Macmillan.

Rothbard, M. (1962), *Man, Economy and State*, Princeton, NJ: Van Nostrand.

Rozman, G. (ed.) (1991), *The East Asian Region: Confucian Heritage and its Modern Adaptation*, Princeton, NJ: Princeton University Press.

Sachs, J.D. (1995), 'Russia's Struggle with Stabilization: Conceptual Issues and Evidence', in World Bank, *Proceedings of the World Bank Annual Conference on Development Economics, 1994*, supplement to *World Bank Economic Review*, Washington, DC: World Bank, 57–92.

Samuels, W.J. (ed.) (1988), *Institutional Economics*, 3 vols, Aldershot, UK, and Brookfield, US: Edward Elgar.

Scherer, F.A. (1984), *Innovation and Growth: Schumpeterian Perspectives*, Cambridge, MA: MIT Press.

Schuck, P. (1992), 'Legal Complexity: Some Causes, Consequences, and Cures', *Duke Law Journal*, vol. 1:3.

Schumpeter, J.A. (1947), *Capitalism, Socialism and Democracy*, 2nd edn, New York: Harper.

Schumpeter, J.A. (1961), *The Theory of Economic Development: An Inquiry into Profits, Capital, Credit, Interest and the Business Cycle*, Oxford and New York: Oxford University Press; first German edition, 1908.

Scobie, G. and S. Lim (1992), 'Economic Reform: a Global Revolution', *Policy*, vol. 8:3, 2–7.

Scully, G.W. (1991), 'Rights, Equity and Economic Efficiency', *Public Choice*, vol. 68, 195–215.

Scully, G.W. (1992), *Constitutional Environments and Economic Growth*, Princeton, NJ: Princeton University Press.

Seldon, A. (1990), *Capitalism*, Oxford and Cambridge, MA: Basil Blackwell.

Shackle, G.L.S. (1972), *Epistemics and Economics: A Critique of Economic Doctrines*, Cambridge: Cambridge University Press.

Shleifer, A. (1995), 'Establishing Property Rights', in World Bank, *Proceedings of the World Bank Annual Conference on Development Economics, 1994*, supplement to *World Bank Economic Review*, Washington, DC: World Bank, 93–128.

Siebert, H. (1991), *The Transformation of Eastern Europe*, Kiel Discussion Papers no. 163, Kiel: Institute of World Economics.

Siebert, H. (ed.) (1993), *Overcoming the Transformation Crisis: Lessons for the Successor States of the Soviet Union*, Tübingen: Mohr-Siebeck.

Siebert, H. (ed.) (1995), *Trends in Business Organization: Do Participation and Cooperation Increase Competitiveness?*, Tübingen: Mohr-Siebeck.

Simon, H.A. (1957), *Administrative Behaviour*, New York: Free Press.

Simon, H.A. (1959), 'Theories of Decision-making in Business Organizations', *American Economic Review*, vol. 49, 253–83.

Simon, H.A. (1976), 'From Substantive to Procedural Rationality', in S.J. Latsis (ed.), *Method and Appraisal in Economics*, Cambridge and New York: Cambridge University Press, 129–48.

Simon, H.A. (1982), *Models of Bounded Rationality and Other Topics in Economic Theory*, 2 vols, Cambridge, MA: MIT Press.

Simon, H.A. (1983), *Reason in Human Affairs*, Oxford and Cambridge, MA: Basil Blackwell.

Simon, J.L. (ed.) (1995), *The State of Humanity*, Oxford and Cambridge, MA: Basil Blackwell.

Simons, H.C. ([1936] 1948), 'Rules versus Authorities in Monetary Policy', in H.C. Simons (ed.), *Economic Policy for a Free Society*, Chicago: University of Chicago Press.

Smith, A. ([1776] 1970–1), *An Inquiry into the Wealth of Nations*, 2 vols, London: Dent.

Sohmen, E. (1959), 'Competition and Growth: the Lesson of West Germany', *American Economic Review*, vol. 49, 986–1003.

Solow, R.E. (1988), *Growth Theory: An Exposition*, Oxford and New York: Oxford University Press.

Soto, H. de (1990), *The Other Path: The Invisible Revolution in the Third World*, New York: Harper & Row.

Soto, H. de (1993), 'The Missing Ingredient', *The Economist*, 11 September.

Sowell, T. (1987), *A Conflict of Visions*, New York: William Morrow.

Sowell, T. (1990), *Preferential Policies: An International Perspective*, New York: William Morrow.

Sowell, T. (1991), 'Cultural Diversity: a World View', *American Enterprise*, vol. 5 (May/June), 44–55.

Sowell, T. (1994), *Race and Culture*, New York: Basic Books.

Sowell, T. (1996), *Migration and Cultures: A World View*, New York: Basic Books.

Sowell, T. (1998), *Conquest and Cultures: A World View*, New York: Basic Books.

Stigler, G.J. (1963), *The Intellectual and the Market Place*, London: Institute of Economic Affairs.

Stigler, G.J. (1967), 'Imperfections in Capital Markets', *Journal of Political Economy*, vol. 75, 287–92.

Stigler, G.J. (1971a), 'The Theory of Economic Regulation', *Bell Journal of Economics and Management Science*, vol. 2:1, 3–21.

Stigler, G.J. (1971b), 'The Economics of Information', in D.M. Lamberton (ed.), *Economics of Information and Knowledge*, Harmondsworth: Penguin, 61–82.

Stigler, G.J. (1975), *The Citizen and the State: Essays on Regulation*, Chicago and London: University of Chicago Press.

Streit, M.E. (1981), 'Demand Management and Catallaxy: Reflections on a Poor Policy Record', *Ordo*, vol. 32, 17–34.

Streit, M.E. (1983), 'Modelling, Managing and Monitoring Futures Trading: Frontiers of Analytical Inquiry', in M.E. Streit (ed.), *Futures Markets*, Oxford and New York: Basil Blackwell, 1–26.

Streit, M.E. (1984), 'The Shadow Economy: a Challenge to the Welfare State?', *Ordo*, vol. 35, 109–19.

Streit, M.E. (1987), 'Economic Order and Public Policy: Market, Constitution and the Welfare State', in R. Pethig and U. Schlieper (eds) *Efficiency, Institutions and Economics Policy*, Berlin and New York: Springer, 1–21.

Streit, M.E. (1988), 'The Mirage of Neo-corporatism', *Kyklos*, vol. 41, 603–24.

Streit, M.E. (1992), 'Economic Order, Private Law and Public Policy: the Freiburg School of Law and Economics in Perspective', *Journal of Institutional and Theoretical Economics*, vol. 148, 675–705.

Streit, M.E. (1993a), 'Cognition, Competition, and Catallaxy: in Memory of Friedrich August von Hayek', *Constitutional Political Economy*, vol. 4:2, 223–62.

Streit, M.E. (1993b), 'Welfare Economics, Economic Order and Competition', in H. Giersch (ed.), *Money, Trade and Competition: Essays in Memory of Egon Sohmen*, Berlin and New York: Springer, 255–78.

Streit, M.E. (1995), *Freiburger Beiträge zur Ordnungsökonomik*, Tübingen: Mohr-Siebeck.

Streit, M.E. (1996), 'Competition among Systems as a Defence of Liberty', in H. Bouillon (ed.), *Libertarians and Liberalism: Essays in Honour of Gerard Radnitzky*, Aldershot, UK, and Brookfield, US: Avebury, 236–52.

Streit, M.E. (forthcoming, 1998), 'Constitutional Ignorance, Spontaneous Order and Rule Orientation: Hayekian Paradigms from a Policy Perspective', in S. Frowen (ed.), *Hayek the Economist and Social Philosopher: A Critical Retrospect*, London: Macmillan.

Streit, M.E. and A. Mangels (1996), *Privatautonomes Recht und grenzüberschreitende Transaktionen*, Jena Discussion Papers 07–96, Jena: Max Planck Institute for Research into Economic Systems.

Streit, M.E. and G. Mussler (1994), 'The Economic Constitution of the European Community: From Rome to Maastricht', *Constitutional Political Economy*, vol. 5:3, 319–53.

Streit, M.E. and S. Voigt (1993), 'The Economics of Conflict Resolution in International Trade', in D. Friedmann and E.-J. Mestmäcker (eds), *Conflict Resolution in International Trade: A Symposium*, Baden-Baden: Nomos Verlag, 39–72.

Streit, M.E. and G. Wegner (1992), 'Information, Transaction and Catallaxy: Reflections on Some Key Concepts of Evolutionary Market Theory', in U. Witt (ed.), *Explaining Process and Change*, Ann Arbor, MI: University of Michigan Press, 125–49.

Sugden, R. (1986), 'Spontaneous Order', *Journal of Economic Perspectives*, vol. 3:4, 85–97.

Syrquin, M. (1988), 'Patterns of Structural Change', in H.B. Chenery and T.N. Srinivasan (eds), *Handbook of Development Economics*, vol. I, Amsterdam and New York: North-Holland, 203–30.

Tanzer, A. (1994), 'The Bamboo Network', *Forbes Magazine*, 18 July, 138–45.

Tanzi, V. and L. Schuknecht (1995), *The Growth of Government and Reform of the State in Industrial Countries*, IMF Working Paper, Washington, DC: International Monetary Fund, mimeo.

Thurow, L.C. (1980), *The Zero-sum Society: Distribution and Possibilities of Economic Change*, Harmondsworth, Middx: Penguin Books.

Tinbergen, J. ([1961] 1965), 'Do Communist and Free Economies Show a Converging Pattern?', in M. Bornstein (ed.), *Comparative Economic Systems: Models and Cases*, Homewood, IL: Irwin, 455–64.

Tollison, R.D. (1982), 'Rent Seeking: a Survey', *Kyklos*, vol. 35, 575–602.

Tullock, G. (1967), 'The Welfare Costs of Tariffs, Monopolies and Theft', *Western Economic Journal*, vol. 5, 224–32.

Tullock, G. (1971), 'Public Decisions as Public Goods', *Journal of Political Economy*, vol. 79, 913–18.

Tullock, G. (1987), 'Public Choice', in Eatwell *et al.* (eds) (1987), *The New Palgrave: A Dictionary of Economics*, London: Macmillan and New York: Stockton Press, 1040–44.

Tullock, G. (1992), 'The Economics of Conflict', in G. Radnitzky (ed.), *Universal Economics*, New York: ICUS Publications, 301–14.

Tumlir, J. (1979), 'International Economic Order and Democratic Constitutionalism', *Ordo*, vol. 34, 71–83.

Tylor, E.B. (1883), *Primitive Culture: Researches into*

the Development of Mythology, Religion, Language, Art and Custom, 2 vols, New York: H. Holt.

United Nations (1995), World Investment Report: Transnational Corporations and Competitiveness, New York and Geneva: United Nations.

Vanberg, V.J. (1988), '"Ordungstheorie" as Constitutional Economics: the German Conceptions of the Social Market Economy', Ordo, vol. 34, 71–83.

Vanberg, V.J. (1992), 'Organizations as Constitutional Systems', Constitutional Political Economy, vol. 3:2, 223–53.

Vaubel, R. (1980), 'Repairing Capitalism', Regulation, July–August, 12–16.

Vaubel, R. (1985), 'Competing Currencies: the Case for Free Entry', Zeitschrift für die gesamten Staatswissenschaften, vol. 105, 547–64.

Vickery, G. and G. Wurzburg (1996), 'Flexible Firms, Skills, and Employment', OECD Observer, no. 202, Oct./Nov., 17–21.

Viscusi, W.K. (1993), 'The Value of Risks to Life and Health', Journal of Economic Literature, vol. 31:4, 1912–76.

Voigt, S. (1993), 'Values, Norms, Institutions and the Prospects for Economic Growth in Central and Eastern Europe', Journal des économistes et des études humaines, vol. 4:4, 495–529.

Voigt, S. (1997), 'Positive Constitutional Economics: a Survey', Public Choice (special issue on constitutional political economy), vol. 90, 11–53.

Wagener, H.J. (ed.) (1994), The Political Economy of Transformation, Heidelberg: Physica-Springer.

Walker, G. de Q. (1988), The Rule of Law: Foundation of Constitutional Democracy, Melbourne: Melbourne University Press.

Weber, M. ([1904] 1985), The Protestant Ethic and the Spirit of Capitalism, London: Unwin Paperbacks.

Weber, M. ([1921] 1978), Economy and Society: An Outline in Interpretative Sociology, 2 vols, Berkeley, CA: University of California Press.

Weber, M. ([1927] 1995), General Economic History, 6th edn, New Brunswick: Transaction Books.

Weber, M. (1951), The Religion of China: Confucianism and Taoism, Glencoe, IL: Free Press.

Weber, M. (1954), Law in Economy and Society, Cambridge, MA: Harvard University Press, original German edition, 1925.

Weede, E. (1990), 'Ideas, Institutions and Political Culture in Western Development', Journal of Theoretical Politics, vol. 2:4, 369–99.

Weede, E. (1995), 'Freedom, Knowledge and Law as Social Capital', in G. Radnitzky and H. Bouillon (eds), Values and the Social Order, vol. I: Values and Society, Aldershot, UK, and Brookfield, US: Avebury, 63–81.

Weede, E. (1996), Economic Development, Social Order, and World Politics, Boulder, CO: Lynne Rienner.

Williamson, O.E. (1975), Markets and Hierarchies: Analysis and Antitrust Implications. A Study in the Economics of Internal Organization, New York and London: Free Press.

Williamson, O.E. (1985), The Economic Institutions of Capitalism: Firms, Market and Relational Contracting, New York and London: Free Press.

Williamson, O.E. (1987), 'Transaction Cost Economics: the Comparative Contracting Perspective', Journal of Economic Behaviour and Organization, vol. 8, 617–25.

Williamson, O.E. (1988), 'The Logic of Economic Organization', Journal of Law, Economics and Organization, vol. 4:1, 65–93.

Williamson, O.E. (1995), 'The New Institutional Economics: the Institutions of Governance of Economic Development and Reform', in World Bank, Proceedings of the World Bank Annual Conference on Development Economics, 1994, supplement to World Bank Economic Review, Washington, DC: World Bank, 171–209.

Wills, I. (1997), Economics and the Environment, Sydney: Allen & Unwin.

Winiecki, J. (1988), The Distorted World of Soviet-type Economics, Pittsburg, PA: University of Pittsburgh Press.

Witt, U. (1991), 'Reflections on the Present State of Evolutionary Economic Theory', in G.M. Hodgson and E. Screpanti (eds), Rethinking Economics: Markets, Technology, and Economic Evolution, Aldershot, UK, and Brookfield, US: Edward Elgar, 83–102.

Witt, U. (1994), 'Evolutionary Economics', in P. Boettke (ed.), The Elgar Companion to Austrian Economics, Aldershot, UK, and Brookfield, US: Edward Elgar, 541–8.

Wohlgemuth, M. (1995), 'Institutional Competition: Notes on an Unfinished Agenda', Journal des économistes et des études humaines, vol. 6:2/3, 277–99.

Wohlgemuth, M. (1997), 'Has John Roemer Resurrected Market Socialism?', Independent Review, vol. 2:2, 193–216.

World Bank (1993), The East Asian Miracle: Economic Growth and Public Policy, Oxford and New York: Oxford University Press.

World Bank (1995), Proceedings of the World Bank Annual Conference on Development Economics 1994, Supplement to the World Bank Economic Review, Washington, DC: World Bank.

World Bank (1997), World Bank Atlas 1997, Washington, DC: World Bank.

World Bank (various), World Development Report, Oxford and New York: Oxford University Press, for World Bank.

World Economic Forum (1996), The Global Competitiveness Report 1996, Geneva: World Economic Forum.

Index

507